THACKERAY'S
CANVASS OF HUMANITY

THACKERAY'S
CANVASS OF HUMANITY

THACKERAY'S
CANVASS OF HUMANITY

An Author and His Public

Robert A. Colby

OHIO STATE UNIVERSITY PRESS : COLUMBUS

Drawing on title page:
Thackeray about age 29. From a drawing by Daniel Maclise (ca. 1840). (Frontispiece to volume 5 of *The Works of William Makepeace Thackeray* [Biographical Edition]; reproduced by kind permission of The National Portrait Gallery, London.)

/ 9 / 9 / 0

Library of Congress Cataloging in Publication Data

Colby, Robert Alan, 1920–
  Thackeray's canvass of humanity.

  Includes bibliographical references and index.
  1. Thackeray, William Makepeace, 1811–1863 —
Criticism and interpretation. I. Title.
PR5638.C6   823'.8   78-27465
ISBN 0-8142-0282-9

CONTENTS

ILLUSTRATIONS

ACKNOWLEDGMENTS

Over the long stretch of time that this book has been in process and in production, I have inevitably incurred many obligations both in this country and abroad, more than can be adequately credited in this brief space.

I am indebted to many curators and staffs of special collections who made their holdings available to me, notably: Dr. William H. Bond, Houghton Library, Harvard University; Marjorie G. Wynne, Beinecke Library, Yale University; Herbert T. Cahoon and Evelyn W. Semler, The Pierpont Morgan Library; Dr. Lola Szladits, Berg Collection, New York Public Library; Dr. Theodore Grieder, Fales Collection, New York University; Kenneth Lohf, Rare Book and Manuscript Library, Columbia University; Clive Driver, The Philip H. and A. S. W. Rosenbach Foundation Library; and Charles Evans, formerly Librarian of the Charterhouse School, Godalming, Surrey. Robert H. Taylor kindly allowed me access to his private collection of Thackeray materials housed in the Firestone Library, Princeton University.

Among fellow Thackerayans I feel especially fortunate to have been able to draw, at various stages of progress, upon the original research of Peter Shillingsburg, Mississippi State University; Edgar F. Harden, Simon Fraser University; and John Sutherland, University College, London, who guided me, to a greater extent than is indicated in footnotes, through the thickets of textual history, manuscript changes, and the economics of publishing. Access to the records maintained by *The Wellesley Index to Victorian Periodicals*, made possible by its editor Walter E. Houghton, has saved me from perpetuating some traditional errors of attribution in *Fraser's Magazine* and other journals to which Thackeray contributed.

Colleagues at Queens College have kindly read portions of the typescript and have given me the benefit of their special competence: Stanley T. Lewis, Library Science Department, and Gerd Muehsam, Art Bibliographer, Paul Klapper Library (chap. 2); Michael Timko, English Department (chap. 3); and Joseph Sungolowsky, Romance Languages Department (chaps. 4 and 8). Outside of Queens College I have consulted with Michael R. Booth, Theatre Studies Department, University of Warwick, on nineteenth-century theater history, and with Donald G. Charlton, School of French Studies, University of Warwick, on Victor Cousin. I have profited in addition from conversations with Raymond Las Vergnas, formerly president of the Nouvelle Sorbonne and doyen of French Thackerayans, and with the late Jean-Albert Bedé, Columbia University, on Victor Cousin and French intellectual history. A former student, Joel Fishman, Librarian, Allegheny County Law Library, was helpful on the seventeenth-century religious background that figures in *Henry Esmond*.

Queens College has been supportive in various ways. A substantial part of the research for and early writing of this book was accomplished during a sabbatical leave granted to me in 1969, and during another leave in 1971. The typing service of the college was made available to me through Mrs. Pearl Sigberman, chief of the Word Processing Division. The typing of the final copy was done mainly by Wendy De Fortuna. Mimi Penchansky, of the staff of the Paul Klapper Library, was instrumental in procuring scarce books for me on interlibrary loan. Maureen Miller, of the Multi-Media Services Department, prepared most of the photographs from which the illustrations in this book are reproduced.

For permission to quote from various Thackeray manuscripts and unpublished letters (individually cited in appropriate places in the book, along with present holders) I am grateful to Mrs. Belinda Norman-Butler, The Thackeray Estate. The following materials are reprinted by permission: a letter in the Maude Morrison Frank Correspondence, the Rare Book and Manuscript Library, Columbia University; a passage from the manuscript "Notes for a Literary Fund Speech," from the Robert H. Taylor Collection, Princeton, New Jersey; a paragraph from the manuscript "Some Unpublished MS Notes by William Makepeace Thackeray For A Life of Prince Talleyrand," by permission of the Houghton Library, Harvard University; passages from the manuscript of Thackeray's Notebook for the Four Georges, The Phillip H. & A. S. W. Rosenbach Foundation, Philadelphia; excerpts from W. M. Thackeray's notebook for

The Virginians in the Beinecke Rare Book and Manuscript Library, Yale University; passages from the manuscript of *The Newcomes*, by permission of the Headmaster of Charterhouse; and quotations from various manuscripts and letters in the collections of The Pierpont Morgan Library. I wish to thank Harvard University Press for permission to quote from *The Letters and Private Papers of William Makepeace Thackeray*, edited by Gordon N. Ray, copyright © 1945 by Hester Thackeray Ritchie Fuller and the President and Fellows of Harvard College. The University of California Press has authorized my quoting from my article on *Barry Lyndon* that appeared in an issue of *Nineteenth-Century Fiction*, as has Oxford University Press to quote from my article on *Catherine* that was published in an issue of the *Review of English Studies*. Notice of permission for reproduction accompanies each illustration.

Various people at Ohio State University merit special mention: Richard D. Altick, Regents Professor of English, for his encouragement; Weldon A. Kefauver, director of the Ohio State University Press, for his considerateness; Robert S. Demorest, editor, for his able assistance during the early stages of the preparation of the typescript; and Carol S. Sykes, assistant editor, for her astuteness and meticulousness in converting it into a finished book.

Finally a word of tribute to my wife, colleague, and collaborator Vineta Colby, who has been with this book from its beginnings, and whose own contribution to it, tangible and intangible, is immeasurable.

NOTE ON DOCUMENTATION

COLLECTED WORKS

The citation *Works* refers to *The Works of William Makepeace Thackeray*, with biographical introductions by his daughter, Anne Ritchie (the Biographical Edition), 13 volumes (London: Smith, Elder; New York: Harper & Bros., 1898–99). Occasionally other collected sets are utilized: *The Works of William Makepeace Thackeray*, with biographical introductions by Lady Ritchie (the Centenary Biographical Edition), 26 volumes (London: Smith, Elder, 1910–11) (cited as Cent. Biog. Ed.); *The Oxford Thackeray*, edited, with introductions, by George Saintsbury, 17 volumes (London: Oxford University Press, 1908) (cited as Oxford Thackeray); and [Works of Thackeray] *Harry Furniss Centenary Edition*, with illustrations by the author and Harry Furniss, 20 volumes (London: Macmillan & Co., 1911) (cited as Furniss Ed.).

INDIVIDUAL WORKS

Most of my citations to Thackeray's individual books are to chapter numbers in *Works* (Biographical Edition). Following are the exceptions: page references to *Catherine* are to the Oxford Thackeray, vol. 3; references to *Barry Lyndon* are to *The Luck of Barry Lyndon*, a critical edition, edited, with an introduction and notes, by Martin J. Anisman (New York: New York University Press, 1970); *Vanity Fair* references are to the Riverside Edition, edited, with an introduction and notes, by Geoffrey and Kathleen Tillotson (Boston: Houghton Mifflin Co., 1963); and chapter references to *Pendennis*, except when otherwise indicated, follow the revised numbering as incorporated in the Penguin English Library text of *The*

History of Pendennis, edited by Donald Hawes, with an introduction by J. I. M. Stewart (Harmondsworth, Middlesex: Penguin Books Ltd., 1972).

CORRESPONDENCE

The citation *Letters* refers to *The Letters and Private Papers of William Makepeace Thackeray*, edited by Gordon N. Ray, 4 volumes (Cambridge, Mass.: Harvard University Press, 1945–46). Unpublished letters are so indicated, with their library location.

MAGAZINE PIECES

For Thackeray's identified contributions to *Fraser's Magazine* and the *Foreign Quarterly Review*, my usual practice is to cite both the original appearance and a reprint in the Biographical Edition or some other collected set, the interval between the two publications usually being fairly long.

For the *Morning Chronicle* pieces I cite the date of original appearance, followed by a page reference to its reprinting in *William Makepeace Thackeray: Contributions to the Morning Chronicle*, edited by Gordon N. Ray (London and Urbana: University of Illinois Press, 1966) (cited as *Contributions*).

For *The Roundabout Papers* I cite only page references to the Biographical Edition, unless I thought it important to establish its context in the *Cornhill Magazine*.

FUGITIVE WRITINGS

Some of Thackeray's essays and miscellaneous journalism that do not appear in standard editions, but which nevertheless have been authenticated, are cited from various posthumous collections. The ones that have been most frequently utilized are *Mr. Thackeray's Writings for the "National Standard" and "Constitutional,"* compiled by Walter Thomas Spencer (London: W. T. Spencer, 1899); *Stray Papers by William Makepeace Thackeray, Being Stories, Reviews, Verses, and Sketches (1821–1847)*, edited, with an introduction and notes, by Louis Melville (Philadelphia: George W. Jacobs & Co., 1901) (cited as *Stray Papers*); and *The New Sketch Book, Essays Collected from the Foreign Quarterly Review*, edited by Robert S. Garnett (London: Alston Rivers, 1906) (cited as *New Sketch Book*).

THACKERAY'S
CANVASS OF HUMANITY

Man, anywhere and under any circumstances, is an object of deep and appalling interest, and from erring man examples of the highest interest have ever been drawn. "Criminals stand forward . . . on the canvass of humanity as prominent objects for our special study." The progress of civilisation and the mutations of manners may be traced to the diversities and fluctuations of crime, for crimes have their cycles. . . . The man who undertakes the truly philosophic task we assign him ought to be patient in research, cool, somewhat sceptical, calmly discriminating between individual guilt and the community of error.

"Hints for a History of Highwaymen,"
Fraser's Magazine, March 1834

INTRODUCTION: THE PROTEAN THACKERAY

In Charles Lever's *Roland Cashel* we are introduced to "a large, high-shouldered spectacled gentleman" as he arrives at a dinner party in Dublin in the phaeton of a society matron. Peering at the company with "glances, at once inquiring and critical," he is identified as Elias Howle of "that numerous horde of Tourist authors held in leash by fashionable booksellers," one, moreover, "of a peculiar class, which this age, so fertile in inventions, has engendered, a publisher's man-of-all-work, ready for anything from statistics to satire, and equally prepared to expound prophecy, or write squibs for 'Punch.'" This was written in 1850 with a backward glance over the previous decade. In Disraeli's last novel, *Endymion*, published in 1880, but based on a hazy memory of impressions some forty years old, we hear a back-biting littérateur named St. Barbe, contributor to a journal called *Scaramouch*, railing at his publishers Shuffle and Screw for paying him less for a novel than a powdered flunky commands in St. James's Square. He takes up society at once as a theater of operations and as a tuft-hunting preserve: "He had the honour of sitting for a time by the side of Mrs. Neuchatel, and being full of good claret, he, as he phrased it, showed his paces: that is to say, delivered himself of some sarcastic paradoxes duly blended with fulsome flattery." Later he sets himself up to the hero as no mere humorist or gossip, as no less in fact than a "literary diplomatist." "The age of mediocrity is not eternal," declares St. Barbe confidently to the budding politician Endymion. "You see the thing offered, and I saw an opening. . . . I will read the 'Debats' and the 'Revue des Deux Mondes,' and make out something. Foreign affairs are all my future, and my views may be as right as anybody else's; probably more correct, not so conventional."

Lever and Disraeli had both squirmed under William Makepeace Thackeray's satirical lash, and in these caricatures they were getting back at him. Yet their portraits of Thackeray as journeyman author struggling for recognition, even if etched in vitriol, testify to his imposing presence, his intelligence, his wit, and his readiness to make all mankind his province—qualities that undeniably contributed to the popularity and prestige he eventually won among the Victorian reading public. Diverse impressions left behind by other fellow writers indicate that he could be many things to many people. To Carlyle he appeared an amalgam of Hogarth and Sterne, "a big fellow, soul and body . . . a big, weeping, hungry man"; to Edmund Yates he was "cold and uninviting" in his manner, "the cool, *suave*, well-bred gentleman, who, whatever may be rankling within, suffers no surface display of emotion"; Dickens complained that Thackeray "too much feigned a want of earnestness, and . . . made a pretence of undervaluing his art" (reflected possibly in the blasé artist Henry Gowan of *Little Dorrit*); Dr. John Brown, to the contrary, bears witness to his "large, acute, and fine understanding," as well as his "great-hearted, and tender and genuine sympathy, unsparing, truthful, inevitable, but with love and the love of goodness, and true loving-kindness over-arching and indeed animating it all." As against Miss Mitford's opinion that Thackeray was "all cynicism with an affectation of fashionable experience," there is on record Mrs. Oliphant's more balanced estimate of him as "a moralist . . . a laughing philosopher, a cynic; yet with a vein of pathos infinitely touching and true," and Charlotte Brontë's resounding tribute to him in her preface to *Jane Eyre* as a modern lion of Judah, "an intellect profounder and more unique than his contemporaries have yet recognized."

His readers appropriated him too under different aspects, most tangibly registered by his succession of pseudonyms. Among his earliest identifiable writings are a series of satires and verses contributed to the Cambridge student reviews the *Snob* and the *Gownsman*, signed simply "T." He was known subsequently as Théophile Wagstaff, Charles Yellowplush, Ikey Solomons, Timothy Titcomb, George Fitz-Boodle, Michael Angelo Titmarsh, Solomon Pacifico, Miss Tickletoby, The Fat Contributor, the Manager of the Performance, and Arthur Pendennis. Furthermore, his delightful habit of intruding himself into the illustrations of his books from time to time impinged on his readers' consciousness in subliminal and elusive ways. To the alert eye he turns up variously as a little boy (on the title page of *The Great Hoggarty Diamond*), as a hookah-smoking vizier (in a sketch in *From Cornhill to Grand Cairo*), now and then as a jester, even as the Reverend Charles Honeyman in *The Newcomes*.

In his lifetime Thackeray must have been among the most sculpted, sketched, painted, and photographed of authors, and this graphic gallery offers us too a choice of Thackerays: the white marble cherub (the nose not yet marred by young Venables' fist) carved by Devile when Thackeray was a schoolboy of eleven, now on view in the library at Charterhouse; the chubby, tousled stripling of James Spedding's pencil sketch; the monocled fledgling journalist posing for Maclise in 1832 with pad on knee; the pudgy, cheeky, rubicund youth preserved in oil at mid-decade by Frank Stone (among the likenesses to be seen in the National Portrait Gallery); the curled, mustachioed dandy peering coolly out of a Maclise drawing of 1840; the silvery, meditative sage of the Samuel Lawrence portraits of the 1850s (contemporaries observed how suddenly he seemed to have aged); the paunchy, bespectacled lecturer, leaning slightly toward his audience with his hands in his pockets, as caught in Sir Edgar Boehm's statuette; the portly bourgeois, frock-coated, white-haired, top-hatted, staring somewhat frozen-faced out of the late photographs, looking at least ten years older than the fifty-two that he was allotted on earth.

Mutability and variety appear to have been the laws of Thackeray's life. "As I travelled through these, to me, enchanting volumes," one of his admirers, George Augustus Sala, recalled late in life of his first acquaintance with Thackeray through the pages of *Fraser's Magazine* chanced upon in a coffee house, "I became aware of a writer, whose name, so I opined, should have been Proteus, since he was continually assuming fresh incarnations." This protean quality asserted itself in a practical way in Thackeray's many talents that made him valuable to editors as a "general hand" before his imaginative genius was recognized—as a critic, travel writer, political correspondent, satirist, poet (well, versifier), and illustrator. In the novel this faculty for "continually assuming fresh incarnations" manifested itself in a unique ability appreciated by his more observant reviewers for "making his men and women talk each in their own voice and tongue" (as John Brown phrased it), for assimilating a myriad of character types, and for expressing an entire diapason of moods. When it turned to creation of fictitious people, Thackeray's nimble, mercurial mind enabled him to act upon humanity, in the words of the editor and critic Richard Holt Hutton, "as a kind of pliant material, a moral india-rubber." What Thackeray's detractors considered dilettantism or opportunism, Sala and others rightly discerned as insatiable intellectual curiosity and interest in all things human, and a virtually universal empathy.

"The more fully his life is made known to the world, the more clearly will the harmony of his works with it appear," wrote James Hannay, a friend and fellow novelist, in one of the first memoirs to appear after Thackeray's death. This prophecy has not been borne out. Thanks to modern scholarship, which has documented the career of Thackeray in greater and greater amplitude, we know far more about his life than did his contemporaries, but, paradoxically, we are in a poorer position than they were to grasp "the harmony of his works." Thackeray must be unique among great Victorian writers in maintaining his major stature on the basis of so small a segment of his vast output. So little of Thackeray's writing being known to the general public, or for that matter to the Victorian scholar, they must take on faith the assertion of David Masson that it has "a more constant element of doctrine, a more distinct vein of personal philosophy than could be found in the work of most other novelists," or George Saintsbury's never disputed (but never proved) observation that Thackeray's work is all of a piece. Although we have seen Thackeray steadily, we cannot be said to have seen him whole.

Obviously a writer of Thackeray's formidable versatility eludes easy capture as much as did Proteus, to whom he has been likened. Apart from this complexity, the fact that Thackeray's success with the great public came late (by contrast with Dickens) has meant that readers now tend to take him up in mid-career with little sense of what came before. *Vanity Fair* and *Henry Esmond*, it stands to reason, did not arise out of a vacuum, nor did Thackeray cease to develop with these two masterpieces. To study Thackeray in full span is to strengthen one's conviction that the caricaturist, artist, critic, traveler, lecturer, historian, and novelist are essentially parts of a continuum. To read through the canon, the "small potatoes" (in his words) as well as the big ones, the "chronicles of small beer" as well as the epical novels, is to discover that although his public recognition was delayed, Thackeray matured early as a writer (it is significant that he was appreciated by intellectuals and by fellow writers before he was taken up by the common reader), and that his progress was not so much an intellectual or artistic development as an expansion of his range and a softening and deepening of his tone.

Even his late works, generally regarded as a creative decline, carry on the curve of his growth, affording him opportunity to reassess himself as man and writer and the age for which he wrote. Early and late, Thackeray never ceases to prod and stimulate us.

"A highly cultured writer, endowed with all the requisites of his calling, a wit reminiscent of Horace, a philosophy as practical as that of Montaigne, but expressed in a language which is as polished and scholarlike as Pope's was in verse, and revealing a knowledge of human nature so wide and comprehensive in its range that it seems unrivalled in the annals of fiction." This eulogy by Charles Eastlake pretty well sums up the esteem in which Thackeray was held on both sides of the Atlantic at the time of his premature death. The philosophic side of Thackeray is perhaps insufficiently appreciated in our age, which generally has responded to his wit more than to his wisdom. Modern critics have been all too ready to take at face value Thackeray's alleged remark that he had "no head above his eyes," but it was his mind above all that impressed his contemporaries. In the memoir appended to the Biographical Edition of the collected works, Leslie Stephen called attention to Thackeray's precocity. His aunt, Mrs. Ritchie, "was alarmed by discovering that the child could wear his uncle's hat, till she was assured by a physician that the big head had a good deal in it." Others besides Charlotte Brontë verified this observation in later life. Dr. John Brown for one wrote: "There was an immense quantity, not less than the finest quality of mind in everything he said. You felt this when with him and when you measured with your eye his enormous brain." A famous drawing by John Leech, in fact, depicts Thackeray as a gigantic, broad-domed head hovering over a lectern. An ample image of the reputation Thackeray attained among Victorian readers and audiences, the Leech sketch can serve as well as an emblem for this study.

Thackeray's assumed modesty about his intellectual ability, the unabashed hackmanship of his early career, his notorious dickering over line rates, have left the impression that he went into literature more under economic necessity than out of any genuine calling. Yet one finds him making an effort, even during his freelancing journalistic days, to establish himself as a writer worthy to be taken seriously. "Ought I take a post script to assure you that I can be as grave as another upon occasion?" he wrote at the end of a letter early in 1842 to the publishers Chapman and Hall. At this time he was making application for an editorial post (unsuccessfully, as it turned out) and put his best foot forward firmly: "I can

"Mr. Michael Angelo Titmarsh as he appeared at Willis' Rooms in his celebrated character of Mr. Thackeray," by John Leech (the artist standing in rear of room, his back to the reader). (From volume 11 of *The Works of William Makepeace Thackeray* [Centenary Biographical Edition]; reproduced by permission of John Murray, Ltd.)

show you performances of mine quite as solemn as need be. What I mean is this, that I can appreciate grave things very soundly I believe and know that the Titmarsh style is occasionally fitted to review writing." If, as Dickens complained, he at times "feigned a want of earnestness," the pose can be attributed partially to his model Montaigne as well as to his gentleman's classical education:

both taught him to eschew pedantry, and to carry learning lightly. His extended apprenticeship in the Victorian literary marketplace, moreover, gradually accustomed him to accommodate himself to minds less cultivated than his own. As a result it became quite natural for him to pose as the average man on "Our Street." Although he had an inquiring mind of unusual acuity, his leaning toward the concrete in preference to the abstract made him additionally suited by temperament to speak to the ordinary reader.

The chapters that follow attempt to set Thackeray more firmly in his time and place as a representative Victorian man of letters than previous critical studies have done. In an earlier book, *Fiction with a Purpose*, I examined several nineteenth-century novels as "repositories of literary history," and urged the importance of seeing their authors in relation to their original sociocultural environment. As I pointed out, the novel, examined in this context, established its respectability through its association with mental and moral cultivation, in common with the more outright didactic forms of literature. The present study extends on its predecessor from a different angle—concentrating on the career of an author who was especially instrumental in elevating the status of both the writer and the novel during the last century. Viewed in this light, Thackeray emerges as a remarkable example of a recurrent Victorian literary type, the high popularizer, who answered, if in an idiosyncratic way, to the needs of a serious kind of reader who had emerged in the nineteenth century, the cultural aspirant, and catered to the strong desire for "improvement" encouraged by adult educators—clerical and lay. This was an age, it must be borne in mind, when such aspiration lacked the kinds of outlet that today we take for granted—public libraries, university extension courses, educational mass media—so that the novel took upon itself an instructional burden that it has tended to cast off in the twentieth century. His versatility and adaptability equipped Thackeray well to assume the role of public educator. To account for his success in this capacity I have explored his particular background; the framework of journalism and popular reading that he worked in; his alertness to literary trends and his endeavors both to imitate and to transcend them; and his continuing dialogue with the reading public.

Early in the year when *Vanity Fair* was published, Thackeray wrote to Mark Lemon, the editor of *Punch*: "I should have sneered at the idea of setting up as a teacher at all . . . but I have got to believe in the business, and in many other things since then." However, in his early "magazinery" we see him "setting up as a teacher," if somewhat deviously, by toying with the vogue for potted learning promoted by the diffusers of useful knowledge. Charles Yellowplush is acquainted with one "Dr. Larnder" who turns up again as Dionysius Diddler in Thackeray's aborted Foolscap Library (an obvious hit at Dr. Lardner's Cabinet Cyclopedia). The garrulous, Münchausen-like narrator of *The Tremendous Adventures of Major Gahagan* claims to be supplementing the military histories of India by Gleig, James Mill, and Thorn. Fitz-Boodle, the editor of the "Men's Wives" series in *Fraser's Magazine* and alumnus of Slaughterhouse, boasts of "that immense fund of classical knowledge which in after life has been so exceedingly useful to him," though he proves something of a noodle in coping with practical life. The anonymous narrator of "Captain Rook and Mr. Pigeon" refers to the "romances of Adam Smith, Malthus, and Ricardo, and the philosophical works of Miss Martineau" presumably as a fitting introduction to his own tale of political economy with its illustrations of the fortuitous ways of money and the misappropriation of wealth. In collecting the papers of Charles Yellowplush, Michael Angelo Titmarsh claims to have enlisted the aid of the learned Doctor Strumpff, an eminent philologist from Bonn, to decipher this "Cockniac dialect." The reader is further informed that Strumpff "has compiled a copious vocabulary and notes, has separated the mythic from the historical part of the volume, and discovered that it is, like Homer, the work of many ages and persons." Miss Tickletoby, the schoolmistress of St. Mary Axe, authoress of a series of *Lectures on English History* printed in *Punch*, prefigures in facetious manner the later Thackeray of Willis's Rooms, the Mechanics Institutes, and the lycea. The role that he mocked while he practiced it is immediately evoked on the title page of one of Thackeray's Christmas stories, *Doctor Birch and His Young Friends*, with its etching of a master in cap and gown, whip in one hand, open book in the other.

Thackeray could be said to have lisped in parody. At Charterhouse he rewrote L.E.L.'s sentimental poem "Violets" as "Cabbages." At Cambridge he wrote a mock prize poem "Timbuctoo." This form of mimicry, which in his maturity brought the resentment of fellow writers down on his head, was really a part of his literary education, a means of finding his own path as author. His better known parodies, such as *Punch's Prize Novels*, expose literary pretension or false sentiment. Many of his "jokes and schoolboy exercises," as we have noted, ape intellectual pretension—pedantry

and pseudolearning of various sorts, perversions of the didactic
purpose of art that he believed in. Thackeray also, along with his
readers, had been brought up on edifying tracts and chapbooks,
and in his magazinery he slyly plays along with the sort of moral
tags with which authors were expected to point their tales. In his
first tale, "The Professor," the title character, "Professor" Dandolo,
is revealed as a lecher and thief; the Seminary of the Misses Pidge
where he taught is ruined by disgrace; and the heroine goes mad.
Yet these disasters have their consolation: "Gentles, my tale is told,"
it concludes with an address to the reader. "If it may have deterred
one soul from vice, my end is fully answered." "Captain Rook and
Mr. Pigeon" ends with this high sentence: "The moral of the above
remarks I take to be this: that blacklegging is as bad a trade as can
be; and so let parents and guardians look to it, and not apprentice
their children to such a villainous, scurvy way of living." In other
rook-and-pigeon tales, Thackeray enjoyed pseudomoralizing, making the worse appear the better cause. "It was charmin to hear this
pair of raskles talking about *honour*," recalls Charles Yellowplush of
his master Deuceace and a crony as they are about to fleece a
hapless young law clerk. "I declare I could have found it in my
heart to warn young Dawkins of the precious way in which these
young chaps were going to serve him. But if they didn't know what
honour was, I did; and never did I tell tails about my masters when
in their service, *out*, in cors, the hobbligation is no longer binding."
This rationalizing of slippery conduct is elaborated in *Barry Lyndon*
and, at its subtlest, underlies Becky Sharp's self-delusion. In his
"comicalities and whimsicalities," Thackeray shows us the farcical
side of the "moral philosopher" who guides our reactions in the
great novels.

Thackeray considered his calling "as serious as the Parson's
own," but he became an unusual parson. He recognized, as with the
Reverend Grimes Wapshot and the Reverend Charles Honeyman,
that a forked tongue can be concealed beneath pious words. The
ultimate point of his satires on moralizing is that no amount of wise
saws and adages can make a man moral whose heart and conscience
remain unchanged. The widow Crawley is still essentially Becky
Sharp even when she writes hymns and becomes a pillar of the
church at Bath and Cheltenham. What the great reading public
needed, as far as he was concerned, was not more and more professions of the good and the right, but more insight into the insidious
sources of evil. Life itself, as he said in his poem "Vanitas Vanitatum," contains many "homilies on human glories" open to the

view of those ready to look into it—and into themselves—with candor and honesty. "I have said this book is all about the world and a respectable family dwelling in it. It is not a sermon, except where it cannot help itself, and the speaker pursuing the destiny of his narrative finds such a homily before him," reads an address to the reader at the end of the first volume of *The Newcomes*. "O friend, in your life, don't we light upon such sermons daily?—don't we see at home as well as amongst our neighbors that battle betwixt Evil and Good?"

This "battle betwixt Evil and Good" is one waged constantly through Thackeray's books, which in their totality constitute a grand epic of the conscience, a continuing moral inquiry into human affairs, jointly participated in by author, reader, and the author's fictitious personages. Even before *Vanity Fair*, as the first chapters of this study will show, Thackeray conceived of life as a moral fable, of mankind as a series of object lessons, and of his history as a series of flashes of truth amidst long stretches of delusion. His Human Comedy therefore is largely a Comedy of Errors. Through its chapters walk criminals, demireps, the shabby genteel, and the respectable; dupes, gulls, coxcombs, and charlatans; cynics, skeptics, and sentimentalists; heroes and ordinary men and women; sinners, saints, and those in between—A Victorian Field Full of Folk. All of these people are caught up in currents larger than themselves, play their brief parts in social history, are molded by forces of which they are but dimly aware, if at all, but which their creator sees as through a glass darkly. His subject is no less than "the hidden and awful Wisdom which apportions the destinies of mankind," as he expressed it in a chapter of *Vanity Fair*. He expounded on this theme later in the poem "Vanitas Vanitatum" inspired by an album containing the autographs of distinguished men from all walks of life:

> What histories of life are here,
>   More wild than all romancers' stories;
> What wondrous transformations queer,
>   What homilies on human glories!
>
> What theme for sorrow or for scorn!
>   What chronicle of Fate's surprises—
> Of adverse fortune nobly borne,
>   Of chances, changes, ruins, rises!

·   ·   ·   ·   ·   ·   ·

How low men were and how they rise!
  How high they were and how they tumble!
O vanity of vanities!
  O laughable, pathetic jumble!

.   .   .   .

Methinks the text is never stale,
  And life is every day renewing
Fresh comments on the old old tale
  Of Folly, Fortune, Glory, Ruin.

Our author's "glances, at once inquiring and critical," then, penetrated wide and deep. The "canvass of humanity" that a fellow Fraserian identified as the proper study of the modern writer seems the phrase most fitting to describe the life work of one who wrought skillfully with both pen and pencil, and whose hand worked busily along with his head. Although I attempt to do justice to Thackeray's achievement as a whole, there are certain limitations to the ensuing study that should be clarified. My concern being principally with the life of Thackeray's mind, I have seen no reason to go over the biographical ground already so thoroughly and so admirably covered by Gordon Ray. Personal events are occasionally alluded to where pertinent, but general knowledge of Thackeray's life history, being so easily accessible, is taken for granted. (For convenience, some highlights are pointed up in the appended Chronology.) I have given only incidental attention also to the political and social issues that form the staple of general histories of the Victorian period, in favor of the cultural environment that I believe more immediately conditioned Thackeray's writing. Fully recognizing that his accomplishment cannot be wholly accounted for by such external causes (there is always the elusive element of "genius"), I have endeavored to relate the novels as far as possible to their various circumstances of publication, to their presumed audiences, as well as to contemporaneous literary vogues and currents of ideas (including some explored by Thackeray himself in reviews and other nonfiction). If to some I may seem to skirt the ultimate question of *evaluation*, I think that what is far more important for Thackeray is *understanding*—particularly of the original motive and intent behind his successive works of fiction. Precisely because he was so deeply rooted in his own times, Thackeray, of all Victorian writers, least lends himself to interpretation by twentieth-century literary, linguistic, and psychological theories.

To scant his position as not only the "Gentle Censor" of his age, but its cultural historian as well, is to miss his essential importance and dimension as a writer.

The unique commingling in Thackeray of thinker, aesthete, and entertainer, his easy familiarity with virtually all levels of Victorian culture—humanistic learning, journalism high and low, the lecture platform, popular arts—dictate to an extent the scope and structure of this book. The first section considers in four interlocking chapters general influences on Thackeray: the reading that shaped his attitudes and turned his interest in particular to what we today call social psychology, the study of man collectively as well as individually; followed by his response respectively to art, theater, and early Victorian progenitors of mass media, aspects of his culture that clearly determined his approach to fiction. The larger part of this study is devoted to a more intensive contextual analysis of individual novels, taken up chronologically within related groups according to their origins and to stages of Thackeray's development. The whole, it is hoped, will convey some sense of the rich, accretive imagination that Thackeray brought to his multiple career: the "natural perversity of vision," as he once put it, that enabled him to move so nimbly from waggery to wisdom, and to view life as through a kaleidoscope; the childlike fondness for fantasy and grotesquerie combined with sophistication and urbanity; the "strange and rare mixture of relish for things of the street and things of the study" (in the words of George Saintsbury) that made him a highbrow of lowbrow sympathies; the cosmopolitan sensibility fed by the triple streams of Great Britain, the continent, and America; and, above all, the sense of humility and mortal fallibility that impelled him, with all his genius, to speak to his audiences "as a man and a brother."

Part One

"THE HUMOROUS EGO"
Panoramic Vision

My dear Sir.

I hardly know what subjects to point out as suited to my capacity—light matters connected with Art, humorous reviews, critiques of novels—French subjects, memoirs, poetry, history from Louis XV downwards and of an earlier period—that of Froissart and Monstrelet. German light literature and poetry—though of these I know but little beyond what I learned in a year's residence in the Country fourteen years ago: finally subjects relating to society in general where a writer may be allowed to display the humorous *ego*, or a victim to be gently immolated. But I am better able to follow than to lead and should hope to give satisfaction in my small way.

Thackeray, letter to Thomas Longman,
proprietor of the *Edinburgh Review*, 6 April 1845

"THE WHOLE EDIFICE OF HUMANITY"

Chapter One

"FURNISH YOURSELF WITH A RICH VARIETY OF ideas; acquaint yourself with things ancient and modern; things natural, civil, and religious; things domestic and national; things of your native land, and of foreign countries; things present, past, and future," reads an early chapter of *Logic; or, The Right Use of Reason*, by Isaac Watts, one of the eighteenth-century authors who retained a place on Thackeray's library shelves alongside his sets of Swift, Fielding, Smollett, and the *Spectator*. "And above all," concludes this sentence, "be well acquainted with God and yourselves; learn animal nature, and the workings of your own spirits."[1] Watts was standard reading for the young at least through the middle of the nineteenth century, and the 1824 imprint of the copy that Thackeray owned suggests that it may have been one of his school texts.[2] Whether on his own inclination or by the persuasion of the Reverend Watts, he certainly followed out the "General Directions" prescribed by this wise doctor for the education of the mind:

> The way of attaining such an extensive treasure of ideas is, with diligence to apply yourself to read the best books, converse with the most knowing and the wisest of men, and endeavour to improve by every person in whose company you are ... visit other cities and countries, when you have seen your own, under the care of one who can teach you to profit by traveling, and to make wise observations: indulge a just curiosity in seeing the wonders of art and nature, search into things yourselves, as well as learn them from others; be acquainted with men as well as books; learn all things as much as you can from first hand; and let as many of your ideas as possible be the

Thackeray at age 21. From a drawing by Daniel Maclise (1832). (Frontispiece to
volume 3 of *The Works of William Makepeace Thackeray* [Biographical Edition]; reproduced by kind permission of the Garrick Club.)

representation of things; and not merely the representation of other
men's ideas; thus your soul, like some noble building, shall be richly
furnished with original paintings, and not mere copies.

Universal curiosity clearly is the prime intellectual virtue that Dr.
Watts hoped to implant in young souls. According to his scheme,

books are but one means to improve each shining hour—others being stimulating society, cosmopolitan travel, and immersion in "the wonders of art and nature." All of these were freely engaged in by the youthful William Makepeace Thackeray, who visited many foreign cities and countries in his double pursuit of culture and a livelihood, knew many men as well as many books, conferred with the great (notably Goethe during his *lehrjahr* in Weimar),[3] and literally attempted "original paintings, and not mere copies." A number of Thackeray's fictitious men and women also follow Watts's program. Colonel Newcome for one believed "It was good for Clive to see men and cities; to visit mills, manufactories, country seats, cathedrals," and Clive, an apt pupil, "asked a hundred questions regarding all things about him."[4] In *Vanity Fair* Dobbin carefully directs Amelia Sedley's observations on her travels, and one plate in illustrated editions shows her sketching "from the life" with his approval.[5] Watts's curriculum for self-education, however, is not intended to make one merely a passive observer of life, but to stimulate the powers of reason, on a firm basis of experience. In religion Watts was no mystic (one of his books is called *A Humble Attempt towards the Revival of Practical Religion among Christians*), and in his logic he tended to follow Locke's empirical principles. In this respect he anticipates the creed that guided Thackeray's practice first in painting and was then transferred to his writing. Watts urged on young students what Thackeray repeatedly advised artists to do: "Copy Nature."[6] Watts's stress on direct contact with phenomena looks forward to Thackeray's own doctrine of "originality" in art and literature. His preference for "things" over "ideas" is also suggestive to those who recall Thackeray's consistent championship of the "real" in favor of the "ideal" in paintings and in books.

Basic also to the cultivation of "right reason" for Watts, and an aid toward understanding the "workings" of the spirit, was a certain critical attitude toward men and things. Cognizant as he was of original sin, he was well prepared for "the disguise and false colours in which many things appear to us in this original state." He knew how prone men were to take the apparent for the real: "We are imposed upon at home as well as abroad; we are deceived by our senses, by our imaginations, by our passions and appetites; by the authority of men; by education and by custom &c; and we are led into frequent errors, by judging according to these false and flattering principles, rather than according to the nature of things." Speaking as a practical man, he attributes such aberrations to the frailty of the flesh, to the slow maturing of judgment, and, speaking as a theologian, to the corruption of our faculties resulting from the primordial fall from grace. Human nature being what it is, we are put on our guard: "There are a thousand things which are not in reality what they appear to be . . . both in the natural and in the moral world." Just as the sun appears to be both small and flat, the moon the same size as the sun, and the rainbow arched and colored, "so knavery puts on the face of justice; hypocrisy and superstition wear the vizard of piety; deceit and evil are often clothed in the shapes and appearances of truth and goodness. Now Logic helps us to strip off the outward disguise of things and behold them, and judge of them in their own nature."[7]

Readers of *Vanity Fair*, to point to the most obvious example, have certainly been made acquainted with the false faces put on by knavery and hypocrisy, and know well how ready Thackeray is to "strip off the outward disguises of things." In one of his first books, Thackeray styled himself as "foe to humbug in all its shapes and hues . . . his smooth brother hypocrisy, or his sickly sister, sentiment,"[8] and his novels all attempt to disentangle the webs men weave, others to deceive. One passage from Watts's *Logic* entitled "The Springs of False Judgment" could almost serve as an epigraph for *The Book of Snobs*, Thackeray's hypothetical anatomy of society:

> We are tempted to form our judgments of persons as well as things by these outward appearances: Where there is wealth, equipage and splendor, we are ready to call that man happy, but we see not the vexing disquietudes of his soul; and when we spy a person in ragged garments, we form a despicable opinion of him too suddenly: we can hardly think him either happy or wise, our judgment is so strangely biassed by outward or sensible things. . . . .
> . . . This prejudice is cured by a longer acquaintance with the world, and a just observation that things are sometimes better and sometimes worse than they appear to be.
> . . . Remember that a grey beard does not make a philosopher; all is not gold that glitters; and a rough diamond may be worth an immense sum.[9]

The better part of wisdom for Watts, as for the ancient Greeks, was the recognition that appearances are deceiving and seeing is not believing. At the same time, in view of the impure state of the world, he urges us to treat our fellow men with forbearance, not, in short, "to judge in the lump."

> There is scarce anything in the world of nature or of art, in the world of morality or religion, that is perfectly uniform. There is a mixture

of wisdom and folly, vice and virtue, good and evil, both in men and in things. We should remember that some persons have great wit and little judgment; others are judicious, but not witty. Some are good humoured without compliment; others have all the formalities of complaisance, but no good humour. We ought to know that one man may be vicious and learned, while another has virtue without learning. That many a man thinks admirable well, who has a poor utterance; while others have a charming manner of speech, but their thoughts are trifling and impertinent. Some are good neighbours, and courteous, and charitable toward men, who have no piety towards God; others are truly religious, but of morose natural tempers. Some excellent sayings are found in very silly books; and some silly things appear in books of value. We should neither praise or dispraise by wholesale, but separate the good from the evil, and judge them apart; the accuracy of a good judgment consists much in making such distinctions.[10]

The inability of mankind in general to discriminate in this way is the purport of Fitz-Boodle's address to the reader that ends the first version of *Barry Lyndon*: "Justice, forsooth! Does human life always exhibit justice . . .? Is it the good always who ride in gold coaches, and the wicked who go to the workhouse? Is a humbug never preferred before a capable man? Does the world always reward merit, never worship cant, never raise mediocrity to distinction? Never crowd to hear a donkey braying from a pulpit, nor ever buy the tenth edition of a fool's book?"[11] Thackeray's own "laughable, pathetic jumble" of a world presents us with a heady "mixture of wisdom and folly, vice and virtue, good and evil." He shows us that charm is not always combined with virtue (v. Becky Sharp), or virtue for that matter with intelligence (Amelia), that one may have the spiritual graces without the social ones (as with Dobbin), that a charitable disposition may be joined to unworldliness and pride (Colonel Newcome), that a glib tongue does not necessarily bespeak wisdom (the Reverend Honeyman), and that a vicious nature can easily conceal itself beneath piety and respectability (Barnes Newcome).

The "Right Use of Reason" then, for Watts, meant a guarded skepticism toward men's pronouncements and pretensions, along with circumspection in judging their characters. "The true method of delivering ourselves from . . . prejudice," he preaches in the section on "The Springs of False Judgement," is "to view a thing on all sides; to compare all the various appearances of the same thing with one another, and let each of them have its full weight in the balance of our judgment."[12] The ideal corrective to prejudice and misjudgment, then, is "a universal acquaintance with things" that should both "keep you from being too positive and dogmatical," and forestall "an excess of credulity and unbelief." In the judicious assessment of men's characters and motives that Thackeray attempted in his writings, both fictitious and nonfictitious, he seems to have taken these words to heart.

There is evidence that Thackeray pursued his interest in what Dr. Watts called "the workings of your own spirits" as a student in Paris, in the midst of painting in various ateliers, visits to art museums, avid theatergoing, and dips into "light literature." In reviewing these years on the basis of a diary he kept, Anne Thackeray singles out three authors who took special hold of her father's imagination—another prominent eighteenth-century English thinker and two French savants. Apart from novels and plays, she informs us, "He also reads in Gibbon and studies old Montaigne and is absorbed by Cousin's 'History of Philosophy.'"[13] These three figures played their parts in Thackeray's intellectual development in demonstrable ways.

"Gibbon was an infidel; and I would not give the end of this cigar for such a man's opinion," fumes Colonel Newcome at Clive and his friends.[14] He is not, we gather, speaking for Thackeray, who was a devotee of this apostle of common sense as far back as his university days. At Cambridge he read the "infidel"'s Decline and Fall of the Roman Empire along with the histories of Hume and Smollett, and a letter of the 1850s indicates familiarity with the Memoirs.[15] His private library included the Miscellaneous Works, edited by Gibbon's friend and literary executor, John Lord Sheffield.[16] In his introduction to the set, Sheffield emphasizes the value in particular of Gibbon's more subjective writings, the Memoirs, as well as of the Letters and Journal: "Few men, I believe, have ever so fully unveiled their own character, by a minute narrative of their sentiments and pursuits as Mr. Gibbon will here be found to have done; not with study and labour—not with an affected frankness—but with a genuine confession of his little foibles and peculiarities, and a good-humoured and natural display of his own conduct and opinions."

Sheffield based this observation on Gibbon's own credo expressed at the beginning of his uncompleted autobiography: "Truth, naked, unblushing truth, the first virtue of more serious history, must be the sole recommendation of this personal narrative." Contributing to the effect of truthfulness is clarity of language, and accordingly the author promises that "the style shall be simple and familiar; but style is the image of character; and the habits of correct writing may produce, without labour or design, the appearance of art and study." Although professing no motive for writing this "personal narrative" beyond his own diversion, Gibbon foresees that it might have a more lasting value: "Yet a sincere and simple narrative of my own life may amuse some of my leisure hours; but it will subject me, and perhaps with justice, to the imputation of vanity. I may judge, however, from the experience both of past and of the present times, that the public are always curious to know the men, who have left behind them any image of their minds: the most scanty accounts of such men are compiled with diligence, and pursued with eagerness; and the student of every class may derive a lesson, or an example, from the lives most similar to his own."

In his apology Gibbon places himself squarely within the tradition of exemplary biography. With no false modesty he speaks of himself as the latest in a long line of illustrious self-portraitists stretching from Pliny the Younger to "the philosophic Hume." Instructive memoirs, he points out, have been conveyed in a variety of forms: in letters, as with Pliny and Erasmus; in essays, as with Montaigne and Sir William Temple; in sermons, as with Huet; in confessions, as with St. Augustine and Rousseau. All of these men, in their different ways, "disclose the secrets of the human heart." Moreover, sinners as well as saints, Gibbon feels, can contribute to our moral education, as, for example, Benvenuto Cellini with his "headstrong passions" and Colley Cibber with his "gay follies."

Thackeray's affinity for "personal history" as a means of character revelation is conspicuous throughout his canon. Not only did he draw freely upon memoirs, journals, diaries, and letters as sources for his novels; he also tended to disguise his "sham histories" as "true accounts," as indicated by the titles of such "comicalities and whimsicalities" as *Cox's Diary*, *The Memoirs of Mr. Charles James Yellowplush*, *Fitz-Boodle's Confessions*, *The History of Samuel Titmarsh and the Great Hoggarty Diamond*, *The Diary of C. Jeames De La Pluche, Esq. . . . with His Letters*, no less than his serious works, such as *The History of Pendennis: His Fortunes and Misfortunes . . .*, *The History of Henry Esmond, Esq.*, *The Newcomes: Memoirs of a Most Respectable Family*, and *The Roundabout Papers*. Along with the form of the memoir, Thackeray cultivated the intimate style of writing favored by Gibbon, with its lucidity, candor, apparent artlessness, and spontaneity. Although he disguised himself behind numerous pseudonyms and alter egos, Thackeray conveyed the "image of character" through language. "Why a man's books may not always speak the truth, but they speak his mind in spite of himself," he confessed, looking back over his career in one of his Roundabout essays.[17] He was not hesitant to "lay bare his own weaknesses, vanities, peculiarities," as he confided to his readers in the preface to *Pendennis*.

"My defects . . . my imperfections, and my natural form, so far as public reverence hath permitted me," was the announced subject of the *Essais* of Montaigne, understandably much admired by Gibbon. "Read in noble old Montaigne," Thackeray recorded in a diary,[18] only one indication of his attraction to the Frenchman's combination of self-centeredness and humility. Montaigne is a bedside book for the meditative Henry Esmond and for the wise Colonel Lambert of *The Virginians,* as he remained for their creator as late as his editorship of *Cornhill Magazine.*[19] Thackeray owned three sets of the *Essays,* two in French, one translated into English "with very considerable amendments and improvements from the most accurate and elegant French edition" of Peter (or Pierre) Coste. Coste was instrumental in the revival of Montaigne's reputation in the early eighteenth century after a period of neglect.[20] First published in 1724, his edition was several times revised and reprinted during the century, and remained in vogue through the early part of the next. Besides addressing himself conscientiously to the editorial tasks of establishing, emending, and annotating the text (which had become badly garbled, as well as obscure to this generation of readers), Coste also set himself up as apologist for the author. Defending the master from a reputation for excessive self-esteem that he had acquired among the general public, Coste, in introducing the *Essays*, stresses the unflagging honesty (in the original, "cette noble candeur . . . qui ne se dément jamais") that is observable throughout the work. In making himself the subject of his book, affirms Coste, Montaigne displays not mere egoism, but a genuine compassion for the human race; he has written about himself, "not so much out of vanity, as to communicate instruction." The reader, Coste argues, is really as much the subject of the book as the author: "'Tis certain . . . that the picture he has here drawn of himself, is in the nature of a faithful mirror, wherein all men may discover some of their features, if they will but take the trouble to view themselves in it attentively, and with an honest design to see what they are in reality." Against those who complain that Montaigne talks too much about himself, Coste hurls back the essayist's own rejoinder that men do not think enough about themselves. Most men, he adds, turn away from the mirror that Montaigne holds up to them, out of cowardice, self-complacence, or sense of shame. The arduous task that Montaigne has imposed upon himself of "painting himself without disguise" offers a challenge to all human beings to do likewise, Coste suggests, adding that there have been a few feeble imitators, but the generality lack the courage even to make the attempt.

Thackeray's latter-day *persona* Mr. Batchelor cannot be so accused. "I may have been wrong, but I am candid," he confides. "I tell my misdeeds; some fellows hold their tongues."[21] In his first novel, *Catherine*, his particularly candid narrator, Ikey Solomons, himself a convicted criminal, upbraids us for a more serious kind of dishonesty, evasion of moral responsibility: "Some call the doctrine of destiny a dark creed; but for me, I would fain try and think it a consolatory one. It is better, with all one's sins upon one's head, to deem oneself in the hands of Fate than to think, with our fierce passions and weak repentances, with our resolves so loud, so vain, so ludicrously, despicably weak and frail, with our dim wavering, wretched conceits about virtue, and our irresistible propensity to wrong, that we are the workers of our future sorrow or happiness."[22] Solomons here has echoed in harsher voice these words of wisdom of Montaigne relating to Good and Evil: "Fortune does us neither good nor hurt; she only presents us the matter and the seed, which our soul, more powerful than she, turns and applies as best she pleases; the sole cause and sovereign mistress of her own happy or unhappy condition. . . . The things are not so painful and difficult of themselves, but our weaknesses or cowardice makes them so. To judge of great and high matters requires a suitable soul; otherwise we attribute the vice to them which is really our own."[23]

The fault is in ourselves, not in our stars. It is understandable, then, that the memoir became for Thackeray what the essay was for Montaigne, an opportunity for probing the self. "Reader, thou hast here an honest book: it doth at the outset forewarn thee that, in contriving the same, I have proposed to myself no other than a domestic and private end . . . ," reads Montaigne's famous prefatory address. "I hope I shall always like to hear men, in reason talk about themselves. What subject does a man know better" declared Thackeray in one of his Roundabout Papers.[24] In some of his "chronicles of small beer," to be sure, he ridiculed the self-conscious narrator revealing himself like the garrulous illiterate Charles Yellowplush, the pompous George Fitz-Boodle, and the gullible Bob Stubbs, who even echoes Montaigne ("Some poet has observed that if a man could write down what has really happened to him in this mortal life, he would be sure to make a good book"),[25] but here he was parodying a role that elsewhere he took seriously. The melancholic clown in cockade looking into a cracked glass who greets us on the title page of *Vanity Fair* in its first publication in book form is a graphic representation of Montaigne's "faithful mirror, wherein all men may discover some of their features."

Montaigne's mirror, however, is supposed to cast its light upon the world, as his editor Coste reminds us in his attempt to justify the egoism of the *Essays* as a form of altruism. Although Montaigne professes no more than "a domestic and private end," his editor asserts that he is really writing about all humanity, that Socrates' famous dictum "know thyself in order to know your fellow man" can justifiably be applied to his "honest book." Such an identity between writer and audience is attempted by the narrator of *Vanity Fair*. In one chapter, alluding to the famous wrapper design accompanying the monthly parts, he assures his readers that "the moralist who is holding forth on the cover (an accurate portrait of your humble servant) professes to wear neither gown nor bands, but only the long-eared livery in which his congregation is arrayed" (chap. 8). The preacher on the barrel top descends to the level of his "congregation" rather than attempting to raise them to his own, thus establishing rapport along with intimacy. So he can be confident that, in speaking for himself, he is speaking for them:

> "I" is here introduced to personify the world in general—the Mrs. Grundy of each respected reader's private circle—every one of whom can point to some families of his acquaintance who live nobody knows how. Many a glass of wine have we all of us drunk, I have very little doubt, hob-and-nobbing with the hospitable giver, and wondering how the deuce he paid for it. (Chap. 36)

> In a word everybody went to wait upon this great man [Lord Steyne]—everybody who was asked: as you the reader (do not say nay) or I the writer thereof would go if we had the invitation. (Chap. 47)

The prophet's admonition "Judge not, lest ye be judged" could well be affixed to Thackeray's books. This spirit of charity and humility joined to moral sensitivity unites him with Montaigne, along with a circuit of response that he sets up through his discourse from narrator to hypothetical personage, to reader, back to narrator:

> It is all vanity to be sure: but who will not own to liking a little of it? I should like to know what well-constituted mind, merely because it is transitory, dislikes roast-beef? That is a vanity; but may every man who reads this have a wholesome portion of it through life, I beg; ay,

though my readers were five hundred thousand. Sit down, gentle-men, and fall to, with a good hearty appetite; the fat, the lean, the gravy, the horse-radish as you like it—don't spare it. Another glass of wine, Jones my boy—a little bit of the Sunday side. Yes, let us eat our fill of the vain thing, and be thankful therefor. And let us make the best of Becky's aristocratic pleasures likewise—for these too, like all mortal delights, were transitory. (Chap. 51)

Thackeray apparently agreed that "A free and generous confes-sion enervates reproach, and disarms slander," as Montaigne ob-serves in his essay called, as it happens, "On Vanity." Toward the end of this essay we read: "If other men would consider themselves at the rate I do, they would, as I do, discover themselves to be full of inanity and foppery; to rid myself of it, I cannot, without making myself away. We are steeped in it, as well one as another; but they who are not aware on't, have somewhat the better bargain; and yet, I know not, whether they have or no." That Victorian disciple of Montaigne, Mr. Batchelor, puts it more racily and succinctly: "I daresay I made a gaby of myself to the world: pray, my good friend, hast thou never done likewise? If thou hast never been a fool, be sure thou wilt never be a wise man."[26]

Thackeray regarded himself as a historian, but, to judge from his favorite reading, the forms of history that interested him most were "private history" and "secret history," works of reflection that helped men and women understand their own natures. "The con-dition of reflection is memory; and the condition of memory is time," wrote the philosopher-educator Victor Cousin in his *Cours de l'histoire de la philosophie*, the book that young Thackeray was "ab-sorbed by" in the reading room of the Palais Royal in Paris, accord-ing to his daughter. Thackeray's own remark at the time is laconic, but enthusiastic: "Read Cousin's History of Philosophy . . . am much pleased with Cousin his style & his spirit. The excitement of metaphysics must equal almost that of gambling."[27] This was trib-ute indeed from a young man about town whose own gambling fever was transferred to the "rooks and pigeons" of his early magazine stories such as Bob Stubbs, Jack Attwood, Algernon Deuceace, and Sam Titmarsh, and for whom the casino wheel and the gaming table attained emblematic significance as prominent as the stage, the masquerade and the ballroom in his "chronicles of fate's surprises." Thackeray came to Cousin in his maturity, and, despite a paucity of references to him in his writing, there is reason to believe that this philosopher was the most significant of all the early influences in the shaping of his mental attitude and in providing a frame of reference for his novels. Thackeray himself invites such conjecture by the words with which his diary entry ends: ". . . I found myself giving utterance to a great number of fine speeches & imagining many wild theories w^h I found it impossible to express on paper."

Contemporary witnesses testify to Cousin's charismatic power as a teacher. The book that Thackeray read grew out of a series of lectures that marked Cousin's resumption of his post at the Faculté des Lettres at the Sorbonne in 1828 after a period of political suppression. When first delivered, these lectures, according to an account by the Scottish philosopher Sir William Hamilton, "excited an unexampled sensation in Paris. . . . Two thousand auditors listened in admiration to the eloquent exposition of doctrines unintelligible to the many, and the oral discussion of philosophy awakened in Paris, and in France, an interest unexampled since the days of Abelard."[28] One member of the original audience, the novelist Stendhal, recorded in a notebook that although the professor's ideas were not altogether clear to him, they "électrisent néanmoins tous nos jeunes de vingt ans." Ernest Renan, who had been one of his students in a seminary, extolled M. Cousin as one who "nous enchantait," and believed him to be "un des exciateurs de ma pensée." Balzac and Sainte-Beuve are among other major literary figures who came under his spell, and such eminent intellectuals as Michelet, Quinet, Jouffroy, and Montalembert were drawn into his orbit in one way or another.[29]

Beyond his audience of students and men of letters, Sir William Hamilton tells us, Cousin's readership was extended by newspapers that printed digests of his lectures, and revised versions of the lectures themselves prepared by Cousin were disseminated in weekly parts throughout the provinces. The first translator of the Cours de l'histoire conveys the impression that the impact of Cousin's ideas was even more far-reaching. In an introduction prepared for his American readers he announced: "It is certain that philosophical views and doctrines are no longer regarded, on the continent of Europe, merely as subjects of literary curiosity or of elegant entertainment. For it is well known that they excite strong emotions of sympathy and approbation, and are listened to and read with that attention and respect which is the most satisfactory evidence of a powerful conviction of their rationality and truth, by a very numerous class of intelligent and well informed young men, who may be fairly considered to represent the flowering of the rising generation of their respective countries."[30]

Thackeray is the one among the "very numerous class of intelligent and well informed young men" whom we can account for. Among the entries in his diary for this period is a sentence from Cousin's lecture on Descartes's *Discourse on Method:* "Douter c'est croire, car doubter c'est penser, celui qui doute croit il qu'il doute ou doute-t-il qu'il doute—S'il doute qu'il doute Il détruit par cela même son scepticisme—& s'il croit qu'il doute il le détruit encore." ("To doubt is to believe; for to doubt is to think. Does he who doubts believe that he doubts, or does he doubt whether he doubt or not? If he doubt whether he doubt or not, he destroys his own skepticism; and if he believes that he doubts, he destroys it again.")[31] The theme of this lecture is brought out in the sentence immediately preceding the one Thackeray copied out, which reads in translation: "What is said of doubt, what Descartes has demonstrated in regard to doubt, applies with greater force to the idea of nothingness." Cousin's teachings, we can gather, have a bearing on Thackeray's own lifelong struggle against cynicism and skepticism—most explicitly dramatized in *Pendennis,* his most personal novel. Other aspects of Cousin's thought too are reflected in his writing.

Cousin was destined to become particularly influential on the education of the "rising generation" of his own country in a series of administrative posts that followed upon his return to the Sorbonne. Something of a persona non grata during the period of the Restoration because of his liberal views, he emerged as an Establishment figure under the July Monarchy that commenced in 1830, serving variously as State Councillor Extraordinary, member of the Royal Council of Public Instruction, Minister of Public Instruction (under Thiers), and Director of the Ecole Normale Supérieure. Although his administration did not go unchallenged, he had a virtually monopolistic control over the school system until the overthrow of the regime of Louis Philippe by the Revolution of 1848 and the subsequent coup d'état that brought in the regime of Louis Napoleon. In the purely intellectual realm, his system of thought, known as Eclecticism, dominated French philosophy until it was displaced by the followers of Auguste Comte's Positivism, demonstrating Cousin's own theory that "each [idea] serves its time; and, after having been useful, it must give place to another whose turn is come."[32]

Victor Cousin's reputation was kept alive after his death in 1867 by a circle of faithful disciples, but it has hardly outlasted his century. In ours there has been a tendency to downgrade him. He "was not a great philosopher, as is clear from any of his philosophical writings," asserts a modern student. "His language was rhetorical, his thought was naively and pompously idealistic, and his general attitude overbearing."[33] But the very affirmative nature of his thought, deplored by this critic, and the fervor with which it was expressed, account for Cousin's appeal to the impressionable youth of Thackeray's generation. His first biographer called him *"Restaurateur De La Philosophie Spiritualiste Au XIX Siècle,"* indicative of his importance in the history of ideas.[34] Cousin at first called his philosophy "the new idealism," signifying his reaction against the materialist tendency of the schools that had preceded him, the *sensualistes* (notably Condillac) of the Enlightenment, and the rationalist circle known as the *idéologues* in vogue during the Napoleonic period. It is true, however, that Cousin was not an original philosopher, his contribution to thought being rather as a historian and synthesizer of philosophies. *Eclecticism*, the overall term he early applied to his system as a whole, puts the emphasis where he wished it, on the process of inquiry itself, rather than on specific doctrines, on aim and purpose, rather than on content. For Cousin the very freedom from absolutism gave philosophy its preeminent position among humane studies. "After having . . . proclaimed the supremacy of philosophy, we hasten to add that it is essentially tolerant," he concluded his introductory lecture. "In fact philosophy is the understanding and the explanation of all things. Of what, then, aside from error and crime, can it be the enemy?"[35]

Cousin's "metaphysics" apparently attracted Thackeray by its comprehensiveness and its attitude of general tolerance, what Cousin called "universal sympathy." For Cousin the primary function of the philosopher in the modern world was to reconcile conflicting positions. As an eclectic he taught "that every system contains a part of the truth; that all systems taken together contain the whole truth, that there is no need to discover truth, only to unite its scattered fragments."[36] Thackeray himself was praised in his time for just this disinterested frame of mind. According to one of his admirers, he "offends no one by the vehemence of his opinions, nor by dogmatism of manner . . . [he] is not a man to create partizans, he espouses no 'cause': has no party." Another characterized his mind as a "hospitable brain . . . tolerant of contradictions." Cousin taught that "each system is true by what it affirms and false by what it denies." Thackeray's most recent biographer, Gordon Ray, in summing up his accomplishment, has written: "In his comprehensive and impartial appraisal of English life, Thackeray praised what was good, while he atttacked what was bad," a succinct enough statement of the eclectic position.[37]

We can understand too why Thackeray, with his introspective temperament, responded to the "philosophie spiritualiste" of Cousin. "The study of consciousness is the study of human nature," concludes the lecture on Descartes that Thackeray quoted in his diary. In "restoring" the mind to the primacy from which the "sensualists" had dislodged it, Cousin employed a term that was novel at the time: "Man is a universe in miniature; *psychology* [*la psychologie*] is universal science concentrated. Psychology contains and reflects everything, both that which is of God and that which is of the world—under the precise and determinate angle of consciousness; everything is brought within a narrow compass, but everything is there."[38] In his intuitive way Thackeray became a practitioner of this "universal science." He wrote once in a letter to an editor that he enjoyed the exercise of "the humorous *ego*," a less exact term than Cousin's "precise and determinate angle of consciousness," but indicating the pleasure he took in the play of mind over what Cousin called "that which is of the world," and which Thackeray referred to simply as "society in general."[39] What Cousin referred to as "that which is of God" also figures in Thackeray's fictional universe. In *Pendennis* he clearly dissociates himself from the law student Paley to whom "All was dark outside his reading lamp," so that "Love, and Nature, and Art (which is the expression of our praise and sense of the beautiful world of God) were shut out from him" (chap. 29). He is more in accord with Cousin, who affirmed in his lecture "The Idea of Philosophy" that "Philosophy does not cut from art its divine wings, but follows it in its flight, measures its reach and aim, Sister of Religion, it draws, from an initmate connection with her, powerful inspirations."[40]

Although he conceived of the mind as a microcosm, Cousin saw it as bounded by man's limitations. He distinguished between the "spontaneous reason" that we all share and the "reflective reason" unique to each individual. The "spontaneous reason" when it operates grasps the nature of reality in a flash of insight, but it is inhibited by the "reflective reason," which "considers the elements of thought successively and not all at once . . . [and] considers each, for a moment at least, in a state of isolation."[41] In one of his addresses to the reader in *Pendennis*, Thackeray describes this solipsistic condition: "O philosophic reader . . . a distinct universe walks about under your hat and under mine—all things in nature are different to each—the woman we look at has not the same features, the dish we eat from has not the same taste to the one and the other—you and I are but a pair of infinite isolations, with some fellow-islands a little more or less near to us?"[42] (chap. 16). The very wrapper design that confronted the first readers of *Pendennis*, showing the hero with chin in hand, puzzled and pondering, torn between the domestic virtues and evil spirits, can be interpreted as an emblem of the "reflective reason" beset with doubts and prone to error.

Because of their limited perspective and their state of isolation, "Men are scarcely ever more than halves and quarters of men; who, unable to understand, accuse each other," Cousin declares in a succeeding lecture. The philosopher, according to Cousin's ideal, transcends these limitations through his capacity to identify himself with all mankind by means of "universal sympathy": "And, do you know the means, gentlemen, by which you may arrive at this tolerance, or rather at this universal sympathy [Cousin addresses his students]? You can arrive at it on one condition only; and that is, that you yourselves get rid of every exclusive prepossession; that you embrace all the elements of thought, and thus reconstruct the whole edifice of humanity in your own minds." This accomplished, Cousin continues: ". . . whosoever of your fellow creatures may present himself to you, and whatever may be the exclusive idea that prepossesses him . . . will not be wanting to you; you will therefore, in him, pardon humanity; for you will comprehend it . . . because you will possess it entirely. This is the only remedy against the malady of fanaticism; which, whatever be its object, proceeds from nothing but the prepossession of the mind by one object exclusively, whilst we are ignorant of, and despise every other."[43]

Arthur Pendennis, in the course of one of his debates with his friend and fellow law student George Warrington, has his say on what Cousin denounced as "the malady of fanaticism": "'Make a faith or dogma absolute, and persecution becomes a logical consequence; and Dominic burns a Jew, or Calvin an Arian, or Nero a Christian, or Elizabeth or Mary a Papist or Protestant; or their father both or either, according to his humour; and acting without any pangs of remorse,—but on the contrary, with strict notions of duty fulfilled. Make dogma absolute, and to inflict or to suffer death becomes easy and necessary'" (chap. 61).

To make dogma absolute is, of course, just what Victor Cousin opposes. "I hope that those youths, who for some time will frequent this lecture room, will there contract different habits," he urged in his lecture entitled "Reflection—the Element of Error," that they will "learn to understand that, as every error should be treated with profound indulgence, and that all those halves of men that we constantly meet with around us, are, nevertheless, fragments of humanity, and that in them, we should still respect that truth and that humanity of which they participate." Arthur Pendennis has taken heed: "'You call me a sceptic because I acknowledge what *is*,'" continues his colloquy with Warrington; "'and in acknowledging that, be it linnet or lark, or priest or parson; be it, I mean, any single one of the infinite varieties of the creatures of God . . . I say that the study and acknowledgement of that variety amongst men especially increases our respect and wonder for the Creator, Commander, and Ordainer of all these minds so different, and yet so united'" (chap. 61).

The "profound indulgence" toward error that Victor Cousin preached called for an eclectic attitude toward men's opinions as well as toward systems of thought. "The truth, friend! . . . where is the truth?" exclaims Arthur Pendennis in another of his philosophic moods. "Show it me. That is the question between us. I see it on both sides. I see it on the Conservative side of the House, and amongst the Radicals, and even on ministerial benches. . . . If the truth is with all these, why should I take side with any one of them?" (chap. 61). Henry Esmond too is eclectic, on matters both spiritual and temporal:

> In the course of his reading (which was neither pursued with that seriousness or that devout mind which such a study requires), the youth found himself at the end of one month, a Papist, and was about to proclaim his faith; the next month a Protestant, with Chillingworth; and the third a sceptic, with Hobbes and Bayle.
>   . . . Harry brought his family Tory politics to college with him, to which he must add a dangerous admiration for Oliver Cromwell, whose side or King James's by turns, he often chose to take in the disputes which the young gentlemen used to hold in each other's rooms, where they debated the state of the nation, crowned and deposed kings, and toasted past and present heroes or beauties in flagons of college ale.[44]

Along with his open-mindedness, Henry, it might be added, displays an unusual disposition to "pardon humanity":

> I look into my heart and think that I am as good as my Lord Mayor, and know I am as bad as Tyburn Jack. Give me a chain and red gown and a pudding before me, and I could play the part of Alderman very well, and sentence Jack after dinner. Starve me, keep me from books and honest people, educate me to love dice, gin, and pleasure, and put me in Hounslow Heath, with a purse before me and I will

take it. "And I shall be deservedly hanged," say you, wishing to put an end to this prosing. I don't say no. I can't but accept the world as I find it, including a rope's end, as long as it is in fashion.[45]

The classical motto *Homo sum; humani nihil a me alienum puto* was invoked by Victor Cousin as the theme of his message of tolerance, the very same motto quoted by Thackeray in one of his early articles on popular literature.[46] Certainly no man was alien to Thackeray as a novelist. His vast gallery of characters, taking in criminals, gamblers, miscreants of various sorts, demireps, the more respectable classes of shopkeepers, professionals, and just ordinary citizens, all the way up to the gentry and the aristocracy, indeed scales the entire "edifice of humanity" from its subbasement to its summit.

In their aggregate Thackeray's novels add up to a cumulative effort on his part to "comprehend" humanity, in Victor Cousin's phrase, to "possess it entirely." His grand company of heroes, heroines, and subsidiary characters, from the naïfs of his early stories to the sophisticates of his later and better known ones, represent diverse "fragments of humanity" each with what Cousin called an "incomplete or partial view of things." He begins at the bottom rung with the ignorant or semiliterate, like Catherine Hayes corrupted by evil companions, and Morgiana (the soubrette of "The Ravenswing," with the voice and brain of a bird), the gullible, like Bob Stubbs, Bob Robinson, and Barber Cox, and assorted primitives, of whom Charles Yellowplush, of the "Cockniack" dialect and outlook on society, remains the most endearing as well as the most enduring. Up the social ladder, but not very far along the scale of intellect, braggarts such as Major Gahagan and Barry Lyndon betray their moral idiocy out of their own mouths. Subtler forms of self-delusion are exposed through the more cultivated or better-educated men and women of the larger books, who are nevertheless hemmed in by various mental blinders: Becky Sharp, a worldling too much in love with her own cleverness; Amelia Sedley, an intransigent sentimentalist; Arthur Pendennis, a selfish epicurean; Henry Esmond, a melancholic; Clive Newcome, who has to learn to discipline his sensibility no less than his father has to learn to curb his pride; Dr. Firmin, charming and gracious, but cold and unfeeling. As omniscient author (or "moral philosopher," as he liked to call himself) Thackeray performs the office of the philosopher that Victor Cousin visualized—to unite the "scattered fragments" of truth possessed by individuals in isolation and to

enlarge their "partial view of things" by a more total conception of
reality.

Thackeray's novels in toto amount to a composite of human nature, the truth of things viewed from varied "angles of consciousness" but in a single novel he tends to shift the angle periodically to
produce a psychological montage. A concise instance occurs in an
episode in *Pendennis* where within a single paragraph we learn the
reactions of the various members of the household at Chatteris to
young Pen's imminent departure for Oxbridge:

> Thus, oh friendly readers, we see how every man in the world has
> his own private griefs and business, by which he is more cast down or
> occupied than by the affairs or sorrows of any other person. While
> Mrs. Pendennis is disquieting herself about losing her son, and that
> anxious hold she has of him, as long as he has remained in the
> mother's nest, whence he is about to take flight in the great world
> beyond—while the Major's great soul chafes and frets, inwardly
> vexed as he thinks what great parties are going on in London, and
> that he might be sunning himself in the glances of Dukes and
> Duchesses, but for those cursed affairs that keep him in a wretched
> little country hole—while Pen is tossing between his passion and a
> more agreeable sensation, unacknowledged yet, but swaying him
> considerably, namely his longing to see the world—Mr. Smirke
> [Pen's tutor, in love with Mrs. Pendennis] has a private care watching
> at his bedside, and sitting behind him on his pony; and is no more
> satisfied than the rest of us. How lonely we are in the world! how
> selfish and secret, everybody! (Chap. 16).

Thackeray enables us to see not only the same events through
different temperaments, but individual characters as well from divers standpoints, through his practice of bringing them back from
novel to novel. A simple example is Barry Lyndon, given to swaggering self-amplification in his own story, but exposed as "an
Irishman of low extraction" by George Warrington during his brief
reappearance in *The Virginians*. A more complex one is Becky
Sharp, on whom we get two more slants after she is removed from
the spotlight, making it possible for us to contrast the face that she
presents to the world with the one that we have already glimpsed
behind her mask. Young Clive Newcome, friend to little Rawdon at
Gown Boys, replies to an inquirer: "I don't know how his
mother—her who wrote the hymns, you know, and goes to Mr.
Honeyman's chapel—comes to be Rebecca, Lady Crawley." Later
in the same novel, we overhear La Duchesse d'Ivry extolling "La
sémillante Becki . . . have you heard, Miladi, of the charming Mistress Becki? Monsieur le Duc describes her as the most *spirituelle*

English woman he ever met." We may retain our private opinion of
Becky, but Beatrix Esmond is allowed to vindicate herself. Long
after we have witnessed Henry's disillusionment with her ("The
roses had shuddered out of her cheeks; her eyes were glaring; she
looked quite old. ... As he looked at her, he wondered that he
could ever have loved her"), we see her in her dotage, grown
coarser and more worldly, but at the same time penitent for her
treatment of Henry, and making up for it to an extent by singing
his praises to his relatives, for whom she feels undisguised contempt.[47] On the other hand, George Brandon, the dashing libertine
of *A Shabby Genteel Story*, when we meet him years later as the suave
Dr. Firmin of *The Adventures of Philip*, seen through the eyes of his
son Philip, has acquired a more sinister character beneath his glossy
exterior. Arthur Pendennis, whose development we watch over a
span of three novels, is seen first as an adolescent through the
critical mind of a detached narrator in *Pendennis*; speaks for himself as an established writer and devoted family man in *The Newcomes*; and finally in *The Adventures of Philip* completes the cycle by
acting as a mentor— if a faulty one— to another growing boy, as
his uncle had been to him.

Thackeray's familiar literary devices—the intrusive narrator, the
constantly switching perspectives, his alter egos, recurring characters, as well as what a modern critic has called his "bufferless
endings"[48]—can now be recognized among the means by which he
impresses upon us the complexity and relativity of truth. He also
endeavors to make the crooked straight by setting the life histories
contained by his novels in a grander context. Victor Cousin, like
Isaac Watts, committed his disciples to large views, suggesting how
they could acquire what Dr. Watts called "an extensive treasure of
ideas." Cousin's prescribed approach to the education of the intellect is at once introspective and panoramic. "Study entire humanity; in yourself first, and in your consciousness, then in that consciousness of the human race which is called history," he advised.[49]
In his lecture entitled "Of the Psychological Method in History," he
establishes the history of civilization as "the pedestal of the history
of philosophy." Just as the mind is a microcosm of the universe, the
history of civilization is the history of man writ large. This history is
spread out through space and time, and takes in all the elements of
culture: "The history of philosophy expresses, in short, the history
of religion, the history of art, the history of legislation, the history
of wealth, and, to a certain point, physical geography itself; for if
the history of philosophy belongs to that of humanity, the history

of humanity belongs to that of nature, the first basis and theatre of humanity, to the constitution of the globe, to its divisions; in a word, to its physical geography."[50]

Man, then, for Cousin, is the proper study of the philosopher, both as individuals with unique consciousnesses and collectively as reflected in their history and in their institutions. Thackeray's historical sense is evident from his first novel, *Catherine*, which opens with a retrospect of continental politics preceding the reign of Queen Anne when this story takes place, giving a grander scope even to this low-life crime story. However, the travel books through which he first reached a substantial readership display at its fullest range his early deep engagement with society and culture. He called these records "Sketch Books," and one tends to look at them now literally as "sketches" for the grand "canvasses" to come. In the first of them, *The Paris Sketch Book*, we are presented immediately with the "theatre of humanity," spectacles of people in the aggregate, all ages and classes thrown together, civilizations intermingling:

> The decks have a strange look; the people on them, that is. Wives, elderly stout husbands, nursemaids, and children predominate, of course, in English steamboats. Such may be considered as the distinctive marks of the English gentleman at three or four-and-forty; two or three of such groups have pitched their camps on the deck. Then there are a number of young men, of whom three or four have allowed their moustaches to *begin* to grow since last Friday; for they are going "on the Continent," and they look, therefore, as if their upper lips were smeared with snuff.
>
> . . . Yonder is a group of young ladies, who are going to Paris to learn how to be governesses: those two splendidly dressed ladies are milliners from the Rue Richelieu, who have just brought over, and disposed of, their cargo of Summer fashions. Here sits the Rev. Mr. Snodgrass with his pupils, whom he is conducting to his establishment, near Boulogne, where, in addition to a classical and mathematical education (washing included), the young gentlemen have the benefit of learning French among *the French themselves.*
>
> . . . There are, of course, many Jews on board. Who ever travelled by steamboat, coach, diligence, eilwagen, vetturino, mule-back, or sledge, without meeting some of the wandering race?[51]

The ordinary "sights" that visitors travel for, Thackeray (or Titmarsh, to use his passport name) is inclined to leave to the Baedekers; he passes up details about Boulogne, for example, which he points out "have all been excellently described by the facetious Coglan, the learned Dr. Millingen, and by innumerable guidebooks besides." He intends for his readers, like the groups of students he observed among his fellow passengers, to learn something from this voyage. They certainly were led to expect something more than meets the eye from a diligence window in the "Allegory" of nine figures designed for the original title page, with its accompanying jingle:

> Number 1's an Ancient Carlist, Number 3 a Paris artist,
> Gloomily there stands between them, Number 2 a Bonapartist;
> In the middle is King Louis-Phillip standing at his ease,
> Guarded by a local Grocer, and a Serjeant of Police;
> 4's the people in a passion, 6 a Priest of pious mien,
> 5 a Gentleman of Fashion, copied from a Magazine.

These members of the Three Estates represent the various areas of civilization that Victor Cousin assigned to the student of "entire humanity": religion (the "Priest of pious mien"); art ("a Paris artist"); government (the Carlist, the Bonapartist, and the Bourgeois King range along the spectrum of politics, and there is that upholder of the law, "the Serjeant of Police"); and wealth (the "local Grocer" at one end of the scale, the "Gentleman of Fashion" at the other). And indeed the attentive reader of *The Paris Sketch Book*, miscellaneous as are its contents, comes away with an introduction to French cultural history, religious ("The Fêtes of July"; "Madame Sand and the New Apocalypse"); political and legal ("Napoleon and His System"), economic ("Meditations at Versailles"), and certainly artistic ("On the French School of Painting," "Caricatures and Lithography in Paris," "On Some French Fashionable Novels," "French Dramas and Melodramas"). Through its pages pass captains and kings, such as Napoleon, Marshal Tallard, and Louis-Philippe; numerous writers, poets, dramatists, and artists; minor functionaries, such as Citizen Schneider (in "The Story of Mary Ancel"); commercial travelers, such as Sam Pogson; shopkeepers, such as the lively but unnamed tradespeople of Paris and Boulogne; servants, such as Beatrice Merger; mountebanks, such as Robert Macaire; jesters, such as Monsieur Poinsinet; gamblers, such as the hapless Jack Attwood; and—out of the sewers of Paris—thieves and murderers, such as Louis Dominic Cartouche and Sebastien Peytel—in short, occupants of every level of M. Cousin's "edifice of humanity."

In Titmarsh's descriptions of the social scene that dominate many of the "sketches," the shadow of history is rarely absent. Past and present intermingle at the entrance to the capital: "But behold us at Paris! The Diligence has reached a rude-looking gate, or *grille*, flanked by two lodges; the French Kings of old made their entry by this gate; some of the hottest battles of the late revolution were fought before it. At present it is blocked by carts and peasants, and a busy crowd of men, in green, examining the packages before they enter, probing the straw with long needles. It is the Barrier of St. Denis, and the green men are the customs-men of the city of Paris."[52] The "movements of thought" that accompany the superseding of one generation by another was one great stimulus to the historical imagination for Cousin. In a few sentences Thackeray has managed to personify the transformation of French society from the fall of the Bourbons to the rise of the bureaucrat. In the final sketch, "Meditations at Versailles," he ponders the passing of the glory that was Louis XIV. Noting that "Tailors, chandlers, tin-men, wretched hucksters, and greengrocers are now established in the mansions of the old peers," he checks any impulse he may have for sentimental nostalgia:

> Why not mourn over it, as Mr. Burke did over his cheap defence of nations and unbought grace of life; that age of chivalry, which he lamented, à propos of a trip to Versailles, some half a century back?
>
> Without stopping to discuss (as might be done in rather a neat and successful manner) whether the age of chivalry was cheap or dear, and whether in the time of the unbought grace of life, there was not more bribery, robbery, villainy, tyranny, corruption, than exists even in our own happy days—let us make a few moral and historical remarks upon the town of Versailles.[53]

The essays that come between the opening "Invasion of France" and the closing "Meditations at Versailles" may be characterized as series of "moral and historical remarks" intended not merely to introduce his countrymen to French culture but to carry on a kind of cross-Channel dialogue. Thackeray had frequent occasion to observe how little these two traditionally enemy nations understood one another, and one aim of the survey of French culture that he attempted here seems to have been to remove what Victor Cousin called "the malady of fanaticism." As he sums it up in one essay: "Tea-parties are the same all the world over, with the exception that, with the French, there are more lights and prettier dresses; and with us a mighty deal more tea in the pot."[54] Weighing the two countries in the balance, he finds good and bad, right and wrong on both sides.

On matters of ethics, he is quick to point out, John Bull has no reason to be smug. "Talk of English morality!—the worst licentiousness, in the worst period of the French monarchy scarcely equalled the wickedness of this Sabbath-keeping country of ours," he observes in comparing the popular prints of the two. The art of

France also shows up the aesthetic blind spots of the English. "Nothing merely intellectual will be popular among us," he complains, "we do not love beauty for beauty's sake, as the Germans; or wit, for wit's sake, as the French; for abstract art we have no appreciation. . . . In France, such matters are far better managed, and the love of art is a thousand times more keen."[55] Through the vivid verbal street scenes to which he treats his readers (the colorful Faubourg St. Denis, for example, which is contrasted with a dingy London street), Titmarsh illustrates what he finds to be a finer quality of life on the continent.[56]

In one area, that of politics, he feels the English can claim superiority, inasmuch as, he concludes in his discussion of government, the English have succeeded better than the French in curbing the powers of the monarchy. The English, too, are on the whole a more prosperous people, and yet, " . . . how much better is social happiness understood [in France]; how much more manly equality is there between Frenchman and Frenchman, than between rich and poor in our own country, with all our superior wealth, instruction, and political freedom! There is, amongst the humblest, a gaiety, a cheerfulness, politeness, and sobriety, to which, in England no class can show a parallel: and these, be it remembered, are not only qualities for holidays, but for working days too, and add to the enjoyment of human life as much as good clothes, good beef, or good wages."[57]

Titmarsh's pictures of street life enable us to participate in this "social happiness" at festivals where all classes intermingle in celebration and entertainment. Particularly in his account of the "humbug" ceremonies commemorating the July Revolution he brings out a shared joie de vivre:

> The sight which I have just come away from is as brilliant, happy, and beautiful as can be conceived; and if you want to see French people to the greatest advantage, you should go to a festival like this, where the manners and innocent gaiety show a very pleasing contrast to the coarse and vulgar hilarity which the same class would exhibit in our own country—at Epsom racecourse, for instance, or at Greenwich Fair . . . . It does one good to see honest heavy épiciers, fathers of families, playing with them in the Tuileries, or, as to-night, bearing them stoutly on their shoulders, through many long hours, in order that the little ones, too, may have their share of the fun. John Bull, I fear, is more selfish: he does not take Mrs. Bull to the public-house; but leaves her, for the most part, to take care of the children at home.[58]

Amid the gay shops and crowds of the Faubourg St. Denis he finds a more somber sign of French enlightenment in a gloomy-looking prison, converted from a Lazarist convent, whose inmates, instead of being confined to cells, are set to useful occupations like baking and sewing. "Was it not a great stroke of the legislature to superintend the morals and linen at once," he quips, "and thus keep these poor creatures continually mending?"[59] This humanitarian motif is sustained through some of the tales and vignettes of *The Paris Sketch Book*—particularly the touching episode of the self-sacrificing servant girl Beatrice Merger—whose effect is to arouse that sympathy with the poor he feels is lacking in his own country, just as the anecdotes of gamblers and criminals bring out the spark of humanity presumably latent in the lowest of creatures.

"With our English notions, our moral and physical constitution, it is quite impossible that we should become intimate with our brisk neighbours," Titmarsh is forced to conclude in one of his comtemplative moments. Despite the abundance of writers, the communications gap is as wide as ever, a situation in which he finds both sides equally at fault, if unwittingly. Just as "a Frenchman might have lived a thousand years in England, and never could have written 'Pickwick,'" he observes in connection with his reading of novels, so "an Englishman cannot hope to give a good description of the inward thoughts and ways of his neighbours."[60] His playgoing in Paris convinces him that English naïveté about the French was well matched by French dramatists' ludicrous misconceptions of English life and history. "Would a Chinese playwright or painter have stranger notions about the barbarians than our neighbours, who are separated from us but by two hours of saltwater?" he asks in dismay.[61] Chauvinism and narrow-mindedness, he discovered, were not the exclusive preserve of either nation. On the positive side, he recognized in the arts one means to bridge the gulf between alien societies and cultures.

The *Irish Sketch Book* (1843) is more truly a travel book than its predecessor in that it records a tour, or series of tours; but here too Thackeray penetrates beyond the conventional visitor's interest in quaint ways and charming people. Ireland, unlike France, was strange and new to him, but it also offers him "opportunity for reflection," as he is quick to inform his readers, not merely scenery and recreation. This Emerald Isle unrolls before his mind's eye as a "strange picture of pleasure and pain, trade, theatre, schools, courts, churches, life and death."[62] The "beauties" of Hibernia are not neglected (in fact, the author takes his readers to task for having ignored them), but these are mainly the backdrop to a cultural pageant. As with France, we are introduced to aspects of Irish civilization in accord with M. Cousin's categories—her religion

("Cork—the Ursuline Convent"); her arts (Carlow cathedral, Mr. Hogan's paintings in the chapels of Dublin and Cork, "Galway-Nights' Entertainments"); her legal institutions ("Roundstone Petty Sessions," the murder trials of Patrick Byrne and John Woods at Tipperary); and her economy ("Cork—the Agricultural Show," the descriptions of the market at Killarney and of the wealth and poverty existing side by side in Dublin). We are taken inside the convent at Cork, living vestige of medieval Christianity across the Irish Sea, with its barren cells, *mementi mori*, and grisly paintings depicting torture and martyrdom. The "smiling beatitude" of the nuns amidst their poverty and mortification leads the philosophical author to ask in awe: "Is it policy, or hypocrisy, or reality?"[63] but he does not stay for an answer. A rainy night at a Galway Inn provides him the chance to relax with some Irish stories and plays, a painless introduction to her bloody history. He was deeply moved by a domestic tragedy, *The Warden of Galway,* commemorating a righteous mayor, James Lynch Fitzstephen, forced by his conscience to hang his own son, who has been found guilty of murder. *The Battle of Aughrim,* based on the defeat of James II by William of Orange, brought him closer to the period he was to make his own with *Henry Esmond.* A lighter side of Gaelic literature that fascinated him were the tall tales, lore of black magic, and legends of bandits, particularly the adventures of that Irish Robin Hood, Captain Freeny, that he utilized for *Barry Lyndon,* the novel that followed upon the Irish journey.[64]

In his *Irish Sketch Book* Titmarsh provides us with generous samples of the famed Irish charm and good humor, but he does not shield us from their less admirable qualities. Their "false magnificence" annoys him in particular. "There is something simple in the way in which these good people belord their clergymen, and respect titles real and sham," he writes. "Take any Dublin paper,—a couple of columns of it are sure to be filled with the movements of the small great men of the world. . . . Have the Irish so much reason to respect their lords that they should so chronicle all their movements; and not only admire real lords, but make sham ones of their own to admire *them*?"[65] He observed a decadent aristocracy clinging to a decayed chivalry here as in France. He assessed his own countrymen against their cousins across the Irish Sea, as he had against their "brisk neighbours" across the Channel. He is ready to concede that the English lack the Irish gusto and wit, "but the bluntness and honesty of the English have well-nigh kicked the fashionable humbug down; and, except perhaps among footmen and about Baker Street, this curiosity about the aristocracy is wearing fast away."[66] *Vanity Fair,* which came out four years later, hardly conveys the impression that the English had "kicked the fashionable humbug down," but then it is set in the Regency. It is more significant perhaps that in the forerunner to *Vanity Fair, The Book of Snobs,* we get only "A Little about Irish Snobs," the rest being taken up with English toadying and belording. "Sham Nobility" and true, then, Thackeray seems to have concluded, were pretty evenly divided among the nations of men. Meanwhile, Ireland, like France, furnished him an "improving" journey—"historical," "topographic," and "descriptive," as he characterized it.[67]

Thackeray's last travel book, *Notes of a Journey from Cornhill to Grand Cairo by Way of Lisbon, Athens, Constantinople, and Jerusalem Performed in the Steamers of the Peninsular and Oriental Company* (1846), is, as its full title indicates, a wide-ranging odyssey by sea and by land into more exotic climes. Titmarsh (still Thackeray's traveling name) appreciates this voyage back into antiquity but is thankful for the technological advance that has made it possible for him within two months to visit "as many men and cities . . . as Ulysses surveyed and noted in ten years."[68] Before long we are involved in "the theatre of humanity," as a civilization is brought to life amongst the busy throng of a Malta seaport:

> The Strada Reale [of Valetta] has a much more courtly appearance. . . . Here are palaces, churches, court-houses, and libraries, the genteel London shops, and the latest articles of perfumery. Gay young officers are strolling about in shell-jackets much too small for them; midshipmen are clattering by on hired horses; squads of priests, habited after the fashion of Don Basilio in the opera, are demurely pacing to and fro; professional beggars run shrieking after the stranger; and agents for horses, for inns, and for worse places still, follow him and insinuate the excellence of their goods. The houses where they are selling carpet-bags and pomatum were the palaces of the successors of the goodliest company of gallant knights the world ever heard tell of.[69]

With his eye for the vitality of the life around him, Titmarsh is also alert to signs of time's ravages. "The present stately houses were built in times of peace and splendour and decay," he observes of the knightly castles of Malta. The progress of history and the movements of thought carry "the perpetual destruction of systems" with them, Victor Cousin pointed out in one of his lectures.[70] Thackeray's journey to the East furnished him with plentiful human evidence:

> There is no cursing and insulting of Giaours now. If a Cockney looks or behaves in a particularly ridiculous way, the little Turks come out and laugh at him. A Londoner is no longer a spittoon for true believ-

ers; and now that dark Hassan sits in his divan and drinks champagne, and Selim has a French watch, and Zuleika perhaps takes
Morison's pills, Byronism becomes absurd instead of sublime, and is
only a foolish expression of Cockney wonder. . . . The paddle-wheel
is a great conqueror. . . . Whole hosts of crusaders have passed and
died, and butchered here in vain. But to manufacture European iron
into pikes and helmets was a waste of metal: in the shape of piston-
rods and furnace-pokers it is irresistible; and I think an allegory
might be made showing how much stronger commerce is than
chivalry, and finishing with a grand image of Mahomet's crescent
being extinguished in Fulton's boiler.[71]

As he had in France and in Ireland, Thackeray bears witness on
these more extended travels to the mortality of power. He reads a
typical sermon in stone on some monuments of magnificence in
Lisbon:

The churches I saw were of the florid periwig architecture—I
mean of that pompous cauliflower kind of ornament which was the
fashion in Louis the Fifteenth's time, at which unlucky period a
building mania seemed to have seized upon many of the monarchs
of Europe, and innumerable public edifices were erected. It seems to
me to have been the period in all history when society was the least
natural, and perhaps the most dissolute; and I have always fancied
that the bloated artificial forms of the architecture partake of the
social disorganisation of the time. Who can respect a simpering
ninny, grinning in a Roman dress and a full-bottomed wig, who is
made to pass off for a hero? or a fat woman in a hoop, and of a most
doubtful virtue, who leers at you like a goddess?[72]

The palaces too echo back the tale of Ozymandias. Titmarsh curls
his lip at the Allegories on the walls and ceilings of one of them
depicting such subjects as Faith, Hope, and Charity restoring Don
Juan to the arms of Lusus; Virtue, Valour, and Victory saluting
Don Emanuel; the Liberal Arts dancing before Don Miguel. "The
picture is there still, at the Ajuda; and ah me! where is poor Mig,"
he sighs in mock sorrow.

This deflation of pretension and air of irreverence that insinuate
themselves through so much of Thackeray's writing can be traced
also to Victor Cousin, whose idealism could be tempered now and
then by iconoclasm. "All great men, closely examined, remind us of
the saying 'There is but one step from the sublime to the ridiculous,'" declared Cousin quoting Napoleon in one of the last lectures
of the *Cours de l'histoire*. "A great man is great, and he is a man: what
makes him great is his relation to the spirit of his times, and to his
people; what makes him a man is his individuality; but separate
these two elements, consider the man in the great man, and the

greatest of men appears small enough."[73] Thackeray furnishes
many a case in point with his general scorn for plaster emperors
and saints. An illustration he designed for *The Paris Sketch Book*
shows the Sun King, Louis XIV, bald, shriveled, pot-bellied, and
bandy-legged, once he has been divested of his wig and robes.[74] In
The Irish Sketch Book he exposes the "small great" among the decayed Aristocracy of Dublin. In the Seraglio of Constantinople he
gives us a closeup of His Highness the Sultan, the Padishah of the
realm, looking "like a young French *roué* worn out by debauch; his
eyes bright, with black rings round them; his cheeks pale and hollow."[75] According to Cousin the heroic element, "the part of the
great man . . . alone belongs to history," while the "vulgar part of
these great destinies," the aspect of the hero, that is, that reduces
him to a mere man, should be "abandoned to memoirs and biography." Thackeray's attraction to memoirs and biographies, Montaigne and Gibbon, as we have noted, to which could be added
other favorite reading such as Walpole's *Letters*, Talleyrand's
Memoirs, Wraxall's *Historical Memoirs of My Own Time*, and a compi-
lation called *Authentic Records of the Court of England*,[76] is evidence
that, contrary to Cousin's advice, he chose the "vulgar part." His
delight in bringing out what Cousin called "the man in the great
man" was to find its fullest release in his historical lectures, such as
his series on the four Georges, and in his historical romances disguised as autobiography, such as *Henry Esmond* and *The Virginians*.

In general, however, Thackeray was one with Cousin in his basically progressive view of history. Much of what man once believed
in has been exposed as folly and self-delusion with the passage of
time, Cousin pointed out at the conclusion of his lecture on "Great
Men," but "this spectacle [of "the perpetual destruction of systems"] instead of producing skepticism, should inspire a faith without limits in this excellent human reason, in this admirable humanity, for which all men of genius labor, which profits by their errors,
their struggles, their defeats, and their victories, which advances
only over ruins, but which continually advances."[77] The improvement of the human condition wrought by historic change was very
much on Thackeray's mind, as he indicates in particular in a review
of a historical study contributed to the *Morning Chronicle* the year
before he began work on *Vanity Fair*. "We reverted to the establishment of the Christian religion, the disruption of ancient empires, the origin and growth of modern nations, the progress of
civil liberties in such and such states, the growth of despotisms in
others," he writes here.[78] The reading of this book—*Historic Fan-*

cies, by the Honorable George Sidney Smythe, M. P.—stirred up his
own thoughts also on such cultural phenomena as "the revival of
letters and the arts, which led to the destruction of the modern
empire of the Popes," the growth of nationalism, the dissemination
of civilization through colonization, the distribution of wealth, the
democratization of society in general, all of which led him to conclude that "without at all going deeply into the dogmas of politics
and political economy, a young man of sound principles, of generous impulses, and of independent feeling, might indulge in 'fancies' by the hour; fancies which could not but prove of interest to
those, having only studied history and facts in the beaten track,
have been hitherto too apt to apply the principles of the old world
to the altered phases of the new."

In his travels Thackeray witnessed the old world being superseded by the new, and his great novels dramatize the continuous
dialectical process of history that Victor Cousin described. A dying
generation lingers on in a once elegant section of Mayfair:

> Gaunt House occupies nearly a side of the Square. The remaining
> three sides are composed of mansions that have passed away into
> Dowagerism;—tall, dark houses, with window-frames of stone, or
> picked out of a lighter red. Little light seems to be behind those lean,
> comfortless casements now: and hospitality seems to have passed
> away from those doors as much as the laced lacqueys and link-boys of
> old times who used to put out their torches in the blank [black] iron
> extinguishers that still flank the lamps over the steps. Brass plates
> have penetrated into the Square—Doctors, the Diddlesex Bank
> Western Branch—the English and European Reunion, &c.[79]

as well as in the rural retreats: "When Colonel Dobbin quitted the
service, which he did immediately after his marriage, he rented a
pretty little country place in Hampshire, not far from Queen's
Crawley, where, after the passing of the Reform Bill, Sir Pitt and
his family constantly resided now. All idea of a Peerage was out of
the question, the baronet's two seats in Parliament being lost. He
was both out of pocket and out of spirits by that catastrophe, failed
in his health, and prophesied the speedy ruin of the Empire."[80]

Habitations loom for Thackeray as emblems of social changes
like the extension of democracy and the rise of the professional
class. A whole village, by its very resistance to change, bears mute
testimony to the coming of the Industrial Revolution: "[Rosebury]
is situated . . . at some five miles from the town of Newcome; away
from the chimneys and smoky atmosphere of that place, in a sweet
country of rural woodlands; over which quiet villages, grey church
spires, and ancient gabled farm-houses are scattered; still wearing

the peaceful aspect which belonged to them when Newcome was as yet but an antiquated country town, before mills were erected on its river banks, and dyes and cinders blackened its stream." Commerce and industry have ushered in the new bourgeoisie and a shifting environment in which the brand new intermingles with the old:

Twenty years since, Newcome Park was the only great house in that district; now scores of fine villas have sprung up in the suburb lying between the town and the park. Newcome New Town, as everybody knows, has grown round the park gates, and the "New Town Hotel" (where the railway station is) is a splendid structure in the Tudor style, more ancient in appearance than the park itself; surrounded by little antique villas with spiked gables, stacks of crooked chimneys, and plate-glass windows looking upon the trim lawns; with glistening hedges of evergreens, spotless gravel walks, and Elizabethan gig-houses. Under the great railway viaduct of the New Town goes the old tranquil winding London highroad, once busy with a score of gay coaches, and ground by innumerable wheels; but at a few miles from the New Town Station the road had become so mouldy that the grass actually grows on it; and Rosebury, Madame de Montecour's house, stands at one end of a village-green which is even more quiet now than it was a hundred years ago.[81]

Now and then an individual epitomizes a passing era for Thackeray, as with the Baroness Bernstein, née Beatrix Esmond, seen momentarily through the eyes of her nephew George Warrington:

Sure 'tis hard with respect to Beauty, that its possessor should not have even a life-enjoyment of it, but be compelled to resign it after, at the most, some forty years' lease. As the old woman prattled of her former lovers and admirers . . . I would look in her face, and, out of the ruins, try to build up in my fancy a notion of her beauty in its prime. What a homily I read there! How the courts were grown with grass, the towers broken, the doors ajar, the fine gilt saloons tarnished, and the tapestries cobwebbed and torn! Yonder dilapidated palace was all alive once with splendour and music, and those dim windows were dazzling and blazing with light! What balls and feasts were once here, what splendour and laughter! I could see lovers in waiting, crowds in admiration, rivals furious. I could imagine twilight assignations, and detect intrigues, though the curtains were closed and drawn . . . and my fancy wandered about in her, amused and solitary, as I had walked about our father's house at Castlewood, meditating on departed glories, and imagining ancient times.[82]

The threnody on "departed glories" sounds its old refrain with variations in Thackeray's novels, where the vestiges of the past and passing leave their traces in deteriorated dwellings, aging belles and beaux, and decadent families, and persist in the clash of generations and ways of life. Thackeray mourns both for what age takes away and what it leaves behind, but there is gain as well as loss. In the spirit of his mentor Victor Cousin, he shows us that mankind in its stumbling way somehow manages to "advance . . . over ruins." With the fading of the eighteenth century and the dawn of the Industrial Age, a new breed has come in, from whom Frederick Lightfoot, formerly *maître d'hôtel* to that seedy aristocrat Lord Clavering, is quick to reap advantage. Under the supervision of this enterprising manager, the old Clavering Arms "has been repaired and decorated in a style of the greatest comfort. Gentlemen hunting with the Dumplingbeare hounds will find excellent stabling and loose boxes for horses. . . . Commercial gentlemen will find the Clavering Arms a most comfortable place of resort: and the scale of charges has been regulated for all, so as to meet the economical spirit of the present times." As Major Pendennis, a leading champion of the old social regime, concedes, however reluctantly, "We are grown doosid republican. Talent ranks with birth and wealth now, begad."[83]

As a holdover from the Age of George, the major is one of Thackeray's most delightful characters, yet one of the most pathetic in his resistance to change. In a moment of reckoning, this habitué of the significantly named Wheel of Fortune Public House "began to own that he was no longer of the present age and dimly to apprehend that the young men laughed at him. Such melancholy musings must come across many a Pall Mall philosopher." The major deplores the passing of the dandies of his youth: ". . . the breed is gone—there's no use for 'em; they're replaced by a parcel of damned cotton-spinners and utilitarians, and young sprigs of parsons with their hair combed down their backs." At this point his creator adds: "And he was not far wrong; the times and manners which he admired were pretty nearly gone. The gay young men 'larked' him irreverently, while the serious youth had a grave pity and wonder at him, which would have been more painful to bear, had the old gentleman been aware of its extent."[84] Major Pendennis represents the Regency giving way to the Age of Victoria, among whose spokesmen is his nephew Arthur. Old systems, old ways of life, pronounced Victor Cousin, "need a momentary dominion in order to develop all that is in them, and at the same time to show what is not in them," and once they have served their time, they must yield place to the new.[85]

"Young men, you who propose to frequent these lectures, love all that is good, all that is beautiful, all that is honest: here is the basis of all philosophy," urged Victor Cousin in the peroration to the first lecture of the *Cours de l'histoire*.[86] Arthur Pendennis, one of these young men, is not disposed, like that "old boy" Major Pendennis, to scorn the "damned cotton-spinners and utilitarians." In one of his philosophical moments, Arthur has a vision of "the earth, where our feet are . . . the work of the same Power as the immeasurable blue yonder, in which the future lies into which we would peer." For him the world of works and days in a source of inspiration, as he confides to his friend Warrington: "'Look, George . . . look and see the sun rise; he sees the labourer on his way a-field; the work-girl plying her poor needle; the lawyer at his desk, perhaps; the beauty smiling asleep upon her pillow of down; or the jaded revel-ler reeling to bed; or the fevered patient tossing on it; or the doctor watching by it, over the throes of the mother for the child that is to be born into the world—to be born and to take his part in the suffering and struggling, the tears and laughter, the crime, re-morse, love, folly, sorrow, rest.'"[87] Along with participation in "both that which is of God, and that which is of the world," Cousin committed his disciples to a stake in mankind's future: "Follow with interest the general movement of the physical sciences and indus-try. Give to yourselves in them, the instructive spectacle of liberty and human intelligence, marching day by day to the conquest and dominion of the sensible world," reads the ringing conclusion to his lecture entitled "The Idea of Philosophy." Young Arthur seems very much a part of this forward movement as we catch sight of him toward the end of *Pendennis* on his walk through Clavering Park, "the once quiet and familiar fields of which were flaming with the kilns and forges of the artificers employed on the new railroad works."[88]

In reviewing the work of another French man of letters, Victor Hugo, Thackeray wrote: "We have read his description of the mul-tifarious duties and accomplishments imposed upon *celui qu'on ap-pelle poète*. He is 'to put his hand to the work,' he is 'never to draw back,' he is a part of his 'decisive century,' 'a light for mankind, feeling all their wants, and their passions; labouring, striving, struggling to understand, and when he has understood to ex-plain.'"[89] He was poking gentle fun at Hugo's grandiosity here, but his conception of the writer's place in society as embodied in Ar-thur Pendennis is close to this ideal. In this same review he evokes the image of "that strange, grotesque, violent, pompous, noble fig-ure of a poet, with his braggart modesty and wonderful simplicity of conceit, his kind heart yearning towards all small things and beauties of nature, small children, birds, flowers, & c., his rich flowing, large eloquence, and his grim humour." Here too he could be speaking for his own elemental love of "small things" that always lay behind his sweeping critiques of mankind in the large. A famous passage from his lecture on Swift delivered some years later confirms this more "primitive" side of Thackeray: "The humorous writer professes to awaken and direct your love, your pity, your kindness—your scorn for untruth, pretension, imposture—your tenderness for the weak, the poor, the oppressed, the unhappy. To the best of his means and ability he comments on all the ordinary actions and passions of life almost."[90]

This sentimental aspect of Thackeray—his elevation of the ordinary and the commonplace—tended to counterbalance the satirist in him, the "scorn of imposture," the iconoclasm, the denigration of the self-styled great and mighty. Arthur Pendennis mingling with the multitudes outdoors stands for Thackeray himself, who on his travels fled the churches and palaces of Paris, Dublin, Lisbon, and the Far East for their streets and marketplaces. Here, too, he may have taken his cue from Victor Cousin, who advised his students in their cultivation of philosophy not to neglect "the authority of those general beliefs which constitute the common sense of mankind."[91] For Cousin these "general beliefs" derived from the "spontaneous reason" by which he set great store. Thackeray's own frequent echoing of "wise saws" from classical authors, together with folk wisdom drawn from such traditional sources as scripture and fables, led one of his admirers in an obituary tribute to label his "a proverbial mind," prone to lean on "the verdict of popular feeling and shrewd common sense on a given line of conduct."[92] The mottoes that make up many of his chapter titles; biblical titles, like his most famous, *Vanity Fair*, taken from Ecclesiastes via *The Pilgrim's Progress*; the humanizing of the bestiaries of Aesop and La Fontaine in *The Newcomes;* the emblematic morals that one can "read" in the historiated initials that head chapters of the novels as originally issued; his frequent Hogarthian allusions—all of these make up a reservoir of "the common sense of mankind," proof against the pretensions and pomposities of civilization.

"In fact what is the philosophy that I teach, but respect for all the elements of humanity and for all things," affirmed Cousin in his concluding lecture. These words probably best express the ultimate aim of Thackeray's inquiries into the "workings" of the souls of men, fictitious and real, historical and contemporary, heroic and commonplace. Eclecticism, as M. Cousin sums it up, "destroys nothing, accepts everything, explains everything, and governs everything." While acknowledging man's fallibility, "our philosophy, gentlemen, is not a melancholy and fanatical philosophy, which being prepossessed with a few exclusive ideas, undertakes to re-form all others upon the same model; it is a philosophy essentially optimistical, whose only end is to comprehend all, and which, therefore, accepts and reconciles all. It seeks to obtain power only by extension; its unity consists only in the harmony of con-trarieties."[93] Among Cousin's disciples may be numbered Arthur Pendennis, significantly an aspiring writer, proud of his "sympathy with all conditions of men," who "had his eyes always eagerly open to its infinite varieties and beauties; contemplating with an unfail-ing delight all specimens of it in all places to which he resorted."[94] Another is Clive Newcome, Thackeray's portrait of himself as young artist, whose "sunny kindly spirit, undimmed by any of the cares, which clouded it subsequently, was disposed to shine on all people alike. The world was welcome to him; the day a pleasure; all nature a gay feast; scarce any dispositions discordant with his own."[95]

In trying to pin down his protean nature, contemporaries of Thackeray used such phrases as "crystal of many facets" and "a strange effervescence of . . . widely differing elements."[96] His friend George Henry Lewes spoke of him as a "Janus bifrons" with a "predominating tendency to antithesis."[97] All of these come close to "the harmony of contrarieties" that Victor Cousin defined as the task of the moral philosopher and one that Thackeray clearly set for himself. Eclecticism is the term that seems best to describe Thackeray's myriad-mindedness, his adroit, nimble, mercurial dis-position, "the variety, the changeableness, the power of rapid transformation which is to be found only in the highest intelli-gences . . . by turns humorous, contemptuous, tender," as one of his fellow novelists put it.[98] His peripatetic spirit, his tendency to view life through a series of sliding lenses, his simulation of a wide range of moods from melancholy to jocularity, his wide empathy, all fall into place as his means of appropriating to himself "entire humanity." Thackeray's moral relativism, an attitude that some have attributed to indifference or pococurantism on his part, is more properly interpreted as part of his eclectic outlook, his at-tempt to illuminate man's confusion out of the cumulated wisdom and folly of the ages, to aid humanity, in Cousin's words, "from incomplete view to incomplete view . . . to arrive at a complete view of itself and of all its substantial elements."[99] Furthermore, what another of his fellow writers called his "literary chameleon" nature indicates that with books too he was eclectic and highly adaptable.

One of Thackeray's admirers went so far to see even in Thackeray's notorious gift for parody evidence of his sympathetic faculty at work, his desire to see the "soul" beneath a work of art, and to "reembody" it in his own.[100] Certainly he learned much from fellow writers, even those he lampooned, showing a remarkable ability, as will appear in later chapters, to extract precious metal from crude ore. That "knowledge of human nature so wide and comprehensive in its nature that it seems unrivalled in the annals of fiction"[101] for which he was praised in the last century was the distillation of a lifetime of self-education spent "with men as well as with books," as one of his first guides, Isaac Watts, advised. But it is evident that from his early years he displayed his special predilection for self-study and confessional writing, curiosity about the vagaries of behavior (those studies known in his time as "mental and moral science"), and a tolerant understanding of human foibles, and that he was further directed in his youth toward the study of man in his social milieu, viewed against the panoramic background of cultural history. Upon this intellectual base he erected, out of his extensive experience—artistic, theatrical, journalistic, literary— the "edifice of humanity" that emerges from his novels.

1. Isaac Watts, *Logic; or, The Right Use Of Reason, In The Inquiry After Truth, With A Variety Of Rules To Guard Against Error, In The Affairs Of Religion And Human Life, As Well As In The Sciences*, pt. 1, chap. 5 ("General Directions Relating to Our Ideas"). This book was first published in 1724, and went through numerous editions. A copy dated 1824 is listed in *Thackerayana: A Catalogue Of Books Forming A Portion Of The Library Of W. M. Thackeray . . . On Sale By Henry Sotheran And Co.* (London, n.d.).

2. The supplement entitled *The Improvement of the Mind* (1743) was printed in later editions together with his *Discourse on the Education of Children and Youth*. An edition of 1822 published in Boston included as an appendix "Questions adapted to the work; for the use of schools and academies." There is on record as late as 1855 a condensation of the entire work entitled *Logic for the Young* prepared by J. W. Gilbart. In chap. 4 of *Pendennis*, "Watts' Catechism" is mentioned among Laura's school books.

3. *Letters*, 3:444; Gordon N. Ray, *Thackeray: The Uses of Adversity* (New York: McGraw-Hill, 1955), pp. 144–45 (hereafter referred to as *The Uses of Adversity*).

4. *The Newcomes*, chap. 15.

5. *Vanity Fair*, chap. 62.

6. See below, pp. 64, 67.

7. Watts, *Logic*, "Introduction and General Scheme."

8. Preface to *Comic Tales and Sketches* (1841).

9. Watts, *Logic*, pt. 2, chap. 3, sec. 1 ("Prejudices arising from Things").

10. Ibid., sec. 1, iii.

11. *The Luck of Barry Lyndon*, p. 387.

12. Watts, *Logic*, "Prejudices arising from Things," sec. 1, iv.

13. Introduction to *Works*, 3:xxx.

14. *The Newcomes*, chap. 4.

15. Ray, *The Uses of Adversity,* p. 119; letter to Kate Perry, 2 July 1855, from Paris, *Letters,* 3:459. His diary for 9 August 1832 mentions having borrowed from a library "Gibbon in one volume" (*Letters,* 1:228).

16. Edward Gibbon, *Miscellaneous Works,* ed. John Lord Sheffield, 3 vols. (Dublin, 1796) (published in London the same year in 2 vols.). The three-volume set is listed in the *Catalogue of the Library of W. M. Thackeray sold by Messrs. Christie, Manson & Woods, March 18, 1864 . . . ,* ed. J. H. Stonehouse (bound together with the Catalogue of Dickens's library from Gadshill) (London: Picadilly Fountain Press, 1935).

17. "Nil Nisi Bonum," *Works,* 12:178–79.

18. 11 August 1846, *Letters,* 2:245.

19. See in particular "On Two Children in Black," *Works,* 12:180. In a number of the Roundabout Papers, notably "Nil Nisi Bonum" and "Ogres," he defends "egotism."

20. After almost a century of frequent publication, the 1669 edition of the *Essays* was the last to appear for fifty-five years. In the eighteenth century Coste had only one rival, Bastien, both of whose editions were frequently reprinted. According to Donald Frame, Montaigne "put such a spotlight on the human psyche as it never had before and was never to lose again. . . . More than anyone else, Montaigne set a whole great literature on the trail of his favorite quarry, human behavior." Frame cites Thackeray among the most prominent nineteenth-century admirers, in the company of Byron, Hazlitt, Landor, FitzGerald, Stevenson, Pater, and Emerson (*Montaigne: A Biography* [New York: Harcourt, Brace, 1965], pp. 315–17).

21. *Lovel the Widower,* chap. 1.

22. *Works* (Oxford Ed.), 3:102–3.

23. "That the relish of good and evil depends in a good measure upon the opinion that we have of them" (*The Essays of Michel de Montaigne,* trans. Charles Cotton, 3 vols. [London: Bohn, 1913], 1:294).

24. "On Two Children in Black," *Works,* 12:180.

25. "The Fatal Boots," *Works,* 3:541. Originally appeared in the *Comick Almanack* for 1839, ed. George Cruikshank.

26. *Essays,* 3:222, 247; *Lovel the Widower,* chap. 1.

27. Diary, 22 August 1832, *Letters,* 1:225.

28. Sir William Hamilton, "M. Cousin's *Course of Philosophy," Edinburgh Review* 50 (October 1829): 194. Quoted in introduction to Victor Cousin, *Course of the History of Modern Philosophy,* trans. O. W. Wight, 2 vols. (New York: Appleton, 1852), 1:9. Cousin had been dismissed from his post in 1820 for alleged antigovernmental opinions (an accusation aroused in part by his interest in German philosophy). For the next several years he traveled to Germany—where he met Hegel, who influenced him—wrote, edited, and translated, notably the works of Plato and Descartes.

29. For a brief survey of Cousin's influence, see Donald G. Charlton, "Victor Cousin and the French Romantics," *French Studies* 17 (October 1963): 311–23, an article to which I am very much indebted. For the essential biographical facts and an introduction to his ideas, see Jules Simon, *Victor Cousin,* trans. Melville S. Anderson and Edward Playfair Anderson (Chicago: A. C. McClurg & Co., 1888).

30. "Translator's Preface" to Victor Cousin, *Introduction to the History of Philosophy,* trans. Henning Gotfried Linberg (Boston: Hilliard, Gray, Little & Wilkins, 1832). Linberg confined himself to the rhetorical first series of lectures tracing the progress of philosophy up to its "present state" in the nineteenth century. The later translation by O. W. Wight (cited above, n. 28) adds the second, more detailed and theoretical series, originally delivered in 1829. I draw on both versions for the passages quoted in English.

31. Diary, 22 August 1831, *Letters,* 1:225–26. The quoted passage is from lecture 5 of the *Cours de l'histoire,* with the translation as given by Linberg (p.138). Some years later Thackeray echoed this passage in reviewing a book on David Hume, "a sceptic and utter worldling, a man entirely without imagination. . . . His life is consistent at least, and he is the same from sixteen to sixty, insensible to a future seemingly, and untroubled by conscience or remorse, or doubt even about his doubts" (review of J. H. Burton's *Life and Correspondence of David Hume, Morning Chronicle,* 23 March 1846; *Contributions,* pp. 113–14).

32. Lecture 10, p. 327 (Linberg trans.). Cousin believed that four great systems of thought—sensationalism, idealism, skepticism, and mysticism—alternate from epoch to epoch (Jules Simon, *Cousin*, p. 52). He thought that his particular age was in need of idealism to offset the sensationalism of the preceding age. Walter M. Simon contends that Cousin and Comte focus the conflict between humanism and scientism in postrevolutionary French thought. See his "The 'Two Cultures' in Nineteenth-Century France: Victor Cousin and Auguste Comte," *Journal of the History of Ideas* 26 (January 1965): 45–58.

33. Frederic Will, *Flumen Historicum: Victor Cousin's Aesthetic and Its Sources* (Chapel Hill: University of North Carolina Press, 1965), p. 1. Will concedes that Cousin's teachings "played a large role in the formation of the Romantic temperament in France," but attributes it to "the post-revolutionary drought of ideas, and . . . the impoverishment of French philosophy at this time." Donald G. Charlton contends to the contrary: "Posterity has indeed been harsh—too harsh . . . in its judgment of Cousin and his school. . . . His achievements in philosophy are well known, but underrated" ("Victor Cousin," p. 312).

34. J. Barthélemy Saint-Hilaire, dedication to *M. Victor Cousin, Sa vie et sa correspondance*, 3 vols. (Paris, 1895). The third volume includes a valuable topic index.

35. Lecture 1, pp. 26–27 (Wight trans). Cousin's thought combines elements of Plato, Descartes, Leibniz, Locke, Kant, Hegel, and (under the influence of his teacher and later colleague Royer-Collard) the Scottish common sense school. Frederic Will traces his aesthetic thought back to the "mythological eclecticism" of the Alexandrians (*Flumen Historicum*, p. 28).

36. Jules Simon, *Cousin*, pp. 55–56.

37. George Henry Lewes, review of *The Book of Snobs, Morning Chronicle*, 6 March 1848, p. 3; [Richard Simpson], "Thackeray," *Home and Foreign Review* 4 (April 1864):405 (author identification provided by *The Wellesley Index*, vol. 1); Ray, *The Uses of Adversity*, p. 418.

38. Lecture 5, p. 147 (Linberg); italics mine.

39. 6 April 1845 to Thomas Longman, editor of the *Edinburgh Review, Letters*, 2:190–91.

40. Lecture 1, p. 27 (Wight)

41. Lecture 6, p. 176 (Linberg)

42. In one of his literary essays, Thackeray wrote with reference to artists: "Is not individuality the great charm of most works of art? Let any two painters make a picture of the same landscape, and the performance of each will differ of course. The distance appears purple to one pair of eyes which is gray to the other's, one man's fields are brown and his neighbour's green, one insists upon a particular feature and details it,while his comrade slurs it over. . . . Every man has a manner of painting, or seeing, or thinking of his own; and lucky it is for us too, for in this manner of every one's work is a new one, and books are fresh and agreeable, though written upon subjects however stale" ("The Rhine, by Victor Hugo," *Foreign Quarterly Review*, April 1842, p. 80; *New Sketch Book*, pp. 8–9). The book under review was Hugo's *Le Rhin, lettres à un ami*.

43. Lecture 7, pp. 198–200 (Linberg).

44. *Henry Esmond*, bk. 1, chap. 10.

45. Ibid., opening of bk. 1.

46. "Horae Catnachianae," *Fraser's Magazine*, April 1839, p. 424.

47. *The Newcomes*, chaps. 13, 33; *Henry Esmond*, bk. 3, chap. 13; *The Virginians*, chap. 2.

48. Geoffrey Tillotson, *Thackeray the Novelist* (Cambridge: Cambridge University Press, 1954), p. 173.

49. Lecture 4, p. 67 (Wight).

50. Lecture 4, p. 66 (Wight).

51. "An Invasion of France," *Works*, 5:8–9.

52. Ibid., p. 14.

53. "Meditations at Versailles," *Works*, 5:254.

54. "On Some French Fashionable Novels," *Works*, 5:83.

55. "Caricatures and Lithography in Paris," *Works*, 5:147.

56. "An Invasion of France," *Works*, 5:14–15. This passage is quoted below, p. 79.

57. "Caricatures and Lithography in Paris," *Works*, 5:148.

58. "The Fêtes of July," *Works*, 5:38–39.

59. "An Invasion of France," *Works*, 5:15.

60. "On Some French Fashionable Novels,". *Works*, 5:84.

61. "French Dramas and Melodramas," *Works*, 5:252.

62. Chap. 1, *Works*, 5:282. The quoted words are Titmarsh's reaction to his sampling of some Irish newspapers.

63. Chap. 6, *Works*, 5:331. The convent stirs up memories of his schoolboy reading of *The Monk, The Romance of the Forest, The Mysteries of Udolpho,* and other Gothic romances.

64. Chaps. 15, 16, *Works*, 5:403–43.

65. Chap. 22, *Works*, 5: 475–76.

66. Ibid., p. 476.

67. Chap. 14, *Works*, 5:399. The words describe a fanciful romance concocted by Titmarsh around the Castle of Bunratty that he visits in Limerick.

68. "Preface," *Works*, 5:587.

69. Chap. 4, *Works*, 5:616.

70. Lecture 10, p. 210 (Wight).

71. Chap. 6, *Works*, 5:633–34.

72. Chap. 2, *Works*, 5:596.

73. Lecture 10 pp. 202–3 (Wight).

74. "Meditations at Versailles," *Works*, vol. 5, facing page 260.

75. See above, p. 42, and chap. 7 below; *From Cornhill to Grand Cairo,* chap. 7, *Works*, 5:643.

76. These are among titles listed in the 1864 catalogue of his library (see above, n. 16). The influence of Cousin's lecture on "Great Men" on Thackeray's antiheroic view of history will be taken up further in the chapter on *Henry Esmond*.

77. Conclusion to lecture 10, p. 210 (Wight). Cousin's theory of history seems to reflect his association with Hegel.

78. Review of *Historic Fancies*. By the Honorable George Sidney Smythe, M. P., *Morning Chronicle*, 2 August 1844; *Contributions*, pp. 47–48.

79. *Vanity Fair*, chap. 47; emendation supplied by the editors.

80. *Vanity Fair*, chap. 67.

81. *The Newcomes*, chap. 57.

82. *The Virginians*, chap. 73.

83. *Pendennis*, chaps. 75, 44.

84. Ibid., chap. 67.

85. Lecture 10, p. 210 (Wight).

86. Lecture 1, p. 27 (Wight). This is the preliminary statement of the theme developed in Cousin's masterwork *Du vrai, du beau, et du bien* (1836; rev. 1853).

87. *Pendennis*, chap. 44.

88. Ibid., chap. 75.

89. "The Rhine," p. 81; *New Sketch Book*, p. 9.

90. "Swift," *The English Humourists of the Eighteenth Century, Works*, 7:423–24.

91. Lecture 13, p. 417 (Linberg).

92. Richard Simpson, "Thackeray," pp. 504–5. His leading French critic of our time, Raymond Las Vergnas, has called him "le saint évangile de l'humble sens commun" (*W. M. Thackeray, l'homme—le penseur—le romancier* [Paris: Librairie Champion, 1932], p. 242).

93. Lecture 13, p. 416 (Linberg).

94. *Pendennis*, chap. 46.

95. *The Newcomes*, chap. 28.

96. Simpson, "Thackeray," p. 405; "Thackeray's Place in English Literature," *Spectator*, 2 January 1864, p. 9.

97. George Henry Lewes, "Pendennis," *Leader*, 21 December 1850, p. 929. Raymond Las Vergnas entitles one chapter of his study "Le dualisme thackerayan. Ses multiples aspects," and organizes his analysis of Thackeray's mind about a series of resolved "Contradictions" (*W. M. Thackeray*, pp. 52–70).

98. Mrs. Oliphant, "Mr. Thackeray's Sketches," *Blackwood's Magazine* 119 (February 1876): 235. In her monograph Barbara Hardy describes him, particularly in relation to *Vanity Fair*, as "an *eclectic* figure, itself a virtuoso performance, shifting roles with the mercurial adaptability of an Elizabethan character-actor . . ." (*The Exposure of Luxury: Radical Themes in Thackeray* [London: Peter Owen, 1972], p. 72; italics mine).

99. Lecture 6, p. 190 (Linberg). Cousin's influence on Thackeray did not extend to the political sphere. Various essays that he contributed to the *National Standard* from May 1833 to the end of January 1834 as editor and correspondent indicate that he did not share Cousin's admiration for Louis Philippe or his enthusiasm for the Charter of 1830 (*La Charte*) that later inspired the Chartist movement in England. Later, as Paris correspondent for the *Constitutional*, he continuously denounced the July Monarchy for its hypocrisy and tyranny. See *Mr. Thackeray's Writings for the "National Standard" and "Constitutional,"* passim.

100. George Augustus Sala, *Things I Have Seen and People I Have Known*, 2 vols. (London: Cassell & Co., 1894), 1:9; Simpson, "Thackeray," pp. 477–78.

101. Charles L. Eastlake, as quoted in James Grant Wilson, *Thackeray in the United States*, 2 vols. (London: Smith, Elder, 1904), vol. 1, verso of dedication page.

"LITERARYTURE AND THE FINE HARTS"

Chapter Two

"THEY TALKED ABOUT LITERARYTURE AND THE fine harts (which is both much used by our gentlemen); and Mr. Mike was very merry," reports Mrs. Barbara, waitress at Morland's Hotel, where Mr. Michael Angelo Titmarsh had taken up temporary residence. "After dinner he was sitten over his punch, when some of our gents came in; and he began to talk and brag to them about his harticle, and what he had for it; and that he was the best cricket in Europe."[1] Titmarsh, of course, is a scarcely disguised alter ego for young William Thackeray himself in the mid-1840s when he was acquiring a reputation in magazine circles as "a good hand for light articles." In 1844, with two short-lived editorial ventures already behind him, Thackeray wrote to his publishers to ask if they would "bring me to London and put me at the head of a slashing, brilliant, gentlemanlike, six-penny aristocratic literary paper?" He had every confidence of its success, especially if authoritative writers could be secured and would sign their articles. As for his own contribution: "I would take the Fine Arts, light literature and the theatre under my charge with the dinner giving (all except *me* paying part) and I know no man in Europe who would handle it better."[2] So Thackeray set himself up in early career as a kind of gourmet of arts and letters, but he was to become something more.

In his "Pictorial Rhapsody," where Mrs. Barbara gives the testimony already quoted, Michael Angelo Titmarsh himself breaks off at a tantalizing point—just as he is about to announce an "Essay on the State of the Fine Arts in this Kingdom, my Proposals for the

General Improvement of Public Taste, and my Plan for the Education of Young Artists."[3] This elaborate title suggests an ambitious program that Thackeray himself might have undertaken had he obtained the editorship he sought at this time, but, as it happened, such a post eluded him until late in life. During these apprentice years he found it necessary to "make a dash at all the magazines," as he advised a young cousin with writing ambitions to do.[4] Since in his capacity of "cricket" Titmarsh had to chirp widely, his various "Proposals" must be pieced together from scattered places.

Some years later, when, as the author of *Pendennis,* Thackeray was vying "at the top of the tree" with the author of *David Copperfield,* one reviewer distinguished Dickens as the more "poetic in style" of the two, whereas Thackeray was regarded as the "more careful artist." To his deftness both with pen and pencil was attributed Thackeray's care and exactness of description. "Being the illustrator of his own works, and accustomed, therefore, to reduce his fancies to visible form and outline," observed this critic, "he attains in the result, greater clearness and precision, than one who works only in language, or who has to get his fancies made visible to himself by the pencil of another."[5] His technical knowledge derived from several periods of training both at the Ecole des Beaux-Arts and at ateliers (particularly the atelier of Antoine-Jean Gros) in Paris, furthermore, provided Thackeray with a special insight in judging the accomplishments of easel painters. However, in the literary preoccupations of his art criticisms—with their emphasis on action, incident, and character—one recognizes the nascent novelist fully as much as the apprentice painter.

Some of the titles of Thackeray-Titmarsh's art criticisms suggest the monocled museum hopper and dilettante: "Strictures on Pictures," "May Gambols," "Picture Gossip," "A Ramble in the Picture Galleries." Although it is true that Thackeray once offered himself to an editor as suited to handle "light matters connected with Art,"[6] there is every evidence that he did not take the painter's vocation lightly. Following him through the numerous exhibitions he viewed and reported on, one is immediately impressed with the quasi-prophetic character he attached to a calling that a good many of his audience at the time were prone to regard as little more than a skilled craft. In one review, for example, Titmarsh referred to artists as "professors at the easel,"[7] a term, one suspects, that he meant in a double sense. At the conclusion of his "Pictorial Rhapsody," he went so far as to propose himself, probably only half in jest, as the head of a projected government college for artists. This, like the "aristocratic literary paper," proved an idle dream, but *Fraser's, Punch,* the *Morning Chronicle,* the *Pictorial Times,* and other journals furnished him with a substitute for an academic chair. These outlets enabled him to promote the moral and social value of "the ingenious arts, which prevent the ferocity of the manners, and act upon them as an emollient,"[8] and much of his critical writing on "the fine harts" was aimed at strengthening the influence of the artist over the public. "What a marvellous power is this of the painter's!" he exclaims in the course of one of his gallery tours, "how each great man can excite us at his will! what a weapon he has, if he knows how to wield it!"[9] For Titmarsh the "professor at the easel," no less than the great orator, is in a position to sway and uplift multitudes, and more. A great painting can produce a spiritual effect: ". . . straightway your mind is carried away in an ecstasy,—happy thrilling hymns sound in your ears melodious,— sweet thankfulness fills your bosom. How much instruction and happiness have we gained from the men, and how grateful should we be to them!"

"Instruction and happiness." The function of delightful teaching that Thackeray's favorite classical critic Horace had assigned to the writer is here applied to the artist. Titmarsh's "Plan for the Education of Artists" was to include (like the course of study at the Ecole des Beaux-Arts under the auspices of the Institut de Paris, which may have been his model) "the benefits of a good literary education without which artists may never prosper." In his sketch "The Artists," which followed shortly after, Thackeray explicitly allied this noble body with the classical ideal of *paideia.* "If we read the works of the Reverend Doctor Lemprière, Monsieur Winckelmann, Professor Plato, and others who have written concerning the musty old Grecians," he observes, "we shall find that Artists of those barbarous times meddled with all sorts of trades besides their own, and dabbled in fighting, philosophy, metaphysics, both Scotch and German, politics, music, and the deuce knows what." He looks back fondly on the times of the "benighted heathens" when "painters were the most accomplished gentlemen—and the most accomplished gentlemen were painters: the former would make you a speech, or read you a dissertation on Kant, or lead you a regiment,—with the very best statesmen, philosopher, or soldier in Athens." He regrets the fall from eminence of the artist in his own time—a decline he blames in part on the art student himself. "Do *our* young artists study anything beyond the proper way of cutting a pencil, or drawing a model?" he asks. "Do you hear of *them* hard at work over books, and bothering their brains with musty learning? Not they forsooth: we understand the doctrine of division of labour, and each man sticks to his trade; and, in revenge, the rest of the world does not meddle with Artists."[10] As one of them, Michael Angelo Titmarsh, very much like his great namesake who also looked to classical antiquity as his ideal, was arguing for recognition of painters as members of a learned professsion rather than mere craftsmen. He was much concerned at this time that "young Artists are not generally as well instructed as they should be; and let the Royal Academy look to it, and give some sound course of lectures to their pupils on literature and history, as well as on anatomy, or light and shade."[11] In good time, Clive Newcome was to incarnate his ideal of the artist as young man. Meanwhile his art criticism served to disseminate his humanism to his fellows of the brush.

As a "professor" at the press as well as at the easel, Thackeray-Titmarsh sought to educate the public of the artist also. One indication of his overriding concern for the status of the painter is his playful device of conferring titles on them—Baron Briggs, Daniel Prince Maclise, Edwin, Earl of Landseer, Lord Charles Landseer, the Duke of Etty, Archbishop Eastlake, and His Majesty King Mulready.[12] Concurrently he tried to remove barriers between the artist and his appreciators. He attributed the greatness of Cruikshank, for one example, to his very freedom from pretension: ". . . living amongst the public, [he] has with them a general wide-hearted sympathy . . . he laughs at what they laugh at . . . he has a kindly spirit of enjoyment, with not a morsel of mysticism in his composition."[13] Behind much of Thackeray's writing on other artists, and on art appreciation in general, lies a tacit endeavor to bring the painter and his public together. Hence he explores along the way such larger issues as the artist's place in society, his utility, his original contribution to basic human needs. As himself a man of wide culture, intellectual curiosity, and versatility, he manages to demonstrate also, if incidentally, how the various arts interpenetrate and enhance each other. Criticism thereby becomes for him a process of mental and moral cultivation at once humanistic and humanitarian.

If his ultimate aim was the improvement of popular taste and of the condition of the arts in general, Titmarsh recognized that the training and practice of artists themselves were fundamental, so that much of his criticism attempted to guide them in what he regarded as the proper choice of subject matter as well as technique. His admiration for the classical curriculum of the Ecole des

Beaux-Arts did not extend to the "antique" mode of representation that was taught there. Some of Titmarsh's caustic reactions to received masterpieces reflect Thackeray's own struggles to throw off the "grand" style that he had been subjected to during his student days, "the bloated, unnatural, stilted, spouting, sham sublime, that our teachers have believed and tried to pass off as real, and which your humble servants and other anti-humbuggists should heartily, according to the strength that is in them, endeavour to pull down."[14] A student tour of the Ecole des Beaux-Arts led him to protest: "Because certain mighty men of old could make heroical statues and plays, must we be told that there is no other beauty but classical beauty?" He complains, moreover, not only of the "pale imitations of the antique" that loom up all over the official exhibitions in Paris, but of "the intolerable stupid classicalities" that clutter up the Royal Academy of London as well, "taught by men who, belonging to the least erudite country in Europe, were themselves, from their profession, the least learned among their countrymen," and, as a result, "only weighed the pupils down, and cramped their hands, their eyes, and their imaginations; drove them away from natural beauty . . . and sent them rambling after artificial grace without the proper means of judging or attaining it."[15]

The "sham sublime" in its various manifestations repeatedly drew Thackeray's scorn both as art student and as art critic. We see him in the Louvre ridiculing such time-hallowed vogues as the "Imperio-Davido-classical school," questioning the value of a "classicism inspired by rouge, gas-lamps, and a few lines in Lemprière, and copied half from ancient statues, and half from a naked guardsman at one shilling and sixpence the hour!" He is just as hard on "this absurd humbug called the Christian or Catholic art," paying tribute instead to "Antichrist" Titian and "Martin Luther" Rubens for freeing the artist's sensibility by substituting "wicked likenesses of men of blood, or dangerous, devilish, sensual portraits of tempting women" for "saints and martyrs, with pure eyes turned heavenward." The Nazarenes, a group of early nineteenth-century German painters active in Rome (and later to influence the Pre-Raphaelite Brotherhood), were to him "the namby-pamby mystical German school."[16] To his friend Edward FitzGerald he confided the opinion from Heidelberg that "what I have seen of the German illuminated school is donkeyism—poor *précieuse* stuff with a sickening sanctified air."[17] He was no more taken with the *style historique* that seems to have abounded on both sides of the Channel. "We have an exhibition here with 2500 pictures in it, of which about a dozen are very good, but there is nobody near Wilkie or Etty or Landseer," Thackeray reported in a letter to his friend and fellow artist Frank Stone in connection with a showing at the Luxembourg Gallery; "lots of history pieces, or what they call here 'école anecdotique,'—little facts cut [out] of history and dressed in correct costumes; battles, murders and adulteries are the subjects preferred. . . . there are lots of six-and-thirty feet canvasses, but not a good one among them."[18] We get one sample from the school in the "Boadishia . . . with the Roman 'elmet, cuirass and javelin of the period" painted by Clive Newcome's master Gandish, and another in Clive's own *General Wellesley at the Battle of Assaye* that he later disowns.[19]

The successful artist for Titmarsh, no less than the successful writer, is dignified without pretension. An unnamed young man who attends a show with him at the Royal Academy described in "Picture Gossip" sounds like Thackeray's spokesman. Like Clive Newcome, this young man has studied "High Art" in Rome, and counterreacts: "At the tragic, swaggering, theatrical-historical pictures he yawned; before some of the grand flashy landscapes he stood without the least emotion; but before some quiet scenes of humor or pathos, or some easy little copy of nature, the youth stood in pleased contemplation."[20] This artist-student turns for refreshment to "little pictures," which to him are "worth a hundred times more than the big ones," whose "heroism is borrowed from the theatre," and whose "sentiment is so maudlin that it makes you sick." "I would sooner have so-and-so's little sketch ('A Donkey on a Common') than What-d'ye-call-'em's enormous picture ('Sir Walter Manny and the Crusaders Discovering Nova Scotia')," he declares, "and prefer yonder unpretending sketch, 'Shrimp Catchers, Morning' (how exquisitely the long and level sands are touched off! how beautifully the morning light touches the countenances of the fishermen, and illuminates the rosy features of the shrimps!) to yonder pretentious illustration from Spencer [sic], 'Sir Botibol Rescues Una from Sir Uglimore in the Cave of the Enchantress Ichtyosaura.'"

Titmarsh obviously shares his friend's predilection toward the "small picture" for a variety of reasons. At times he is simply the antisnob. "'Bertrand de Gourdon pardoned by Richard' is a work of some merit," he concedes about a prize historical painting of the time, "but why kings, Mr. Cross? Why kings, Messieurs artists? Have men no hearts, save under the purple? Does sorrow only sit upon thrones?"[21] As he says elsewhere: "A man, as a man, from a dustman up to Aeschylus, is God's work, and good to read, as all works of Nature are."[22] At other times he cautions the budding artist to scale down his ambition, as Clive Newcome learns to do. Unlike Browning's Andrea del Sarto, Titmarsh believes that a man's reach should not exceed his grasp. "I see no symptoms of thought, or of minds strong and genuine enough to cope with elevated subjects," complains the disenchanted disciple of "High Art" before the "heroic" paintings at the Royal Academy. "If, however, the aspiring men don't succeed, the modest do," he adds, "and what they have really seen or experienced, our artists can depict with successful accuracy and delightful skill."[23] Fundamentally, however, size, great or small, for Titmarsh was related to the principle of *economy*—the artist's ability to make much of little. "It is absurd you will say . . . for Titmarsh, or any other Briton, to grow so politically enthusiastic about a four-foot canvas, representing a ship, a steamer, a river, and a sunset," he interrupts his praise of Turner's *Fighting Téméraire;* "But herein surely lies the power of the great artist. He makes you see and think of a great deal more than the objects before you; he knows how to soothe or intoxicate, to fire or to depress by a few notes, or forms, or colours, of which we cannot trace the effect to the source, but only acknowledge the power." "It is a grand and touching picture; and looks as large as if the three-foot canvas had been twenty," he remarks of William Etty's *The Prodigal Son,* concluding "what a world of thought can be conjured up out of a few inches of painted canvas." In a museum in Brussels he is struck by a little Rubens portrait of a governess: " . . . just the finest portrait that was ever seen. Only a half-length; but such a majesty, such a force, such a splendor, such a simplicity about it. . . . Here stands the majestic woman in her every day working dress of black satin, *looking your hat off,* as it were."[24]

From such reactions one infers that Titmarsh's rejection of "the ancient, heroic, allegorical subjects," as he denounces them in one sweeping anathema,[25] is part of his campaign for the contemporary, domestic, realistic subject matter he considers more suitable to the modern artist. For one thing, such subjects brought the artist closer to what he was painting than was possible with models, making for that quality he prized above all else in art—a spontaneity of response that can readily be transferred to the viewer. "These pictures come straight to the heart, and then all criticism and calculation vanishes at once," he writes of a genre piece that touched him. "Not one of these figures but has a grace and soul of his own; no conventional copies of the stony antique; no distorted caricatures, like those of your 'classiques,'" he notes with pleasure about William Mulready's *Seven Ages*, " . . . but such expressions as a great poet would draw, who thinks profoundly and truly, and never forgets . . . grace and beauty withal."[26] Thackeray seems here to have carried with him one lesson he learned from his schoolboy reading in Watt's *Logic*: " . . . and let as many of your ideas as possible be the representation of things, and not merely the representation of other men's ideas. . . . thus your soul, like some noble building, shall be furnished with original paintings, and not with mere copies." Various judgments show his inclination toward "original" work in favor of "copies."[27] Holman Hunt's portrait heads impress him with their "real nature, real expression, real startling home poetry"; on the other hand, "What could Monsieur Laffond care about the death of Eudamidas? What was Hecuba to the Chevalier Drolling, or Chevalier Drolling to Hecuba?" he asks, as he turns away from two derivative products of the "Imperio-Davido-classical" school in the Louvre. Far more appealing to him are *La prière* by Monsieur Trimolet, "a quiet little painting" depicting a missal painter and his wife praying for the life of a sickly child; Madame Juillerat's representation of Saint Elizabeth of Hungary leading a little beggar boy into her house, with its "pleasant, mystic, innocent look," which leaves one "all the better for regarding it"; Monsieur Biard's *Slave Trade,* judged "as fine as Hogarth"; Monsieur Meissonier's *The Chess Players,* "about four-inches square . . . truly an astonishing piece of workmanship. No silly tricks of effect, and abrupt startling shadow and light, but a picture painted with the minuteness and accuracy of a daguerreotype. and as near as possible perfect in its kind . . . every one of them [chess players and chessmen] an accurate portrait, with all the light, shadow, roundness, character, and colour belonging to it."[28]

The social and artistic milieu he moved in as well as his temperament conditioned Thackeray's "plebianism" toward painting. As art student, critic, and observer of the social scene, he came of age in a period of the democratization and popularization of the arts, an era characterized, according to a recent art historian, by "the co-existence of many different genres, often of a highly specialized nature, the relative indifference to mythology, the corresponding love of landscape and seascape, the interest in domestic scenes, mild anecdotic pleasantries, in still life, in very highly finished surfaces, and very minute naturalism, the emphasis on people rather than ideas, on psychological and moral problems, rather than on

theoretical programmes."[29] In his *Paris Sketch Book*, Thackeray
shows that he was very much aware of the new trend. Here he
relates "the little pictures" to which he responded with so much
pleasure to "that agreeable branch of the art for which we have I
believe no name, but which the French call *genre*." He attaches
other labels to these pictures of which "there are at Paris several
eminent professors"—such as "small history subjects," "the serious
melodramatic," and, with a nod toward the new patrons for the
emergent artists of the 1830s and 1840s, "the *bourgeois* style."[30] In
1843, in a fictitious letter addressed to a hypothetical artist, one
Sanders McGilp, Esq., he expresses his satisfaction with the analogous trend in his own country toward what came to be known as
"Dutch painting." "They paint from *the heart* more than of old, and
less from the old heroic, absurd, incomprehensible, unattainable
rules. They look at Nature very hard, and match her with the best
of their eyes and ability," he reports of the new English school.
"They do not aim at such great subjects as heretofore, or at subjects
which the world is pleased to call great, viz., tales from Hume or
Gibbon of royal personages under various circumstances, of battle,
murder, and sudden death. . . . The heroic, and peace be with it!
has been deposed; and our artists, in place, cultivate the pathetic
and the familiar."[31]

In espousing the "pathetic and familiar" or "bourgeois art"
through his alter ego Titmarsh and other mouthpieces such as
Professor Byles and M. Gobemouche, or sounding boards such as
M. Anatole Victor de Bricabrac and the young dropout from the
Academy at Rome, Thackeray obviously was endeavoring to raise
not only the status of modern artists but also the prestige of the
ordinary, the local, and the temporal as their proper subjects.
"Now, as Nature made every man with a nose and eyes of his own,
she gave him a character of his own too," he muses on one of his
gambols among the galleries of Paris, "and yet we, O foolish race!
must try our very best to ape some one or two of our neighbours,
whose ideas fit us no more than their breeches!"[32] Accordingly he
finds his delectation in scenes taken from popular literature (e.g.,
Leslie's "Vicar of Wakefield," Maclise's "Gil Blas") as well as from
everyday life (e.g., Redgrave's depiction of a governess in sorrow as
she reads a black-edged note; Stone's representation of a rustic
young lover proposing; Charles Landseer's country drinking party;
McNee's "young person musing in a quiet nook and thinking of her
love").[33] In the Louvre he is moved by *The Two Friends,* by a minor
genre artist, M. Debay, which concentrates attention on a nursing

mother who has taken on the additional burden of feeding the infant of a feeble companion. "Monsieur Debay's pictures are not bad, as most of the others . . . appertaining to the *bourgeois* class," he observes somewhat condescendingly, "but, good or bad, I can't but own that I like to see these honest, hearty representations which work upon good simple feeling in a good, downright way; and if not works of art, are certainly works that can do a great deal of good, and make honest people happy." As one who, he was to write in *Henry Esmond,* "would have History familiar rather than heroic," he responds with equal emotion to the "human" side of great men, represented in painting. A picture in the Louvre showing Napoleon reading military dispatches while his infant son sleeps on his knee evoked this reaction from the worldly Titmarsh: "What a contrast! The conqueror of the world, the stern warrior, the great giver of laws and ruler of nations, he dare not move because the little baby is asleep and he would not disturb him for all the kingdoms he knows so well how to conquer." This may not be art either, he concludes, "but it is pleasant to see fat, good-natured mothers and grandmothers clustered round this picture and looking at it with solemn eyes."[34]

With such responses we find Titmarsh shedding the sophistication of the critic and connoisseur to put himself in the place of the naïve appreciator. In this role he displays, like his hero Philip Firmin, a "childish sensibility for what was tender, helpless, pretty, or pathetic; and a mighty scorn of imposture, wherever he found it."[35] Out of these twin impulses issue both his denunciation of the "sham sublime" and his championship of the "true pathetic" in art as well as in life. The combination of inclination, trial and error, and circumstance drew Thackeray toward "low art." His recognition of the rarity of transcendent genius and his own modest accomplishment as a painter have already been suggested as influences on his taste, together with his desire to improve the rapport between the artists and the general public. Above all, however, Thackeray became convinced that the modern artist's principal function was to interpret his world as his predecessors had interpreted theirs, and much of his writing on art, accordingly, is directed toward stimulating the alertness of his fellow artists to their environment.

"It is the study of Nature, surely, that profits us, and not of these imitations of her," is the credo advanced by Titmarsh to the copiers of Michelangelo in Saint Peter's and of Poussin and David in the Louvre.[36] As Thackeray pointed out in an essay on a literary man of his acquaintance, "originality" should be the primary goal of the creative artist, to be achieved not so much by inventiveness as by working from fresh sources of inspiration: "The very characteristic of genius is to be imitative—first of authors, then of nature. Books lead us to fancy feelings that are not yet genuine. Experience is necessary to record those which colour our own existence; and the style becomes original in proportion as the sentiment it expresses is sincere."[37] *Punch's Prize Novelists,* which followed this essay by a year, seems to have been intended to demonstrate, among other things, the absurdity of "fancy feelings" produced by reading untested by experience. Books, we gather from this famous series of parodies, can carry the creative mind just so far and no farther. The same goes for pictures and the toadies after the "false antique" and the "sham sublime" in painting. Thackeray once confided to a friend, after attempts to copy two Titians, a Leonardo portrait, and some Dutch masters in the Louvre: "They are all of them very bad, but I don't despair—tonight I begin at the life academy."[38] One has the feeling that here Thackeray meant "life academy" in other than the art student's sense. Here he seems to be in accord with the plein-air creed of the Barbizon painters who anticipated the impressionists.

"Copy Nature," Thackeray-Titmarsh admonished his fellow artists, a doctrine that goes back at least as far as Aristotle—and one always easier to pronounce than to put into practice. What Thackeray meant beyond the classical mimesis can be inferred, if not precisely pinned down. The influence has already been suggested of Watts's *Logic,* which urged the learning "as much as possible at first hand."[39] Along these lines, some of Titmarsh's "strictures on pictures" are of interest mainly for what they tell the artist *not* to do. He finds the "humbug" of David and Girodet less deplorable than that of the German Nazarenes, for one instance, because the first, he contends, is "founded on Nature at least," while the latter is "made up of silly affectations and improvements upon Nature."[40] *"On n'embellit pas la nature,* my dear Bricabrac," he declares to a supposed Parisian confidant concerning one of his more controversial countrymen; "one may make pert caricatures of it, or mad exaggerations like Mr. Turner in his fancy pieces. O ye gods! why will he not stick to copying her majestical countenance, instead of daubing it with some absurd antics and fard of his own?"[41] Distortion and mannerism, it appears from such remarks, are to be avoided. Thackeray himself freely indulged in "mad exaggerations" when it came to satire and parody, and was not above "pert caricatures" in his cartoons and decorated initials, but he looked for correct representation in scenes and portraits from life.[42]

On the positive side, the artist's great gift, according to Titmarsh, seems to be the ability to bring out the qualities inherent in nature. The successful artist, we gather from some pictures that he praises, stimulates our sensuous response to things of this world. Among painters in the grand style, Titian and Rubens are hailed as the harbingers of a new dawn in art "with their brilliant colours and dashing worldly notions." As for contemporaries: "Look for a while at Mr. Etty's pictures and away you rush, your 'eyes on fire' drunken with the luscious colours that are poured out for you on the liberal canvas. . . . You fly from this . . . and plunge into a green shady landscape of Lee or Creswick, and follow a quiet stream babbling beneath whispering trees, and chequered with cool shade and golden sunshine; or you set the world—nay the Thames and the ocean—on fire with the incendiary Turner." Titmarsh's enthusiasms extend also to those artists who stir the elemental emotions: ". . . you laugh with honest, kind-hearted Webster, or you fall a-weeping with Monsieur Biard for his poor blacks."[43] Although a follower of nature, the artist, for Titmarsh, is no literalist. Far from being a mere transcriber of the external world, it is the artist's "great end . . . to strike far deeper than the sight," Titamarsh proclaims in one of his critical pieces.[44] Accuracy of drawing combines with spontaneity of feeling in his conception of "nature." A good picture is at once eye-filling and, in his own term, "rhapsodic."

Titmarsh certainly did not believe that technique alone made a painter, as in his judgment, for one example, of Charles Landseer's biblical picture *Pillage of a Jew's House,* in his opinion "a very well and carefully painted picture, containing a great many figures and good points; but we are not going to praise it: it wants vigour to our taste, and what you call *actualité.*"[45] A similar fault is found with one of Charles Eastlake's illustrations from the Bible: "The scene is not represented with its actual agony and despair; but it is, as it were, a sort of limning to remind you of the scene."[46] From these and other remarks one can easily gather that for Titmarsh, vitality—the illusion of living people—is the greatest value that the artist can impart to his work—and one that can make up for lack of skill. In some of his criticisms he tries to get to the root of this quality. The figures in the Landseer painting, he complains, look "as if they were in a tableau and paid for standing there; one longs

to see them all in motion and naturally employed." Charles Robert
Leslie, a rival painter, is congratulated on the other hand for his
illustration of a scene from *Roderick Random,* in which each character "acts his part in the most admirable unconscious way—there is
no attempt at a *pose* or a *tableau* . . . everybody is busied, and
perfectly naturally, with the scene, at which the spectator is admitted
to look."[47] For Titmarsh dynamism and the sense of motion are
among the artist's means for conveying the illusion of actuality in a
picture, whether the scene is in the present or the past, the person
king or commoner. "You want something more than a composition,
and a set of costumes and figures decently posed and studied," he
observed of a historical episode painted by Charles Leedseer,
Charles I Before the Battle of Edge Hill, in which the doomed monarch
is shown relaxing by an inn on the eve of battle, watching a young
girl munch on a ham bone. "Now all this is very well, but you want
something more than this in a historic picture, which should have
its parts, characters, varieties, and climax like a drama. You don't
want the *Deus intersit* for no other purpose than to look at a knuckle
of ham."[48] To this "cricket" the art of painting, no less than the art
of story telling, means involving the audience in active life.

Young Clive Newcome, once he is removed from Gandish's
studio, is thus engaged as he plants himself in the streets of Rome
to observe the passing parade: "By this time Clive's books were full
of sketches. . . . Ruins imperial and medieval; peasants and bag-
pipemen; Passionists with shaven polls; Capuchins and the equally
hairy frequenters of the Café Greco; painters of all nations who
resort there; Cardinals and their queer equipages and attendants;
the Holy Father himself . . . the dandified English on the Pincio
and the wonderful Roman members of the hunt—were not all
these designed by the young man and admired by his friends in
after days?"[49] Not destined himself for great success as a painter,
Thackeray turned his alert eye, sensitivity to color, and heightened
tactile sense—all the faculties he endeavored to train in himself and
in his fellow art students—to good use in the word pictures and
living dioramas that distinguish his novels. Some of his most im-
pressive effects can be attributed to verbal translation of techniques
he admired among the pictorial realists and "bourgeois" painters of
his time.

One minor French genre painter to whom Thackeray gave what
may now seem exaggerated praise was Mme Juillerat, whose paintings on medieval subjects he much preferred to the work of the
then more celebrated Nazarene school. He was impressed in par-

ticular with the convincing illusion of her religious subjects, an
effect he traces to her adoption of the methods of medieval
miniaturists: "What a fine instinct or taste it was in the old missal
illuminators to be so particular in the painting of the minor parts of
their pictures!" he exclaims; "the precise manner in which the
flowers and leaves, birds and branches, are painted, gives an air of
truth and simplicity to the whole performance, and makes nature,
as it were, an accomplice and actor in the scene going on." He is
speaking here of Mme Juillerat's representation of Saint Elizabeth
of Hungary succoring a beggar boy, the appeal of which is enhanced by such details as bright-colored roses and chirping
blackbirds. In his opinion, "if the flowers on the young ladies'
heads had been omitted, and not painted with their pleasing *minuteness* and *circumstantiality,* I fancy that the effect of the piece
would have been by no means the same."[50] Monsieur Servan,
another "artist of the mystical school," is commended for employing these "same adjuncts" with the result that the viewer's perceptions are quickened and he is drawn into the picture almost despite
himself: "One of his pictures represents Saint Augustin meditating
in a garden; a great cluster of rose-bushes, hollyhocks, and other
plants is in the foreground, most accurately delineated; and a fine
rich landscape and river stretch behind the saint. . . ."[51]

In his own verbal landscapes Thackeray applies this same "minuteness," "circumstantiality," and accuracy of delineation, as in
this description of Colonel Newcome's birthplace at Clapham:

> When his father married, Mr. Thomas Newcome, jun. and Sarah
> his nurse were transported from the cottage where they had lived in
> great comfort to the palace hard by, surrounded by lawns and gar-
> dens, pineries, graperies, aviaries, luxuries of all kinds. This
> paradise, five miles from the Standard at Cornhill, was separated
> from the outer world by a thick hedge of tall trees, and an ivy-
> covered porter's gate, through which they who travelled to London
> on top of the Clapham coach could only get a glimpse of the bliss
> within. It was a serious paradise. . . . The rooks in the elms cawed
> sermons at morning and evening; the peacocks walked demurely on
> the terraces; the guinea-fowls looked more quaker-like than those
> savoury-birds usually do.[52]

The author (through his alter ego Arthur Pendennis) has indeed
made nature "an accomplice and an actor in the scene going on,"
the very birds taking on the character of this "serious paradise." In
another such "set piece" from *The Virginians*—the estate of the
Lambert family, which we see for the first time in company with
Harry Warrington—tangible detail helps to identify home and
owner:

Two tall gates, each surmounted by a couple of heraldic monsters, led from the high-road up to a neat broad stone terrace, whereon stood Oakhurst House: a square brick building, with windows faced with stone, and many high chimneys, and a tall roof surmounted by a fair balustrade. Behind the house stretched a large garden, where there was plenty of room for cabbages as well as roses to grow; and before the mansion, separated from it by the high-road, was a field of many acres, where the Colonel's cows and horses were at grass. Over the centre window was a carved shield supported by the same monsters who pranced or ramped upon the entrance-gates; and a coronet over the shield. The fact is, that the house has been origi- nally the jointure-house of Oakhurst Castle, which stood hard by,— its chimneys and turrets appearing over the surrounding woods, now bronzed with the darkest foliage of summer. (chap. 22).

This being a literary landscape, the author has supplied us with a historical note.

In his criticisms of portraits—another form of genre piece that he much admired—Thackeray looked for accuracy of sartorial de- tail. "A painter should be as careful about his costumes as an histo- rian about his dates, or he plays the deuce with his composition," he declared on one of his visits to the Royal Academy. On this occasion his eye is caught by George Richmond's *The Children of Colonel Lindsay:* "Such satins and lace, such diamond rings and charming little lapdogs, were never painted before,—not by Watteau, the first master of the *genre,*—and Lancret, who was scarcely his in- ferior."[53] Not surprisingly, Thackeray clothes his own personages fastidiously:

At a quarter past ten the Major invariably made his appearance in the best blacked boots in all London, with a checked morning cravat that never was rumpled until dinner time, a buff waistcoat which bore the crown of the sovereign on the buttons, and linen so spotless that Mr. Brummel himself asked the name of his laundress, and would probably have employed her had not misfortunes compelled that great man to fly the country. Pendennis's coat, his white gloves, his whiskers, his very cane, were perfect of their kind as specimens of the costume of a military man *en retraite.*[54]

He takes pains even with supernumerary figures: "Of the other illustrious persons whom Becky had the honour to encounter on this her first presentation to the grand world, it does not become the present historian to say much. There was his Excellency the Prince Peterwaradin, with his Princess; a nobleman tightly girthed, with a large military chest, on which the *plaque* of his order shone magnificently, and the red collar of the Golden Fleece round his neck. He was the owner of countless flocks."[55] No admirer of still life or static pose, as we have seen, Thackeray is most noteworthy for his ability literally to animate a portait, as in our introduction to Henry Esmond's aunt, Lady Isabella, at home:

> My Lady Viscountess's face was daubed with white and red up to the eyes to which paint gave an unearthly glare: she had a tower of lace on her head, under which was a bush of black curls—borrowed curls. . . . She sate in a great chair by the fire-corner; in her lap was a spaniel-dog that barked furiously; on a little table by her was her ladyship's snuff-box and her sugar-plum box. She wore a dress of black velvet, and a petticoat of flame-coloured brocade. She had as many rings on her fingers as the old woman of Banbury Cross; and pretty small feet which she was fond of showing, with great gold clocks to her stockings, and white pantofles with red heels; and an odour of musk was shook out of her garments whenever she moved or quitted the room, leaning on her tortoiseshell stick, little Fury barking at her heels.[56]

Visual and kinetic stimuli join to bring My Lady Viscountess to life. She does not merely "sit" for her portrait, but gets up out of her chair and casts off perfume. Even her lap dog is active.

Titmarsh was equally sensitive to the surroundings amidst which his persons sit and move, as indicated in one of his gallery talks by his admiration for the "curious fidelity and skill" of Douglas Morison's Windsor and Buckingham Palace sketches:

> There is the dining-hall in Buckingham Palace with all the portraits, all the candles in all the chandeliers; the China gimcracks over the mantlepiece, the dinner-table set out; the napkins folded mitre-wise, the round water-glasses, the sherry-glasses, the champagne ditto. . . . There is the Queen's own chamber at Windsor, her Majesty's piano, her Royal writing-table, an escritoire with pigeon-holes, where the august papers are probably kept; and very curious, clever, and ugly all these pictures of furniture are too, and will be a model for the avoidance of upholsterers in coming ages.[57]

In his own "interiors" Thackeray succeeds in giving solidity and density to decor. For one notable instance we are quickly made to feel the massiveness and stuffiness of the Brian Newcomes' mansion on Park Lane, as we enter it alongside Clive and his father the Colonel:

> A splendid portrait of the late Earl of Kew in his peer's robes hangs opposite his daughter and her harp. We are writing of George the Fourth's reign; I daresay there hung in the room a fine framed print of that great sovereign. The chandelier is in a canvas bag; the vast sideboard, whereon are erected open frames for the support of Sir Brian Newcome's grand silver trays, which on dinner days gleam on that festive board, now groans under the weight of Sir Brian's bluebooks. An immense receptacle for wine, shaped like a Roman

sarcophagus, lurks under the sideboard. Two people sitting at that large dining-table must talk very loud so as to make themselves heard across those great slabs of mahogany covered with damask. The butler and the servants who attend at the table take a long time walking around it. I picture to myself two persons of ordinary size sitting in that great room at that great table, far apart, in neat evening costume, sipping a little sherry, silent, genteel, and glum.[58]

Furthermore, in Thackeray's remarkable ability to give texture to objects and surfaces, one can recognize the literary equivalent of a technique that he observed among French artists as a further aid to the illusion of actuality. During one of his strolls through the Louvre, he noticed that some landscape painters had "laid aside the slimy weak manner formerly in vogue, and perhaps have adopted in its place a method equally reprehensible—that of plastering their pictures excessively." This method, known technically as *impasting (impasto)* is effective in the representation of solid masses, "a piece of old timber, or a crumbling wall, or the ruts and stones in a road," but he felt that it was being employed to excess in some of the works he was looking at: ". . . here the skies are trowelled on; the light-vapouring distances are as thick as plum-pudding, the cool clear shadows are mashed-down masses of sienna and indigo." Still, he concedes that "by these violent means, a certain power is had."[59]

Thackeray himself liked at times to "plaster" on detail, particularly to suggest human "old timber" or a "crumbling wall" like the well-named Lady Castlemouldy:

A stout countess of sixty, *décolletée,* painted, wrinkled, with rouge up to her drooping eyelids, and diamonds twinkling in her wig, is a wholesome and edifying, but not a pleasant sight. . . . If even Cynthia looks haggard of an afternoon, as we may see her sometimes in the present winter season, with Phoebus staring her out of countenance from the opposite side of the heavens, how much more can old Lady Castlemouldy keep her head up when the sun is shining full upon it through the chariot windows, and showing all the chinks and crannies with which time has marked her face?[60]

As the party went down the great staircase of Gaunt House, the morning had risen stark and clear over the black trees of the square; the skies were tinged with pink; and the cheeks of some of the people at the ball,—ah, how ghastly they looked! That admirable and devoted Major [Pendennis] above all,—who had been for hours by Lady Clavering's side, ministering to her and feeding her body with everything that was nice, and her ear with everything that was sweet and flattering,—oh! what an object he was! The rings round his eyes were of the colour of bistre; those orbs themselves were like the plovers' eggs whereof Lady Clavering and Blanche had tasted; the wrinkles in his old face were furrowed with deep gashes; and a silver stubble, like an elderly morning dew, was glittering on his chin, and alongside the dyed whiskers, now limp and out of curl.[61]

Human habitations at times appear three dimensional under Thackeray's trowel-like pen. Queens Crawley looms up ponderously before Becky and Rawdon as they approach the ancestral hall after an absence of nine years: "They were going through the lodge-gates kept by old Mrs. Lock, whose hand Rebecca insisted upon shaking, as she flung open the creaking old iron gate, and the carriage passed between the two moss-grown pillars surmounted by the dove and serpent. . . . The gravel walk and terrace had been scraped quite clean. A grand painted hatchment was already over the great entrance, and two very solemn and tall personages in black each flung open a leaf of the door as the carriage pulled up at the familiar steps."[62] This method of "laying-on" can be seen in full play in a lesser novel where tactile imagery is employed to evoke an unhappy household with an impact that is as much physical as visual:

> Everything in Dr. Firmin's house was as handsome as might be, and yet somehow the place was not cheerful. One's steps fell noiselessly on the faded Turkey carpet; the room was large, and all save the dining-table in a dingy twilight. The picture of Mrs. Firmin looked at us from the wall, and followed us about with wild violet eyes. Philip Firmin had the same violet odd bright eyes, and the same coloured hair of an auburn tinge; in the picture it fell in long wild masses over the lady's back as she leaned with bare arms on a harp. Over the sideboard was the Doctor, in a black velvet coat and a fur collar, his hand on a skull, like Hamlet. Skulls of oxen, horned with wreaths, formed the cheerful ornaments of the cornice. On the side-table glittered a pair of cups, given by grateful patients, looking like receptacles rather for funereal ashes than for festive flowers or wine. . . . The drawing-room had a rhubarb-coloured flock paper . . . a great piano, a harp smothered in a leather bag in the corner, which the languid owner now never touched; and everybody's face seemed scared and pale in the great looking-glasses, which reflected you over and over again into the distance, so that you seemed to twinkle off right through the Albany into Piccadilly.[63]

This thickening of verbal paint is employed by Thackeray in his living portraits, vivified landscapes, and vitalized interiors to represent the excesses of affectation, pomposity, and ornamentation indulged in by his personages. The technique, in its particular application here, might be called the impasto of imposture.

Thackeray's ability to bring his leading characters to life is widely acclaimed, but not so much, perhaps, the pains he takes with the

numerous "extras" in his novels. As art critic he complained of one
of Sir David Wilkie's large-scale paintings that the men and women
in it "seem to be painted with snuff and tallow-grease: the faces are
merely indicated, and without individuality; the forms only half-
drawn, and almost always wrong."[64] As literary painter Thackeray
could not be accused of such negligence. He manages to give precise identity even to figures whom we meet but fleetingly at Lord
Steyne's ball in Gaunt House: "There was Mr. John Paul Jefferson
Jones, titularly attached to the American Embassy, and correspondent of the New York Demagogue. . . . He and George
[Lord Steyne] had been most intimate at Naples, and had gone up
Vesuvius together. Mr. Jones wrote a full and particular account of
the dinner, which appeared duly in the Demagogue."[65] Mr. Jones
has been particularized, not so much by painterly means in this
instance, but through the narrative artist's medium of time—past,
present, and future fused in one moment. Other subsidiary figures
are individualized through names and genealogy:

> Here, before long, Becky received not only "the best" foreigners
> (as the phrase is in our noble and admirable society slang), but some
> of the best English people too . . . such as the great Lady Fitz-Willis,
> the Patron Saint of Almack's, the great Lady Slowbore, the great
> Lady Grizzel Macbeth (she was Lady G. Glowry, daughter of Lord
> Grey of Glowry), and the like. When the Countess of Fitz-Willis (her
> ladyship is of the King-Street family, see Debrett and Burke,) takes
> up a person, he or she is safe. There is no question about them any
> more. Not that my Lady Fitz-Willis is any better than anybody else,
> being, on the contrary, a faded person, fifty-seven years of age, and
> neither handsome, nor wealthy, nor entertaining; but it is agreed on
> all sides that she is of the "best people."[66]

Always diverting, as well as revealing how close he was to the best
practices of the genre painters of his time, are the ways in which
Thackeray met the challenge, inevitably posed by the panoramic
scale of his novels, of "placing" large assemblages. The care he took
with such scenes can be exemplified by the episode where Arthur
Pendennis goes to dine with "The Knights of the Temple":

> In term-time, Mr. Pen showed a most praiseworthy regularity in
> performing one part of the law-student's course of duty, and eating
> his dinners in Hall. Indeed, that Hall of the Upper temple is a sight
> not uninteresting, and with the exception of some trifling im-
> provements and anachronisms which have been introduced to the
> practice there, a man may sit down and fancy that he joins in a meal
> of the seventeenth century. The bar have their messes, the students
> have their tables apart; the benchers sit at the high table on the
> raised platform, surrounded by pictures of judges of the law and
> portraits of royal personages who have honoured its festivities with

their presence and patronage. Pen looked about, on his first introduction, not a little amused with the scene which he witnessed.
Among his comrades of the student class there were gentlemen of all
ages, from sixty to seventeen; stout grey-headed attorneys who were
proceeding to take the superior dignity,—dandies and men-about-
town who wished for some reason to be barristers of seven years'
standing,—swarthy, black-eyed natives of the Colonies,who came to
be called here before they practiced in their own islands,—and many
gentlemen of the Irish nation, who make a sojourn in Middle Temple Lane before they return to the green country of their birth.
There were little squads of reading students who talked law all
dinner-time; there were rowing men, whose discourse was of sculling
matches, the Red House, Vauxhall, and the Opera; there were
others great in politics, and orators of the students' debating clubs;
with all which sets, except the first, whose talk was an almost unknown and a quite uninteresting language to him, Mr. Pen made a
gradual acquaintance, and had many points of sympathy.[67]

One of Thackeray's American admirers rightly pointed out that
his people "are never portrayed in isolation . . . the mutuality of
their numerous and vital relations furnishes an important strand in
the texture of the very story in which they figure."[68] In deploying
the large populations of his huge novelistic canvases Thackeray
seems to have learned something from contemporaneous artists
who turned their attention to groups of people. "I wish you could
see the wonderful accuracy with which all these figures are drawn,"
writes Titmarsh to Monsieur Anatole Bricabrac in praise of Daniel
Maclise's *Christmas.* He marvels at the "extraordinary skill with
which the artist has managed to throw into a hundred different
faces a hundred different characters and individualities of joy."
Every one of the "five hundred merry figures painted on this canvas, gobbling, singing, kissing, carousing," he notes, "has his own
particular smile."[69] Thackeray achieves an analogous variety within
unity in one of his big partying scenes—Harry Warrington's ball at
the Assembly Rooms in Tunbridge Wells:

> Mr. Warrington had the honour of a duchess's company at his
> tea-drinking—Colonel Lambert's and Mr. Prior's heroine, the
> Duchess of Queensberry. And though the Duchess carefully turned
> her back upon a Countess who was present, laughed loudly, glanced
> at the latter over her shoulder, and pointed at her with her fan, yet
> almost all the company pushed, and bowed, and cringed, and smiled,
> and backed before this Countess, scarcely taking any notice of Her
> Grace of Queensberry and her jokes, and her fan, and her airs. Now
> this Countess was no other than the Countess of Yarmouth-
> Walmoden, the lady whom his majesty George the Second, of Great
> Britain, France, and Ireland, King, defender of the Faith, delighted
> to honour. . . . And everybody congratulated the youth on his good

fortune. At night, all the world, in order to show their loyalty doubtless, thronged round my Lady Yarmouth; my Lord Bamborough
was eager to make her *partie* at quadrille; my Lady Blanche Pendra-
gon, that model of virtue; Sir Lancelot Quintain, that pattern of
knighthood and valour; Mr. Dean of Ealing, that exemplary divine
and preacher; numerous gentlemen, noblemen, generals, colonels,
matrons, and spinsters of the highest rank, were on the watch for a
smile from her, or eager to jump up and join her card-table. Lady
Maria waited upon her with meek respect, and Madame de Bernstein treated the Hanoverian lady with profound gravity and courtesy.[70]

One notices here how Thackeray has managed to give each partici-
pant in this scene (incidental as it is to the novel as a whole) "his own
particular smile" or specific motivation, united as they all are in
their deference to George the Second's current paramour. He has
also avoided making this group just so many figures in a tableau,
but practiced his own principle by seeing to it that they are "all in
motion and naturally employed."[71]

This ability to differentiate individuals within a heterogeneous
assembly also impressed Titmarsh in one of Maclise's more serious
studies. "A large part of this vast picture Mr. Maclise has painted
very finely," he writes of this painter's representation of the banquet scene from *Macbeth*. "The lords are all there in gloomy state,
fierce stalwart men in steel; the variety of attitude and light in
which the different groups are placed, the wonderful knowledge
and firmness with which each individual figure and feature are
placed down upon the canvas will be understood and admired by
the public, but by the artist still more, who knows the difficulty of
these things, which seem so easy." Furthermore, "The effect, as far
as we know, is entirely new; the figures drawn with exquisite minuteness and clearness, not in the least interrupting the general
harmony of the picture."[72] From this appreciation one turns to a
sombre scene in *The Newcomes*, the Founder's Day chapel service at
Grey Friars, as recollected by Arthur Pendennis:

The boys are already in their seats, with smug fresh faces, and shining white collars; the old black-gowned pensioners are on their
benches, the chapel is lighted, and Founders' Tomb, with its grotesque carvings, monsters, heraldries, darkles and shines with the
most wonderful shadows and lights. There he lies, Fundator Noster,
in his ruff and gown, awaiting the great Examination Day. We old-
sters, be we ever so old, become boys again as we look at that familiar
old tomb, and think how the seats were altered since we were here,
and how the doctor—not the present doctor, the doctor of *our*
time—used to sit yonder, and his awful eye used to frighten us
shuddering boys, on whom it lighted; and how the boy next us *would*

kick our shins during service time, and how the monitor would cane us afterwards because our shins were kicked. Yonder sit forty cherry-cheeked boys, thinking about home and holidays to-morrow. Yonder sit some three score old gentlemen pensioners of the Hospital, listening to the prayers and the psalms. You hear them coughing feebly in the twilight,—the old reverend blackgowns. Is Codd Ajax alive, you wonder . . . or Codd Soldier? or kind old Codd Gentleman? or has the grave closed over them? A plenty of candles lights up this chapel, and this scene of age and youth, and early memories, and pompous death. (Chap. 75)

While he has employed the narrator's privilege of extending "this scene of age and youth" back into the past, and enters into the minds of his figures as no purely graphic artist could, we can catch Thackeray working in the manner of the scene painter to impart a "general harmony" to this mingled group, united by a sense of religious awe in the midst of their various worldly concerns. Evocative detail together with imagery of color and shadow combine to create "the variety of attitude and light in which the different groups are placed."

The precision, meticulousness, and carefully wrought scenic effects of Thackeray's novels were not lost on contemporaneous reviewers, some of whom in fact praised him in the very terms he applied to genre painters. Such phrases as "minute accuracy," "minute anatomy," and "telling minuteness of detail" recur in the critical journals of the time. A memorial tribute connnected his "scrupulous fidelity to nature" to realistic painting. Graphic analogies occur here and there, as in an American review that spoke of his "pre-Raphaelite school of novel writing" (meant in compliment to his detailism), and Walter Bagehot's reference to his last completed novel, *The Adventures of Philip*, as "a sort of annotated picture."[73] The popularity of paintings based on scenes from great novels and dramas, together with the widespread diffusion of fiction in parts "with illustrations on wood and steel," helped to bring the worlds of the artist and writer together in the general mind and made such analogy natural.

For Thackeray books and paintings alike were camera obscura in which reader or viewer beheld himself. The copiousness and density of his literary portraiture and landscape painting serve not as ends in themselves, as some of his detractors have contended, but as means of imitating the dynamic quality of life (*"vis,"* "vigour," *"actualité,"* as he referred to it at various times), which he considered it the supreme function of the artist to reproduce.[74] Hence his emphasis on the present moment (or the presentness of the past in his historical subjects) and on life in process. After his death, Anne Thackeray wrote of her father: "Mr Titmarsh was for ever observing and recording what he saw. . . . He wrote it down, and he drew the pictures and sketches—specially the sketches—abroad, where shadows are crisper than with us, and houses are quainter, and the people and the scenes more pleasantly varied."[75] The verbal record of this student tour and apprenticeship is left behind in several colorful *tableaux vivants*.

> The street which we enter, that of the Faubourg St. Denis, presents a strange contrast to the dark uniformity of a London street, where everything, in the dingy and smoky atmosphere, looks as though it were painted in India-ink—black houses, black passengers, and black sky. Here, on the contrary, is a thousand times more life and colour. . . . on each side are houses of all dimensions and hues; some, but of one storey, some as high as the Tower of Babel. From these the haberdashers (and this is their favourite street) flaunt long strips of gaudy calicoes, which give a strange air of rude gaiety to the street. Milk-women, with a little crowd of gossips round each, are, at this early hour of the morning, selling the chief material of the Parisian *café-au-lait*. Gay wine-shops, painted red, and smartly decorated with vines and guilded railings are filled with workmen taking their morning's draught. . . .
>
> It is a strange, mongrel, merry place, this town of Boulogne: the little French fishermen's children are beautiful, and the little French soldiers four feet high, red-breeched, with huge *pompons* on their caps, and brown faces, and clear sharp eyes, look, for all their littleness, far more military and more intelligent that the heavy louts one has seen swaggering about the garrison towns in England. Yonder go a crowd of barelegged fishermen; there is the town idiot, mocking a woman who is screaming "Fleuve du Tage," at an inn-window, to a harp, and there are the little gamins mocking *him*. Lo! these seven young ladies with red hair and green veils, they are from neighbouring Albion, and going to bathe. Here come three Englishmen, *habitués* evidently of the place—dandy specimens of our countrymen: one has got a marine dress, another has a shooting dress, a third has a blouse and a pair of guiltless spurs—all have as much hair on the face as nature or art can supply, and all wear their hats very much on one side.[76]

Nature and art combine too in this description, which with its prominence of color and line suggest the sketcher at his drawing board. But for Thackeray, the student of Victor Cousin, the visual is but the outward manifestation of a society and a culture. Light and shade, costume and decor, unfold the spectacle of a people viewed both in aggregate and as "specimens" of cultural types. Paris and Boulogne have been vividly pictured, not merely for the delectation of the tourist, but as living, working cities, represented through characteristic habitations, occupations, and amusements. This same eye for color combined with insight into ethnic character reveal themselves in this record of a visit to Holland, a literal representation of the kind of convivial gathering that becomes a central image in his best-known novel:

> It is fair time—and the town is illuminated with a hundred thousand of extra lights and swarming with people. . . .
> The people . . . have a coarse and somewhat ruffianly physiognomy. They look by no means as innocent as a multitude of French or Germans met together for pleasure. The women have bright complexions, twinkling little eyes, and great fresh healthy grinning mouths, w^h as they smile upon the passer-by shew rows of gleaming white teeth that are more useful than beautiful. A spotless cap of white lace sits closely round these full-moon countenances; and over the head & skull and terminated by a pair of enormous corkscrew ornaments that butt out at either ear like ram's horns, lies a glistening plate of gold or silver—exceedingly fine. A tight sleeved divinity jacket w^h descends as far as a pair of enormous hips, and a pair of splay feet paddling in flat shoes and crumpled stockings, completed the costume of the Friezeland women who were here by thousands.[77]

On another tour the Maltese seaport of Valetta is caught on canvas in work, play, and worship:

> The streets are thronged with a lively, comfortable-looking population; the poor seem to inhabit handsome stone palaces with balconies and projecting windows of heavy carved stone. The lights and shadows, the cries and stenches, the fruit shops and fish-stalls, the dresses and chatter of all nations; the soldiers in scarlet and women in black mantillas; the beggars, boat-men, barrels of pickled herrings and macaroni; the shovel-hatted priests and bearded capuchins; the tobacco, grapes, onions, and sunshine; the signboards, bottled-porter stores, the statues of saints and little chapels which jostle the stranger's eyes as he goes up the once famous stairs from the Water-gate, make a scene of such pleasant confusion and liveliness as I have never witnessed before. . . . [The] ornaments are stately; castle and palaces are rising all around; and the flags, towers, and walls of Fort St. Elmo look as fresh and magnificent as if they had been erected only yesterday.[78]

Clive Newcome, sketching in the midst of the moving hordes in the streets of Rome, can be taken for a surrogate of Thackeray as author. Having planted himself amongst the throngs and the bustle of many a busy town years before he created his artist-hero, he anticipated Clive's progress from studio to the life academy to the academy of life. Humanity in juxtaposition, emergent life, the recording of events as they are taking place—these are the proper subjects for the creative imagination—literary or artistic—for

Thackeray. One of the first reviewers of *The Newcomes* wrote: "The world of 'fable-land' will never be exhausted; each generation will supply new materials for the novelist no less than for the historian, and whoever has the cunning to reproduce truly what is passing before his eyes will by that very circumstance be an original writer."[79] He understood well Thackeray's instinct for recapturing the sense of "only yesterday," the "minuteness" and "circumstantiality" that set "people and scenes" in their original environments— moment and milieu rendered eternal. Titmarsh's "Plan for the Education of Young Artists," as we have seen, was intended to turn them away from mere "artificial grace" toward that "natural beauty" that is "fresh and attainable by us all, to-day, and yesterday, and to-morrow.'[80] Even the comic artist, he believed, "ties you to all these grotesque ways by a certain lurking human kindness," and manages to insinuate "in the midst of the fun a feeling of friendliness and beauty."[81] Particularly in his famous eulogy of George Cruikshank, he upheld the position of the artist in society as friend to man. One part of his early "Proposals for the General Improvement of Public Taste" called for the breaking down of barriers among classes and degrees of society. The artist works toward this ideal through a generalized sympathy by which he directs the sensitivities of us all to "what is real, and natural, and unaffected."[82] Universal rapport therefore was essential to the artist's success, according to Titmarsh's program for "literaryture and the fine harts." "Some clever artists will do no harm in condescending . . . to suit the general taste," he wrote in one critical article. Elsewhere he expressed the conviction that in art, as in literature, "there is a higher ingredient in beauty than mere form: a skilful hand is only the second artist's quality, worthless without the first, which is a great heart."[83]

"Dexterity" remained subordinate to "sincerity" and truth to life for Thackeray in his sketches and in the novels for which they proved a preparation. As writer and artist, moreover, Thackeray seems to have had one eye on his own times, as he believed the responsible painter of life should, but the other on posterity. "Personalities are odious; but let the British public look at the pictures of the celebrated Mr. Shalloon—the moral British public," he exclaims in contemplating the work of an imaginary contemporary, "and say whether our grandchildren (or the grandchildren of the exalted personages whom Mr. Shalloon paints) will not have a queer idea of the manners of their grandmamas, as they are represented in the most beautiful, dexterous, captivating water-colours that ever were?"[84] As against the artificial attractions of the Shalloons of the art world:

> Now, any one who looks over Mr. Leech's portfolio must see that the social pictures that he gives us are authentic. What comfortable little drawing-rooms and dining-rooms, what snug libraries we enter; what fine young-gentlemanly wags they are, those beautiful little dandies who wake up gouty old grandpapa to ring the bell; who decline aunt's pudding and custards, saying that they will reserve themselves for an anchovy toast with the claret. . . . Look well at everything appertaining to the economy of the famous Mr. Briggs: how snug, quiet, appropriate all the appointments are! What a comfortable, neat, clean, middle-class house Briggs' is . . . . How cozy all the Briggs party seem in their dining-room: Briggs reading a treatise on Dog-breaking by a lamp; Mama and Grannie with their respective needleworks; the children clustering round a great book of prints—a great book of prints such as this before us, which at this season must make thousands of children happy by as many firesides!

This scene, like so many that Thackeray admired and emulated, is solid with detail, replete with actuality, and moreover,

> The inner life of all these people is represented: Leech draws them as naturally as Teniers depicts Dutch boors, or Morland pigs and stables. It is your house and mine: we are looking at everybody's family circle. Our boys coming from school give themselves such airs, the young scapegraces! our girls, going to parties, are so tricked out by fond mamas—a social history of London in the middle of the nineteenth century. As such, future students—lucky they to have a book so pleasant—will regard these pages: even the mutations of fashion they may follow here if they be so inclined.[85]

This tribute to John Leech sums up the model popular artist for Thackeray. Leech in his view did for the Age of Victoria what Hogarth had done for the Age of the Georges: "To the student of history, these admirable works must be invaluable, as they give us the most complete and truthful picture of the manners, and even the thoughts, of the past century," he had already said in praise of the painter of *The Rake's Progress* in his lectures on the eighteenth-century humorists.[86] Hogarth was a favorite of Clive Newcome, if not of his father the colonel, and through his portrait of the artist as young man Thackeray may well have been looking forward to the role he hoped to fulfill for our century. His essay on Leech was based on a picture book that brought the lithographer of *The Rising Generation* to the attention of the great public. In Thackeray's own books, word supplanted picture, but they could just as truly be called "a social history of London in the middle of the nineteenth century."

1. "A Pictorial Rhapsody: Concluded" ("Statement by Mrs. Barbara"), *Fraser's Magazine*, July 1840, pp. 124–25; *Works*, 13:356–58.

2. 26 February 1844 to Bradbury and Evans, *Letters*, 2:163. The full title of the first journal Thackeray edited was *The National Standard and Journal of Literature, Science, Music, Theatricals and the Fine Arts*.

3. "A Pictorial Rhapsody: Concluded," p. 123; *Works*, 13:355.

4. 21 December 1843 to Richard Bedingfield, *Letters*, 2:137.

5. [David Masson], "Pendennis and Copperfield," *North British Review*, May 1851, p. 76. In this article Masson also called attention to the names of Thackeray's characters as a sign of his distinctness of visual perception (e.g., Dr. Slocum, Mrs. Mactoddy, Glowry).

6. 6 April 1845 to Thomas Longman, editor of the *Edinburgh Review*, *Letters*, 2:190–91.

7. "On Men and Pictures," *Fraser's Magazine*, July 1841, p. 102; *Works*, 13:368. In the Paris ateliers, which Thackeray knew as an art student, teachers of anatomy and perspective were called *professeurs*.

8. This Ovidian phrase is quoted by Thackeray in his essay "On the Genius of George Cruikshank," *Westminster Review*, June 1840, p. 4; *Works*, 13:285.

9. "A Pictorial Rhapsody," *Fraser's Magazine*, June 1840, p. 720; *Works*, 13:340.

10. *Works*, 3:536. Originally published in *Heads of the People; or, Portraits of the English*, Drawn by Kenny Meadows (London, 1841). For details on Parisian art education throughout this chapter, I have drawn on Albert Boime, *The Academy and French Painting in the Nineteenth Century* (London: Phaidon; New York: Praeger, 1971), in addition to what I could infer from Thackeray's observations.

11. Cf. a qualifying remark he once made about Daniel Maclise, generally one of his favorites among contemporary painters: "What might not this man do, if he could read and meditate a little, and profit by the works of men whose taste and education were superior to his own" ("Strictures on Pictures," *Fraser's Magazine*, June 1838, p. 763; *Works*, 13:267).

12. "Strictures on Pictures," *Works*, 13:262–63; "A Second Lecture on the Fine Arts," *Fraser's Magazine*, June 1839, p. 743; *Works*, 13:273. "Strictures on Pictures" in its magazine appearance was accompanied by a sketch of Titmarsh placing a laurel wreath on Mulready's brow.

13. "George Cruikshank," p. 10; *Works*, 13:291.

14. "On the French School of Painting," *Paris Sketch Book*, *Works*, 5:48. This essay was incorporated into the *Paris Sketch Book* from its initial appearance in *Fraser's Magazine*, December 1839.

15. Ibid., pp. 45–46.

16. "Strictures on Pictures," *Works*, 13:265; "On the French School of Painting," *Works*, 5:50.

17. October 1841, *Letters*, 2:38.

18. 17 April 1835, from Paris, *Letters*, 1:279–80.

19. *The Newcomes*, chaps. 17, 22.

20. "Picture Gossip," *Fraser's Magazine*, June 1845, p. 714; *Works*, 13:448–49.

21. "Professor Byles's Opinion of the Westminster Hall Exhibition," *Punch*, July 1847, p. 8, referring to John Cross (1819–61); rpt. in *Contributions to "Punch"* (London: Smith, Elder, 1886), p. 165. This painting, *The Clemency of Coeur-de-Lion*, won first prize at an exhibition in 1847, and was purchased for £1,000 by the royal commissioners (Bryan's *Dictionary of Painters and Engravers*).

22. "On the French School of Painting," *Works*, 5:45.

23. "Picture Gossip," *Works*, 13:449. Presumably Thackeray would not have regarded it as inappropriate that he came to be judged in such terms as a writer. The critic Theodore Martin, commenting on a remark by the historian Archibald Alison that Thackeray lacked imaginative power and elevation of thought, wrote in a general evaluation: "But what right have we to expect to find the qualities of a Raphael in a Hogarth, or of a Milton in a Fielding?" ("Thackeray's Works," *Westminster Review*, April 1853, p. 371; rpt. in *Thackeray: The Critical Heritage*, ed. Geoffrey Tillotson and Donald Hawes [London: Routledge & Kegan Paul, 1968], p. 178).

24. "A Second Lecture on the Fine Arts," p. 744; *Works*, 13:274; "Strictures on Pictures," p. 763; *Works*, 13:268, 270; "From Richmond . . . To Brussels," *Little Travels and Roadside Sketches, Fraser's Magazine*, May 1844, p. 526; *Works*, 6:281.

25. "Letters on the Fine Arts: The Royal Academy" *Pictorial Times*, 13 May 1843; rpt. in *Stray Papers*, p. 214.

26. "Strictures on Pictures," *Works*, 13:263.

27. See above, p. 17.

28. "On the French School of Painting," *Works*, 5:48; "On Men and Pictures," passim. François-Henri Alexandre Lafond (1815–1901), a pupil of Ingres, was eminent at the time for his paintings based on classical and historical subjects; Michel-Martin Drolling (1786–1851), pupil of David, was the leading master of an atelier, and gained fame for his works based on ancient legend and the Bible; Louis Joseph Trimolet (1812–43) was associated with Daubigny; his *La prière* was exhibited in the Salon of 1841; Mme Paul Juillerat, née Clothilde Gerard (1806–1905?), pupil of Paul Delaroche, was known for her pastels; her *Sainte Elizabeth, reine de Hongrie, ramenant au chateau un petit mendiant* was also exhibited in 1841; François-Auguste Biard (1799–1882) was popular during the July Monarchy for his familiar scenes as well as his historical and military pictures, and scenes based upon his travels in Egypt, Syria, and other exotic lands; Jean-Louis-Ernest Meissonier (1815–91) was a genre painter and engraver and successful imitator of the Dutch style; Thackeray refers here to his *La partie d'échecs* (1841), one of his several highly esteemed pieces on this subject (Bénézit, *Dictionnaire critique et documentaire des peintres, sculteurs, dessinateurs et graveurs); Gabet, Dictionnaire des artistes de l'école française au xixe siècle).*

29. Quentin Bell, *Victorian Artists* (London: Routledge & Kegan Paul, 1967), p. 7. Bell compares Victorian England in this respect with seventeenth-century Holland.

30. "On Men and Pictures," *Works*, 13:371, 373, 379.

31. "Letters on the Fine Arts," *Stray Papers*, p. 214.

32. "On the French School of Painting," *Works*, 5:45.

33. "Letters on the Fine Arts," *Stray Papers*, p. 215. The Frank Stone picture referred to presumably is *An Interior with Figures*, showing a young man seated before a sweet-faced maiden in a country cottage (photograph in Frick Reference Library).

34. "On Men and Pictures," *Works*, 5:372. Cf. Thackeray's apology to his readers in *Vanity Fair*, chap. 1, following the description of Amelia's leave-taking of her friends at Chiswick Hall: "All which details, I have no doubt, JONES, who reads this book at his Club, will pronounce to be excessively foolish, trivial, twaddling, and ultra-sentimental. . . . Well, he is a lofty man of genius, and admires the great and heroic in life and in novels; and so had better take warning and go elsewhere."

35. *The Adventures of Philip*, chap. 6.

36. "On the French School of Painting," *Works*, 5:45.

37. "A Brother of the Press on the History of a Literary Man . . . ," *Fraser's Magazine*, March 1846, p. 338; *Works*, 13:475. Here Thackeray is quoting from Bulwer's biographical sketch of his subject, Laman Blanchard.

38. 8 October 1834 to Edward FitzGerald, from Paris, *Letters*, 1:276.

39. See above, p. 17.

40. "On the French School of Painting," *Works*, 5:50.

41. "A Second Lecture on the Fine Arts," *Works*, 13:275. In the piece he later contributed for Turner to Louis Marvy's *Sketches After English Landscape Painters* (London: Bogue, 1850), Thackeray called his late pictures "those blazing wonders, whose blood-red shadows, those whirling gamboge suns—awful hieroglyphics which even the Oxford Graduate, Turner's most faithful priest and worshipper, cannot altogether make clear."

42. Cf. his diatribes against the popular Keepsake books of the 1830s with their "artificial grace" and embellishment. One group of prints was condemned as "bad in artistical feeling, careless in drawing, poor and feeble in effect." Furthermore, "There is not one of these beauties, with her great eyes, and slim waist, that looks as if it had been painted from a human figure. It is but a slovenly, ricketty, wooden imitation of it, tricked out in some tawdry feathers and frippery, and no more like a

real woman than the verses which accompany the plate are like real poetry" ("A Word on the Annuals," *Fraser's Magazine*, December 1837, p. 761; *Works* [Cent. Biog. Ed.], 25:81). See also "The Annuals," *Times*, 2 November 1838; *Works* (Cent. Biog. Ed.), 25:125–26. On the background of Thackeray's ridicule of these confections, see Donald Hawes, "Thackeray and the Annuals," *Ariel* 7 (January 1976): 3–31.

43. "A Pictorial Rhapsody," *Works*, 13:340. References are to Joseph Lee (1780–1859), Thomas Creswick (1811–69), and Thomas Webster (1800–1886).

In his piece on Creswick contributed to Louis Marvy's *Sketches After English Landscape Painters*, Thackeray commented that he, "Perhaps, more than any other landscape painter, ancient or modern, . . . has united the perfection of aerial perspective in his distances, with a precision in the foregrounds only equalled by the pictures formed in convex glasses, and, we believe, frequently used by artists, to see how nature is 'done.' . . . The beholder has a perfect confidence in the painter whose happy gift it is to translate nature with an admirable fidelity and truthfulness."

44. "A Second Lecture on the Fine Arts," *Works*, 13:277 (on Charles Eastlake's *Our Lord and the Little Children*).

45. Ibid., p. 278 (on Landseer's *Pillage of a Jew's House*).

46. "Letters on the Fine Arts," *Stray Papers*, p. 217 (on Eastlake's *Hagar*).

47. "The Exhibition of the Royal Academy," *Morning Chronicle*, 5 May 1846; rpt. in *Contributions*, pp. 144–45.

48. "Picture Gossip," *Works*, 13:460.

49. *The Newcomes*, chap. 39.

50. "On Men and Pictures," *Works*, 13:369–70.

51. Ibid., p. 370. Florentin Servan (1810–79) was a landscape painter.

52. *The Newcomes*, chap. 2.

53. "A Pictorial Rhapsody," *Works*, 13:334–35. George Richmond (1809–96) was in great demand as a portrait painter. His likenesses of George Eliot and Mrs. Gaskell hang in the National Portrait Gallery.

54. *Pendennis*, chap. 1.

55. *Vanity Fair*, chap. 49.

56. *Henry Esmond*, bk. 1, chap. 3.

57. "May Gambols," *Fraser's Magazine*, June 1844, pp. 714–15; *Works*, 13:442–43.

58. *The Newcomes*, chap. 14.

59. "On Men and Pictures," *Works*, 13:382. Among English painters, Titmarsh finds an effective use of impasting in Turner's work: "The rain, in the astounding picture called 'Rain-Steam-Speed' is composed of dabs of dirty paint *slapped* on to the canvas with a trowel; the sunshine scintillates out of the very smeary lumps of chrome yellow" ("May Gambols," *Works*, 13:439). This technique is best known to present-day art viewers through the landscapes and interiors of van Gogh.

60. *Vanity Fair*, chap. 48.

61. *Pendennis*, chap. 45.

62. *Vanity Fair*, chap. 41.

63. *The Adventures of Philip*, chap. 2.

64. "A Second Lecture on the Fine Arts," *Works*, 13:276 (on Wilkie's *Sir David Baird*).

65. *Vanity Fair*, chap. 49.

66. Ibid., chap. 51.

67. *Pendennis*, chap. 29.

68. W. C. Brownell, *Victorian Prose Masters* (New York: Scribner, 1902), p. 29.

69. "Strictures on Pictures," *Works*, 13:267.

70. *The Virginians*, chap. 34.

71. See above, p. 69 (comment on Charles Landseer).

72. "A Pictorial Rhapsody Concluded," *Works*, 13:343. In another essay he praises Cattermole's *Monks in a Refectory* as "rich, original and sober in colour;

excellent in sentiment and general grouping," but faults it because it is "in individual attitude and grouping not sufficiently correct" ("May Gambols," *Works*, 13:442).

73. *Westminster Review*, October 1860 (Francis T. Palgrave); *Spectator*, 9 August 1862 (Walter Bagehot); *Charleston Mercury*, 27 February 1856 (William Gilmore Simms); *Daily News*, 30 December 1859; Peter Bayne, "The Modern Novel: Dickens-Bulwer-Thackeray," *Essays in Biography and Criticism* (Boston, 1857), pp. 363–92. For these citations I am indebted to Dudley Flamm, *Thackeray's Critics* (Chapel Hill: University of North Carolina Press, 1967).

74. See especially "On the French School of Painting," *Works*, 5:56; "A Second Lecture on the Fine Arts"; "A Pictorial Rhapsody"; "May Gambols"; "Picture Gossip," *Works*, 13:278, 329, 435–36, 460.

75. Introduction to *The Paris Sketch Book*, *Works*, 5:xx.

76. "An Invasion of France," *Paris Sketch Book*, *Works*, 5:12, 14–15. This essay originally appeared in the *Corsair* (New York), 24 August 1839, as the first part of his "Letters from London, Paris, Pekin, Petersburgh, & C."

77. "An Evening in Rotterdam," *Notes of a Tour in the Low Countries, Letters*, 2:833 (from MS in the Huntington Library).

78. "Gibraltar," *Notes of a Journey from Cornhill to Grand Cairo*, *Works*, 5:615.

79. Whitwell Elwin, in *Quarterly Review*, September 1855, p. 358.

80. "On the French School of Painting," *Works*, 5:46.

81. "The Exhibition of the Royal Academy," *Morning Chronicle*, 5 May 1846; *Contributions*, p. 145 (on Charles Robert Leslie).

82. "Picture Gossip," *Works*, 13:449. See also "A Pictorial Rhapsody," ibid., p. 328.

83. Quoted in Lewis Melville, *Life of William Makepeace Thackeray*, 2 vols. (London: Hutchinson, 1899), 2:219, 221. See also "Letters on the Fine Arts," *Stray Papers*, p. 215.

84. "The Artists," *Works*, 3:529–30.

85. "John Leech's Pictures of Life and Character," *Quarterly Review*, December 1854, pp. 83–84; *Works*, 13:488–89.

86. "Hogarth, Smollett, and Fielding," *English Humourists of the Eighteenth Century*, *Works*, 7:562. Lidmilla Pantučková, in her survey "W. M. Thackeray as a Critic of Literature" *(Brno Studies in English.* nos. 10–11, 1972), suggests the importance of Thackeray's art criticism in the development of his literary practice—particularly his ideas of realism and his conception of the beautiful (chap. 1, "Thackeray's Qualifications as a Literary Critic," pp. 35–37).

"THE GREAT DRAMA OF THE WORLD"

Chapter Three

THACKERAY MIGHT BE CHARACTERIZED AS A born artist, a developed writer, and a suppressed actor. In offering himself to Bradbury and Evans as a pundit on theater as well as on graphic arts and "light literature," he was seeking expression for one essential part of his many-sided talent—a mimetic gift that was oral as well as visual. A boyhood friend has left a recollection of young William Makepeace amusing his cousins the Ritchies and their children in their house in Southhampton Row by drawing caricatures as well as performing in little plays that the two of them produced.[1] One of the roles that young Thackeray played, according to this companion, was Dr. Pangloss in "a wig capitally got up." More in anticipation of the future parodist was his playing a character named Fusbos in a performance at Charterhouse of a burlesque tragic opera called *Bombastes Furioso*.[2] From Cambridge he wrote gleefully to his mother: "I am going to take part I believe in a play; to be acted at a Dr. Jermyns at Swaffham a little distance from Cambridge. I am to be the heroine! . . . Dr. J[ermyns] has got scenes & c. My dress I shall make myself with the aid of your needle & thread, & some silver paper tucked to my white trousers. My bedmaker is going to lend me a white gown."[3] The letter is accompanied by a drawing of himself in apron and crinolines, topped by a feathered headdress, dwarfing a fellow student actor identified simply as "my lover and Dr. Faustus." In his adult life, an artist friend recalled Thackeray regaling a group of other artists in a tavern in Rome by improvising a grisly ballad, and an Irish acquaintance has recorded a jolly evening in Dublin when Thackeray entertained some fellow writers by acting out, with song and pirouette, a scene from a trashy music drama he had seen, called "Belshazzar's Feast."[4]

Thackeray's participation in the theater, as events turned out, proved to be more as spectator than actor, but his love of the stage never flagged. A letter written to his mother while he was still in his teens reports: "I went to Matthews on Saturday night—I was very much amused indeed—he performed the Trip to Paris."[5] A diary entry made nine months before his death reads: "St James's Theatre. Lady Audley's Secret & Effie Deans."[6] In the richly reminiscential *The Adventures of Philip*, his last completed novel, Thackeray's persona Arthur Pendennis recalls theatergoing in Old Parr Street, where "The yellow fogs didn't damp our spirits—and we never thought them too thick to keep us away from the play: from the chivalrous Charles Kemble . . . my Mirabel, my Mercutio, my princely Falconbridge . . . from the classic Young; from the glorious Long Tom Coffin; from the unearthly Vanderdecken . . . from the sweet 'Victorine' and 'The Bottle Imp.'" Of pleasant memory also was a place near Covent Garden where he "heard the most celestial glees, over a supper of fizzing sausages and mashed potatoes, such as the world has never seen since" (chap. 2).

In these jottings Thackeray conveys an omnivorous relish for the art of performance, extending from classical and Shakespearean tragedy down to melodrama and vaudeville, and a musical ear ranging from grand opera to burletta. This wide tolerance can easily be documented from his school days, professional life, and travel. While a student at Cambridge, Thackeray heard the tragic actor Charles Reece Pemberton read Shylock; that summer he was excited by the acting of Mlle Mars (recalled fondly by Major Pendennis) in Dumas's *Henri III et sa cour* at the Comédie-Française; later this same season he enjoyed the French comic actor Adrien Perlet at the Théâtre de Madame, and raved to his mother about the "divine" Leontine Fay. ("It gives me the best French lesson possible," he rationalized, feeling on the defensive with his mother about attending the theater, as did his hero Arthur Pendennis much later.)[7] There were other continental Miss Fotheringays, notably the great soprano Giulia Grisi, the "beautiful creature" whom he heard at the Italian opera in Paris during the season of 1833 and intermittently during the next fifteen years, both in Paris and in London.[8] Another passion was Mlle Déjazet, who "looked as mignon as a China image, and danced fought sang and capered in a way that w^d have set Walpole mad could he have seen her." *Gentil*

Bernard; ou, l'art d'aimer, a vaudeville in which Mlle Déjazet appeared, struck him as " . . . the wickedest I ever saw and one of the
pleasantest—adorably funny and naughty."[9]

During his *lehrjahr* in Weimar, in line with his triple pursuit of
"study, or sport, or society" (as he later characterized this interlude
to George Henry Lewes),[10] young Thackeray kept a scrapbook into
which he pasted playbills, pictures of costumes, and critical notices.
His theatergoing, at least as set down here, appears to have been
suited to the Olympian atmosphere of this cultural capital—Hugo's
Hernani (in German translation), Schiller's *Die Räuber*; Shylock,
Hamlet, and Falstaff, as interpreted by Ludwig Devrient, "the
Kean of Germany"; operas, such as *Medea in Corinto*, a then popular
work in the bel canto style by Johann Simon Mayr, and the more
enduring *The Magic Flute, The Barber of Seville*, and *Fidelio*. Here his
hand kept busy, along with his eyes and ears, as he engaged in his
typical activity of translating mental impressions into visual images,
and fixing scenes on paper as they were transpiring before him.
One letter includes a sketch of the composer-conductor Hummell.
Another catches him in a characteristic absorption with the criminal mentality: a drawing of Devrient as Franz Moor in *Die Räuber*,
praying while his castle is burning, and uttering the words "I am no
common murderer Mein Herr Gott."[11]

We have more extensive records of Thackeray's theatergoing in
Paris, where he was an avid attender at "the play," both classical
and popular. Among his most vivid impressions is curtain time at
the Théâtre Ambigu-Comique: "Presently the prompter gives his
three heart-thrilling slaps, and the great painted cloth moves upwards: it is always a moment of awe and pleasure. What is coming?
First you get a glimpse of legs and feet; then suddenly the owners
of the limbs in question in steady attitudes, looking as if they had
been there one thousand years before; now behold the landscape,
the clouds, the great curtain vanishes altogether, the charm is dis-
solved, and the disenchanted performers begin."[12] As "cricket" or
as correspondent he sometimes displays pleasure, at other times
disenchantment, with the spectacles that passed before his eyes at
the Ambigu-Comique and other Parisian theaters. An article sent
to the American journal the *Corsair* bubbles over with joy at the
comedians of the season "who make a French farce the most
sparkling, joyous delightful thing in the world," leading one to
"love [them] with their merriment, and their wit, and their follies,
and their delightful absurd affectation." The tragedies fall somewhat heavier on his ear: "Bajazet is only a bawling bore (let it be

said in confidence), Athalia is a great imperious Mademoiselle Georges of a woman—the Cid himself, the largest and noblest figure of French tragedy, would talk more nobly still, if he would but talk in prose, and get rid of that odious jiggling rhyme."[13] In *The Paris Sketch Book* he has occasion again to scoff at the "old tragedies in which half-a-dozen characters appear, and spout Alexandrines for half-a-dozen hours."[14] Before the curtain, as at the easel, Titmarsh regards himself as a deflater of the "sham sublime." Obviously Thackeray had not forgotten these "old tragedies" when he was writing *The Newcomes*. One of the minor characters of this domestic chronicle, the intriguing continental adulteress Madame la Duchesse d'Ivry, could almost be a disciple of Mademoiselle Georges: "Like good performers, she flung herself heart and soul into the business of the stage, and *was* what she acted. She was Phèdre, and if, in the first part of the play, she was uncommonly tender to Hippolyte, in the second she hated him furiously. She was Medea, and if Jason was *volage*, woe to Creusa!" (chap. 34). The Duchesse may feel grand classical thoughts and gesture in the grand manner, but in line with a bourgeois tragedy set in modern Paris, she talks in prose, not in alexandrines.[15]

On his rounds of the Paris theaters, Titmarsh is not much drawn either to French classical comedies "wherein the knavish valets, rakish heroes, stolid old guardians, and smart free-spoken servingwomen discourse in Alexandrines, as loud as the Horaces or the Cid."[16] An advocate of the "bourgeois style" in drama as well as in painting, he would have all actors, serious and comic, speak, like M. Jourdain, in prose. As author Thackeray practices what he preaches with his own versions of "knavish valets," like Charles Yellowplush and Jeames De La Pluche, who, whatever their pretensions, discourse in "Cockniac dialect," just as his "rakish heroes," like Algernon Deuceace, George Brandon, and Barry Lyndon, devious as they may be in thought and deed, speak in plain language. The same may be said for his equivalents of "old guardians," like the Earl of Crabs in "Dimond Cut Dimond," and "outspoken servingwomen," like Becky, the cook in *A Shabby Genteel Story*.

Posing as the ordinary visitor from across the Channel, Titmarsh seeks refuge in the popular theater from the stuffiness of the Comédie-Française. "For my part," he affirms, "I had rather go to Madame Sacqui's, or see Durburan dancing on a rope; his lines are quite as natural and poetical." An etching that accompanies the original edition of *The Paris Sketch Book* is entitled "The Gallery at Deburau's Theatre. Sketched from Nature." Here the reader is absorbed by the real-life comedy acted out in the facial expressions and gestures of the commonplace audience—a boy leaning, rapt, over the gallery railing; a sleeping mother with a toddler seated before her on the railing; a young man flirting with her, the husband visibly resenting these attentions; a gendarme with an eye peeled for possible disturbances; others looking at the stage apathetically.[17]

For Thackeray accessible humanity obviously meant far more than "fine words and grand sentences."[18] One might have expected him, therefore, to respond more enthusiastically to the new romantic drama that emerged during the July Monarchy, which proudly proclaimed its freedom from the classical rules, but this too left him unmoved. "In the time of Voltaire the heroes of poetry and drama were fine gentlemen; in the days of Victor Hugo they bluster about in velvet and mustachios and gold chains," he wrote in a diary he kept during his youth. For him the change did not bring about improvement. "The poets and the dramatists of the old time had to combat ag[ainst] the coldness of custom, & yet circumscribed in metre time and subject they occasionally produced true poetry," continues this entry. "The gentlemen of the Ecole Romantique have thrown away all these prejudices, but still seem no wise better or more poetical than their rigid predecessors."[19]

If Titmarsh found classical drama for the most part cold and rigid, though sometimes poetical, the romantic drama for him was unpoetical and all too "warm." He denounces Hugo's *Marion Delorme* in words that look forward to *Catherine*, his satire of the following year on criminal romances: "I . . . am so disgusted and sick with the horrid piece that I have hardly heart to write," reads a letter from Paris to his wife, Isabella. "The last act ends with an execution, & you are kept waiting a long hour listening to the agonies of parting lovers, & grim speculations about head chopping, dead-bodies, coffins & what not—Bah! I am as sick as if I had taken an emetic."[20] He is repelled by all the "heroes" of Hugo's dramas since *Hernani:* "Triboulet, a foolish monster; Lucrèce Borgia, a maternal monster; Mary Tudor, a religious monster: Monsieur Quasimodo, a hump-backed monster, whose monstrosities we are induced to pardon—nay, admiringly to witness—because they are agreeably mingled with some exquisite display of affection." Not to be outdone, Hugo's rival in the new drama, "the great Dumas," usually includes in his cast of characters "half-a dozen [monsters] to whom murder is nothing; common intrigue, and simple breakage of the [seventh] commandment nothing; but who

live and move in a vast, delightful complication of crime that cannot easily be conceived in England, much less described."[21]

For his English audiences Thackeray, after *Catherine*, preferred
to scale down his monsters, maternal, adulterous, religious, and
otherwise, but he seems to have taken a cue or two from this French
theater of cruelty. "Such tragedies are not so good as a real downright execution; but in point of interest, the next thing to it," he
observed in reaction to Mlle George's portrayals of some of these
villainesses; "with what a number of moral emotions do they fill the
breast; with what a hatred for vice, and yet a true pity and respect
for that grain of virtue that is to found in us all: our bloody,
daughter-loving Brinvilliers; our warm-hearted, poisonous Lu-
cretia Borgias." Significantly, he found a "grain of virtue" in the
uxoricidal Catherine, "heroine" of his first novel, who is shown to
be capable of a sincere maternal feeling. He could easily swing to
the other side of the scale, as in his summing up of the human
comedy at the conclusion of *Pendennis*, where he refers to both
"flowers of good blooming in foul places" and "in the most lofty
and splendid fortunes, flaws of vice and meanness, and stains of
evil."

Despite his own preference for "mixed characters," Thackeray
could still ask (in the voice of his alter ego Titmarsh), when speaking of "small pictures" that "can do a lot of good, and make honest
people happy," "Who is the man that despises melodramas? . . .
Away with him who has no stomach for such kind of entertainments, where vice is always punished, where virtue always meets its
reward."[22] This toleration of sentimentality eventually was expressed by the narrator of *Pendennis*, commenting on a play by
Kotzebue enjoyed by the hero at the theatre where Miss Fotheringay holds forth: "The Stranger's talk is sham, like the book he reads
and the hair he wears, and the bank he sits on, and the diamond
ring he makes play with—but in the midst of the balderdash, there
runs the reality of love, children, and the forgiveness of wrong,
which will be listened to wherever it is preached, and sets all the
world sympathising" (chap. 4). In his roundabout of the Parisian
theaters, Titmarsh notices that the more popular dramatists "do
not deal in descriptions of the agreeably wicked, or ask pity and
admiration for the tender-hearted criminals, and philanthropic
murderers, as their betters do." No,

> vice is vice on the Boulevard; and it is fine to hear the audience, as a
> tyrant king roars out cruel sentences of death, or a bereaved mother
> pleads for the life of her child, making their remarks on the circum-
> stances of the scene. "Ah, le gredin!" growls an indignant country-

man. "Quel monstre!" says a grisette in a fury. You see very fat old men crying like babies; and, like babies, sucking enormous sticks of barley-sugar. Actors and audiences enter warmly into the illusion of the piece. . . . Surely there is fine hearty virtue in this, and pleasant childlike simplicity.[23]

On the whole, concludes Titmarsh, "while the drama of Victor Hugo, Dumas, and the enlightened classes is profoundly immoral and absurd, the drama of the common people is absurd, if you will, but good and right-hearted."[24] Confronted with a choice, Titmarsh sides with the Jacobins over the "enlightened classes" among theater audiences, but the implication is clear that the drama, at its best, should be "good and right-hearted" without absurdity. One lesson, at any rate, that Titmarsh carried back home from his student tour of the continent was that the stage afforded a vivid medium to bring images of vice and virtue before a wide public. It is not surprising, therefore, that devices of the theater should figure so prominently in the illusion of actuality provided by his novels.

Thackeray-Titmarsh was not, of course, oblivious to the pure diversion offered by stage spectacle, as we can see in Arthur Pendennis's reaction to the delight that Fanny Bolton expresses at her first view of Vauxhall: "'. . . O-O-law, how beautiful!' She shrank back as she spoke, starting with wonder and delight, as she saw the Royal Gardens blaze before her with a hundred million of lamps, with a splendour such as the finest fairy tale, the finest pantomime she had ever witnessed at the theatre, had never realised. Pen was pleased with her pleasure, and pressed to his side the little hand which clung so kindly to him. 'What would I not give for a little of this pleasure?' said the *blasé* young man."[25] Immersing himself in the popular theater of Paris, he can identify himself with the naïve, childlike populace, as in this rhapsody on vaudeville: "The classic drama may pale before the romantic, and the romantic, after assuming a thousand extravagant shapes, may go down in brimstone and red and blue lights; but the vaudeville, will mount up, light as a champagne bubble, coloured with the gay rays of wit and animal spirits, and immortal as France, its own sunny land."[26] But there are always two sides to him as theatergoer and drama critic, just as with all the arts, and the more prudential part of his nature complains of the decline of the theater as a moral force: "Your modern dramatists are mechanics, not artists: cobblers, not creators; wanting in imagination, and destitute of nice perceptions." Viewing with alarm what has happened to comedy now that it has fallen into the hands of the popular "cobbler" Scribe, he looks back with nostalgia on the classic comedy at its height: "How hearty, and kind, and

natural and generous is Molière, even in his occasional extravagance. How coldly quick, how smartly pretty, how shallow in the
fulness of his pretension is his successor! But the age has always
much to do with the creation of its oracles. Molière lived in an age
of great men and brilliant deeds. Scribe lives in an age of commonplace actions and commonplace men . . . and Scribe is the poet
laureate of the Financiers of the Chausée d'Antin."[27]

"Good heavens! with what a number of gay colonels, smart
widows, and silly husbands has that gentleman peopled the play
books!" a jaded Titmarsh had reacted earlier to this "father" of "the
comedy of the day." "How that unfortunate seventh commandment has been maltreated by him and his disciples! . . . When is
this joke to cease?"[28] Subsequently he was amazed to discover that
this playsmith was turning his superficial talents to more elevated
subjects: "The atmosphere of the French Acádemy, which has always been an unhappy influence upon the genius of dramatic writers, has lately transformed Eugène Scribe, the Vaudevilliste, into a
Professor of English History. . . . The Sorbonne is transferred to
the Théâtre Française, and Scribe takes the place of Guizot," begins
a review article covering several historical dramas that Thackeray
attended at the national theater.[29] Here he is annoyed by the
numerous misrepresentations of his nation's history and distortions
of English character by alien dramatists, but he is most disturbed by
Scribe's lapses in taste. A certain "indelicacy," which he regards as
the sign of a "dull moral sense," leads him to ask: "Does the presence of these in a play from the most popular of living dramatic
writers exhibited upon the boards of the most classic theatre, demonstrate a vice in the social state of society? or do a careless people
seek to be amused without reflecting upon the means provided
only they are novel?"

This question, of course, has a significance beyond its immediate
occasion. In his attack on one of France's most popular purveyors
at the time of not so innocent merriment, Thackeray is raising the
larger issue of the pleasure principle versus the didactic function of
art. We catch him here engaged in debate with himself whether the
writer merely serves the public, or can in some way influence it. As
far as Scribe is concerned,

> it will be said that he does not aspire to be either [a teacher of morals
> or history]. If so, let him remove his enervating pictures of an ill
> drawn and worse imagined society from beside the rich comedy of
> Molière. . . . Let Scribe return to the Gymnase, now under the ban
> of the displeasure of the authors' society. Let him fix again in some

new combination his never-changing personages. The old colonel of
the empire; the rich young widow; the banker; the gallant sea
lieutenant; and the half-sentimental heiress. In his hands these are
"marionettes" to be shifted about at his pleasure: without character,
colour, or physiognomy, it is true, but exciting curiosity by varying
changes of position, and still appearing to talk from themselves,
though it be the author's voice which is heard in one unchanged
tone, cutting his jokes upon the passing occurrences of the day. In this
light walk of the drama M. Scribe could not do much harm.[30]

"Better dost thou think it to serve at the feet of Molière's statue,
than to reign in a paradise of repartee and chansonette?" he
queries Scribe, subtly deviating the dilemma of Milton's Satan to
express the plight of the public entertainer torn between intellectual pride and the need to court the populace. Since Thackeray
himself never quite deserted the "paradise of repartee and chansonette" even in his most serious novels,[31] he proved that he was
really posing a false dilemma, that it is in fact possible to move
through the "light walk of drama" without a light head. As he later
wrote, in tribute, to the editor of *Punch,* the "fun" magazine that
provided him with the framework for *Vanity Fair:* "When the future inquirer shall take up your volumes, or a bundle of French
plays, and contrast the performance of your booth with that of the
Parisian theatre, he won't fail to remark how different they are,
and what different objects we admire or satirise."[32]

Actually, for the "performance" of his own booth, Thackeray,
much as he emulated the serious comedy of Molière and Congreve,
was not above borrowing some of the "personages" that he had
picked out as Scribe's stock-in-trade. Certainly the "old colonel of
the empire" turns up in Thackeray's own writings with variations,
gay (Major Gahagan, Major Pendennis, Colonel O'Dowd) and
grave (Colonel Newcome, the elderly Colonel Esmond); as do
"smart widows," if not always rich ones (Mrs. Ensign Macarty, later
Mrs. Gann of *A Shabby Genteel Story,* Aunt Hoggarty of *The Great
Hoggarty Diamond,* and, of course, Mrs. Rawdon Crawley); the
banker appears in various moral shadings from the swindling Mr.
Brough to the "respectable" Brian and Hobson Newcome; Blanche
Amory, with her diary called *Mes larmes* and her suicide complex,
is a more than "half-sentimental" heiress; Ensign Dobbin comes
close to the figure of the "gallant sea-lieutenant," and Denis Duval
actually seeks his career in the Navy, though that is as far as we are
able to follow him. The "puppets" in the booths of Vanity Fair are
"shifted about at his pleasure" by the "Manager of the Performance" here no less than are the "marionettes" of M. Scribe,

though this puppet master, to be sure, gives more "character, colour [and] physiognomy" to his dolls. Moreover, even before *Vanity Fair,* we get much of "the author's voice . . . cutting his jokes upon the passing occurrences of the day."[33]

Thackeray cast himself in the role of dramatist as early as his study year in Germany. In a letter to Frau von Goethe written in Weimar, he tells her of a German book he was than translating, and admits, " . . . but the Theatre is still my rage (don't think me conceited or say anything about it). I intend fully to try my hand at farce, tragedy or comedy, w^h I cannot yet say, all three perhaps."[34] On his travels the world seems naturally to assemble for him into what Victor Cousin called a "theatre of humanity."[35] In the port of Valetta, "The streets are thronged with a lively, comfortable looking population . . . and the effect of the group of multitudinous actors in this busy cheerful drama is heightened as it were by the decorations of the stage."[36] The soldiers of the town square of a Spanish port appear ". . . ludicrously young and diminutive for the most part, in a uniform at once cheap and tawdry,—like those supplied to the warriors at Astley's, or from still humbler theatrical wardrobes: indeed the whole scene was just like that of a little theatre; the houses curiously small, with arcades and balconies."[37] The port of Constantinople calls to mind "Drury Lane, such as we used to see it in our youth, when to our sight the grand last pictures of the melodrama or pantomime were so magnificent as any objects of nature we have seen with maturer eyes. Well, the view of Constantinople is as fine as any of Stanfield's best theatrical pictures, seen at the best period of youth, when fancy had all the bloom on her."[38]

So far as the professional theater was concerned, Thackeray was destined for even less success than Henry Esmond, whose comedy runs but three nights and sells all of nine copies. The only performance that Thackeray achieved for his one comedy, *The Wolves and the Lamb,* was a private one for a home theatrical. Not surprisingly, *Lovel the Widower,* the novel that Thackeray retrieved from this failure, retains the proscenium frame of its origins, from the narrator who announces himself as "The Chorus of the Play" to the stagy entrances and exits, props, dialogue, even to the concluding *"Valete and plaudite,* you good people, who have witnessed the little comedy. Down with the curtain; cover up the boxes; pop out the gas lights." *Lovel the Widower* is the most sustainedly dramatic of Thackeray's novels, but the author as impresario apppears as early as his first novel, *Catherine,* with its bloody Grand Tableau, and Ikey

Solomons's valedictory address: "Ring ding ding! the gloomy green
curtain drops, the *dramatis personae* are disposed of, the nimble-
candle snuffers put out the lights, and the audience goeth pondering home." In more than one of the early stories his fictitious
people are treated as stage figures. Part of *A Shabby Genteel Story* is
written in play form, and in its magazine version, one installment
ends: "To sum up, in six short weeks after the appearance of the
two gentlemen we find our chief *dramatis personae* as follows:
Caroline, an innocent young women in love with Brandon. Fitch, a
celebrated painter, almost in love with Caroline. Brandon, a young
gentleman in love with himself."[39] Andreas Fitch, the impecunious
young painter of this tale, is characterized at one point as "a fantastic youth, who lived but for his art; to whom the world was like the
Coburg Theatre, and he in a magnificent costume acting the principal part." The theatricality of *The Bedford-Row Conspiracy*, another
early magazine farce, is established by its chapter headings ("Shows
How The Plot Began To Thicken In Or About Bedford Row,"
"Behind The Scenes") and is sustained by such devices as sol-
iloquies and overheard private conversations. The "Speech Before
the Curtain" that opens *Vanity Fair* in its first edition in book form,
along with the assumption of the role of "Manager of the Performance," came quite naturally to its author, and was familiar to the
fit though few readers who knew his earlier work.

Theater conventions remain prominent in Thackeray's work
even after *Vanity Fair,* though after this point they tend to be subsumed more into the narrative. The narrator of *Pendennis* refers
intermittently to his "sentimental scenes," and some chapter headings read like stage directions: "In Which Pen Is Kept Waiting At
The Door, While The Reader Is Informed Who Little Laura Was";
"In Or Near The Temple Garden"; "In Which The Decks Begin
To Clear"; "Exeunt Omnes." One chapter heading echoes a drama
by Victor Hugo ("Monsigneur s'amuse"); another is taken from
Congreve ("The Way Of The World"). In a late episode, Blanche
Amory and Arthur Pendennis parry with each other in mock stage
dialogue, well befitting a young man who has been infatuated with
an actress and a young lady who has made a pageant of her "sham
enthusiasm, sham hatred, sham love." *The Newcomes,* too, is redo-
lent of the performing arts, with its opening chapter entitled "The
Overture—After Which The Curtain Rises Upon A Drinking
Chorus," followed by others like "In Which Thomas Newcome
Sings His Last Song" and "In Which We Hear a Soprano And A
Contralto." The chapter entitled "Two Or Three Acts Of A Little

Comedy" is made up of a series of "conversations" set off as scenes in a play with assigned speeches. The decorated initial to the chapter entitled "Family Secrets" depicts Barnes Newcome as Macbeth visiting Lady Kew got up as Hecate. In *The Virginians,* Colonel and Mrs. Lambert enact a scene from *Tartuffe.*

Children's theater, as we know from *Vanity Fair,* also furnishes a backdrop to Thackeray's fiction. Two years before *Vanity Fair* was published, Thackeray, in reviewing Dickens's *The Cricket on the Hearth,* likened this tale to a "Christmas frolic," and "As a Christmas pageant which you witness in the armchair—your private box by the fireside—the piece is excellent, incomparably brilliant, and dexterous. It opens with broad pantomime, but the interest deepens as it proceeds. The little rural scenery is delightfully painted. Each pretty, pleasant, impossible character has his *entrée* and his *pas.* The music is gay or plaintive, always fresh and agreeable. The piece ends with a grand *pas d'ensemble,* where the whole *dramatis personae* figure high and low, toe and heel, to a full orchestra crash, and a brilliant illumination of blue and pink fire."[40] *The Rose and the Ring,* his "Fireside Pantomime for Great and Small Children," is derived from the plot and characters of the traditional Christmas fairy play. He returns to this setting at the end of *The Adventures of Philip* to prepare his readers for the happy turn in the hero's fortunes after his tribulations: "You know—all good boys and girls at Christmas know—that before the last scene of the pantomime, when the Good Fairy ascends in a blaze of glory, and Harlequin and Columbine take hands, having danced through all their tricks and troubles and tumbles, there is a dark brief, seemingly meaningless, penultimate scene, in which the performers appear to group about perplexed, while the music of bassoons and trombones, and the like, groans tragically." At times he is in the position of "grumbler" Warrington in *Pendennis,* who vicariously enjoys the gay spirits of his young friend Arthur "as a man who has long since left off being amused with clown and harlequin, still gets a pleasure in watching a child at a pantomime" (chap. 37).

Thackeray liked not only to frame scenes of his novels as stage settings, but also to surround the stories themselves in a theatrical ambience. More specifically, the deftness of his characterization surely owes something to his sense of theatre, and the raciness of the speech he puts into the mouths of his men and women indicates that his ear was fully as sensitive as his eye. The opening of *Pendennis,* which introduces Major Pendennis during a typical morning in his club, is a playlet in itself, though a silent one: "The major sate down at his accustomed table then, and while the waiters went to bring him his toast and his hot newspaper, he surveyed his letters through his gold double eye-glass, and examined one pretty note after another, and laid them by in order . . . all of which letters Pendennis read gracefully, and with the more satisfaction, because Glowry, the Scotch surgeon, breakfasting opposite to him, was looking on, and hating him for having so many invitations, which nobody ever sent to Glowry." In a later episode of this same novel, the hand of a theatrical director seems to impart a gathering momentum to a crowd scene:

> "The consequences are, that I will fling you out of the window, you—impudent scoundrel," bawled out Mr. Pen; and darting upon the Frenchman, he would very likely have put his threat into execution, for the window was at hand, and the artist by no means a match for the gentleman—had not Captain Broadfoot and another heavy officer flung themselves between the combatants,—had not the ladies begun to scream,—had not the fiddles stopped,—had not the crowd of people come running in that direction,—had not Laura, with a face of great alarm, looked over their heads and asked for Heaven's sake what was wrong,—had not the opportune Strong made his appearance from the refreshment-room, and found Alcide grinding his teeth, and jabbering oaths in his Gascon French, and Pen looking uncommonly wicked, although trying to appear as calm as possible, when the ladies and the crowd came up. (Chap. 27).

In *The Virginians* the worldly society of Castlewood presents itself simultaneously to us and to the young Virginian Harry Warrington in a living tableau:

> Parson Sampson formed the delight of the entertainment, and amused the ladies, with a hundred agreeable stories. . . . My Lord's chaplain poured out all this intelligence to the amused ladies and the delighted young provincial, seasoning his conversation with such plain terms and lively jokes as made Harry stare, who was newly arrived from the colonies and unused to the elegancies of London life. The ladies, old and young, laughed quite cheerfully at the lively jokes. . . . 'tis certain that their Ladyships at Castlewood never once thought of being shocked, but sat listening to the parson's funny tales until the chapel bell, clinking for afternoon service, summoned his reverence away for half-an-hour. There was no sermon. He would be back in the drinking of a bottle of Burgundy. Mr. Will called a fresh one, and the chaplain tossed off a glass ere he ran out. (Chap. 15)

Thackeray's dramatic portraits are vocal as well as kinetic. With an ability at impersonation outdoing that of Becky Sharp, he can make a wide range of characters come to life merely by speaking for themselves. Be it a cockney footman:

"The less I say about my parint the better, for the dear old creatur was very good to me, and, I fear, had very little other goodness in her. . . . We led a strange life; sometimes ma was dressed in sattn and rooge, and sometimes in rags and dutt; sometimes I got kisses and sometimes kix; sometimes gin, and sometimes shampang."[41]

Or a parvenu banker:

"I'm a plain man . . . and eat a plain dinner. I hate your kickshaws, though I keep a French cook for those who are not of my way of thinking. I'm no egotist look you; I've no prejudices and Miss there has her béchamels and her fallals according to her taste. Captain, try the *volly-vong*."[42]

Or, up the social ladder, a country baronet:

"Come as Lady Crawley, if you like. . . . There will that zatusfy you? Come back and be my wife. Your vit vor't. Birth be hanged. Your as good a lady as ever I see. You've got more brains in your little vinger than any baronet's wife in the country. Will you come? Yes or no?" . . .
"Say yes, Becky. . . . I'm an old man, but a good'n. I'm good for twenty years. I'll make you happy, zee if I don't. You shall do what you like; spend what you like; and av it all your own way. I'll make you a zettlement, I'll do everything reglar. Look year!"[43]

His phonographic ear for dialect reproduces an Irish captain's bluster:

"Your hand, young man! for ye speak from your heart. . . . Thank ye, sir, and old soldier and a fond father thanks ye. She *is* the finest actress in the world. I've seen the Siddons, sir, and the O'Nale—They were great, but what were they compared to Miss Fotheringay? I do not wish she should ashume her own name while on the stage. Me family, sir, are proud people; and the Costigans of Costiganstown think that an honest man, who has borne Her Majesty's colours in the Hundtherd and Third, would demean himself by permitting his daughter to earn her old father's bread."[44]

as easily as the Franglais of an expatriate:

"En Angleterre je me fais Anglais, vois-tu, mon ami. . . . Demain c'est Sunday, et tu vas voir! I hear the bell, dress thyself for the dinner—my friend! . . . It do good to my 'art to 'ave you in my 'ouse! Heuh!" . . .
"Il est vrai . . . I comprehend neither the suicide nor the chaise-de-poste. What will you? I am not yet enough English, my friend. We made marriages of convenance in our country, que diable, and what follows follows; but no scandal afterwards."[45]

More remarkable is his accuracy in rendering the speech of women of all ranks and ages. A match for Mrs. Barbara, waitress at

Morland's Hotel, whom we heard from at the beginning of the previous chapter, is Firkin, maid to Miss Crawley:

> "Miss B[riggs], they are all infatyated about that young woman. . . . Sir Pitt wouln't have let her go, but he daren't refuse Miss Crawley anything. Mrs. Bute at the Rectory jist as bad—never happy out of her sight. The Capting quite wild about her. Mr. Crawley mortial jealous. Since Miss C. was took ill, she wouldn't have nobody near her but Miss Sharp, I can't tell for where nor for why; and I think somethink has bewidged everybody."[46]

Equally spontaneous is the voice of a "bewidge"-ing lady from the teens of the previous century:

> "Who are you? I shall go my own way, sirrah, and that way is towards a husband, and I don't want *you* on the way. I am for your betters, Colonel, for your betters: do you hear that? You might do if you had an estate and were younger; only eight years older than I, you say! pish you are a hundred years older. You are an old, old Graveairs, and I should make you miserable, that would be the only comfort I should have in marrying you." . . .
>
> "Yes . . . I solemnly vow, own, and confess, that I want a good husband. Where's the harm of one? My face is my fortune. Who'll come—buy! buy! buy! I cannot toil, neither can I spin, but I can play twenty-three games on the cards. I can dance the last dance. I can hunt the stag, and think I could shoot flying. I can talk as wicked as any woman of my years, and I know enough stories to amuse a sulky husband for at least one thousand and one nights. I have a pretty taste for dress, diamonds, gambling, and old china. I love sugar plums, Malines lace (that you bought me, cousin, is very pretty), the opera, and everything that is useless and costly. I have got a monkey and a little black boy—Pompey, sir, go and give a dish of chocolate to Colonel Graveairs,—and a parrot and a spaniel, and I must have a husband, Cupid, you hear?"
>
> "Iss, Missis!" says Pompey, a little grinning negro Lord Peterborough gave her, with a bird of paradise in his turbant, and a collar with his mistress's name on it.
>
> "Iss, Missis . . . And if husband not come, Pompey must go fetch one."[47]

We hear from her again, grown old and stout, trying to forestall time and death:

> "Ha! . . . Did not Adam live near a thousand years, and was not Eve beautiful all the time? I used to perplex Mr. Tusher with that—poor creature! What have we done since, that our lives are so much lessened, I say?" . . .
>
> . . . "Who loves me in heaven? I am quite alone, child—that is why I had rather stay here. . . . You are kind to me, God bless your sweet face! Though I scold, and have a frightful temper, my servants will do anything to make me comfortable, and get up at any hour of

the night, and never say a cross word in answer. I like my cards still. Indeed life would be a blank without 'em. Almost everything is gone except that. I can't eat my dinner now, since I lost those last two teeth. Everything goes away from us in old age. But I still have my cards—thank Heaven, I still have my cards! . . . Don't go away, I can't bear to be alone. I don't want you to talk. But I like to see your face, my dear! It is much pleasanter than that horrid old Brett's [her servant], that I have had scowling about my bedroom these ever so long years."[48]

The autumn of life is contrasted with its spring more movingly in the faltering but firm voice of Lady Kew:

"Stay a little, Ethel . . . I am older than your father, and you owe me a little obedience, that is if children *do* owe any obedience to their parents nowadays. I don't know. I am an old woman—the world perhaps has changed since my time; and it is you who ought to command, I daresay, and we to follow. Perhaps I have been wrong all through life, and in trying to teach my children to do as I was made to do. God knows I had very little comfort from them: whether they did or whether they didn't. You and Frank I had set my heart on; I loved you out of all my grandchildren—was it very unnatural that I should want to see you together? For that boy I have been saving money these years past. He flies back to the arms of his mother, who has been pleased to hate me as only such virtuous people can; who took away my own son from me; and now his son—towards whom the only fault I ever committed was to spoil him and be too fond of him. Don't leave me too, my child. Let me have something that I can like at my years. And I like your pride, Ethel, and your beauty, my dear; and I am not angry with your hard words; and if I wish to see you in the place in life which becomes you—do I do wrong? No. Silly girl! There—give me the little hand. How hot it is! Mine is as cold as a stone—and shakes, doesn't it?—Eh! It was a pretty hand once!"[49]

"In fact, what is that philosophy that I teach, but respect for all the elements of humanity and for all things. . . . It is a philosophy . . . whose only end is to comprehend all, and which, therefore, accepts and reconciles all," young Thackeray had read in Victor Cousin's *Cours de l'histoire de la philosophie* during his student days in Paris.[50] One way to understand humanity for Cousin, it will be recalled, is to enter into the consciousness of men: "When that is done . . . whosoever of your fellow creatures may present himself to you . . . you will sympathise with him; for the idea that subdues him, will not be wanting in you; you will therefore in him pardon humanity; for you will comprehend it, because you will possess it entirely." As the examples above attest, along with numerous others that could be added, Thackeray was uniquely equipped to "possess" humanity through his dramatic ability to speak for men and women of various ages, degrees of education, and cast of mind.

Thackeray's sense of theater is displayed more amply in dramatic scenes that could serve as episodes in a play. An outstanding one occurs in *Pendennis,* when Blanche Amory learns that the man she has known as Colonel Altamont is really her father, heretofore supposed dead:

> Bonner [Blanche's maid] still looked quite puzzled at the sound of the voice which she had heard.
>
> The bedroom door here opened, and the individual who had called out "Grady, my coat," appeared without the garment in question.
>
> He nodded to the women, and walked across the room. "I beg your pardon, ladies. Grady bring my coat down, sir! Well, my dears, it's a fine day, and we'll have a jolly lark at _____"
>
> He said no more; for here Mrs. Bonner, who had been looking at him with scared eyes, suddenly shrieked out, "Amory! Amory!" and fell back screaming and fainting in her chair.
>
> The man so apostrophised looked at the woman in an instant, and, rushing up to Blanche, seized her and kissed her. "Yes, Betsy," he said, "by G—— it is me. Mary Bonner knew me. What a fine gal we've grown! But it's a secret, mind. I'm dead, though I'm your father. Your mother don't know it. What a pretty gal we've grown! Kiss me—kiss me close, my Betsy! D—— it, I love you: I'm your old father."
>
> Betsy or Blanche looked quite bewildered, and began to scream too—once, twice, thrice; and it was her piercing shrieks which Captain Costigan heard as he walked the court below.
>
> At the sound of these shrieks the perplexed parent clasped his hands (his wristbands were open, and on one brawny arm you could see letters tattooed in blue), and, rushing to his apartment, came back with the eau-de-Cologne bottle from his grand silver dressing case, with the fragrant contents of which he began to sprinkle Bonner and Blanche.
>
> The screams of these women brought the other occupants of the chambers into the room: Grady from his kitchen, and Strong from his apartment in the upper story. The other at once saw from the aspect of the two women what had occurred.
>
> "Grady, go and wait in the court," he said, "and if anybody comes—you understand me."
>
> "Is it the play-actress and her mother?" said Grady.
>
> "Yes—confound you—say that there's nobody in chambers, and the party's off for to-day."
>
> "Shall I say that, sir? and after I bought them bokays?" asked Grady of the master.
>
> "Yes," said Amory, with a stamp of his foot; and Strong going to the door, too, reached it just in time to prevent the entrance of Captain Costigan, who had mounted the stair. (Conclusion of chap. 65)

This dramatic impulse Thackeray retained down to his last works when, by his own admission, his powers of invention and character creation were on the wane. In *The Adventures of Philip*, the most saintly of his characters, the Little Sister, confronts one of his most deep-dyed villains, the blackmailing Reverend Tufton Hunt, in a suspenseful scene that Sardou might have envied:

> The wretch was suiting actions to his words, and rose once more advancing towards his hostess, who shrank back, laughing half-hysterically, and retreating as the other neared her. Behind her was that cupboard which had contained her poor little treasure and other stores, and appended to the lock of which her keys were still hanging. As the brute approached her, she flung back the cupboard-door smartly upon him. The keys struck him on the head; and bleeding, and with a little curse and cry, he fell back on his chair.
>
> In the cupboard was that bottle which she had received from America not long since; and about which she had talked with [Doctor] Goodenough on that very day. It had been used twice or thrice by his direction, by hospital surgeons, and under her eye. She suddenly seized this bottle. As the ruffian before her uttered his imprecations of wrath, she poured out a quantity of the contents of the bottle on her handkerchief. She said, "Oh, Mr. Hunt, have I hurt you? I didn't mean it. But you shouldn't—you shouldn't frighten a lonely woman so! Here, let me bathe you! Smell this! It will—it will do you—good—it will—it will, indeed." The handkerchief was over his face. Bewildered by drink before, the fumes of the liquor which he was absorbing served almost instantly to overcome him. He struggled for a moment or two. "Stop—stop! you'll be better in a moment," she whispered. "Oh, yes! better, quite better!" She squeezed more of the liquor from the bottle on to the handkerchief. In a minute Hunt was quite inanimate. (Chap. 38)

Consistent with the biblical imagery that pervades this novel, the illustration to this incident of the chloroforming of the Reverend Hunt, in order to retrieve a document that might incriminate Philip's father, is entitled "Judith and Holofernes." However, by his method of relating it—pantomime, monologue, brief narrative details that read like stage directions in a promptbook—Thackeray reveals a flair for melodrama equal to his more celebrated finesse in high comedy.

As late as *Denis Duval*, the novel Thackeray was working on at his death, of which only a few chapters were completed, one finds his dramatic power fully engaged. In one episode in particular, where Denis recollects the funeral of the Comtesse de Saverne attended by, among others, her lover, who had previously murdered her husband, setting, character, gesture, and speech fuse into a memorable stage picture:

I imagine the scene before me now—the tramp of the people, the flicker of a torch or two; and then we go in at the gate of the Priory ground into the old graveyard of the monastery, where a grave had been dug, on which the stone still tells that Clarissa, born De Viomesnil, and widow of Francis Stanislas, Count of Saverne and Barr in Lorraine, lies buried beneath.

When the service was ended, the Chevalier de la Motte (by whose side I stood, holding by his cloak) came up to the Doctor. "Monsieur le Docteur," says he, "you have acted like a gallant man; you have prevented bloodshed—"

"I am fortunate, sir," says the Doctor.

"You have saved the lives of these two worthy ecclesiastics, and rescued from insults the remains of one—"

"Of whom I know the sad history," says the Doctor, very gravely.

"I am not rich, but will you permit me to give this purse for your poor?"

"Sir, it is my duty to accept it," replied the Doctor. The purse contained a few hundred louis, as he afterwards told me.

"And may I ask to take your hand, sir?" cries the poor Chevalier, clasping his own together.

"No, sir!" said the Doctor putting his own hands behind his back. "Your hands have that on them which the gift of a few guineas cannot wash away." The Doctor spoke very good French. "My child, good-night; and the best thing I can wish thee is to wish thee out of the hands of that man."

"Monsieur!" says the Chevalier, laying his hand on his sword mechanically.

"I think, sir, the last time it was with the pistol that you showed your skill!" says Doctor Barnard, and went in at his own wicket as he spoke, leaving poor La Motte like a man who has just been struck with a blow; and then he fell to weeping and crying that the curse— the curse of Cain was upon him. (Chap. 4)

It is significant that this episode almost tells itself, with but a minimum of narration by Denis. We feel cheated by the accident of fate that leaves us deprived of the outcome.[51]

When he wrote to Frau Goethe, during his youthful cultural fling in Weimar, that he did not know whether he would write farce, tragedy, or comedy, Thackeray's most premonitory words were, "all three perhaps."[52] He might have added that he would write all three not just intermittently, but sometimes simultaneously—with the addition of melodrama. It may seem incongruous that Thackeray's most solemn hero, Henry Esmond, writes a comedy (though its title, "The Faithful Fool," has an ironical appropriateness to Henry's situation), whereas his gentle, retiring grandson George Warrington writes the "terrible and pathetic" *Carpezan,* and the poetic tragedy *Pocahantas;* but both reflect from different an-

gles their creator's divergent temperament. In Thackeray's one
overt play, *The Wolves and the Lamb,* Captain Touchit, discovering
Lady Kicklebury and Mrs. Bonnington on their knees before the
eligible widower Horace Milliken, asks: "What is this comedy going
on, ladies and gentlemen? The ladies on their elderly knees—Miss
Prior with her hair down her back. Is it tragedy or comedy—is it a
rehearsal for a charade?" (act 2). Mr. Batchelor, Captain Touchit's
counterpart in *Lovel the Widower,* the novel derived from the play,
significantly a writer, observes: "What a queer little drama was
unfolding itself before me! What struggles and passions were going
on here—what *certamina* and *motus animorum!*" He displays a certain
psychological amphibiousness in his debate with himself whether
or not to leave Lovel's house, where he is a weekend guest: "I could
finish a scene or two of my tragedy at my leisure; besides there
were one or two little comedies going on in the house which inspired me with no little curiosity" (chap 3). These two "stage mana-
gers" reflect not only Thackeray's mercurial moods but his disposition also to see the same human situations under shifting emotional
lights.

Thackeray would have agreed with T. S. Eliot that "drama is a
mixed form; pure magnificence will not carry it through."[53] But
with Thackeray the mixtures vary in their contents and proportions, from the "comic and sentimental" *The Great Hoggarty
Diamond,* to the farcical "romance" of *Barry Lyndon* (one chapter of
which, nevertheless, "Contains The Tragical History Of The Princess of X——"), to the "sentimental and cynical" *Vanity Fair* (also
called in places a "comic history"), to *Pendennis,* a comedy of manners "in the pathetic key," to the "melancholic" *Henry Esmond,*
which, however, intercalates a comic paper from the *Spectator* and is
brought to its climax by a cloak-and-dagger escapade imitative of a
Dumas-Scribe melodrama. The chapter in *The Newcomes* entitled
"Contains Two Or Three Acts Of A Little Comedy" is balanced by
one entitled "Has A Tragical Ending," indicative of the oscillations
of mood in that predominantly tragic tale. One of Pendennis's
addresses to the readers of this family chronicle indeed compares
this fictitious world to "a fair, where time is short and pleasures
numerous [and so] the master of the theatrical booth shows you a
tragedy, a farce, and a pantomime, all in a quarter of an hour,
having a dozen new audiences to witness his entertainments in the
course of the forenoon" (chap. 34). Furthermore, observes the narrator of *The Virginians:* "Why, what tragedies, comedies, interludes,
intrigues, farces, are going on under our noses in friends' drawing

rooms where we visit everyday, and we remain utterly ignorant, self-satisfied, and blind!" (chap. 23).

Literary forms were scrambled by Thackeray as readily as virtue and vice were mixed in his heroes and villains. He felt, for one thing, the need of the impresario to provide "something for everyone." But there is a more serious intent behind his pasticcios. "My Dear—, It is no easy task in this world to distinguish between what is great in it, and what is mean," begins one of his iconoclastic essays.[54] Ikey Solomons, the narrator and producer of the Grand Tableau in *Catherine*, expresses a similar sense of resignation: "My dear sir, when you have well studied the world—how supremely great the meanest thing in the world is, and how infinitely mean the greatest, I am mistaken if you do not make a strange and proper jumble of the sublime and the ridiculous, the lofty and the low."[55] The Preacher of Cornhill phrases it more sententiously in "Vanitas Vanitatum":

> How low men were, and how they rise!
> How high they were, and how they tumble!
> O vanity of vanities
> O laughable, pathetic jumble![56]

For Thackeray such seeming incompatibles as farcical melodrama (*Catherine*), melodramatic farce (*Barry Lyndon*), children's pantomime fused with high comedy and history (*Vanity Fair*), and domestic tragedy with an admixture of bacchanalia (*The Newcomes*) were the "strange and proper" means of imitating the "laughable, pathetic jumble" that is the human comedy.

Past as well as present took on for Thackeray the aspect of the theater, and for him its glamor too was soon dispelled:

> In our orthodox history-books [he writes in a review] the characters move on as a gaudy play-house procession, a glittering pageant of kings and warriors, and stately ladies, appearing and passing away. Only he who sits very near to the stage can discover of what stuff the spectacle is made. The kings are poor creatures, taken from the dregs of the company; the noble knights are dirty dwarfs in tin foil; the fair ladies are painted hags with cracked feathers and soiled trains. One wonders how gas and distance could ever have rendered them so bewitching.[57]

Thackeray's own quite unorthodox histories, of his own times as well as of times gone by, were at this time still in the offing. In them we are in effect brought "near to the stage," the better to see the actors on it at close range, but with "gas and distance" both removed. We can agree with an admirer of Thackeray who remarked late in the century that "the theatre, indeed occupies an important part in his writings," adding that "while his literary manner was wholly untheatrical, owned no odour of the stage lamps, his stories are often found to be rich in dramatic qualities."[58] This critic confirms one's general impression that what Thackeray chiefly emulated from the theater was its vigor and liveliness, rather than its histrionics. For him a representation of life, like a painted picture, "should have its parts, characters, varieties, and climax like a drama."[59] In a "sham history," just as in a sketch, a portrait, or a painting, people, so far as Thackeray was concerned, should appear au naturel, not in greasepaint, and not posed or grouped in tableaux, but "busied, and perfectly naturally, with the scene at which the spectator is admitted to look."[60]

Thackeray's lifelong devotion to the theater was attended from time to time with twinges of conscience inevitable to one of evangelical upbringing. A dip into Restoration comedy, in preparation for his lecture series on the eighteenth-century wits, alternately fascinates and repels him: "Congreve's comic feast flares with lights, and, round the tables, emptying their flaming bowls of drink, and exchanging the wildest jokes and ribaldry, sit men and women, waited on by rascally attendants and valets as dissolute as their mistresses—perhaps the very worst company in the world. There doesn't seem to be a pretence of morals." His excursion into this roisterous, bawdy world of rakish Mirabels and Belmours, of ravishing Millamants, of nubile young wives easily won away from their gouty old husbands, leaves him quickly sated: "All this pretty morality you have in the comedies of William Congreve, Esquire. They are full of wit. Such manners as he observes, he observes with great humor: but ah! it's a weary feast, that banquet of wit where no love is."[61] Even ridicule, Thackeray believed, should have "a certain lurking kindness behind it."[62] "It was his wont to laugh at the stage," a commentator on Thackeray has observed, "but his laughter was very kindly, and but thinly disguised his love."[63] Whatever compunction he may occasionally have had about utilizing the amusements of the populace to transmit his wisdom, Eugène Scribe, vaudevilliste turned professor of history at the Académie française, the Guizot of the Gymnase, as Thackeray styled him, had, among others, shown the way to capture both the Chausée d'Antin and "commonplace men." Moreover, his studies of predecessors of the eighteenth century taught Thackeray that "pleasure is always warring against self-restraint. . . . A man in life, a humourist, in writing about life, sways over to one principle or the other, and laughs with the reverence for right and the love of truth in his heart, or laughs at these from the other side. Didn't I tell you that dancing was a serious business to Harlequin?"[64]

Transmitting his enthusiasm and mingled emotions for the performing arts to his audiences, Thackeray assumes a position toward them comparable to that of Dobbin with relation to Amelia as he accompanies her to the opera in Germany:

> Here [at the Pumpernickel Staats-Theatre] it was that Emmy found her delight, and was introduced for the first time to the wonders of Mozart and Cimarosa. . . . A new world of love and beauty broke upon her when she was introduced to those divine compositions: this lady had the keenest and finest sensibility and how could she be indifferent when she heard Mozart? The tender parts of *Don Juan* awakened in her raptures so exquisite that she would ask herself when she went to say her prayers of a night, whether it was not wicked to feel so much delight as that which "Vedrai Carino" and "Batti Batti" filled her gentle little bosom? But the Major, whom she consulted upon this head, as her theological advisor (and who himself had a pious and reverent soul) said that, for his part, every beauty of art and nature made him thankful as well as happy; and that the pleasure to be had in listening to fine music, as in looking at the stars in the sky, or at a beautiful landscape or picture, was a benefit, for which we might thank Heaven as sincerely as for any other worldly blessing.[65]

Thackeray was reliving here the thrill of soul he had enjoyed during his *lehrjahr* in the Weimar theater, by this time elevated into a form of worship. He was now teaching his readers how to turn delight into a sacrifice.

In his next novel, *Pendennis*, where the hero becomes absorbed early in life by the theater of his provincial village, one suspects that Thackeray sees himself not only in young Pen but also in Mr. Bingley, the stage manager of Miss Fotheringay's company, ". . . reading out of the stage-book—that wonderful stage-book—which is not bound like any other stage-book in the world, but is rouged and tawdry like the hero or heroine who holds it; and who holds it as people never do hold books: and points with his finger to a passage, and wags his head ominously to the audience, and then lifts up his eyes and finger to the ceiling professing to derive some intense consolation for the work between which and heaven there is a strong affinity" (chap. 4). The role of the theater manager as surrogate for God came as naturally to Thackeray as did his vision of the creation as the "theatre of humanity," all the men and women in it merely players, performing a variety of parts, deceiving themselves and each other sometimes, but not their Maker. His stage was not confined to the proscenium, nor was its action confined to Time the Present. As he wrote once, in reviewing a work of history for one of the numerous papers he served as "cricket": "We instinctively ran over in our minds the principal salient periods of history, which—most dramatic in themselves—have been of most notable influence over posterity, the early acts as it were of the great drama of the world, of which the succeeding scenes are yet passing before us."[66] For this harlequin the comedy was never finished.

1. Gerald Ritchie, *The Ritchies in India* (London: John Murray, 1920), p. 12 (quoted in *Letters*, 1:clx–xi). The friend, Richmond Shakespear, lived for a time with the Ritchies, along with young Thackeray, who stayed with them when he first arrived in London from India.

2. See letter of 4–8 February 1828 to his mother, *Letters*, 1:16.

3. 1 November 1829 to his mother, *Letters*, 1:106. Ray identifies the master referred to as "Probably the Rev. George Britton Jermyns of Trinity Hall, Cambridge."

4. Samuel Bevan, *Sand and Canvas* (London: Bennett, 1849), pp. 336–37. The ballad was "The Three Sailors," later published as "Little Billie" (W. J. Fitzpatrick, *The Life of Charles Lever* [London: Chapman & Hall, 1879], 2:405–10). The play, not specified by Fitzpatrick, was seen by Thackeray at the Théâtre Ambigu-Comique while he was editing the *National Standard*, and reported on to that paper as "a scandalous parody of Scripture, made up of French sentiment and French decency [*sic*; indecency?]" (6 July 1833; *Stray Papers*, p, 37). See also Gordon N. Ray, *The Uses of Adversity* (New York: McGraw-Hill, 1955), pp. 298–300, 293–94.

5. 20 June 1827, *Letters*, 1:14.

6. 28 April 1863, *Letters*, 4:411. The plays referred to were dramatizations of M. E. Braddon's sensational novel and of Scott's *Heart of Midlothian*.

7. 26–28 March 1829, *Letters*, 1:48; 18? July 1829, ibid., p. 88; 20–28 August 1829, ibid., pp. 92–93. In *Pendennis* Harry Foker tells his credulous mother, Lady Agnes Foker, that "he went to the French play because he wanted to perfect himself in the language, and there was no such good lesson as a comedy or vaudeville" (chap. 40).

8. 22–30 October 1833 to Mrs. Carmichael-Smyth, *Letters*, 1:266, and n. 13.

9. 26–28 July 1848 to Mrs. Brookfield, from Brussels, *Letters*, 2:407.

10. "Goethe in His Old Age," a letter of 28 April 1855 to Lewes for inclusion in his biography of Goethe (*Works*, 13:640–42).

11. 28 September 1830, *Letters*, 1:127; 18 January 1831, ibid., p. 142; additional details from "Goethe in His Old Age." Some sketches from a Weimar playbill, including Devrient as Shylock and Franz Moor, are reproduced in *Works* (Cent. Biog. Ed.), 24:xxxii–xxxiv.

12. "Dickens in France," *Fraser's Magazine*, March 1842, p. 342; *Works* (Cent. Biog. Ed.), 26:501.

13. "Letters from London, Paris, Pekin, Petersburgh, Etc." (signed T. T. for "Timothy Titcomb"), *Corsair*, 26 October 1839; *Stray Papers*, pp. 178–79. The use of initials may have been in imitation of Jules Janin, who signed his reviews in the *Journal des débats*, J.J.

14. "French Dramas and Melodramas," *Paris Sketch Book*, *Works*, 5:235.

15. Thackeray's acquaintance with French drama seems to have begun with his student days at Charterhouse. The Fales Library, New York University, owns a

wrapper from an edition of *Athalie* dated 1825, with the signature "W. Thackeray, Esqre" on the back. This was one of a series edited by A. Gombert entitled *The French Drama Illustrated By Arguments In English At The Head Of Each Scene, With Notes, Critical And Explanatory For The Use Of Schools.*

16. "French Dramas and Melodramas," *Works,* 5:235.

17. Ibid., facing p. 244.

18. A phrase used by Thackeray in disparagement of Byron's verse drama *Werner* in his letter of 19 February 1838 to Edward FitzGerald, *Letters,* 1:349.

19. Diary, 16 August 1832, *Letters,* 1:224.

20. 20 March 1838, *Letters,* 1:362.

21. "French Dramas and Melodramas," *Works,* 5:236.

22. "On Men and Pictures," *Works,* 13:373. See above, p. 66.

23. "French Dramas and Melodramas," *Works,* 5:245–46. Thackeray reverts to these dramas in *Vanity Fair* during a discourse to his readers on villainy: "At the little Paris theatres . . . you will not only hear the people yelling out '*Ah gredin! Ah monstre!*' and cursing the tyrant of the play from the boxes; but the actors themselves refuse to play the wicked parts, such as those of the *infâmes Anglais,* brutal Cossacks, and what not, and prefer to appear at a smaller salary, in their real characters as loyal Frenchmen" (chap 8).

24. "French Dramas and Melodramas," *Works,* 5:245–46. On one of the plays cited as an example of popular taste, *Hermann l'ivrogne,* by J. Bouchardy and E. Deligny, in which the villains are aristocratic libertines, Titmarsh comments: "Vulgar prejudice against the great . . . is only a rude expression of sympathy with the poor."

25. *Pendennis,* chap. 46.

26. "English History and Character on the French Stage," *Foreign Quarterly Review,* April 1843, p. 153; rpt. in *New Sketch Book,* p. 157.

27. "English History and Character on the French Stage," p. 148; *New Sketch Book,* pp. 150–51.

28. "French Dramas and Melodramas," *Works,* 5:235.

29. "English History and Character on the French Stage," p. 140; *New Sketch Book,* p. 139. One of Scribe's historical dramas unfavorably reviewed here, *Le verre d'eau,* which deals with the downfall of the Duke and Duchess of Marlborough, bears a devious relationship to *Henry Esmond,* as will be brought out in a later chapter.

30. "English History and Character on the French Stage," pp. 167–68; *New Sketch Book,* pp. 177–78.

31. For example, the Cave of Harmony episode that opens the most tragic of his novels, *The Newcomes.*

32. "Two or Three Theatres at Paris," *Punch,* 24 February 1849, p. 75; rpt. in *Contributions to "Punch,"* (London: Smith, Elder, 1886), pp. 208–12.

33. In later years a French admirer, Amédée Pichot, conjectured that Thackeray's "types comiques" owed something to Scribe. See his introduction to *La diamant de famille et la jeunesse de Pendennis* (Paris: Librairie Hachette, 1855), p. vi.

34. 26? August 1831, *Letters,* 1:154.

35. See above, p. 37.

36. "Gibraltar," *Notes of a Journey from Cornhill to Grand Cairo, Works,* 5:615.

37. "Vigo," *Notes of a Journey from Cornhill to Grand Cairo, Works,* 5:592–93.

38. "Constantinople," *Notes of a Journey from Cornhill to Grand Cairo, Works,* 5:636. A few years later Thackeray paid tribute to Clarkson Stanfield in his friend Louis Marvy's *English Landscape Painters,* referring to him as an artist who "for many years taught the public from the stage—taught the pit and gallery to admire landscape art and the boxes to become connoisseurs." For a number of years, Stanfield was chief of the Drury Lane scene room.

39. Cf. the end of the opening paragraph of *Vanity Fair,* chap. 6: "The argument stands thus—Osborne, in love with Amelia, has asked an old friend to dinner and to Vauxhall—Jos Sedley is in love with Rebecca. Will he marry her? That is the great subject now in hand."

40. *Morning Chronicle*, 24 December 1845; rpt. in *Contributions*, pp. 90–91.

41. *The Memoirs of Mr. C. J. Yellowplush*, chap. 1.

42. *The Great Hoggarty Diamond*, chap. 7 (Mr. Brough as host).

43. *Vanity Fair*, chap. 14 (Sir Pitt Crawley's proposal to Becky).

44. *Pendennis*, chap. 5 (Captain Costigan introducing himself to Arthur).

45. *The Newcomers*, chap. 57 (M. Florac on Lady Clara's elopement).

46. *Vanity Fair*, chap. 14.

47. *Henry Esmond*, bk. 3, chap. 3 (Beatrix to Henry; Beatrix to her servant, as recalled by Henry).

48. *The Virginians*, chap. 83 (the Baroness Bernstein to George Warrington and his wife, Theo).

49. *The Newcomes*, chap. 38.

50. See above, pp. 50–51.

51. This incident foreshadows de la Motte's eventual execution for treason and other crimes. Denis, it appears from notes Thackeray left behind, develops an admiration and compassion for this culprit, despite what he suffers through de la Motte's intrigues (see "Notes on Denis Duval," *Works*, 12:565).

52. See above, p. 96.

53. T. S. Eliot, "John Dryden," in *Selected Essays*, 1917–32 (New York: Harcourt, Brace, 1932), p. 273.

54. "The Second Funeral of Napoleon," *Works*, 4:273.

55. *Works*, 4:642.

56. *Cornhill Magazine* 2 (July 1860): 59–60; *Works*, 13:101.

57. Review of *The Private Correspondence of Sarah, Duchess of Marlborough*, *Times*, 6 January 1838; rpt. in *Works* (Furniss Ed.), 12:49–57.

58. Dutton Cook, "Thackeray and the Theatre," *Longman's Magazine* 4 (August 1884): 410–11.

59. "Picture Gossip," *Works*, 13:460. See above, p. 69.

60. "The Exhibition of the Royal Academy," *Morning Chronicle*, 5 May 1846. See above, p. 69.

61. "Congreve and Addison," *English Humourists of the Eighteenth Century*, *Works*, 7:464.

62. See above, p. 81, in connection with his essay on Cruikshank.

63. Cook, "Thackeray and the Theatre," p. 410.

64. "Congreve and Addison," *Works*, 7:462.

65. *Vanity Fair*, chap. 62.

66. Review of *Historic Fancies*, by the Honorable George Sidney Smythe, M. P., *Morning Chronicle*, 2 August 1844; *Contributions*, p. 47.

"OUR DARLING ROMANCES"

Chapter Four

In 1850 Thackeray, by now established with the reading public, addressed them in the preface to *Pendennis*, stressing the high seriousness of his calling: "Does he tell the truth in the main? Does he seem activated by a desire to find out and speak it? Is he a quack, who shams sentiment, or mouths for effect? Does he seek popularity by claptraps or other arts? I can no more ignore good fortune than any other chance which has befallen me. I have found many thousands more readers than I ever looked for. I have no right to say to these, You shall not find fault with my art, or fall asleep over my pages; but I ask you to believe that this person writing strives to tell the truth. If there is not that, there is nothing."

Here Thackeray has put the novelist on a pedestal, but only two years before he had been quite ready to address this same public as a clown from a barrel top. It is amusing to see how quickly the ingenuous narrator of *Pendennis* has superseded the "quack, who shams sentiment" of *Vanity Fair:* "As the Manager of the Performance sits before the curtain on the boards, and looks in the Fair, a feeling of profound melancholy comes over him." This "Manager" is also one to "seek popularity by claptraps or other arts," priding himself in fact on his borrowings from crowd-pleasing shows: "The famous little Becky Puppet has been pronounced to be uncommonly flexible in the joints, and lively on the wire"; "There are scenes of all sorts; some dreadful combats, some grand and lofty horse-riding . . . some love-making for the sentimental, and some light comic business." In *Vanity Fair,* as in its predecessors, Thackeray was quite openly role playing, mocking not merely his readers, but the writer who has to woo the public. The "Manager" of *Vanity Fair* cajoles his "kind friends" while pretending to cater to them: "Every reader of a sentimental turn (and we desire no other) must have been pleased with the *tableau* with which the last act of our little drama concluded": "The present number will be very mild—others, but we will not anticipate these"; "I know that the tune I am piping is a very mild one (although there are some terrific chapters coming presently)." As reader, critic, and eventually writer of novels, Thackeray was well aware of the struggles of the serious writer (the "philosopher," or "man of reflective turn of mind," as he refers to him from time to time) getting through to the "lazy, novel-reading, unscientific world."

He had been a part of this world himself as a "lazy idle boy" long before he became either a professional reader or writer. "Oh delightful novels well remembered! Oh, novels, sweet and delicious as the raspberry open-tarts of budding boyhood!" exclaims the silver-haired editor of *Cornhill Magazine* becoming momentarily as a child again. "Figs are sweet, but fictions are sweeter," he affirms in another of his Roundabout Papers where he savors again some of the "jam tarts" of his school days, rendered more piquant by their contraband nature: "What was it that so fascinated the young student as he stood by the river shore? Not the *pons asinorum*. What book so delighted him, and blinded him to all the rest of the world, so that he did not care to see the apple-woman with her fruit, or (more tempting still to sons of Eve) the pretty girls with their apple cheeks, who laughed and prattled round the fountain? What was the book? Do you suppose it was Livy, or the Greek grammar? No; it was a NOVEL that you were reading, you lazy, not very clean, good-for-nothing, sensible boy!"[1]

Memory brings back the primal appeal of some of these early acquaintances peeped at surreptitiously behind more stately tomes. "O Scottish Chiefs, didn't we weep over you!" recalls this old boy of the first romance that came his way, and others made even more lasting impression. "O Mysteries of Udolpho, didn't I and Briggs Minor draw pictures out of you. . . . Efforts, feeble indeed, but still giving pleasure to us and our friends. . . ."[2] These "efforts" are among the stray items inherited by Thackeray's daughter, along with a figure of Sir Aymer de Valence of *Scottish Chiefs* drawn on the title page of a Latin grammar he used as a boy. "'Peregrine Pickle' we liked, our fathers admiring it, and telling us (the sly old boys) it was capital fun: but I think I was rather bewildered by it,

though 'Roderick Random' was and remains delightful," he confided to his readers of 1860 of two old favorites that he had ransacked for his own picaresque novel, *Barry Lyndon*. Also of happy
memory were "Walter Scott, the kindly, the generous, the pure—
the companion of what countless delightful hours," and "brave,
kind, gallant olde Alexandre," to both of whom he had paid the
tribute of loving ridicule. He has a mellow spot in his heart too for
G. P. R. James, "the veteran, from whose flowing pen we had the
books which delighted our young days," a favorite whipping boy of
his adult years, parodied even in the *The Rose and the Ring*. The fun
of Pierce Egan's *Life in London*, with its bumptious heroes Jerry
Hawthorne, Corinthian Tom, and Bob Logic, had somewhat diminished when he returned to it in middle age, but he looked back
on these "Days and Night Scenes" fondly as his first introduction to
the bucks and blacklegs of Regency London recreated in *Vanity Fair*
and *Pendennis*.[3]

"But as surely as the cadet drinks too much pale ale, it will dis-
agree with him; and so surely, dear youth, will too much of novels
cloy on thee," the editor of *Cornhill* warns the rising generation.
But Thackeray himself in his youth imbibed freely of the literary
springs, from witches' brew like *Melmoth the Wanderer* to the claret
of T. H. Lister. He kept up with most of the new novelists of the
1820s and the early 1830s, like John Galt ("very clever, though
rather dull . . . a man may write very wisely & be no Solomon," he
observed after reading *Stanley Buxton; or, The Schoolfellows*); Mrs.
Gore (*The Fair of May Fair* was "a sensible book enough"); Bulwer
(*Pelham* was to young Thackeray "rather dull & very impertinent");
William Pitt Scargill (*Rank and Talent* is rated "poor"); and Captain
Marryat (*The Bravo* is "poor"; *The King's Own* is "very fair"; *Newton
Forster* is "better still").[4] As a law student he recorded a "day spent
in seediness repentance & novel reading—dined in Hall. . . . I did
nothing else all day except eat biscuits, a very excellent amusement
& not so expensive as some others."[5] One supposes that many other
such days went unrecorded. In one of Thackeray's last novels, *The
Virginians*, the serious-minded George Warrington, also a law student, defends this indulgence: "O blessed Idleness! Divine lazy
Nymph! Reach me a novel as I lie in my dressing-gown at three
o'clock in the afternoon; compound a sherry-cobbler for me, and
bring me a cigar! Dear slatternly smiling Enchantress! They may
assail thee with bad names—swear thy character away, and call thee
mother of Evil; but, for all that, thou art the best company in the
world!" (chap. 29).

Nor was Thackeray's reading as an art student in Paris confined to Montaigne and Victor Cousin. Along with the heady volumes of history and philosophy that he chewed and digested at the Palais Royal, he nibbled also at the fiction of the day supplied by such shops as Galignani's and Baudry's. Here, too, he exercised his early developed critical instincts. His diary for 1832 records judgments on Balzac, whose *La peau de chagrin,* a moral fable on the root of all evil, "possesses many of the faults & the beauties of the school— plenty of light & shade, good colouring and costume, but no character;" and Hugo, whose historical epic *Notre-Dame de Paris* he rated "most highly as a work of genius, though it is not perhaps a fine novel." He shows more than a nodding acquaintance with the light risqué novels of Paul de Kock, whom later he palmed off on Major Pendennis. He also dipped into such curiosities as the *Roi des ribauds,* a historical romance by Paul Lacroix, and the salacious *Chroniques de l'Oeil-de-Boeuf,* a "secret" history of the reigns of Louis XIV and his successors, analogous to the sources he later drew on for *Henry Esmond* and for his portraits of the four Georges.[6]

It therefore came to Thackeray quite naturally to put his name forward to the editor of the *Edinburgh Review* as a contributor on "light matters connected with Art, humorous reviews, critiques of novels," as well as on "French subjects, memoirs, poetry, history from Louis XV downwards, and of an earlier period."[7] This was in 1845, when *The Luck of Barry Lyndon,* his masterpiece to date, had concluded its run in *Fraser's* without applause, and *Vanity Fair* was only barely projected. At this time Thackeray was a kind of professor of things in general, still not sure of his direction, and feeling out his own conception of fiction.

Thackeray's beloved "French subjects" were indeed the center of his first volume published in England, *The Paris Sketch Book* (1840), and here, significantly, he wrote his most extended apology for "novels, sweet and delicious." The essay in this book called "On Some French Fashionable Novels" begins with "a Plea for Romances in General," in which the "lazy idle boy" grown up now takes the side of "all who, from laziness as well as principle, are inclined to follow the easy and comfortable study of novels." He tries to assure these readers that "they are studying matters quite as important as history," and that one can learn as much from a duodecimo as from a quarto. "If then, ladies," continues Titmarsh's defense, "the bigwigs begin to sneer at the course of our studies, calling our darling romances foolish, trivial, noxious to the mind, enervators of intellect, fathers of idleness, and what not, let us at once take a high ground and say,—Go to your own employments, and to such dull studies as you fancy; go and bob for triangles, from the Pons Asinorum; go enjoy your dull black draughts of metaphysics; go fumble over history books and dissert upon Herodotus and Livy; *our* histories are, perhaps, as true as yours."[8] Following upon the "pale ale" of youth, ". . . our drink is the brisk, sparkling champagne drink, from the presses of Colburn, Bentley, & Co.; our walks are over such sunshiny pleasure-grounds as Scott and Shakespeare have laid out for us; and if our dwellings are castles in the air, we find them excessively splendid and commodious;—be not you envious because you have no wings to fly thither."

The "bigwigs," of course, are the preachers and pedants, from whose prying eyes many a reader besides Thackeray presumably remembered having hidden away their favorite little books. This fledgling novelist may seem to be saying "a fig for your ancient history and metaphysics," but it is possible to read behind his scorn an attempt at a modus vivendi between "our darling romances" and "dull studies." Thackeray had discovered, like Sir Philip Sidney before him, how "sham histories" draw old men from their chimney corners and children from play, and he seems to be renewing in a nineteenth-century context the Renaissance apologist's alliance of fiction with the time-hallowed disciplines of history and philosophy. "The novelist has a loud, eloquent, instructive language, though his enemies may despise or deny it ever so much," he argues in the voice of Titmarsh. He goes further: "sham histories" can teach better than true histories, which are "mere contemptible catalogues of names and places that can have no moral effect on the reader."

Titmarsh has in mind not merely the older histories, but the modern "catalogues of names and places" that were rapidly accumulating in this era of potted "useful knowledge," like the *Biographie universelle,* the *Cabinet Cyclopedia* of Dionysius Lardner (or "Diddler," as he is called in one of Thackeray's satires),[9] Walker's *Gazeteer,* and the periodical *Court Guide.* As a modernist concentrating his attention primarily on "the study of humanity," Thackeray is implicitly promoting the novel as a more effectual means of "keeping up with the world" than ancient history, metaphysics, or new encyclopedias, in the spirit of Isaac Watts's advice to "learn all things as much as you can from first hand." Dr. Watts also prescribed that students "visit other cities and countries when you have seen your own, under the care of one who can teach you to profit by travelling." The novel, from Titmarsh's viewpoint, is, among other things, a less expensive substitute for the Grand Tour, and a more personalized kind of travel book: "On the wings of a novel, from the next circulating library [the reader] sends his imagination a gadding, and gains acquaintance with people and manners, whom he could not otherwise hope to know." The novelist promises, in other words, not mere escape to "sunshiny pleasure-grounds" and "castles in the air," but educational travel that may give his readers knowledge of their fellow men more practical and more up to date than the ancient historians and metaphysicians can supply them.

Thackeray's apprenticeship in France, which opened his eyes to the joys and pathos of genre painting and of "the drama of the common people" at the Théâtre Ambigu-Comique, awakened him also to the power of the novelist to fix "ordinary people" in their natural setting:

> . . . Passing from novels in general to French novels, let us confess . . . that we borrow from these stories a great deal more knowledge of French society than from our own personal observation we ever can hope to gain: for, let a gentleman who has dwelt two, four, or ten years in Paris . . . let an English gentleman say, at the end of any given period, how much he knows of French society, how many French houses he has entered, and how many French friends he has made? . . .
>
> He has, we say, seen an immense number of wax candles, cups of tea, glasses of orgeat, and French people, in best clothes enjoying the same; but intimacy there is none: we see but the outsides of the people.[10]

Important as firsthand knowledge is to mankind, Thackeray is suggesting where it may fall short and how a good novel may extend direct experience:

> Year by year we live in France, and grow grey, and see no more. We play écarté with Monsieur de Trèfle every night; but what know we of the heart of the man—of the inward ways, thoughts and customs of Trèfle? If we have good legs, and love the amusement, we dance with Countess Flicflac, Tuesdays and Thursdays, ever since the Peace: and how far are we advanced in acquaintance with her since we first twirled her round a room? We know her velvet gown, and her diamonds (about three-fourths of them are sham, by the way); we know her smiles, and her simpers, and her rouge—but no more; she may turn into a kitchen wench at twelve on Thursday night, for aught we know; her *voiture*, a pumpkin; and her *gens* so many rats; but the real rougeless, *intime* Flicflac, we know not. This privilege is granted to no Englishman: we may understand the French language as well as Monsieur de Levizac; but never can penetrate into Flicflac's confidence.

Whereas the mere traveler may be confined to the surface of life, in Titmarsh's view, the novelist can make us more intimately acquainted with human nature. It is through his understanding of "the heart of the man" that the novelist has the advantage over the historian, the travel writer, and the journalist.

In his letter to Thomas Longman, editor of the *Edinburgh Review*, Thackeray added to his qualifications probably the most significant one: "finally subjects relating to society in general where a writer may be allowed to display the humorous *ego*," an indication of the large context in which he viewed fiction along with the other arts. To him the responsibility of the novelist as social historian extended beyond his own generation:

> . . . A hundred years hence (when, of course, the frequenters of the circulating library will be as eager to read the works of Soulié, Dumas, and the rest, as now), a hundred years hence, what a strange opinion the world will have of the French society of today! Did all married people, we may imagine they will ask, break a certain commandment?—They all do in the novels. Was French society composed of murderers, of forgers, of children without parents, of men consequently running the risk of marrying their grandmothers by mistake; of disguised princes, who lived in the friendship of amiable cut-throats and spotless prostitutes; who gave up the sceptre for the *savate*, and the stars and pigtails of the court for the chains and wooden shoes of the galleys? All these characters are quite common in French novels, and France in the nineteenth century was the politest country in the world. What must the rest of the world have been?[11]

Thackeray assumed, as this passage emphasizes, that one function of the serious writer, as of the painter, is to leave a record of his times to posterity, but what kind of a record is it to be? From this composite, based mainly on Sue's *Les mystères de Paris*, it is easy to gather that Thackeray was not taken with the sensational writers who were then enlivening the *feuilletons*. He was less interested in *les mystères* than in what the French called *les moeurs,* or what he referred to as the "inward thoughts and ways," the "manners" and the "customs" of people. "To a person inclined to study these in the light and amusing fashion in which the novelist treats them," Titmarsh writes in his essay "On Some French Fashionable Novels," "Let us recommend the works of a new writer . . . who has painted actual manners, without those monstrous and terrible exaggerations in which late French writers have indulged; and who, if he occasionally wounds the English sense of propriety (as what French man or woman alive will not?), does so more by slighting than by outraging it, as, with their laboured descriptions of all sorts of imaginable wickedness, some of his brethren of the press have done."[12] He is speaking of Charles de Bernard, descendant of a noble family who, like Thackeray, had given up law studies for a literary career, and anticipated his move from journalism into the novel of society. M. de Bernard, Titmarsh was pleased to observe, drew his characters from "men and women of genteel society— rascals enough, but living in no state of convulsive crimes; and we follow him in his lively malicious account of their manners, without risk of lighting upon such horrors as Balzac and Dumas have provided for us." Thackeray generally admired de Bernard for the "ease, grace, and *ton* in his style," and about the time when these words were written he adapted (or had "stolen" as he put it), de Bernard's *Le pied d'argile* for his own sociopolitical tale *The Bedford-Row Conspiracy*.[13] Later he wrote in praise of *Gerfaut*, de Bernard's more serious tale of adultery: "It is full of fine observation and gentle feeling; it has a gallant sense of the absurd, and is written—rare quality for a French romance—in a gentlemanlike style."[14] Thackeray had already had his bout with "convulsive crimes," as we shall see later in connection with *Catherine*, and was opting now for "genteel society" as his subject and the "gentlemanly style" as his language, though with his "natural perversity of vision," the "horrors" and "monstrous and terrible exaggerations" of the more sensational writers remained on the periphery of his pictures of society.

Charles de Bernard's pinioning of more elegant sin furnished Thackeray with one agreeable model for his own broad canvases. He enjoyed the refinements of intrigue—amorous, social, political—that wind their way beneath the bubbly surface of such *nouvelles* as *La femme de quarante ans*, with its superannuated belle who plays several former lovers off against one another; *Les ailes d'Icaire*, with its provincial young man who rapidly accustoms himself to the ways of the big city; and *Un acte de vertu*, with its hero who starts out as a radical firebrand and ends up as a stuffy bureaucrat. He admired in particular the "accurate picture of the actual French dandy" in *Les ailes d'Icaire*, an indication to him of de Bernard's facility for capturing the life of social man in process. "The fashions will change in a few years, and the rogue, of course with them," Titmarsh predicts, "Let us catch this delightful fellow ere he flies."[15]

In his essay on French society novels, Thackeray contrasts de Bernard and some of his colleagues with traveling English women writers such as Mrs. Trollope and Lady Morgan, who, "having frequented a certain number of tea-parties in the French capital, begin to prattle about French manners and men—with all respect for the talents of those ladies we do not believe their information to be worth a sixpence: They speak to us not of men, but of tea-parties." In *The Book of Snobs* several years later he ridiculed these and other literary "fashnabbles" of his own land:

> If anybody wants to know how intimately authors are connected with the fashionable world, they have but to read the genteel novels. What refinement and delicacy pervades the works of Mrs. Barnaby! What delightful good company do you meet with in Mrs. Armytage! She seldom introduces you to anybody under a marquis! I don't know anything more delicious than the pictures of genteel life in "Ten Thousand a Year," except, perhaps the "Young Duke" and "Coningsby." There's a modest grace about *them*, and an easy high fashion, which only belongs to blood, my dear sir—to true blood.[16]

This flippant passage serves as an introduction to the "pictures of genteel life" reproduced in "Novels by Eminent Hands" that appeared in *Punch* the following year, where the distinct impression is conveyed that these authors are anything but intimate with the life they write about. We overhear the "prattle" of the "delightful good company" provided for us by "Mrs. Armytage" in her new novel "Lords and Liveries":

> "Corpo di Bacco," he said, pitching the end of his cigar on to the red nose of the Countess of Delawaddymore's coachman—who, having deposited her fat ladyship at No. 236 Piccadilly, was driving the carriage to the stables, before commencing his evening at the "Fortune of War" public-house—"what a lovely creature that was! What eyes! What hair! Who knows her? Do you, mon cher prince?"
> "E bellissima, certamente," said the Duca di Montepulciano, and stroked down his jetty moustache.[17]

But they "speak to us not of men, but of tea-parties," or in this case stag parties. We are indeed confined here to the "outsides" of this fabled countess, "her velvet gown, and her diamonds ... her smiles, and her simpers, and her rouge."

We meet with a similar frustration in "Codlingsby" by one D. Shrewsbury, Esq. This author gives us the dimensions of a dwelling ("They entered a moderate-sized apartment—indeed Holywell Street is not above a hundred yards long, and this chamber was not more than half that length") and a full inventory of its furnishings:

> The carpet was of white velvet—(laid over several webs of Aubusson, Ispahan, and Axminster, so that your foot gave no more sound as it trod upon the yielding plain than the shadow did which followed you)—of white velvet, painted with flowers, arabesques, and

classic figures. . . . The edges were wrought with seed-pearls, and fringed with Valenciennes lace and bullion. The walls were hung with cloth of silver, embroidered with gold figures, over which were worked pomegranates, polyanthuses, and passion-flowers in ruby, amethyst and smaragd. . . . Divans of carved amber . . . went round the room, and in the midst was a fountain, pattering and bubbling with jets of double-distilled otto of roses.[18]

But nothing of the "heart of the man" Raphael Mendoza who occupies this Xanadu in Holywell Street. In his serious review of *Coningsby*, Thackeray generalized: "Not an unremarkable characteristic of our society-novelists is that ardour of imagination which sets them so often to work in describing grand company for us. They like to disport themselves in inventing fine people for us, as we to sit in this imaginary society. There is something *naif* in this credulity on both sides: in these cheap Barmecide entertainments, to which author and reader are content to sit down. Mr. Disraeli is the most splendid of all feast-givers in this way—there is no end to the sumptuous hospitality of his imagination."[19]

Disraeli's imagination, moreover, with all its "sumptuous hospitality," seemed to dwell in a hothouse. By comparison with de Bernard's "accurate picture of the actual French dandy," the dandyism of *Coningsby* was to Thackeray "intense, but not real; not English, that is. It is vastly too ornamental, energetic and tawdry for our quiet habits. The author's coxcombry is splendid, gold-land, refulgent, like that of Murat rather than that of Brummell." He vastly preferred the "refined observation" of de Bernard and other disciples of Balzac who were recording for future generations the emergent society of the *juste milieu*. As against what he regarded as the preoccupation with externals of "our society-novelists," Thackeray translates passages from de Bernard's stories to illustrate the French writer's ability to penetrate beyond costume and decor to reveal the "inner man." Dambergeac, the student activist of *Un acte de vertu*, in particular is presented to us vividly individualized and representative of his times. We see him first as a youth:

> He was then a young man of eighteen, with a tall slim figure, a broad chest, and a flaming black eye, out of all which personal charms he knew how to draw the most advantage; and though his costume was such as Staub might probably have criticized, he had, nevertheless, a style peculiar to himself—to himself and the students, among whom he was the leader of fashion. A tight black coat, buttoned up to the chin, across the chest, set off that part of his person; a low-crowned hat, with a voluminous rim, cast solemn shadows over a countenance bronzed by a southern sun: he wore, at

one time, enormous flowing black locks, which he sacrificed
pitilessly, however, and adopted a Brutus, as being more revolutionary: finally, he carried an enormous club, that was his code and
digest: in like manner, De Retz used to carry a stiletto in his pocket,
by way of a breviary.[20]

and subsequently in middle age, settled into a provincial subprefec-
ture:

> In fact a great change, and such a one as many people would call a
> change for the better, had taken place in my friend: he had grown
> fat, and announced a decided disposition to become what French
> people call a *bel homme:* that is, a very fat one. His complexion,
> bronzed before, was now clear white and red: there were no more
> political allusions in his hair, which was, on the contrary, neatly frizzed
> and brushed over the forehead, shell-shape. This head-dress, joined
> to a thin pair of whiskers, cut crescent-wise from the ear to the nose,
> gave my friend a regular bourgeois physiognomy, wax-doll like.[21]

Thackeray reveals here his own preoccupation with the novelist's
medium of time and the changes wrought by the years. He was
beguiled too by the round of "bets, breakfasts, riding, dinners at
the 'Café de Paris,' and delirious Carnival balls" that occupy the
young boulevardiers of M. de Bernard. Especially amusing to him
was the manner in which "our author describes a swindler imitating
the manners of a dandy" as exemplified by Blondeau de Gustan of
Les ailes d'Icaire; he could not help adding: "and many swindlers
and dandies be there, doubtless, in London as well as in Paris."
Charles Yellowplush is well acquainted with one of them:

> The name of my nex master was, if posbil, still more ellygant and
> youfonious than that of my fust. I now found myself boddy servant
> to the Honrabble Halgernon Percy Deuceace, youngest and fifth son
> of the Earl of Crabs. . . .
> When I say that Mr. Deuceace was a barrystir, I don't mean that he
> sent sesshuns or surcoats (as they call 'em), but simply that he kep
> chambers, lived in Pump Cort, and looked out for a commissionar-
> ship or a revisinship, or any other place that the Wig guvvyment
> could give him. His father was a Wig pier (as the landriss told me),
> and had been a Toary pier. The fack is his Lordship was so poar, that
> he could be anythink or nothink, to get provisions for his sons and an
> inkum for himself.[22]

Another, who hails from Dublin rather than London, introduces
himself:

> I presume that there is no gentleman in Europe that has not heard of
> the house of Barry of Barryogue, of the kingdom of Ireland, than

which a more famous name is not to be found in Gwillim or D'Hozier; and though, as a man of the world, I have learned to despise heartily the claims of some *pretenders* to high birth who have no more genealogy than the lackey who cleans my boots, and though I laugh to utter scorn the boasting of many of my countrymen, who are all for descending from kings of Ireland, and talk of a domain no bigger than would feed a pig as if it were a principality; yet truth compels me to assert that my family was the noblest of the island, and, perhaps, of the universal world.[23]

The most famous of his rogues has "arrived" in London from obscure Paris origins, claiming descent from the Entrechats, "a noble family of Gascony;"

> Becky felt as if she could bless the people out of the carriage windows, so elated was she in spirit, and so strong a sense had she of the dignified position which she had at last attained in life. Even our Becky had her weaknesses, and as one often sees how men pride themselves upon excellencies which others are slow to perceive . . . so to be, and to be thought, a respectable woman, was Becky's aim in life, and she got up the genteel with amazing assiduity, readiness, and success. We have said, there were times when she believed herself to be a fine lady, and forgot that there was no money in the chest at home—duns round the gate, tradesmen to coax and wheedle—no ground to walk upon, in a word. And as she went to Court in the carriage, she adopted a demeanour so grand, self-satisfied, deliberate, and imposing, that it made even Lady Jane laugh. She walked into the royal apartments with a toss of the head which would have befitted an empress, and I have no doubt had she been one, she would have become the character perfectly.[24]

Thackeray frequently allows his scamps and charlatans to betray themselves through letters or memoirs, in the manner of the continental models he admired, but for him the novelist as student of the "inward thoughts and ways" of man should transcend language. "There is a great deal of matter for curious speculation in the accounts here so wittily given by M. de Bernard," he wrote in commendation of this elegant farceur still unknown at the time to English readers, "but, perhaps, it is still more curious to think what he has *not* written, and to judge of his characters, not so much by the words in which he describes them, as by the unconscious testimony that the words altogether convey."[25] Certainly in some of Thackeray's own most memorable episodes, it is the "unconscious testimony" that ultimately is most revealing:

> Easy and pleasant as their life at Paris was, it was after all only an idle dalliance and amiable trifling; and Rebecca saw that she must push Rawdon's fortune in their own country. She must get him a place or appointment at home or in the colonies; and she deter-

mined to make a move upon England as soon as the way could be cleared for her. As a first step she had made Crawley sell out of the Guards and go on half-pay. His function as aide-de-camp to General Tufto had ceased previously. Rebecca laughed in all the companies at that officer, at his toupee . . . at his waistband, at his false teeth, at his pretensions to be a lady-killer above all. . . . Becky had a dozen admirers in his place to be sure; and could cut her rival to pieces with her wit. But as we have said, she was growing tired of this idle social life: opera boxes and restaurateur-dinners palled upon her: nosegays could not be laid about as a provision for future years: and she could not live upon knick-knacks, laced handkerchiefs, and kid gloves. She felt the frivolity of pleasure, and longed for more substantial benefits.[26]

We enter the consciousness of Major Pendennis in the midst of a scene that could be one of the Parisian Carnival balls described by M. de Bernard, where "men of all classes high and low . . . congregate and give themselves up to the disgusting worship of the genius of the place," but the setting is May Fair:

There he stood, with admirable patience, enduring, uncomplainingly, a silent agony; knowing that people could see the state of his face (for could he not himself perceive the condition of others, males and females, of his own age?)—longing to go to rest for hours past; aware that suppers disagreed with him, and yet having eaten a little so as to keep his friend, Lady Clavering, in good-humour; with twinges of rheumatism in the back and knees; with weary feet burning in his varnished boots,—so tired, oh, so tired and longing for bed! If a man, struggling with hardship and bravely overcoming it, is an object of admiration for the gods, that Power in whose chapels the old Major was a faithful worshipper must have looked upwards approvingly upon the constancy of Pendennis's martyrdom. There are sufferers in that cause as in the other: the negroes in the service of Mumbo Jumbo tattoo and drill themselves with burning skewers with great fortitude; and we read that priests in the service of Baal gashed themselves and bled freely. You who can smash the idols, do so with good courage; but do not be too fierce with the idolators,— they worship the best thing they know.[27]

Turning from the "jam tarts" of his boyhood to French pastries enhanced Thackeray's appreciation for the more substantial fare that the novel offered beyond vicarious excitement for the idle mind. His sojourns in Paris gave him opportunity also to observe that fiction writing was a going enterprise. "Their fecundity is so prodigious that it is impossible to take any account of their progeny," he wrote in an article entitled "French Romancers on England" in 1843, "and a Review which professes to keep its readers *au courant* on French light literature, should be published, not once a quarter, but more than once a day." The popular press, one by-

product of the late revolution, cultural as well as political, now
offered a new presumably inexhaustible outlet for the wares of the
"romancers": ". . . Since the invention of the *Feuilleton* in France,
every journal has its six columns of particular and especial report.
M. Eugène Sue is still guillotining and murdering and intriguing in
the *Débats*. . . . M. Dumas has his tale in the *Siècle*; Madame Gay is
pouring out her eloquence daily in the *Presse*; M. Reybaud is en-
deavouring with the adventures of Jean Mouton in the *National*, to
equal the popularity he obtained with "Jérôme Paturot"; in a word,
every newspaper has its different tale."[28] The teller of tales has
discovered the way to the great public. Moreover, these organs with
such resounding names as *Débats, Siècle, Moniteur*, and *National* can
accommodate under one fold anything conveyable by the printed
word—gossip, sensation, persuasion, and instruction.

One of the novels referred to in this article, Louis Reybaud's
Jérôme Paturot à la recherche d'une position sociale (1842), made a special impression on Thackeray, and he devoted a critical article to it
in *Fraser's Magazine* during the same season. Reybaud gave him "a
curious insight into some of the social and political humbugs of the
great nation," Titmarsh told his readers, and impressed him with
his ability to inculcate a "wholesome moral . . . with much
philosophical acumen."[29] This wise and witty satire is wide in its
sweep, casting ridicule on virtually all aspects of political and cultural life under the July Monarchy through its ineffectual hero,
prototype of the eternal bungler, "who imagines himself fitted for
everything and cannot make a lasting success of anything." After a
series of aborted careers as social reformer, poet, journalist, politician, and soldier, Jerome eventually settles down in the humdrum
family business, a happy mediocrity. Jerome's charming aggressive
wife Malvina, an ex-grisette who enjoys a brief whirl in the *haut-
monde*, is, as we shall see in a later chapter, among the literary sisters
of Becky Sharp. Of more immediate interest is Jerome's attempt,
early in life, to become a man of letters, an experience fraught with
sociological significance. The chapter entitled "Paturot Feuilletoniste" is an amusing, if cynical and hard-headed, excursion into
the politics and economics of the writing life, focusing our attention
on the emergent bourgeois public and the way to their hearts and
pocket books. Titmarsh translates some advice to Jerome by the
editor of a popular paper whom the aspiring young writer has
approached with his wares:

> "You must recollect, sir, that the newspaper, and in consequence,
> the *Feuilleton*, is a family affair. The father and mother read the story
> first, from their hands it passes to the children, from the children to

the servants, from the servants to the house porter, and becomes at once a part of the family. . . ."

"Well, granting that the *Feuilleton* is a necessity nowadays [replies Jerome], what sort of *Feuilleton* must one write in order to please all these various people?"[30]

Jerome's question is one that many a nineteenth-century novelist must have asked himself as he reached out to the variegated audience that George Meredith was to refer to as "the republic of the fireside." In his preceding colloquy with the editor, which Titmarsh did not translate but must have read, Jerome, recognizing that the *feuilleton* "a pris dans notre ordre social une importance au moins égale à celle de la tasse de café et du cigare de la Havane," is inspired with a sense of mission. "Je crois que j'ai trouvé une veine encore inexploitée dans le domaine de l'art," he declares. The editor puts him down quickly enough:

> "Sir . . . come off it, please. What you call the domain of art must take second place when you address a large public. Look, let's not take leave of reality. What makes up the mass of readers of newspapers? landlords, farmers, merchants, manufacturers, with a sprinkling of a few men of the law and of the sword; moreover, these are the most enlightened. Now ask yourself what is the average intelligence of this clientele. Do you think that your theories of art will have any effect on them? that they will respond to them? that they will even understand you? When one speaks to everybody, sir, one must speak like everybody."[31]

Jerome, standing by his principles, replies that the great artist lifts the public up to his level; he does not descend to theirs. He reminds the jaded journalist that not everybody in ancient Greece was a Phidias, but that all Greeks came to admire that sculptor's work; that Cicero, speaking in the Roman Forum, did not mold his rhetoric on that of his fellow senators, but imposed his own style on them. "The true artist does not obey, he rules," affirms the idealistic Paturot. Our sophisticated editor has his rejoinder ready:

> "My dear sir, when one writes for a newspaper, one is neither orator nor sculptor. One aims at a great number of subscribers, and the best theory is the one that makes them come to you. You speak besides of two ages eminently artistic, of two peoples who sucked up the taste for grand things with their mothers' milk. Nothing like that here. We live in a bourgeois age, sir, in the midst of a nation that is attracted more and more to trumpery. What to do? Resist? To climb up Mount Hymettus and live off the honey of poetry? One has to be very young to have such ideas, and you will get over them."

The audience of the writer of the nineteenth century, this editor reminds young Paturot, extends beyond the family circle to embrace a heterogeneous, respectable, but uncultivated multitude. The fundamental issue raised here is: Who calls the tune, the writer or the reader? "The true artist does not obey, he rules," pronounces the serious writer trying to reach his unknown audience through popular organs.[32] The modern writer must join the multitude, not try to lead them, replies his editor: "When one speaks to everybody, one must speak like everybody" ("Quand on parle à tout le monde, môsieur, il faut parler comme tout le monde"), Thackeray himself had to confront this situation, and it is possible to some extent to infer his position. As one who deplored the "prodigious pomposity" and "fine writing" of some of his more "literary" rivals, parodied in *Catherine* and in *Punch's Prize Novelists*, and liked to refer to his own as "a sort of confidential talk between writer and reader," he seems to side with Jerome's editor on the matter of style. On the other hand, the author of *Jérôme Paturot*, which itself originated as a *feuilleton*, offered sufficient evidence that one can write to entertain "la masse de lecteurs" without producing claptrap (what the editor calls "le camelotte"). "I have heard that 'Jerome Paturot' is a political novel. . . . Perhaps it *is* a political novel," comments Titmarsh at the conclusion of his review, "perhaps there is a great deal of sound thinking in this careless, familiar, sparkling narrative, and a vast deal of reflection hidden under Jerome's ordinary cotton nightcap."[33] He recommended this "course of French humbug, commercial, legal, literary, political" heartily to "all lovers of the Pantagruelian philosophy." He could not help adding that "if there be any writer in England who has knowledge and wit sufficient, he would do well to borrow the Frenchman's idea, and give a similar satire in our own country," and he followed suit.

In his own country, Thackeray could not help noticing, equivalents to the French *feuilleton* had proliferated since the teens of the century, providing the popular instructor with cheap and easy access to the cultural new masses. "It must be confessed that the controversialists of the present day have an eminent advantage over their predecessors in the days of folios," he observes in another essay in *The Paris Sketch Book*. Whereas the compiling of folios required erudition, intellectual labor, and time, he continues, "now, in the age of duodecimos . . . a male or female controversialist draws upon his imagination, and not his learning; makes a story instead of an argument, and in the course of 150 pages . . . will prove or disprove you anything."[34]

One result is "those detestable mixtures of truth, lies, false sentiment, false reasoning, bad grammar, correct and genuine philan-
thropy and piety," disseminated in tracts, "which any woman or
man, be he ever so silly, can take upon himself to write, and sell for
a penny." In *The Book of Snobs* we are introduced to the Reverend
Lionel Pettipois offering his "awakening" little books at half-a-
crown a hundred, "which dribble out of his pockets wherever he
goes," and we realize how far the little books themselves travel from
one of Thackeray's drawings in *Punch* showing a castaway on a
desert island holding up to a fellow in misery a sheaf of tracts from
a bottle washed up on shore.[35] In *Vanity Fair* Mrs. Kirk, disciple of
the Reverend Doctor Ramshorn, puts "three little penny books
with pictures," entitled "Howling Wilderness," "The Washerwoman of Wandsworth Common," and "The British Soldier's Best
Bayonet," into the hands of Amelia Sedley for her bedside enlightenment. Off the same press may have plumped "Crumbs from
the Pantry," "The Frying Pan and the Fire," "The Livery of Sin,"
Lady Emily Southdown's "Washerwoman of Finchley Common,"
and her mother's "Fleshpots Broken; or, the Converted Cannibal,"
which are intended to draw Miss Crawley away from Pigault-
Lebrun and closer to salvation (chaps. 27, 33).

Wherever he turned Thackeray saw himself surrounded by professors with the pen. "Since the days of Aesop, comic philosophy
has not been cultivated so much as at present. The chief of our
pleasant writers—Mr. Jerrold, Mr. Dickens, Mr. Lever—are as-
siduously following this branch of writing," he wrote in a review for
the *Morning Chronicle*, "and the first-named jocular sage, whose
apologues adorned our spelling-books in youth, was not more careful to append a wholesome piece of instruction to his fable than our
modern teachers now are able to give their volumes a moral bal-
last."[36] Before long the faculty was joined by the "dandiacal" author
of *Coningsby*. "It will not be the fault of the romantic writers of the
present day if the public don't perceive that the times are out of
joint, and want setting right very sadly," begins Thackeray's review
of *Sybil*. To the *feuilleton*, the tract, and the "little penny books with
pictures" could now be added Mr. Disraeli's "three-volume parable," a proper key to which would require "a history of the Refor-
mation, the Revolution, and of parties since the advent of the
House of Hanover—a digest of the social, political, and commercial
life of the Normans and Anglo-Saxons—a history of agriculture,
manufacture, banking, and credit."[37]

In these reviews Thackeray seems to be deploring the compound of fact and fiction, the insinuating of teaching and preaching into books that readers turn to for amusement. In one of his reviews he puts himself in the place of those who would prefer to keep pleasure and instruction on separate shelves: "We like to hear sermons from his reverence at church; to get our notions of trade, crime, politics and other national statistics, from the proper papers and figures; but when suddenly, out of the gilt pages of a pretty picture book, a comic moralist rushes forward, and takes occasion to tell us that society is diseased, the laws unjust, the rich ruthless, the poor martyrs, the world lop-sided, and *vice-versa*, persons who wish to lead an easy life are inclined to remonstrate against this literary ambuscadoe."[38] As with religion and politics, so with metaphysics and science, Thackeray suggests in an extreme hypothetical case:

> If Professor Airy, having particular astronomical discoveries to communicate, should bring them forward through Mr. Colburn's duodecimo medium, with, let us say, Newton for a hero—(the apple tumbling on the sleeping philosopher's nose might be made a thrilling incident of romance . . .)—[but] if the professor, lecturing to a class, should so mingle astronomy and sentiment together, it is needless to say his pupils would not have a very high respect for him; and as they would have a right to doubt and grumble, because upon a matter of astronomy their professor introduced a novel, so conversely, have novel readers good cause to complain, if their teacher, in an affair of romance, think fit to inflict upon them a great quantity of more or less wholesome philosophy.[39]

Thackeray's position on this question seems to be summed up near the beginning of his review of *Sybil*: "We stand already committed as to our idea of the tendency and province of the novel. Morals and manners we believe to be the novelist's best themes; and hence prefer romances which do not treat of algebra, religion, political economy, or other abstract science. We doubt the fitness of the occasion, and often (it must be confessed) the competency of the teacher."[40] Yet this self-styled "week-day preacher" had himself demonstrated that these areas were not necessarily incompatible. In his first novel, *Catherine*, he drew upon none other than Professor Airy's hero to adorn the tale and point a moral of his own: "A fit of indigestion puts itself between you and honours and reputation; an apple plops on your nose, and makes you a world's wonder and glory; a fit of poverty makes a rascal of you, who were, and are still, an honest man; clubs, trumps, or six lucky mains at dice, makes an honest man for life of you, who ever were, will be, and are a rascal. Who sends the illness? who causes the apple to fall? who deprives you of worldly goods? or who shuffles the cards, and brings trumps, honour, virtue, and prosperity back again?" "The excitement of metaphysics must equal almost that of gambling," young Thackeray had remarked in reaction to his reading of Victor Cousin's *Cours de l'histoire de la philosophie*,[41] and he seems to have felt the same way about some of the other "dull studies" he had ruled out of the novelist's province. In the "magazinery" that followed *Catherine*, such as *The Bedford-Row Conspiracy* and *The Great Hoggarty Diamond*, politics and economics affect the ups and downs of the characters' fortunes. *Barry Lyndon*, along with a swashbuckling, swindling, card-playing hero, offers us a "near view" of the political and military history of Europe during the Seven Years' War. Religion is intruded into *Vanity Fair* with the author's apologies: "Sick-bed homilies and pious reflections are, to be sure, out of place in mere story-books, and we are not going (after the fashion of some novelists of the present day) to cajole the public into a sermon, when it is only a comedy that the reader pays his money to witness. But, without preaching, the truth may surely be borne in mind, that the bustle, and triumph, and laughter, and gaiety which Vanity Fair exhibits in public, do not always pursue the performer into private life" (chap. 19). Certainly by the time the reader has finished this "comedy," he has had a vivid impression of people who live "without God in the world." As for the subsequent "mere story-books," Arthur Pendennis freely discusses religion, philosophy, and politics with his friend George Warrington, and the narrators of *Henry Esmond* and *The Newcomes* do not hesitate to cast their lots with "the parson's own."

Whatever a superficial reading of his pronouncements on novels and novelists may suggest, Thackeray himself did not separate fact from fiction or teaching and preaching from entertainment. Speaking for the kind of reader who resists tub thumping or finger pointing, he advocates "amusing by means of amiable fiction, and instructing by kindly satire, being careful to avoid the discussion of abstract principles, beyond those of the common ethical science which forms a branch of all poets' and novelists' business."[42] Himself more attracted to "actual manners" than to "abstract principles," Thackeray set great store by the power of the imagination, combined with observation, to "illustrate" character (in the parlance of the day). Significantly he points out in one of his pieces on Disraeli that "the great success of 'Coningsby' arose—not from the Caucasian theory, and discovery of the Venetian origin of the English constitution—but from those amusing bitter sketches of Tadpole, Rigby, Monmouth, and the rest, of which the likenesses were irresistible, and the malice tickled everybody." In *Sybil*, on the other hand, he complains, "there is very little personality . . . very little pleasant caricaturing, or laughable malice, or Gillray grotesqueness; but there is more Venetian theory, more high-flown Young England mystery."[43] The novelist's contribution to "common ethical science," in other words, is not through "abstract principles," but through principles *personified* and *exemplified*. As a student of the visual as well as literary arts, Thackeray drew freely on graphic analogies to make his own points. "Parson . . . if you come for cards, 'tis mighty well, but I will thank you to spare me your sermons," shouts the Baroness Bernstein to her chaplain Mr. Sampson in one delightful episode of *The Virginians*. But earlier we have caught her in a rare moment of truth when she sighs before her portrait painted by Godfrey Kneller in the sunshine of her days: "Ah! Here is a sermon!"

"If truth is not always pleasant, at any rate truth is best, from whatever chair—from whence graver writers or thinkers argue, as from that at which the story-teller sits as he concludes his labour, and bids his kind reader farewell," are Thackeray's parting words in the preface to *Pendennis*. These words can be taken as the upshot of his continuous campaign in the writings before *Pendennis* to reconcile "the story-teller" with "graver writers or thinkers." Having allowed the story-teller to speak for himself before the curtain in *Vanity Fair*, he gives equal time to the more earnest writer in "A Plan for a Prize Novel" that appeared in *Punch* the year after *Pendennis* was completed. This satire takes the form of a "Letter from the eminent Dramatist Brown to the eminent Novelist Snooks," a young author whose "work is eagerly read by the masses." The letter is supposedly addressed from the Café des Aveugles in Paris. Knowing of Thackeray's own saturation in the popular Parisian press, we are not surprised that Brown's plan is "taken from the French . . . in the law report of the *National Magazine*," and credited to "a French literary gentleman, M. Emanuel Gonzales." Brown suggests to Snooks how the French example can be adapted to suit the tastes of the English public:

> "Unless he writes with a purpose, you know, a novelist in our days is good for nothing. This one writes with a socialist purpose; that with a conservative purpose: this author or authoress with the most delicate skill insinuates Catholicism into you, and you find yourself all but a Papist in the third volume: another doctors you with Low-Church remedies to work inwardly upon you, and which you swallow

down unsuspiciously, as children do calomel in jelly. Fiction advocates all sorts of truths and causes—doesn't the delightful bard of the Minories find Moses in everything?"[44]

Both the curtain lecture of *Vanity Fair* and the "Plan for a Prize Novel" of the "eminent Dramatist Brown" wax jocular, in their converse ways, over the dilemma, shared by Thackeray with his rivals, of the serious novelist caught between his desire to educate his readers and his need to amuse them. Although he made fun of neatly packaged nostrums in the form of fiction that "advocates all sorts of truths and causes," he recognized that "wholesome philosophy" needed to be made palatable in order to go down. In one of his first published books, he had characterized satire as a curative medicine, "often sharp, but wholesome, like the bark that is bitter to the palate, but that helps to brace and strengthen the frame."[45] He learned how to sweeten the medicine. As a fellow novelist, Anthony Trollope, was to write in his book on Thackeray: "The palpable and overt dose the child rejects; but that which is cunningly insinuated by the aid of jam and honey is accepted unconsciously, and goes upon its curative mission. So it is with the novel. It is taken because of its jam and honey. But unlike the jam and honey of the household cupboard, it is never unmixed with physic."[46] He was speaking of a writer for whom the "raspberry open tarts" of boyhood had given way to "calomel in jelly." By transforming the cotton nightcap of the French satirist into a cap and bells, Thackeray convinced his public that a "funny book" can "add to one's knowledge of the world" and of mankind.

Thackeray's various critiques of novels and other popular reading show that he was concerned with the medium, as we say today, as well as the message. With the extension of the writer's audience, he saw himself competing not only with the tract writers and the "comic philosophers," but also with what he referred to as the "scandal and ribaldry organs" that had also sprouted up as an outgrowth of the steam press and were further abetted by the reduction of the stamp laws. He has a word to say on this phenomenon also in *The Paris Sketch Book*: ". . . Why does this immorality exist? Because the people *must* be amused and have not been taught *how*; because the upper classes, frightened by stupid cant, or absorbed in material wants, have not as yet learned the refinement which only the cultivation of art can give; and when their intellects are uneducated, and their tastes are coarse, the tastes and amusements of classes still more ignorant must be coarse and vicious likewise, in an increased proportion."[47] He was referring specifically to the two-penny papers that had emerged in England in the 1830s, which he found inferior to their French equivalents, the *feuilletons* and the cartoons through which Parisian polemicists were educating the masses. The former had already been the subject of an article, "Half-a Crown's Worth of Cheap Knowledge," that appeared in 1838 in *Fraser's Magazine* (published anonymously, but since identified as Thackeray's). "We have our penny libraries for debauchery as for other useful knowledge," he wryly concluded this omnibus review of a dozen of the most widely circulated "periodical works" of the time, carrying such titles as *The Poor Man's Friend, Livesey's Moral Reformer, The Penny Story-Teller, The Penny Satirist, Cleave's Penny Gazette of Variety,* and *The Town.* "Blessed be the press, and the fruits thereof!" proclaims this critic, extending mock congratulations to the camp followers of the "March of Intellect." "In old times (before education grew general)," he continues, "licentiousness was considered as the secret of the aristocracy. Only men enervated by luxury, and fevered by excess of wealth, were supposed to indulge in vices which are now common to the poorest apprentice or the poorest artisan."[48] But now, thanks to the energies of Lord Brougham and his printers, "'this schoolmaster is abroad,' and the prejudices of the people disappear." His sarcasm was not, of course, directed to popular education as such, in which he wholeheartedly believed, but at what "the people" were being taught in these rabble-rousing penny guides and gazettes. It is evident from a sequel article, "Horae Catnachianae," that he was not altogether discouraged with the prospects of teaching the populace through "cheap literature." Here his subject is broadside ballads. "Our public has grown to be tired of hearing great characters, or extraordinary ones, uttering virtuous sentiments," he observes in this review of the "literature" that emanated from Seven Dials, "but put them in the mouth of a street-walker straightaway they become agreeable to listen to."[49] Thackeray himself uttered some of his own "virtuous sentiments" in ballad form, in "numbers" if not in broadsheets. Nor did he find it beneath him to play jester and, at least in spirit, wander among the crowd in the streets as the wrapper design for *Vanity Fair* shows.

Critical as he was of the literature aimed at the working-class reader, some of Thackeray's most delicious diatribe was directed at that eyewash of genteel ladies, the illustrated gift books, the Albums, Annuals, Books of Beauty, and Keepsakes, which he once flung aside in one heap as: "such a display of miserable mediocrity, such a collection of feeble verse, such a gathering of small wit," in which "a little sham sentiment is employed to illustrate a little sham art." In one of his "Annual Executions," he asks the readers of *Fraser's:*

> But seriously . . . is this style of literature to continue to flourish in England? Is every year to bring more nonsense like this, for foolish parents to give to their foolish children; for dull people to dawdle over till the dinner-bell rings; to add something to the trash on my lady's drawing-room table, or in Miss's bookcase? *Quousque tandem* How far, O keepsake, wilt thou abuse our forbearance? How many more bad pictures are to be engraved, how many more dull stories to be written, how long will journalists puff and the gulled public purchase?[50]

Indefinitely, to judge by the way Arthur Pendennis's publisher, Mr. Bacon of Paternoster Row, kowtows to the Lady Violet Lebas, editor of the Spring Annual, "daintily illustrated with pictures of reigning beauties, or other prints of a tender and voluptuous character."[51] Arthur Pendennis contributes a poem to Lady Violet's Annual, as indeed Thackeray wrote for the Keepsake edited by her namesake Lady Blessington. Lady Violet's *Spring Annual,* we are told, "has since shared the fate of other vernal blossoms, and perished out of the world," but it blossomed anew in other forms. Thackeray showed what he could do with the genre in *Mrs. Perkins's Ball,* one of his Christmas books in pink wrappers, where, incidentally, are introduced Miss Bunion, the heavy-set poetess of such delicate lyrics as "Heartstrings," "The Deadly Nightshade," and "Passion Flowers," along with Poseidon Hicks, the aesthetic young author of Greek lyrics and epics "in the Byronic manner." His next work was a yellow-wrappered compendium of wit, sentiment, verse, and art called *Vanity Fair.* As critic Thackeray may have scorned the "pretty picture book," but as author he took it in stride. *Vanity Fair,* in fact, received a posthumous tribute that he would have appreciated as "one of the best illustrated books in the world."[52]

"Poor fellows of the pen and pencil! we must live. The public likes light literature, and we must write it. Here I am writing magazine jokes and follies, and why? Because the public like such, will purchase no other," laments Titmarsh in the midst of a gallery tour during the season of 1844.[53] Yet the following year he defends these very "magazine jokes and follies" to one of his hypothetical readers: "What a quantity of writings by the same hand have you, my dear friend, pored over! How much delicate wit, profound

philosophy (lurking hid under harlequin's black mask and spangled jacket, nay under clown's white lead and grinning vermillion)
how many quiet wells of deep-gushing pathos, have you failed to
remark as you hurried through those modest pages, for which the
author himself here makes an apology. . . ."[54] A month later, reading Dickens's "Christmas frolic," *The Cricket on the Hearth*, Thackeray cannot help admiring how "the author is at high jinks with that
half-million of the public which regards him and sympathises with
him," over whom he has "such a kindly, friendly hold . . . as
perhaps no writer ever had before." He likens the tale to a theatrical piece: "It interests you as such—charms you with its grace,
picturesqueness and variety—tickles you with its admirable grotesque." He tries to probe to the source of this magician's power
over readers: "We fancy that we see throughout the aim of the
author—to startle, to keep on amusing his reader; to ply him with
brisk sentences, rapid conceits, dazzling pictures, adroit inter-
changes of pathos and extravaganza."[55] Thackeray was working at
this time on *Vanity Fair*, certainly one of the most "adroit inter-
changes of pathos and extravaganza" that he ever achieved. He had
come to recognize that the public instructor needed a bag of tricks
in addition to a well-stuffed portfolio. If it was possible to convey
religion through tracts, politics through broadsheets and ballads,
parables in pink boards, and art in gilt-edged picture books, why
not "common ethical science" under "gaudy yellow wrappers"?
When one speaks to everybody, one speaks like everybody. To
these wise words of Jerome Paturot's editor Thackeray might have
added that the author who would speak to everybody must also
catch everybody's eye first.

But Thackeray was not merely making a virtue of necessity. The
flimsy, if attractive, dress in which much of his wisdom for the ages
originally appeared may be taken as emblematic of his own fascination with the transitory and the mundane. Realism for him meant
not merely writing about what one is familiar with, but becoming
familiar with what one chooses to write about. The notebooks he
gathered for his novels are crammed with jottings from contemporaneous newspapers and magazines, government documents,
court records, diaries, guidebooks, maps—indicative of his passion
for primary sources, for what is "fresh from the press," as he
phrased it on one occasion.[56] He was encouraged along these lines,
one gathers from its influence on his first novel, *Catherine*, by an
essay-review that appeared in *Fraser's Magazine* in the mid-1830s
called "Hints for a History of Highwaymen." This writer, calling

attention to the sheets and broadsides that in the last century and his own disseminated "hot newes" of the streets, courts, prisons, and gallows to the populace, declared: "We have ourselves not seldom obtained an insight into the realities of life through the rude language of these ephemeral repertories of sorrow and crime." Toward the end of his review he throws out a challenge: "Have we not opened out a wide and rich field of labour for a philosophic, literary, legal observer? He must combine some law with a larger portion of literature, to secure for his readers those ballads and pamphlets of the passing hour which, though light in themselves, show most surely the settings of current opinion; and for the satisfactory completion of the task he should possess more moral discrimination than either law or literature."[57]

A "philosophic, literary, legal observer" is an apt enough description of an aspiring young writer, who, as he was to write of one of his heroes, "behaved to Themis with a very decent respect and attention, but he loved letters more than law always."[58] By this time Thackeray himself had left the Middle Temple behind for Fleet Street, with Paternoster Row still beckoning. The "light" literature of the hour, the "ephemeral repertories of sorrow and crime," are, according to the author of "Hints for a History of Highwaymen," grist alike to the mills of the lawyer, the news reporter, and the novelist. Although the specific context of the *Fraser's* article is the literature of outlawry, it emphasizes that the real concern of the "philosophic" writer is "erring man" in general. This writer seems to anticipate Thackeray's succession of fictitious "histories," in which men and women of all sorts and conditions are called before the bar of judgment, though a moral rather than a legal one. Certainly he helps define what was to be Thackeray's dual function—documentalist of his age to future generations, and moral teacher to his own.

It was to his own age, of course, that Thackeray immediately addressed himself, not as one of the "graver writers or thinkers" but as a "laughing philosopher," the label he used for himself in the preface to his *Comic Tales and Sketches*. "The best humour that we know of has been as eagerly received by the public as by the connoisseur," he proclaimed in his essay on Cruikshank. "Some may have a keener enjoyment of it than others, but all the world can be merry over it, and is always ready to welcome it." He likens Cruikshank to a charismatic leader such as Napoleon who has "*fait vivre la fibre populaire*," and attributes the success of his favorite artist to a "general wide-hearted sympathy" that at once "pities and loves the poor, and jokes at the follies of the great . . . and addresses all in a perfectly sincere and manly way."[59] Although his own brand of comedy appealed at first mainly to "the connoisseur," his whole career can be characterized as an attempt to address "all the world"—or, in his own terms, "leaders of public opinion," "genteel people," "the bourgeois," "people of the working sort," and "low-bred creatures," as he designated the divers elements of the reading public at various times.[60]

Thackeray's fundamental conception of his function as author was dominated by an elitist sociology of culture, more readily assumed in his century than in ours. "People in their battles about public matters forget the greatest good of all, social-good, I mean fine arts and civilization, dandyism as you call it," he wrote as a young man to his mother; "We owe this to the aristocracy, and we must keep an aristocracy (pure & modified as you wish) in order to retain it."[61] Like many "leaders of public opinion" of the age, Thackeray conceived the progress of culture as a filtering down of "literaryture and the fine harts" from the top to the bottom of "the edifice of humanity." In time he came to see the writer as taking over the duty, abandoned by the aristocracy, of educating the public intellect and refining their taste. We catch a glimpse of this idealistic side of young Thackeray in his satirical playlet on the literary marketplace called "Reading a Poem" (1841), where he represents a crusading young journalist, one Percy Dishwash, all afire with his vision of "the great republic of genius." In this utopia the writer is expected to "rank with the foremost of the land."[62] Quixotic as it may have appeared at the time, this vision seemed to materialize in the person of one citizen of this republic greeted by Thackeray in 1843 as "the first literary man in this country who has made himself honourably and worthily the equal of the noblest and wealthiest in it." The nation at large, he wrote, owed a debt of gratitude to "this accomplished scholar from the unlettered public . . . for laying open his learning to all, and bidding the humble and the great alike welcome to it."[63] Like Macaulay, whom he was eulogizing here, Thackeray aspired to "open his learning to all," to become "a man of letters and of the world, too." In one of his last novels, *Lovel the Widower*, his surrogate, Mr. Batchelor, recalls of his journalistic days: "I daresay I gave myself airs as editor of that confounded *Museum*, and proposed to educate the public taste, to diffuse morality and sound literature throughout the nation, and to pocket a liberal salary in return for my services" (chap. 1). In this noble cause Thackeray joined forces with Lord Macaulay as well as that other literary aristocrat, Lord Brougham.

Much as he may have complained from time to time of the exploitation of the drivers of the quill by the lords of the press, or hinted at the indifference of Parliament to the welfare of authors, or grumbled over his lack of acclaim by the vox populi, Thackeray became convinced that the lot of the literary man was a happy as well as beneficial one. In a late chapter of *The Newcomes*, he has Arthur Pendennis say that, in contrast to other professions, including the learned ones and the artistic calling, "I have been grateful for my own more fortunate one, which necessitates cringing to no patron; which calls for no keeping up of appearances; and which requires no stock-in-trade save the workman's industry, his best ability, and a dozen sheets of paper" (chap. 74). Even before he found his way to the "many thousands more readers than I ever looked for" whom he greets in the preface to *Pendennis*, Thackeray expressed his satisfaction with this career open to talents: "Let men of letters stand for themselves," he writes in 1846. "Every day enlarges their market, and multiplies their clients. The most skilful and the most successful among the cultivators of light literature have such a hold upon the public feelings, and awaken such a sympathy, as men of the class never enjoyed until now: Men of science and learning who aim at other distinction, get it: and . . . I believe there was never a time when so much of the practically useful was written and read, and every branch of book-making pursued, with an interest so eager."[64]

Although he identifies himself here with "the cultivators of light literature," Thackeray had already, in his essay "On Some French Fashionable Novels," established "our darling romances" among "the practically useful":

> Twopence a volume bears us whithersoever we will—back to Ivanhoe and Coeur de Lion, or to Waverley and the Young Pretender, along with Walter Scott; up to the charming enchanters of the silver-fork school; or, better still, to the snug inn-parlour, or the jovial tap-room, with Mr. Pickwick and his faithful Sancho Weller. . . . [A novel] contains true character under false names; and, like "Roderick Random" . . . and "Tom Jones" . . . gives us a better idea of the state and ways of the people than one could gather from any more pompous or authentic histories.[65]

With our hindsight we can see Thackeray laying out here the range of his own "histories"—rogue tales, travel books, "silver-forks," historical romances, and domestic novels—even one of his parodies. The relish for "jam-tarts," he discovered, extends beyond childhood, as he reminds the readers of *Cornhill* at the zenith of his career:

Novels are sweets. All people with healthy literary appetites love
them—almost all women;—a vast number of clever hard-headed
men. . . . Judges, bishops, chancellors, mathematicians are notorious
novel-readers; as well as young boys and sweet girls, and their kind
tender mothers. Who has not read about [Lord] Eldon and how he
cried over novels every night when he was not at whist? . . .
    And pray what is the moral of this apologue? The moral I take to
be this: the appetite for novels extending to the end of the world—
far away in the frozen deep, the sailors reading them to one another
during the endless night; far away under the Syrian stars, the solemn
sheikhs and elders hearkening to the poet as he recites his tales; far
away in the Indian camps, where the soldiers listen to ___'s tales, or
___'s, after the hot day's march; far away in little Chur yonder,
where the lazy boy peers over the fond volume, and drinks it in with
all his eyes;—the demand being what we know it is, the merchant
must supply it as he will supply saddles or pale ale for Bombay or
Calcutta.[66]

"I wonder, do novel-writers themselves read many novels?" the
editor of *Cornhill* asks in this same Roundabout Paper.[67] Biting as
he could be as a critic and parodist of the novel, he never lost his
tolerance even for the kind of fiction that "provides the *ne plus ultra
of indolence*," that one can "go through . . . with a gentle, languid,
agreeable interest,"[68] and he conjectures the same about some of
his notable rivals, such as Dickens, Ainsworth, Bulwer, Lever, Sur-
tees, and the Trollopes, Frances and Anthony. "Dear youth of ingenuous countenance and ingenuous pudor!" he addresses the rising generation, "I make no doubt that the eminent parties above
named all partake of novels in moderation—eat jellies—but mainly
nourish themselves upon wholesome roast and boiled."[69] Shortly
before, he wrote to Anthony Trollope, in the course of confirming
his publishers' invitation to contribute a tale to *Cornhill:* "Don't
understand me to disparage our craft, especially *your* wares. I often
say I am like the pastry-cook, and don't care for tarts, but prefer
bread and cheese; but the public love the tarts (luckily for us), and
we must bake and sell them."[70] To apply his own image, Thackeray
did not confine himself to the dessert course in his own novels. The
opposition he set up between "jellies" and "wholesome roast and
boiled" was his homely way of expressing his perennial conflict
between the entertaining and the useful. But both were well ac-
commodated within the scope of the novel as he defined it in a
review: the "ways of work and pleasure," of men and women, "their
feelings, interests and lives, public and private."[71] Arthur Pendennis, Thackeray's prototype of the writer, certainly manages to unite
his vocation with his avocation, "contemplating with an unfailing

delight all specimens of [humanity] in all places to which he resorted, whether it was the coquetting of a wrinkled dowager in a
ballroom, or a high-bred young beauty blushing in her prime
there; whether it was the hulking guardsman coaxing a servant-girl
in the Park—or innocent little Tommy that was feeding the ducks
whilst his nurse listened."[72] Not long after, Thackeray affirmed in
his own voice in a role that he found especially congenial, that of
public lecturer: "Our business is pleasure, and the town, and the
coffee-house, and the theatre, and the mall."[73] This "lazy idle boy"
had borne witness to, and had himself played an important part in,
the metamorphosis of "our darling romances" into "our society
novels."

1. "On A Peal Of Bells"; "On A Lazy Idle Boy," *Works*, 12:384, 169.

2. "De Juventute," *Works*, 12:237.

3. Ibid., pp. 231, 237–38; "On A Lazy Idle Boy," pp. 169, 171. Some of the sketches based on his early reading that Thackeray drew in school books are reproduced in *Thackerayana*, comp. Joseph Grego (London: Chatto & Windus, 1901), chap. 2.

4. *Letters*, 3:444 (28 April 1855 to G. H. Lewes); 1:22 (12–21 February 1828 to Mrs. Carmichael-Smyth); 1:187, 203, 206, 224, 228 (diary, 2 April–23 November 1832).

5. *Letters*, 1:206 (diary, 5 June 1832).

6. Ibid., pp. 222, 224, 225, 228, 234.

7. 6 April 1845 to Thomas Longman, *Letters*, 2:190–91.

8. *Works*, 5:80.

9. "The History of Dionysius Diddler," *Works*, 13: 652–70.

10. "On Some French Fashionable Novels," *Works*, 5:82.

11. "Jerome Paturot. With considerations on Novels in General," *Fraser's Magazine*, September 1843, p. 350; *Works*, 13:386.

12. "On Some French Fashionable Novels," *Works*, 5:84.

13. March 1840 to Mrs. Carmichael-Smyth, *Letters*, 1:433.

14. "Jerome Paturot," *Works*, 13:385.

15. "On Some French Fashionable Novels," *Works*, 5:84.

16. "On Some Literary Snobs," *Punch* 10 (1846):271; *Works*, 6:358. Mrs. Trollope was author of *The Widow Barnaby*, and among Mrs. Gore's novels was *Mrs. Armytage; or, Female Domination*. The *Young Duke*, as well as *Coningsby*, was written by Disraeli, and *Ten Thousand a Year* was Samuel Warren's most popular novel.

17. *Punch*, 12 June 1847, pp. 237–38; *Works*, 6:511.

18. *Punch*, 22 May 1847, pp. 213–14; *Works*, 6:484–85.

19. *Morning Chronicle*, 13 May 1844; *Contributions*, p. 40. Thackeray also reviewed *Coningsby* in the *Pictorial Times*, 25 May 1844; rpt. in *Stray Papers*, pp. 22–23. Here he remarked that the "coxcombries" of Disraeli are "quite unlike the vapid, cool coxcombries of the English dandy; they are picturesque, wild, and outrageous."

20. "On Some French Fashionable Novels," *Works*, 5:87–88.

21. Ibid., pp. 90–91.

22. "Dimond Cut Dimond," *Memoirs of Mr. Charles J. Yellowplush, Works*, 3:256.

23. *Barry Lyndon*, chap. 1.

24. *Vanity Fair*, chap. 48.

25. "On Some French Fashionable Novels," *Works*, 5:92.

26. *Vanity Fair*, chap. 36.

27. *Pendennis*, chap. 45 (Major Pendennis at Lady Clavering's evening party at Gaunt House).

28. "French Romancers on England," *New Sketch Book*, p. 204.

29. "Jerome Paturot," *Works*, 13:396. For a useful introduction to this delightful book, see D. P. Scales, "French Manners under the July Monarchy, Louis Teybaud's Humorous Novel . . .," *AUMLA*, August 1954, pp. 21–30. The quotation about Jerome that follows is taken from this article.

30. "Jerome Paturot," *Works*, 13:390. The formula set out by the editor will be taken up in the chapter on *Vanity Fair*.

31. Chap. 7, my translation (as in succeeding passages). In an illustrated edition of 1846, this passage is accompanied by a cut showing a kitchen maid reading a newspaper while the kettles are boiling on the stove.

32. In his essay "May Gambols," Thackeray, possibly with this episode in mind, takes artists to task who "paint down to the level of the public intelligence, rather than seek to elevate the public to them" (*Works*, 13:423).

33. Jerome eventually goes into the family business of manufacturing nightcaps—used emblematically in the novel. The headpiece to the illustrated edition of 1846 shows a winged cotton nightcap arched by a rainbow, bearing the label "Au Bonnet Du Grand Romantique." At the end of the introduction, the author is shown at his desk dozing with a nightcap on his head.

Prior to his success with *Jérôme Paturot*, Reybaud had tried to reach the public with a serious political treatise, *Etude sur les réformateurs ou socialistes modernes*.

34. "Madame Sand and the New Apocalypse," *Paris Sketch Book*, *Works*, 5:191; originally appeared in the *Corsair*, 14 September 1839.

35. "On Some Country Snobs," *Works*, 6:409; *Punch* (reproduced in Lewis Melville, *Life of William Makepeace Thackeray*, 2 vols. [London: Hutchinson, 1899], 2:184).

36. Review of Charles Lever's *St. Patrick's Eve*, *Morning Chronicle*, 3 April 1845; *Contributions*, pp. 70–71.

37. Review of *Sybil*, *Morning Chronicle*, 13 May 1845; *Contributions*, pp. 77–79.

38. Review of *St. Patrick's Eve*.

39. Review of *Sybil*. The reference is to Sir George Biddell Airy, eminent at this time as a professor of astronomy and director of the Cambridge observatory; in 1835 he had been appointed Astronomer Royal.

40. Ibid.

41. See above, p. 27.

42. Review of *St. Patrick's Eve*.

43. Review of *Sybil*. In reviewing *Coningsby* for the *Pictorial Times*, Thackeray pointed out the numerous figures in the book representing real people under fictitious names, adding that the author "paints his own portrait in this book in the most splendid fashion; it is the queerest in the whole gallery of likenesses" (*Stray Papers*, p. 222).

44. *Punch* 20 (1851): 75; *Works*, 6:535. The "bard of the Minories" is, of course, Disraeli.

45. Preface, *Comic Tales and Sketches*.

46. Anthony Trollope, *Thackeray*, English Men of Letters (London: Macmillan, 1879), pp. 202–3.

47. "Caricature and Lithography in France," *Works*, 5:147 (revised from "Parisian Caricatures," *Westminster Review*, April 1839).

48. "Half-a Crown's Worth of Cheap Knowledge," *Fraser's Magazine*, March 1838, p. 290; rpt. in *Works* (Furniss ed.), 8:75–94. For details on the fiction contained in some of these magazines, and especially in their more lurid successors, see Louis James, *Fiction for the Working Man* (London: Oxford University Press, 1963).

49. "Horae Catnachianae," *Fraser's Magazine*, April 1839, p. 408.

50. "A Word on the Annuals," *Fraser's Magazine*, December 1837, p. 761; rpt. in *Works* (Cent. Biog. Ed.), 25:80–81.

51. *Pendennis*, chap. 31. "An Interesting Event. By Mr. Titmarsh" appeared in the *Keepsake* for 1849 (rpt. in *Stray Papers*, pp. 259–65).

52. Russell Sturgis in *Scribner's Monthly*, June 1880; quoted in *Vanity Fair*, p. xxxix.

53. "May Gambols," *Works*, 13:422.

54. "Barmecide Banquets," *Fraser's Magazine*, November 1845, p. 584 (under the pseudonym of George Savage Fitz-Boodle); *Works* (Furniss Ed.), 10:423.

55. "Christmas Books, No. I: Dickens's *Cricket on the Hearth*," *Morning Chronicle*, 24 December 1845; *Contributions*, pp. 88–90.

56. "Anybody who will take the trouble of looking back to a file of newspapers of the time, must, even now, feel at second hand this breathless pause of expectation. . . . Think what the feelings must have been as these papers followed each other fresh from the press" (*Vanity Fair*, chap. 35, in connection with his account of the Battle of Waterloo); while working on *The Virginians*, Thackeray wrote to his friend Dr. John Brown: "I read no new books, only Newspapers and Magazines of 1756" (*Letters*, 4:64). His passion for what was "fresh from the press" persisted to the end. The manuscript of *Denis Duval* cites, among many other sources, the Session Papers of the Old Bailey, the *Gentleman's Magazine*, and the *Annual Register*.

57. *Fraser's Magazine*, March 1834, p. 287. This article has been attributed to Thackeray by several bibliographers, first by C. P. Johnson in *The Early Writings of William Makepeace Thackeray* (London: E. Stock, 1888), p. 41, followed by Harold S. Gulliver in *Thackeray's Literary Apprenticeship* (Valdosta, Ga.: Southern Stationery and Printing Co., 1934), pp. 75–76, and Miriam Thrall, *Rebellious Fraser's* (New York: Columbia University Press, 1934), pp. 254–56. This attribution was vigorously disputed for the first time by Edward M. White in his "Thackeray's Contributions to *Fraser's Magazine*," *Studies in Bibliography* 19 (1966): 74–75. Since White's piece appeared, a rereading of the article in connection with research for vol. 2 of the *Wellesley Index* has resulted in the rejection of it as Thackeray's on the basis of some biographical data supplied by the author that do not jibe with the known facts about Thackeray. Although it can no longer be included in the Thackerayan canon, "Hints" is, I believe, seminal in the formation of his ideas on the moral purpose of fiction, as will be brought out in the chapter on *Catherine*.

58. George Warrington in *The Virginians*, chap. 63.

59. "George Cruikshank," *Works*, 13:291.

60. See in particular "On Men and Pictures" and "May Gambols," *Works*, 13:365, 421; and "George Cruikshank," ibid., passim.

61. Fragmentary manuscript letter of 1836–37, quoted in Gordon N. Ray, *The Uses of Adversity* (New York: McGraw-Hill, 1955), p. 192.

62. *Works*, 13:536. This sketch originally appeared in *Britannia*, 1 and 8 May 1841.

63. "Mr. Macaulay's Essays," *Pictorial Times*, April 1843; *Works* (Cent. Biog. Ed.), 13:266.

64. "A Brother of the Press on the History of a Literary Man . . .," *Works*, 13:478–79.

65. "On Some French Fashionable Novels," *Works*, 5:83–84.

66. "On A Lazy Idle Boy," *Works*, 12:170–71.

67. Ibid., p. 171.

68. "A Brighton Night's Entertainment," *Punch*, 18 October 1845.

69. "On A Lazy Idle Boy," *Works*, 12:171.

70. 28 October 1859, *Letters*, 4:158–59. Quoted in Trollope's *An Autobiography* (London: Oxford University Press, 1923), p. 126.

71. Review of *Sybil*, *Contributions*, p. 80.

72. *Pendennis*, chap. 46.

73. "George the First," *The Four Georges*, *Works*, 8:640.

Part Two

"THE LAUGHING PHILOSOPHER"
Fraser's Period

CATHERINE; OR, "UNMIXED RASCALITY"

Chapter Five

For his first extended work of fiction, Thackeray turned to one of those "ephemeral repertories of sorrow and crime" much admired by a fellow Fraserian for their elementary appeal and fresh insight into human nature.[1] *Catherine: A Story*, a "horrific" account of a husband murderess and her execution drawn from the *Newgate Calendar*, remained a "pamphlet of the passing hour" not reprinted in Thackeray's lifetime[2] (owing, it appears, to both reader apathy and the author's own dissatisfaction with his story), but he humorously recalled the grisly events in an imitation folk ballad that appeared years later in his *Lyra Hibernica:*

> In the reign of King George and Queen Anne,
>   In Swift's and in Marlborough's days,
> There lived an unfortunate man,
>   A man by the name of John Hayes.

> A decent respectable life,
>   And rather deserving of praise,
> Lived John, but his curse was his wife
>   —His horrible wife Mrs. Hayes.

> A heart more atrociously foul
>   Never beat under any one's stays:
> As eager for blood as a ghoul
>   Was Catherine the wife of John Hayes

By marriage and John she was bored
(He'd many ridiculous traits);
And she hated her husband and lord,
This infamous, false Mrs. Hayes.

When madness and fury begin
The senses they utterly craze;
She called two accomplices in,
And the three of 'em killed Mr. Hayes.

And when they'd completed the act,
The old *Bailey Chronicle* says,
In several pieces they hacked
The body of poor Mr. Hayes.

This bloody saga continues with the discovery of Hayes's remains in the Thames and the posting of his head in a churchyard, leading to the discovery and exposure of the murderers. In true ballad form, it concludes with a moral and an envoy:

And sooner or later 'tis plain
For wickedness every one pays
They hanged the accomplices twain,
And burned the foul murderess Hayes.

And a writer who scribbles in prose,
And sometimes poetical lays,
The terrible tale did compose
Of Mr. and Mrs. John Hayes.[3]

In this version the "terrible tale" that Thackeray took from the *Newgate Calendar* is reduced literally to its bare bones, and conveyed in the form of one of the cheap broadsides through which many of these real-life crime stories were popularly disseminated. Thackeray does not mention here any of the characters he added in his own retelling of the story, such as the Count von Galgenstein and Tom Billings, who thicken the plot, or the brigands Brock and Macshane, who lighten it. Neither does he introduce any of the antecedent incidents or subsidiary themes that he engrafted, for reasons of his own to be discussed later, upon the original sordid events. In these rhymes Thackeray skips lightly over the ground that he had trod upon with scorn and anger when he was out to attack the so-called Newgate novelists.

It is as an anti-Newgate novel that *Catherine* is chiefly remembered, and because it remains the most widely unread of Thack-

eray's stories, even historians of fiction are content to leave it at
that. To be sure he continually impales on its pages such contemporary masters of literary Grand Guignol as Ainsworth, Dickens,
and "Mr. Bulwig" (as Charles Yellowplush calls him). He apologizes
at the outset for presuming "to take a few more pages from the Old
Bailey calendar, to bless the public with one more draught from the
Stone Jug" (a popular name for Newgate Prison), justifying himself
only on the ground that he will exceed his predecessors in "scenes
of villainy, throat-cutting, and bodily suffering in general" (p. 4).
He conceived his "draught" as an emetic, relieving surfeit through
excess. Quite early in the novel, the author himself confesses that
he is beginning to feel queasy: "And here, though we are only in
the third chapter of this history, we feel almost sick of the characters that appear in it, and the adventures they are called upon to go
through. But how can we help ourselves? The public will hear of
nothing but rogues; and the only way in which poor authors, who
must live, can act honestly by the public and themselves, is to paint
such thieves as they are; not dandy, poetical, rose-water thieves; but
real downright scoundrels, leading scoundrelly lives, drunken,
profligate, dissolute, low; as scoundrels will be." If readers must
have criminals, then "Ikey Solomons" will oblige, but not with the
literary-aesthetic kind they are accustomed to:

> They don't quote Plato, like Eugene Aram; or live like gentlemen,
> and sing the pleasantest ballads in the world, like jolly Dick Turpin
> [hero of Ainsworth's *Rookwood*]; or prate eternally about το καλόν like
> that precious canting Maltravers, whom we all of us have read about
> and pitied; or die whitewashed saints, like poor "Biss Dadsy" in
> "Oliver Twist." No, my dear madam, you and your daughters have
> no right to admire and sympathise with any such persons, fictitious
> or real: you ought to be made cordially to detest, scorn, loathe,
> abhor, and abominate all peoples of this kidney. . . . Keep your
> sympathy for those who deserve it: don't carry it, for preference, to
> the old Bailey, and grow maudlin over the company assembled
> there. (P. 46)

And so Solomons keeps up the dosage of his "Catherine cathartic,"
making it more and more violent.

One motive behind Thackeray's deliberate choice of such shocking matter was obviously to ridicule his more successful rivals ("The
other popular novelists of the day," he wryly refers to them at one
point), but a more important one was to advance his own ideas on
fiction. In one respect his first novel is a comment on, and reaction
to, popular taste. His addresses to readers needle them for their
low appetites fully as much as his fellow writers for catering to
them:

These points being duly settled, we are now arrived, O public, at a point for which the author's soul hath been yearning ever since this history commenced. We are now come, O critic, to a stage of the work when this tale begins to assume an appearance so interestingly horrific, that you must have a heart of stone if you are not interested by it. O candid and discerning reader, who art sick of the hideous scenes of brutal bloodshed which have of late come forth from pens of certain eminent wits, if you turn away disgusted from the book, remember that this passage hath not been written for you, or such as you, who have the taste to know and hate the style in which it hath been composed; but for the public, which hath no such taste:—for the public, which can patronise four different representations of Jack Sheppard,—for the public whom its literary providers have gorged with blood and foul Newgate garbage,—and to whom we poor creatures, humbly following at the tail of the great high-priests and prophets of the press, may, as in duty bound, offer some small gift of our own: a little mite truly, but given with goodwill. Come up, then, fair Catherine and brave Count;—appear, gallant Brock, and faultless Billings;—hasten hither, honest John Hayes: the former chapters are but flowers in which we have been decking you for sacrifice. Ascend to the altar, ye innocent lambs, and prepare for the final act: lo! the knife is sharpened, and the sacrificer ready! Stretch your throats, sweet ones,—for the public is thirsty, and must have blood! (Conclusion of chap. 13)

On the continent, as we already have noticed, Thackeray was equally revolted by the "drames brutales" of Hugo and Dumas, with their "monstrosities, adulteries, murders, and executions." Also, a dosage of the novels of Sue and Soulié had led him to ask: "Was French society composed of murderers, of forgers, of children without parents . . . of disguised princes, who live in the friendship of amiable cut-throats and spotless prostitutes?"[4] From *Catherine* one might easily infer that English society during the Age of Anne was composed largely of outlaws, adulterers, bastards, and murderers, but the cut-throats whom Count (not Prince) Galgenstein lives among are not very amiable, and the prostitute he consorts with is far from spotless. Writing early in 1833 for the *National Standard*, which he edited at the time and contributed to as Paris correspondent, Thackeray complained of even lower depths of taste: "Young France requires something infinitely more piquant than an ordinary hanging matter, or a commonplace *crim con.* To succeed, to gain a reputation, and to satisfy La jeune France, you must accurately represent all anatomical peculiarities attending the murder, or crime in question; You must dilate on the clotted blood, rejoice over the scattered brains, particularise the sores and bruises, the quavering muscles and the gaping wounds."[5] Thackeray seems to have learned something from the *feuilletonistes* as well as from the writers for the *Newgate Calendar* about how to represent "real down-right scoundrels" rather than "dandy, poetical, rose-water thieves." For the benefit of Young England, "Ikey Solomons" is lavish with details about the decapitation of John Hayes (including the collection of the blood in a bucket), the hanging of Tom Billings in chains, and the burning of Catherine (including the battering out of her brains by the executioner before the flames reach her). Furthermore, for the delectation of audiences of all ages "which can patronise four different representations of Jack Sheppard," Solomons provides this scenario:

A Grand Tableau
MRS. CATHERINE CUTTING OFF HER HUSBAND'S HEAD

———————————

1. The Carrying of the Pail.
2. The Thames at Midnight. The Emptying of the Pail.
3. The Thames at Low-Water. Discovery of the Head.
4. St. Margaret's by Moonlight. The Head on the Pole!

* * * * * * * * * * * *

CATHERINE BURNING AT THE STAKE! BILLINGS
HANGING IN THE BACKGROUND! THE THREE SCREAMS
OF THE VICTIM!!!
The Executioner dashes her brains out with a billet.

———————————

The Curtain falls to slow Music.
God save the Queen!   No money returned.[6]
Children in arms encouraged, rather than otherwise.

It appears also that Thackeray got other ideas from the Parisians. During his student days, the "famous and witty French critic" Jules Janin[7] excoriated the popular melodramas of the day that were packing in crowds at the Porte St. Martin:

And when evening came, I used to find again a cruel pleasure; I was accustomed to go out alone, and at the door of the theatres I used to see wretched people struggling for a place to applaud a poisoner or a devil, a parricide or a leper, an incendiary or a vampire; in the theatre I saw men moving about who had nothing better to do than to become by turns brigands, gendarmes, peasants, great lords, Greeks, Turks, white bears, black bears, whatever one wanted them to become, without realizing that they exposed to these unwholesome boards their wives and small children, and their old grandparents. . . . This dramatic pleasure, stirred up by such means, repelled me; but it became my practice to watch these low-bred people amusing themselves, laughing, living, experiencing in the theatre, among comedians, comediennes, and men with a talent completely devoted to distilling vice and horror for them.

Janin sets out to compete with these masters of vice and horror in the story where these words appear, a mock sensational novel entitled *L'âne mort et la femme guillotinée* (1829).[8] The heroine is a provincial girl who falls in with bad company, becomes a prostitute, bears an illegitimate child (the product of her seduction by her jailer), and eventually is executed for murdering her lover (a public hangman whimsically nicknamed Charlot by his intimates). In following the downward course of Henriette, we are treated not only to graphic descriptions of life in the Bastille and death by the guillotine, but to visits as well to an abattoir and to a morgue, in keeping with the author's determination to induce terror by realistic means.[9] Janin's "heroine" is a model at once of cold-bloodedness and of warped feeling, expressing no regret for her deeds, only compassion for a pet donkey who has been cruelly slaughtered.[10] There are surface resemblances between her and Thackeray's Catherine—apart from their eventual fates. Both meet their lovers at country inns, are dazzled by them with false ideas of glamor, and enjoy brief entrées into high society. Thackeray was in fact acquainted with the story,[11] and one suspects that he read Janin's tongue-in-cheek apology (in the preface) to his critics for the "fracas de style" of his ghastly joke, which he defends as "une parodie sérieuse, une parodie malgré lui" written in the cause of "la verité dans l'art."

The specific targets of the two authors differed, but Thackeray also aimed at truth in art in his serious parody, in which, like Janin, he ridicules popular fiction and theater while he wields them to his own ends. Janin compared himself to a physician probing society with his scalpel to expose the raw nerves of human nature. Thackeray preferred to use his scalpel to dissect his characters' souls. "Criminals stand forward . . . on the canvass of humanity as prominent objects for our special study," a brother Fraserian had already written,[12] leading us to expect Thackeray to begin his reconstruction of the "edifice of humanity" at "the bottom of the dried-up, weed-choked well,"[13] even if the excesses of the Newgate novelists had not provoked him to it. As is clear from the remarks on *Jack Sheppard* and *Oliver Twist* that concluded the original version of *Catherine,* his quarrel with Ainsworth and Dickens is based not so much on their making heroes of criminals, as for their failure to turn these figures into complete human beings. "As no writer can or dare tell the *whole* truth concerning them, and faithfully explain their vices, there is no need to give *ex-parte* statements of their virtues," he declares (p. 185). It is not the place of the novelist,

Solomons implies, to defend or to condemn criminals, but to represent them, like all men, as a "mixture of wisdom and folly, vice and
virtue, good and evil," as Dr. Watts put it.[14] In other words, if one is
to deal with criminals, their vices should be explained as a good
biographer or historian would do, not explained away in the manner of the romancer.

This is just what Solomons attempts to do with Catherine, and, to
a lesser extent, with other characters in the novel. Basically he
addresses himself to the sources of moral evil in the world, the
serious import behind the wry reference, early in the story, to a
certain "dark angel" who seems to have the heroine in thrall, as she
flees from Count Galgenstein after her unsuccessful attempt to
poison him:

> I do not mean to say that, in this strait, he appeared to her in the
> likeness of a gentleman in black, and made her sign her name in
> blood to a document conveying over to him her soul, in exchange for
> certain conditions to be performed by him. Such diabolical bargains
> have always appeared to me unworthy of the astute personage who is
> supposed to be one of the parties to them; and who would scarcely be
> fool enough to pay dearly for that which he can have in a few years
> for nothing. It is not, then, to be supposed that a demon of darkness
> appeared to Mrs. Cat, and led her into a flaming chariot harnessed
> by dragons, and careering through the air, at the rate of a thousand
> leagues a minute. No such thing; the vehicle that was sent to her aid
> was one of a much more vulgar description. (P. 53)

Thackeray's literary allusions—the flaming chariot, the man in
black, the diabolical bargain—are, presumably, to the sensationally
popular Faustian tale *Melmoth the Wanderer*.[15] The vehicle that carries Catherine to the Bugle Inn and to her doom in the form of
John Hayes is the humdrum "Liverpool carryvan" out of Birming-
ham. So the author reminds his readers that in this world, unlike
Maturin's Gothic world, evil is natural, not supernatural, in origin,
and that all men are accountable for their sins.

Having disposed of a romantic conception of evil, Solomons addresses himself to what he regards as another false notion about
human nature, in connection with young Tom, the illegitimate son
of Catherine and Count Galgenstein, who has been adopted by
Goody Billings, a benevolent housewife of the village:

> A celebrated philosopher—I think Miss Edgeworth—has
> broached the consolatory doctrine, that in intellect and disposition
> all human beings are entirely equal, and that circumstance and edu-
> cation are the causes of the distinctions and divisions which after-
> wards unhappily take place among them. Not to argue this question

. . . let us simply state that Master Thomas Billings . . . was in his long-coats fearfully passionate, screaming and roaring perpetually, and showing all the ill that he *could* show. At the age of two, when his strength enabled him to toddle abroad, his favourite resort was the coal-hole or the dung-heap; his roarings had not diminished in the least, and he had added to his former virtues two new ones—a love of fighting and of stealing; both which amiable qualities he had many opportunities of exercising every day. (Pp. 98–99)

In probing the corrupted soul, Solomons himslf rejects the sentimental theory of natural innocence reflected in Miss Edgeworth's much imitated *Moral Tales* and *Early Lessons,* where children, who are at worst unruly, are properly conditioned by exemplary tutelage and salutary environments. He seems to be more on the side of original sin: "As I have heard the author of Richelieu, Natural Odes, Siamese Twins, &c. ["Bulwig" again] say, 'Poeta nascitur non fit,' which means, that though he had tried ever so much to be a poet, it was all moonshine; in the like manner I say, 'Roagus nascitur non fit.' We have it from nature, and so a fig for Miss Edgeworth" (p. 100). Had Tom simply followed the cottage-lined walks of Miss Edgeworth's children, or Fatherless Fanny, Mrs. Hofland's beggar boys—and Oliver Twist—presumably he would have been led up the path of righteousness under the guidance of amiable adopted parents. But fresh country air fails to purify Tom's bad blood. His road leads to Tyburn, like that of another apprentice fallen on evil ways, Jack Sheppard. However, unlike Ainsworth, who blames society for his hero's downfall, Solomons makes Tom fully culpable for his crimes.[16]

Moral responsibility, then, is the fundamental theme of *Catherine: A Story,* with the most heinous of sinners set out as prominent object lessons. However, Solomons's dedication to truth in art commits him to painting all men, not merely thieves, "as they are." His parody, therefore, is not confined to the Newgate novel, but takes in all manner of fictitious representations of life that romanticize or sentimentalize human nature. To make his point about "sham" versus "true" history, he anticipates "George de Barnwell" of the later Punch Prize Novels series: "Had we been writing novels instead of authentic histories we might have carried them [Catherine and her husband] anywhere else we chose," he declares in connection with the false threat of impressment of Hayes by the vagabonds Brock and Macshane, "and we had a great mind to make Hayes philosophising with Bolingbroke, like a certain Devereux; and Mrs. Catherine *maîtresse en titre* to Mr. Alexander Pope, Dr. Sacheverel, Sir John Reade the oculist, Dean Swift, or Marshal

Tallard; as the very commonest romancer would under such circumstances." The "very commonest romancer" was Bulwer with his well-known capacity for historical name-dropping and over-coloring of the past. To be sure, with *Henry Esmond* Thackeray was to teach Bulwer how to bring this sort of thing off more convincingly, but for now he is determined to adhere closely to the line of the Newgate Calendar, and "not for the sake of the most brilliant episode—no, not for a bribe of twenty guineas per sheet, would we depart from it" (p. 79). Here too is an early swipe at glorified war heroes that Thackeray was to repeat with variations in "Phil Fogarty," the parody of Lever that first appeared in *Punch,* and in *Barry Lyndon* and *Vanity Fair.* Brock and Macshane, the brigands of *Catherine,* deflate the pseudoepical style of the military novelists then in vogue—among whom the names chiefly remembered are Gleig,[17] Maxwell, and Glascock. A typical figure in Gleig's tales in particular was the peninsular *miles gloriosus,* and it is with one of these in mind that Ensign Macshane is best appreciated: "He was perfectly ready with his sword, and when better still, a very little tipsy, was a complete master of it; in the art of boasting and lying he had hardly any equals." Furthermore, "it was a fact that he had been in Spain as a volunteer, where he had shown some gallantry, had had a brain fever, and was sent home to starve as before." As to the present life of the two ex-soldiers: "[Macshane] and Brock took to their roving occupation, he cheerfully submitted to the latter as his commanding officer, called him always major, and, bating blunders and drunkenness, was perfectly true to his leader. He had a notion—and, indeed, I don't know that it was a wrong one—that his profession was now, as before, strictly military, and according to the rules of honour. Robbing he called plundering the enemy; and hanging was, in his idea, a dastardly and cruel advantage that the latter took, and that called for the sternest reprisals" (pp. 80–81). Brock and Macshane, in other words, may have changed their uniforms, but not their way of life. The criminal code, according to Ikey Solomons, is merely the obverse side of the code of war upheld by society.

Owing to the delicious irony that the depraved Tom Billings is in fact the son of an aristocrat, the upper classes also come in for their share of the satire in the story. Before he created gentleman criminals, Bulwer created gentleman fops, for which he had already been exposed to public ridicule in *Fraser's* pages by *Sartor Resartus.* It is not surprising, therefore, that Thackeray makes sport also of what he was to label the Silver-Fork novel. "It is not our purpose to make a great and learned display here," he declares when he is about to describe the ball at Marylebone Gardens, where Catherine meets Galgenstein after years of separation; "otherwise the costumes of the company assembled at this fête might afford scope for at least half a dozen pages of fine writing; and we might give, if need were, specimens of the very songs and music sung on the occasion" (p. 138). Thackeray assumes that the refined readers of *Fraser's Magazine for Town and Country* have grown as weary as he has of *Pelham* and *Devereux* as well as of Lady Morgan's *Dramatic Scenes* and Lady Charlotte Bury's *Diary of a Lady in Waiting to the Court of George IV.*[18] No matter that he was to do something like these, and more, in *Vanity Fair*. For now, "leave we these trifles to meaner souls! Our business is not with the hoops and patches, but with the divine hearts of men, and the passions which agitate them," he writes, echoing Professor Teufelsdröckh.[19]

In large part a pasticcio of the popular fiction of the 1830s, *Catherine* might have been subtitled *"Fraser's* Prize Novelists," for it adds up to the same sort of farrago as the famous *Punch* series of the following decade. But beyond its topicality, the sweep of its satire—taking in a cross section of humanity, respectable citizens as well as criminals, old and young, soldiers and civilians, aristocrats and commoners—moves it in the direction of the panoramic novel of society that we associate with the mature Thackeray. Ikey Solomons's immediate intention, however, is to make his history something more than an "Old Bailey Chronicle." In carrying out this objective he seems to contradict himself. "Now if we *are* to be interested by rascally actions, let us have them with plain faces, and let them be performed not by virtuous philosophers, but by rascals. . . . We say let your rogues in novels act like rogues, and your honest men like honest men, don't let us have any juggling and thimblerigging with virtue and vice," he affirms early in the story, with an obvious hit at Bulwer's *Eugene Aram* and *Ernest Maltravers* (chap. 1). Yet in a later address to the reader he says: "Surely our novel-writers make a great mistake in divesting their rascals of all gentle human qualities: they have such," concluding that "the only sad point to think of is, in all private concerns of life, abstract feelings, and dealings with friends, and so on, how dreadfully like a rascal is to an honest man" (chap. 5). This last jab of course cuts two ways, and Solomons demonstrates his point quite amply in the "strange and proper jumble" that he creates, where rascals and honest people—thieves, whores, bourgeois, and nobility—are thrown together and scrambled. So we do indeed get "juggling and thimblerigging with virtue and vice" from Solomons, if in unexpected ways.

A comment on *The Beggar's Opera* that appeared in the serial version of *Catherine* helps us read between the lines of Solomons's rather cryptic pronouncements. Here he praises the "bitter wit" of Gay's comedy that "hits the great by showing their similarity with the wretches that figure in the play" (p. 187). This tradition was carried forward by "Gur"-lyle and many another contributor to *Fraser's Magazine,* no respecter of persons, as is well known, either in its literary or political assaults.[20] During the year when *Catherine* was running, a number of poems appeared in the magazine, laden with innuendo about the character of the ruling classes. Among these were "Robyn Hode and Kynge Richarde" that implied in no uncertain terms an affinity between the two title characters, and a sonnet, "Triumph of the XXII," in which the current Whig ministry was likened to convicts awaiting hanging.[21] Very much in line with this antiestablishment tone of the magazine in general is the belittling historical introduction to *Catherine:*

> At that famous period in history, when the seventeenth century (after a deal of quarrelling, king-killing, reforming, republicanising, restoring, re-restoring, play-writing, sermon-writing, Oliver Cromwellising, Stuartising, and Orangising, to be sure) had sunk into its grave, giving place to the lusty eighteenth; when Mr. Isaac Newton was a tutor of Trinity, and Mr. Joseph Addison Commissioner of Appeals; when the presiding genius that watched over the destinies of the French nation had played out all the best cards in his hand, and his adversaries began to pour in their trumps; when there were two kings in Spain employed perpetually in running away from one another; when there was a queen in England, with such rogues for Ministers as have never been seen, no, not in our own day, and a General [Marlborough], of whom it may be severely argued whether he was the meanest miser or the greatest hero in the world; when Mrs. Masham had not yet put Madam Marlborough's nose out of joint; when people had their ears cut off for writing very meek political pamphlets; and very large full-bottomed wigs were just beginning to be worn with powder; and the face of Louis the Great, as his was handed in to him behind the bed-curtains, was, when issuing thence, observed to look longer, older, and more dismal daily. . . .

This burlesque version of history from the Commonwealth to Queen Anne anticipates in more scurrilous voice the iconoclasm of *Henry Esmond:* "Why shall history go on kneeling to the end of time? I am for having her rise up off her knees, and take a natural posture: not to be forever performing cringes and congees like a Court-chamberlain, and shuffling backwards out of doors in the presence of the sovereign. In a word, I would have History familiar rather than heroic."[22] The "familiar" history that *Catherine* presents to us, however, serves to bring royalty uncomfortably close to roguery—showing nobles, ministers of state, generals, and court ladies engaged in the very activities pursued so vigorously by the vagabonds and wenches of the story that follows—gambling, thievery, and murder. As we see that might makes right in high places as in low, and that intriguers and imposters prosper in both spheres, we recognize indeed "how dreadfully like a rascal is to an honest man."

In addresses to readers between the events of the story, Solomons tends to reverse this formula by stressing how an honest man resembles a rascal. In writing about French fashionable novels, Thackeray was to express a preference for "men and women of genteel society—rascals enough, but living in no state of convulsive crimes,"[23] but in his prankish first novel he shows us genteel society reflected as in a crazy glass in the criminal underworld. Ikey Solomons's sermons, like his capsule history of modern Europe, enlarge the moral context of this crime story: "Who has not felt how he works, the dreadful conquering Spirit of Ill?" he asks in a particularly saturine mood. "Who cannot see in the circle of his own society, the fated and the foredoomed to woe and evil?" (chap. 7). In the midst of predicting Catherine's doom, he admonishes us: "You call it chance; ay, and so it is chance, that when the floor gives way, and the rope stretches tight, the poor wretch before St. Sepulchre's clock dies. Only with us, clear-sighted mortals as we are, we cannot *see* the rope by which we hang, and know not when or how the drop may fall" (chap. 7).[24] By the time he has completed his bill of indictment, crime becomes, as in *The Beggar's Opera,* a gross image of the evil that pervades society.[25]

Since Solomons obviously means for us to cry for all humanity through our laughter, more attention might be given to the story he manages to tell in the midst of his various feints, false starts, and digressions. Among the ways in which this convict narrator[26] fools us is by leading us to suppose that he is following his chronicle source slavishly. As things turn out, he introduces characters for whom he had no factual source, the most important being Count von Galgenstein,[27] Catherine's lover and Tom's natural father. Others are the misguided humanitarians Dr. Dobbs, Mrs. Dobbs, and Goody Billings, and the roles of the brigands Brock and Macshane were expanded from mere allusions in the *Newgate Calendar.* Solomons seems then to be doing what he upbraids Ainsworth,

Bulwer, and company for doing—embroidering upon reality—but he does it with a difference. The incidents that he takes over from documentary evidence—the tumultuous marriage of Catherine and John Hayes, the murder of Hayes, and the execution of the culprits—make his point that stark fact is more stirring than romance can make it. On the other hand, the author's unique additions to the record—which precede these climactic episodes— illustrate his conception of the novelist's proper function and purpose.

Actually, the documented fact in *Catherine* is virtually confined to the end of the story, where the narrator reprints contemporaneous accounts from newspapers of the discovery of Hayes's head (at the time unidentified) in a churchyard, and of the execution of Catherine and Tom.[28] The first of the items reads: "'Yesterday morning, early, a man's head, that by the freshness of it seemed to have been newly cut off from the body, having its own hair on, was found by the river's side near Millbank, Westminster, and was afterwards exposed to public view in St. Margaret's Churchyard, where thousands of people have seen it; but none could tell who the unhappy person was, much less who committed such a horrid and barbarous action. There are various conjectures relating to the deceased; but there being nothing certain, we omit them. The head was much hacked and mangled in the cutting off.'"[29]

"Various conjectures relating to the deceased" make up the bulk of the story up to this point. Thackeray's later, and lighter (or, in his terms, "facetious"), account of these events in the form of imitation broadside verse has already been quoted. In the story itself we get a pseudo-Gothic (or "romantic") version, where the churchyard becomes the scene of a rendezvous between the heroine and her lover, Count Gustavus Adolphus Maximilian von Galgenstein. At this midnight meeting Catherine, muffled in a cloak, extending her hand "clammy and cold" to the fear-ridden libertine Galgenstein, is the mischevous author's means of injecting a strain of the *schrecksroman* into what is supposed to be a realistic crime narrative. Catherine, the slatternly murderess, is made to speak like a tragic princess. Of course, "the wind was very cold, and the piteous howling was the only noise that broke the silence of the place." Max von Galgenstein's reaction to the head, as it is revealed in a flood of moonlight, is true to the "tale from the German": "On a sudden his face assumed a look of the most dreadful surprise and agony. He stood still, and stared with wild eyes starting from their sockets; he stared upwards at a point seemingly above Catherine's head. At last he raised up his finger slowly, and said, 'Look, Cat,—*the head!—the head!*' Then, uttering a horrible laugh, he fell down grovelling among the stones, gibbering and writing in a fit of epilepsy" (p. 174). The hapless count never regains his sanity. "He was taken up a hopeless idiot, and so lived for years and years, clanking the chain, and moaning under the lash, and howling through long nights when the moon peered through the bars of his solitary cell, and he buried his face in the straw." The reference is once more to *Melmoth the Wanderer,* this time taking the form of a travesty of Stanton's narrative of his ordeal in prison, which recalls to him the cries of maniacal prisoners clanking their chains in tune with the pitiless lashing of their sadistic guards.

At this point Ikey Solomons turns to his readers and apologizes for teasing them. "There—the murder is out!" he exclaims after the mock-Gothic graveyard episode. "And having indulged himself in a chapter of the very finest writing, the author begs the attention of the British public towards it; humbly conceiving that it possesses some of those peculiar merits which have rendered the fine writing in other chapters of the works of other authors so famous." "Fine writing" (the equivalent in fiction of the "sham sublime" in art) is actually what this author has been castigating throughout his novel-on-novels where the idiocies of popular romance are whipped like the wretched Count Galgenstein.

Against this "sham history" Ikey Solomons sets his "true history," for which we can see the way prepared in the previously mentioned review essay in *Fraser's Magazine* called "Hints for a History of Highwaymen." The book under review, a series of biographies of outlaws by a writer named Charles Whitehead, becomes the occasion for a discourse on crime, past and present. The main thesis of the reviewer is that crimes have become reduced in explosiveness since the last century, but in the process have become more sinister. "The age of highwaymen is gone—that of cheats and swindlers has succeeded," he begins, echoing Burke. "Let us with earnest solemnity ask whether the violences of the past century were productive of more misery than the frauds of the present."[30] Although it is true that "the pistol shot no longer rings in our streets," still he asks, "has the voice of wailing ceased in the secret chamber? Blood now seldom flows openly on our highways, battered brains rarely besprinkle our pavements, castle-spectre horrors have fled away like night-walking ghosts at break of day; is the amount of silent suffering lessened?"

Relating crime to sin, and regarding both as rooted in human instincts that are sublimated but never wholly obliterated in civilized society, this anonymous reviewer expresses deep curiosity about the psychology of the renegades of society—just what he finds lacking in the biographies under review, which he considers not only cursory and superficial as narratives, but lacking as well in character analysis. To him Whitehead's histories of crimes and criminals (like the Newgate novels later denounced in *Catherine*) were less effective than the raw accounts to be found in newspapers and in the ballads vended in the streets. There is a job to be done:

> The history of English highwaymen yet remains to be written, and in competent hands the subject would not only be striking, interesting and affecting, but convey important instruction. Man, anywhere and under any circumstances, is an object of deep and appalling interest, and from erring man examples of the highest interest have ever been drawn. "Criminals stand forward," to use the words of Burke, "on the canvass of humanity as prominent objects for our special study." The progress of civilisation and the mutations of manners may be traced by the diversities and fluctuations of crime, for crimes have their cycles. . . . Hitherto the English criminal has been exhibited amidst the incidents of a novel, or his personal beauty lauded, and his untimely fate deplored in the stanzas of a song. It would be well to have him displayed as he really is in action, and in principle; recount if you can his education and his first associates, his first temptations, and all that may palliate or aggravate his first yielding to the tempter; exclude poetic adornment and speculative reverie. The man who undertakes the truly philosophic task we assign him ought to be patient in research, cool, somewhat sceptical, calmly discriminating between individual guilt and the community of error.

A history of English highwaymen meeting with these ambitious specifications still remains to be written. Nevertheless, in *Catherine* Thackeray seems to be attempting the "philosophic task" projected in this review. Behind his satire there certainly lurks the serious intention to convey instruction through examples of "erring men." The capsule history that begins the story traces "the progress of civilization" through the "diversities and fluctuations of crime," placing the ugly story of Catherine in a larger tradition of iniquity.[31] Subsequently, Thackeray does all he can to point up the moral significance of the case of Catherine Hayes. His superadditions upon the *Newgate Calendar* are concerned precisely with the "education . . . first associates . . . first temptations" of Catherine, all the influences, that is, that led her to transgress. Her schooling in the village poorhouse and her early enforced apprenticeship are both guaranteed to keep her in a state of semiliteracy and in a primitive stage of moral feeling. Other episodes and characters invented by Thackeray are meant to motivate further her eventual downfall. She is taken in by a relative, the coarse tavern keeper Mrs. Score, who only encourages her coquettish inclinations and generally abets her in unscrupulousness. It is Catherine's further misfortune to run in with the unprincipled derelict Corporal Brock, and the handsome but rotten Count von Galgenstein. (In the original magazine version, the first meeting with the heroine was accompanied by an illustration captioned "Mrs. Catherine's Temptation.") Galgenstein easily succeeds in seducing her, not only because of her inherent looseness of character, but also through catering to her naïve ideas of glamour and social status. John Hayes, the rustic carpenter whom Catherine is prevailed upon to marry after Count Galgenstein deserts her (and after, be it added, her attempt to poison the count), is shown up to be mean and unlovable, so that Catherine's continued longing for her first lover is made plausible. By such details Thackeray makes us understand the causes that lie behind Catherine's crime without condoning it.

In an often quoted letter to his mother, Thackeray expressed dissatisfaction with the way in which he has allowed his story to develop: "It was not made disgusting enough. . . . the triumph of it would have been to make readers so horribly horrified as to cause them to give up or rather throw up the book and all of its kind, whereas you see the author had a sneaking kindness for his heroine, and did not like to make her utterly worthless."[32] It is true that, without ever going so far as to make his heroine likeable, he makes some attempt to humanize her. A certain *joie de vivre* draws her to Galgenstein in the first place and makes her cling to his memory. Her maternal instinct leads her to take her son home to live with her after his adoption by the Billings family,[33] a decision that proves fateful, for young Billings eventually aggravates the rift between Catherine and her husband. Furthermore, one motive for her seeking out Galgenstein once more, after a separation of several years, is her ambition to make a gentleman out of Tom. A lingering fondness for Brock, her early companion in evil, leads her to take him into her home as a lodger after his return from forced labor in Virginia. This proves to be another mistake in judgment, inasmuch as Brock stirs up dissension between Catherine and her husband. As Thackeray rewrites Catherine's history, he even has her balk momentarily at the murder of Hayes, making Brock and Billings more the aggressors in the act. In her

eventual complicity in the murder, anger over Hayes's alleged infidelity (as falsely reported by Brock) is added to her original motives of lust and hate. However, if these softening touches made
Catherine's story less disgusting, as Thackeray thought, they presumably enhanced its value as a cautionary tale. It fits in with his
moral scheme for the novel that she should be driven by instincts
that, however perverted and misdirected, are recognizable human
ones. Although Catherine is depicted far too sketchily and spas-
modically to affect us as either a coherent or a sympathetic character, it is clear that Thackeray intended her to be a woman sinned
against as well as sinning. Her sins, though far greater in degree,
are related to those that all flesh is heir to as fallible creatures
exercising freedom of will and choice.

In the long run, Thackeray's probing of Catherine's past is supposed to help us in "discriminating between individual guilt and
the community of error." He manages, without diminishing
Catherine's culpability, to make us recognize the part that others
have played in her undoing. The slatternly Mrs. Score, by her very
efforts to separate the two lovers, goads Count Galgenstein into
carrying off Catherine. Hayes, impelled by his passion for "Miss
Cat," pursues her, even though he knows she loathes him. Brock, to
further his own gain, fans up Catherine's jealousy of the count to
the point where she attempts to poison him. But Thackeray's real
skill in irony is employed in his exposure of the evil wrought by
"do-gooders" like Doctor Dobbs, who naïvely accepts Catherine as a
repentant Magdalen after her unsuccessful attempt to poison
Galgenstein; Mrs. Dobbs, whose matchmaking propensity leads her
to bring Catherine and John Hayes together; and Goody Billings,
whose indulgence of young Tom only feeds his basically evil instincts.

The effect of all of this wisdom of Solomons is to extend the
"community of error" even beyond the population of the story. "De
te fabula" reads a passage in the original version. Yet along with the
recognition of our own frailty we are supposed to learn to "pardon
humanity." A review contributed by Thackeray to another journal
a month before *Catherine* began its run in *Fraser's* contains a caveat
that might have served as an epigraph to this fable:

> Our purpose here is not to preach up the refinement of morality,
> or to exercise that cheap virtue which consists in laying bare the
> faults of our neighbour. To grow angry with the cant of patriotism,
> the thousand meannesses of party, the coarse lies with which ambi-
> tion is obliged to feed the fools on whom it lives in return,—to grow

angry with these would be to pass through life in a fury; and we might as well be wroth at any other of the diseases to which Providence has subjected the children of men. Our passions, our wants, the dire struggles of necessity, the blindness of vanity, offer, if not an excuse for worldly dishonesty, at least a palliation; and a wise man will look at them not so much with anger as with humble pity, and pray that he himself may not be led into temptation.[34]

The specific occasion for these remarks was the trial of Queen Caroline for adultery, with the political chicanery and moral confusion it engendered, but the application obviously was intended to be universal. Here, in the course of criticizing the statesmanship of Lord Brougham, whose speeches before Parliament, the bar, and various educational institutions he was reviewing, Thackeray seems to be charting his own literary path:

> When the history of those days [the times of George IV] comes to be written, when some future Swift or Fielding shall take upon himself to describe the facts and characters which Lord Brougham has *not* described—which he might describe if common honesty would allow him, and common decency would not prevent him—the tale will not be an uninstructive one, and the moral wholesome, though bitter. In the annals of human folly, is there a page more strangely ludicrous and despicable? In the history of human baseness, is there a story more base? Which is the more contemptible, the immaculate accuser or the spotless accused?[35]

In this light, *Catherine* can be read as a kind of preface to Thackeray's "annals of human folly," in which he tries to remove human obloquy from the courts of law to the tribunal of the conscience, identifying plaintiff and defendant, judge and culprit. On its serious side, then, the effect of his parody of crime novels is to reverse their drift. The Newgate novels of Ainsworth and Bulwer were in part polemical tracts against capital punishment (an aspect of them that Ikey Solomons does not consider). Therefore it suited their purpose to *elevate* the criminal by revealing his better nature, that is, his affinity with respectable citizens.[36] The object of the author of *Catherine*, on the contrary, was to *lower* the respectable of society by exposing what they had in common with criminals. This was a strange way to "pardon humanity," but Thackeray's concern then and thereafter was not so much with unjust laws and penal institutions, as with "what is false within." Readers were expected to shudder more at the contemplation of themselves than at the deeds of murderers. No wonder that the subscribers to *Fraser's* found the story repulsive.

Readers of the time undoubtedly were thrown off also by a novel without a hero—with nothing in fact but villains. Then, too, what were they to make of the pompous exhortations in the midst of farce, of the chameleonlike narrator who is successively jester, lay prophet, chronicler, and theater manager, of the kaleidoscopic movement in time and place, of the false leads, of narratives begun and dropped, of humor mixed with horror, of so much space given to how the story is to be told, but so relatively little to the telling of it? As if in apology for this chaos of narration, Solomons declares at one point: "My dear sir, when you have well studied the world— how supremely great the meanest thing in the world is, and how infinitely mean the greatest—I am mistaken if you do not make a strange and proper jumble of the sublime and the ridiculous, the lofty and the low" (p. 149).[37] But out of this "jumble" he was to make order. If it is a youthful perversity that asserts itself predominantly in his first novel, this perversity was to be mellowed by compassion for "erring man."

"Hints for a History of Highwaymen," it has already been suggested, also contains a pointer or two for the would-be novelist. Certainly Thackeray remained firm in his conviction, in kinship with the "philosophic, literary, legal observer" projected by the writer of "Hints," that the novelist, no less than the historian, builds upon fact, not fancy, upon the world as it is, not as one would wish it to be. Consequently he always valued primary sources—records, documents, letters, memoirs—for the texture of actuality that they conveyed. At the same time he thought that their value was enhanced if interpreted by a moral philosopher with the poised attitude of the skeptic toward human character and motive. True representation of character meant "the whole truth"—vices as well as virtues—tracing the sources of both, placing blame where blame is due, while giving due attention to extenuating circumstances. And he always interested himself in the "canvass of humanity" rather than mere individuals, seeking insight into human behavior in the worst as well as in the best of men.

"That he has not altogether failed in the object he had in view, is evident from some newspaper critiques which he has had the good fortune to see; and which abuse the tale of 'Catherine' as one of the dullest, most vulgar, and immoral tales extant," reads Ikey Solomons's last address to the reader. He is, of course, rationalizing the failure of his medicinal "dose" to go down. His demonstration of how the novelist-historian-philosopher can draw instruction for

mankind from the fleeting records of the day went generally un-
appreciated. The public was not yet ready for his peculiar "jumble"
of the sublime and the ridiculous and of "sham" history and true.
Especially lost on its first readers were the intricate linking of cause
and effect and painstaking psychology, particularly in the probing
of the warped minds of the doomed "Mrs. Cat" and Hayes:

> But no mortal is wise at all times: and the fact was, that Hayes, who
> cared for himself intensely, had set his heart upon winning
> Catherine; and loved her with a desperate greedy eagerness and
> desire of possession, which makes passions for women often so fierce
> and unreasonable among very cold and selfish men. His parents
> (whose frugality he had inherited) had tried in vain to wean him
> from this passion, and had made many fruitless attempts to engage
> him with women who possessed money and desired husbands; but
> Hayes was, for a wonder, quite proof against their attractions; and,
> though quite ready to acknowledge the absurdity of his love for a
> penniless alehouse servant-girl, nevertheless persisted in it doggedly.
> "I know I'm a fool," said he; "and what's more, the girl does not care
> for me; but marry her I must, or I think I shall just die; and marry
> her I will." For very much to the credit of Miss Catherine's modesty,
> she had declared that marriage with her was a *sine quâ non*, and had
> dismissed, with the loudest scorn and indignation, all propositions of
> a less proper nature. (Chap. 1)

> "A fool, a miser, and a coward! Why was I bound to this wretch?"
> thought Catherine: "I, who am high-spirited and beautiful (did not
> *he* tell me so); I who born a beggar, have raised myself to compe-
> tence, and might have mounted—who knows whither?—if cursed
> Fortune had not balked me!"
> As Mrs. Cat did not utter these sentiments, but only thought them,
> we have a right to clothe her thoughts in the genteelest possible
> language: and, to the best of our power, have done so. If the reader
> examines Mrs. Hayes' train of reasoning he will not, we should think,
> fail to perceive how ingeniously she managed to fix all the wrong
> upon her husband, and yet to twist out some consolatory arguments
> for her own vanity. This perverse argumentation we have all of us,
> no doubt, employed in our time. How often have we—we poets,
> politicians, philosophers, family-men—found charming excuses for
> our own rascalities in the monstrous wickedness of the world about
> us; how loudly have we abused the times and our neighbours! All
> this devil's logic did Mrs. Catherine, lying wakeful in her bed on the
> night of the Marylebone fête, exert in gloomy triumph. (Chap. 11)

This analysis unfortunately tends to swamp incident, and ultimately is wasted on shallow people and a repellent story.
    "His poem may be dull—ay and probably is," the author is ready
to concede. "Be it granted, Solomons *is* dull; but don't attack his
morality; he humbly submits that, in his poem, no man shall mis-

take virtue for vice, no man shall allow a single sentiment of pity or admiration to enter his bosom for any character of the piece: it being, from beginning to end, a scene of unmixed rascality performed by persons who never deviate into good feeling." Subsequently he made more concession not only to "good feeling" but to the pleasure principle in general. His fictitious children after Tom Billings do not exactly trail clouds of glory, but neither do they reek so heavily of brimstone. In his novels of society he provided those "hoops and patches" he had deliberately left out of the ball at Marylebone Gardens, the ball at Gaunt House in particular showing off "the costumes of the company" and resounding with "specimens of the very songs and music sung on the occasion." Furthermore he indulged more in that "pathos" in which he thought his chief rival Dickens excelled.[38]

Most significant for Thackeray's development after *Catherine* was his abandonment of "unmixed rascality." A year after the appearance of his first novel, we find him backing away from a vivid picture in the Louvre of human depravity: "Oh Eugenius Delacroix! how can you manage with a few paint-bladders, and a dirty brush, and a careless hand, to dash such savage histories as these, and fill people's minds with thoughts so dreadful."[39] Thackeray's own "savage histories" were behind him, but they furnished him with the scaffolding for his "edifice of humanity." If *Catherine* represents crime and sin in their starkest forms, Thackeray's maturer works represent them in their finer mutations and subtler shadings. A Catherine toned down and endowed with charm becomes a Becky Sharp engaged in a more refined husband murder. The bastard making his way through a corrupt society becomes a hero in *Henry Esmond,* the high-born exchanging roles with the base-born. The antiheroic theme undergoes a variety of modulations in *Barry Lyndon, Vanity Fair, Henry Esmond,* and *The Virginians,* where too we get history from the viewpoint of the ordinary person caught up in its currents. The social climber and the parvenu, which Catherine and her son are, among other things, stalk and strut through virtually all of the novels. And with his first novel Thackeray began his exploration through fiction of the phenomenon called Snobbism, which he defined for himself as the mean aspiration after mean things. The historian of Vanity Fair is contained in the Newgate Chronicler.

Not "unmixed rascality," in low life, but, as he indicates in an essay on French satire, "the ridicules and rascalities of common life"[40] were what really fascinated Thackeray. Ten years later, established with the public, he reverts to the subject of "gallows fiction" in the preface to *Pendennis:*

> Perhaps the lovers of "excitement" may care to know, that this book began with a very precise plan, which was entirely put aside. Ladies and gentlemen, you were to have been treated, and the writer's and the publisher's pocket benefited, by the recital of the most active horrors. What more exciting than a ruffian (with many admirable virtues) in St. Giles's, visited constantly by a young lady from Belgravia? What more stirring than the contrasts of society the mixture of slang and fashionable language? the escapes, the battles, the murders? Nay, up to nine o'clock this very morning, my poor friend, Colonel Altamont, was doomed to execution, and the author only relented when his victim was actually at the window.
>
> The "exciting" plan was laid aside (with a very honourable forbearance on the part of the publishers) because, on attempting it, I found that I failed from want of experience of my subject; and never having been intimate with any convict in my life, and the manners of ruffians and gaol-birds being quite unfamiliar to me, the idea of entering into competition with M. Eugène Sue was abandoned. To describe a real rascal, you must make him so horrible that he would be too hideous to show; and unless the painter paints him fairly, I hold he has no right to show him at all.

In between *Catherine* and *Pendennis* there had been Thackeray's survey of "The Thieves' Literature of France," following upon Janin's *L'âne morte*, and his abortive translation of Sue's *Les mystères de Paris.*[41] These fixed him in his preference for those living "in no state of convulsive crimes." He implies in his preface to *Pendennis* that he was more familiar with the villainy of "genteel society" than with "the manners of ruffians and gaol-birds." After all, as Thackeray's audience could have read in the pages of *Fraser's Magazine* before he became a novelist, and as he had reminded them subsequently in his novels and was to continue to remind them: "Fraud is more frightful than force, to those who know the history of the past and the present centuries."[42]

---

1. See above, p. 137.

2. "Catherine: A Story," by "Ikey Solomons, Jr. Esq." first appeared in *Fraser's Magazine* intermittently from May 1839 through February 1840. It did not reach book form until thirty years later, six years after Thackeray's death, first in America (Boston: Appleton, 1869), then later the same year in England (London: Smith, Elder). Virtually all reprints follow the practice of these two first editions of cutting out the most ghastly episodes, including the murder of Hayes, the subsequent execution, the Grand Tableau, in which readers are invited to participate in a blood bath, and the graphic newspaper accounts that Thackeray drew on among hs primary sources, so that modern readers may easily be left wondering why its first readers were so revolted by the story. Only in the Oxford Thackeray, vol. 3, and in

the Furniss Ed., vol. 6, can a modern reader readily get any conception of Thackeray's first novel in the form in which it originally appeared. The Oxford Thackeray reprints also the charmingly crude drawings that Thackeray made for the magazine version (presumably in reaction against the inanity of the Keepsakes that he also campaigned against in the pages of *Fraser's*). These are redrawn in most editions. Harry Furniss, an artist in his own right, prepared new illustrations for the edition he supervised.

3. *Works*, 13:107–8. This ballad is coupled in this collection with a contrasting one on the "beautiful singer" of the same name whose "voice was so sweet and so loud." In the second of these poems Thackeray recalls the trouble he got into over this coincidence of names with Irish patriots who, unaware of the notorious murderess, thought that Thackeray was slandering their countrywoman. Subsequently he got into similar difficulty when he referred to his "heroine" Catherine Hayes in *Pendennis*. See Anne Thackeray's introduction to *Catherine* in *Works*, 4:xxix–xxx.

4. See above, p. 119.

5. "Foreign Correspondence," 27 June 1833; rpt. in *Mr. Thackeray's Writings in "The National Standard" and "Constitutional"* (London, 1899), pp. 27–30. Among popular works cited is *Champavert: Immoral Tales*, by Petrus Borel the Lycanthrope, which abounds in rape, murder, and bloodshed of all sorts.

6. The Grand Tableau is preceded by Solomons's suggestions for equally lurid illustrations depicting the murder of Hayes in his bed. These plans do not appear to have been carried out.

7. So referred to by Thackeray years later in "Small Beer Chronicle," *Roundabout Papers*, *Works*, 12:305. Janin conducted a regular department of theater criticism in the *Journal des débats* for forty years, through which he became influential and widely known.

8. The quoted passage is from chap. 3 (my translation). This proved to be Janin's most popular work of fiction, reaching four editions by 1837 and fifteen over the next forty years. In 1851 it appeared in English translation as *The Guillotined Woman*.

9. Janin's satire was aimed mainly at the Gothic novel.

10. Janin was poking fun also at sentimental pastorals.

11. He refers to it in his article "Dickens in France," *Fraser's Magazine* 25 (March 1842): 349; *Works* (Cent. Biog. Ed.), 26:514, with a note: "Some day the writer meditates a great and splendid review of J.J.'s works." In the article Thackeray complains of Janin's prejudices against the English, but subsequently they became close friends, especially during Janin's visit to England in 1850. Other literary connections will be pointed out in later chapters.

12. In "Hints for a History of Highwaymen." See above, pp. 136–37.

13. Phrase used by Dickens in defense of his characterization of Nancy in his preface to *Oliver Twist*.

14. See above, p. 20.

15. For reference to Thackeray's youthful reading of *Melmoth*, see Lewis Melville, *William Makepeace Thackeray* (Garden City, N.Y.: Doubleday Doran, 1928), p. 79. Thackeray seems also to have in mind here a grotesque tale, James Dalton's *The Gentleman in Black*, which was illustrated by Cruikshank. See his essay "On the Genius of George Cruikshank," *Westminster Review*, June 1840, p. 37; *Works*, 13:308–9.

16. Like Ainsworth's hero, Billings is conceived as a variant of Hogarth's "idle apprentice," but, unlike Jack Sheppard, who attributes his turning to crime to maltreatment by his master's wife, Tom is pampered by Goody Billings. Thackeray also turns about another of Ainsworth's fictitious details of characterization. "The conceit of making Jack Sheppard the son of a woman of high family, and connected with a house of long descent, is rather droll," states the writer of the article "William Ainsworth and Jack Sheppard," which appeared simultaneously with the conclusion of *Catherine*; "Jack was a blackguard, blood, bone, and sinew; and any refining does his character perfect injustice" (*Fraser's Magazine*, February 1840, p. 237). Thackeray makes Tom the son of a *man* of noble family, but of ignoble character, thereby negating Ainsworth's sentimental fallacy.

17. Gleig was among Thackeray's fellow contributors to *Fraser's*.

18. These are among books reviewed by Thackeray for *Fraser's* or the *Times* during the years preceding the publication of *Catherine*.

19. Carlyle was one of the few of Thackeray's contemporaries to profess an unqualified admiration for *Catherine* (see *Letters*, 1:421). One can understand why in view of the unmistakable evidence of his influence. One satirical device employed in the story—the ease with which the criminal characters pass themselves off as aristocrats merely by dressing in elegant clothes—illustrates the basic idea of *Sartor Resartus* that "Society is founded upon Cloth." The encounter between Tom Billings and his father, Count Galgenstein, toward the end of the story also plays on the Teufelsdröckh theme. Young Tom has become a tailor's apprentice working under "one Beinkleider, a German . . . skilful in his trade (after the manner of his nation, which in breeches and metaphysics—in inexpressibles and incomprehensibles—may instruct all Europe)." Beinkleider is induced to fashion a waistcoat for Tom out of brocade furnished by Catherine, and thus accoutred, he is thought fit to go forth to meet his father (chap. 8).

20. See Miriam Thrall, *Rebellious Fraser's: Nol Yorke's Magazine in the Days of Maginn, Thackeray, and Carlyle* (New York: Columbia University Press, 1934). Miss Thrall's discussion of the influence of Maginn on Thackeray (pp. 55–80) is interesting, if probably overstated. A number of her Thackeray attributions have since been seriously questioned.

21. *Fraser's Magazine* 19 (1839): 593–603, 638. The sonnet was composed by Maginn under the pseudonym of "Sir Morgan O'Doherty." Also related to *Catherine* are two articles on popular ballads attributed to Thackeray, "Half-a-Crown's Worth of Cheap Knowledge" (ibid. 17 [1838]: 275–90) and "Horae Catnachianae" (ibid. 19 [1839]: 407–24), along with one of his damning reviews of Keepsakes, "Our Annual Execution" (ibid., pp. 182–201). A kind of forerunner of *Catherine* is "Elizabeth Brownrigge" (ibid. 6 [1832]: 67–88, 127–48), which satirizes criminal stories by romanticizing the career of the notorious eighteenth-century exploiter of child apprentices and murderess. This tale was for a long time attributed to Thackeray, but is now believed to be the work of Maginn, possibly in collaboration with Lockhart. Edward M. White disputes this attribution as well as other traditional ones in his "Thackeray's Contributions to *Fraser's Magazine*," *Studies in Bibliography* 19 (1966): 67–78.

22. *Henry Esmond*, beginning of bk. 1, preceding chap. 1.

23. See above, p. 120.

24. Cf. the following anecdote relating to Louis Philippe, found among Thackeray's notes for a projected essay: "A woman with the aid of her daughter had killed her husband—the crime was a most monstrous and cruel one and the King was called upon to sign the death-warrant of the criminals—he would not—he could not—he had rather he said resign his crown than sign—then he asked for a week's delay, then when pressed by the Council for eight and forty hours more, then he flung himself into the arms of Lafitte [President of the Council] and bursting into tears said—'My father died on the scaffold'" ("Some Unpublished MS Notes by William Makepeace Thackeray For A Life of Prince Talleyrand" [1836?], Houghton Library, Harvard University, MS Eng 951.6).

25. It is among the ironies of literary history that Thackeray did not recognize Dickens's similar satirical intention in *Oliver Twist*, one of the novels lampooned in *Catherine* (see Robert A. Colby, *Fiction with a Purpose* [Bloomington: Indiana University Press, 1967], pp. 119, 326, n. 27).

26. Solomons slyly interposes this autobiographic detail in a footnote to chap. 6 in connection with the temptations to crime induced by poverty ("The author, it must be remembered, has his lodgings and food provided for him by the government of his country"). It adds a nuance to his ultimate identification of his readers with criminals, and of course joins him with his real-life counterpart, the prototype also of Fagin in *Oliver Twist*. For further discussion of this point, see John Christopher Kleis, "Dramatic Irony in Thackeray's *Catherine*: The Function of Ikey Solomons, Esq., Jr.," *Victorian Newsletter* 33 (Spring 1968): 50–53.

27. His name possibly was suggested by a minor character in *Jack Sheppard*, the Dutch conjuror Van Galgebrok, who predicts that the hero will die by hanging.

28. In all editions I have examined except the Oxford Thackeray and the Furniss Ed., the following anonymous note is inserted before the climactic episodes: "The description of the murder and the execution of the culprits, which here follows in the original, was taken from the newspapers of the day. Coming from a source, they have, as may be imagined, no literary merit whatever. The details of the crime are simply horrible, without one touch of that sort of romance which sometimes gives a little dignity to murder. As such they precisely suited Mr. Thackeray's purpose at the time—which was to show the real manners of the Sheppards and the Turpins who were then the popular heroes of fiction. But nowadays there is no such purpose to serve, and therefore these too literal details are omitted." This note may have been written by W. S. Williams, an editor for Smith, Elder, who prepared the first collected edition of Thackeray's works (1867–69). See introduction to *Catherine, Works* (Cent. Biog. Ed.), 24:xvii n.

29. *Daily Post*, 3 March 1726, as quoted in *Fraser's Magazine*, February 1840, p. 205; Oxford Thackeray, 3:175–76. The authenticity of the account was verified by C. E. Crouch, an assistant to W. S. Williams (Cent. Biog. Ed.).

30. Although it is no longer possible to attribute this article to Thackeray, it is evident that it made an impression on him, apart from its influence on *Catherine*. He echoes its phraseology in "Meditations at Versailles," one of the essays that went into the *Paris Sketch Book*, where the context is once more Edmund Burke's views on historical change: "But the age of horseflesh is gone—that of engineers, economists, and calculators has succeeded" (*Works*, 5:254).

31. "The opening sentences to the melancholy history of Catherine are like the chords to an overture, which tell of what is yet to come. The sordid story is lifted to its place in destiny by the irresible order of the events thus indicated" (Anne Thackeray, introduction to *Catherine, Works* [Cent. Biog. Ed.], 24:xv).

32. *Letters*, 1:433. Janin confesses to a similar lapse in one of his digressions in *L'âne mort:* "J'étais plus morose que jamais; inquiet pour moi-même, je ne sauvais pas si, en effect, malgré tout mon mépris, je n'étais pas amoureux de cette femme" (beginning of chap. 7).

33. This part of the story is related to a polemical article, "The Custody of Infants Bill," that appeared in *Fraser's* earlier that year (19 [1839]: 205–14). The writer of this article protests against the tyranny of the law that permits a husband to deprive his wife of her child, whether she be innocent or guilty of any wrong. He argues that this practice, condoned by English courts, is a barbarous cruelty, for it thwarts the natural maternal instinct that God has implanted in the hearts of all women, poor and rich, savage and civilized.

34. Review of *Speeches of Henry, Lord Brougham, British and Foreign Review* 8 (April 1839): 517; rpt. in *Stray Papers*, p. 142.

35. *British and Foreign Review* 8 (April 1839): 501; *Stray Papers*, pp. 125–26.

36. For detailed discussion of the relation between the crime fiction of this period and developments in penal institutions and in the criminal law, see Joseph Keith Hollingsworth, *The Newgate Novel, 1830–1847* (Detroit: Wayne State University Press, 1963), especially chaps. 1 and 2. Not long after the publication of *Catherine*, Thackeray attended the execution of the murderer François Courvoisier. His sensitive report on this event shows strong sympathy with the condemned man as well as revulsion against capital punishment. See "Going to See a Man Hanged," *Fraser's Magazine* 22 (August 1840): 150–58; *Works*, 3:635–49, a fitting pendant to the sanguinary spectacles deplored in *Catherine*. For the background of this essay, see Albert I. Borowitz, "Why Thackeray Went to See a Man Hanged," *Victorian Newsletter* 48 (Fall 1975): 15–21.

37. Cf. the discussion of Cousin's ideas on history, pp. 44–45.

38. In some concluding critical remarks in the original version of *Catherine*, Thackeray betrayed a "sneaking kindness" for two of the novels he had satirized— *Oliver Twist* and *Jack Sheppard*. He confesses, for example, to having felt a vicarious excitement in reading *Oliver Twist:* "The power of the writer is so amazing, that the reader at once becomes his captive, and must follow him withersoever he leads" (p. 185). To this power Thackeray would join a dedication to truth. He conceded to Ainsworth a certain vigour and descriptive ability, but found the author of *Jack Sheppard* wanting in sophistication and the art of "banter" (p. 187)—lacking, in other words, Thackeray's skeptical mind, irony, and detachment.

39. "On Men and Pictures," *Fraser's Magazine* 24 (July 1841): 111; *Works*, 13:382. This painting, entitled *Le naufrage de Don Juan*, first shown at the Salon of 1841, is based upon an episode in Byron's *Don Juan*, canto 2. It depicts a group of starving men in an open boat, survivors of a shipwreck, drawing lots to determine who shall be the first to be eaten. (For a comic treatment of this subject, see Thackeray's ballad "Little Billie," *Works*, 13:103–4.)

40. "Caricatures and Lithography in France," *Westminster Review* 30 (April 1839) (as "Parisian Caricatures"); *Works*, 5:151.

41. *Foreign Quarterly Review* 31 (April 1843): 231–45. The translation of Sue will be taken up in connection with *Vanity Fair*. At the end of this decade, a French critic, Philarete Chasles, referred to Thackeray's "satirical novel for *Fraser's Magazine*, directed against the extravagantly philanthropical novels then in vogue in England, and which since have been imported by ourselves; novels filled with very amiable jail birds and metaphysical hangmen" ("A Personal Sketch of Thackeray," *Literary World* 4 [23 June 1849]; translated and condensed from his "Le roman de moeurs en Angleterre," *Revue des deux mondes*, 6th ser., no. 1 [15 February 1849]: 537–71).

42. "Hints for a History of Highwaymen," *Fraser's Magazine*, March 1834, p. 285.

THE GREAT HOGGARTY DIAMOND: A MORAL AND ECONOMICAL TALE

Chapter Six

AFTER THE "BITTER BARK" OF "CATHERINE," Thackeray was determined for a time to leave a sweeter taste in readers' mouths. "The Judges stand [up] for me: Carlyle says Catherine is wonderful, and many more laud it highly, b[ut it is] a disgusting subject & no mistake. I wish I had taken a pleasanter one," he wrote to his mother,[1] as his "romance of Mrs. Cat" was dropping its "gloomy green curtain." For the next year and a half or so he seems to have been floundering about for a congenial subject. After his attempt to make moral philosophy out of popular melodrama, he switched to the farcical treatment of politics with *The Bedford-Row Conspiracy,* "stolen from the French" of Charles de Bernard, and transplanted to an English borough, with the altercations of Whigs and Tories furnishing a backdrop of intrigue to an appealing tale of love and courtship.[2] *A Shabby Genteel Story,* a sophisticated and somewhat acrid modern adaptation of the Cinderella story set in a Margate rooming house, was left dangling in mid-course, owing to Thackeray's own domestic difficulties, not to be taken up again until *The Adventures of Philip.*[3] The direction in which Thackeray was moving is indicated, perhaps, in another letter to his mother, written early in 1840; "I don't see why you should not care a fig for ordinary people w^h is what . . . I wanted to paint. . . . I hope to get to something stabler and better, and not fritter away time as now."[4]

In September of the following year, readers of *Fraser's Magazine* were greeted with the first installment of *The History of Samuel Titmarsh and The Great Hoggarty Diamond.*[5] Thackeray's biographer has suggested that *The Bedford-Row Conspiracy* may have led him to attempt in this "history" a comparable story purely English in background and inspiration.[6] Like its predecessor, *The Great Hoggarty Diamond* is tough in fiber, but tender at its core, dealing with the triumph of pure young love over the corruptions of the world. However, for its richness of humor and depth of characterization it may well qualify as the "something stabler and better" that Thackeray promised his mother. It is a tale of swindling and of unselfish devotion, of candor as well as of self-delusion. Domestic in setting, and with a quite "ordinary" clerk for its hero, it is at the same time panoramic in sweep, taking in town and country, Fulham, the West End, and Fleet Prison, and its population ranges among peers, parvenus, and poor. In tone it is at once more cheerful and more plaintive than Thackeray's readers had been accustomed to from him, resembling those songs sung by its hero, Samuel Titmarsh, and his friend Gus Hoskins in a relaxed moment—"both comic and sentimental."

On its surface *The Great Hoggarty Diamond* is an elementary fable about gold (in this instance a jewel) turning to dust and ashes in its owner's hands. It also illustrates the familiar maxim about touching pitch. The hero (a cousin of Michael Angelo Titmarsh, who has "edited" the story), struggling along on his pittance as thirteenth clerk of the West Diddlesex Fire and Life Insurance Company in Cornhill, and aspiring to marry his country sweetheart, Mary Smith, receives from his wealthy Aunt Hoggarty of Dublin a diamond pin, a family heirloom. At first disappointed in not receiving a more substantial gift of money, Sam finds to his joy that this treasure enhances him in various material ways. First it raises him in eminence among his fellow employees; then his employer Mr. Brough, hoping to add Aunt Hoggarty to his list of investors, plays up to Sam, promoting him to third clerk and introducing him to his family; eventually, as the rumor of Sam's aristocratic connection spreads, he gains entrance into higher society.

Ultimately, however, Sam's good fortune boomerangs. To keep up his position in society he buys fine clothes and fine furniture, plunging himself thereby into debt. When Aunt Hoggarty comes to live with him and his young bride, he is led into more extravagant living habits. Aunt Hoggarty is inveigled by Brough into investing in the West Diddlesex Association, which proves to be a paper empire and collapses. Mr. Brough flees to the continent, leaving Sam to bear the brunt for his boss's misdeeds. After a period in prison, Sam is exonerated, obtains another position, and feels well rid of the diamond, which he had pawned. The patience of his long-suffering wife, Mary (whose ordeals have included the death of their infant child), elicits the moral set forth in the concluding chapter, entitled "In Which It Is Shown That A Good Wife Is The Best Diamond A Man Can Wear In His Bosom." Thackeray was out to make amends for Catherine indeed!

The basic human vanities—greed, social climbing, and braggadocio—that motivate so many of Thackeray's characters are set down here in good spirits rather than in malice. There is a purposive naïveté about the characters, who have the well-marked attributes of figures in chapbooks or from popular theater. Young Samuel Titmarsh is the essence of clerkdom—obsequious, gullible, eternally optimistic. His young bride, Mary, is the country girl of solid rural virtues—simple, staid, and sterling in her loyalty. The shrewish Aunt Hoggarty combines the raucous biddy of Irish farce with the fairy godmother of children's stories (the godmother in this tale proving to be a stepmother-witch). Mr. Brough, chairman of the directors of the Independent West Diddlesex Fire and Life Insurance Company, which "did a tremendous business in the fig and sponge way," is a model Mr. Moneybags. The Reverend Grimes Wapshot, his accomplice, who marries Aunt Hoggarty for her "protection" and eventually makes her a widow once more, is an evangelical Tartuffe.[7] Subsidiary figures, such as the clerk Roundhand, Lord Bagwig, Lady Drum (Doldrum in the magazine version), Lady Fanny Rakes, the tailor Von Stiltz (Abednego in the magazine version), and generic place names such as Slopperton and Squishtail evoke the world of the didactic fable.

Various chapter headings sustain this fantasy motif: "Tells How The Diamond Is Brought Up To London And Produces Wonderful Effects Both In The City And At The West End"; "How The Possessor Of The Diamond Is Whisked Into A Magnificent Chariot, And Has Yet Further Good Luck"; "How Samuel Titmarsh Reached The Highest Point Of Prosperity." This sense of a charmed life is carried forward intermittently by allusion. Sam considers himself to be favored by Providence: "See, thought I, what I have gained by Aunt Hoggarty giving me a diamond-pin! What a lucky thing it is that she did not give me the money, as I hoped she would! Had I not the pin—had I even taken it to any other person but Mr. Polonius [the jeweler who mounts the pin], Lady Drum [who introduced him into society] would never have noticed me; had Lady Drum never noticed me, Mr. Brough never would, and I never should have been third clerk of the West Diddlesex" (chap.

6). He refers in this episode to "the magic of the pin." The sparkle
and illumination of the diamond put him in mind of "the history of
Coggia Hassan Alhabbal in the 'Arabian Nights'" (chap. 5), in
which a diamond found by accident brings a poor man prosperity.[8]

As Sam comes to recognize that his hopes have been buoyed up
by a bubble no more substantial than Mr. Brough's business empire, *The Great Hoggarty Diamond* expands into a real-life parable of
the delusive fancy that cheats itself. One chapter heading, "In
Which It Appears That A Man May Possess A Diamond And Yet
Be Very Hard Pressed For A Dinner," is typical of the common
sense interposed here and there that prepares us for Sam's rude
awakening. More subtle is the superimposing throughout the story
of the everyday world of getting and spending upon the timeless
universe of fable. Concrete detail pins Sam's adventures precisely
down to time and place. The years covered are from 1822 to 1825,
a fact of significance, as will be brought out later. The diamond pin
presented to Sam by his aunt originated as a locket "of Dublin
manufacture in the year 1795" and was worn by Sam's uncle at the
battle of Vinegar Hill. The Independent West Diddlesex Fire and
Life Insurance Company, where Sam goes to work, is given not
only a name but a local habitation—in Crutched Friars, in Cornhill,
in the City. The assets of the firm of Brough and Hoff are opened
to audit: "I was told in the strictest confidence that the house one
year with another divided a good even thousand pounds: of which
Brough had half, Hoff two-sixths, and the other sixth went to old
Tudlow, who had been Mr. Brough's clerk before the partnership
began." Sam's mother "had sunk a sum of four hundred pounds in
the purchase of an annuity at this office, which paid her no less
than six-and-thirty pounds a year, when no other company in London would give her more than thirty-four." Sam has a well-marked
niche in the hierarchy of Brough and Hoff—thirteenth clerk in a
retinue of twenty-four.

As for sense of place, residences are located with the exactness of
a London guide, not only that of the Titmarshes (No. 3, Bell Lane,
Salisbury Square, near St. Bride's Church, Fleet Street), but also the
Roundhands' domicile in Myddleton Square, Pentonville, the
Broughs' *rus in urbe* at Fulham, and Lady Jane Preston's great
house in Whitehall Street. We learn not only where these storied
people live and work, but where they shop as well. The jewelry
establishment of Mr. Polonius is in Coventry Street, off St. Martin's
Lane. Mr. Von Stiltz, the tailor, is in Clifford Street; the ices and
supper that furnish forth the Broughs' soirée, even the footmen

borrowed for the occasion, are supplied by the quite palpable Mr. Gunter of Berkeley Square; Sam purchases his black satin stock at Ludlam's in Piccadilly.[9] We even know where some of our friends carouse, for example at the Yellow Lion and at the Poppleton Arms in Grumpley.

Witnessing Sam's precipitate rise in life allows us also a brief glimpse at the sartorial fashions of the early 1820s. Sam remembers precisely what he was wearing when he met Lady Jane and the Countess of Drum: "I had on that day my blue coat and brass buttons, nankeen trousers, a white sprig waistcoat, and one of Dando's silk hats, that had just come in in the year '22, and looked a great deal more glossy than the best beaver" (chap. 3); later, bolstered up by Mr. Brough and his own apparent prosperity, he orders from Von Stiltz "two of the finest coats ever seen, a dress-coat and a frock, a velvet waistcoat, a silk ditto, and three pairs of pantaloons, of the most beautiful make." There is also much mouth-watering gustatory detail: the gift of red peaches, luscious grapes, and venison from Lady Jane's garden and park; the "turbitt and sammon with immense boles of lobster sauce" enjoyed by Aunt Hoggarty at the Brough mansion. The "illustrations" promised, but not delivered, by Michael Angelo Titmarsh are supplied by the graphic narrative.[10]

We learn something also of the family background of the genealogy-conscious figures in this "History." Aunt Hoggarty qualifies for Thackeray's gallery of the "small great" Irish Snobs, with her stickpin heirloom and the legendary Castle Hoggarty. Lady Jane claims to know "all the Hoskinses in England," presumed ancestors of Sam's friend Gus, third son of a leatherseller in Skinner Street. At Brough's establishment in Fulham, Sam confronts "a grave gentleman out of livery . . . in a chocolate coat and gold lace, with Brough's crest on his button" (chap 7). Captain Fitzigig, suitor to Mr. Brough's daughter Belinda, claims kinship with such peers of the realm as the Duke of Doncaster, the Earl of Crabs, and the Earl of Cinqbars (the second and third of whom some readers might have remembered conducting themselves rather ignobly in, respectively, "The Amours of Mr. Deuceace" and "A Shabby Genteel Story"). We are thus early plunged into the Thackerayan social swim of toadies and tuft-hunters.

Just as young Samuel Titmarsh has his head in the clouds, but his feet firmly planted in the City and in the West End, so his "history," with its plethora of factual information on finance, clothing, and home economy, fixes its readers' eyes on the London of the

Scheherazades of the press—the writers for *John Bull,*[11] the *Morning Post*—and *Fraser's Magazine for Town and Country.* The line between fact and fiction could be a thin one indeed in the last-named journal, to judge by the titles of some of the articles that surrounded *The Great Hoggarty Diamond* on its original publication. Among pieces that appeared earlier in the year that are pertinent to matter of the tale were: "On Manners, Fashion, and Things in General . . . The Philosophy of Fashion," by Captain Orlando Sabertash; and "Memorials of Gormandizing. In a Letter to Oliver Yorke, Esq.," By M. A. Titmarsh. Political and religious issues debated in such editorials as "Our Foreign Policy and Home Prospects"; "The Literary Labours of Daniel O' Connell, Esq., M.P."; and "Dissent, 1841"[12] find their echoes in the fulminations of Aunt Hoggarty and in the preachment of the Reverend Grimes Wapshot. The collapse of the West Diddlesex Empire of Mr. Brough is anticipated in "The Condemned Cells. From the Notebooks of the Ordinary . . . The Confessions of a Swindler."[13]

The background events to *The Great Hoggarty Diamond* are very much in the foreground in the lead article, "The End of the Beginning," that opened the issue of *Fraser's* in which the first chapters of the story also ran.[14] This article sounds a general hurrah over the latest elections, which brought the Conservative party back into power after a ten-year rule by the Whigs, a decade marked, according to this commentator, by a continuous course of political and financial bungling. Among other things, this leader writer shares Aunt Hoggarty's disdain for her countrymen. "As for those odious Irish people . . . don't speak of them: I hate them, and everyone of their mothers," she exclaims, according to Sam's report, in a moment of pique over a lawsuit connected with her family property (chap. 1). The writer of "The End of the Beginning" was also finding the Irish "odious," though for political rather than personal reasons. Among his sources of irritation with the outgoing Melbourne administration was its "truckling," as he regarded it, to O'Connell and his repeal movement. Reference to O'Connell's agitation for repeal of the Union of 1798 evokes memories here of the late civil war, as does the Dublin brooch that Sam receives from his aunt at the beginning of his "history." In the middle of this jewel, we soon learn, is represented Uncle Hoggarty dressed in "the scarlet uniform of the corps of Fencibles to which he belonged." This very brooch, according to family tradition, was worn by Sam's uncle at the battle of Vinegar Hill and miraculously preserved his life in the bloody fray that saw the defeat of the Irish by General Lake. The resultant Union, we infer from the editorial pages of *Fraser's*, has proved as unstable as Aunt Hoggarty's temper.

Closer to the nerve center of Sam Titmarsh's predicament is the denunciation in this article of the late unlamented Whig government for their mismanagement of finances. Lord John Russell is labeled unequivocally as *"facile principe charlatonorum."* The occasion for the abuse is the administration of the New Poor Law, rather than investment or speculation, but this writer conveys the vivid impression that a whole new generation has been victimized, as Sam Titmarsh turns out to be, into a delusive hope for a quick rise of fortune. "When the Whigs entered upon office," the leader writer recalls, "we all expected such economy from their management, and their luminous political theories, that ere long the national debt would only afford matter of speculation to the historian, whilst everything would become so cheap that our paupers could afford to take houses in St. James's Square, and live on French wines and *pâtés de foie gras de Strasbourg.*" But, we are informed, the event proved otherwise, as a good number of humble folk suffered a fate that sounds very much like that wrought on Sam Titmarsh, his aunt, and his mother by Mr. Brough: "Let us render them [the Whigs] full justice. How they did squeeze poor old dowagers. . . . Many a poor clerk who thought his hard earnings and scanty living had taught him what economy was, learned that Whig economy was to make those who were poor already poorer still, and teach them who lived on cheese to be content in the future with cheese-parings."[15]

Titmarsh's comeuppance, however, occurs, he reminds us, "some score of years ago, when, as the reader may remember, there was a great mania in the City of London for establishing companies of all sorts; by which many people made pretty fortunes" (chap. 2)—while many others were wiped out, he might have added. For the benefit of those who might have forgotten this "great mania," the writer of "The End of the Beginning" joggles their memories of "the panic of 1825," mainly to credit the Conservative party for pulling the country out of the resultant depression, which he lays at the door of the Whig administration. This panic came along in the wake of the wild wave of speculation recalled by Sam Titmarsh, investor in Mr. Brough's enterprises, capitalized at five million sovereigns, and paying off (in its brief heyday) 6½ percent a year. Sam hints at other sources of Brough's income: "He was a great

man on 'Change, too. . . . . the young stockbrokers used to tell us
of immense bargains in Spanish, Greek, and Columbians, that
Brough made" (chap. 2).

Sam Titmarsh was not, of course, the only young man temporarily ruined by ill-advised speculation during this era of stock watering and unregulated currency. Among his better-known contemporaries who shared his fate was Benjamin Disraeli, whose first
publication was not a novel or a political tract, but a pamphlet entitled *An Enquiry Concerning the Plans, Progress and Policy of the American Mining Companies* (1825), one of a series promoting what proved
to be worthless companies. The Mr. Brough in young Disraeli's
life was J. D. Powles, principal partner of a leading firm of South
American merchants, who prevailed on the future statesman to
speculate in shares of new mining companies, particularly in emergent Latin American republics, such as the Anglo-Mexican Mining
Association and the Columbian Mining Association.[16] One recognizes here at least two of Mr. Brough's "Spanish, Greek, and Columbians." This line of investment had been abetted by the policy
of George Canning, the Foreign Minister, to encourage the new
republics of the Western Hemisphere, but dissentient voices were
raised, mainly those of Lord Liverpool, the prime minister, and
Lord Eldon, the lord chancellor, who issued warnings against the
spreading gambling fever. Disraeli's pamphlets were intended to
counteract Lord Eldon's alarms, but Eldon proved to be all too
accurate a prophet of doom. The unhealthy financial situation was
further aggravated by the incompetence of Lord Vansittart, who
succeeded Eldon as chancellor of the exchequer, and during the
spring of 1825, almost simultaneously with the collapse of the West
Diddlesex Association, the bottom fell out of the mining-share
market.

This embarrassing episode in Disraeli's life is alluded to in that
semiautobiographical fantasia on the follies of youth *Vivian Grey,*
where Powles is disguised as Mr. Millions, and Isaac D'Israeli (who
had been unhappy about his son's paper schemes) as Mr. Grey.
Vivian is duly warned by his father: "Here dashed by the gorgeous
equipage of Mrs. Ormulu, the wife of a man who was working all
the gold and silver mines in Christendom. 'Ah! my dear Vivian,'
said Mr. Grey, 'it is this which has turned all your brains. . . . This
thirst for sudden wealth it is, which engenders the extravagant
conceptions, and fosters that wild spirit of speculation which is now
stalking abroad. . . . Oh, my son, the wisest has said, "He that
maketh haste to be rich shall not be innocent.""[17] So Vivian Grey

learns too late along with Sam Titmarsh, but the financial embarrassment of Thackeray's hero (like his own, which always hovers
behind any of his situations involving money) proves temporary,
unlike that of the creator of Vivian Grey, who was saddled with
debt for years after the misadventures of his early years.

The "thirst for sudden wealth," the quest after paper El Dorados,
spins the plots of much of the fiction of the 1830s that elevated
financial speculation into matter for moral speculation. Sitting in
the British Museum early in 1840 "casting about for some other
subject" now that *Catherine* was off his hands, Thackeray had one of
the most popular of these tales very much in mind. While waiting
for some books to be delivered to him, he wrote to his mother:
"There is a story called Ten thousand a year in Blackwood that all
the world attributes to me, but it is not mine—only better: it is
capital fun: of a good scornful kind."[18] Samuel Warren's "tallow-
faced counter jumper" of a hero, Tittlebat Titmouse, clerk in Mr.
Tag-rag's drapery shop, living wretchedly on his thirty-five pounds
a year while he dreams of pennies from heaven, sprang from the
pages of *Maga* in the fall of 1839 to become the quintessential
cockney upstart to many an early and mid-Victorian reader.[19] The
author makes clear very early that he meant his book for more than
"capital fun," as he breaks into his naïve young hero's daydreams
with a sermon:

> "Hope springs eternal in the human breast." And probably, in
> common with most who are miserable from straitened circum-
> stances, he often conceived, and secretly relied upon, the possibility
> of some unexpected and accidental change for the better. He had
> heard and read of extraordinary cases of LUCK. Why might he not
> be one of the LUCKY? A rich girl might fall in love with him—that
> was, poor fellow! in his consideration, one of the least unlikely ways
> of luck's advent; or some one might leave him money; or he might
> win a prize in the lottery;—all these, and other accidental modes of
> getting rich, frequently occurred to the well-regulated mind of Mr.
> Tittlebat Titmouse; but he never once thought of one thing, viz., of
> determined, unwearying industry, perseverance, and integrity in the
> way of his business, conducting to such a result!
> Is his case a solitary one?—Dear reader, *you* may be unlike poor
> Tittlebat Titmouse in every respect except *one*! (Chap. 1)

As one might expect, the histories of Titmouse and the similarly
named Titmarsh[20] bear a resemblance, in outline if not in detail.
Both young clerks enjoy a sudden windfall which proves an ill
wind. Titmouse, like Titmarsh, tastes an illusory prosperity,

brought about in his case through the manipulations of an unscrupulous lawyer who leads the ignorant draper's assistant to believe himself true heir to an estate and income of ten thousand a
year illegally held by a distant kinsman. His aristocratic connections, as with Titmarsh, open doors previously closed to him, but he
goes young Sam one better by entering the ranks of the squirearchy
and marrying an earl's daughter.[21] Titmouse outdistances Titmarsh also in his pseudodandyism: "figged out in his very utter-
most best, with satin stock and double breastpins; his glossy hat
cocked on one side of his head, his tight blue surtout, with the
snowy handkerchief elegantly drooping out of the breast pocket;
straw-coloured kid gloves, tight trousers, and shining boots, his
ebony silver-headed cane held carelessly under his arm!" (bk. 1,
chap. 10).[22] Sam Titmarsh, arriving at Mr. Brough's country house
in Fulham in his dress, coat, silk stockings, and pumps, is riding for
a fall no less than Tittlebat Titmouse, arriving at the house of Mr.
Tag-rag, and subsequently at the more stately mansion of the Earl
of Dreddlingcourt, bedecked in his foppery, but Titmouse suffers a
heavier one. The ground gives out under young Tittlebat's feet
when his claim to his ancestral estate is voided through discovery of
his illegitimacy, and he ends his days in a madhouse.

    Ten Thousand a Year and *The Great Hoggarty Diamond* both illus-
trate the folly of what Carlyle called Mammonism, but Thackeray's
fable has a buoyancy lacking in Warren's more grisly exemplum.
Thackeray had reason at this time, as has already been observed, to
avoid Warren's "scornful kind" of humor. Also, he had a basic
sympathy with his erring young clerk (whose experience, after all,
to an extent paralleled his own), whereas Warren never conceals his
utter contempt for his shop man. Sam is naïve, but basically good;
Tittlebat Titmouse, on the other hand, is both ignorant and mean,
a "pint pot," according to his creator, and perpetrator of "gentlemanly frauds." Oily Gammon, the shyster lawyer who victimizes
Titmouse, is likened to a snake wrapped around a monkey. Warren
condemns materialism and social climbing out of strong moral convictions, but also from a viewpoint that strikes one as somewhat
patronizing and patrician. His antihero is conceived as "no more
than an average sample of his kind," that is, of the working-class
man who overreaches, and as such he is contrasted with "true nobility" as represented by the ideal squire Mr. Aubrey, the rightful
owner of the estate at Yatton from which he is temporarily displaced by the presumptuous cockney, Titmouse. It is noteworthy
that the Aubrey family along with their only begetter were later
inscribed in Thackeray's *Book of Snobs*.[23]

The sharpies and charlatans who frisk through *The Great Hoggarty Diamond* place this story among Thackeray's "rook and pigeon" tales (Mr. Brough's country house, in fact, is called "The Rookery"). At the beginning of one of them, "Captain Rook and Mr. Pigeon," Thackeray refers to "the romances of Adam Smith, Malthus and Ricardo, and the philosophical works of Miss Martineau,"[24] in recognition presumably of the reputation the last-named lady then enjoyed as priestess of the mysteries of political economy. Harriet Martineau also had witnessed the financial crisis of 1825, her father's bombazine manufacturing business in Norwich being one of the numerous enterprises that went under at that time. She thus acquired a rough education in economics early in life, refined through a study of James Mill's writings (which helped her to understand what happened to her father), and was determined to pass her hard-earned wisdom to the reading public in a more easily accessible form.[25] So were conceived her *Illustrations of Political Economy,* a series of tales launched in 1832, extending eventually, with the addition of two more groups, to some thirty-four volumes, in which she set out literally to "illustrate" the recondite laws of the free marketplace through "pictures of what these principles are actually doing in communities."[26]

What Hannah More had sought to do for the common man's spiritual salvation in the *Repository Tales,* Harriet Martineau attempted to do for his material weal through the gospels of the Manchester school of economics. As she has a curate remark in one of the tales: "All fair means of improving the temporal condition are, or ought to be, means for improving the moral state of the people."[27] She had for precedent Mrs. Marcet's *Conversations on Political Economy* (1829), in which a young girl is instructed by her tutor on such topics as savings banks and land allotments through a series of questions and answers (on the order of Mangnall's *Questions*).[28] This format of the secular catechism was extended by Miss Martineau into lengthy dialogues on wealth and poverty, accompanied by incidents dramatizing the working out of Malthusian and Ricardian doctrine, particularly as expounded in James Mill's *Elements of Political Economy.* Her *Illustrations* span the range of economic phenomena as they were then understood, subsumed under the production, distribution, and consumption of wealth. There are tales to represent a Hobbesian "state of nature" (the Crusoe-like "Life in the Wilds"); the benefits of the enclosure movement ("Brooke of Brooke Farm"); the immorality of slavery ("Demerara"); the need for Malthusian celibacy and "preventive" checks on population growth ("Ella of Garveloch'"); the evils of low wages and factory working conditions ("A Manchester Strike"); and the advantages of free trade ("For Each and For All").[29]

Whether Thackeray exerted the patience to plow through Miss Martineau's entire five-foot shelf of ready economics education is doubtful, but he seems to have read at least one of the more delightful of the tales, "Berkeley the Banker," intended to bring out the havoc of unrestricted currency issue. A leading figure in the story, set in the period preceding Napoleon's defeat at Waterloo, is a shady investment banker named Mr. Cavendish who brings ruin down on his head, and on a number of people who have put their trust in him, when he is detected in the forgery of notes.[30] However, before his disgrace he has enriched himself by underselling grain merchants and extending his paper trading to a point where his cash reserve is dangerously low (in the manner of Hoff, partner to Brough, who brings the West Diddlesex Corporation to bankruptcy by endorsing bills for the Jamaica Ginger Beer Company and the Patent Pump Company, both of which prove insolvent). The immediate cause of the demise of Mr. Cavendish is the introduction of foreign corn on the English market at the conclusion of the Napoleonic wars, not the failure of mines, banks, and ginger beer firms, as with Mr. Brough, but the outcomes of their manipulations are similar. Both escape from England, leaving a young assistant to face the music.[31] Mr. Cavendish transfers his operations across the sea: "The family are now flourishing at New York," we are told in the epilogue, "where, by their own account, are concentrated all the talents and virtues requisite of the genius of Mr. Cavendish, the accomplishments of Mrs. Cavendish, and the respective brilliant qualities of all the Masters and Misses Cavendish." As for the destiny of Mr. Brough, we learn through the edited account of Sam Titmarsh: "Since he vanished from the London world, he has become celebrated on the Continent, where he has acted a thousand parts, and met all sorts of changes of high and low fortune" (chap. 13). Here, to judge by the success of Robert Macaire and other mountebanks as already recounted by Sam Titmarsh's cousin Michael in The Paris Sketch Book, Mr. Brough must have found as ready a market for his wares as did Mr. Cavendish.[32]

The Great Hoggarty Diamond and Berkeley the Banker both expose human gullibility and cupidity, but Miss Martineau traces Cavendish's success to infraction of economic order more than of moral order: "Such were his means and such the principles of his profit, means which could be plausibly acted upon, only in the times of banking run mad, when the currency having been desperately tampered with, the door was opened to abuses of every sort; and the imprudence of some parties encouraged the knavery of others, to the permanent injury of every class of society in turn" (chap. 4). Along with such dicta interspersed through the tales, her general practice, lest her "pictures" were not in themselves sufficiently instructive, was to end each volume with a "Summary of Principles."[33] And so the fate of Mr. Cavendish's victims leaves its indelible sermon on paper: "Great evils, in the midst of many advantages, have arisen out of the use of paper money, from the neglect of measures of security, or from the adoption of such of those as have. Issues of controvertible money have been allowed to a large extent, unguarded by any restriction as to the quantity issued."[34]

Nevertheless Miss Martineau was convinced that "Example is better than precept," as stated in the motto attached collectively to the *Illustrations of Political Economy*. Thackeray later put this motto in the mouth of one of his fictitious elderly mentors, Mr. Brown, who had been commenting to his nephew on a "silly and sentimental book which I looked over at the Club, called the 'Foggarty Diamond' (or some such vulgar name)."[35] So in *The Great Hoggarty Diamond*, together with other "magazinery" such as "Cox's Diary," a tale of the rise and fall of a barber temporarily enriched by an inheritance he is not legally entitled to; "The Amours of Mr. Deuceace" and "Mr. Deuceace in Paris," Charles Yellowplush's sagas of gambling dandies; and "The Fatal Boots," a fable of a debt incurred at school that plagues a man through life, Thackeray drew his own "illustrations of political economy," or at least of the fortuitous ways of money.[36] Furthermore, in *The Great Hoggarty Diamond* the "editor" appends the "principles" illustrated by the tale, in the manner prescribed by Miss Martineau, as he takes his farewell, "bidding all gents who peruse this, to be cautious of their money, if they have it; to be still more cautious of their friends' money; to remember that great profits imply great risks; and that the great shrewd capitalists of this country would not be content with four per cent for their money, if they could securely get more: above all, I entreat them never to embark in any speculation, of which the conduct is not perfectly clear to them, and of which the agents are not perfectly open and loyal." It might be argued that one need not have journeyed to Manchester or sat at the feet of Ricardo to come to these conclusions, but such is Thackeray's perfunctory nod to "fable-books, where you are obliged to accept the story with the inevitable moral corollary that *will* stick close to it."[37]

In his offhand way with the moral fable, Thackeray betrays some kinship with Theodore Hook, a fellow contributor both to *Fraser's Magazine* and the *New Monthly Magazine*. Among Hook's more popular writing was his series of tales with the collective title *Sayings and Doings* (1824–28), whose purpose was set forth in the Shakespearean motto that originally adorned the title pages of its nine volumes: "Full of Wise Saws and Modern Instances." His avowed purpose in these "Sketches from Life" was "to judge, by the events of real life, the truth or fallacy of those axioms which have been transmitted to us with a character for 'usefulness and dignity: as conducive to the understanding of philosophy, of which they are the very remains, and of which they are adapted to persuade.'"[38] A devotee of the Parisian stage before Thackeray made its acquaintance, Hook claimed to have derived the scheme for *Sayings and Doings* from the popular French plays known as *proverbes*, in which maxims were acted out by illustrative incidents.[39] Feeling that the point of these *proverbes* was all too frequently blunted in English translation, Hook decided (as he indicates in a preface) to produce their equivalent in fiction, while drawing his examples from English life. Far from suggesting that life be regulated by proverbs, Hook stated that his intention was to select from his experience events in which people unconsciously exemplify proverbs in their conduct. In brief—as the covering title for the series signifies—the "doings" of modern men and women are compared with the "sayings" of the ancient sages.

Its plots concocted out of intrigues, counterintrigues, mischances, and the fortuities of fate, *Sayings and Doings* can be candidly described as a series of devious tales with dubious morals. To illustrate the motto "There's many a slip twixt the cup and the lip" Hook fabricated an ironical and somewhat chilling story of a young man who rescues his sweetheart from an unwanted marriage, is prevented himself from marrying her by the young lady's scheming mother, and finally, when, after numerous obstacles, they are free to wed, his beloved dies. Another story, bearing the twin mottoes "Look before you leap" and "Marry in haste, repent in leisure," concerns two brothers, a sentimental one who marries an Irish beauty purely for love, and a more circumspect one, who makes a "prudent" match with the wealthy, but unattractive and phlegmatic, daughter of a nabob. Both brothers, it turns out, are "done," for the two wives turn out to be equally disagreeable.[40]

The world of these moral fables, as these samples may indicate, is a rather harsh one. The narrator is generally a tough-minded worldling, cynical about men and their motives. One of the author's spokesmen is the significantly, if not subtly, named Mr. Humbug, head of a family whose various members are given to some foolish excess or other (the mother is addicted to romantic literature; Humbug himself tries futilely to preserve his youth; the eldest daughter is snobbish, the middle one prudish, the younger one pedantic), altogether exemplifying the maxim, "All is not gold that glitters."[41] Declares Humbug at the end of this story: "'Tis the way of the World . . . where there is most pretension, there is the least merit," and so most of the stories confirm. All manner of humbugs flit through the sleazy society conjured up by Hook, made up in equal part of gulls who fly too high and the cormorants who prey on them. Here are swindlers, parasites, parvenus, maneuvering mothers, snobs, hypocrites, opportunists, and innocents—often young lovers and newlyweds.

Hook's coarse-grained social world is not far removed from that of Thackeray's "rook and pigeon" stories, and one of the tales in *Sayings and Doings*, called "Danvers," is, in fact, quite close to *The Great Hoggarty Diamond*.[42] Thomas Burton, the hero of this story (intended to illustrate the saying "Too much of a good thing is good for nothing"), is an up-and-coming young lawyer newly married to the daughter of a Somerset baronet.[43] The smooth course of their marriage is ruffled by the young wife's wealthy and crotchety uncle Frumpington Danvers, who indulges the young couple in extravagant gifts that turn out to be white elephants. Upon the death of the uncle, the Burtons inherit most of his fortune, a curse, as things develop, rather than a blessing. In order to receive the uncle's money, Burton has to adopt the name of Danvers, which he is pleased to do, but adopting the style expected of them with their new affluence forces the newlyweds to live beyond their means. The estate they purchase becomes a constant drain on their finances; they accumulate expensive pictures, furniture, gold plate, and ornaments (including diamonds). Worse still, their attempts to move in the "best" society involve them in all manner of gaucheries.

In time the prosperity of the Burtons brings about a series of disasters. Young Danvers tries to go into politics, engaging in a campaign that amounts to a costly failure. The combination of a drop in the market and crop failure in the West Indies, together with his overextended speculations, ruins him financially. After a year in prison, he is happy to return to his own class of society and resume his former simpler way of life. With a few divergences, the basic pattern of Sam Titmarsh's history is anticipated here, down to the sentimental conclusion. "How fervently do I thank my God that by His Providence I have been taught what to value in this transitory world and what reject," declares the chastened Thomas Danvers (né Burton), "that I have seen the worthlessness of wealth, and find the real value of virtue and religion." To this amen is added a benediction, as the hero passes his hard-earned wisdom on to his seven daughters:

> "It is here, my children," said Danvers, pointing to his wife, "it is here that I possess my Treasure; to your mother I owe not only the means by which I have purchased the experience so beneficial to myself and these my dearest and best beloved, but to her I am indebted for the correction of all my indiscretions, for the excitement and encouragement of every right feeling which I possess.
> "It is," continued he, "in the possession of a fond, faithful and amiable wife, and such dear pledges as these which now surround me with the power of doing good, and the blessings of that peace of mind which the Disposer of all events vouchsafes to those who devoutly seek it, that man possesses real happiness upon earth."

Young Danvers's tribute to his Mary is directly echoed in the title of the last chapter of *The Great Hoggarty Diamond*, where Mary Titmarsh is praised as "the best diamond a man can wear in his bosom." Hook and Thackeray both revert to homiletics to assert the triumph of spiritual goods over those things that moths and rust corrupt. However, one detects a hollow ring in the preachments of the sly Hook. Mary Danvers is indeed the "means" by which he learns his lesson, her uncle having started them on their unfortunate course. We infer besides that young Burton is henpecked and that his wife uses her humility as a guise to dominate him. His concluding sermonette, then, could be taken as a sign of her success. One does not doubt the sincerity of Titmarsh (Mary Smith, after all, was based in part on Thackeray's Isabella), but, as will appear later, the conclusion of his history is not without its tinge of irony either.

Thackeray is at one with Hook in the ridicule of those who seek quick and easy ways to wealth, eminence, and social position, and both authors mock false aspiration in general. The narrator of "Danvers" remarks of the efforts of the newly rich young couple to break into society: "In short there is always some drawback, some terrible qualifier in the affair, which it would be difficult distinctly to define, but which invariably gives the *air bourgeois* to all the attempts of upstart wealth to imitate the tone and manner of the aristocracy of our country." A certain amount of the comedy of *The Great Hoggarty Diamond*, too, is derived from mudlarks adopting the plumage of peacocks. Titmarsh, to his credit, knows his limitations:

> And now I should be glad to enlarge upon that experience in genteel life which I obtained through the perseverance of Mrs. Hoggarty;

but it must be owned that my opportunities were but few, lasting only for the brief period of six months: and also, genteel society has been fully described already by various authors of novels, whose names need not be here set down, but who, besides being themselves connected with the aristocracy, viz., as members of noble families, or as footmen or hangers-on thereof, naturally understand their subject a great deal better than a poor young fellow from a fire-office can. (Chap. 10)

Through his alter ego Thackeray pelts away at what was to be a favorite target—the society novelists then in vogue. In a sarcastic article that had appeared earlier that year in *Fraser's*, "On Manners, Fashions, and Things in General" by one Captain Orlando Sabertash, the writers of "Mr. Colburn's menage" are lumped together with parvenus as social gate crashers:

> To place myself at once on the elevated pedestal which belongs to me, let me here explain the great difference existing between these, my compositions, and the works of all others who, from Dandy Bulwer to Dowdy [Frances] Trollope, have written on modern manners: it is easily shewn out, and settles at once the value of our relative pretensions. The fashionable novel-writers cannot distinguish just tact and real elegance of manners from what I am forced to term *vulgar gentility:* from the half breeding that an ordinary intercourse with society will bestow, even on the ignorant, illiterate and vulgar minded. Like all others, these writers can distinguish between the polished gold and the *unpolished* brass; but they cannot, like the skilful metallist, distinguish between the pure metal, and the base but superficially polished ore.[44]

Thackeray had already introduced readers of *Fraser's* to such "members of noble families" as Count von Galgenstein, the Earl of Crabs, and Lord Cinqbars. They also had seen society through the eyes of one of the "footmen or hangers-on of noble families," Charles Yellowplush, who has moved in "exquizzit suckles" and has been inside "Holmax and Crockfuds." Samuel Titmarsh gives us still more pictures of "vulgar gentility," if necessarily fleeting ones. He runs into none other than Charles Yellowplush, who by now has left the employ of "the Honrabble Halgernon Percy Deuceace, youngest and fifth son of the Earl of Crabs" to become servant in livery to Lord and Lady Preston. As guardian of this domicile, Yellowplush refuses admittance to Aunt Hoggarty, unimpressed by her descent from "the Hoggartys of Castle Hoggarty." Sam's aunt is a particularly blatant specimen of the Irish snobs who, as Thackeray was to write later, "are on their knees still before English fashion—these simple wild people; and indeed it is hard not to grin at some of their *naive* exhibitions."[45] Sam reports with a straight face her attempts at playing the *grande dame* with her "*shy dewvers*," "bongtong" and "ally mode de Parry." He also bears witness to her wearing of "yellow satn" at "two ellygant (though quiet) evening-parties by my *hospattable* host" Mr. Brough, where "Lord Scaramouche handed me to table" and "everything was in the most *sumptious* style"—on the basis of her unique epistolary accounts (chap. 9). One taste of fashion is sufficient to set Aunt Hoggarty off on a binge of "trumpery imitations" of the mode—hiring a fly, donning a wig, and applying the rouge, which, according to Sam resulted in "such a pair of red cheeks as Nature never gave her." Other indulgences by her strain the Titmarsh economy, such as her forcing her nephew and his young wife to set up a servant in livery wearing buttons representing "the united crests of the Titmarshes and Hoggartys, viz., a tomtit rampant and a hog in armour" (chap. 10). Her madcap course is finally brought to a halt by her futile efforts to gain entrée into the Preston establishment and her snub by Lady Drum at the Opera House. These setbacks turn her from "the vanities of this wicked world" to the ministering attentions of her rescuer from "the bottomless pit," the Reverend Grimes Wapshot.

Aunt Hoggarty is only one of many examples in this story of brass passing itself off for gold. Through Sam Titmarsh's ingenuous eyes we also meet the coronet-worshipping clerk Gus Hoskins, with his imitation gold neck chain; Mrs. Roundhand of Pentonville, wife of another of Sam's fellow clerks, who regularly consults the Peerage and lives in memory of waltzing with Count de Schloppenzollern at the City ball; Mrs. Brough, with her French cook and gold-epauleted butler in chocolate livery; her affected daughter Belinda who likes to drop French phrases; the pseudodandy Tidd, with his Byron ribands and turned-down collars; his rival, the foppish Captain Fitzigig, ever busy with his quizzing glass. Needless to say, most of the gold that glitters in this story proves to be fool's gold, from the silly, garrulous Lady Drum, to her grandson-in-law, the pompous, vicious-tempered Lord Preston, to the down-at-heels son of Lord Deuceace (another holdover from Yellowplush's memoirs), whom Sam finds in debtors' prison being kowtowed to by fellow inmates as though they themselves were Bond Street bucks. "I have seen sauntering dandies in watering-places ogling the women, watching eagerly for steamboats and stage-coaches as if their lives depended upon them, and strutting all day in jackets up and down the public walks," Sam recalls. "Well there are such fellows in prison: quite as dandified and foolish, only a little more shabby—dandies with dirty beards and holes at their elbows" (chap. 12). The paths of glory and fashion lead to the Fives Court, where the shabby dandy rubs tattered elbows with the shabby genteel.

Whatever Thackeray's opinion of fable books with moral tags, he pays lip service to the practice, if with tongue in cheek. Along with aphoristic chapter headings and Sam's little economics lessons, the proper moral atmosphere is set by "exemplary" characters. Besides the Reverend Grimes Wapshot, there is that model financier John Brough, "a great man among the Dissenting connection," charitable with his purse, who will accept no clerk "without a certificate from the school master and clergyman of his native place, strongly vouching for his morals and doctrine," and whose firm, moreover, was looked upon by city and country "for order, honesty, and good example" (chap. 2). He is the paragon of prudence, at least according to his own lights: "Those who know John Brough, know that ten years ago he was a poor clerk like my friend Titmarsh here, and is now worth half a million. Is there a man in the House better listened to than John Brough? Is there any Duke in the land that can give a better dinner than John Brough; or a larger fortune to his daughter than John Brough?"; "I'm a *man*,—a plain, downright citizen of London, without particle of pride. . . . This is the way that we live, Titmarsh, my boy: ours is a happy, humble, Christian home, and that's all" (chap. 7). Sam himself is given to finger wagging, as when he cautions his friend Gus against idling on Sunday, and reads to him from Blair's sermons (chap. 4). Now and then he addresses a wise saw to the reader ("When rogues fall out, honest men come by their own" [chap. 10]).

Yet such morals as are to be gleaned from the story itself are far from comforting ones. The most important lesson that Sam learns from Mr. Brough is the vast distance between precept and practice, or, as Hook might have put it, between men's sayings and their doings. Sam himself offers ample evidence that the armor of commonplace wisdom does not shield one from folly. Moreover, it is certainly no conventional moral tale whose villain not only goes unpunished, but for whom his victim acquires a certain amount of respect. Learning of Mr. Brough's resettlement and temporary rehabilitation on the continent, Sam remarks: "One thing we may at least admire in the man, and that is, his undaunted courage; and I can't help thinking, as I have said before, that there must be some good in him, seeing the way in which his family are faithful to him."

As for "the best diamond" Sam is left with, it is made clear that his good wife has been as much a material as a spiritual benefit to him. Sam is quick to throw his wife into the struggle for existence, as nurse in the home of Lord and Lady Tiptoff, when his own fortunes are on the wane: "And though some gents who read this, may call me a poor-spirited fellow for allowing my wife to go out to service, who was bred a lady and ought to have servants herself," Sam rationalizes, "yet, for my part, I confess I did not feel one minute's scruple or mortification on the subject. If you love a person, is it not a pleasure to feel obliged to him? And this, in consequence, I felt. I was proud and happy at being able to think that my dear wife should be able to labour and earn bread for me, now misfortune had put it out of my power to support me and her" (chap. 13). Mary's endearing herself to the Tiptoff family has the collateral result of helping Sam find new employment. Eventually, despite all his blunders and gaucheries, Sam becomes a rich man again, but through a whim of Aunt Hoggarty rather than by his own efforts. After cutting him out of her will, Sam's aunt decides to leave him her estates when she learns of his connection with Lord Tiptoff. Hence he benefits in the long run from Aunt Hoggarty's social climbing ambitions, an outcome that may seem to undercut traditional bromides about Mammon worship. As Sam Titmarsh basks in unearned prosperity, at the happy conclusion of his history readers of the time may well have been left wondering just what sort of a moral his misadventures are supposed to convey. The best answer seems to be "that dubious one . . . which every man may select according to his own mind."[46]

Samuel Titmarsh is certainly no model of that "determined, unwearying industry, perseverance, and integrity in the way of business," the Hogarthian ideal promoted by Samuel Warren in *Ten Thousand A Year*, any more than is Warren's own "hero" Tittlebat Titmouse, but the consequences are not so dire for Sam. Both young men, however, are the sport of "the blind jade Fortune in her mad vagaries," whom Warren invokes as he foretells the doom of poor Titmouse. This deity, as Warren reminds us, has a way of bestowing "her shifty boons benign" haphazardly and unpredictably (bk. 1, chap. 2), and we also watch her alternately smile and frown on Titmarsh. Sam himself tends to attribute his weal and his woe alike, not so much to prudence and the deficiency thereof, as to that intangible influence he refers to from time to time as "luck." It brings him the diamond in the first place, with temporary prosperity and social success, and at the end Sam concludes that "the disappearance of that ornament had somehow brought a different and better sort of luck into my family," and appreciates "the great good fortune my dear wife's conduct procured for me" (chap. 13). Luck then appears in this history to be as capricious as the fluctuations of the paper market and of Aunt Hoggarty's moods. In his poem "Vanitas Vanitatum," Thackeray was to characterize the Goddess Fortune as both irrational and amoral:

> . . . .
> How strange a record here is written!
> Of honours dealt as if in joke;
> Of brave desert unkindly smitten.
>
> . . . .
> O Vanity of vanities!
> How wayward the decrees of Fate are;
> How very weak the very wise,
> How very small the very great are!

Are we to conclude from *The Great Hoggarty Diamond* that mankind is entirely at the mercy of blind chance? Sam himself, who, with all the foolishness he has been capable of, is at heart sensible, seems to feel that we are at least as much the victims of our own natures. The "mania" for speculation that he recalls is only one of the excesses illustrated in his story. Lady Drum, for one, "had, it appeared, the mania for fancying all the world related to her" (chap. 3). "Mania" too is the word for Aunt Hoggarty's obsession with imitating fashion, her subsequent (and short-lived) religious fanaticism, and her various mental storms and rages. High society is an inflated bubble no less than high finance in this fable that fuses the Arabian Nights with the Silver Fork novel and *Illustrations of Political Economy*. Against the delusions of fancy so delightfully represented here are posed the virtues of common sense, the "regularity" and "honesty" exemplified by Sam Titmarsh and his wife Mary. To this tale of a diamond lost and won Thackeray might have appended the subtitle of Dr. Watts's treatise on logic that he seems to have taken to heart—*The Right Use of Reason*.

Just how much or how far reason prevails among men either in life or in fiction remains a moot question. It is the Commissioner of the Bankruptcy Court who suggests to the victimized Sam, as he passes sentence on him, that "your story is not likely to get into the newspapers; for, as you say, it is a private affair. . . . But if it *could* be made public, it might do some good and warn people, if they *will* be warned, against the folly of such enterprises, as that in which you have been engaged" (chap 12). Sam's story eventually is made public, though in a half-hearted way and not at his own behest. "Though I am no literary man myself," he writes in conclusion, "my cousin Michael (who generally, when he is short of coin, comes down and passes a few months with us) says that my Memoirs may be of some use to the public (meaning, I suspect, to himself); and if so, I am glad to serve him and them, and hereby take farewell."

Titmarsh's memoirs, however, seem to have been generally ignored by "the public" on their first appearance. As Thackeray's own luck had it, at least two rejections preceded their publication in *Fraser's*, and there was no immediate call for a reprint.[47] To be sure, the story had its early admirers, notably John Sterling: "What is there better in Fielding and Goldsmith? The man is a true genius; and, with quiet and comfort, might produce masterpieces that would last as long as any we have, and delight millions of unborn readers," he predicted in a letter to his friend Thomas Carlyle.[48] But his praise did not at this time secure a wide audience for *The Great Hoggarty Diamond* any more than Carlyle's had for *Catherine*. Thackeray himself retained a soft place in his heart for this little gem, referring to it on one occasion as "the best story I ever wrote."[49] To a French friend he recommended it for translation as "un joli petit livre a mon idée d'une bonhommie et simplicité affectées peut être."[50] To Mrs. Brookfield he confided: "I have been rereading the Hoggarty Diamond—upon my word and honour if it does not make you cry I shall have a mean opinion of you. It was written at a time of great affliction when my heart was soft and humble."[51] He was referring to the death of one of his and Isabella's children that had occurred in 1839, paralleled by an episode in the story (chap. 12), which to one of its late reviewers "surpasses in beauty and pathos . . . anything by Dickens."[52]

As it happened, this story that provokes such mixed emotions, written for money and for love, uniting much that was personal to Thackeray with so much that was at the time topical, did not reach book publication until 1849, when his publishers, Bradbury and Evans, were, as he says in the preface, "bold enough to venture upon producing the 'Hoggarty Diamond' in its present connected shape."[53] By this time they were hardly taking a risk, as Thackeray insinuates, for he was now the celebrated author of *Vanity Fair*, and *Pendennis* was beginning to appear. *The Great Hoggarty Diamond* was, in fact, advertised in the last number of *Vanity Fair*, and one disadvantage of its reaching the larger public so belatedly is that critics tended to measure it against this epic, next to which it naturally fell short. One critic, however, noted a "family likeness" to the later cynical-sentimental history, and another regretted that it had not attracted more attention when it first came out, for to him it loomed as "a Mountain of Life" above its class of periodical writing.[54]

"My kind friends, the publishers of this little book, appear to have a very high opinion of the virtue of prefaces, and demand one for the present occasion in terms so urgent, that it is impossible to refuse a compliance with their petition," Thackeray explained to his enlarged public of 1849. So from the well-rewarded author we get more tacked-on "principles" à la Miss Martineau:

> Those enterprising men are anxious that the moral of the tale, viz., that speculations are hazardous, and that honesty is the best policy, should be specially pointed out to the British public. But that moral is spoken a thousand times every year. Are not the newspapers full of advertisements about California? Have we not the Railway Share List as a constant monitor? It was after paying a call, with a very bad grace, that I thought to myself ruefully,—why did I not remember the last page of The Great Hoggarty Diamond?[55]
> Because prudence sometimes comes a little too late, and parsons do not practice what they preach, shall there be no more advice, and no more sermons? Profit by it or not; at least the present discourse is not very long.

A different "moral corollary" is offered about this time by the worldly Mr. Brown to the nephew whose social education he is supervising through the pages of *Punch* in time for him to take notice of "this little book":

> Magnificence is the decency of the rich—but it cannot be purchased with half-a guinea a day, which, when the rent of your chambers is paid, I take to be pretty nearly the amount of your worship's income. This point, I thought, was rather well illustrated the other day, in an otherwise silly and sentimental book which I looked at over at the Club, called the 'Foggarty Diamond.' . . . Somebody gives the hero, who is a poor fellow, a diamond pin: he is obliged to buy a new stock to set off the diamond, then a new waistcoat, to correspond with the stock, then a new coat, because the old one is too shabby for the rest of his attire;—finally the poor devil is ruined by the diamond ornament, which he is forced to sell, as I would recommend you to sell your waistcoat studs, were they worth anything.[56]

There are other repercussions. Becky Sharp claims to have rented the diamonds she wears to her presentation at court from none other than Mr. Polonius of Coventry Street. As for Lady Clavering, the nabob's daughter in *Pendennis:* "Her account at her London banker's was positively known, and the sum embraced so many cyphers as to create many O's of admiration in the wondering hearer. It was a known fact that an envoy from an Indian Prince, a Colonel Altamont, the Nawaub of Lucknow's prime favourite, an extraordinary man, who had, it was said, embraced Mahometanism, and undergone a thousand wild and perilous adventures, was at present in this country, trying to negotiate with the Begum Clavering, the sale of the Nawaub's celebrated nose-ring diamond, 'the light of the Dewan'" (chap. 7). Such rumors are sufficient to win the Begum entrée into circles normally barred to those with her infra dig manners and grammar. Nor does the trail of the diamond end there. Sam Titmarsh's story seems to be starting all over again on a loftier plane and more than a century earlier with Henry Esmond, whose aunt, the Viscountess Esmond, intercedes for him at Court: "My lady made feasts for him, introduced him to more company, and pushed his fortunes with such enthusiasm and success, that she got a promise of a company for him through the Lady Marlborough's interest, who was graciously pleased to accept of a diamond worth a couple of hundred guineas, which Mr. Esmond was enabled to present to her ladyship through his aunt's bounty, and was promised that she would take charge of Esmond's fortune" (bk. 2, chap. 5).

Thackeray obviously did not forget *The History of Samuel Titmarsh and the Great Hoggarty Diamond*, and he did not let his readers forget it either, however much they may have taken its "sermon" to their bosoms. But the last word seems to have been pronounced by the Commissioner of the Bankruptcy Court, who originally urged Sam to make his story public: "But what's the use of talking . . . here is one rogue detected, and a thousand dupes made; and if another swindler starts tomorrow, there will be a thousand more of his victims round this table a year hence; and so, I suppose, to the end. And now let's go to business, gentlemen, and excuse this sermon" (chap. 12). Or, in the immortal words of Robert Macaire, who, like Mr. Brough, has managed to combine the careers of financial swindler and moralist, "Le jour va passer, mais les badauds ne passeront pas."[57] Do as I say, not as I do, saith the preacher. "*O mea culpa, mea maxima culpa!*" Thackeray was to write twenty years later. "But though the preacher trips, shall not the doctrine be good?"[58] For now he had in mind for the readers of *Fraser's Magazine* another story of Irish luck, and this a quite unsentimental one.

1. 11–15 February 1840, *Letters*, 1:421.

2. *The Bedford-Row Conspiracy* first appeared in the *New Monthly Magazine* 58 (January, March, April 1840) and was reprinted the following year in *Comic Tales and Sketches*, vol. 2.

3. *A Shabby Genteel Story* appeared in *Fraser's Magazine* 21 (June 1840); 22 (July, August, October 1840). The setting is probably owing to Thackeray's having taken his wife, Isabella, to Margate for a rest early that year when she displayed alarming mental symptoms. He cut the story short abruptly with the October number, unable to sustain the mood when it became necessary for him to take Isabella to the continent for medical aid. This story will be considered in a later chapter in connection with *The Adventures of Philip*.

4. March 1840, *Letters*, 1:433.

5. 21 (September–December 1841). Its subsequent publishing history will be taken up later in the chapter.

6. Gordon N. Ray, *The Uses of Adversity* (New York: McGraw-Hill, 1955), p. 238.

7. He is based in part on the Reverend Cartwright, the title villain of Frances Trollope's *The Vicar of Wrexhill* (1837), which quotes from Molière's play on its title page. Thackeray reviewed this novel, among several others, in "Our Batch of Novels for Christmas," *Fraser's Magazine* 17 (January 1838): 79–92.

8. In this tale a ropemaker, having lost two gifts of money from one benefactor, receives a piece of lead from another. He gives the lead to a neighbor, a fisherman, to weight a net. In return the neighbor gives him a fish that turns out to have a diamond inside its belly, and through the diamond the ropemaker becomes wealthy. In time the diamond finds its place in the treasury of the Caliph Haroun Alraschid, to whom the ropemaker narrates the story. It is intended to illustrate the truism that "money is not always a certain means to get money and become rich." Thackeray twists the tale about by having the diamond bring his hero to poverty.

9. In his "Plan for a Prize Novel," Thackeray later satirized this device in an "advertisement novel," in which he demonstrates how novels can join in collusion with merchants. Here is a sample paragraph: "Lady Emily was reclining on one of Down and Eider's voluptuous ottomans, the only couch on which Belgravian beauty now reposes, when Lord Bathershins entered, stepping noiselessly over one of Tomkin's elastic Axminster carpets. 'Good heavens, my Lord!' she said—and the lovely creature fainted. The Earl rushed to the mantelpiece, where he saw a flacon of Otto's eau-de-cologne, and, &c." (*Punch* 20 [1851]; *Works*, 6:536).

10. When the story first appeared in *Fraser's Magazine*, it was announced as "Edited and Illustrated by Sam's Cousin Michael Angelo," but no cuts or plates accompany this version. The uniformity of the original heading with "*Comic Tales and Sketches*. Edited and Illustrated by Michael Angelo Titmarsh," published earlier that year by Hugh Cunningham, suggests that Thackeray was hoping to reprint *The Great Hoggarty Diamond* as a third volume in that series. In a letter of 1 June 1841 to Richard Bentley, Thackeray writes: "Have the goodness to give my MS. of the Diamond to my friend Mr. Cunningham. I can't get any answer from you good bad or indifferent" (Fales Library, New York University; Ray, *The Uses of Adversity*, p. 478, n. 3). One infers from this letter that Thackeray tried to place the story in *Bentley's Miscellany* before *Fraser's* accepted it, but why Cunningham might have turned it down for book publication is unknown—possibly because *Comic Tales and Sketches* was not a success.

11. Edited at the time when the story takes place by Theodore Hook, one of the writers imitated by Thackeray.

12. January, June, February, May, and June 1841, respectively. "Orlando Sabertash" is identified by Miriam Thrall, the historian of *Fraser's*, as John Mitchell. "Titmarsh," of course, is Thackeray writing to Maginn as "Oliver Yorke."

13. February, March, and April 1841.

14. September 1841, pp. 253–68.

15. Ibid., pp. 256–57.

16. Robert Blake, *Disraeli* (New York: St. Martin's Press, 1966), p. 26. This ur-

bane biography is the source of much of the detail that follows. Of these early pamphlets Blake remarks: "For one destined to be a master of the art of fiction, this literary debut was perhaps not inappropriate, but it is an odd beginning for a future Chancellor of the Exchequer."

17. Disraeli, *Vivian Grey* (London, 1826), bk. 1, chap. 9.

18. 18 January 1840, *Letters*, 1:412.

19. *Ten Thousand a Year* was published in book form immediately after its conclusion in *Maga* in August 1841. Mrs. Oliphant, the historian of the Blackwood firm, recalled late in the century that it "attracted a great deal of attention, and combined caricature with sentiment, the ridiculous with the exalted, in a manner which delighted the public" (*Annals of a Publishing House*, 2 vols. [Edinburgh and London: William Blackwood & Sons, 1897], 2:32). It was revised by its author several times, and reprinted intermittently through the century, both in England and in America. In his introduction to the final version of 1854, Warren characterizes the book as "exhibiting in the course of natural events the aspect socially, professionally, politically, and religiously of English society," and considers it "an enormous engine for developing and testing the character of man, individually and collectively." He quotes a letter from an admirer in Kentucky who attributed his rise from mechanic to an important position in society to the example of Warren's model gentleman Charles Aubrey, and who had named his daughter after Mr. Aubrey's daughter Kate.
Although Warren clearly thought of himself as a contributor to the literature of "self-help," Thackeray's references to *Ten Thousand a Year* call attention mainly to its humor. See in particular his essay "The Dignity of Literature," where he alludes to "the famous history of the firm of Quirk, Gammon and Snap," and "De Finibus," where he recalls the episode of Titmouse's green hair produced by a dye palmed off on him by an unscrupulous perruquier.

20. Thackeray had introduced the name Titmarsh as an alter ego before Warren's story began its run in *Maga* (October 1839), but he may have given it to Sam with Warren's hero in mind. In one episode of *Ten Thousand a Year*, a character mistakenly refers to Titmouse at a dinner as "Titmash" (bk. 1, chap. 10). A letter indicates that Thackeray tried to place *The Great Hoggarty Diamond* in *Maga*, but was rejected (2 January 1847 to William Edmounstone Aytoun, *Letters*, 2:262).

21. There are also analogous characters, e.g., the merchant Mr. Tag-rag, a forerunner of Sam's employer Mr. Brough, who also has an affected wife and daughter; and the dissenting minister, the Reverend Dismal Horror, who anticipates the Reverend Grimes Wapshot, Aunt Hoggarty's spiritual counselor.

22. Titmarsh and Titmouse are juxtaposed as examples of early Victorian "Gents" or pseudodandies in Ellen Moers, *The Dandy: Brummell to Beerbohm* (New York: Viking Press, 1960), pp. 217–18.
Michael Steig suggests that Warren modeled his hero in part on his rival Dickens, who was conspicuous at the time for his showy dress. See his "Subversive Grotesque in Samuel Warren's *Ten Thousand a Year*," *Nineteenth-Century Fiction* 24 (September 1969): 163. If so, the reincarnation of Titmouse in Pip of *Great Expectations* is an outstanding case of literary cross-fertilization.

23. For his "pictures of genteel life," Warren is placed, along with Bulwer, Disraeli, Mrs. Gore, and Mrs. Trollope, among the "Literary Snobs" (chap. 16). Because of their longing for their dinners with great families in the midst of their temporary indigence, the Aubreys are included among *déclassé* snobs in "Snobs and Marriage" (chap. 34). See *Works*, 6:358, 420–21.

24. *Corsair*, 28 September 1839; *Works*, 3:495–96.

25. R. K. Webb has pointed out that Miss Martineau also followed the discussions of economic problems in her local newspaper the *Globe*, and suggests that she may have heard reports of Cobbett's lectures in Norwich (*Harriet Martineau* [New York: Columbia University Press, 1960] pp. 59–60).

26. Preface to *Illustrations of Political Economy* (London: Charles Fox, 1834).

27. "Berkeley the Banker," chap. 1 (Mr. Craig speaking).

28. Harriet Martineau, *Autobiography*, ed. Maria Weston Chapman (London, 1877), 1:105–6; Vera Wheatley, *The Life and Works of Harriet Martineau* (Fair Lawn, N.J.: Essential Books, 1957), pp. 60–61.

29. Prior to the launching of the *Illustrations*, she had written two tales on economics subjects for the publisher Houlston—"The Rioters," suggested by an account of machine breaking in the *Globe*, and "The Turn-Out," on the subject of wages (Webb, *Harriet Martineau*, p. 99), but the method of the *Illustrations* was suggested by her reading of Mrs. Marcet.

30. Although set early in the century, the story is based in part on her memory of her father's tribulations with a Norwich bank (Martineau, *Autobiography*, 1:181).

31. Edgar Morrison, of "Berkeley the Banker," however, is a weak-willed accomplice, not an innocent dupe like Sam Titmarsh.

32. See "Caricatures and Lithography in Paris." On Robert Macaire and his success, Michael Angelo Titmarsh remarks: "Will this satire apply anywhere in England? Have we any Consolidated European Blacking Associations amongst us? Have we penniless directors issuing El Dorado prospectuses, and jockeying their shares through the market? For information on this head, we must refer the reader to the newspapers; or if he be connected with the City, and acquainted with commercial men, he will be able to say whether *all* the persons whose names figure at the head of the announcements of projected companies are as rich as Rothschild, or quite as honest as heart could desire" (*Works*, 5:159). Another analogue is the hero of *Jérôme Paturot*, a favorite novel of Thackeray's (see above, pp. 126–28), whose hero is inveigled into becoming the treasurer of the Imperial Bitumen Company, the manager of which subsequently disappears with the treasury of the firm (see "Jerome Paturot," *Works*, 13:390).

33. R. K. Webb has pointed out that these summaries are taken almost verbatim from James Mill's *Elements of Political Economy*.

34. Conclusion to vol. 5.

35. "On Friendship," *Mr. Brown's Letters to His Nephew, Punch* 28 (28 April 1849): 165; *Works*, 6:619.

36. His two cartoons contributed to the *Anti–Corn Law Circular* (1839), ed. Richard Cobden, entitled "Illustrations of the Rent Laws," suggest parodic echoes of Miss Martineau's later series *Poor Laws and Paupers Illustrated* (1833) and *Illustrations of Taxation* (1834).
The first of these, with the caption "Poles Offering Corn," shows foreign grain merchants prevented from bringing their sheaves ashore by a minister and military officers, with dead and starving figures behind them. The second, bearing the legend "The Choice of a Loaf," shows a poor man being forced at gun point to purchase a loaf of bread at 1s, while at the next booth Polish bread is offered at 4d a loaf (partially rpt. in *Stray Papers*, frontispiece; pp. 167–68). So much for "free trade"!

37. *Irish Sketch Book*, chap. 15; *Works*, 5:405 (relating to *The Adventures of Captain Freeny*, which Thackeray admired for its straightforward amorality). See below, chap. 7.

38. Theodore Hook, from advertisement to the first edition, *Sayings and Doings* (London: Henry Colburn, 1824).

39. In chap. 3 of "The Ravenswing" (one of the "Men's Wives" series originally published in *Fraser's*, June 1843), Thackeray appended this note: "A French *proverbe* furnished the author with the notion of the rivalry between the barber and the tailor [Mr. Eglantine and Mr. Woolsey]." A French scholar has traced this allusion to a *proverbe* acted out by characters in Charles de Bernard's novel *La chasse aux amants* (1841). See R. Maître, "Nouvelles sources françaises de Thackeray," *Etudes anglaises* 17 (January–March 1964): 56–61.

40. "Merton," *Sayings and Doings*, first series; "The Sutherlands," ibid., second series.

41. "The Friend of the Family," ibid., first series.

42. Hook died while *The Great Hoggarty Diamond* was running in *Fraser's*. An obituary article on him appeared in the October issue.

43. Sam's wife comes from Somerset, the locale of chap. 1 of *The Great Hoggarty Diamond*.

44. January 1841, p. 53. The author of this article is identified as John Mitchell in *Wellesley Index*, 2:370.

45. "A Little about Irish Snobs," *Book of Snobs, Works*, 6:360.

46. *Irish Sketch Book*, chap. 15.

47. See above, nn. 10, 20.

48. Quoted in Carlyle, *Life of John Sterling, Works*, ed. Henry Duff Traill (London: Chapman & Hall, 1899–1900), 11: 223.

49. Letter to Aytoun, *Letters*, 2:262.

50. September 1850? to Louis Marvy (Morgan Library, unpublished).

51. 14 October 1848, *Letters*, 2:440.

52. *Godey's Lady's Book* 38 (February 1849).

53. The book was attractively designed, with simulated vellum boards, green flowered borders, and, for its centerpiece, a medallion containing the Hoggarty locket. The title page represents four children (one resembling Thackeray) holding up the diamond stick pin. The text includes the illustrations promised in the title of the magazine version. These alternate between the comic (Sam drinking the rosolio with his aunt; Gus Hoskins looking enviously at Sam riding in an open carriage with Lady Drum and Lady Jane; Mrs. Roundhand rattling away to an obviously bored Sam; and Sam literally walking on air at Mr. Brough's ball) and the sentimental (Sam courting Mary Smith by a hay rick; Mary holding the baby of Lord and Lady Tiptoff in her arms; and an especially stark one called "The Common Lot" showing Sam and Mary weeping over the cradle of their dead child).
The first book publication occurred in America (New York: Harper, 1848), about two months before that of Bradbury and Evans, but was not so elaborate.

54. *Athenaeum*, 10 February 1849, pp. 137–38; *Literary Gazette*, 17 March 1849, p. 190.

55. Ill-fated railway speculations bring ruin to the hero of Thackeray's "The Diary of C. Jeames De La Pluche, Esq" (*Punch*, 2 August 1845), published in America in Appleton's Popular Library with the subtitle *A Tale of the Panic of 1845*.

56. 24 March 1849, p. 115; *Works*, 6:607.

57. *Works*, 5:165.

58. "On A Hundred Years Hence," *Roundabout Papers, Works*, 12:298.

BARRY LYNDON: IRISH HEROES AND DEMIREPS

Chapter Seven

A "POOR DAY-LABOURER IN THE WINYARD," Thackeray called himself in a letter to a friend at the end of 1843, concluding in the same vein with reference to his recent tour of Ireland: "As an agriculturalist I should wish that the Humbug crop should not be quite so plenteous in 1844 as it has been in '43."[1] Humbuggery had been Thackeray's announced subject from the outset, and the particular Irish variety already introduced in the persons of Major Gahagan and Aunt Hoggarty. Since then, Thackeray had extended opportunity to look at "the dashing, daring, duelling, rollicking, whiskey-drinking people"[2] up close, recording his impressions of them and their surroundings in *The Irish Sketch Book,* the first work to come out under his own name. A by-product of this trip was "The Luck of Barry Lyndon," Thackeray's last tale for *Fraser's Magazine,* which began its run there a month after the letter relating to the "Humbug crop."[3] In this later incarnation the Irish braggart has become more swashbuckling and more cosmopolitan if no less naïve, and is allowed to tell his own story at length in a consummate display of "the humorous ego."

Thackeray seems to have had *Barry Lyndon* in mind as early as the summer of 1841, following his first and shorter trip to Ireland. At this time, in a letter to James Fraser, he writes of a semilegendary figure of Irish literature who had captivated his imagination, Captain Freeny, a peripatetic highwayman who ran away from home as a boy: "I have in my trip to the country, found materials (rather a character) for a story, that I'm sure must be amusing."[4] Thackeray

admired in particular "the noble *naïveté* and simplicity of the hero
as he recounts his own adventures, and the utter unconsciousness
that he is narrating anything wonderful. It is the way of all great
men, who recite their great actions modestly, and, as if they were
matters of course; as indeed to them they are."[15]

On his return to Ireland, Thackeray resumed interest in Captain
Freeny's history, together with other "ephemeral repertories" from
the wild past of his host nation, accounts of rogues and vagabonds,
"suited to the meanest as well as the highest capacity, tending both
to improve the fancy and enrich the mind." On a rainy night at an
inn he regaled himself with a few "Galway-Nights' Entertainments"
(by analogy with his favorite *Arabian Nights*). These, he writes,
"have the old tricks and some of the old plots that one has read in
many popular legends of almost all countries, European and Eastern: successful cunning is the great virtue applauded; and the
heroes pass through a thousand wild extravagant dangers, such as
could have been invented when art was young and faith was
large."[6] Barry Lyndon carries on the tradition:

> There was much more liveliness and bustle on the king's highroad
> in those times, than in these days of stage-coaches, which carry you
> from one end of the kingdom to another in a few score hours. The
> gentry rode their own horses or drove in their own coaches, and
> spent three days on a journey which now occupies ten hours; so that
> there was no lack of company for a person travelling towards Dublin.
> I made part of the journey from Carlow towards Naas with a well-
> armed gentleman from Kilkenny dressed in green and a gold cord,
> with a patch on his eye and riding a powerful mare. He asked me the
> questions of the day, and whither I was bound, and whether my
> mother was not afraid on account of the highwaymen to let one so
> young as myself travel? But I said, pulling out one of them from a
> bolster, that I had a pair of good pistols that had already done
> execution, and were ready to do it again; and here a pock-marked
> man coming up, he put spurs into his bay mare and left me. She was
> a much more powerful animal than mine, and besides, I did not wish
> to fatigue my horse, wishing to enter Dublin that night, and in repu-
> table condition. (Chap. 4)

This "civilized" brigand is obviously well endowed with the blarney and bravado that distinguished his forerunners. By the time he
has returned to his native land after his continental escapades, we
are quite ready to go along with his characterization of his countrymen: "There was a simplicity about this Irish gentry which
amused and made me wonder. If they tell more fibs than their
downright neighbours across the water, on the other hand they
believe more" (chap. 15). These words of course are equally appli-

cable to Barry himself, who really proves more gullible in the long run than do any of his victims, or the reader. Another instance of Thackeray's sly parody is his inversion of the Freeny formula. Unlike that outlaw's disposition to recite "great actions modestly," Barry, who has much to be modest about, is prone to amplify ordinary achievements:

> I am not going to entertain my readers with an account of my professional career as a gamester, any more than I did with anecdotes of my life as a military man. I might fill volumes with anecdotes of this kind were I so minded, but at this rate my recital would not be brought to a conclusion for years, and who knows how soon I may be called upon to stop? I have gout, rheumatism, gravel, and a disordered liver. I have two or three wounds in my body, which break out every now and then, and give me intolerable pain, and a hundred more signs of breaking up. Such are the effects of time, illness, and free-living, upon one of the strongest constitutions and finest forms the world ever saw. Ah! I suffered from none of these ills in the year '66, when there was no man in Europe more gay in spirits, more splendid in personal accomplishment, than young Redmond Barry. (Chap. 11)

> Nor need I mention my successes among the fairer portion of the creation. One of the most accomplished, the tallest, the most athletic, and the handsomest gentleman of Europe, as I was then, a young fellow of my figure could not fail of having advantages, which a person of my spirit knew very well how to use. But upon these subjects I am dumb. (Chap. 14)

In keeping with the interplay between "sham history" and "true history" carried out through so much of Thackeray's fiction, in *Barry Lyndon* fantasy—here taking the form of the Irish tall tale—is constantly intruded upon by the rude world of fact. Originally subtitled "A Romance of the Last Century," Thackeray's rogue tale could have been called "A Romance of Real Life," like many a novel of its time, and with more justification than most, for it is grounded more firmly than his previous fiction in biography, history, journalism, and contemporary politics.

Besides personal observations based on his travels, Thackeray drew on various records to limn out Barry Lyndon's story. It is known that the latter part, concerned with Barry's stormy marriage to Lady Lyndon, is based on the career of the notorious adventurer Andrew Robertson Stoney-Bowes, who wheedled a wealthy countess into marriage and subsequently made her life miserable until she was able to wrench herself free from him by divorce.[7] For the repulsive intrigue involving the Princess of X—Thackeray himself indicates that he drew upon a "silly little book," *L'Empire*, by the

Baron de la Mothe-Langon, which contains an account of the execution of Princess Caroline by the King of Wurtenberg after she was taken in adultery.[8] These two disparate incidents seem to have bound themselves together in Thackeray's mind by analogy, both involving tyrannical husbands, hysterical wives, and adultery played out against a background of corrupt society.

The somberness that hangs over Barry's last years echoes the sad demise of that real-life Irish hero William Maginn. "Maginn a famous subject for moralising," Thackeray commented on reading an obituary on the late editor of *Fraser's Magazine*, whose death occurred at the time when "The Luck of Barry Lyndon" was beginning to appear.[9] It is hardly Maginn's learning, scholarship, and wit that are carried over into Thackeray's vulgar, semiliterate hero, but one detects about Barry something of Maginn's facile charm, slippery morality, and sense of doom. There is also a suggestive parallel between Barry's death in prison in a *non compos* state and the ignominious end of Beau Brummell, whose career was just then being widely publicized through Jesse's biography.[10] Generally Thackeray's way of proceeding with his rogue hero resembles his handling of his criminal heroine Catherine Hayes—pushing back from effects to causes, from what is known about the later life of his character, as recorded in biography, history, or chronicle, to the reconstruction of his early days. Such an approach is anticipated in "Hints for a History of Highwaymen," the *Fraser's* review that influenced *Catherine*, where it is proposed that when one sets down the life history of a malefactor: "It would be well to have him at last displayed as he really is in action and in principle; recount if you can his education and his first associates, his first temptations, and all that may palliate or aggravate his first yielding to the tempter."[11]

Modern readers who know Thackeray's Irish hero only through the revised and retitled version of his narrative called *The Memoirs of Barry Lyndon, Esq.* can easily lose sight of its Fraserian roots. In the revised version prepared for the *Miscellanies*, a number of the discursive essays and moralizings (useful to maintain rapport with monthly readers) were dropped, and the role was virtually eliminated of Thackeray's favorite *persona* of the time, the staid, smug, snobbish, somewhat humorless bachelor George Savage Fitz-Boodle who is nominally the editor of Barry's papers. Barry's opening words, "Since the days of Adam, there has been hardly a mischief done in this world but a woman has been at the bottom of it," line his tale up with "Men's Wives," a rather harsh series of narratives that had appeared in *Fraser's* during the previous year under the editorship of Fitz-Boodle centering on a number of young husbands wheedled, henpecked, or otherwise victimized by grasping wives or mothers-in-law.[12] Barry's pretension to being a displaced aristocrat ("I would assume the Irish crown over my coat-of-arms, but that there are so many silly pretenders to that distinction who bear it and render it common"), along with his concern with getting on in the world, makes his memoir also a kind of continuation of Fitz-Boodle's "Professions," in which this man-about-town offers ideas for new vocations for "younger sons of the nobility" thrown upon their own resources.[13] Old faces turn up from "F—a magazine of wit"—such as Deuceace and the Earl of Crabs from *The Yellowplush Papers*, and the Irish expatriate who had figured in "Denis Haggerty's Wife" in the "Men's Wives" series, as well as in *The Great Hoggarty Diamond*—but readers were brought up to date as well on "topics of the day." To one following its progress month by month, "The Luck of Barry Lyndon" must have read like an extension of *Fraser's* editorial and review pages.

"I presume that there is no gentleman in Europe that has not heard of the House of Barry of Barryogue, of the Kingdom of Ireland, than which a more famous name is not to be found in Gwillim or D'Hozier . . . the noblest of the island, and, perhaps of the universal world," declares Barry at the beginning of his memoirs. His preoccupation with lineage, and with the character of the gentleman, is one that of course transcends nationalities, and was shared quite explicitly, at the time when these words were written, by a *Fraser's* reviewer. Genealogy and gentility are the very themes of the long article that precedes the first number of "The Luck of Barry Lyndon"—a review of a contemporary book on great families.[14] Despite occasional touches of humor, the article is a straight-faced discussion of family pride and hereditary aristocracy. In *Barry Lyndon* one finds Thackeray both echoing and parodying it, tapping early in his career a vein of social satire that he was to make his own. "Political ethics tells us," affirms the reviewer, himself quoting Gibbon, "that 'wherever the distinction of birth is allowed to form a superior order in the state, education and example should always, and will often, produce among them a dignity of sentiment and propriety of conduct, which is guarded from dishonour by their own and the public esteem.'" The Hatfield and McCoy history of his family that occupies the first several pages of Barry Lyndon's narrative seems calculated to demonstrate just the opposite:

> That very estate which the Lyndons now possess in Ireland was once the property of my race. Rory Barry of Barryogue owned it in Elizabeth's time, and half Munster beside. The Barry was always in

feud with the O'Mahonys in those times; and, as it happened, a certain English colonel passed through the former's country with a body of men-at-arms, on the very day when the O'Mahonys had made an inroad upon our territories, and carried off a frightful plunder of our flocks and herds.

This young Englishman, whose name was Roger Lyndon . . . having been most hospitably received by the Barry, and finding him just of the point of carrying an inroad into the O'Mahonys' land, offered the aid of himself and his lances, and behaved himself so well, as it appeared, that the O'Mahonys were entirely overcome, all the Barry's property restored, and with it, says the old chronicle, twice as much of the O'Mahonys' goods and cattle.

It was the setting in of the winter season, and the young soldier was pressed by the Barry not to quit his house of Barryogue, and remained there during several months, his men being quartered with Barry's own gallow-glasses, man by man in the cottages round about. They conducted themselves, as is their wont, with the most intolerable insolence towards the Irish; so much so, that fights and murders continually ensued, and the people vowed to destroy them. (Chap. 1)

At the same time Barry's family history does illustrate, if in a negative way, another generalization made by the reviewer, bolstered again by a traditional source: "We have the authority of the Jewish legislator Moses, that every creature begets its like; and that may be understood in the most extensive sense, for although there may not be two persons so alike as not to be known apart from each other, the characteristics of families are often very clearly marked and continued for generations." Barry Lyndon, very much a product of his heritage, serves as a clear case in point. His inherited sense of values is revealed in his eulogy of his father, Roaring Harry Barry, who, we are told, might have distinguished himself as a lawyer "had not his social qualities, love of field-sports, and extraordinary graces of manner, marked him out for a higher sphere" (chap. 1). "Peace be to his ashes!" reads Barry's memorial. "He was not faultless, and dissipated all our princely family property; but he was as brave a fellow as ever tossed a bumper or called a main, and he drove his coach-and-six like a man of fashion." Like father, like son, even to the next of kin, Bryan Lyndon, who is carefully nurtured by his father in the family traditions of extravagance, hooliganism and sadism, but whose untimely death extinguishes the line.[15]

Barry Lyndon's "Pedigree and Family," from Barry of Barryogue through Simon de Bary and Rory Barry to Roaring Harry Barry, recapitulates the sanguinary history of Anglo-Irish relations down through the ages. Before Barry's Irish eyes, his loyal ancestors were "puling knaves who bent the knee to Richard II"; Oliver Cromwell was a "murderous ruffian"; "Our unhappy race had lost its possessions a century earlier, and by the most shameful treason"; "the dastardly English had prevented the just massacre of themselves by falling upon the Irish" (chap. 1). Thackeray himself was fresh from a rapid retrospect of Irish history in the course of reviewing books for the *Morning Chronicle*, which included J. Venedey's *Ireland* and D. Owen Madden's *Ireland and Its Rulers since 1829*.[16] His review of the Venedey book opens with the observation that one "visited Scotland for its romantic recollections and beauty—England for the wonders of its wealth—Ireland for the wonders of its poverty. For poverty and misery have, it seems, their *sublime*, and that sublime is to be found in Ireland. What a flattering homage to England's constitutional rule over a sister country." At the same time he complains that the author "makes too little allowance for the difficulties attending the linking together of two such unequally advanced countries . . . and, instead of making it a matter of historical research, he treats it as a romance, personifying England as the villain of the tale, and Ireland as the heroine and the victim." The drift of Thackeray's own "romance" is to reverse the relation through the English heiress Lady Lyndon and the usurping Barry. The Madden book, described as "a somewhat irregular history of Irish politics, from the passing of the Catholic Relief Bill to the time of the Mulgrave government," is praised for its eloquence and faulted for its dogmatism in exposing the causes of the current agitation in Ireland and accounting for the seemingly irreconcilable differences among his countrymen. Also related to *Barry Lyndon* is an earlier book that Thackeray had reviewed, *Memoirs of Joseph Holt, General of the Irish Rebels in 1798*, a "lively and picturesque account," in his opinion, by an eyewitness to the late revolt that had brought about the Act of Union.[17]

Barry was born long before this insurrection, but his first readers were well aware that the resultant forced marriage between the two nations (like that between Barry and Lady Lyndon) was a turbulent and unstable one. In fact, the troubles were flaring up again just as *Barry Lyndon* was beginning its run in *Fraser's*, despite several conciliatory moves by Parliament during the years immediately preceding. In 1838 the Irish Poor Law extended the privileges of the New Poor Law, recently passed in England, to the sister nation, and the Commutation of Tithes ended the forced payment by Irish Catholics to support the Anglican Church. In 1840 Catholics in Irish cities were given a share in municipal government. Nevertheless, the Repeal Association was founded in the spring of that year and carried on a compaign for the dissolution of the Union under the leadership of the newly elected Lord Mayor of Dublin, Daniel O'Connell, of which readers of *Fraser's Magazine* were kept informed.[18] Particularly during the six months before "The Luck of Barry Lyndon" was introduced, there was not an issue that failed to touch in some way on the Irish situation. "God forbid that we should witness a civil war!" wrote one of the more alarmed commentators. "God forbid that the scenes of 1798 should ever again be enacted in that unhappy land. . . . All things are tending to that point, and if that point be not reached ere long, both England and Ireland will be very mercifully dealt with." In the next issue a political article entitled "Parliamentary Pickings; or the Wonders and Marvels of the Session of 1843," took that body to task for its ineptitude in dealing with the Irish problem. In the November issue, the article "O'Connell and the Government" expressed relief over the ending of the agitation for Repeal as the result of a government proclamation. At year's end the perennial question was raised, "What is to be done with Ireland now?" and Parliament was strongly urged to make a "searching inquiry" into the state of affairs there.[19]

This threat was temporarily removed with the quelling of the repeal agitation and the arrest of O'Connell at the end of 1843. However, in 1844, while O'Connell was in prison, the movement for repeal of the Union was sustained by the Young Ireland Party, and O'Connell himself eventually reverted to this position (after briefly entertaining the compromise position of the Federalists). Barry Lyndon is made to comment laterally on this new outburst of shillelagh rattling. Returning to his homeland from the glamorous continent, he finds that Dublin in the year 1771 "was as savage as Warsaw almost, without the regal grandeur of the latter city." He looks down his patrician nose at the ragged people and the ruffians who roam the streets, to say nothing of the squalid houses and run-down inns. "I know this description of them will excite anger among some Irish patriots, who don't like the nakedness of our land abused, and are angry if the whole truth be told concerning it," he adds. His readers were perusing these lines at a time when O'Connell's fanatical intolerance of any criticism of Ireland or the Irish (which extended even to Charles Lever's novels) was a frequent object of ridicule among journalists. Barry returns to the topic later when he describes his travels in connection with his status as landed gentleman:

I went to reside at the Trecothick estate and the Polwellan Wheal, where I found, instead of profit, every kind of pettifogging chicanery. . . . I passed over in state to our territories in Ireland, where I entertained the gentry in a style the lord-lieutenant himself could not equal; gave the fashion to Dublin (to be sure it was a beggarly, savage city in those days, and, since the time there has been a pother about the Union, and the misfortunes attending it, I have been at a loss to account for the mad praises at the old order of things, which the fond Irish patriots have invented); I say I set the fashion to Dublin, and small praise to me, for a poor place it was in those times, whatever the Irish party may say. (Pt. 2, chap. 1)

In one adroit stroke, Thackeray indirectly has his say about the Young Ireland Party and allows Barry unconsciously to deflate his own pretensions.[20]

Barry Lyndon gives free voice to Thackeray the urbane traveler as well as to Thackeray the detached political and social commentator. Simultaneously it offers further scope to his abilities as literary parodist and critic. A generic connection has been established between Barry and the hero of Fielding's *Jonathan Wild* ("the dreadful satire" mentioned at the end of the serial version of *Catherine* in connection with which the narrator, Ikey Solomons, comments that "no reader is so dull as to make the mistake of admiring, and can overlook the grand hearty contempt of the author for the character he has described"),[21] though it suits Thackeray's specific satirical purpose that his "hero" is not a professional criminal and pays lip service to the code of genteel society. Also hovering in the background of *Barry Lyndon* are Smollett's *Ferdinand Count Fathom* and *Peregrine Pickle*.[22] But whatever are its links with rogue literature on both sides of the Irish Sea, the first readers of *The Luck of Barry Lyndon* undoubtedly connected it with the heroes of Charles Lever, Samuel Lover, and other Irish novelists then in vogue. Barry himself announces at one point that "once free [of military service], with my fine person and good family, I will do what ten thousand Irish gentlemen have done before, and will marry a lady of fortune and condition" (chap. 8). To Thackeray's contemporaries, "ten thousand Irish gentlemen" meant Hardress Cregan, Valentine McClutchey, Rory O'More, Ned Corkery, Harry Lorrequer, Tom Burke, Charles O'Malley, and their rapidly proliferating literary tribe.

Thackeray certainly points us in this direction through having dedicated *The Irish Sketch Book* to Charles Lever, "a good Irishman (the hearty charity of whose visionary redcoats, some substantial personages in black might imitate to advantage) . . . a friend from whom I have received a hundred acts of kindness and cordial hospitality." The original version of this dedication, which he cut down for publication, says more about Lever's popularity:

> It was pleasant in travelling through the country to see in a thousand humble windows the familiar pink wrapper which covers the gallant adventures of Harry Lorrequer and Tom Burke; to hear their merits canvassed by rich and poor; and to find that there was, at any rate, one subject in Ireland about which parties were disposed to agree. While political patriots are exposing the wrongs under which the people labour, and telling them as in duty bound to quarrel for their rights, you have found a happy neutral ground, whither you lead them to repose between their quarrels, and where you keep a nation in good humour.
>
> In the honour of their craft, all literary men are surely bound to admire *your* kind of patriotism and its effects.[23]

Indeed, when he first apprised James Fraser of his forthcoming novel, Thackeray wrote: "I want to write and illustrate it, and as you see how Harry Lorrequer succeeds both in the Dublin Magazine & out of it, why should not my story of BARRY-LYNN (or by what name so ever it may be called) answer in as well as out of Regina."[24]

As happened more than once with Thackeray, admiration and envy are compounded with mockery as *Barry Lyndon* develops, Lever becoming more a butt than a model. Superficially Barry Lyndon's adventures follow the course pursued by Lever's heroes—escape from poverty, depression, and oppression in Ireland, soldiering on the continent, return to "that land of punch, priests and potatoes," as Harry Lorrequer calls it, capped by an affluent marriage. However, as Thackeray tells the story, Lorrequer's high spirits are somewhat dampened; his military bravado is undercut, and his sentimentality is purged with an acid shower bath. This antiromantic approach to the kind of material that had offered all too ample leeway for Irish gusto and capacity for exaggeration is anticipated in the omnibus review "A Box of Novels" that Thackeray published in *Fraser's* along with the second installment of *Barry Lyndon*.

In his article Thackeray sets out to correct some of the stereotyped notions held by the English with respect to the Irish, owing to lack of direct contact with them. He denies, in refutation of popular representations of them, that the Irish are unvaryingly gay and high-spirited either in their writing or in real life. "All Irish stories are sad, all humorous Irish songs are sad," he declares;

"there is never a burst of laughter excited by them but, as I fancy, tears are near at hand; and from *Castle Rackrent* downwards, every Hibernian tale I have ever read is sure to leave a woeful tender impression."[25] Moreover, Thackeray discovers this plaintive note not only in a serious writer like William Carleton and a melodramatic one like Gerald Griffin, but even in so basically humorous a one as Lever. One understands, therefore, why Barry Lyndon's gaiety proves to be merely on the surface, with an undercurrent of melancholy. In other ways Thackeray drives home his point by exaggeration. He makes Barry sentimental to the degree of mawkishness; with his tendency to burst into tears over memories of his land, people, mother, and family, and his histrionic emotionalism over the death of his son Bryan rivals Dickens at his most lachrymose.

Thackeray finds the vaudeville Irishmen then enjoying wide popularity partially to blame for the spread of false ideas about Dubliners. The success of such farces as *The Irishman in London,* he complains, has "led Cockneys to suppose . . . that Paddy was in a perpetual whirl of high spirits and whiskey; for ever screeching and whopping mad songs and wild jokes; a being entirely devoid of artifice and calculation."[26] For the benefit of those to whom Handy Andy and such *naïfs* represented the typical Son of Erin, he offers Sheridan's Sir Lucius O'Trigger as a stage character closer to life—a complete hypocrite, "and his fun no more real than his Irish estate." Sir Charles Lyndon may mistakenly address Barry as "my artless Irish rustic" (chap. 14), but Fitz-Boodle is not so taken in, nor are we likely to be, as we see what unscrupulous, deep-laid intrigues Barry is capable of.

Barry Lyndon is Thackeray's "real Irishman" in contrast with the "sham Irishman" he denounces in his review. He holds novelists as responsible as farce writers and actors for the distorted image, and certain details of Barry's character and adventures were intended to offset in particular the Lever-Lover kind of Irish hero with whom his readers had grown familiar. Thackeray was especially amused at the stolid incorruptibility of Lever's young men: "there is no reader of Mr. Lever's tales but must admire the extreme, almost woman-like delicacy of the author, who amidst all the wild scenes through which he carries his characters; and with all the outbreaks of spirits and fun, never writes a sentence that is not entirely pure." Moreover, life does nothing to quench the "spirits and fun" of Lever's heroes. Like Barry Lyndon, Lever's Harry Lorrequer is "now—alas that I should say it—somewhat in the 'sere and yellow'" though looking back nostalgically over his salad days.

However, as Harry remembers these times, "I gained all my earlier experiences of life in very pleasant company—highly enjoyable at the time, and with matter for charming souvenirs long after."[27]

The men and women with whom Barry Lyndon mingles, it has already been suggested, are not "very pleasant company," and "charming" is hardly the word for his scandal-ridden past. Lever's heroes, besides, are more patriotic than Barry Lyndon. Lorrequer recalls with fervor his return to Cork with His Majesty's 4th Regiment after eight years of war, "the tattered flag of the regiment proudly waving over our heads, and not a man among us whose warm heart did not bound behind a Waterloo medal." As for that soldier in spite of himself, Barry Lyndon: "I am not going to give any romantic narrative of the Seven Years' War. At the close of it, the Prussian army, so renowned for its disciplined valour, was officered and under-officered by native Prussians, it is true, but was composed for the most part of men hired or stolen, like myself, from almost every nation in Europe. The deserting to and fro was prodigious" (chap. 7).

In his preface to *Charles O'Malley*, Lever accounts for the prominence of warfare in his fiction: "When . . . my publishers asked me could I write a story in the Lorrequer vein, in which active service and military adventure could figure more prominently than mere civilian life, and where the achievements of a British army might form the staple of the narrative—when this question was propounded to me, I was ready to reply: Not one—but fifty." And he came close to keeping his word. The success in turn of *Charles O'Malley* led Lever to attempt in *Tom Burke of "Ours,"* the particular novel that Thackeray reviewed for *Fraser's*, "a great tableau of the Empire from its gorgeous celebrations in Paris to its numerous achievements on the field of battle." In protest against "the Lorrequer vein," Thackeray chose to reverse the proportion of civilian to army life.

Later on, in one of his Punch's Prize Novels, "Phil Fogarty. A Tale of the Fighting Onety-oneth. By Harry Rollicker," Thackeray caricatured Lorrequer's unabashed swagger, braggadocio, and name-dropping.[28] In *Barry Lyndon* he simply has his blatantly unmilitaristic hero remark: "Were these memoirs not characterized by truth, and did I deign to utter a single word for which my own personal experience did not give me the fullest authority, I might easily make myself the hero of some strange and popular adventures, and, after the fashion of novel-writers, introduce my reader to the great characters of this remarkable time" (chap. 5). Barry reminds his readers that a poor, lowly corporal, such as he was, is not generally privileged to enter into the company of commanding officers. Nevertheless:

> I saw, I promise you, some very good company on the *French* part, for their regiments of Lorraine and Royal Cravate were charging us all day; and in *that* sort of *mêlée* high and low are pretty equally received. I hate bragging, but I cannot help saying that I made a very close acquaintance with the colonel of the Cravates; for I drove my bayonet into his body, and finished off a poor little ensign, so young, slender, and small that a blow from my pigtail would have dispatched him, I think, in place of the butt of my musket, with which I clubbed him down. I killed, besides, four more officers and men, and in the poor ensign's pocket found a purse of fourteen louis-d'or, and a silver box of sugar-plums, of which the former present was very agreeable to me. If people would tell their stories of battle in this simple way, I think the cause of truth would not suffer by it. (Chap. 5)

So much for Lorrequer's gaiety under fire, his picnics on the battlefield with provender ransacked from corpses, and his numerous decorations by distinguished generals for bravery in bloodless battles.[29]

The military satire in *Barry Lyndon* was motivated by Thackeray's objection to what he called "the pugnacious and horse-racious parts of the Lorrequer novels." He lodged a similar complaint in his review article against £. *S. D.*, Samuel Lover's "romance of war, and love, and fun, and sentiment, and intrigue, and escape, and rebellion . . . with war's alarms ringing in the ear the whole way, and we are plunged into sea-fights, and land-fights, and shipwrecks, and chases, and conspiracies without end." With Lover's story Thackeray in addition made fun of its historical setting in the time of Bonnie Prince Charlie. This was a period, Thackeray remarks, "when men, instead of bandying compliments and congées in Belgrave Square, flying thither in hack-cabs, with white kid gloves on, and comfortable passports in their pockets, turned out on the hillside, sword in hand, and faced Cumberland's thundering dragoons, and saw the backs of Johnny Cope's grenadiers. . . . *O vanitas!* O woeful change of times! Who dies for kings now?" That Thackeray had his tongue in his cheek is obvious from *Barry Lyndon,* subtitled "A Romance of the Last Century" in its first version, and set, in fact, in the very period of Lover's romance. Yet what does Barry choose to remember about these fateful times? "We wore silk and embroidery then," he recollects happily. "Then it took a man of fashion a couple of hours to make his toilette, and he could shew some taste and genius in the selecting it. What a blaze of splendour was a drawing room, or an opera, of a gala night! What sums of money were lost and won at the delicious faro-table! . . . Gentlemen are dead and gone. The fashion has now turned upon your soldiers and sailors, and I grow moody and sad when I think of thirty years ago" (pt. 2, chap. 1).

In £. S. D., Lover defines the character type that Thackeray imitated and satirized in *Barry Lyndon*—the Irish Heir—and also indicates the type of "luck" he enjoys. "There is nothing to be said of a man who inherits a fortune smoothly, lives a regular respectable life, and dies decently and quietly in his bed," asserts Lover in his preface. "Out on all such! Were the world made up of these, what an unromantic world it would be! As Irish Heirs seldom have the luck to be such uninteresting persons as those who have raised my indignation, they are heirs after an author's heart; and as their patrimonies mostly departed with their forefathers, waifs and strays and money found must be considered legitimate Irish Heirships." The fortunes of Thackeray's fugitive hero are indeed repaired, like those of Lover's pauper-heir Ned Corkery, by "money found" in the viable form of a wealthy young lady, except that Thackeray has Barry win by guile what good-hearted Ned wins by selfless courage and devotion.[30]

Ever the eclectic as well as the antiromantic, Thackeray took what appealed to him in the Irish novel of his time—its humor, liveliness and adventure—while rejecting its chauvinism and toning down its excess euphoria. He also brought discipline to a genre that was threatening to run amuck. Some of the tales in his "Box of Novels" he found too wanton in their picaresqueness. While praising £. S. D., for example, for its narrative interest and descriptive power, he found fault with its author's garrulousness, as well as with the proliferation of incident and too frequent change of scene in the novel. No wonder that he has Barry remark with unusual peremptoriness, as he is about to return to the "ould sod":

> I find I have already filled up nearly half of the space which is usually allotted to modern authors for their books, and yet a vast deal of the most interesting portion of my history remains to be told, *viz.*, that which describes my sojourn in the kingdoms of England and Ireland, and the great part I played there; moving among the most illustrious of the land, myself not the least distingushed of the brilliant circle. In order to give due justice to this portion of my memoirs, then—which is more important than my foreign adventures can be (though I could fill volumes with interesting descriptions of the latter),—I shall cut short the account of my travels in

Europe, and of my success at the Continental courts, in order to speak of what befell me at home. Suffice it to say that there is not a capital in Europe, except the beggarly one of Berlin, where the young Chevalier de Balibarri was not known and admired; and where he has not made the brave, the high-born, and the beautiful talk of him. (Chap. 14)

With Lever's stories, Thackeray admitted to enjoying the Irish episodes, but concluded that these novels "show no art of construction; it is the good old place of virtue triumphant to the end of the chapter, vice being woefully demolished some pages previously."[31] The chapter titles of *Barry Lyndon* in themselves indicate the structure that Thackeray imposed on the traditionally loose-woven rogue's tale: "In which the hero Makes a false start in the Genteel World"; "More Runs of Luck"; "In which the Luck goes against Barry"; "Barry provides for his family and attains the Height of his Luck"; "Barry appears at the summit of Fortune"; "In which the Luck of Barry Lyndon begins to Waver," and so forth. The plot thus turns upon the rise and fall of the "hero," his changes of fortune, to which all the episodes contribute their part.

As Thackeray contrives Barry Lyndon's history, his "luck," including his marrying a lady of fortune, proves his undoing. This is among the contrivances by which Thackeray upsets the formula of the popular Irish novel, along with imposing a "tragic" plot on comic subject matter. In keeping with his antiheroic nature, Barry's fate takes a series of devious turns that make mockery of his ambitions. Just as Barry is constantly making virtue out of vice, it is fitting that when he thinks his fortunes are on the rise, they are actually on the downgrade. It is this series of upsets that keeps his villainy on the side of the comic and makes him, to our eyes, a worm instead of a snake. When Barry leaves the military service, he proclaims as his goal in life: "I sighed to be out of slavery. I knew I was born to make a figure in the world" (chap. 8). As it turns out, his moves to cast off his chains only fasten them on more securely. He does succeed in wiving it wealthily in Dublin, but this marriage leads him into debt, poverty, and imprisonment. His denunciation of women as the cause of all the mischief in the world proves only too true in his case, for the sons of his childhood sweetheart, Nora Brady, and his wife, Lady Lyndon, help to bring about his downfall. The formula for the "luck" of Barry Lyndon, as it develops, is that whenever fortune appears to be *with* him (the supposed killing of Captain Quin, escape from the army, the wooing of the Countess Ida, the attempted blackmail of de Magny, the wooing and winning of Lady Lyndon, running for Parliament, establishment in London society, the "deaths" of Lord Poynings and Viscount Bullingdon), it is really *against* him. Barry observes of the intrigues at the court of Ludwigslust: "Those sharp tools with which great people cut out their enterprise are generally broken in the using" (chap. 13). However, he is too obtuse to apply this wisdom to his own situation, and his own arrows fly back in his face. "Alas! we are the sport of destiny," exclaims Barry in one of his sententious moments. "When I consider upon what small circumstances all the great events of my life have turned, I can hardly believe myself to have been anything but a puppet in the hands of Fate, which has played its most fantastic tricks upon me" (chap. 4).

An antiheroic hero, a comic figure with a tragic fate, Barry Lyndon is the most deliberately paradoxical character in the Thackerayan cabinet of oddities. Compounding the curious mixture, he is a moral fool given to offering moral advice to readers, presumably because he deems it obligatory to do so. "These books were evidently written before the useful had attained its present detestable popularity," Titmarsh had written of the collection of tales that diverted him in a Galway inn. "There is nothing useful *here,* that's certain: and a man will be puzzled to extract a precise moral out of the 'Adventures of Mr. James Freeny'; or out of the legends in the Hibernian Tales." This prompts him to ask the perennial question, "But are we to reject all things that have not a moral tacked to them? 'Is there any moral shut within the bosom of the rose?'" And he has his reply ready: "And yet as the same noble poet sings (giving a smart slap to the utility people the while), 'useful applications lie in art and nature,' and every man may find a moral suited to his mind in them; or, if not a moral, an occasion for moralising."[32]

Barry for one proves particularly adept at finding in his sordid past many "a moral suited to his mind":

> Some prudish persons may affect indigation at the frankness of these confessions, but Heaven pity them! Do you suppose that any man who has lost or won a hundred thousands pounds at play will not take the advantages which his neighbour enjoys? They are all the same. But it is only the clumsy fool who *cheats,* who resorts to the vulgar expedients of cogged dice and cut cards. Such a man is sure to go wrong some time or other, and is not fit to play in the society of gallant gentlemen; and my advice to people who see such a vulgar person at his pranks is, of course, to back him while he plays, but never—never to have anything to do with him. (Chap. 9)

> I do not defend this practice of letter-opening in private life, except in cases of the most urgent necessity, when we must follow the

examples of our betters, the statesmen of all Europe, and, for the sake of a great good, infringe a little matter of ceremony. My Lady Lyndon's letters were none the worse for being opened, and a great deal the better, the knowledge obtained from the perusal of some of her multifarious epistles enabling me to become intimate with her character in a hundred ways. (Chap. 17)

His ingenuity at making a virtue of opportunism is matched by his worldly code of ethics—on life adjustment, for example: "Many a gallant man of the highest honour is often not proof against these [calamities of life], and has been known to despair over a bad dinner, or to be cast down at a ragged-elbow coat. *My* maxim is to bear all, to put up with water if you cannot get burgundy, and if you have no velvet, to be content with frieze. But burgundy and velvet are the best, *bien entendu,* and the man is a fool who will not seize the best when the scramble is open" (chap. 7). Or, on speculation as a way to wealth: "One never is secure in these cases; and when one considers the time and labour spent, the genius, the anxiety, the outlay of money required, the multiplicity of bad debts that one meets with (for dishonourable rascals are to be found at the play-table, as every where else in the world)—I say, for my part, the profession is a bad one; and, indeed, scarcely ever met a man who, in the end, profited by it" (chap. 9). And eventually on reward and punishment: "And now, if any people should be disposed to think my history immoral (for I have heard some assert that I was a man who never deserved that so much prosperity should fall to my share), I will beg those cavillers to do the favour to read the conclusion of my adventures, when they will see that it was no great prize that I had won, and that wealth, splendour, thirty thousand per annum, and a seat in parliament, are often purchased at too dear a rate, when one has to buy those enjoyments at the price of personal liberty, and saddled with the charge of a troublesome wife" (pt. 2, chap. 2).

Barry's slippery life is made to yield its "useful applications" in the open-ended manner that Titmarsh had suggested to readers of the adventures of the free booter James Freeny "[in which] one may see the evil of drinking, another the harm of horse-racing, another of the danger attendant on early marriage, a fourth the exceeding inconvenience as well as hazard of the heroic high-wayman's life."[33] But in line with those "fable books, where you are obliged to accept the story with the inevitable moral corollary that *will* stick close to it," that Titmarsh recalls from his youthful reading,[34] Barry offers a bonus in the form of advice of the "don't steal—it will land you in jail" sort. So his creator manages to attack platitudinous morals while baiting the type of reader who expects them. The mess that Barry makes of his own life sufficiently points up how much easier it is to preach "wisdom" than to practice it.

Not the least of the feats of bravado practiced by Barry is his setting himself up, with his scrappy education, to be a writer. Yet, however unreliable he may be as a moral guide, his literary credo is not far removed from that of his creator. He too can put down sentimentality: "If the truth must be told—and every word of this narrative of my life is of the most sacred veracity—my passion for Nora began in a very vulgar and unromantic way," he recalls of his first love. "I did not save her life . . . I did not behold her by moonlight playing on the guitar, or rescue her from the hands of ruffians, as Alonso does Lindamira in the novel" (chap. 1). This allusion to the world of Mme de Scudéry, however incongruous, is Barry's way of reminding us that he is a flesh-and-blood, not an idealized, man. Where he does indulge himself in poetry and flowery rhetoric, for purposes of wooing, it is with a cynical calculation, about which he is characteristically blunt to the reader. He is quite open, for example, about his motive for pursuing the Countess Ida: "Was it on account of her personal charms or qualities? No. She was quite white, thin, short-sighted, tall and awkward, and my taste is quite the contrary. . . . It was her estate I made love to" (chap. 11). As for his future wife, because "authors are accustomed to describe the persons of the ladies with whom their heroes fall in love . . . I perhaps should say a word or two respecting the charms of Lady Lyndon. . . . truth compels me to say that there was nothing divine about her at all" (chap. 14). Candor, truth to life, freedom from illusion—these make up Thackeray's code as a writer no less than that of Barry Lyndon, even if Barry fails to apply it to himself as well as he does to others.

In other ways, as we have seen, Thackeray makes his hero something of a surrogate for himself as author. Barry refuses to write about what he has not known at first hand, so he forswears battle scenes, however much his readers may expect them. Though he has more than a trace of the Irish blarney in his composition, he generally avoids the temptation toward garrulousness and the telling of pointless stories. Among his other Thackerayan characteristics are his penchant for the memoir form and attraction to primary sources—eyewitnesses, letters, documents—even if in his own case he is willing to stoop to spying and intercepting mail to suit his purposes. And both Thackeray and Barry Lyndon, be it added, are iconoclasts. Thackeray then carries his literary joke to the point of spoofing his own chosen vocation, making his hero-villain, among other things, a comic analogue of the society novelist and social historian.

Through George Savage Fitz-Boodle, who is more conspicuous in the serial version of *Barry Lyndon* than in the later revision, Thackeray mocks his other literary roles—the editor and the commentator on human affairs. In his own "Confessions" contributed to *Fraser's Magazine,* a record of youthful indiscretions, Fitz-Boodle had written: "If I did not write with a moral purpose, and because my unfortunate example may act wholesomely upon other young men of fashion, and induce them to learn wisdom, I should not say a single syllable about . . . all the blunders I committed, nor the humiliation I suffered."[35] With a similar rationalization he offers up Barry as another "unfortunate example." By now Fitz-Boodle has mellowed from man of the world to one of those "rigid moralists" whom Barry himself scoffs at. Thackeray utilizes him as another sop to the literal-minded (the "judicious reader" to whom Charlotte Brontë was to refer at the end of *Shirley,* "putting on his spectacles to look for the moral"). Fitz-Boodle's interpolations vary from pedantic ("Mr. Barry's story *may* be correct; but we find in the autobiography of Captain Freeny, that it was not he, but a couple of associates, who were acquitted from a bribe of five guineas distributed amongst the jury" [chap. 4]) to obtuse ("In another part of his memoir Mr. Barry will be found to describe this mansion as one of the most splendid palaces in Europe, but this is a practice not unusual with his nation" [chap. 1]) to simply gratuitous ("It never seems to have struck Mr. Barry that had he not represented himself to be a man of fortune none of the difficulties here described would have happened to him" [chap. 4]). In a discourse to his readers toward the end, he manages at once to pique their prurient curiosity: "It must be manifest to the observer of human nature that the honourable subject of these memoirs has never told the whole truth about himself, and, as his career comes to a close, perhaps is less to be relied on than ever. We have been obliged to expunge long chapters about his town and Paris life, which were by no means edifying; to omit numbers of particulars of his domestic career, which he tells with much *naïveté*" and to hit them over the heads with the "message" of the book:

> But though, in one respect, he communicates a great deal too much, he by no means tells all, and it must be remembered that we are only hearing his, the autobiographer's side of the story. Even that is sufficient to shew that Mr. Barry Lyndon is as unprincipled a personage

as ever has figured at the head of a history, and as the public will
persist in having a moral appended to such tales, we beg here re-
spectfully to declare that we take the moral of the story of Barry
Lyndon, Esquire, to be—that worldly success is by no means the
consequence of virtue; that if it is effected by honesty sometimes, it is
attained by selfishness and roguery still oftener; and that our anger
at seeing rascals prosper and good men frequently unlucky, is
founded on a gross and unreasonable idea of what good fortune
really is. (Pt. 2, chap. 2)

This sport with readers seems to have missed its point, both with
those who found the story shocking, even with Fitz-Boodle's moral
balm, and with those (including some of the present day) who have
objected to Fitz-Boodle's comments as trite and obvious. It is easy to
understand why, in the shorter and tighter version that appeared
almost ten years later in the *Miscellanies,* Fitz-Boodle obtrudes
much less and Barry is allowed to speak for himself more—so that
one reviewer could observe: "The book has a moral . . . but it is
kept in its proper place."[36] If the early Fitz-Boodle may be taken as
Thackeray's "unfortunate example" of a commentator—a super-
fluous one—by the time the revised version of Barry's memoir
came out, he had demonstrated in the novels that followed the
proper function of the "intrusive" narrator—to expose those
whose deceit is not so obvious as that of the Chevalier de Balibarri
né Redmond Barry, and to point out what is *not* evident from
appearances.

"Our anger at seeing rascals prosper" is properly diminished as
we recognize that the luck of Barry Lyndon proves to be misfortune. Along with his lady of fortune he loses his estate, which reverts eventually to Lady Lyndon's heirs. "The trees in Brackton
Park are all about forty years old," Fitz-Boodle informs us in a
postscript, "and the Irish property is rented in exceedingly small
farms to many thousands of the thrifty, cleanly, orderly, loyal
peasantry of Ireland, who still entertain the stranger with stories of
the daring, and the devilry, and the wickedness, and the fall of
Barry Lyndon." Barry's story then becomes part of the public domain to the tenants of the rack-renters, along with the "Galway
Night's Entertainments" and other lore of Hibernia. We are reminded of the Irish tendency toward hyperbole by the narrator of
The Virginians, who recalls:

> My happy chance in early life led me to become intimate with a
> respectable person who was born in a certain island, which is pro-
> nounced to be the first gem of the ocean by, no doubt, impartial
> judges of maritime jewellery. The stories which that person im-

parted to me regarding his relatives who inhabited the gem above mentioned, were such as to make my young blood curdle with horror to think that there should be so much wickedness in the world. Every crime which you can think of; the entire Ten Commandments broken in a general smash: such rogueries as Thurtell or Turpin scarce ever perpetrated;—were by my informant accurately remembered and freely related, respecting his nearest kindred to any one who chose to hear him. . . . The family of Atreus was as nothing compared to the race of O'What-d'ye-call-'em, from which my friend sprang; but no power on earth would, of course, induce me to name the country whence he came. (Chap. 38)

Our hero is effectively put down by George Warrington who, toward the end of this same novel, gives us a passing glimpse of "A notorious adventurer, gambler, and *spadassin,* calling himself the Chevalier de Barry, and said to be a relative of the mistress of the French king, but afterwards turning out to be an Irishman of low extraction," who "was in constant attendance upon the Earl and Countess [of Castlewood] at this time, and conspicuous for the audacity of his lies, the extravagance of his play, and somewhat mercenary gallantry towards the other sex, and a ferocious bravo courage, which, however, failed him on one or two awkward occasions, if common report said true" (chap. 92).

In *The Book of Snobs,* Barry and his countrymen are eventually assimilated among the "small great" of the world. "The Irish snobbishness develops itself not in pride," Thackeray wrote here, "so much as in servility, and mean admirations and trumpery imitations of their neighbours." Moreover, "Two penny magnificence, indeed, exists all over Ireland and may be considered as the great characteristic of the snobbishness of that country.[37] Barry Lyndon, the very model of the "two penny" hero, takes his place in Thackeray's long procession of those who "meanly admire mean things."[38] As a representative of vulgar conceptions of gentility, Barry ultimately crosses national borders. It is most significant that he is more interested in *looking* like a gentleman than in *being* one. As he candidly admits: "The great and rich are welcomed, smiling, up the grand staircase of the world; the poor but aspiring must clamber up the wall, or push and struggle up the back stair, or *pardi,* crawl through any of the conduits of the house, never mind how foul and narrow, that lead to the top. . . . What is life good for but honour? and that is so indispensable, that we should attain it any how" (chap. 11). No wonder that he is dazzled by the mere accoutrements of class, such as clothes and jewels, and knows the price of everything but the value of nothing as he sets about "improving" Hackton Hall, the ancient residence of the Lyndon family, and gets swindled for his pains. To our persistent questioning of his pretensions to aristocracy he has a ready retort: "I warrant the legends of the Heralds' Colleges are not more authentic than mine was" (chap. 10). We are left to infer that ours is a world where appearance is generally taken for reality, as one of Thackeray's early masters, Isaac Watts, had warned,[39] and where bogus and authentic nobility are pretty much interchangeable.

Such certainly is the purport of Fitz-Boodle's peroration in the original version ("Is it the good always who ride in gold coaches, and the wicked who go to the workhouse? Is a humbug never preferred before a capable man? Does the world always reward merit, never raise mediocrity to distinction?").[40] With his "story of Barry-Lynn," accordingly, Thackeray shifted to the debatable land between sin and virtue, moving up the scale of "the edifice of humanity" from the outright criminal to the demirep, from those who cheat others to those who also delude themselves. More to the point, however, are Fitz-Boodle's concluding words to his readers, for here we may be sure that he speaks for the true begetter of Barry Lyndon in forecasting things to come:

> If this be true of the world, those persons who find their pleasure or get their livelihood by describing its manners and the people who live in it are bound surely to represent to the best of their power life as it really appears to them to be; not to foist off upon the public figures pretending to be delineations of human nature,—gay and agreeable cut-throats, otto-of-rose murderers, amiable hackney-coachmen, Prince Rodolphos and the like, being representatives of beings that never have or could have existed. At least, if not bounden to copy nature, they are justified in trying; and hence in describing not only what is beautiful, but what is ill-favoured too, faithfully, so that each may appear as like as possible to nature. It is as right to look at a beauty as at a hunchback; and, if to look, to describe too: nor can the most prodigious genius improve upon the original. Who knows, then, but the old style of Molière and Fielding, who drew from nature, may come into fashion again, and replace the terrible, the humorous, always the genteel impossible now in vogue? Then, with the sham characters, the sham *moral* may disappear. The one is a sickly humbug as well as the other. I believe for my part Hogarth's pictures of "Marriage à la Mode" in Trafalgar Square to be more moral and more beautiful than West's biggest heroical piece, or Angelica Kaufmann's most elegant allegory!

Thackeray seems to be signaling to his readers, through his alter ego, his intention to "paint" the world they know rather than artificially reconstruct the past and to replace "the genteel impossible" with the domestic and the familiar.

Thackeray does not cease his games with his audience, certainly, but he does make more conscious efforts to catch their hearts and consciences along with their pennies. Toward this end he was prompted alike by a vanity of his own and by conviction. Fitz-Boodle's question, "Does the world always reward merit, never raise mediocrity to distinction?" could well have been his own as he continued to find himself cast in the shade in favor of lesser rivals. A case in point is "The Luck of Barry Lyndon," which was widely ignored by the public and by critics alike. It received acclaim enough when it appeared in book form in America in 1853 and in its later version in the *Miscellanies* in 1856, by which time Thackeray was the celebrated author of *Vanity Fair, Pendennis, Henry Esmond,* and *The Newcomes.* Some of the praise perhaps is attributable more to hindsight than to perspicacity. "Bears the image and superscription of Thackeray, and this is enough to recommend it," wrote a reviewer in Washington, D.C.[41] According to the *Saturday Review,* it was "in some respects . . . the most characteristic and best executed of Thackeray's works."[42] One is not surprised that this tour de force was highly regarded by Thackeray's fellow writers. "And if Dickens showed the best of his power early in life, so did Thackeray the best of his intellect," proclaimed Anthony Trollope in the first extended biography.[43] "In no display of mental force did he rise above *Barry Lyndon.* I hardly know how the teller of a narrative shall hope to mount in simply intellectual faculty above the effort there made." William Dean Howells called it "the most perfect creation of Thackeray's mind . . . a stupendous feat in pure irony."[44] Such tributes testify to the appeal of *Barry Lyndon* to the connoisseur. Thackeray himself doubted its popular appeal. "My father once said to me when I was a girl: 'You needn't read *Barry Lyndon,* you won't like it,'" recalled Anne Thackeray in her introduction prepared for the Biographical Edition of the collected works. "Indeed it is scarce a book to *like,*" she continued, "but one to admire for its consummate power and mastery."[45] Her very encomium suggests why her father's miracle of rare device did not exactly grab hold of the common readers of the time—those, that is, who only know what they like and are not particularly equipped to admire virtuosity.

For sheer inventiveness *Barry Lyndon* is unsurpassed in Thackeray's canon. The creation by a genius of wide sympathies of his direct opposite, a complete egotist—self-centered, amoral, and stupid—is indeed a supreme act of imagination, but such a product by the same token cannot be very close to humanity. After this, he kept promise "not to foist off upon the public figures pretending to

be delineations of human nature,—gay and agreeable cut-throats."
By now his imagination had been stirred by a demirep closer to his
experience—a female one this time, a grisette named Mlle Pauline
who had known respectability as governess in an English household. He was also more inclined to temper scorn with compassion,
as revealed by a stray confidence to be found in one of his art
reviews contributed to *Fraser's* six months after *Barry Lyndon* had
ended its run: "I began to find the world growing more pathetic
daily, and laugh less every year of my life. Why laugh at idle hopes,
or vain purposes, or utter blundering self-confidence? Let us be
gentle with them henceforth; who knows whether there may not be
something of the sort *chez nous?*"[46]

His next novel is called in places a "comic history," but also a
"sentimental and cynical" one. It is to be a "Novel without a Hero,"
but also without a villain passing himself off for a hero. He found
his way to the general public through characters they could recognize, moving through a tangible world they knew. In the writing of
Barry Lyndon, Thackeray was even more peripatetic than his hero,
and his tale of Irish luck and cunning encompasses the Germany of
his youth, Paris, where he began it, and the Orient, where he ardu-
ously brought it to its conclusion.[47] The new novel is no less cosmopolitan, but when he first submitted it for publication, Thackeray pointedly gave it the subtitle *Pen and Pencil Sketches of English
Life.* He had some second thoughts about the main title, as we
know. Almost simultaneously with the issue of its first yellow-
covered part, his audience could read in *The Snob Papers* then appearing in *Punch:* "Man is a Drama—of Wonder and Passion . . .
Each Bosom is a Booth in Vanity Fair."[48]

1. Christmas Day 1843 to Peter Purcell, *Letters,* 2:138; original examined in
Fales Library, New York University.

2. *Irish Sketch Book,* chap. 15; *Works,* 5:403.

3. "The Luck of Barry Lyndon" ran in *Fraser's Magazine* continuously from
January through December 1844, except for October (when presumably Thackeray, who was working against deadlines, failed to supply copy). The first edition in
book form, published in America (New York: Appleton, 1853) is based on the
magazine version. It was first reprinted in England in 1856, considerably revised
(whether by Thackeray or not is unknown), tightened, and retitled (over Thackeray's objection) *The Memoirs of Barry Lyndon, Esq.* In this form it appeared both as a
separate book and as vol. 3 of Thackeray's *Miscellanies.* Subsequently most reprints
have been based upon the later version, but the two versions are intercalated (with
passages bracketed that were omitted in the second version) in the Oxford Thackeray, vol. 6. The Bison Book reprint on *The Memoirs of Barry Lyndon, Esq.,* ed.
Robert L. Morris (Lincoln: University of Nebraska Press, 1962) brings together in
an appendix many passages from *Fraser's Magazine* left out of the revision. The

more recent critical edition of *The Luck of Barry Lyndon*, ed. Martin J. Anisman (New York: New York University Press, 1970), restores (imperfectly) the text as it appeared in *Fraser's*, with the passages bracketed that were cut in the book publication. This edition, although faulty, is the fullest one easily available, and my chapter references consequently will be based upon it.

4. 24 July 1841, *Letters*, 2:29.

5. *Irish Sketch Book*, chap. 15; *Works*, 5:406.

6. Ibid., chap. 16; *Works*, 5:430.

7. Thackeray was a school friend of John Bowes Bowes, grandson of the victimized heiress, from whom he first heard of the affair (see *Letters*, 1:91.) He also had access to Jesse Foot's detailed account, *Lives of Andrew Robertson Bowes and the Countess of Strathmore* (London, 1812).

8. *Letters*, 2:139. The main point of the digression (the story is related years later to Barry by a superannuated courtesan), besides its analogy with Barry's own situation, is that it exposes his lack of moral feeling. His only reaction to this horrifying story is to remind his readers that this intrigue resulted in his leaving Ludwigslust sooner than he had expected, with the consequence that he had to terminate abruptly his pursuit of the Countess Ida.

9. "Our Portrait Gallery—No. XXIV. William Maginn, LLD," *Dublin University Magazine*, January, 1844, p. 72. The writer, Edward Kenealy, expressed deep regret that "the Hope, which in the morning of his manhood rose resplendently in the distance, and cast around his path imaginary triumphs, trophies and applause, had disappeared as he proceeded, and like the mirage of the desert, left only wretchedness and disappointment." Thackeray's comment appears in the letter to James Fraser quoted above (p. 201).

10. Captain William Jesse, *The Life of George Brummell, Esq., Commonly Called Beau Brummel* (London, 1844). Thackeray reviewed this book for the *Morning Chronicle*, 6 May 1844; rpt. in *Contributions*, pp. 31–39. "As for his wit," Thackeray wrote of Brummell, "all his compositions show prodigious pains, but likewise that he was an entire ninny." Barry writes disparagingly of the Beau from a contemporary viewpoint: "There is no elegance, no refinement, none of the chivalry of the old world, of which I form a portion. Think of the fashion of London being led by a Br—mm—ll! a nobody's son! a low creature, who can no more dance a minuet than I can talk Cherokee" (chap. 14). It is possible that Thackeray drew also upon the memoirs of Casanova, whom Barry refers to in chap. 9. (See discussion of sources by Anisman in his edition, p. 29.)

11. See above, pp. 161–62.

12. This series is made up of "Mr. and Mrs. Frank Berry," March 1843; "The Ravenswing," April–June, August–September 1843; "Denis Haggerty's Wife," October 1843; and "The [Executioner]'s Wife," November 1843.

13. "Professions. By George Fitz-Boodle. Being Appeals to the Unemployed Younger Sons of the Nobility," *Fraser's Magazine*, July 1843. This and the "Men's Wives" series are collected together with *Barry Lyndon* in *Works*, vol. 4.

14. "Drummond's Noble English Families," *Fraser's Magazine*, January 1844, pp. 25–34.

15. The reviewer of Drummond's *Histories of Noble Families* complained in passing that the science of genealogy was being widely neglected by heads of great families. Barry, on the other hand, boasts: "My uncle, like a noble gentleman as he was, knew the pedigree of every considerable family in Europe. He said it was the only knowledge befitting a gentleman; and when we were not at cards, we would pass hours over Gwillim and D'Hozier, reading the genealogies, learning the blazons, and making ourselves acquainted with the relationships of our class!" He too complains: "Alas! the noble science is going into disrepute now; so are cards, without which studies and pastimes I can hardly conceive how a man of honour can exist" (chap. 10).

Despite his emphasis upon the preservation of great heritage, the reviewer points out that "mere birth is an accident not within the control of humanity." His article concludes with a distinction pertinent to *Barry Lyndon:* "Let every one remember that a *gentleman* includes *nobility*. A *nobleman* may be made, a *gentleman* must be born so."

16. 16 March 1844; 20 March 1844; *Contributions*, pp. 1–8, 9–13.

17. *Times*, 31 January 1838; *Works* (Furniss Ed.), 12:68–74.

18. See above, p. 178.

19. August 1843, p. 242; September 1843, pp. 337–45; November 1843, pp. 615–30; December 1843, pp. 729–48. In his critical article "Jerome Paturot. With Considerations on Novels in General . . . ," which he contributed to the September issue, Thackeray took occasion to refer to "Mr. O'Connell's Irish romances," in relation to that leader's polemics. A reviewer of *The Irish Sketch Book* for an Irish journal considered Thackeray's reporting prejudiced, representing the views of "an English liberal, a thorough Cockney, a Protestant, a hater of controversy . . . and Repeal" (*Tablet*, 13 May 1843, pp. 291–92).

20. Near the time when this episode ran in *Fraser's*, Thackeray reported to the *Calcutta Star*, an Indian paper he served briefly as European political correspondent: "We have been trying to get up some sympathy for O'Connell in his durance, but the old gentleman himself put an end to any tender feelings one might have had regarding him by his outrageous comfortableness and good humour" (7 August 1844; rpt. in "Letters from a Club Arm Chair . . . ," ed. Henry Summerfield, *Nineteenth-Century Fiction* 18 [December 1963]: 218). Thackeray goes on to speak of O'Connell's attempts at conciliation among the Irish factions and his good will, despite imprisonment. He was released the following month.

21. *Fraser's Magazine*, February 1840, p. 211.

22. Thackeray reread *Peregrine Pickle* while he was composing *Barry Lyndon*, describing it in a letter as "excellent for its liveliness and spirit and wonderful for its atrocious vulgarity" (*Letters*, 2:144). Such characters as the swindling couple the Fitzsimons, whom Barry runs into on the road (chap. 4), and the pedantic German pastor whom he meets in the army (chap. 7) suggests Smollett. For the influence of *Ferdinand Count Fathom*, see Anisman, pp. 36–38. Another possible source is *The Life of Tiger Roche* that appears in a volume called *Ireland Sixty Years Since* (see *Notes and Queries*, 25 April 1936, p. 296, and Anisman, pp. 27–28).

23. Quoted by Anne Thackeray, from the manuscript then in her possession, in her introduction to *The Irish Sketch Book*, *Works*, 5:xxix.

24. 24 July 1841, *Letters*, 2:29.

25. February 1845, pp. 153–69; *Works*, 13:400.

26. Thackeray refers specifically to the actor Tyrone Power, who was virtually unrivaled during this period as a performer of Irish characters, particularly shrewd servants. He appeared on the London stage at the Haymarket, Adelphi, and Covent Garden theaters from the mid-1820s on in such roles as Murtoch Delany in *The Irishman in London*, Sir Patrick Plenipo in *The Irish Ambassador*, and Tim More, the traveling tailor, in *The Irish Lion*. He also wrote Irish farces such as *Born to Good Luck, or the Irishman's Fortune* (possibly echoed in the original title of *Barry Lyndon*).

27. Preface to *Charles O'Malley* (Dublin: William Curry, 1841), supposedly "edited" by Harry Lorrequer; Charles Lever, *The Confessions of Harry Lorrequer* (Dublin: William Curry, 1839), chap. 1.

28. *Works*, 6:489–500 (with general title changed to "Novels by Eminent Hands"). Thackeray meant the satire good-humoredly, but it strained the friendship that had existed between the two authors and led Lever to retaliate with the caricature of Thackeray as Elias Howle in *Roland Cashel*.

29. In reviewing *The Memoirs of Joseph Holt* (see above, p. 207), Thackeray praised that veteran for his accurate and vigorous descriptions of the horrors of battle and the plundering of corpses, with no attempt to flinch at actuality: "We may learn admirably to understand the character of this war by details such as these, which are told by honest Holt, as things of quite common occurrence." Barry emulates Holt's straightforwardness in his account of the Seven Years' War, though hardly the "strength, courage, and fortitude" that Thackeray also commends in this old soldier.

30. Reviewing this romance before its conclusion as a serial, Thackeray expressed a playful curiosity about its denouement. He wondered how the high-class heroine could take such a commonplace name as Corkery, and forecast that some way would be found to get her out of this predicament, either by the young people's dying before they can be married or by Ned learning that he is somebody else's son.

Thackeray proved to be right about the outcome, but failed to anticipate how it was brought about. Ned Corkery married Ellen, but takes her name. (Cf. Barry's adopting the name of Lady Lyndon.)

31. Lever himself described *The Confessions of Harry Lorrequer* as "little more than a farrago of absurd and laughable incidents" (see preface to *Charles O'Malley*).

32. *Irish Sketch Book*, chap. 15; *Works*, 5:405. Thackeray here slightly misquotes Tennyson's "The Day Dream: Moral," which had appeared for the first time in the poet's 1842 volume.

33. Ibid., pp. 405–6.

34. Ibid., p. 405.

35. "Fitz-Boodle's Confessions: Miss Löwe," *Fraser's Magazine*, October 1842; *Works*, 4:297.

36. *Saturday Review*, 27 December 1856, p. 785. The reviewer is identified by Dudley Flamm as James Fitzjames Stephen.

37. "A Little More about Irish Snobs," *Punch*, 15 August 1846; *Works*, 6:360.

38. "The Snob Royal," *Punch*, 14 March 1846; *Works*, 6:310.

39. See above (discussion of Watts), pp. 19–20.

40. For the full text of this passage, see above, p. 21.

41. *National Era*, 3 February 1853, p. 18.

42. Fitzjames Stephen's review (see p. 220 and n. 36).

43. Anthony Trollope, *Thackeray*, English Men of Letters (London: Macmillan, 1879), p. 18.

44. Howells, "Thackeray," *My Literary Passions* (New York: Harper, 1895), p. 102. Quoted in introduction to *Barry Lyndon*, ed. Charles Elbert Rhodes (New York: Gregg, 1920).

45. *Works*, 4:xxxiii.

46. "Picture Gossip," *Fraser's Magazine*, June 1845; *Works*, 13:450.

47. Here and there Thackeray manages to intrude references to the Eastern voyage that resulted in the book *From Cornhill to Grand Cairo*, published in the same year. During his sojourn in Ludwigslust, for example, Barry is accompanied sultan-like by a negro boy, Zamor, habited like a Turk, and his pavilion is "fitted up in the Eastern manner very splendid" (chap. 11). Back home in Ireland, Lord Tiptoff "issued his mandates as securely as if he had been the Grand Turk, and the Tippletonians no better than so many slaves of his will" (pt. 2, chap. 1). This exotic journey enters more subliminally into *Vanity Fair*, as will be brought out in the next chapter.

48. "Club Snobs, III," *Punch*, 16 January 1847; *Works*, 6:440. In its original appearance in *Punch*, this sketch is preceded by a squib entitled "The Triumph of Pantomime" illustrated with a clown figure, relating to the opening of Parliament, with the legend "Lord John Russell as *Harlequin*, jumping through the House of Commons hoop and sticking halfway, when Peel as *Pantaloon* comes behind him and pushes him through."

Part Three

"THE PUNCH CONNEXION"
The Moralist of the Booths

VANITY FAIR; OR, THE MYSTERIES OF MAYFAIR

Chapter Eight

A SPECIAL PRESENTATION COPY OF THE FIRST issue of *Vanity Fair* in book form that Thackeray gave to an aristocratic friend bore on its inside cover a sketch drawn by the author depicting Punch in livery handing out the book with a bow.[1] So he called attention to its origins— evident enough to the growing number of readers who followed it initially through its part publication. As the first of Thackeray's "independent" novels—published, that is, separately rather than in the pages of a magazine—it marks an important milestone in his career, but in the yellow-wrappered form in which it first emerged, it obviously had not fallen far from the Mahogany Tree.[2] In its first version, the title of *Vanity Fair* was set in twig-shaped capitals recalling the first masthead of *Punch*. The grotesque illustrations and decorated initials resembled those that had loomed up before the eyes of subscribers to *Punch's Almanack*. Nor could the clown figure along with the framework of the children's pantomime and puppet show come as a surprise to those who had been with this magazine from its beginnings. "Pantomime . . . may be considered as the natural form of the visible language,—literature being taken as the artificial. This is the most primitive, as well as the most comprehensive of all," proclaimed the first number of *Punch; or, The London Charivari.* "Indeed, if we consider for a moment that all existence is but a Pantomime, of which Time is the harlequin changing to-day into yesterday, summer into winter, youth into old age, and life into death, and we but the clowns who bear the kicks and buffets of the scene, we cannot fail to desire the general cultivation of an art

which constitutes the very existence of life itself."[3] At the same
time, these opening words of the debut number warned subscribers
not to be misled by the title into "a belief that we have no other
intention than the amusement of the thoughtful crowd." The
Merry Master Punch may have a traditional reputation as a creature of "a rude and boisterous mirth," the editor notes, but "when
we have seen him parading in the glories of his motley, flourishing
his baton . . . in time with his own unrivalled discord, by which he
seeks to win the attention and admiration of the crowd, what visions of graver puppetry have passed before our eyes!"[4]

Graver puppetry indeed. In reviewing Eugène Sue's *The Mysteries
of Paris,* the future stage manager likened the elemental appeal of
innocence threatened by villainy as dramatized in this thriller to
"that exciting contest between the white-robed angel of good and
the black principle of evil, which, as children we have seen awfully
delineated in the galanty-show, under the personifications of the
devil and the baker."[5] He would be as a child again: "And the
subject *is* interesting, let us say what we will: if galanty-shows are
not now what they were some scores of years since, that is: still is it a
stirring and exciting theme." To be sure, in Thackeray's version the
white robe is not spotless, and the black one is greyed, but what he
was to refer to as "that strange and awful struggle of good and
wrong which takes place in our hearts and in the world" renews
itself in *Vanity Fair.* Of another French writer, the dramatist Scribe,
he complained, as we have noticed, that "in his hands [characters]
are 'marionettes' to be shifted about at his pleasure: without character, colour, or physiognomy."[6] As implied in the curtain speech
that provides the prologue to *Vanity Fair,* such criticism was not
leveled at this puppet master, whose dolls "have given satisfaction
to the very best company in this empire."[7] Furthermore, "The famous little Becky Puppet has been pronounced to be uncommonly
flexible in the joints, and lively on the wire; the Amelia doll, though
it has a smaller circle of admirers, has yet been carved and dressed
with the greatest care by the artist." In reviewing Scribe he accused
that popular comedian of turning history into "a sad farce," and of
bringing "art into contempt" by his flippancy. "If any subject might
thus be trifled with," he objected, "fictitious writing would cease to
be regarded as a medium of truth of any kind. Fiction should
assume the cap and bells, and Imagination go out as a pantomime
clown."[8] Exactly. What he learned from Reybaud and other masters of "comic philosophy" was confirmed by his colleagues around
the Mahogany Tree who convinced him that the Merry Master
Punch can be "a teacher of no mean pretensions."[9]

The various "performances" promised by the manager-author in his curtain speech also bear a close relationship to the "Heads" announced in the opening number of *Punch* and maintained by subsequent issues: Politics ("with no party prejudices"); Fashions ("information on the movements of the Fashionable World" furnished by Mrs. Punch, who is acquainted with the "elite"); and Police News ("under the direction of an experienced nobleman"). Along with the serious business of life, Master Punch also gives due attention to its recreative side, as subsumed under the Fine Arts, Music and the Drama, Sporting, and Facetiae. In *Vanity Fair,* accordingly, we are offered "laughing and the contrary, smoking, cheating, fighting, dancing, and fiddling . . . bullies pushing about, bucks ogling the women, knaves picking pockets, policemen on the lookout." Thus at the outset we are led to expect an amalgam of politics, social life, crime, and sport, and an admixture of the serious and the humorous. The "scenes of all sorts" presumably are intended to meet all wants and needs: "some dreadful combats" for those interested in diplomacy or its continuation on the battlefield; some "grand and lofty horseriding" for the sportsmen in the audience; "some scenes of high life" for the fashionables and their hangers-on; for ordinary folk, "some of very middling indeed." In addition there is "some love making for the sentimental," "some light comic business" for the light-minded, and the artistic should be pleased with the assurance that "the whole [is] accompanied by appropriate scenery, and brilliantly illuminated with the Author's own candles."

Whatever the pretensions of *Punch,* its "light comic business" was undoubtedly what drew most readers. "Ah! . . . nothing now succeeds unless it's in the comic line," complains Mr. Cobbington, the fictitious bookseller in G. W. M. Reynolds's *The Mysteries of London*—which in going about its night business is not without its own lighter moments:

> "We have comic Latin grammars, and comic Greek grammars; indeed I don't know but what English grammar, too, is a comedy altogether [continues Cobbington]. All our tragedies are made into comedies by the way they are performed; and no work sells without comic illustrations to it. I have brought out several new comic works which have been very successful. For instance 'The Comic Wealth of Nations': 'The Comic Parliamentary Speeches'; 'The Comic Report of the Poor Law Commissioners,' with an Appendix containing the 'Comic Dietary Scale,' and the 'Comic Distresses of the Industrious Population.' I even propose to bring out a 'Comic Whole Duty of Man.' All these books will sell well: they do admirably for the nurseries of the children of the aristocracy. In fact they are as good as manuals and text-books."[10]

Reynolds's mouthpiece could well be describing some of the *facetiae* advertised in the monthly parts of *Vanity Fair*, such as Percival Leigh's *Comic Latin Grammar* and *Comic English Grammar*. Corresponding to the "Comic Wealth of Nations" is Douglas Jerrold's *Twiddlethumb Town*, concerned with "the speculations, sayings and doings of the Twiddlethumblings—their social and political condition—their customs and manners."[11] One of Thackeray's closest friends among the *Punch* humorists was Gilbert Abbott A'Beckett, whose specialty was the illustrated comic textbook. Himself a barrister and presumably knowing whereof he spoke, A'Beckett manages in *The Comic Blackstone* (1846) to make the law an ass in a manner worthy of W. S. Gilbert after him. As he makes darkness of Blackstone in this book, he makes light of Hume and Lingard in *The Comic History of England* (1847), an unbuttoned chronicle extending from the landing of Julius Caesar and the Roman legions through the reign of George III. Convinced that the "food is certainly not the most wholesome which is the heaviest and least digestible," A'Beckett is determined "to blend amusement with instruction by serving up in as palatable a shape as he could, the facts of English history." His device of a children's primer for adults is suggested immediately by the woodcut on the title page representing "Clio Instructing the Young British Lion in History," the lion depicted literally as a cub in the lap of the muse. The plates designed by John Leech are the visual counterpart of the author's iconoclastic view of the great captains and kings: a phalanx of Roman soldiers is beaten down by a single barbarian with a club; William the Conqueror falls flat on his face as he lands on the English shore; a roly-poly Henry VIII greets a hook-nosed Francis I on the Field of the Cloth of Gold, while beneath them a French poodle sniffs an English bull.[12]

One of Thackeray's biographers has suggested that A'Beckett borrowed a leaf or two from Thackeray's earlier (and unsuccessful) *Punch* series *Miss Tickletoby's Lectures on English History*.[13] If so, in his invocation to "The Muse, whoever she be, who presides over this Comic History" in *Vanity Fair* (chap. 50), Thackeray could well be returning the compliment. A'Beckett deliberately did not carry forward his history beyond the reign of George III on the ground that "we are very desirous to avoid taking any liberty with the names of living persons, and perhaps giving pain or offence, which might be the result were we to venture nearer to our own times than the reign of the grandfather of her Present Majesty."[14] The less reticent comic historian of Vanity Fair begins his account "while the present century was in its teens" as the opening reads. To an extent he carries forward his *Punch* colleague's *Comic History of England* through the Regency. Like its predecessor, it is "illuminated" with historiated initials, caricatures, cuts, and plates. The wrapper drawing, with its upside-down statue on Nelson's Pillar and the Punch figure occupying the place of the Duke of Wellington in the monument at Hyde Park, both dimly perceptible in the background, prepared readers for a somewhat cockeyed view of history.[15] Their expectations were borne out by the pictures inside some of the initials, like the one introducing "Crawley of King's Crawley" (chap. 7), where we see an Elizabethan courtier kneeling before an obese queen drinking beer from a pitcher. A later one shows Napoleon pacing in his prison cell, a clown bowing before him (chap. 18). Becky herself is transformed into Napoleon with a spy glass looking out over the sea in the initial picture that opens "A Vagabond Chapter" (chap. 64). At the beginning of the chapter called "Georgy Is Made A Gentleman" (chap. 56), little Georgy Osborne, presumably in line with his pampered upbringing, is represented in the crown and robes of the Prince Regent.

In this "comic history," moreover, history is reduced as well as caricatured. The epical title of chapter 2, "In Which Miss Sharp And Miss Sedley Prepare To Open The Campaign," introduces early the "dreadful combats" promised by the manager. The mock military motif is repeated by other chapter headings: "Rebecca Is In Presence Of The Enemy," referring to the launching of her attack on Jos Sedley; "In Which Amelia Joins Her Regiment," and "In Which Amelia Invades The Low Countries," announcing the Brussels episodes. "Venus Preparing The Armour of Mars," the subject of one of the full-page plates, turns out to be a short, lumpy Mrs. O'Dowd packing the war implements of the sleeping (and inaudibly snoring) Major O'Dowd. The end of the Battle of Waterloo is represented in another plate by a fat-faced, short-legged, and visibly uncomfortable Jos Sedley fleeing on a horse. Consistent with this petticoat history, it is Becky Sharp's victory at Waterloo (the Duchess of Richmond's ball) rather than the triumph of the Duke of Wellington in the field that this chronicler chooses to narrate, just as later we witness her Elba rather than that of Napoleon. So at once, the great is diminished and the commonplace magnified.

The publishers of *Vanity Fair: Pen and Pencil Sketches of English Society,* Bradbury and Evans, made a particular point of Thackeray's connection with their magazine, identifying the clown figure depicted on the cover as "Author of . . . the 'Snob Papers' in 'Punch' &c &c." One of the early reviewers dubbed the author "Thack the Snob Killer," and others too were quick enough to connect the "Papers" with the *Pen and Pencil Sketches*. "The 'Snob Papers' in *Punch* have before evinced the author's knowledge of the springs of action," affirmed a review used to promote the novel, "but we were hardly prepared, though our expectations were warm on the subject, for such a deep insight into the human heart as is here represented."[16] In format, certainly, "The Snobs of England" (later reprinted as *The Book of Snobs*) prefigured *Vanity Fair,* with its monthly installments also decorated by pictorial initials of the author's design. From the literary standpoint the novel extends the papers by giving soul and specific personality to the generic abstractions of the "Snobbium Gatherum."

Vanity Fair qualifies as a *Book of Snobs* no less than the series that was coming to an end just as *Vanity Fair* was beginning. Here too are Respectable Snobs (Lord Steyne, Lord and Lady Huddlestone-Fuddlestone), Clerical Snobs (the Bute Crawleys), Great City Snobs (Sedley, Osborne), Country Snobs (the Crawleys), Military Snobs (George Osborne, General Tufto), Irish Snobs (Mrs. O'Dowd), Continental Snobs (The Prince of Pumpernickel and his court), and all manner of Party-Giving and Dining-Out Snobs (including the antisocial but politically ambitious Sir Pitt Crawley). Hardly anybody, in fact, in the world of this novel is free from the taint of snobbery in one form or another, defined in Thackeray's dictionary as "the mean admiration of mean things."[17] One of the papers, "Snobs and Marriage," in its sweeping indictment of the "ephemeral repertories" that were then drawing readers, looks forward in particular to *Vanity Fair:* "Does not the world love *Court Guides,* and millinery, and plate, and carriages? Mercy on us! Read the fashionable intelligence; read the *Court Circular;* read the genteel novels; survey mankind, from Pimlico to Red Lion Square, and see how the Poor Snob is aping the Rich Snob; how the Mean Snob is grovelling at the feet of the Proud Snob; and the Great Snob is lording it over his humble brother."[18] Among the snobs of *Vanity Fair,* Miss Osborne, we notice, is addicted to the "Fashionable Reunions" section of the *Morning Post* (chap. 42); the *Court Guide* is conspicuous on Sir Pitt Crawley's desk, alongside his blue books, pamphlets, and Bible (chap. 54); and Jos Sedley consults the Travelling Peerage during his tour of the continent with Dobbin and Amelia (chap. 63). The "genteel novel" itself, as it surveys mankind from Pimlico to Bloomsbury Square and plummets through the pecking order of society from the rich to the down-at-heel, serves as a reasonable facsimile of *Punch's* "fashionable intelligence" for all curious readers.

As for the principal social climber of this grand assemblage, it is additionally worth nothing that a writer for *Punch* commented during the summer of 1845, when Thackeray was writing *Vanity Fair*, on an advertisement (signed by one A.B.) currently appearing in the *Times* seeking a "lady wishing for a situation as GOVERNESS in a gentleman's family residing in the country, to instruct two little girls in music, drawing and English; a thorough knowledge of the French language is required." The position, according to this account offered a comfortable home, but no salary. Observes Master Punch: "Does he regard the governess as a horse that he would work her like one, and in terms corresponding to keep and stabling? And lastly on what principle or pretence does he presume to call his family 'a *gentleman's?*' Answer that, A.B. Answer that!"[19] This last certainly is one question the author of *Vanity Fair* raises.

The situation publicized by *Punch* was far from an unusual one, the plight and social status of the governess figuring prominently both in fiction and in journalism during this decade. Back toward the onset of the century, the "celebrated philosopher . . . Miss Edgeworth" (as Thackeray refers to her in his first novel) had urged in her treatise *Practical Education:* "It is surely the interest of parents to treat the person who educates their children, with that perfect equality and kindness, which will conciliate her affection, and which will at the same time preserve her influence and authority over her pupils."[20] Writing of a period closer to the time when *Vanity Fair* takes place than when it was written, Miss Edgeworth is sanguine on the whole about the circumstances of these parents' assistants: "And it is with pleasure we observe, that the style of behaviour to governesses, in well bred families, is much changed within these few years. A governess is no longer treated as an upper servant, or as an intermediate being between a servant and a gentlewoman; she is now being treated as the friend and companion of the family, and she must, consequently, have warm and permanent interest in its prosperity: she becomes attached to her pupils from gratitude to their parents, from sympathy, from generosity, as well as from the strict sense of duty." She cautions affluent families, therefore, not against exploiting governesses, but against the opposite excess of over-indulging them—encouraging intimate social relations, making the teachers of their children "their companion in all their amusements" to the extent that the young charges are neglected. Becky writes to her friend Amelia from Queen's Crawley that "I am to be treated as one of the family except on company days" (chap. 8), a situation that undoubtedly would have met with the approval of Miss Edgeworth, but probably little else about the regimen at this arcadian retreat would have. When it comes to cribbage with the young Miss Crawleys, as against the young Sir Pitt's sermons and pamphlets, we can easily guess what choice Miss Edgeworth would have proposed for Becky. The celebrated philosopher says nothing about the master of the household ogling and pinching the children's governess and is silent too about the said young gentlewoman's eloping with the master's son.

Practical Education also warns parents against choosing a governess from the ranks of entertainers. In one passage that we can imagine Thackeray's reading with amused interest, Miss Edgeworth cites the example of an opera dancer who applied for this coveted position with a genteel family. "Do I not speak good Parisian French? Have I any provincial accent?" asks the would-be lady in attempting to overcome the natural resistance of her prospective employer. "I will undertake to teach the language grammatically. And for music and dancing, without vanity, may I not pretend to teach them to any young person?" This case offers Miss Edgeworth occasion to raise the issue that concerned many early nineteenth-century parents—the value of exclusive attention to "accomplishments":

> Without alarming those mothers, who declare themselves above all things anxious for the rapid progress of their daughters in every fashionable accomplishment, it may be innocently asked, what price such mothers are willing to pay for these advantages. Any price within the limits of our fortune! they will probably exclaim.
>
> There are other standards by which we can measure the value of objects, as well as by money. "Fond mother, would you, if it were in your power, accept of an opera dancer for your daughter's governess, upon condition that you should live to see that daughter dance the best minuet at a birthnight ball?"
>
> "Not for the world," replies the mother. "Do you think I would hazard my daughter's innocence and reputation, for the sake of seeing her dance a good minuet? Shocking! Absurd! What can you mean by such an outrageous question?"[21]

Thackeray for his part was acquainted with real-life counterparts of Miss Edgeworth's hypothetical opera dancer. For one example, there was the life history of his friend Lady Morgan, still a garrulous gadabout in the 1840s, who was of theatrical ancestry, and whose rise from governess to an upper-class marriage and glittering social success on the continent bore a suggestive resemblance to the progress of Becky Sharp, which has been duly noted.[22] He was on more intimate terms with a former governess "in a very sober, worthy family in England," identified simply as Pauline, whose story he tells briefly in one of his accounts from Paris sent to the *Britannia* in 1841. Here he relates how he renewed acquaintance with her at a masked ball during carnival time, when she tapped him on the shoulder, and subsequently he visited her in her quarters in the Rue Neuve St. Augustin, where, despite her wretched surroundings, she comported herself "with the air and politeness of a duchess." He muses on her eventual fate:

> Madame or Mademoiselle Pauline must be now five-and-forty years old, and I wonder whether she still goes to the Carnival balls? If she is alive, and has a gown to pawn, or a shilling to buy a ticket, or a friend to give her one, or is not in the hospital, no doubt she was dancing away last night to the sound of Monsieur Dufrêsne's trumpets, and finished the morning at the Courtille.

and reviews her past:

> *Que voulez-vous?* it is her nature. Before she turned Protestant, and instructed the respectable English family in whose bosom she found a home, where she became acquainted with all the elegancies of life, and habituated to the luxuries of refinement, where she had a comfortable hot joint every day with the children, in the nursery, at one. and passed the evening deliciously in the drawing room, listening to the conversation of the ladies, making tea, mayhap, for the gentlemen as they came up from their wine, or playing quadrilles and waltzes when her lady desired her to do so—before this period of her genteel existence, it is probable that Madame Pauline was a grisette.[23]

At any rate, it is to the life of the grisette that she returns, even though, conjectures Thackeray (in the voice of Titmarsh), she could have found another situation as governess, with the good recommendation she received from her upper-class employer, "or have seized upon a promise of marriage from young Master Tom, at college, if she had been artful; or, better still, from a respectable governess have become a respectable stepmother, as many women with half her good looks have done."

In this essay Thackeray leads us to expect that we have not heard the last of this grisette, and thanks to the freedom allowed to the "sham historian," he eventually scrambled life and art in order to allow her to miss out on a chance to become a "respectable stepmother," but yet to marry "Master Tom," to slip back to Bohemia, but to ascend once more to "respectability." As his account further proceeds, Thackeray makes clear that her life furnished him with more than the material of romance:

> A fierce, honest moralist might, to be sure, find a good deal to blame in Madame Pauline's conduct and life; and I should probably offend the reader if I imparted to him secrets which the lady told me with the utmost simplicity, and without the slightest appearance of confusion. But to rightly judge the woman's character, we must take the good and the bad together. It would have been easy for us to coin a romantic, harrowing story of some monstrous seducer, in three volumes, who, by his superior blackness of character, should make Madame Pauline appear beside him as white as snow; but I want to make no heroine of her. Let us neither abuse her nor pity her too much, but look at the woman as we find her, if we look at her at all. Her type is quite unknown in England; it tells a whole social history, and speaks of manners and morals widely different from those which obtain in our own country. There are a hundred thousand Paulines in Paris, cheerful in poverty, careless and prodigal in good fortune, but dreadfully lax in some points of morals in which our own females are praiseworthily severe.[24]

When the opportunity arose to impart Madame Pauline's "secrets" to the English public, Thackeray indeed made no "heroine" of her (the account was pointedly subtitled *A Novel Without A Hero*). Like the tolerant eclectics that this honest, but not fierce, moralist has trained us to be, we "take the good and the bad together." Moreover, to properly assess her character we must reconstruct her past, go back to her "education . . . first associates . . . first temptations," as with her predecessor Catherine Hayes.[25] "On the wings of a novel," furthermore, we are propelled into the future of this demimondaine victim of fate and her own nature.

So we are reminded that Thackeray conceived his novel-without-a-hero as a "cynical and sentimental history" in addition to a comic one. Though his principal nonheroine was drawn from life, the scenario of her adventures was suggested, at least in part, by a novel—appropriately a French one. During one of his Paris visits Thackeray was much delighted, it will be recalled, by a satire he read and reviewed—Louis Reybaud's *Jérôme Paturot*. Among his short-lived careers, Jerome attempts writing, of which something has already been said, seeking advice from the editor of a *feuilleton*. Here is Thackeray's translation of the formula proposed by the editor for a tale suitable for family reading: "My dear, nothing easier. After you have written a number or two, you will see that you can write seventy or a hundred at your will. For example you take a young woman, beautiful, persecuted, and unhappy. You add, of course, a brutal tyrant of a husband or father; you give the lady a perfidious friend, and introduce a lover, the pink of virtue, valour, and manly beauty. What is more simple? You mix up your characters well, and can serve them up hot in a dozen or fourscore numbers as you please."[26] Jerome, who considers himself above such crowd pleasing, scorns the editor's advice, but not Thackeray, who was at this time still trying to find his way to the great public. We now know how he proceeded to "mix up" these characters in his own score of numbers. Amelia Sedley certainly answers to the "beautiful, persecuted, and unhappy" maiden, as does our darling Becky to her "perfidious friend." There is a "brutal tyrant" of a father-in-law, if not father. Dobbin stands for the "pink of virtue [and] valour," the "manly beauty" reserved for that "padded booby" George Osborne, who also qualifies as a cruel husband—if unwittingly so.

Reybaud's satire seems also to have helped Thackeray limn out the character of the "perfidious friend." Jerome marries a grisette named Malvina, and at one point we are told that once Jerome has risen to become a captain in the National Guard, "Ambition . . . seized upon the captain's wife, who too was determined to play her part in the world, and had chosen the world of fashion for her sphere of action. A certain Russian Princess, of undoubted grandeur, had taken a great fancy to Madame Paturot, and under the auspices of that illustrious hyperborean chaperon, she entered the genteel world."[27] Becky, also a product of the bohemia of Paris and married to a captain, crashes the genteel world, like her counterpart, through charm, facility with words, and by the aid of patrons—in her instance a *grande dame* and a lord.

Just as Becky earns her introduction to court, Malvina, through her aristocratic connection, wins an invitation for herself and her husband to a Tuilleries ball, in anticipation of which she prepared "une resplendissante toilette." This episode impressed Thackeray as "a description of the affair so accurate, that, after translating it, I for my part feel as if I were quite familiar with the palace of the French king." The power of the novelist thus enables readers to enter genteel society along with the heroine.

And how much easier it is to enjoy this Barmecide dance in the description of honest Paturot than to dress at midnight, and pay a guinea for a carriage, and keep out of one's wholesome bed, in order to look at King Louis Philippe smiling! What a mercy it is not to be a gentleman! What a blessing it is not to be obliged to drive a cab in white kid gloves, nor to sit behind a great floundering racing-tailed horse of Rotten Row, expecting momentarily that he will jump you into the barouche full of ladies just ahead! What a mercy it is not to be obliged to wear tight lacquered boots, nor to dress for dinner, nor to go to balls at midnight, nor even to be a member of the House of Commons, nor to be prevented from smoking a cigar if you are so minded! All which privileges of poverty may Fortune long keep to us! Men do not know half their luck, that is the fact. If the real truth were known about things, we should have their Graces of Sutherland and Devonshire giving up their incomes to the national debt and saying to their country, "Give me a mutton chop and a thousand a year!"[28]

It follows then that the Barmecide feast that we enjoy at Saint James's Palace, ushered into the midst of "the very best of company," should be treated by the narrator as a vicarious experience: "We are authorized to state that Mrs. Rawdon Crawley's *costume de cour* . . . was of the most elegant and brilliant description"; "This may be said, that in all London there was no more loyal heart than Becky's after this interview"; "The particulars of Becky's costume were in the newspapers—feathers, lappets, superb diamonds, and all the rest." The author belongs not with those "who wear stars and cordons," but with those "who, in muddy boots, dawdle up and down Pall Mall, and peep into the coaches as they drive up with the great folks in their feathers." He even questions the ability of "such a feeble and inexperienced pen as mine to attempt to relate" the interview between Becky and her Imperial Master: "The dazzled eyes close before that Magnificent Idea. Loyal respect and decency tell even the imagination not to look too keenly and audaciously about the sacred audience-chamber" (chap. 48). "Loyal respect and decency," however, do not prevent this Asmodeus of Mayfair turned "fashionable intelligencer" to insinuate much about what goes on behind the dazzling exteriors into which we are offered tantalizing peeps. As already noted, his reading of that "course of French humbug" called *Jérôme Paturot* led him to conclude that "if there be any writer in England who has knowledge and wit sufficient, he could do well to borrow the Frenchman's idea and give a similar satire on our own country."[29]

In concocting his "similar satire," Thackeray had at hand, of course, those "pictures of genteel life," composed by "authors . . . connected with the fashionable world," the fine company of "literary snobs" to which he had introduced readers of *Punch*.[30] In reviewing one of these "pictures," Disraeli's *Coningsby*, Thackeray remarked that the "secrets of high life" seemed to have a natural appeal to all readers from squires down to lady's maids.[31] Some of the chapter headings of *Vanity Fair* promise more "secrets of high life": "Private and Confidential"; "Family Portraits"; "A Quarrel About An Heiress"; "A Marriage And Part Of A Honeymoon"; "Gaunt House"; "In Which The Reader Is Introduced To The Very Best Of Company"; "Returns To The Genteel World." These and other such titles subliminally recall the scandal chronicles disguised as society novels that had swamped readers between *Vivian Grey* and *Vanity Fair*—such as *The Exclusives, A Marriage in High Life, Family Records, Memoirs of a Peeress, The Debutante; or, The London Season, The Man of Fortune,* and *The Woman of the World.* The authors of "the genteel novels" whom Thackeray mildly needles in *The Book of Snobs* intrude themselves in various ways, obvious and subtle, in *Vanity Fair.* Mrs. Guy Flouncey, the charming, witty social climber of *Coningsby,* has been suggested as one of the prototypes of Becky Sharp, as Lord Monmouth, the cynical aristocrat of that sociopolitical fantasy, anticipates Lord Steyne. The title of Mrs. Gore's *Peers and Parvenus* clearly pinpoints the targets of Thackeray's satire. In a review Thackeray referred to her *Sketches of English Character* as a series of "worldly lectures" bearing the implicit moral that "the world is the most hollow, heartless, vulgar, brazen world, and those are luckiest who are out of it."[32] This title, yoked with her *Sketch Book of Fashion,* a series of vignettes looking back to Regency London and Brighton, and *The Fair of May Fair,* a cynical-sentimental anthology of marital manoeuvering, flirtation, and adultery in which love matches are contrasted with marriages of convenience, almost yields the first title that Thackeray gave to his "worldly lectures"—*Vanity Fair: Pen and Pencil Sketches of English Society.* Among other of his so-called literary snobs, Samuel Warren's still popular *Ten Thousand a Year* is echoed in the most famous of the chapter headings of *Vanity Fair*—"How To Live Well On Nothing A Year." The concluding chapter, "Which Contains Births, Marriages, and Deaths" copies the newspaper columns of the day, but also twists about the subtitle of Theodore Hook's *All in the Wrong; or, Births, Deaths, and Marriages.*

A number of these novelists belonged to the ménage of Henry Colburn, who early laid claim to be the first to give the reading public "delineations of the most refined society, by its most refined members," and thereby to have "rescued the annals of Polite Life from the Swiss, the valet, and the lady's-maid, the rip, the roué, and the blackleg."[33] Colburn's rescue operation was not so thorough-going as he had hoped, for fictitious autobiographies of servants purportedly exposing the "secrets" of their betters continued to abound, as variously represented by the journal *Figaro in London* (1831–38), edited by Gilbert A'Beckett before he went to *Punch,* Matthew James Higginson's *Peter Priggins the College Scout* (1841), and Lady Blessington's *Memoirs of a Femme de Chambre* (1846). In the face of Colburn's claim, Charles Yellowplush's editor affirms that this literary footman offers *"the only authentic picture of fashionable life* which has been given to the world in our time."[34] That later rein-carnation of Yellowplush, Charles Jeames De La Pluche, Esq, pre-sents a disenchanted view of the *haut monde* through the pages of *Punch.* Aspiring to form "a noble kinnexion" with "Harrystoxy," this cockney manservant comes a cropper through some unfortu-nate "muccantile speclations," and reconciles himself to becoming just plain James Plush, manager of the aptly named Wheel of For-tune Public House, frequented by butlers and footmen of the nobil-ity. Hence he knows whereof he speaks: "People phansy it's hall gaiety and pleasure the life of us fashnabble gents about townd," he confides to his diary. "But I can tell 'em it's not hall goold that glitters. They dont know our moments of hagony, hour ours of studdy and reflechshun. . . . they little think that leader of the tong, seaminkly so reckliss, is a careworn mann! and yet so it is."[35]

Among the "fashnabble gents" with whom De La Pluche claims acquaintanceship during his brief foray into society is one "Mr. Mills, my rivle in Halbany."[36] This gentleman is none other, one presumes, than John Mills, author of *D'Horsay; or, The Follies of the Day* (1844), probably the most sensational scandal chronicle of the decade, published in the same year as *Coningsby.*[37] In his book Mills deplores the various reminiscences of "high life below stairs" that had been foisted on the public, and the signature "A Man of Fash-ion" on the title page was obviously intended to give his own ac-count the stamp of authenticity. Ostensibly based upon the career of Lady Blessington's consort, this novel gained notoriety in its day because of its open and often malicious representation of other well-known aristocrats—notably the Marquess of Hertford, pro-totype of both Disraeli's Lord Monmouth in *Coningsby* and Thack-eray's Lord Steyne, here depicted as a debauchee in the last stages of moral and physical degeneracy.[38] Striking similarities in point of view and tone with *Vanity Fair* indicate that Thackeray must have had more than a casual acquaintance with the book, if not with the author.

The author of this murky calendar of calumny professes a serious aim, to distill "the essence of the age in which we live" out of a series of "cursory glances at life" (preface). His somewhat ramshackle epic of the *ton,* which sweeps through London and its environs, taking in Curzon Street, Hyde Park, Crockford's, Tattersall's, the Queen's Bench, along with assorted taverns, race tracks and gambling halls, is intended as a warning to the unwary. His heightened and metaphorical language is in keeping with this end. Hyde Park on a July afternoon is denounced as "a hot-bed of vanity" where "the votaries of fashion were thronging the ring . . . to flit their painted wings in the hour prescribed" (chap. 6). To this philosophical man of fashion who veers between "the vein sentimental" and scorn for human vanity, "effects are so often the reflection of such secret and hidden causes, that to attempt to dive beneath the surface and peep at their source and spring, is a futile expenditure of exertion and labour." Nevertheless, "as far as within the compass of our abilities to lay bare the machinery working the woof of the adventures, and pulling the strings of our puppets on the stage, we will to the work with a will, and make them dance a jig to as merry a tune as was ever scraped on a catgut" (chap. 16). In line with his moral purpose, this puppet master justifies even the invasion of privacy: "Shall we, with the power of Asmodeus, skip o'er wall and roof, and, stripping the substantial curtain of bricks and mortar from all its inward secrets,—lay them bare to the prying, peeping eyes of our companions? Yes, or how can we expose 'follies of the day' and vices of the night?" (chap. 10). In the long run, he declares, "should the result . . . prove to a single sceptic how fruitless it is to join the gaudy train of Folly, how painful to make pleasure the business of existence, they [the author's efforts] will meet with a reward more than commensurate to the exertion." The way clearly was prepared for the melancholic theater manager who takes over in *Vanity Fair* and is ready to stoop even to "the Tom Eavesian way of life" to make his point.[39]

In his own "delineations of the most refined society," Thackeray adopts neither the "below stairs" vantage point nor that of the "man of fashion." Lady Blessington, a fashionable authoress who had pushed her way into society, has a character remark: "The middle class is indeed, most estimable, possessing much of the quality of its favourite beverage, beer, having neither the froth attributed to the fashionable portion of the highest class, nor the dregs which appertain to the lower."[40] The historian of *Vanity Fair,* following her lead, identifies himself neither with the froth nor the dregs, addressing

himself rather to "our gracious public—situated between Saint
Giles's and Saint James's." Posing as a solid member of the middle
class, he dissociates himself from the ranks of the society novelists
when he approaches Gaunt House, as emphatically as he had from
those of the military novelists at Waterloo. Appropriately, at the
great ball at Lord Steyne's mansion, he places himself not with the
guests inside, but with the outsiders looking in, "the honest newspaper fellow who sits in the hall and takes down the names of the
great ones who are admitted to the feasts." At other times, he is the
snapper up of trifles "at second hand," out of the gossip sheets
beloved by "Party-Giving and Dining-Out Snobs." "It is only by
inquiry and perseverance that one sometimes gets hints of these
secrets," he affirms, "and by a similar diligence every person who
treads the Pall Mall pavement and frequents the clubs of the metropolis, knows either through his own experience or through some
acquaintance with whom he plays at billiards or shares the joint,
something about the genteel world of London" (chap. 37). Playing
on the title of a popular exemplary memoir of the day, "The pursuit of fashion under difficulties,"[41] he suggests, "would be a fine
theme for any great person who had the wit, the leisure, and the
knowledge of the English language necessary for the compiling of
such a history." Thackeray announces his credentials for the un-
dertaking, along with his intention to elevate the general readers'
passion for gossip into moral teaching, while he appeals adroitly
both to their social climbing instinct and their desire for self-
improvement.

With the mock awe he expresses from time to time, the narrator
of *Vanity Fair* brings his readers to the threshold of Gaunt House,
but draws back: "Dear brethren, let us tremble before those august
portals. I fancy them guarded by grooms of the chamber with
flaming silver forks with which they prong all those who have not
the right of the *entrée*" (chap. 51). This Hadean image had been
rendered more vivid by the grotesquely designed initial that originally headed chapter 47 ("Gaunt House") containing two spread-
out silver forks, a tiara suspended between them, dangling from
the hands of a horned imp. Here too is an emblem for the kind of
novel Thackeray was parodying and improving in *Vanity Fair*. We
are enabled to scale "the heights of fashion with the charming
enchanters of the silver-fork school," he had written in *The Paris
Sketch Book*. These words appear in his essay "On Some French
Fashionable Novels," which generally gave him more delight, as we

have already observed, than their counterparts in his own country.[42] The qualities that attracted him in French fashionable novels appear in some remarks in his review of *Lettres parisiennes*, an intimate diary by Mme Emile de Girardin, that sound like a slap at Henry Colburn and his stable:

> And hence the great use of having real people of fashion to write their own lives, in place of the humble male and female authors, who, under the denomination of the Silver Fork School, have been employed by silly booksellers in our own day. They cannot give us any representation of the real authentic genteel fashionable life, they will relapse into morality in spite of themselves, do what they will they are often vulgar, sometimes hearty and natural; *they have not the unconscious wickedness, the delightful want of principle, which the great fashionable man possesses, none of the grace and ease of vice.*[43]

This "delightful want of principle . . . grace and ease of vice" is certainly a part of the make-up of Becky Sharp ("I'm no angel," she remarks early in her story, and her creator readily agrees). Candid self-revelation is among the literary qualities Thackeray typically singles out for admiration in his review of the *Lettres parisiennes*, together with naturalness and spontaneity of feeling, expressed

Vanity Fair, chapter 47, initial letter *A* (imp dangling two silver forks). (From volume 2 of *The Works of William Makepeace Thackeray* [Centenary Biographical Edition]; reproduced by permission of John Murray, Ltd.)

with grace and urbanity. The "sermon" contained in these letters is to him moral without dullness: "every page, on the contrary, is lively and amusing—it sparkles with such wit as only a Frenchman can invent—it abounds with pleasing anecdote, and happy turns of thought. It is entirely selfish and heartless, but the accomplished author does not perceive this: Its malice is gentlemanlike and not too ill-natured: and its statements, if exaggerated, are not more so than good company warrants." Here one can almost feel Thackeray groping his way toward his own mode of social satire, lively and witty like his French model, but more engaged morally. He does suggest in this review that "for the benefit of the vulgar and unrefined, the vicomte's work ought to be translated, and would surely be read with profit." Furthermore he conjectures the sort of readers who might benefit from such a work: "Here might the country gentleman's daughter who, weary of her humdrum village retirement, pines for the delights of Paris, find those pleasures chronicled of which she longs to take a share . . . and . . . ask is this the fashionable life that I have been sighing after—this heartless, false, and above all, intolerably wearisome existence, which the most witty and brilliant people in the world consent to lead?"[44]

Thackeray supplied his bourgeois readers with *morceaux choisis* culled from some of his favorite fictitious memoirs in "On Some French Fashionable Novels" and other essay-reviews, from which it is easy to infer his predilection for panoramas of social life and manners, written with wit, verve, and moral sophistication. It is customary to compare Thackeray with Balzac because of the extensive compass of *La comédie humaine* and the device the two writers shared of carrying over characters from novel to novel, but from available evidence Thackeray seems to have preferred two of Balzac's lesser disciples,[45] whom he considered more refined. We know of Thackeray's admiration for Charles de Bernard, shared by Mrs. Gore, who edited several of his novels for the British public and praised him as "the philosophic satirist of a state of society, unhinged by revolutions and characterised by demoralization, wearing the smoothest and most tempting surface."[46] Thackeray also devotes some space in his essay on French society novels to another literary aristocrat, le Comte Horace de Viel-Castel, great-nephew of Mirabeau, author of several novels of manners (*Le faubourg Saint-Germain, Le faubourg Saint-Honoré, La noblesse de la province*) that attempted to survey the peerage of the realm as Balzac had the middle classes, along with cultural history (*Collection de costumes, armes, et meubles, pour servir à l'histoire de France depuis le commencement de la monarchie jusqu'à nos jours*) and historical studies of the period of the French Revolution. Speaking for his readers, whose easy shockability he well understands, Thackeray expresses an embarrassed delight over "that remarkable *naïf* contempt of the institution called marriage" reflected in Monsieur de Viel-Castel's novels, and "the wonderful rascality which all the conversationists betray."[47]

The population of Viel-Castel's books, as Thackeray characterized it, is the *"crème de la crème de la haute volée,"* whose quality this
historian finds considerably diluted under the new regime. *Le
faubourg Saint-Honoré* and its successors can be described as a series
of requiems for an aristocracy cut off from both its glorious past
and its rural roots, frittering away their lives in ostentation and
dissipation "dans ce grand bazar que l'on nomme Paris."[48] Le
Comte de Viel-Castel transforms the faubourgs into the glorious
and decadent sort of spectacle that Thackeray was to make of
Mayfair. In *Le faubourg Saint-Germain* (1837–38) he poses as a jaded
ennuyé, warning a young country cousin away from the metropolis
where people die old and worn out ("vieux et usés"). To this disenchanted Parisian, the provinces are infinitely preferable to the capital, which somehow freezes the natural impulses and affections,
makes people overly civilized and sophisticated, vying to outshine
one another in society, engaged in dissimulation and role playing.
The dazzling jewels of the matrons and belles of this society are just
so many overvalued "faux semblants." Thackeray is not as prone to
find virtue among the rural gentry (v. "Arcadian Simplicity," in
which we dine with the Crawleys) as is the Count de Viel-Castel,
who was descended from a prominent provincial aristocratic family, but *Vanity Fair* makes us equally aware of urban vice. In sounding his funeral knell over the faubourg Saint-Germain, Viel-Castel
invokes, as Thackeray does from time to time, the passing of the
ancient kingdoms of the East ("C'est le Bas-Empire, dont passe le
convoi. . . . C'est Sardanaple sur son bûcher de mort"). Here,
impervious to their impending fate, the inhabitants live, like the
citizens of Vanity Fair, without God in the world ("ne croyant plus
aux lois divines, il ne peut plus croire aux lois humaines").[49]

Viel-Castel having turned to the comedy of manners as the vehicle for his jeremiad, one can enjoy the "wonderful rascality" betrayed by his characters, as did Thackeray who translated some of
their conversation for his readers. The count introduces us into the
homes as well as the ballrooms of the Faubourg Saint-Germain. We
overhear the gossip and the backbiting in the salons of the
Blacourts, where diplomats mingle with the demimondaine, where
state business is conducted, and where reputations are made and
unmade. Scenes are carefully set, the personages are elegantly
dressed, and their "paroles flétrissantes" wing past us. (Thackeray
translated a chapter entitled "Un bal," whose epigraph is "Vanitas
Vanitatum.")[50] Viel-Castel propelled his plots through the kinds of
characters—innocents from the provinces, young wives, old husbands, superannuated flirts, worldly mistresses—and situations—

marriages of convenience, misalliances, philandering, and adultery—that later deteriorated into boulevard farce, but for him they reflect a corrupt society. As critic of society, the author lectures intermittently to the reader on conventions, rails against the hypocrisy of the marriage laws, and denounces the tradition of female education that leaves young ladies completely unprepared for life. One thinks of Amelia Sedley while reading that "pendant vingt ans, la vie des femmes s'écoule entourée d'un mensonge perpetuel; elles doivent, pendant vingt ans, marcher sourdes, aveugles et insensibles au milieu de nos villes corrompues."[51] The publisher's title for Viel-Castel's massive novel—*Etude sur les moeurs du faubourg Saint-Germain*—clearly aligns it with the collective title of Balzac's great series—*Etudes de moeurs au XIXe siècle*—and establishes its claim to be taken seriously as social history. Furthermore, the function that Viel-Castel assigned himself as "sténographiant la chronique contemporaine"[52] interestingly anticipates Balzac's famous anouncement in the "Avant-propos" to the collected *Comédie humaine:* "La société française allait être l'historien, je ne devais être que le secrétaire."

Thackeray's Paris experience, it becomes increasingly obvious, furnished him with models aplenty of the novelist as both sociologist and chronicler, anatomist and diagnostician of social and moral ills. In his review of the aforementioned "lively, witty, and unwise" *Lettres parisiennes* of Mme de Girardin, he raises some leading questions:

> And is it so? Is it true that the women of Madame de Girardin's country, and of fashionable life, are the heartless, odious, foolish, swindling, smiling, silly, selfish creatures she paints them? Have they no sense of religious duty, no feeling of maternal affection, no principle of conjugal attachment, no motive except variety, for which they will simulate passion (it stands to reason that a woman who does not love husband and children, can love nobody) and break all law? Is it true—as every French romance that has been written time out of mind, would have us believe? Is it so common that Madame de Girardin can afford to laugh at it as a joke, and talk of it as a daily occurrence?[53]

Since these are among the questions that Thackeray was to ask and attempt to answer in his probing of English society, living "without God in the world," his conclusion to these remarks has an ironical ring: "If so, and we must take the Frenchman's own word for it—in spite of all the faults, and all the respectability, and all the lord-worship, and all the prejudice, and all the intolerable dulness of Baker Street—Miss . . . had much better marry in the Portman

Square, than in the Place Vendôme quarter." In *Vanity Fair*, as we know, he was to offer clear evidence that marriages in Portman Square are not necessarily made in heaven any more than those in the Place Vendôme.

The principal marriage whose tribulations we follow in *Vanity Fair* that unites a governess of nondescript French origin with an English buck signalizes Thackeray's grandest achievement in this book—the wedding of the Silver Fork novel of England with the French *Etudes de moeurs*. As critic, translator, and eventually transplanter to English soil of French novels, Thackeray allied himself with fellow writers who were endeavoring to overcome an endemic English literary Gallophobia. One of these was Mrs. Gore, who in 1841, in her introduction to translations of two of Charles de Bernard's novels, acknowledged that these tales of Parisian high life "as full of truth as of polished and deliberate corruption" may seem to represent life "in a form somewhat too naked" for its present audience. In extenuation she asserted that these novels are no franker than those of Fielding, Richardson, and Smollett or widely read dramas that deal with illicit love or adultery, such as *Romeo and Juliet, Othello, Jane Shore,* and *Venice Preserved*. She offered a basic reason for the greater frankness of contemporary French writers over English in dealing with such matters: "In France, young persons are not permitted to read novels, and the middle classes have little taste for works of this nature. It is probably a safeguard to the purity of our own schools of fiction, though a consideraeble injury to all others, that novels are placed in the hands of persons of immature judgment and experience. On the Continent fiction is considered a recreation for persons careworn with the business of life, and too firm of principle to be injured by light or frivolous pastimes."[54] Here Mrs. Gore urged not so much a liberalizing of English moral standards regarding literature, as a wider tolerance of French ones. If English readers could overcome their antipathy, they would be richly rewarded, she promised, for French novels offered valuable insight into French society and politics.

Two years before, the more belligerent G. W. M. Reynolds had openly castigated the English public for their prudery toward the French. Reynolds was well informed on the writers of France, having spent a number of years as a journalist there, and in 1839 he compiled an anthology of excerpts in translation entitled *The Modern Literature of France* with the hope of overcoming the prejudices engendered in readers by what he regarded as an unduly hostile press.[55] In his preface to this collection he attributed this animus to both political and ethical causes—a lingering bitterness from Napoleonic days, fear of a repetition in England of the violence of 1830 that brought Louis Philippe to the throne, as well as the alleged immorality of the novels. Reynolds took particular umbrage at a *Quarterly Review* article that went so far as to lay the blame for the 1830 revolution on "a depraved taste in literature" rather than on social oppression.[56] In general he defends both the French character and French literature, contrasting the honesty and open-mindedness of both with English hypocrisy.

"Because we read in French Novels of intrigues, adulteries and murders, do they exist the more in France than in England on that account?" Reynolds asks. "Or does the critic in the *Quarterly* mean to argue that every *wife* is unfaithful to the marriage-bed in France, that every *husband* revenges her wrongs, and that every *lover* kills himself in despair? Are English women always pure, is vengeance unknown in Britain?" He proceeds to answer his own question:

> No—we never take up a paper without reading a case of *crim con*, we see, alas! too often terrible instances of the most deadly vengeance. . . . Perhaps the critic whose terrible misrepresentations we have taken some pains to correct, is not aware that the average amount of crime in England preponderates over that in France; and that there are more murders, more robberies, more infanticides, and more unnatural crimes registered in the annals of turpitude and delinquency in the former than in the latter country. An appeal to the "Newgate Calendar" and to a collection of the "Gazette des Tribunaux" will bear us out in our assertion.[57]

As we shall see presently, Reynolds set out to write a Newgate Calendar for his own times in his scurrilous and scandalous novel *The Mysteries of London,* quite detailed in its "annals of turpitude and delinquency," particularly among the upper classes. This is the kind of matter, Reynolds implies in his introduction to *The Modern Literature of France,* that the polite novelists of England avoid, but that journalists batten on. So Thackeray insinuates in his backhanded way in *Vanity Fair:* "The novelist, it has been said before, knows everything, and as I am in a situation to be able to tell the public how Crawley and his wife lived without any income, may I entreat the public newspapers . . . *not* to reprint the following narrative and calculations" (chap. 36).

Reynolds attacked English novelists en masse for their evasiveness, complaining that English fiction was still as prim and unrealistic as the serious novel had been in France before 1830 when "moral lessons were taught through the medium of almost impos-

sible fictions." But *nous avons changé tout cela.* "Now the French
author paints the truth in all its nudity; and this development of the
secrets of nature shocks the English reader, because he is not yet
accustomed to so novel a style. To depict truth, in all its bearings,
consistently with nature, is a difficult task; and he who attempts it
must occasionally exhibit deformities, which disgust the timid
mind." A balanced representation of life, Reynolds insisted, includes
"much to please" together with "much that will be abhorrent to the
virtuous imagination," but "the strict conventional usages of English society prevent the introduction of highly-coloured pictures
into works of fiction; and thus in an English book which professes
to be a history of man or of the world, the narrative is but half told.
In France the whole tale is given at once; and the young men, and
young females do not there enter upon life with minds so circumscribed and narrow that the work of initiation becomes an
expensive or ruinous task."[58] Assuming, along with the more conventional novelists of his age, that the novel is a handy instrument
for the moral education of the young, he questioned the received
view that reading about sin will make one sinful, or that the cause
of morality is served by prettifying life. The French writers, he was
convinced, better prepared young readers for life by freeing them
of false illusions. Against the English tendency to represent good
invariably overcoming evil, he much preferred the unflinching
honesty of French writers, who "carry their system to such an extent, that they do not hesitate to represent vice triumphant, and
virtue levelled with the dust; for they assert that the former invariably prospers, and the other languishes without support; whereas
the English points to a different moral in his fiction."
    Thackeray too had occasion to observe that "a French satirist has
a certain advantage which, with our modest public, an English
novelist cannot possess. The former is allowed to speak more freely
than the latter."[59] This "modest public" is treated to a certain
amount of condescension in *Vanity Fair:* "The times are such that
one scarcely dares to allude to that kind of company which
thousands of our young men in Vanity Fair are frequenting every
day, which nightly fills casinos and dancing-rooms, which is known
to exist as well as the Ring in Hyde-Park or the Congregation at St.
James's" (chap. 49); "We must pass over a part of Mrs. Rebecca
Crawley's biography with that lightness and delicacy which the
world demands—the moral world that has, perhaps, no particular
objection to vice, but an insuperable repugnance to hearing vice
called by its proper name" (chap. 64). At times he deliberately

leaves the story "but half told," in Reynolds's words, leaving it to his readers to supply the other half: "And so, when Becky is out of the way, be sure that she is not particularly well employed, and that the less that is said about her doings is in fact the better" (chap. 64); "Whether my lord [Steyne] really had murderous intentions towards Mrs. Becky . . . and the factotum objected to have to do with assassination; or whether he simply had a commission to frighten Mrs. Crawley out of a city where his lordship proposed to pass the winter . . . is a point which has never been ascertained" (chap. 64). What Reynolds condemns—the prudishness of the English audience—provides Thackeray with his main satirical thrust as he adroitly manages to sustain "that lightness and delicacy of touch which the world demands" in presenting his sordid subject matter, and maintains a moral tone proper to the "congregation" of all ages that he represents on his "gaudy yellow cover."

Thackeray's remarks on the greater liberty of expression enjoyed by French writers occurred in his review of Eugène Sue's *Les mystères de Paris*, a work that alternately fascinated and repelled him. In a letter to Chapman and Hall, publishers of the *Foreign Quarterly Review* where this essay appeared, he suggested that it should be done "in a moral tone, with thanks for the cessations of the kind of thing in England,"[60] but in the review he wrote that "perhaps the best parts of M. Sue's books are the most hideous."[61] The next year Thackeray was commissioned by a publisher named Giraldon to do a translation of Sue's crime story, a project that fell through when he was not promptly paid.[62] Others jumped in, however, and by mid-decade this scabrous tale was available to a wide public in weekly numbers, with illustrations. Moreover, Sue spawned innumerable imitators, and shortly every capital in Europe, as well as many a town in America, had its "mysteries."[63] Thackeray's own "sneaking kindness" for this underworld fantasia, whose taste and style he had felt obliged to condemn, creeps into a passage in the manuscript version of the "Vauxhall" episode of *Vanity Fair* (subsequently excised): "[Our gracious public] has never been hanged before Newgate any more than it has danced at the Queen's ball, hence accounts either of the prison or the palace are the most welcome to it: and a novel w^h should be made to bring these two buildings together, and w^h should pass abruptly from the Queen's boudoir to Bow Street and vice versâ—such a novel as the famous French 'Mystères de Paris' for instance should be sure of acquiring great success, and creating a general sympathy."[64]

Thackeray does manage the circuit between "palace" and "prison" to an extent in *Vanity Fair,* elevating us to the "extreme heights" of society when we go along with Becky on her presentation at court, and dropping us to its depths, as we accompany Rawdon to "Mr. Moss's mansion in Cursitor Street," as it is euphemistically called (chap. 53). But where Thackeray peeps, Sue's English disciple G. W. M. Reynolds plunges. *The Mysteries of London* juxtaposes Disraeli's "Two Nations" in a series of "highly colored pictures" of his own illustrating the stark contrasts of life in the metropolis, "the most gorgeous pomp . . . placed in strong relief by the most deplorable squalor," as Reynolds points out in his introduction, all revealing a "mighty panorama of grandeur and misery." Accordingly chapters entitled "The Boudoir," "The Masquerade," "The Royal Breakfast," and "Crockford's" are interspersed among others entitled "Newgate," "The Dungeon," "The Old Bailey," and "The Road to Ruin." To complete the span we are introduced not only to high life and low life, but also to some of what Thackeray calls the "middling" areas—"A City Man-Smithfield Scenes"; "The House of Commons"; "The Ex-Member for Rottenborough"; "Alderman Sniff-Tomlinson and Greenwood."

Even to students of the period, the prurience of *The Mysteries of London* has tended to live after it, whereas its polemics are buried with its bones. Reynolds had serious enough reasons for writing the book. Knowing of his ardent championship of French "naked" realism, one readily understands why he served up his meat raw to what he regarded as a pabulum-fed public. His radical politics further motivated his shock tactics, one of his intentions being to awaken the apathetic multitude to social injustice.[65] He is explicit on this point in the epilogue to the first volume: "For we have constituted ourselves the scourge of the oppressor, and the champion of the oppressed; we have taken virtue by the hand to raise it, and we have seized upon vice to expose it; we have no fear of those who sit in high places; but we dwell as emphatically upon the failings of the educated and the rich, as on the immorality of the ignorant and poor." Although Reynolds claims a sense of balance, a reader may easily conclude that he weighs the scales of iniquity in the direction of the top levels of society, especially in such chapters as "Scenes in Fashionable Life," which looks in on the unhappily married Harboroughs of Tavistock Square (an episode following close on "The Wrongs and Crimes of the Poor" dealing with girls forced into prostitution because of poverty); "The Forger and the Adulteress," taken up with the characteristic recreations of the Harboroughs; and "Aristocratic Morals," in which this unexemplary pair catch one another with paramours. Depravity is flushed out in high places in other episodes, such as "The Intrigues of a Demirep"; "The Fall" (in which the Rector of Saint David's is seduced by Lady Harborough); "The Mysteries of Helmesford House"; "The Aristocratic Villain and the Low Miscreant," "The History of a Gamester," and "The Tortures of Lady Ravensworth." In the course of the two "series" and hundreds of pages of *The Mysteries of London,* Reynolds certainly bludgeons home his message: "Crime is abundant in the city; the lazar-house, the prison, the brothel, and the dark alley, are rife with all kinds of enormity, in the same way as the palace, the mansion, the club house, the parliament, and the parsonages are each and all characterized by their different degrees and shades of vice."[66]

Thackeray must have had in mind the audience of Sue and Reynolds, who by this time were legion, in a teasing address to his readers intruded early in *Vanity Fair:* "I warn my 'kyind friends,' then, that I am going to tell a story of harrowing villainy and complicated—but, as I trust, intensely interesting—crime. My rascals are no milk-and-water rascals, I promise you. When we come to the proper places we won't spare fine language—No, no! But when we are going over the quiet country we must perforce be calm. A tempest in a slop-basin is absurd. We will reserve that sort of thing for the mighty ocean and the lonely midnight. The present Number will be very mild. Others—But we will not anticipate *those"* (chap. 8). He was acquainted undoubtedly with Reynolds's habit of addressing his readers as "my kind friends," and two of the chapter headings in *The Mysteries of London* are "The Thames Pirates" and "A Midnight Scene of Mystery."[67] On the surface Thackeray seems here to be reopening his attack on the Newgate novelists begun in *Catherine:* "The public will hear of nothing but rogues; and the only way in which poor authors, who must live, can act honestly by the public and themselves, is to paint such thieves as they are: not dandy, poetical, rose-water thieves; but real downright scoundrels, leading scoundrelly lives, drunken, profligate, dissolute, low, as scoundrels will be." The subject is still the candid treatment of crime and sin, it is true, but by now the author has shifted his emphasis. He is no longer faced with the "rose-water thieves" of Ainsworth and Bulwer, or "whitewashed saints" like "Poor Biss Dadsy" of *Oliver Twist,* but with the "downright scoundrels" of Sue,

Reynolds, and company. In 1847 his point about "fine language" refers not to the Plato-quoting villains of Bulwer, but to that master of thieves' argot, Reynolds. The parody crime story "The Night Attack," included in the first version of the "Vauxhall" chapter of *Vanity Fair*, meets Reynolds on his ground, particularly in the dialogue of the two brigands:

> "Mofy! is that your snum?" said a voice from the area. "I'll gully the dag and bimbole the clicky in a snuffkin."
> "Nuffle your clod, and beladle your glumbanions," said Vizard, with a dreadful oath. "This way, men; if they screak; out with your snickers and slick! Look to the pewter room, Blowser. You, Mark, to the old gaff's mopus box! and I," added he in a lower but more horrible voice, "I will look to Amelia!"

The manuscript version in addition explains one of these sentences, in imitation, one suspects, of Reynolds's numerous footnote glossaries of the obscure underworld slang that riddles much of his text.[68]

By the time *Vanity Fair* was published in book form, the thief talk had disappeared. The author has covered his tracks, presumably in keeping with his new role as "fashionable intelligencer." In *Catherine*, Thackeray, through his mouthpiece "Ikey Solomons," was determined to shock his audience out of their too easy responsiveness to the sentimentalization of criminals; in the more "civilized" world inhabited by the population of *Vanity Fair*, he feels obligated instead to tone down the sensationalism of the "mysteries." In this rarefied world, after all, it is appearance mainly that counts. As against Reynolds's frontal attack, therefore, Thackeray chooses to sideswipe. He is deferential to "madam" and to "the most squeamish immoralist," working within their confined code. Becky, we are assured, "did everything that was respectable, and that is why we dwell upon this part of her career with more fondness than upon subsequent parts of her history, which are not pleasant" (chap. 64). Of course there is talk: "Some people, who took the trouble to busy themselves in the matter [of her separation from Rawdon], said that she was the criminal, while others vowed that she was innocent as a lamb, and that her odious husband was in fault" (chap. 64). When Rawdon finds himself in Mr. Moss's establishment in Cursitor Street, it is clearly implied that he is no stranger to the place: "We have not thought it necessary in the previous course of this narrative to mention these trivial little domestic incidents," the author apologizes, "but the reader may be assured that they can't unfrequently occur in the life of a man who

lives on nothing a-year" (chap. 53). There is more than an intima-
tion of immorality in the past history of the Steynes of Gaunt
House: "And let us, my brethren who have not our names in the
Red Book, console ourselves by thinking comfortably how miserable our betters may be, and that Damocles, who sits on satin cush-
ions, and is served on gold plate, has an awful sword hanging over
his head in the shape of a bailiff, or an hereditary disease, or a
family secret, which peeps out every now and then from the embroidered arras in a ghastly manner, and will be sure to drop one
day or the other in the right place" (chap. 47).

If Thackeray prefers to hide behind the damask what Reynolds
exposes under the glare of gaslight, the gentler writer after all is
tactfully addressing an audience given to evasion and concealment,
as he reminds them in the opening of the last monthly number:

> There are things we do and know perfectly well in Vanity Fair,
> though we never speak them, as the Ahrimanians worship the devil,
> but don't mention him: and a polite public will no more bear to read
> an authentic description of vice than a truly-refined English or
> American female will permit the word breeches to be pronounced in
> her chaste hearing. And yet, madam, both are walking the world
> before our faces every day, without much shocking us. . . . It is only
> when their naughty names are called out that your modesty has any
> occasion to show alarm or sense of outrage, and it has been the wish
> of the present writer, all through this story, deferentially to submit to
> the fashion at present prevailing, and only hint at the existence of
> wickedness in a light, easy, and agreeable manner, so that nobody's
> fine feelings may be offended. (Chap. 64)

The author of *Vanity Fair* may choose to address himself to the
prudent rather than to the prurient, like the author of *The Mysteries
of London,* but he is no less vehement than his rival in his castigation
of hypocrisy and humbug, and the two writers employ equally vivid
imagery to embody evil. "The transition from the young man about
town to the man upon the town is as natural as that of a chrysalis to
a butterfly," writes Reynolds. This vivarium is transformed before
our eyes into a swamp: "These men *upon* the town constitute as
pestilential a section of male society as the women *of* the town do of
the female portion of the community. They are alike the reptiles
produced by the great moral dung-heap." Moreover, the entire city
is infested:

> The visitor to the Polytechnic Institution, or the Adelaide Gallery,
> has doubtless seen the exhibition of the microscope. A drop of the
> purest water, magnified by that instrument some thousands of times,
> appears filled with horrid reptiles and monsters of revolting forms.

Such is London.

Fair and attractive as the mighty metropolis may appear to the superficial observer, it swarms with disgusting, loathsome, and venemous objects wearing human shapes.[69]

One of these could be that "syren" Becky Sharp, but her creator stands by his faith to the social code: "In describing this syren, singing and smiling, coaxing and cajoling, the author, with modest pride, asks his readers all round, has he once forgotten the laws of politeness, and showed the monster's hideous tail above water? No! Those who like may peep down under waves that are pretty transparent, and see it writhing and twirling, diabolically hideous and slimy, flapping amongst bones, or curling round corpses; but above the water line, I ask, has not everything been proper, agreeable and decorous, and has any the most squeamish immoralist in Vanity Fair a right to cry fie?" (chap. 64).[70] In accordance with his assumed virtue, Thackeray poeticized his reptilian imagery with mythological associations. Here mermaids "twanging their harps and combing their hair" as they bask upon their rocks are contrasted with

Vanity Fair, chapter 44, initial letter *O* (Becky as a Lorelei). (From volume 2 of *The Works of William Makepeace Thackeray* [Centenary Biographical Edition]; reproduced by permission of John Murray, Ltd.)

these same creatures beneath the surface transformed into "fiendish marine cannibals, revelling and feasting on their wretched pickled victims." Several numbers before, readers had encountered a Lorelei adorning a chapter heading, here shown with her tail underneath the water. Other chapter emblems are more grisly, like one showing Dobbin on a charger defending himself against a winged serpent (chap. 14), another whose initial is made up of coiled snakes (chap. 23), and still another representing Hecate brandishing her snaky wand (chap. 63).

One episode of *The Mysteries of London* evokes the gaudy luxury of Crockford's, where "the whole magic scene was brilliantly lighted up with innumerable wax candles, the lustre of which was reflected in the immense mirrors."[71] The manager of Vanity Fair prefers to "illuminate" his scene with his "own candles," and they do light up some of the byways and hidden alleys that G. W. M. Reynolds had stalked. There are "mysteries" in Vanity Fair, most of which remain so. One relates to how the Sedleys' prosperity has been built up. While Mrs. Sedley enjoys her customary round of social life and shopping, we are informed that "Papa conducted his mysterious operations in the city—a stirring place in those days when war was raging all over Europe, and empires were being staked" (chap. 12). Just as mysteriously, but presumably bearing some connection with the necromancy of high finance and high statesmanship, this prosperity suddenly collapses. Later the author admits to his readers certain limitations to his omniscience: "With regard to the world of female fashion and its customs, the present writer can only speak at second hand. A man can no more penetrate or understand these mysteries than he can know what the ladies talk about when they go upstairs after dinner" (chap. 37). Tom Eaves, one of the author's sources of information, on the other hand, is said to be well up on "all the great folks of London, and the stories and mysteries of each family" (chap. 47). As for Becky's successful seasons in the social world: "We must be brief in descanting upon this part of her career. As I cannot describe the mysteries of freemasonry, although I have a shrewd idea that it is a humbug: so an uninitiated man cannot take it upon himself to pourtray the great world accurately and had best keep his opinions to himself whatever they are" (chap. 51). When we pick up Becky in Germany, having lost sight of her for a time following upon her fall in fortune, our curiosity about her is squelched by the narrator: "Her history was after all a mystery. Parties were divided about her" (chap. 64).

Such phrases indicate that with *Vanity Fair* Thackeray meant to make his own unique contribution to the numerous "mysteries" that had been crowding the bookstalls since Eugène Sue conducted readers of the *Journal des débats* on a vicarious tour of the sinister streets of Paris. Thackeray might have given to his version the title of that "admirable novel" by the "eminent" writer Snooks, whose "Mysteries of Mayfair" he later recommended to the readers of *Punch,* though his own fell short of the 281,000 a week sale of that delectation in numbers.[72] In his essay "On Some French Fashionable Novels," it is true, Thackeray had professed a preference for "men of genteel society" over those "in a state of convulsive crime," but it is evident from the "mysteries" he refers to with their hints of hidden evil that the urban and the suburban (in the French sense) worlds are not really so far apart. The most dramatic incident in *Vanity Fair* involves *crim con,* whether in word, or in deed (Becky may be technically correct in affirming "I am innocent," but that is hardly the point). The devious working out of Becky's intrigue with Lord Steyne, leading to her repudiation by her husband and the "wicked nobleman" both, is Thackeray's dusty answer to Reynolds's question: "Are English women always pure, is vengeance unknown in Britain?" Becky is certainly not among the English women Reynolds alludes to who have committed infanticide, but she is guilty of the more insidious sin of child neglect. As for other "French" themes like murder, the fact that Becky could be accused of poisoning Jos Sedley, whether or not she actually had, says sufficient for her reputation. Of the lesser crimes registered by Reynolds, outright robbery may not be committed in Vanity Fair, but its citizens are not above cheating at cards, welshing on debts, and depriving tradespeople of their just due. By allowing himself French license in subject matter but employing English reticence in treating it, this "manager" in effect obtains the best of both worlds—as we have come to expect from his eclectic outlook. Moreover his mincing tone is admirably suited to a world where sin is sublimated and concealed, where cruelty tends to be mental rather than physical, where people think thoughts that they do not speak out and do things that "good" people just do not talk about. "Quand on parle à tout le monde, il faut parler comme tout le monde," he had learned from the editor whom Jerome Paturot meets.[73] Our adaptable author consequently speaks to the men and women of Vanity Fair in the language of Vanity Fair—innuendo.

It is not of course the Mysteries of Mayfair alone that engage this Snooks of Vanity Fair. His "survey of the bustling place" ranges wide, beginning at a girls' school in Chiswick Mall, ending at a fair somewhere in London, stopping off at Queen's Crawley, Brighton, Brussels, and the Rhine country in between. Its span encompasses town and country, the continent, even India. Socially it plumbs all the ranks of society, but scrambles them with snobbish servants, parvenu merchants, penurious baronets, and corrupt peers. It is a world that seems on its surface to be governed by fortuity and mischance. A sudden downturn in the city following Napoleon's defeat brings poverty to the Sedleys of Bloomsbury and transfers them to genteel poverty in the Fulham Road.[74] The whim of a maiden aunt defeats the expectations of Captain and Mrs. Crawley. It is a world too where people are difficult to fathom. A Rawdon Crawley unexpectedly demonstrates pride, tenderness, and courage; the meek and simple Lady Jane Sheepshanks reveals unsuspected reserves of moral strength. The calculating Becky Sharp, herself tripped up by so many miscalculations, eventually proves capable of a selfless act in bringing Dobbin and Amelia together. The "mysteries" exposed in Thackeray's universe are the mystifications of life itself—sudden rises and falls, unaccountable turns in fortune, the "chronicle of Fate's surprises" as he was to express it in his poem "Vanitas Vanitatum," and the greater surprises of human character. "Man is a Drama—of Wonder and Passion, and Mystery and Meanness, and Beauty and Truthfulness, and Etecetera," his audience read in one of the Snob Papers.[75]

The sense of an audience as heterogeneous and variegated as the world of Vanity Fair dominates the manager throughout the performance. His addresses appeal to different kinds of readers: "If Miss Rebecca Sharp had determined in her heart upon making a conquest of this big beau [Jos Sedley], I don't think, ladies, we have any right to blame her" (chap. 3); "All which details, I have no doubt, JONES, who reads this book at his Club, will pronounce to be excessively foolish, trivial, twaddling, and ultra-sentimental" (chap. 1); "Every reader of a sentimental turn (and we desire no other) must have been pleased with the *tableau* with which the last act of our little drama concluded" (chap. 15, referring to Sir Pitt's proposal); "'We don't care a fig for her [Amelia],' writes some unknown correspondent with a pretty little handwriting and a pink seal to her note" (chap. 12); "Perhaps some infatuated swain has ere this mistaken insensibility for modesty, dullness for maiden-reserve, mere vacuity for sweet bashfulness, and a goose, in a word, for a swan" (chap. 13, referring to George Osborne's courtship of Amelia); "I throw out these queries for intelligent readers to answer" (chap. 23).

The Manager does not address children and adolescents openly, but the audience gathered around the long-eared clown-moralist on the wrapper includes a little boy in a military suit and a baby in its mother's arms. Our "week-day preacher" seems to have recognized along with Mrs. Gore that English novels, unlike French, "are

placed in the hands of persons of immature judgment and experience," and he is certainly aware of young ears in his congregation.
The toy box on the title page of the first edition in book form
continues the children's show framework of the speech "Before the
Curtain" ("The famous little Becky Puppet," "the Amelia Doll,"
"the Dobbin Figure," "the Little Boys' Dance," "the Wicked Nobleman," "Old Nick"). This motif was sustained for the first readers of
the narrative that follows by scattered "illuminations" in initial letters, such as two boys in paper hats playing soldier (chap. 5); two
children peeping through the holes of a picture box (chap. 20); or a
tot in a clown suit walking on stilts (chap. 20). With the world of
children's fun and games the Manager began, and to it he reverts in
his farewell to the reader, which is, however, on a note far removed
from the "happy ever after" of children's fantasies: "Ah! *Vanitas
Vanitatum*! Which of us is happy in this world? Which of us has his
desire? or, having it is satisfied?—Come, children, let us shut up
the box and the puppets, for our play is played out." This comedy
is finished now that "the famous little Becky Puppet" has had her
Jos by the "leading strings," and that "the Dobbin Figure" has at
long last captured his "Amelia Doll." The clown holding forth on
the barrel has not only reduced war, politics, and society to the level
of "comic history"; he has also brought his deep fable within the
comprehension of "Great and Small Children" (to whom that
"Fireside Pantomime" *The Rose and the Ring* later was
addressed)—be they actually children, like little Georgy or little
Rawdon; merely child-minded, like Amelia Sedley, and Rawdon
Crawley, before his eyes are opened; retarded adults, like Lord
George Hunt of the Straight Waistcoat, kinsman of Lord Steyne,
who is given to playing with the dolls belonging to his keeper's
baby; or those who would become as children again, like virtually
all of us.

In the midst of the frolic we are offered hints aplenty that the
child's world is not all sugar plums—particularly in a grisly cut
showing a little boy and girl crouched under two crossed swords on
a wall, accompanying the comparison of the ill-starred family of
Gaunt House to the household of Damocles (chap. 47). So evil
threatens innocent minds, as the sins of the fathers are visited upon
the children, and it is forced on our minds that *Vanity Fair,* in
common with many didactic novels of the age, addresses itself to
the nature and nurture of the young idea. Opening in a school and
ending with a call to children from play, it superimposes the class-

room upon its more obvious theatrical frame. The author's educational qualifications are established by the titles scattered about here and there of the "improving" books beloved of early nineteenth-century parents and teachers. Fenelon's *Télémaque* is given as a prize to Dobbin at Doctor Swishtail's Academy. Amelia purchases *The Parent's Assistant* of Miss Edgeworth and Thomas Day's *Sandford and Merton* for Little Georgy. Polly Clapp, daughter of the Sedleys' landlady, reads *Fatherless Fanny* along with *The Scottish Chiefs*. Addressing his readers early in the novel where he has been describing the schooling of Dobbin and George Osborne under the supervision of Doctor Swishtail, the author seems to undercut all such guidance: "If people would but leave children to themselves; if teachers would cease to bully them; if parents would

Vanity Fair, chapter 47, cut of children playing under the family escutcheon at Gaunt House. (From volume 2 of *The Works of William Makepeace Thackeray* [Centenary Biographical Edition]; reproduced by permission of John Murray, Ltd.)

not insist upon directing their thoughts and dominating their feelings—those feelings and thoughts which are a mystery to all (for how much do you and I know of each other, of our children, of our fathers, of our neighbour, and how far more beautiful and sacred are the thoughts of the poor lad or girl whom you govern likely to be, than those of the dull world-corrupted person who rules him?)" (chap. 5). The "world-corrupted" Becky Sharp, to be sure, hardly answers to the model "Good French Governess" of Miss Edgeworth's *Moral Tales*. In a subsequent novel, we find Becky reading the kind of pamphlets that Lady Emily Southdown writes and outwardly performing those acts of charity that this religious peeress would approve of.[76] If there seems to be a lack of inner conviction to the conversion of this "Fatherless Fanny," so much for the moral effects of books, our worldly teacher seems to be saying. He appears to set more store by living example—as with little Rawdon under the care of Lady Jane, and even the spoiled Georgy, once he is adopted by Dobbin. Ultimately "those feelings and thoughts which are a mystery to all" were the "mysteries" that most fascinated Thackeray, and so we are led to expect that the theme of the influence of parents on children for good and bad, latent in *Vanity Fair*, will become central in the more purely domestic novels that follow.

It is amply demonstrated that the world is "a very vain, wicked, foolish place, full of all sorts of humbugs and falsenesses and pretensions," in this cynical-sentimental-comic history. Yet in some ways we seem to "advance over ruins," to invoke Victor Cousin once more. Gaunt House may go the way of the Seraglio occupied by the decaying Padishah of Constantinople[77] and Hyde Park Gardens the way of the Hanging Gardens of Babylon; Sir Pitt Crawley, "both out of pocket and out of spirits" after the passage of the First Reform Bill, "prophesied the speedy ruin of the Empire"; and the preacher in cap and bells likened all humanity in a passage (which he subsequently canceled) to Homer's "race of leaves"; but Dobbin's country place, in Hampshire, we note, is called "the Evergreens." There are other signs of life and hope stirring. We learn that there was "a perpetual crossing of pony-chaises" between Dobbins' establishment and the adjacent one of Queen's Crawley, now superintended by Lady Jane, who inherits the title of Lady Crawley that Becky Sharp had aspired to. We learn also that Lady Jane becomes godmother to the child of Dobbin and Amelia, and that both young Rawdon and young Georgy are rivals for the hand of Lady Jane's daughter. It appears to be in the union of those enfranchised by the Reform Bill (Dobbin is the son of a grocer become the "best of gentlemen") and the squirearchy rooted in the land and in Christian principle that Thackeray pins his hopes for the regeneration of the realm. He seems, at any rate, willing to retain the best elements of the aristocracy and the middle class alike, while rejecting the worst.

All in all, in what he chooses as well as in what he avoids, the author of *Vanity Fair* could say, along with his fellow contributor to *Punch*, the author of *The Comic History of England,* that far from having "a contempt for what is great and good," he has "so much real respect for the great and good that he is desirous of preventing the little and bad from continuing to claim admiration on false pretenses."[78] Both satirists remained faithful to the credo of the Punch figure, who announced on his first appearance in motley, flourishing his baton: "The noble in his robes and coronet—the beadle in his gaudy livery of scarlet and purple, and gold—the dignitary in the fulness of his pomp—the demagogue in the triumph of his hollowness—these and other visual and oral cheats by which mankind is cajoled, have passed in review before us, conjured up by the magic wand of *Punch.*"[79]

Some years before Thackeray conceived *Vanity Fair,* a friend of his had defined satire as "a glass in which the beholder sees every face but his own."[80] To the contrary Thackeray, who, as we have already observed, shows us on the title page of the first edition in book form a clown looking at himself in a cracked glass; nor did he intend to exclude himself from his bill of indictment in *The Book of Snobs,* which was signed "By One of Themselves." "Do I wish all Snobs to perish? Do I wish these Snob Papers to determine?" he asks at the end of one of them. "Suicidal fool! art not thou, too, a Snob and a brother?"[81] He echoes these words in a chapter in *Vanity Fair* where he requests the permission of his readers, "as a man and a brother, not only to introduce them [my characters], but occasionally to step down from the platform, and talk about them" (chap. 8). He makes a point too about being dressed not in clerical garb, but in the same way as his "congregation," and indeed clown suits and foolscaps are perceptible among the listeners, old and young, gathered around the barrel, as depicted on the yellow cover.

Identifying himself with his audience is one means by which this satirist attempts to soften the blows of Master Punch's castigating rod. His disposition is another. "The world is a looking-glass, and gives back to every man the reflection of his own face," as he explicates the picture on the title page, following Montaigne's philosophy, to which he adds: "Frown at it, and it will in turn look sourly upon you; laugh at it and with it, and it is a jolly kind companion; and so let all young persons take their choice" (chap. 2). The choice that our "laughing philosopher" makes here, in keeping with this world where all is vanity, is to abandon the sour visage of the clown on the title page in favor of the urbane smile. He is prepared, moreover, to accommodate his mood to suit the mingled throng at the booths. At the beginning of one chapter, Vanity Fair is described as a place where "Satire and Sentiment can visit arm in arm together; where you light on the strangest contrasts laughable and tearful: where you may be gentle and pathetic, or savage and cynical with perfect propriety" (chap. 17). Emotional attitudes that had tended to be dissociated in Thackeray's previous writings are here brought together in a nimble fusion of his "genteel," "romantic," "facetious," and "terrific" manners, providing "something for everyone."

"My dear sir, when you have well studied the world—how supremely great the meanest thing in the world is, and how infinitely mean the greatest—I am mistaken if you do not make a strange and proper jumble of the sublime and the ridiculous, the lofty and the low," to recall once more the curtain lines of Ikey Solomons, the putative narrator of *Catherine*.[82] Transmuted into the Manager of the Performance from the erstwhile master of Grand Guignol tableaux, he has by now indeed "well studied the world," its humbugs and its honest men, its poor, rich, and shabby genteel, its preoccupation with getting and spending, and brings to the little universe of Bloomsbury and Mayfair the cosmopolitan outlook of the traveler. The result is another "strange and proper jumble," but of different elements—the naïveté of the children's play blended with the sophistication of the society novelist, the *haut monde* linked with the underworld of thieves' literature, all "illuminated" with the whimsicality, diablerie, and grotesquerie of the comic magazine. But we are led to the same conclusion: "Well, Snobbishness pervades the little Social Farce as well as the great State Comedy," Thackeray's audience had already read in *The Book of Snobs*.[83] Those who had been with him from the beginning of his writing career knew his various versions of the "little Social Farce." With *Vanity Fair* he graduated to "the great State Comedy." From now on there was to be more of the pathos and tragedy of humanity. "I have corrected the last corrections: and say now Amen and Good Luck to Vanity Fair," Thackeray wrote to his publisher in the letter that accompanied the final proofs. "May the public relish it, may the publishers profit, may the author be always honest and kind hearted."[84] The publishers did profit from it eventually, the public relished it gradually,[85] though at first they noticed the honesty more than the kind heart lurking beneath. "I am beginning to see the folly of my ways & that people are a hundred times more frank, kind and good-natured than a certain author chooses to paint them," he wrote to a friend a year after *Vanity Fair* made its debut and while it was still running in monthly parts. "He shan't wear yellow any more: it is he who is jaundiced and not the world that is bitter: in fine . . . I will have my next book in rose colour and try and amend."[86] As things turned out, he retained the yellow cover, but he modified his "jaundiced" view of the world.

1. To Lady Normanby (see Ray, *The Uses of Adversity*, between pp. 366 and 367, illustration 22).

2.
Here let us sport,
Boys, as we sit;
Laughter and wit
Flashing so free.
Life is but short—
When we are gone,
Let them sing on
Round the old tree.

From "The Mahogany Tree," *Punch*, 9 January, 1847; *Works*, 13:51 (referring to the tree around which the *Punch* staff gathered for their weekly dinners).

3. "On the Introduction of Pantomime into the English Language," *Punch*, 17 July 1841, p. 10.

4. "The Moral of Punch," ibid., p. 1.

5. "The Thieves' Literature of France," *Foreign Quarterly Review*, April 1843, p. 239; *New Sketch Book*, p. 190.

6. "English History and Character on the French Stage," *Foreign Quarterly Review*, April 1843, p. 168; *New Sketch Book*, p. 178. In "The Puppet Frame of *Vanity Fair*," *English Language Notes*, September 1968, pp. 40–42, Myron Taube contends that this device as well as the "Before the Curtain" speech were "afterthoughts" for Thackeray, suggested by a chance conversation with a friend while he was at work on the last number, but it seems obvious that both puppets and clowns were very much on his mind earlier. The additional detail of the barrel top possibly owes its origin to a piece of light verse, "The opinions of one fond of liquor," found in Thackeray's Commonplace Book dating from his year in Weimar. The last lines of the first stanza read:

I rate him an ass, who despising his glass
For place & preferment will quarrel
My creed I do hold with the Cynic of old
For he stuck all his life to the barrel!
(Weimar MS, 1830–31, Morgan Library, New York City)

This presumably is the first version of the drinking song attributed to Thackeray in *Das Chaos*, a literary magazine edited by Goethe's daughter-in-law Ottilie von Goethe, See Walter Vulpius, "Thackeray in Weimar," *Century Magazine* 53 (April 1897): 920–28. Vulpius refers to the MS in the Poet-Archives in Weimar.

7. Advertisements in the various numbers quote laudatory reviews from newspapers outside London such as the *Western Times, Bristol Courier*, and *Chester Courant*, as well as from Ireland (*Cork Examiner*) and Scotland (*Dumfries Courier* and *Edinburgh Weekly Register*).

8. "English History and Character on the French Stage," p. 149; *New Sketch Book*, p. 152. See above, pp. 94–95.

9. "The Moral of Punch," p. 1.

10. G. W. M. Reynolds, *The Mysteries of London*, 4 vols. (London: George Vickers, 1846), vol. 1, chap. 11.

11. Advertised in *Vanity Fair*, no. 12 (December 1847).

12. Gilbert Abbott A'Beckett, *The Comic History of England*, 2 vols. (London: Punch, 1847–48), vol. 1, preface, chaps. 1, 7; vol. 2, bk. 5, chap. 2. A'Beckett also wrote a *Comic History of Rome*.

13. Lewis Melville, *Life of William Makepeace Thackeray*, 2 vols. (London: Hutchinson, 1899), 1:169.

14. A'Beckett, *Comic History of England*, preface, vol. 1.

15. *Punch*, 22 August 1846, p. 78, contains a cartoon captioned "Proposed Statue of Punch at Hyde Park Corner" representing the Punch figure in place of the statue of the Duke of Wellington. For further details on the topicality of this drawing, see Joan Stevens, "*Vanity Fair* and the London Skyline," *Costerus*, n.s. 2 (1974): 13–41. This article is copiously illustrated, showing the real counterparts of monuments caricatured by Thackeray.

16. *Felix Farley's Journal, Western Times;* both quoted in no. 13 (January 1848).

17. As a modern critic puts it: "Almost every sin in Vanity Fair can be traced, beyond personal weakness, to the fundamental laws of money and class; to fawn upon the rich and kick the poor is a Christian law of the land. The poison in Vanity Fair infects even the servants" (A. E. Dyson, "Vanity Fair: An Irony Against Heroes," *Critical Quarterly*, Spring 1964, p. 20).

18. *Punch*, 26 December 1846, p. 261; *Works*, 6:432.

19. *Punch*, 12 July 1845, p. 25.

20. Maria Edgeworth, *Practical Education, Works*, 13 vols. (Boston: S. Parker, 1825), vol. 1, chap. 20.

21. Ibid.

22. In particular by Lionel Stevenson in his article "*Vanity Fair* and Lady Morgan," *PMLA* 48 (June 1933): 547–51. Glorvina O'Dowd bears the first name of the heroine of *The Wild Irish Girl*, and in *Florence Macarthy* appears a family named Crawley who name their children after viceroys and secretaries of state. Lady Morgan reviewed *The Irish Sketch Book* in the *Athenaeum*, 13 May 1843. That Thackeray was closely acquainted with her at this time is further attested by a letter of 4 December 1847 in the Fales Library, New York University (unpublished), in which he declines her invitation to dinner.

23. "Shrove Tuesday in Paris," *Britannia*, 5 June 1841, p. 475; *Works*, 13:568.

24. "Shrove Tuesday in Paris," pp. 476–77; *Works*, 13:568–69. In pointing out the anticipation of Becky Sharp in Mlle Pauline, Gordon Ray suggests that Thackeray presents here a "laundered" version of his relations with her for prudential reasons (see *The Uses of Adversity* [New York: McGraw-Hill, 1955], p. 126). Titmarsh states that he visited her rooms to fetch some shirts she had made for him.

25. See above, p. 161.

26. "Jerome Paturot," *Works*, 13:391. Here Thackeray has translated a portion of chap. 7 ("Paturot feuilletoniste").

27. Ibid., p. 394.

28. Ibid., p. 396.

29. See above, p. 128.

30. "The Snobs of England," chap. 16, *Punch*, 20 June 1846, p. 271; *Works*, 6:357–59.

31. *Pictorial Times*, 25 May 1844; *Works* (Furniss Ed.), 12:310–11.

32. *Morning Chronicle*, 4 May 1846; *Contributions*, p. 142. Her novel *The Hamiltons* (1834) expresses the moral indignation with the corruption of George IV found in *Vanity Fair*. There also are analogous characters, e.g. the sweet, innocent young wife Susan (Amelia), betrayed by her self-centered husband Augustus (George Osborne) who has an affair with the hypocritical Caroline Cadogan (Becky). However, Thackeray's first recorded reference to this novel is in a letter to Mrs. Gore in 1850 (*Letters*, 2:724–25) commenting on the reprint that came out that year.

33. Henry Colburn, *The Court Journal*, 23 May 1829. Quoted in Matthew Whiting Rosa, *The Silver-Fork School: Novels of Fashion Preceding Vanity Fair* (New York: Columbia University Press, 1936).

34. "Fashnable Fax And Polite Annygoats. By Charles Yellowplush, Esq," *Fraser's Magazine*, November 1837; *Works*, 13:260 (comment by "Oliver Yorke").

35. "Jeames's Diary," *Punch*, 15 March 1845, p. 210; *Works*, 3:392.

36. "Jeames's Diary," p. 210; *Works*, 3:393.

37. According to Michael Sadleir, Mills "was certainly a member of the very world whose antics he therein describes. Undoubtedly, therefore, his story was founded on fact, and we may assume it to have reflected current gossip, if nothing more substantial" (*The Strange Life of Lady Blessington* [New York: Farrar, Straus, 1947], p. 261). D'Horsay is, of course, the notorious dandy Count D'Orsay, who in this novel rather improbably reforms after a wild course of gambling, debt, and dissipation. The book was reprinted in 1902 with a "Key" supplied by Joseph Grego. According to Grego, it was "instantly suppressed" when first published. Sadleir comments that "one is less surprised that it should have been withdrawn than that in 1844 it should ever have been published."

38. In one episode the marquis, knowing that he is on the point of death from an unnamed disease, has a valet arrange a tryst with two prostitutes at a hotel in Richmond as a last fling. So feeble has he become that he can only recline in a moribund state while the ladies of the evening cavort naked before him. "Poor old man! What, pity *him*!" comments the author, "the debauched sensualist, the heartless *roué*, the gamester—he who never evinced a latent spark of virtue among his glaring vice, revelling in crime even in his impotent age and dotage" (chap. 14). Thackeray merely hints at an Italian mistress after Lord Steyne breaks off his affair with Becky, and also implies that he is not above hiring assassins to exact revenge.

39. Kathleen Tillotson has pointed out that Mills's novel "occasionally anticipates" *Vanity Fair* (*Novels of the Eighteen-Forties* [Oxford: Clarendon Press, 1954], p. 85, n. 2).

40. Lady Blessington, *Strathern* (1845), chap. 1 (Lord Wyndermere speaking). In chap. 1 of *Memoirs of a Femme de Chambre*, one of Lady Blessington's characters adopts a point of view we associate with Thackeray, purporting to reveal "*en déshabillé*" the minds and characters of society figures normally seen by the world "only in full costume, with their manners as scrupulously got up for the occasion as is their dress." In this same chapter the author thinks of herself, like Thackeray, as Asmodeus, and justifies authorial omniscience.

41. The allusion is to George Lillie Craik's *The Pursuit of Learning under Difficulties* (1830). In this same chapter Thackeray refers to "the apprentices in the Park" among those who envy the dandies strolling with their *chères amies* in this popular place of assembly, a far cry from the industrious apprentice extolled by Craik.

42. See above, pp. 122–23.

43. "New Accounts of Paris," *Foreign Quarterly Review*, January 1844, p. 470; *New Sketch Book*, p. 232. Italics mine.

44. "New Accounts of Paris," p. 471. In the book Thackeray reviewed, Mme de Girardin used the male pseudonym of le Vicomte de Launay.

45. The influence of Balzac remains a vexed, tantalizing, and unresolved question. Although Thackeray was generally unenthusiastic about Balzac in his public pronouncements, the two authors have frequently been linked, both in Thackeray's time and in our own. The year after his death, for one outstanding example, the *Dublin University Magazine* (December 1864) made an extended comparison. W. C. D. Pacey, in "Balzac and Thackeray," *Modern Language Review* 36 (April 1941):

213–24, suggests several analogies, but also cites an article that appeared in the *Revue des deux mondes* of 1849, calling attention to the difference that Balzac reveled in details of corruption, whereas Thackeray merely suggested it. The tendency to couple their names is further indicated in the first French translation of *Vanity Fair* (*La foire aux vanités*, 1855), where it is referred to, in the preface, as "cette comédie humaine." (The translator, however, likens Becky to la Baronne d'Ange, a figure in a light risqué comedy then in vogue.) The Balzac novel closest to *Vanity Fair* is *Cousine Bette*, published in book form about the same time, but it has been pointed out that Thackeray could have read it the year before in *Le constitutionnel*, one of the papers taken at the Reform Club, where he did some of his writing (see A. Carey Taylor, "Balzac et Thackeray," *Revue de littérature comparée* 34 [July–September 1960]: 354–69). However, Raymond Maître, in "Balzac, Thackeray, et Charles de Bernard," *Revue de littérature comparée* 24 (April–June 1950): 278–93, emphasizes Thackeray's affinities with de Bernard in such matters as urbanity of tone, grace of style, and delicate feminine psychology.

46. Preface to *The Lover and the Husband* (English version of de Bernard's *Gerfaut* [London, 1841]).

47. "On Some French Fashionable Novelists," *Works*, 5:97.

48. Dedication to *Cécile de Vareil*, the first part of *Le faubourg Saint-Honoré* (Paris: Librairie de Charles Gosselin, 1839). Gosselin also published several of Charles de Bernard's novels, including *Les ailes d'Icaire*, part of which Thackeray translated in *The Paris Sketch Book*. *Les ailes d'Icaire*, as well as *Le faubourg Saint-Honoré*, it might be added, were first issued in yellow wrappers.

49. Introduction to *Le faubourg Saint-Germain* (Paris: Chez Ladvocat, 1837).

50. "On Some French Fashionable Novelists," *Works*, 5:95–97. The passage is from chap. 2 of part 1 (*Gérard de Stolberg*). Thackeray does not give the chapter title or epigraph.

51. *Le faubourg Saint-Germain*, vol. 1, chap. 5.

52. *Le faubourg Saint-Germain*, vol. 2 (*Madame la duchesse*), introduction. It is amusing to see that Viel-Castel encountered some of the kind of audience response Thackeray was to meet. In this introduction he confides to a patron that he has been accused of immorality, of abusing his privilege of entering society for his own profit, of malicious caricature, of betraying secret confidences, and of all manner of inaccuracy and distortion. He hastens to assure his confidante that he paints "d'après nature."

53. "New Accounts of Paris," p. 486; *New Sketch Book*, p. 250.

54. Mrs. Gore, preface to *The Lover and the Husband* (London: Richard Bentley, 1841).

55. Reynolds's coverage is comprehensive, taking in virtually all the novelists then in vogue (e.g., George Sand, Balzac, Sue, Soulié, Dumas, Ricard, Merimée, de Kock, Janin, Hugo, Lacroix) as well as important poets such as Lamartine and Béranger and intellectuals such as de Tocqueville and Michael Chevalier; his concluding chapter is devoted to national airs and songs.

56. "French Revolution of 1830," *Quarterly Review*, July 1833, pp. 464–85. Attributed to John Wilson Croker in *Wellesley Index*, vol. 1.

57. G. W. M. Reynolds, *The Modern Literature of France* (London: George Henderson, 1839), p. vii.

58. Ibid., pp. xvii–xviii.

59. "The Thieves' Literature of France," p. 241; *New Sketch Book*, p. 193.

60. 19 January 1843, from Paris, *Letters*, 2:92.

61. "The Thieves' Literature of France," p. 241.

62. Diary, 6 January 1844, 21 January 1844, *Letters*, 2:139 (and n. 4), 2:141; letter of 2 February 1844 to M. Giraldon, *Letters*, 2:159.

63. Among the numerous on record are *Mysteries of Berlin*, *The Mysteries of Marseilles* (attributed to Emile Zola), and *Mysterios de Napoles* (published in Lisbon); in America there were *Mysteries of New Orleans*, *Mysteries and Miseries of New York* (both by "Ned Buntline," the promoter of Buffalo Bill), *Mysteries and Miseries of San Francisco*, by a Californian, *Mysteries of Three Cities—Boston, New York, and Philadelphia*,

and *The Mysteries of Nashua; or, Revenge Punished and Constancy Rewarded*. Perhaps the coup de grace was rendered by James Buel's *Mysteries and Miseries of America's Great Cities* (1883). For an account of the tremendous vogue of this book, see Pierre Chaunu, *Eugène Sue et la seconde république* (Paris: Presses Universitaires, 1948), p. 16.

64. Reprinted in *Vanity Fair*, Riverside ed. (1963), appendix B, p. 676.

65. George H. Ford is misleading in calling Reynolds "the Mickey Spillane of the Victorian Age" (*Dickens and His Readers* [Princeton, N.J.: Princeton University Press, 1955], p. 79). According to his own testimony, Spillane had no other intention than to write the kind of books he himself could enjoy, whereas it becomes immediately clear that Reynolds had a "purpose" in his sensationalism.

Thackeray appears to have had regard for Reynolds as both man and author. While *Vanity Fair* was appearing in monthly parts, Thackeray reported on a meeting of the working classes at Kennington Common presided over by Reynolds, for the *Morning Chronicle* (14 March 1848). In this article he characterized Reynolds's speech championing the Chartist cause as "temperate." At a dinner of the Royal Literary Fund on 10 May 1858, Thackeray referred to Reynolds as "a great Novelist, a member of my own profession . . . standing upon Kennington Common in the van of liberty, prepared to assume any responsibility, to take upon himself any direction of government, to decorate himself with the tricolour sash, or the Robespierre waistcoat" (Melville, *Life*, 2:66–67; cited by Ray, *Contributions*, p. 94 n).

66. The devious windings of the story defy synopsis, but it has a framework of sorts in the moral trials of two brothers, Richard and Eugene Markham, the first of whom proves incorruptible, despite the sordid environment in which he moves, while the other progressively deteriorates and eventually dies a violent death.

67. Thackeray's acquaintance with Reynolds goes back to his student-journalist days in Paris. In his autobiography James Payn recalled: "Thackeray told me that the first money he ever received in literature . . . was from G. W. M. Reynolds" (*Some Literary Recollections* [London: Smith, Elder, 1884], p. 34). The exact nature of their association, long a matter for scholarly conjecture, has recently been clarified by the discovery of a file of the *Paris Literary Gazette* edited by Reynolds, in which are to be found five articles contributed during 1835, signed "W.M.T." See Jean Guivarc'h, "Deux journalistes anglaises de Paris en 1835 (George W. M. Reynolds et W.M.T.)," *Etudes anglaises* 28 (April–June 1975): 203–12. Here reprinted for the first time is one of Thackeray's pieces, "England," from the *Gazette* of 10 November 1835.

68. "The Night Attack" is reprinted, minus the "gloss," in the Riverside ed., appendix B, pp. 672–73. As is suggested by the Tillotsons, this parody is a complicated pastiche. Apart from the atmosphere of Sue and Reynolds, there are definite echoes of the opening of Bulwer's *Paul Clifford* (reissued in 1848), as well as the perennial *Pelham* (chap. 82). In addition, John Sutherland has pointed out a verbal correspondence between the opening words of "The Night Attack" and the beginning of G. P. R. James's *Agincourt*, first published in November 1844 (see his "A Date for the Early Composition of *Vanity Fair*," *English Studies*, February 1972, p. 4). There may be a further guying of G. P. R. James in the cartoon Thackeray drew in the manuscript of this chapter showing a masked highwayman holding up a kneeling fat lady on the road. James's *The King's Highway* is advertised in part I of *Vanity Fair*.

69. Reynolds, *The Mysteries of London*, vol. 1, chaps. 9, 23.

70. Cf. also: "Every schoolboy, pre-admonished that the Syrens were scaly monsters with soft faces and sweet voices, is enabled to jest upon the folly of their victims. But the danger of the temptation consisted in the glassy waters, which, concealing their deformities, allowed them to be perceived only as the fairest of the fair" (Mrs. Gore, *Cecil a Peer* [1841], chap. 1).

71. Reynolds, *The Mysteries of London*, vol. 2, chap. 241.

72. "A Plan for a Prize Novel," *Punch* 20 (1851): 75; *Works*, 6:535.

73. See above, pp. 127–28.

74. This turn in the Sedleys' fortunes is anticipated in "The Second Funeral of Napoleon," where high politics and war are juxtaposed with ordinary life in connection with an intrigue involving Turkey, England, and France at the time of the removal of Napoleon's remains from Saint Helena: "You, my dear, must know as

well as I, that the balance of power in Europe could not possibly be maintained in any such way; and though, to be sure, for the last fifteen years, the progress of the old robber [Sultan Mehemet Ali] has not made much difference to us in the neighbourhood of Russell Square, and the battle of Nezib did not in the least affect our taxes, our homes, our institutions, or the price of butcher's meat, yet there is no knowing what *might* have happened had Mehemet Ali been allowed to remain quietly as he was; and the balance of power in Europe might have been—the deuce knows where" *(Works,* 4:685).

75. *Works,* 6:470.

76. *The Newcomes,* chap. 13. Miss M. T. Wigglesworth, the genteel authoress of *The Orphan of Pimlico; a Moral Tale of Belgravian Life,* identifies herself as "many years Governess in the Nobilitys families." Her writing furthermore is endorsed by "The Rev. Mr. Oriel, The Rev. Mr. Thurifer and other revered clergy of the district." This sport was brought out posthumously in 1876 under her father's name by Anne Thackeray. Its date of composition is unknown.

77. Lord Steyne is depicted as an oriental potentate, reclined on a sofa in turban and Persian slippers, leering, teeth bared, in the picture inside the initial that begins chap. 52. In chap. 49 the intimidated female entourage of Gaunt House is referred to as "Lord Steyne's Hareem." These are among reminders of Thackeray's Eastern voyage of 1844, a more extended one being the charade played out in Turkish costume at the ball at Levant House (chap. 51) led by that "elegant dandy and Eastern traveller" Bedwin Sands, acting as master of revels.

78. Preface, *Punch,* vol. 1.

79. Conclusion to "The Moral of Punch."

80. *The Tin Trumpet; or, Heads And Tales, For The Wise And Waggish* . . . By The Late Paul Chatfield, M.D. [Horace Smith]. (London: Printed for Whittaker & Co., 1836), 2:135. This was among humorous books in Thackeray's library, and was actually attributed to him until the belated revelation of its authorship.

81. "Snobs and Marriage," *Works,* 6:432.

82. See above, p. 165.

83. "Snobbium Gatherum," *Works,* 6:413–14.

84. Undated letter to Bradbury and Evans in Morgan Library, New York City (MA 2011 ex/V/9/A). Since this chapter was completed, the letter has been printed in Edgar Harden's "Thackeray and His Publishers . . .," *Papers on Language & Literature* 12 (Spring 1976): 170.

85. The most specific account of its economic fortunes is Robert L. Patten, "The Fight at the Top of the Tree: *Vanity Fair* versus *Dombey and Son,*" *Studies in English Literature* 10 (Autumn 1970): 759–72. According to Patten, *Vanity Fair* actually lost money during its serial run, not making up the 1,200 pounds contracted by the publishers until 1850. However, the bound volumes and the cheap edition of 1853 were successful, and by 1859 Thackeray had earned over 1,700 pounds for his first popular novel. It appears that the successors to *Vanity Fair* with which Thackeray took firm hold of the public boosted its sales.

86. 28 March 1848, to Lady Holland; quoted in Gordon N. Ray, *The Age of Wisdom* (New York: McGraw-Hill, 1958), p. 40.

PENDENNIS; OR, THE MAN OF THE WORLD

Chapter Nine

As "Vanity Fair" was drawing to its close in July 1848, the *Advertiser* attached to its last number was able to announce the first number of a new novel from its author's pen and pencil for the coming fall. *The History of Pendennis: His Fortunes and Misfortunes, His Friends and His Greatest Enemy* had a "hero" in its title, unlike its predecessor, but issued in the familiar yellow wrappers, in twenty-two monthly numbers concluded by a double number, and "illuminated" by its author "on wood and steel," it looked like more of the same. One of its first reviewers, in fact, complained that "it cannot be described as an advance of 'Vanity Fair.' It is rather like a pair of volumes added to that story,—containing the results of a second ramble among the booths, the wild-beast shows, and the merry-go-rounds of that chaos of folly, vice and charlatanry."[1] "Why must Mr. Thackeray be always 'going to the fair?'" asked this reviewer. "His authorship seems in some danger of becoming a performance on one string with several variations, but all in the same key, and all on the same theme of 'Humbug everywhere.'"

Thackeray's publishers, Bradbury and Evans, certainly emphasized this continuity in associating the author of *Pendennis* with *Punch*, connecting his name in the first number (November 1848) not only with *Vanity Fair* but with *The Book of Snobs* as well. The characters of the new novel indeed move about in the *Punch* orbit, particularly that described in a panoramic series by Richard Doyle entitled "Mr. Pips His Diary. Manners and Customs of Ye Englyshe in 1849,"[2] which includes glimpses of "Ye Fashionable Worlde

Takynge Its Exercyse In Hyde Parke," "A Drawynge Room Day. Saynte James His Streete," "A Prospect Of Greenwich Fair," "Kensyngton Gardens With Ye Bande Playing There," "'Socyete' Enjoying Itself At A Soyree," "A Theatre Showynge Ye House Amused By Ye Comycke Actor," "Ye National Sporte!!! Of Steeple Chasynge," "A Prospect Of An Election," and "A Weddynge Breakfast," all of which have their counterparts in Arthur Pendennis's gadabout social history (in such chapters as "Mrs. Haller," "Contains some Ball-Practising," "Where Pen appears in Town and Country," "Carries the Reader both to Richmond and Greenwich," "Miss Amory's Partners," "In or Near the Temple Garden," "In which Pen Begins his Canvass," "A Chapter of Match-Making").

To more discerning readers, however, a certain shift of focus must have been evident in the new novel, superficially defined by some features of the *Punch Almanack for 1849*. This annual opens with "The Young Man's Almanack" dispensing tips to the real-life Arthur Pendennises and Harry Fokers on how to conduct oneself in fashionable places: "The fashion varies with every place you visit. For instance, you may keep your hat on at the casino; but it is scarcely considered good manners to do so at the Opera. . . . A cigar may be lighted with good effect in the corridor of the Adelphi, when the audience is coming out; but you would hardly attempt such a thing in the crush-room of her Majesty's Theatre." Bachelors are warned not to be too smug: "It is a sure sign of a cruel disposition if You see a person standing outside of St. George's, Hanover Square, deriving pleasure in watching the poor bridegrooms take the fatal leap from their carriages into the church. He who has no pity for others, depend upon it, will receive none himself, when his own fate is sealed!" Pearls of "wisdom" are strewn about: "Staring at a lady under her bonnet, is considered very much beneath a gentleman"; "A 'rising young man' is one who rises regularly—not later than eight o'clock; a 'promising young man' is one who pays his tailor not later than a twelvemonth after he has promised him"; "The old pay with money—the young with compliments."

In a matching "Lady's Almanack," the inevitable man trap opens its jaws wide, with marriage manoeuvering as rife as in a novel by Mrs. Gore. Young female readers are advised as to *The Best Partners:* "The oldest for whist, the youngest for dancing, and for marriage, which-ever you can"; and on *The Matrimonial Market:* "Buy in the cheapest, and sell in the dearest." As for *Courtship:* "A lover should be treated with the same gentleness as a new glove.

The young lady should pull him on with the utmost tenderness at first, only making the smallest advance at a time, till she gradually gains upon him, and twists him ultimately round her little finger." At Christmas time the real-life Laura Pendennises, Blanche Amorys, and Fanny Boltons were greeted by the cheery face of Punch presenting a bouquet of mistletoe to a pretty maiden with this "Caution": "Mr. Punch, desirous of combining the best counsel with the best mirth, is tremblingly anxious to inform the Young—especially Young Ladies—that, of those very Mistletoe Berries that seem so bead-like and so innocent, BIRDLIME IS OFTEN MANUFACTURED, wherewith unconscious Birds of Paradise are frequently caught, and what is dreadful to reflect upon—caged for the natural term of their life!"³

This tone of urbane banter accompanying advice to youth, "combining the best counsel with the best mirth," is set by the opening of *Pendennis*, where Major Pendennis finds among his morning mail at his club in Pall Mall a letter from the young hero's mother, his sister-in-law, entreating this sophisticate to extricate "my dearest boy" from his childish infatuation with an actress. Readers were into the fifth number of *Pendennis* (March 1849)—by which time Miss Fotheringay was out of young Pen's life—when a new series was inaugurated by Thackeray in *Punch* entitled "Mr. Brown's Letters to His Nephew."⁴ In these social vignettes the elder Brown stands in much the same relationship with his nephew Robert ("My dear Bobby") as Major Pendennis continues with his nephew Arthur. "As you have now completed your academical studies and are about to commence your career in London," writes Mr. Brown in his first letter to young Bob Brown, now reading law at the Inner Temple, "I propose, my dear Nephew, to give you a few hints for your guidance." Uncle Brown, like Uncle Pendennis, addresses himself more to his young ward's avocations than to his vocation. "It is not . . . with regard to your duties as a law-student that I have a desire to lecture you," he assures young Bob, "but in respect of your pleasures, amusements, acquaintances, and general conduct and bearing as a young man of the world."⁵

"It is not learning, it is not virtue, about which people inquire in society. It is manners," affirms this old man of the world (letter 2). The worldly concerns of Mr. Brown pretty well circumscribe also the social side of *Pendennis*: "On Tailoring—And Toilettes In General" (*Pendennis* opens with a description of the major's attire); "The Influence of Lovely Women Upon Society" ("An influence so vast, for good or for evil," affirms Mr. Brown, and so Pen, along with other Thackerayan heroes, discovers); "On Friendship"; "A Word About Balls In Season"; "Great And Little Dinners" (on which Mr. Brown, presumably speaking for his author, observes: "I would have a great deal more hospitality practised than is common among us—more hospitality and less show"); and in three letters out of the eighteen Mr. Brown holds forth on "Love, Marriage, Men and Women," a prominent theme also in *Pendennis*, which requires a penultimate "Chapter of Match-Making" to tie up its strands.[6]

Although to an extent a "second ramble among the booths," this successor to *Vanity Fair* views society not as a peepshow gaped at by an interloper, but from the more secure vantage point of the insider. In general, *Pendennis* conveys the impression sought by Captain Shandon, editor of the *Pall Mall Gazette*, on whose staff Pen serves his journalistic apprenticeship, of being "written by gentlemen for gentlemen," and moreover by "men famous at the Universities . . . known at the Clubs, and of the Society which they described" (chap. 32). In this man's world (as against the predominantly woman's world of *Vanity Fair*), seen from the windows of Bays's, the Wheel of Fortune, and other such male establishments, gossip is superseded by the overheard conversation, and the "fashionable intelligencer" of *Vanity Fair* gives way to the "accomplished man about town" that our Victorian middle-class Lord Chesterfield seeks to make of his nephew Bobby, the mold after which that superannuated Regency beau Major Pendennis tries to fashion his nephew Arthur.

"And so, my dear lad, you are at this moment enduring the delights and tortures, the jealousy and wakefulness, the longing and raptures, the frantic despair and elation, attendant upon the passion of love," writes the elder Brown sympathetically to Bob toward the end of his budget of letters.[7] (By the time these lines appeared in *Punch*, Arthur Pendennis had turned his attentions from Miss Fotheringay to the "femme incomprise" Blanche Amory, and had been refused, after a half-hearted marriage proposal, by Laura.) "I myself went through some of these miseries and pleasures which you now, O my Nephew, are enduring. I pity and sympathise with you. I am an old cock now, with a feeble strut and a faltering crow. But I was young once: and remember the time very well," muses Mr. Brown. The sense of time remembered, and the passing on of hard-won wisdom from the old to the young, also run through the meditative memoir that is *Pendennis*. Some further words of "old cock" Brown to his fledgling protégé anticipate what

Arthur Pendennis learns from his youthful trials and tribulations: "If you lose the object of your desires, the loss won't kill you; you may set that down as a certainty. If you win, it is possible that you will be disappointed; that point also is to be considered. But hit or miss, good luck or bad—I should be sorry, my honest Bob, that thou didst not undergo the malady. Every man ought to be in love a few times in his life, and to have a smart attack of the fever. You are better for it when it is over: the better for your misfortune if you endure it with a manly heart; how much the better for success if you win it and a good wife into the bargain!"

Having been summoned by his sister-in-law Helen, Major Pendennis remains *in loco parentis* for Pen, as counselor on deportment as well as on affairs of the heart. Like Mr. Punch in various guises, he incarnates the elder mentor, a familiar figure of the Victorian novel inherited from the illustrated school books and conduct books that Thackeray and his generation were nurtured on.[8] But the major is quite a remove from the pedants of those enlightening tomes:

> It can't be said that Mr. Pen's new guide, philosopher, and friend discoursed him on the most elevated subjects, or treated the subjects which he chose in the most elevated manner. But his morality, such as it was, was consistent. It might not, perhaps, tend to a man's progress in another world, but it was pretty well calculated to advance his interests in this; and then it must be remembered that the Major never for one instant doubted that his views were the only views practicable, and that his conduct was perfectly virtuous and respectable. He was a man of honour, in a word; and had his eyes, what he called, open. He took pity on this young greenhorn of a nephew, and wanted to open his eyes too. (Chap. 9)[9]

Becky Sharp, we have noticed, did not correspond precisely with Miss Edgeworth's notion of "The Good French Governess." Neither is the major the sort of Parent's Assistant calculated to please the "celebrated philosopher" any more than he does Pen's mother Helen, who squirms in shock and dismay through the "anecdotes of the great George, the Royal Dukes, of the statesmen, beauties, and fashionable ladies of the day," that hold Arthur in thrall. As we learn upon this adolescent's entrance into Boniface College, "the world had got hold of Pen in the shape of his selfish old Mentor" (chap. 17). The major, so long as he retains this hold, represents one distinct kind of teaching that Arthur is subjected to in the academy of life. "Flames and darts and passion, and that sort of thing, do very well for a lad: and you were but a lad when that affair with the Fotheringill—Fotheringay—(what's her name?)

came off," admonishes the major, visiting Pen in his rooms at Pump Court:

> "But a man of the world gives up those follies. You may still do very well. You have been hit, but you may recover. You are heir to a little independence, which everyone fancies is a doosid deal more. You have a good name, good wits, good manners, and a good person—and begad! I don't see why you shouldn't marry a woman with money—get into Parliament—distinguish yourself. . . . Remember, it's as easy to marry a rich woman as a poor woman. . . . Look out: I shall be on the watch for you: and I shall die content, my boy, if I can see you with a good ladylike wife, and a good carriage, and a good pair of horses, living in society, and seeing your friends like a gentleman." It was thus this affectionate uncle spoke, and expounded to Pen his simple philosophy.[10] (Chap. 28)

But there are more things in heaven and earth than are dreamt of in uncle Pendennis's simple philosophy, as the major himself is dimly aware, of which Pen has lingering intimations: "'What would my mother and Laura say to this, I wonder?' thought the lad. Indeed old Pendennis's morals were not their morals, nor was his wisdom theirs." Readers had already witnessed a touching little episode where Pen as a boy was introduced to Keble's *The Christian Year:* "The son and the mother whispered it to each other with awe—faint, very faint, and seldom in after life Pendennis heard that solemn church-music; but he always loved the remembrance of it, and of the times when it struck on his heart" (chap. 3). Not surprisingly, Helen's prognostication of her son's future runs in a contrary direction to that of her brother-in-law:

> Helen Pendennis by the force of sheer love divined a great number of her son's secrets. But she kept these things in her heart (if we may so speak), and did not speak of them. Besides she had made up her mind that he was to marry little Laura, who would be eighteen when Pen was six- and twenty: and had finished his college career; and had made his grand tour; and was settled either in London, astonishing all the metropolis by his learning and eloquence at the bar, or better still in a sweet country parsonage surrounded with hollyhocks and roses, close to a delightful romantic ivy-covered church, from the pulpit of which Pen would utter the most beautiful sermons ever preached. (Chap. 3)

So the sacred and the profane spirits wrestle for the soul of this Victorian Nice Wanton.

The original wrapper design on the monthly parts—representing allegorically a young man surrounded on one side by a siren and evil sprites, on the other by a sweet-faced mother and innocent-looking children (a church looming in the

background)—announces immediately matter of greater seriousness than anything contained in *Punch's* "Young Man's Almanack,"
however they may be related. The opposed self is personified
graphically throughout. The cut that concludes chapter 3 (the end
of part 1 in the monthly numbers), entitled "Youth Between Pleasure
And Duty," shows the hero standing next to his friend Harry
Foker, a young buck and heir to a brewer's fortune, while being
confronted in the Cathedral Yard by the voice of conscience in the
form of the stern parson, Doctor Portman. Such evocative chapter
headings as "Rake's Progress," "Prodigal's Return," "Babylon," and
"Temptation" mark fluctuations in Pen's unequal bout with the
fleshpots of London. Hogarth had his Victorian successors, as we
are reminded in one authorial digression: "A committee of mar-
riageable ladies, or of any Christian persons interested in the prop-
agation of the domestic virtues, should employ a Cruikshank or a
Leech, or some other kindly expositor of the follies of the day, to
make a series of Designs representing the horrors of a bachelor's
life in chambers, and leading the beholder to think of better things,
and a more wholesome condition" (chap. 51). These words, of
course, are a jibe more at predatory young women than at spry
young bachelors, but in the absence of Cruikshank and Leech, this
illustrator provides enough examples of "follies of the day": Pen
confronting his creditors at Oxbridge in the plate entitled "A Few
Little Bills" (chap. 19), and a later plate showing "Pen Pursuing His
Law Studies" in a rather desultory fashion (chap. 28). One cut
shows Pen "dandifying himself in the glass" (chap. 17); another
shows him succumbing to the siren song of Blanche Amory at the
spinet (chap. 22). Among the ornamented initials is one representing an imp curled around an overturned wine glass (chap. 19),
while other more literal ones discover various assignations and flirtations (chaps. 27, 32, 34, 44). With its intercalation of grotesque
imagery and pictures of real life, the whole novel seems to have
been designed as a nineteenth-century version of an old morality
play (even concluding with the stage direction "Exeunt Omnes"),
with more modern angels and devils engaged in "that strange and
awful struggle of good and wrong."

The figure of the uncle as worldly mentor was not of course
original with Thackeray. He appears among other places in some
French novels that Thackeray knew. In *Jérôme Paturot* the hero's
uncle comes to his rescue when his fortunes are at low ebb, a turn
of events that led Thackeray to comment: " . . . alas! it is only in

novels that these uncles are found—living literary characters have no such lucky relationships."[11] A more pernicious uncle appears in one of the novels Thackeray refers to in his essay "On Some French Fashionable Novels"—Charles de Bernard's *La femme de quarante ans*. Here young Edward de Mornac, torn (like Octavian in *Der Rosenkavalier*) between his love for an aging demimondaine and the prospect of marriage to a wealthy young *paysanne*, is urged by an uncle to take the practical course. The author comments that the young man's relative "poured into every fresh wound some drops of that seductive science, materialism, with which the good faith of the youth of the nineteenth century is poisoned at the fountain head."[12] Closer to Major Pendennis is the Baron Dumesnil of Jules Janin's *Le chemin de traverse* (1836), a didactic novel which may well have come to Thackeray's attention even before he became an intimate friend of its author during the writing of *Pendennis*.[13] It was highly praised by the *Times* when it first came out, and received tribute as well from that champion of the French novel G. W. M. Reynolds as "one of the finest books in the French language . . . a great moral lecture constructed on a slender ground-work of fiction . . . [teaching] the necessity of pursuing a direct path in our journey through life."[14] Early in the 1840s when an English version appeared in the Romancist and Novelist Library, the anonymous translator hailed it as work in which "wit, wisdom, eloquence, the purest morality, the most profound knowledge of the human heart alike in the sunny brightness of its virtues, and the dark and terrible depths of its prejudices and vices, are to be found on every page," and placed the author in the company of Chateaubriand and Victor Hugo.[15]

The title of the English translation of Janin's novel, *The Cross Roads. A Romance of Real Life*, clearly poses the dilemma of its youthful hero Prosper Chavigni, pulled, like Arthur Pendennis, in contrary directions, designated by the original divisions of the tale into "L'éducation du village"[16] and "L'éducation de la ville," with a concluding section entitled "La ligne droite." We follow the progress of young Prosper from provincial *naïf* to Parisian *homme fait*. In his birthplace in Ampuy, in the Rhone Valley, he is brought up somewhat like Arthur Pendennis: "Happy was it, that he, Prosper, had his mother. A mother is a supreme intelligence; she comprehends at once, with mind, and with soul, and with heart; the most hidden mysteries of her child are to her visible as the sunbeam. What no one else had forseen or observed in the education, so suddenly, and unluckily completed . . . his mother alone had seen and understood" (chap. 6). We are witnesses to one moment of communion between the two:

> It was just at the beginning of autumn. The leaves had not yet fallen, the trees were still green, but the green had begun to be mingled with some yellowish tints. The sky was calm but dark; the Rhone ran sadly but not angrily. Prosper and his mother sat together beneath the paternal elm, and gazed upon the other's face, without venturing to break the sad and boding silence, until at length Prosper, unable to restrain his sufferings, and his desire to ease his full heart, threw himself into his mother's arms, and wept as he embraced her. (Chap. 6)

With a change of season and country, this description could almost accompany the cut entitled "Calm Summer Evenings" that appears in illustrated editions of *Pendennis* (chap. 2), showing Pen in his mother's embrace looking pensively out over a placid river at the church of Clavering. These are paradises about to be lost. With his literary education it soon becomes evident that Ampuy can no longer contain Prosper, and he goes to Paris to seek his career, with his mother's blessing. The serpent in Prosper's garden is the aforementioned uncle who, as Reynolds noted, "undertakes to educate him as a man of the world, or in other words a selfish man." This bon vivant is characterized by his creator as "the man in all France, and perhaps in the whole world, the best qualified to write and publish a book, which is far more needed than the *Dictionnaire de l'Académie* . . . this mundane gospel which would snatch from poverty and despair so many young and ardent intelligences which are abandoned to themselves . . . this book should be entitled *The Art of Rising in the World*." Instead of writing this book, however, the uncle determines to make a living exemplum of Prosper:

> It was the Baron Dumesnil who, finding Prosper still encrusted with his village simplicity, slowly and step by step despoiled him of his last vestige of virtue and innocence. It was the Baron Dumesnil who replaced the vulgar education of Brother Christophe [Prosper's devout clerical tutor] by the true Parisian education which, as doubtless you are well aware, is the best possible education, past, present, or to come. To say the truth, the worthy uncle took no small pains to elevate his pupil to his own level. And if he did not altogether succeed, you must charge his partial failure upon the perverse nature of the pupil, who without knowing or wishing it, was constantly influenced by the first impressions of the paternal home. (Chap. 14)

The baron is further described at one point as one of those social parasites who "have all their lives great joy, good cheer, fine clothes, convenient houses—every luxury, love, of a sort, not excluded, without ever having a brick in the street, an acre under the sun, an idea in their heads, a virtue in their hearts, or a pursuit at their fingers' ends" (chap. 14). Major Pendennis, who tries to erase his nephew's "first impressions of the paternal home," is endowed with some of the superficial panache of the Baron Dumesnil, but stops short of the unscrupulousness of his prototype, who opens mail to compromise enemies, spies for the government, and even goes so far as to lead Prosper to kill a rival in a duel as a proof of gallantry. Consistently with his toning down the sensationalism and sexual intrigue of French fiction, Thackeray mellows his portrait of a roué from its French source. He even has the major succumb eventually to the "sentimental" way of life, together with Arthur, unlike the Baron Dumesnil who remains true to his corrupt code, dying an impenitent failure.[17]

Inevitably the Baron Dumesnil had his literary kinfolk in English society. One of the "charming enchanters of the silver-fork school," Lady Blessington (the Lady Violet Le Bas of *Pendennis*) kept her name before the reading public during the 1840s with an undistinguished series of "confession" memoirs. Among these were *Meredith* (1843) and *Marmaduke Herbert; or, The Fatal Error* (1847), in both of which a young man is torn, like the hero of *Le chemin de traverse*, by the conflicting influences of a religious mother and a polished, but morally sleazy, uncle. Not included in the company at Bacon's or Bungay's entertainments was Mrs. Catherine Gore, a steady contributor nevertheless to the lists of their real-life counterparts Colburn and Bentley. Thackeray's friendship with and respect (despite "Lords and Liveries") for this queen of the chroniclers of the "thrice filtered filtration of the fashionable world" is already well known, and attention has been called to analogies between the character and amours of the hero of her best known novel, *Cecil; or, The Adventures of a Coxcomb* (1841), and those of young Pen.[18] Additionally worth noting is her *Preferment; or, My Uncle the Earl*, issued by Colburn a year before *Cecil*. In this novel the title character, a forty-five-year-old roué named Adolphus Egerton, exerts an insidious influence over a nephew, who, as a result of expert tutelage, "attained that sort of *ignis fatuus* brilliancy, the result of a species of malaria, generated by the fashionable quarters of London—the mere phosphorescence of corruption" (bk. 1, chap. 14). As these words indicate, Uncle Adolphus succeeds all too well in dandifying his nephew Dick, though he turns his disciple into something less than a gentleman in the process. After being extricated from an adulterous affair through the interceding of a cousin, this protégé is obliged to flee England, leaving his debts and promising parliamentary career behind. The young man we are supposed to admire in this novel is Dick's unassuming high-minded country cousin Julius, who manages to withstand the temptations of the world and rises by his own merit rather than by aristocratic patronage. Against a background of Regency decadence, contrasting town and country morality, the *mode* and the simple domestic life, Mrs. Gore raises anew and more in earnest Falstaff's question—also posed in *Pendennis*—"What Is Honor?"

In this quest, young Arthur Pendennis, true to the character of the neophyte of the didactic fables, comes under the surveillance of a variety of mentors. Counteracting the influence of the major are, as has already been observed, the pious mother and the exemplary young "sister" (as Laura is called from time to time by Helen because of her devotion to the young lady destined to become Pen's bride). There are also the traditional "Parents' Assistants"—the schoolmaster Dr. Portman, and the curate Mr. Smirke. But in the midst of the various moral pressures this youth is subjected to, his creator intrudes a plea for self-development. As he reminds the parents among his readers: "[Pen] had a world of his own. What generous, ardent, imaginative soul has not a secret pleasure-place in which it disports. Let no clumsy prying or dull meddling of ours try to disturb it in our children." And so, he cautions them, "Leave him occasionally alone, my good madam, if you have a poet for a child. Even your admirable advice may be a bore sometimes. Yonder little child may have thoughts too deep even for your great mind, and fancies so coy and timid that they will not bare themselves when your ladyship sits by" (chap. 3). Helen Pendennis, cut off, like the mother of Prosper Chavigni, from her son's mental development, tries by intuition to read his "inmost heart." But, as his creator says, Pen has "a world of his own" permanently shut out from his mother's vision. He is indeed an unusual child—an incipient man of letters, as his name indicates. From his boyhood lessons in construing Greek plays (however reluctantly) at Greyfriars to his poring over headier volumes of religion and philosophy on the steps of Dr. Portman's library and his subsequent study of ancient poets and "the charming wicked Aristophanes" under the rather lax supervision of Mr. Smirke, young Pen is clearly in training for the literary life.

Since *Pendennis* is to a large extent the story of the author as a young man,[19] other writers for a time supersede "Home Influence" on his growth. Among the fans who watch Miss Fotheringay perform Mrs. Haller at the Chatteris theater, and subsequently a caller on Helen Pendennis, is one Mr. Wagg, a popular novelist of the day (now generally identified with Theodore Hook). We first catch him engaged in a typical activity: "Mr. Wagg noted everything that he saw; the barometer and the letter-bag, the umbrellas and the ladies' clogs, Pen's hats and tartan wrapper, and old John opening the drawing-room door to introduce the new-comers." Wagg is ever the practicing novelist, even away from his desk: "Such minutiae attracted Wagg instinctively; he seized them in spite of himself" (chap. 25). Helen, ever the polite hostess, professes admiration for Wagg's books, though privately she cannot abide them. Nor is she taken with the man himself, as "he poured out a flood of fashionable talk, introducing the names of a score of peers, and rattling on with breathless spirits," a continuation presumably of the major's name-dropping chatter that had left this refined rural widow "so sadly bored and perplexed." "What a man! she thought; are all the men of fashion like this? I am sure Pen will never be like him" (chap. 25). Pen, according to Laura's report, "laughs at Mr. Wagg's celebrity . . . and says he is a dunce, and that everybody could write his books." Pen, no less than his creator at his age, has indeed been following this eminent writer's sayings and doings,[20] and recognizes that it is possible to gain celebrity from writing about contemporary society with observation and wit. In fact his decision to invade Paternoster Row is prompted largely by his confidence that he can surpass Mr. Wagg—a bit of self-esteem bolstered by Laura ("If Pen can write better than this gentleman . . . He ought to go away, indeed he ought").

Captain Shandon, the editor of the *Pall Mall Gazette*, who launches Pen on his career of literary journalism, "spoke of the characters of the day, and great personages of the fashion with easy familiarity and jocular allusions, as if it is his own habit to live amongst them." In the midst of his own embarrassed circumstances, Shandon "told anecdotes of their private life, and of the conversations he had had, and entertainments, and at which such and such a thing occurred." The incongruity of the situation is not lost on Shandon's visitor: "Pen was amused to hear the shabby prisoner in a tattered dressing-gown talking glibly about the great of the land" (chap. 32). He derives similar amusement from watching Jack Finucane, the subeditor "with a plate of meat from the cookshop, and a glass of porter from the public-house, for his meal, recounting the feasts of the great, as if he had been present at them; and in tattered trousers and dingy shirt-sleeves, cheerfully describing and arranging the most brilliant *fêtes* of the world of fashion" (chap. 35).

In the Upper Temple, meanwhile, Pen falls in with another struggling young law student with literary aspirations, George Warrington. He comes to admire George's contributions to law reviews, as well as his newspaper articles, for their "strong thoughts and curt periods, the sense, the satire, and the scholarship" (chap. 31). This sounds like a challenge indeed to the potential novelist who has ambitions beyond mere entertainment, who would describe the world he lives in, yet rise above the mere "minutiae" and gossip of Mr. Wagg, and, unlike Jack Finucane, prefers to know the people he writes about. Hence George Warrington exerts a firmer guiding hand on Pen, at least subliminally, than any of this young dandy's other friends, as he sets about revising and expanding his first effort at a novel, "Leaves from the Life-book of Walter Lorraine," transforming it from an effusion of adolescent weltschmerz into a "picture of real life," to borrow a familiar kind of subtitle of the time. In plotting his hero's career, Thackeray steers an adroit course between depicting an average youth "no better nor worse than most educated men" promised in his preface and in some of the archetypal chapter headings ("Shows First Love may Interrupt Breakfast": "In which Pendennis Appears as a Very Young Man Indeed") and yet a unique specimen of the genus author. Consequently we become witnesses not only to a rake's progress, but to a work in progress.

"You have been bred up as a mollycoddle, Pen, and spoilt by the women," remarks George candidly during one of their conversations (chap. 31), but at the same time he renews Pen's confidence in himself, which has begun to flag in the course of his removal from the shelter and loving care of Fairoaks to the harsh competition of Fleet Street. Simultaneously he applies the bit and spur to Arthur's Pegasus, catering to his authorial vanity and yet openly criticising his early efforts ("The Prize Poem is so pompous, that I'm positively surprised, sir, that it didn't get the medal. You don't suppose you are a serious poet, do you, and are going to cut out Milton and Aeschylus?" [chap. 31]). At this point Warrington does not know the extent of Arthur's abilities, or the direction they will take, but he turns Pen's literary sights toward the workaday world and makes him aware that this world owes the writer a living no more than it does any other profession ("If a lawyer, or a soldier, or a parson, outruns his income, and does not pay his bills, he must go to gaol, and an author must go, too"). More importantly, Warrington inspires him with a sense of disinterested dedication: "If fortune favours me, I laud her; if she frowns, I resign her," he meditates to himself following his conversation with his friend. "I pray Heaven I may be honest if I fail, or if I succeed. I pray Heaven I may tell the truth as far as I know it: that I mayn't swerve from it through flattery, or interest, or personal enmity, or party prejudice" (chap. 32).[21]

Warrington serves a double function in *Pendennis*, alternating between confidant and sounding board to the hero, and Thackeray's own second self. "I am a prose labourer. . . . you, my boy, are a poet in a small way, and so, I suppose, consider you are authorised to be flighty," says Warrington to Pen on one occasion, this time over brandy and water in one of their favorite haunts, the Back Kitchen (chap. 32). So the hack engages with the creative artist. Pen and Warrington join various disparate elements of Thackeray's temperament as writer—the man of reflection and the bon vivant, the idealist and the skeptic, the topical journalist and the writer for the ages, the seasoned sophisticate and the eternal youth to whom the world is ever new.[22] These come together with Arthur's discovery, during his perambulations about Saint Paul's Churchyard as he awaits the outcome of his "agent" Warrington's offer of his first fruits to Mr. Bacon, that the Corporation of the Goosequill offers a career open to all talents:

> Pen looked at all the windows of all the shops, and the strange variety of literature which they exhibit. In this were displayed black-letter volumes and books in the clear pale types of Aldus and Elzevier: in the next, you might see the "Penny Horrific Register;" the "Halfpenny Annals of Crime," and "History of the most celebrated Murderers of all Countries," "The Raff's Magazine," "The Larky Swell," and other publications of the penny press; whilst at the next window, portraits of ill-favoured individuals, with facsimiles of the venerated signatures of the Reverend Grimes Wapshot,[23] the Reverend Elias Howle,[24] and the works written and the sermons preached by them showed the British Dissenter where he could find mental pabulum. Hard by would be . . . books of controversial theology, by which the faithful of the Roman opinion might learn a short way to deal with Protestants . . . whilst in the very next window you might see "Come out of Rome," a sermon preached at the opening of the Shepherd's Bush College, by John Thomas Lord Bishop of Ealing. Scarce an opinion but has its expositor and its place of exhibition in this peaceful old Paternoster Row, under the toll of the bells of Saint Paul. (Chap. 31)

In his ramble among the booths of the book fair, Arthur in effect reviews the history of modern print, from the introduction of the small book aimed at the purse of the common reader (Aldines and Elzeviers), to the emergence of the penny press that brought "mental pabulum" to the millions. His own career seems cut out for him. Moreover, the topics represented here among the shops of Paternoster Row—crime, the affairs of the "raffs" and "swells" of society, and religion—somehow become amalgamated in his book.

The form that his own book takes, as apart from its matter, is conditioned to an extent by fiction that Arthur sees is capturing the market. Fishing up his adolescent trifle from its storage box, he concludes that it did not add up to much, "but it was as good as most books of the kind that had the run of the circulating libraries and the career of the season." He has had opportunity, that is, to observe that others besides that modern Asmodeus Mr. Wagg have been converting silver forks into lucre. "He had critically examined more than one fashionable novel by the authors of the day then popular, and he thought that his intellect was as good as theirs, and that he could write the English language as well as those ladies and gentlemen" (chap. 41). Pen does not name names, but we have already noticed his creator's sly habit of introducing "authors of the day then popular" into the novel, slightly disguised. Others are alluded to: "It was the period when the novel called the 'fashionable' was in vogue among us," we are informed at one point, "and Warrington did not fail to point out [to Mr. Bungay] . . . how Pen was a man of the first fashion himself, and received at the houses of some of the greatest personages of the land" (chap. 41). At this time there was, of course, more than *one* novel called "The Fashionable," or some variant thereof. *Fashionables and Unfashionables*, by Rosalia St. Clair (an offering of A. K. Newman of Minerva Press fame), and *English Fashionables Abroad* (a product of Colburn's factory) preceded *Pelham* by a year. These were followed by such scandal chronicles as *Russell; or, The Reign of Fashion* (1830), Mrs. Gore's *Sketch Book of Fashion* (1833), and the Misses Beauclerks' *Tales of Fashion and Reality* (1836).[25] In the very year when *Pendennis* began to appear, though the vogue was beginning to spend itself, readers could have renewed their acquaintance with "fashion and its votaries" through the Honorable Catherine Charlotte Maberly's novel of that title.

We do not learn much specifically about the published version of Arthur's novel that (unlike any of Thackeray's own early efforts) catches on with the public sufficiently to require a second edition within two months. "The rubbish is saleable enough," was Warrington's opinion as he looked over the first version, but he advised Pen to "give [it] a more modern air, prune away . . . some of the green passages, and add a little comedy, and cheerfulness, and satire, and that sort of thing, and then we'll take him to the market and sell him" (chap. 41). Pen succeeds, at least in the eyes of another of his literary companions, the aspiring hack Percy Popjoy, who puffs Pen's book to Mrs. Bungay, the publisher's wife, as "full of wit, genius, satire, pathos, and every conceivable good quality" (chap. 41). He could be speaking for *Pendennis* itself, in which something of Warrington's "strong thoughts," "sense," and "scholarship" is engrafted upon the romantic sensibility of Pen's salad days and the social reportage that makes up the stock-in-trade of the silver-fork novelist. With *Pendennis*, that is to say, Thackeray carries the fashionable novel beyond gossip chronicle into living social history.

Mrs. Gore had led the way, to an extent, in the aforementioned *Preferment*, in which the managing uncle, Adolphus Egerton, is represented as a relic of a passing age: "Adolphus had, in fact, cherished occasional misgivings that the legitimate school, of which he was so distinguished a professor, was on the decline, and the temple of fine gentlemanism, reared under the auspices of Carlton House, tottering to its fall. Of the great men illustrating the dandy epoch of his youth. . . . Some were in exile—some in the grave. . . . George Robins had disposed of the paraphernalia of a dozen or so, whose place remembered them no longer . . . whose names were forgotten amid their daily haunts and ancient neighbourhood, except in the defaulter-lists of the clubs" (bk. 1, chap. 5). Major Pendennis can be numbered among the legion of those "whose names were forgotten amid their daily haunts and ancient neighbourhood":

> As became a man of fashion, Major Pendennis spent the autumn passing from house to house of such country friends as were at home to receive him. . . . To say the truth, the old gentleman's reputation was somewhat on the wane: many of the men of his time had died out, and the occupants of their halls and the present wearers of their titles knew not Major Pendennis: and little cared for his traditions of the wild Prince and Poins and of the heroes of fashion passed away. It must have struck the good man with melancholy as he walked by many a London door, to think how seldom it was now open for him, and how often he used to knock at it—to what banquets and welcome he used to pass through it—a score of years back. (Chap. 67)

The major shares the regret felt by his prototype Adolphus Egerton for the dear dead teens of the century gone beyond recall:
"The men, thinks he, are not such as they used to be in his time; the
old grand manner and courtly grace of life are gone." In a rare
moment of reckoning he muses: "'I'm getting old: they're getting
past me: they laugh at us old boys'" (chap. 67).

Earlier we have had a glimpse at the major through the eyes of
two of "the men of the new time" (as this "old boy" refers to the
rising generation):

> In the course of that very day, it chanced that the Major had
> stationed himself in the great window of Bays's Club in Saint James's
> Street at the hour in the afternoon when you see a half-score of
> respectable old bucks similarly recreating themselves (Bays's is rather
> an old-fashioned place of resort now; and many of its members more
> than middle-aged; but in the time of the Prince Regent, these old
> fellows occupied the same window, and were some of the very
> greatest dandies in this empire)—Major Pendennis was looking from
> the great window, and spied his nephew Arthur walking down the
> street in company with his friend Mr. Popjoy.
> "Look!" said Popjoy to Pen, as they passed, "did you ever pass
> Bays's at four o'clock without seeing that collection of old fogies? It's
> a regular museum. They ought to be cast in wax, and set up at
> Madame Tussaud's—"
> "—In a chamber of horrors by themselves," said Pen laughing.
> (Chap. 36)

Popjoy's analogy suggests one aspect of this novel itself—a kind of
animated museum of ways of life passed and passing, set up for the
delight and instruction of that hypothetical reader the author looks
forward to, "the antiquary of future generations." The impression
of a portrait gallery is further conveyed by the window frame in
which the major and fellow "old fogies" are momentarily caught,
transformed in the illustration that originally accompanied this
dialogue into a picture frame. This is the frame that Pen is determined to burst free of as he strives to become a "man of the world"
in a wider sense than that envisaged in the major's "simple philosophy."

The "history" of Arthur Pendennis is essentially his evolution
from man-about-town to man of letters. As Thackeray widened the
span of the silver-fork novel to take in social life, manners, and
morals in general, not merely those of "society," so his hero's wanderings take him beyond the clubs of Pall Mall and Saint James.
Shortly after his arrival in the metropolis, "elated with the idea of

seeing life, Pen went into a hundred queer London haunts. He liked to think he was consorting with all sorts of men—so he beheld coalheavers in their tap rooms; boxers in their inn-parlours; honest citizens disporting in the suburbs or on the river; and he would have liked to hob and nob with celebrated pickpockets, or drink a pot of ale with a company of burglars and cracksmen, had chance afforded him an opportunity of making the acquaintance of this class of society" (chap. 30). Here too Pen follows the lead of War-rington, who enjoys the company of the proprietors of public houses and their customers "to that of his own class, whose man-ners annoyed him, and whose conversation bored him." In society, Warrington affirms, "everybody is the same, wears the same dress, eats and drinks, and says the same things; one young dandy at the club talks and looks just like another, one Miss at a ball exactly resembles another, whereas there's character here. . . . I like gin-and-water better than claret. I like a sanded floor in Carnaby Mar-ket better than a chalked floor in Mayfair" (chap. 30).

A "social republican" Thackeray calls Warrington, and one to whom "it never entered his head while conversing with Jack and Tom that he was in any respect their better," adding the sly qualifi-cation that "perhaps the deference which they paid him might secretly please him." Pen at this point, more in conformity with one of Thackeray's "Respectable Snobs," conducts himself like "a young prince in disguise, visiting the poor of his father's kingdom." There is distance on both sides: "They [the frequenters of the public houses] respected him as a high chap, a fine fellow, a regular young swell. He had somehow about him an air of imperious good-humour, and a royal frankness and majesty, although he was only heir apparent to twopence halfpenny, and but one in descent from a gallipot." Pen has been an apt pupil in the school of deportment conducted by Major Pendennis. As he is weaned away from the major's influence under the supervision of George Warrington, he approaches the ideal of the writer as "social republican."

Pen's education by society thereby becomes a means of defining the social role of the writer. In one respect Thackeray was carrying on a crusade already underway. The year before *Pendennis* began to appear, George Henry Lewes, who was to be one of its most favorable reviewers,[26] spoke out in his own novel *Ranthorpe* (like *Pendennis* a *Bildungsroman* concerned with vocation and the literary life)[27] on the importance and responsibilities of authorship. In one chapter, significantly entitled "The Aristocracy of Intellect," Lewes complained that this class, no less than the aristocracy of birth, has its pretenders, "presumptuous parvenus, despicable and despised . . . men who aspire to qualities they have no claim to: eunuchs of ambition!" "Authors, consent to be authors," Lewes exhorts his fellows of the writing fraternity, "and before attempting to 'move in the first circles,' unless your position calls you there, rigidly scrutinize *what* it is you want: what is your aim, and whether this society and its demands be compatible with the mission of your lives. . . . Either there is dignity in intellectual rank, or there is not; if there is, no other rank is needed; if there is not, no other rank can give it; for dignity is not an accident, but a quality" (bk. 3, chap. 1). While *Pendennis* was in mid-course, Thackeray himself felt called upon to affirm the dignity of literature, having come under critical attack for his apparent ridicule of writers: "The literary profession is not held in disrepute [he wrote]; nobody wants to disparage it, no man loses his social rank, whatever it may be, by practising it. On the contrary: the pen gives a place in the world to men who had none before, a fair place, fairly achieved by their genius, as any other degree of eminence is by any other kind of merit. Literary men need not, as it seems to me, be in the least querulous about their position any more, or want the pity of anybody."[28] This observtion seems to be confirmed by that arch snob Major Pendennis. "You have got yourself a little reputation by your literary talents, which I am very far from undervaluing," he deigns to concede to his nephew, "though in my time, begad, poetry and genius and that sort of thing were devilish disreputable. There was poor Byron, for instance, who ruined himself and contracted the worst habits by living with poets and newspaper-writers, and people of that kind. But the times are changed now—there's a run upon literature—clever fellows get into the best houses in town, begad!" (chap. 36). "We are grown doosid republican," as this old boy is forced to admit (chap. 44).

By now the newly respectable Arthur is not contented merely to "get into the best houses in town." Returning with Warrington to the Back Kitchen, he "had the pleasure of seeing as many different persons of his race as the most eager observer need desire to inspect." Here come together "healthy country tradesmen and farmers . . . squads of young apprentices and assistants . . . rakish young medical students, gallant, dashing, what is called 'loudly' dressed, and (must it be owned?) somewhat dirty . . . young university bucks . . . with that indescribably genteel simper which is only learned at the knees of Alma Mater;—and handsome young guardsmen, and florid bucks from the St. James's Street Clubs;—nay, senators English and Irish; and even members of the House of Peers." In short, "men of all sorts and conditons entered and quitted the house of entertainment" (chap. 30).

The Back Kitchen can be taken as a microcosm of society from top to bottom—and of Arthur's potential readership. His wanderings take him also to Shepherd's Inn, in the vicinity of the Inns of Court, where Fanny Bolton and her family dwell: "Ballad-singers come and chant here, in deadly guttural tones, satirical songs against the Whig administration, against the bishops and dignified clergy, against the German relatives of an august royal family: Punch sets up his theatre, sure of an audience, and occasionally of a half-penny from the swarming occupants of the houses" (chap. 42). These audiences Arthur too hopes to capture for his more refined criticism of society, once he "sets up his theatre." Among Fanny's neighbors are Blanche Amory's vagabond father (as yet unbeknownst to her), Colonel Altamont, Altamont's trusty Ned Strong, and their boisterous company: "A strange and motley set they were, these friends of the Chevalier [Strong]; and though Major Pendennis would not much have relished their company, Arthur and Warrington liked it not a little, and Pen thought it as amusing as the society of the finest gentlemen in the finest houses which he had the honour to frequent" (chap. 42).

Presumably Thackeray here means as much to cast reflection on the "finest houses" as to compliment Shepherd's Inn. He also seems to be recalling for us whence he has come as a writer and indicating whither he is going. The "set" surrounding Altamont and Strong look familiar. Jack Holt, the mercenary from Don Carlos's army,[29] engaged now in smuggling tobacco, is reminiscent of Captain Brock of *Catherine*. Keightley, manager of the Polwheedle and Tredyddlum Copper Mines, "which were as yet under water," as well as of a sponge company and "a little quicksilver operation . . . which would set him straight wth the world yet," would have fit well with Brough and Hoff, proprietors of the West Diddlesex Company in *The Great Hoggarty Diamond;* and Filby, an Irish ex-soldier and peripatetic ne'er-do-well whose father "left him that famous property from which he got no rents now, and of which nobody exactly knew the situation," could be a kinsman of Barry Lyndon. Seedy as the company assembled here may be, it is significant that Blanche Amory's stepfather, Lord Clavering, one of the "finest gentleman in the finest houses" that Arthur has gained entrée to, finds it quite congenial. Clavering "liked their society, although he did not add much to their amusements by his convivial powers," we are told, and in turn "he was made much of by the company now, on account of his wealth and position" (chap. 42). Moreover, as we learn shortly afterward, this noble was "as destitute of honesty as the people who cheated him, and a dupe chiefly because he was too mean to be a successful knave. . . . Had he been a Crown Prince— he could not have been more weak, useless, dissolute, or ungrateful" (chap. 43).

So high touches low in the course of Arthur Pendennis's forays through society, and at times they seem to be mirror images. It must have been with tongue in cheek that Thackeray apologized to his readers in the preface, in explanation for his laying aside a more "exciting" plan for the book in favor of the one he adopted: " . . . never having been intimate with any convict in my life, and the manners of ruffians and gaol-birds being quite unfamiliar to me, the idea of entering into competition with M. Sue was abandoned." To the contrary we encounter plenty of gaol-birds in the story that follows. Sir Francis Clavering, for one glittering example, "had had his own history . . . before his accession to good fortune, and had seen the inside of more prisons than one, and written his name on many a stamped paper" (chap. 42). Pen's first meeting with his editor, Shandon, is in a cell in the Fleet where that down-at-the-heels journalist has been confined for debt. The ex-convict Colonel Altamont, when last heard from (and as seen in the drawing that originally accompanied this episode), has jumped out of a window in Shepherd's Inn to escape arrest from a constable.[30]

The implication behind Thackeray's preface, however, is that not all of society's transgressors are behind prison bars. And so we are led to gather from some further conversation between Pen and his friend Percy Popjoy before the great window of Bays's Club:

> ". . . They *are* old rogues, most of 'em; and no mistake [says Popjoy]. There's old Blondel; there's my Uncle Colchicum, the most confounded old sinner in Europe; there's—hullo! there's somebody rapping the window and nodding at us."
> "It's my uncle, the Major," said Pen. "Is he an old sinner too?"
> "Notorious old rogue," Pop said, wagging his head. . . . "He's beckoning you in; he wants to speak to you."
> "Come in, too," Pen said.
> "——Can't," replied the other. "Cut uncle Col. two years ago, about Mademoiselle Frangipane—Ta, ta," and the young sinner took leave of Pen, and the club of the elder criminals, and sauntered into Blacquière's, an adjacent establishment, frequented by reprobates of his own age.

This club in Saint James's, already likened to a museum and chamber of horrors, here takes on the semblance of a classy prison house, emblematic of the thin line Thackeray enjoys drawing between respectability and rascality.

"To describe a real rascal, you must make him so horrible that he would be too hideous to show; and unless the painter paints him fairly, I hold he has no right to show him at all," further declares Thackeray in the preface to *Pendennis,* echoing the manifesto of Ikey Solomons in *Catherine.* He keeps his promise to his readers, sparing them "the most active horrors," preferring, in the civilized world defined by Pall Mall, Kensington, and the Royal Gardens of Vauxhall, to speak in "dark suggestions and generalities," as he says in one place. Dire enough predictions are made for Arthur's future by his earliest "parents' assistants" (as with his prototype Tom Jones). "Miserable trifler!" exclaims Dr. Portman, angry at little Pen's resistance to the niceties of classical grammar: "A boy, sir, who does not learn his Greek play cheats the parent who spends money for his education. A boy who cheats his parent is not very far from robbing or forging upon his neighbor, A man who forges upon his neighbor pays the penalty of his crime at the gallows" (chap. 2). Pen's infatuation with Miss Fotheringay leads the local parson to prepare a sermon "in which he spoke of Jezebel, theatrical entertainments . . . and of youth going to perdition, in a manner which made it clear to every capacity that Pen was the individual meant, and on the road alluded to." Hard upon his punishment of a village yokel who has made fun of his discomfiture, "Pen was pronounced to be a murderer as well as a profligate, and his name became a name of terror and a byword in Clavering."[31] At Oxbridge Pen does not seem to learn much, but he gets a forcible lesson on how evil companions can corrupt good manners. "A man may have a very good coat-of-arms, and be a tiger my boy," Major Pendennis, with all his toadying, is shrewd enough to observe during a visit with Pen at Boniface College (chap. 19). He is speaking of the flashy Bloundell-Bloundell of the Suffolk Bloundells (offspring of the roguish "old Blondel" whom Percy Popjoy gossips about. "One such diseased creature as this is enough to infect a whole colony," it is observed in passing, "and the tutors of Boniface began to find the moral tone of their college lowered and their young men growing unruly and almost ungentlemanlike, soon after Mr. Bloundell's arrival at Oxbridge."[32] Bloundell is a good example of the man of the world that Pen might have become, but as it happens he is drawn only temporarily into that scapegrace's net, just long enough to gain, in the author's double entendre, "a knowledge of the odds at hazard." Nevertheless Pen's conduct continues to be open to question. His carryings on in "Babylon" provoke a rival to characterize him as "an abandoned criminal, a regular Don Juan, a fellow who when he *did* come into the country, ought to be kept out of *honest people's houses*" (chap. 50).[33] And subsequently "Pen formed the subject for a second sermon at the Clavering chapel of ease: where the dangers of London, and the crime of reading and writing novels, were pointed out on a Sunday evening, to a large and warm congregation. They did not wait to hear whether he was guilty or not. They took his wickedness for granted" (chap. 50).

This last bit of sarcasm snipes implicitly at the didactic moral fable that Thackeray has been imitating in *Pendennis*. Earlier he had addressed, by implication, the "large and warm congregation" so ready to condemn the hero:

> Who among us has not given a plenty of the very best advice to his friends? Who has not preached, and who has practised? To be sure, you, madam, are perhaps a perfect being, and never had a wrong thought in the whole course of your frigid and irreproachable existence; or you, sir, are a great deal too strong-minded to allow any foolish passion to interfere with your equanimity in chambers or your attendance on "Change": you are so strong that you don't want any sympathy. We don't give you any, then; we keep ours for the humble and the weak, that struggle and stumble and get up again, and so march with the rest of mortals. What need have *you* of a hand that never fall? Your serene virtue is never shaded by passion, or ruffled by temptation, or darkened by remorse. . . . Good bye, then; our way lies with the humble folks, and not with serene highnesses like you; and we give notice that there are no perfect characters in this history.[34]

Nor presumably are there any perfect characters among the readers of "this history." In describing his hero as "a gentleman of our age . . . no better nor worse than most educated men," Thackeray means to expose the moral taint from which no human being is free. At one point Pen is characterized as "very weak as well as very impetuous, very vain as well as very frank, and if of a generous disposition, not a little selfish in the midst of his profuseness, and also rather fickle," to which is added, "as all eager pursuers of self-gratification are" (chap. 17). Those prone to cast a stone have it flung back in their faces, as when the author defends Arthur's plan to marry Blanche Amory's fortune: "And, if like many a worse and better man, Arthur Pendennis, the widow's son, was meditating an apostasy, and going to sell himself . . . at least the renegade did not pretend to be a believer in the creed to which he was ready to swear. And if every woman and man in this kingdom, who has sold her or himself for money, or position, as Mr. Pendennis was about to do, would but purchase a copy of his memoirs, what tons of volumes Messrs. Smith and Elder would sell!" (chap. 64).[35] Moral evil is traced to its fount and source—in the school and in the home. "Before he was twelve years old and while his mother fancied him an angel of candour, little Pen had heard talk enough to make him quite awfully wise upon some points," the author informs the mothers of England with reference to his hero's education at Greyfriars, adding for their benefit: "—and so, Madam, has your pretty rosy-cheeked son, who is coming home for the ensuing Christmas holidays" (chap. 2).[36] "I don't say that the boy is lost, or that the innocence has left him which he had from 'Heaven, which is our home,'" the narrator continues, "but that the shades of the prison-house are closing very fast over him,[37] and that we are helping as much as possible to corrupt him."

The main effect then of Thackeray's adroit turnabout of the Parent's Assistants and conduct books of his era was to make mentors and their pupils equally blameworthy. On the positive side, they become joint witnesses of this Victorian Rake's Progress. "Yes, it was the same Pendennis, and time had brought to him, as to the rest of us, its ordinary consequences, consolations, developments," the author reminds his readers, as Pen is contemplating his "sensible" marriage to Blanche, under the prodding of the major: "We alter very little. When we talk of this man or that woman being no longer the same person whom we remember in youth, and remark . . . changes in our friends, we don't, perhaps, calculate that circumstance only brings out the latest defect or quality, and does not create it" (chap. 59). There is something of interest for everybody in the vicissitudes that govern young Pen's life—for parents who might easily be presumed to share the central interest of this book in the maturing of a pampered youth, and for their sons and daughters as well, involved in love problems of their own: "What don't you sacrifice to it, indeed, young gentlemen and young ladies of ill-regulated minds. . . . Life, business, family ties, all things useful and dear once, become intolerable, and you are never easy except when you are in pursuit of your flame" (chap. 45): "Yes, you must go through the hot fits and the cold fits of that pretty fever. . . . As the gambler said of his dice, to love and win is the best thing, to love and lose the next best" (chap. 39). The "constant communication with the reader" promised in the preface is intended primarily to urge sweet reasonableness in human relations as against the irrationality ("fever," "passion," "ill-regulated minds") amply illustrated in Pendennis's history.

The audience for this history extends beyond the family circle. The author addresses also those "who have a real and heartfelt relish for London society, and the privilege of an *entrée* into its most select circles" (chap. 9). In one of his digressions he speaks to the "philosophic reader" (chap. 16); in another it is the "friendly reader . . . taking up the page for a moment's light reading" who engages his attention (chap. 59); in connection with the Epsom Downs episode he is reminded of "our sporting readers" (chap. 59); and in another reflective mood he turns his words to "each man who lives by his pen" (chap. 71). All readers—old and young, married and unmarried, "philosophical" and "sporting"—are supposed to see something of themselves in this glass of fashion that is Arthur Pendennis. By the end of his history, once they are assured that Arthur has not "sold himself," but is joined in holy matrimony with his angel in the house, Laura, all of these readers are supposed to take to heart the author's parting words: "knowing how mean the best of us is, let us give a hand of charity to Arthur Pendennis, with all his faults and shortcomings, who does not claim to be a hero, but only a man and a brother." The author makes every endeavor to transfer his own disposition to "pardon humanity" to his readers.

The creator of Arthur Pendennis is no upholder, certainly, of a cloistered virtue. Once his hero is launched on his literary career, he asks his readers: "Was Pendennis becoming worldly, or only seeing the world, or both? and is a man very wrong for being after all only a man? Which is the most reasonable and does his duty best: he who stands aloof from the struggle of life, calmly contemplating it, or he who descends to the ground, and takes his part in the contest" (chap. 44). In raising this question and answering it, Thackeray at once comes to the defence of his hero's moral character and of the vocation of the novelist, both of which are condemned by the "large and warm congregation" at the Clavering chapel. In the course of his adventures, during which he is beset by the temptations to which youthful flesh is heir, Pen proves that a man of the world can be also a man of honor. At the same time, we watch this progress as man of letters out of a self-centered romanticism and indulgence in social lionizing to devote his pen to humanity.[38] Despite his apparent world weariness following upon his introduction to the *haut monde,* we are assured that he retains "a constant desire for society, which showed to be anything but misanthropical" (chap. 46). His snobbishness toward the cook Mirobolant and a certain condescension toward the habitués of the Back Kitchen and the Shepherd's Inn notwithstanding, his tolerance surfaces in moods of relaxation: "If he could not get a good dinner he sate down to a bad one with entire contentment; if he could not procure the company of great or beautiful persons, he put up with any society that came to hand." Significantly it is in a public park where we watch his convivial faculty expand:

> [In the Royal Gardens of Vauxhall] he was on terms of friendship with the great Simpson, and . . . shook the principal comic singer or the lovely equestrian of the arena by the hand. And while he could watch the grimaces or the graces of these with a satiric humour that was not deprived of sympathy, he could look on with an eye of kindness at the lookers-on too; at the roystering youth bent upon enjoyment, and here taking it; at the honest parents with their delighted children laughing and clapping their hands at the show: at the poor outcasts, whose laughter was less innocent though perhaps louder, and who brought their shame and their youth here, to dance and be merry till the dawn at least; and to get bread and drown care. Of this sympathy with all conditions of men Arthur often boasted: he was pleased to possess it: and said that he hoped thus to the last he should retain it. (Chap. 46).

In entitling this chapter "Monseigneur s' amuse," Thackeray obviously intends a witty analogy between the philandering of Victor Hugo's Francis I and Arthur's impending "affair" with the porter's daughter Fanny Bolton, whom he meets for the first time here. More fundamental is the juncture of the grave and the gay, of amusement with edification exemplified in this episode—essential to the literary credo that Thackeray imparts to his hero. What starts out as a light-hearted flirtation proves to have serious enough implications, almost leading to a rift between Pen and his mother and Laura, and testing his moral strength. Vauxhall itself, though a random gathering of pleasure seekers, represents various elements of the population that crisscross in the novel itself—entertainers (Miss Fotheringay; her father, Captain Costigan; and Bows, the musician, who loves her in vain); parents and children (the Pendennises obviously, as well as the Claverings, the Fokers, and the Huxters); as well as "poor outcasts" (Colonel Altamont, Ned Strong, and their cohorts); all treated with "a satiric humour that was not deprived of sympathy."

This evolution of the hero as author proceeds against a background of society itself in development. Arthur's mingling among all the degrees of men and women is one among many evidences of the general social motility in operation throughout his "history." It is announced immediately in the ostentation of that arch-climber Major Pendennis, who in turn devotes himself to making a successful parvenu of his nephew. The major has his low comedy counterpart in Johnny Armstrong–Mr. Amory–Colonel Altamont, who manages easy leaps from one rung of the social ladder to another through a glib tongue and slick manners aided by human gullibility. Marriages as well as characters in this novel are "mixed," another manifestation of a dynamic society. Pen's own father, we learn early, was an apothecary who tried to seal his pretensions to gentility by his second marriage to Helen Thistlewood (eventually Pen's mother). Helen comes out of a faintly genteel background as "a very distant relative of the noble house of Bareacres" (whose acquaintance we made in *Vanity Fair*). Occupying central stage is the marriage of the high-born wastrel Lord Clavering to Blanche Amory's ignorant and commonplace but kind-hearted mother. With his "predominating tendency to antithesis"[39] Thackeray gives us the converse situation also, with the marriage of Harry Foker's father, a wealthy brewer, to a lady. Blanche Amory, who loses out both on Arthur and Harry Foker, marries a Parisian of dubious title (ironically appropriate to her dubious legitimacy), allowing her to proclaim herself to Mr. Bungay's readers as Madame la Comtesse de Montmorenci de Valentinois. Occasionally extremes meet, as with the scholarly George Warrington, saddled to his grief with his "female boor," and the matching of Pen's adolescent passion, the illiterate actress Miss Fotheringay, to that peer of the realm Charles Mirabel.[40] Outside the circle of marriage and giving in marriage, there is Major Pendennis's blackmailing valet, Morgan, who manages somehow to become "one of the most respectable men in the parish of St. James's, and in the present political movement has pronounced himself like a man and a Briton" (chap. 75). Another *arriviste* is the erstwhile *maître d'hôtel* of the Clavering household, Frederick Lightfoot, who when last heard from "has begged leave to inform the nobility and gentry of ——shire that he has taken that well-known and comfortable hotel, the 'Clavering Arms' in Clavering, where he hopes for the continued patronage of the gentlemen and families of the county" (chap. 75).

This scrambling of the social classes, of the respectable with the less so, these pictures of people struggling upwards, of men and women from various walks of life juxtaposed, are all tangible evidence of those "chances and changes" that Thackeray sees as part of the modern human condition Arthur Pendennis bears witness to and tries to capture for his growing audience—life in flux, as a constant state of becoming. *Pendennis,* like all of Thackeray's novels, is a "chronicle of Fate's surprises" whose emblem is the Wheel of Fortune, the name of one of the clubs that Pen frequents. The quirks of fortune are signalized in turns of plot that may strike the casual reader as mere contrivance, notably the yoking and unyoking of Colonel Altamont and Lady Clavering and the delayed revelation that Blanche Amory is illegitimate rather than the product of a bigamous union. It is also consistent with Thackeray's Hericlitean concept of life that couples shift so readily throughout the novel (e.g., Fanny Bolton from Bows, to Pen, to Sam Huxter; Blanche from Pen, to Foker, to her French count), with the result that we are kept guessing to the end as to who marries whom. Significantly, readers are deprived of the conventional "and they lived happily ever after" ending, even when they know that Pen has abandoned any idea of a "sensible" marriage once and for all and has settled down with the girl of his mother's choice. "And what sort of husband would this Pendennis be?" the author anticipates his readers' asking, involving them with his hero's development even beyond the confines of this story. "The querists, if they meet her, are referred to that lady herself, who, seeing his faults and wayward moods—seeing and owning that there are better men than he—loves him always with the most constant affection" (chap. 75). So our hero and heroine are left not exactly in a bower of bliss, but in a habitable house. Character, moreover, like plot is openended as Thackeray conceives it, being pretty much a function, as he says at one point, of "circumstance" (chap. 59).[41] That Pen's character is by no means "fixed" could have been apparent to a sharp-eyed reader of *Pendennis* in its first publication in book form where the revised version of the wrapper drawing shows him looking in the direction of the serpent woman, having shifted his gaze from the good wife, as represented in the monthly parts. To those hot for certainties in a world where all is uncertain there remains the "constant affection" of Laura, a sustained sweet note to lighten the burden of "Humbug everywhere" that Thackeray's critics had complained of.

Neither Helen Pendennis nor the major quite predicts how Pen will turn out, but both prove partially right. He manages to distinguish himself socially, as Major Pendennis hopes, but not with "a good carriage, and a good pair of horses." He opts for the "sweet country parsonage surrounded with hollyhocks and roses" and marries Laura, as Helen wishes, though he does not carry her fond dream so far as to take a pulpit. He ends up somewhat like his French prototype Prosper Chavigni of Jules Janin's *Le chemin de traverse*, another chastened cynic who, we learn, returns to Ampuy after disillusionment with Paris, marries his childhood sweetheart Laetitia (the Laura of his life), and thereafter "happiness, repose, and the esteem of all around them, were their possessions." Janin concludes his novel with these words, which could also have been tacked on to the end of *Pendennis*, had Thackeray been given to such sampler wisdom: "And of all the lessons [Prosper and Laetitia] inculcated upon their children, they inculcated none more carefully than this—that *Cross Roads* in life are to be avoided, and that in this world there is only one road by which we can arrive at fortune without incurring regret and self-upbraiding; the high

Pendennis, allegorical design that appeared on wrapper of the monthly parts. (From volume 3 of *The Works of William Makepeace Thackeray* [Centenary Biographical Edition]; reproduced by permission of John Murray, Ltd.)

Pendennis, variant of allegorical design that appeared on the title page of volume 1 of the first edition in book form. (From volume 3 of *The Works of William Makepeace Thackeray* [Centenary Biographical Edition]; reproduced by permission of John Murray, Ltd.)

road of honesty, labour, patience, and virtue." For those following Pen's fortunes beyond the concluding monthly part, as has been noted, Thackeray had a coup-de-grace in store to remind them that the flesh is still weak even where the spirit is willing.

"A man and a brother" no more and no less is all that Thackeray claims for his hero, but one equipped to speak for and on behalf of humanity. His wisdom, however, is to find its outlet in the *Pall Mall Gazette,* and to be contained in wrappers and boards rather than spoken out from bar, bench, or pulpit. It is through the novel that he will capture "all conditions" of audiences, the Fanny Boltons addicted to the "darling greasy volumes" from Miss Minifer's circulating library, the Blanche Amorys immersed in "Mes larmes" and the *Journal des modes,* the Madame Fribsbys who sigh over sentimental romances, the Helen Pendennises, who "melt right away" at the reading of Bishop Heber and Felicia Hemans. He would win Sir Francis Clavering away from *Bell's Life in London* if he could, as well as Major Pendennis from Paul de Kock, and Foker from his sporting prints, and would like at the same time to provide nutriment substantial enough to impress even Paley buried in his law books and Dr. Portman surrounded by the folios of his private library. Young Pen, we learn early in his history, "never read to improve himself out of school-hours, but, on the contrary, devoured all the novels, plays, and poetry, on which he could lay his hands" (chap. 2). But, as his creator affirms in the preface to *Pendennis,* truth should be welcomed "from whatever chair—from those whence graver writers or thinkers argue, as from that at which the story-teller sits."

"To myself and to many of my own generation it has always seemed as if there was a special music in 'Pendennis,' and the best wisdom of a strong heart beating under its yellow waistcoat," recalled Anne Thackeray in the introduction she prepared for the Biographical Edition.[42] The esteem in which it was held at the time is indicated by her placing it second to *Vanity Fair* in this collection. If its "special music" has not proved particularly attuned to the ears of this generation, that is probably because, of all of Thackeray's major novels, *Pendennis* is best savored in connection with its original circumstances and milieu. It is highly significant in Thackeray's career in a number of ways. His latest biographer has pointed out that the success of *Vanity Fair* relieved Thackeray from economic struggle, leaving him free to appraise his own youth and early manhood, and meditate over its significance.[43] In an earlier chapter of this study it was suggested that Thackeray's self-confidence as a novelist made it possible for him to speak out to his readers more straightforwardly and seriously, in *propria persona* rather than in the guise of a popular entertainer—though theater hovers in the background and theatrical metaphor persists. But success brought its perils too, as Thackeray was aware in a letter he wrote to his mother when he was about to begin the writing of *Pendennis:* "May God Almighty keep me honest and keep pride and vanity down. In spite of himself a man gets worldly and ambitious in this great place: with every body courting and flattering. I am frightened at it and my own infernal pride and arrogance. . . . What I mean is that all of a sudden I am a great man. I am ashamed of it: but yet I can't help seeing it—being elated by it trying to keep it down, etc." So this most personal of Thackeray's novels becomes a stocktaking of himself both as man and as author, achieving identity of writer and readers, because he is able to look into their hearts with a knowledge of his own.

Amalgamating guide to youth, fashionable novel, and literary *Bildungsroman, Pendennis,* moreover, is the culminating novel of "the Punch connexion," just as *Barry Lyndon* had marked the zenith of his career with "F a magazine of wit." Its growth out of humorous "fashionable intelligence" and popular moral advice parallels Thackeray's own evolution from journalist to novelist-educator-philosopher. Now that his eminence in fiction was assured, Thackeray was, moreover, not so dependent upon magazines for themes, and he tended after *Pendennis* to seek his subject matter elsewhere. For his next venture, in view of the complaint of one of the reviewers of *Pendennis* that he was tending to "play on one string with several variations, but all in the same key," it is not surprising that he changed his tune and also removed himself far from "the booths, the wild-beast shows, and the merry-go-rounds," he had become associated with. "I've got a better subject for a novel than any I've yet had," he wrote to his mother late in 1850, on the day that he finished *Pendennis.*[44] We can almost see the new novel shaping itself in the chapter of *Pendennis* entitled "The Knights of the Temple," where the author muses: "I don't know whether the student of law permits himself the refreshment of enthusiasm, or indulges in poetical reminiscences as he passes by historical chambers . . . but the man of letters can't but love the place which has been inhabited by so many of his brethren, or peopled by their creations as real to us at this day as the authors whose children they were—and Sir Roger de Coverley walking in the Temple Garden, and discoursing with Mr. Spectator about the beauties in hoops and patches who are sauntering over the grass, is just as lively a figure to me as old Samuel Johnson" (chap. 29). In his heart he shared with that "Pall Mall philosopher" Major Pendennis a wistful nostalgia for the more genteel, less hurried era before the railroads, whose coming, among other economic developments, is documented in *Pendennis:* "The men, thinks [the major], are not such as they used to be in his time: the old grand manner and courtly grace of life are gone: what is Castlewood House and the present Castlewood compared to the magnificence of the old mansion and owner? The late lord came to London with four post-chaises and sixteen horses: all the North Road hurried out to look at his cavalcade: the people in London streets even stopped as his procession passed them" (chap. 67).

Thackeray could not bring back the old Castlewood House, but he could do the next best thing. At the time he wrote to his mother about the new novel he had in mind, he was returning to the period of *Barry Lyndon* in his reading, presumably in preparation for the series of lectures on eighteenth-century humorists that he launched the following spring. Henceforth the aura of the public lecturer and popular historian, the literary situation he found most congenial, was to dominate his fiction. In other ways too he was shifting his ground. "I must tell you that a story is biling up in my interior, in w^h there shall appear some very good lofty and generous people," he wrote to Mrs. Brookfield early in 1851. "Perhaps a story without any villain in it would be good, wouldn't it?"[45] He had swung full round from "A Novel without a Hero." As for the nature of the new hero, Thackeray may have taken to heart the suggestion of another reviewer of *Pendennis* that "we should like to see him in the future diminish the Pen a little and develop the Warrington."[46] What we do know now is that Henry Esmond was destined to become the ancestor of George Warrington through his daughter Rachel. With change of tone and color came also a transformation of mode. "Pathos I hold should be very occasional indeed in humorous works and indicated rather than expressed or expressed very rarely," Thackeray wrote a friend in the fall of 1848, before *Pendennis* had begun to appear. "We shouldn't do much more than that I think in comic books," the letter continues; "In a story written in the pathetic key it would be different & then the comedy should be occasional. Some day—but a truce to egotistical twaddle."[47] In *Pendennis* we can see pathos overtaking comedy, but in the next novel we find ourselves with Henry, returned to Castlewood after his student days at Cambridge, "in the midst of this actual tragedy of life."[48]

    1. *Athenaeum*, 7 December 1850, p. 1273.

    2. *Punch* 16 (January-June 1849), 17 (July-December 1849), practically concurrent with the first twelve numbers of *Pendennis*, the first of which appeared in November 1848. In her introduction to *Pendennis*, Anne Thackeray refers to this series and quotes a letter written by her father to a friend in imitation of its style, signed "Samuel S. Pips" (*Works*, 2:xxxviii–ix). This letter of October 1850 (to Lady Eddisbury) is reprinted in *Letters*, 2:699–70. Doyle's cartoon "A Cydere Cellare During a Comyck Songe," which illustrated the episode of this series in *Punch*, 17 March 1849, is reproduced in *Letters*, 2:442 (facing). "Mr. Pips" was Percival Leigh, who wrote the text illustrated by the cartoons.

    3. Conclusion of preface to vol. 17 (July–December 1849).

    4. It began on 24 March 1849 and ran through 18 August of that year. *Pendennis* was not concluded until December 1850.

    5. Despite surface similarities, the two uncles differ fundamentally in character. The elder Brown is a widower, not a bachelor like Major Pendennis, has read law, tends toward restraint in matters of dress, unlike the foppish major; and though worldly and opportunistic, he deplores tuft-hunting and chasing after "swells." In some ways he serves as a corrective to the major.

6. A direct connection is established with the novel in one of the numbers (12 May 1849; letter 7 in reprints), in which Mr. Brown visits a club with his nephew where a member is discovered dozing over part 7 of *Pendennis*. Book and reader are clearly shown in the headpiece that originally preceded this episode.

7. The first of the group entitled "On Love, Marriage, Men, and Women" (letter 14 in reprints).

8. Thackeray specifically mentions *The Parent's Assistant, Ami des enfans, Evenings at Home,* and Dr. Dilworth's illustrated spelling books as part of the reading of his own childhood in his essay "John Leech's Pictures of Life and Character," *Quarterly Review* 96 (December 1854); *Works,* 13:481.

9. My chapter references generally follow the revised numbering as incorporated in the Penguin English Library reprint, but there will be occasional quotations from the first edition. Beginning with the unillustrated one-volume edition of 1855 (dated 1856), considerable cuts were made (whether by Thackeray or not is unknown). Chapter numbers and titles do not diverge between the two versions of the text until after chap. 15; with the 1855 edition the telescoping of the original chaps. 16 and 17 resulted in the dropping of one heading ("More Storms in the Puddle," chap. 16 in the early editions) and the reduction of the number of chapters from seventy-six to seventy-five. Minor revisions were made in the text (largely changes in punctuation and corrections of typographical errors) in the first book issue. See Peter L. Shillingsburg, "The First Edition of Thackeray's *Pendennis*," *Publications of the Bibliographical Society of America* 66 (First Quarter 1972): 35–49.

10. The less materialistic Mr. Brown, on the other hand, advises nephew Bob to marry "a lady not very much above or below your station" (letter 15). This letter appeared almost concurrently with the ninth number of *Pendennis* (July 1849), in the last chapter of which the major expresses the wisdom quoted in the text.

11. "Jerome Paturot," *Works,* 13:389.

12. Chap. 5 (as quoted from an anonymous translation, London, n.d.)

13. His meeting with Janin in London is mentioned in letters to W. Raymond Sams, 4 February 1849, and to Mrs. Brookfield, 4 February 1849 (*Letters,* 2:499, 500). In October 1853 he wrote to Lord Holland from Paris in anticipation of seeing Janin in a cafe the next day: "Have you met JJ? He is the most wonderful company more amusing than 20 vaudevilles" (*Letters,* 3:309). The friendship kept up practically to the end of Thackeray's life, his diary recording a visit on 8 March 1863 (*Letters,* 4:409). In "Small-Beer Chronicle" he recalls wandering about the streets of London with this "famous and witty French critic" (*Roundabout Papers, Works,* 13:305).

14. G. W. M. Reynolds, *The Modern Literature of France* (London: George Henderson, 1839), vol. 2, chap. 3. The *Times* review is mentioned in the preface to the English version.

15. "Translator's Preface," *Prosper Chavigni & Letitia Laferti* (thus on the title page, but the running title is *The Cross Roads*) (London: J. Clements, n.d. [though one of the stories bound up with it is dated 1842]).

16. "The happy village," a phrase used to describe the hero's birthplace, is the title of chap. 15 of *Pendennis*. Blanche Amory, on her first meeting with Pen in London, remarks: "How different from Arthur Pendennis of the country! Ah! I think I like Arthur Pendennis of the country best, though!" (chap. 40).

17. "'Ho, ho!' they will exclaim, 'so you are going to begin at the beginning, with the education of this young provincial!'" writes Janin at the beginning of his narrative, addressing his readers, with whom he seems to have enjoyed bantering as much as did Thackeray. Janin too tries to fob off charges of deliberately setting out to shock readers: "You are going, then, to show him systematically how to become a liar, a coward, a cheat, a duellist, a scamp—in a word you are going to teach him to become something. . . . It is thus that I hear many voices exclaiming around me, in spite of all the precautions with which I encircled the second part of my recital. Morality has made such immense progress in our days!" (chap. 2). Cf. Thackeray's testimony in the preface to *Pendennis:* "Many ladies have remonstrated and subscribers have left me, because, in the course of this story, I described a young man resisting and affected by temptation."

18. See my *Fiction with a Purpose* (Bloomington: Indiana University Press, 1967), pp. 162–66.

19. In his introduction to the Penguin English Library reprint, J. I. M. Stewart compares *Pendennis* in this respect to Joyce's *A Portrait of the Artist as a Young Man*, pointing out the difference that in *A Portrait* "the mature Joyce *is* Joyce the adolescent as he writes, so that his work is a masterpiece . . . of self-empathy," whereas in *Pendennis*, Thackeray "is looking back, so that the boy comes to us, as it were, refracted through the gaze of the man" (p. 8). Also, as I point out in this chapter, Thackeray is not concerned so much with the artist sui generis, as with what the artist has in common with the humanity at large.

In "Michael Angelo Titmarsh and the Knebworth Apollo" *(Costerus,* n.s. 2 [1974]: 77), Anthea Trodd asserts that *Pendennis* is in part a rebuttal to Bulwer's conception of the writer as a superior being in *Ernest Maltravers*.

20. See above, pp. 185–88, and Colby, *Fiction with a Purpose*, pp. 159–62.

21. Cf. letter to his mother, 18 July 1848 *(Letters,* 2:401), quoted below (p. 304).

22. In his *W. M. Thackeray, l'homme—le penseur—le romancier* (Paris: Librairie Champion, 1932), Raymond Las Vergnas analyzes Thackeray's resolution of such dualities in his temperament as bohemianism and gentility, cynicism and tenderheartedness, melancholy and gaiety, insularity and cosmopolitan, realism and romanticism (see the chapter entitled "Contradictions," pp. 52–70).

23. The evangelical clergyman in *The Great Hoggarty Diamond* (see above, p. 175 and 195 n. 7).

24. The name Lever gave to his caricature of Thackeray in *Roland Cashel* (1850).

25. See Colby, *Fiction with a Purpose,* pp. 156–57.

26. *Leader,* 21 December 1850, pp. 929–30.

27. With much quotation from *Faust* on the strivings of the imagination, appropriate to the future biographer of Goethe.

28. *Works,* 13:630–31. This essay originally was published in the *Morning Chronicle,* 12 January 1850, in reply to a leading article that had appeared in the previous number, as well as a comment in the *Examiner* that had taken issue with the views on the literary profession expressed by Thackeray in *Pendennis.*

29. Thus in the first edition; subsequently changed to "Queen Christina's army."

30. Altamont is best appreciated as a parodic character, a spoof at once of the "high-souled convict" who figures in the French romances read by his daughter Blanche (chap. 23) and of the swashbuckling characters of Sue and Dumas.

31. Chap. 16 in first edition, cut out in 1855 when chaps. 15 and 16 were telescoped.

32. Among matter relating to Bloundell that was cut out in 1855.

33. The rival is the gruff but generally good-natured young medical student Sam Huxter, prompted at this point by his own interest in Fanny Bolton.

34. Chap. 46 in first edition, excised in 1855.

35. "Bradbury and Evans" in monthly parts and first book issue, as well as in revision of 1855.

36. This passage appeared in the first number that came out in November 1848.

37. Wordsworth was poet laureate at the time.

38. Further parallels are pointed out with *Ranthorpe* in Colby, *Fiction with a Purpose,* pp. 143, 168.

39. George Henry Lewes, review of *Pendennis, Leader,* 21 December 1850, p. 929. See above, p. 51.

40. "Beware how you marry out of your degree," Warrington warns Arthur (chap. 57), apparently more in agreement with Mr. Brown than with Major Pendennis (see above, n. 10). Mixed marriages on the whole do not fare well in this novel; v. Warrington, who is married to the ignorant daughter of a yeoman, and Mr. Pynsent and Sam Huxter, who marry respectively above and below their stations, to not altogether happy result.

41. See above, p. 294.

42. *Works*, 2:xxxvi. According to Peter Shillingsburg, who has studied the records, *Pendennis* "established its popularity . . . at a faster rate than did *Vanity Fair*." He indicates that initial printings of the first twelve parts ranged from eight thousand to ten thousand, and that reader demand necessitated printing of additional copies. He conjectures further that parts may still have been run off by Bradbury and Evans even after the book issue ("The First Edition of Thackeray's *Pendennis*," pp. 38–39).

43. Gordon N. Ray, *Thackeray: The Age of Wisdom* (New York: McGraw-Hill, 1958), p. 109 (hereafter referred to as *The Age of Wisdom*).

44. *Letters*, 2:708.

45. Ibid., p. 736.

46. [David Masson], *"Pendennis* and *Copperfield:* Thackeray and Dickens," *North British Review* 15 (May 1851): 87. Author identification supplied by *Wellesley Index*, vol. 1.

47. 3 September 1848 to Robert Bell, *Letters*, 2:424–25.

48. *Henry Esmond*, bk. 1, chap. 11.

Part Four

"THE WEEK-DAY PREACHER"
The Novelist as Public Educator

HENRY ESMOND; OR, THE COMPLETE CAVALIER

Chapter Ten

"HARLEQUIN WITHOUT HIS MASK IS known to present a very sober countenance, and was himself . . . a man full of cares and perplexities like the rest of us, whose Self must always be serious to him, under whatever mask or disguise or uniform he presents it to the public," declared Thackeray to the first audience gathered for his lectures on the humorists of the eighteenth century.[1] "And as all of you here must needs be grave when you think of your own past and present, you will not look to find, in the histories of those whose lives and feelings I am going to try and describe to you, a story that is otherwise than serious, and often very sad." So Thackeray prepared readers for *Henry Esmond,* which grew out of these lectures (and in which a number of the "humorists" appear), for his own metamorphosis from fantastical clown on a barrel top to frock-coated "week-day preacher" on a platform, and for a voice of deeper plangency than they had been used to from him.

It may well be that at this time Thackeray was taking his cue from one of the then most distinguished members of this audience, his friend and neighbor at Kensington, Leigh Hunt. Some months before Thackeray announced to his mother that he had a "better subject ! . . . than any I've yet had," Hunt's one novel, *Sir Ralph Esher; or, Memoirs of a Gentleman of the Court of Charles II,* first published in 1832, was briefly revived through Bentley's Standard Novels.[2] In its genesis *Sir Ralph Esher* is similar to that of *Esmond.* As Hunt recalls in his "Advertisement to the Reader" that introduces the 1850 edition, his original intention had been to compile a book

on the wits of the age of Charles II, but, discouraged by the licentiousness of the wit of the "gentry" of the age, he decided to use the
material he had gathered as the basis for a fictitious memoir. In the
novel that resulted, Hunt indicates that " . . . while it is hoped that
the animal spirits of the times are not absent, and divers of the
scapegraces are to be found, an attempt has been made to portray
the good-heartedness that was still beating in the bosoms of some of
their associates, and the wisdom which a more serious and suffering nature had produced in some of their friends, notwithstanding
the pangs that caused it by the mistakes both of levity and bigotry."[3]
The novel itself illustrates both the "levity" and "bigotry" of
Caroline England, an aspect of the clash of Miltonic mirth and
melancholy. Its young hero (of whom more later), in reaction
against a strict religious upbringing, tries to steer a middle ground
between Cavalier laxity and Puritan rectitude. These dual impulses
in the English character of hedonism and morality ("pleasure warring against self-restraint")—what Matthew Arnold was later to
identify as Hellenism and Hebraism—surge also through Thackeray's lectures on the eighteenth-century wits. As he remarks, for
example, on the comedies of Congreve and contemporaries who
bridge the period from the Restoration to the Age of Anne:

> Reading in these plays now, is like shutting your ears and looking
> at people dancing. What does it mean? The measures, the grimaces,
> the bowing, shuffling, and retreating, the *cavalier seul* advancing
> upon those ladies—those ladies and men twirling round at the end
> in a mad galop, after which everybody bows and the quaint rite is
> celebrated. Without the music we can't understand that comic dance
> of the last century—its strange gravity and gaiety, its decorum or its
> indecorum. It has a jargon of its own quite unlike life; a sort of moral
> of its own quite unlike life too. I'm afraid it's a Heathen mystery,
> symbolising a Pagan doctrine; protesting . . . against the new, hard,
> ascetic pleasure-hating doctrine whose gaunt disciples, lately passed
> over from the Asian shores of the Mediterranean, were for breaking
> the fair images of Venus and flinging the altars of Bacchus down.[4]

Appropriately the "music" with which our humorist of the
nineteenth century is to quicken the "comic dance of the last century" into life is to be rich, but not solemn. Other writings, recalled
for the audiences of his lectures, provide him with the dancers and
their backdrops: "As we read in these delightful volumes of the
Tatler and *Spectator* the past age returns, the England of our ancestors is revivified. The Maypole rises in the Strand again in London;
the churches are thronged with daily worshippers; the beaux are
gathering in the coffee-houses; the gentry are going to the Draw-

ing-room; the ladies are thronging to the toy-shops; the chairmen are jostling in the streets; the footmen are running with links before the chariots, or fighting round the theatre doors."[5] And quite typically he turns to the "ephemeral repertories" of the age to supply its special "jargon": "I have looked over many of the comic books with which our ancestors amused themselves. . . . The slang of the taverns and the ordinaries, the wit of the bagnios, form the strongest part of the farrago of which these libels are composed."

In seeking the proper tone for his historical romance, Thackeray looked also to the trend of historical writing in his own time. "It takes as much trouble as Macaulay's *History* almost," Thackeray remarked in a letter to his mother while he was at work on *Esmond*.[6] It was the function of the historian to make us see "ordinary men as they appear in their ordinary business and in their ordinary pleasures," Macaulay had affirmed in an early essay. "[He] must mingle in the crowds of the exchange and the coffee-house." In a famous passage of his *History* that did so much to popularize this study among mid-Victorian common readers, Macaulay declared: "I should very imperfectly execute the task which I have undertaken if I were merely to treat of battles and sieges, of the rise and fall of administrations, of intrigues in the palace, and of debates in parliament. It will be my endeavour to relate the history of the people as well as the history of government."[7] So Henry Esmond's famous query was pertinent: "I wonder shall History ever pull off her periwig and cease to be court-ridden? Shall we see something of France and England besides Versailles and Windsor?" Shall we, in other words, see something of the last century besides what can be gleaned from Captain Jesse's *Memoirs of the Court of England from 1688 to the Death of George II*, Boyer's *Annals*, or James Macpherson's *Secret History of Great Britain*—to mention but a few of Thackeray's primary sources?[8] Among Thackeray's rivals, Harrison Ainsworth, in his romance *Saint James's; or, The Court of Queen Anne* (1845), had treated this period almost exclusively as a succession of rises and falls of the mighty—Marlborough, Bolingbroke, and Oxford—interspersed with a series of female palace intrigues, but in *Esmond* these notables become supernumeraries, not the chief actors.

Thackeray thought his hero Henry overly grave at times ("I wish the new novel wasn't so grand and melancholy," he wrote to his mother while he was writing it, "the hero is as stately as Sir Charles Grandison—something like Warrington—a handsome likeness of an ugly son of yours"),[9] but he makes him far from stuffy or humorless in his opening remarks where he describes his task as chronicler of the past: "Why shall History go on kneeling to the end of time? I am for having her rise up off her knees, and take a natural posture: not to be for ever performing cringes and congees like a Court-chamberlain, and shuffling backwards out of doors in the presence of the sovereign. In a word, I would have History familiar rather than heroic." Henry adopts in general what Thackeray had called in *Barry Lyndon* a "near" view of history. A few years before, Archibald Alison, another highly respected historian of the time, although asserting as one requirement of the historical romance "that the subject should be of an *elevating and ennobling kind*," added that "we by no means intend to assert that the author is always to be on stilts, that he is never to descend to the description of low or even vulgar life, or that humour and characteristic description are to be excluded from his composition. We are well aware of the value of contrast in bringing out effect; we know that the mind of the reader requires repose even from the most exalted emotions; we have felt the weariness of being satiated with beauty."[10] Henry Esmond echoes him in the more sonorous manner of his own age:

> The actors in the old tragedies, as we read, piped their iambics to a tune, speaking from under a mask, and wearing stilts and a great head-dress. 'Twas thought the dignity of the Tragic Muse required these appurtenances, and that she was not to move except to a measure and cadence. . . . The Muse of History hath encumbered herself with ceremony as well as her Sister of the Theatre. She too wears the mask and the cothurnus, and speaks to measure. She too, in our age, busies herself with the affairs only of kings; waiting on them obsequiously and stately, as if she were but a mistress of court ceremonies, and had nothing to do with the registering of the affairs of the common people.

In *Henry Esmond,* Thackeray does not actually "descend to the description of low or even vulgar life," having already done so in *Catherine,* aptly described by a reviewer when it was concluding its run in *Fraser's* as "strong, coarse, literal painting of men and manners in the profligate classes of the profligate times of Queen Anne."[11] In the later novel we get a subdued, stylish picture of the upper classes of this period, but one that illustrates how "the great historical figures" of Queen Anne's Court "dwindle down into the common proportions as we come to view them so closely," to quote one of Thackeray's own early reviews.[12] In keeping with Henry's conviction that history be "familiar rather than heroic," he gives us a brief glimpse of Queen Anne herself, unperiwigged and unlaced, "a hot, red-faced woman, not in the least resembling that statue of her which turns its stone back upon St. Paul's . . . neither better bred nor wiser than you and me, though we knelt to hand her a letter or a wash-hand basin."

For his somewhat irreverent attitude toward the high and mighty Thackeray could lean also on the precedent of Scott, at the time still preeminent among historical romancers. Unlike contemporaries, notably Bulwer, who tended to think of the Waverley Novels as picturesque fustian, to Thackeray,

> [Scott] was, if we mistake not, the first romantic author who dealt with kings and princes familiarly. Charles and Louis are made to laugh before us as unconcernedly as schoolboys; Richard takes his share of canary out of the cup of Friar Tuck; and the last words we hear from James are, that the cockaleeky is growing cold. What is it that pleases us in the contemplation of these royal people so employed? Why are we more amused with the notion of a king on the broad grin than with the hilariousness of a commoner? That mingling of grandeur and simplicity, that ticklish conjunction of awe and frivolity, are wonderfully agreeable to the reader.[13]

He carried this "ticklish conjunction" to its absurd extreme in *Rebecca and Rowena,* his long-threatened parodic sequel to *Ivanhoe* published in the year *Esmond* was begun, where Richard the Lion-Hearted is caught unhorsed, as a fat, blustering, ill-tempered, vain, quite undivine monarch. As we have seen, *Henry Esmond* too deals with "kings and princes familiarly." As the story progresses, we find that his opinion of Marlborough and the "rogues" who surround Queen Anne does not differ from that of Ikey Solomons. Prince James the Pretender is shown up as just that in more than the political sense. "Would you know how a prince, heroic from misfortunes, and descended from a line of kings . . . was employed, when the envoy who came to him through danger and difficulty beheld him for the first time?" asks Henry, and gives us the answer. "The young King, in a flannel jacket, was at tennis with the gentlemen of his suite, crying out after the balls, and swearing like the meanest of his subjects" (bk. 3, chap. 8). The next time we glimpse the prince through Henry's eyes, he is visibly in his cups and playing cards with Miss Oglethorpe, his mistress of the hour.

"We must paint our great Duke . . . not as a man, which no doubt he is, with weaknesses like the rest of us but as a hero," affirms Henry's literary friend Joseph Addison (bk. 2, chap. 11). In his poem *The Campaign,* Addison feels compelled to "follow the rules of my art, and the composition of such a strain as this must be harmonious and majestic, not familiar, or too near the vulgar truth." Addison, however, is writing a commemorative ode, whereas Henry is writing a memoir, which Victor Cousin defined as "the vulgar part of these great destinies . . . the ridiculous and comic part of the majestic drama of history."[14] Thackeray showed an inclination toward the "vulgar part" in his series on the eighteenth-century humorists. Certainly his various wits fell short of "The Hero as Man of Letters" as visualized in the more idealistic historiography of Carlyle—another fellow writer in attendance at the opening lecture on Swift.[15] Much earlier, in reviewing *The French Revolution*, Thackeray had contrasted Carlyle, "our mystical poet" for whom "the little actors of this great drama [of history] are striving towards a great end and moral," with his rival "sharp sighted and prosaic Thiers" for whom "the whole story is but a bustling for places."[16] By temperament Thackeray was inclined more toward the worldly Thiers, "the *valet de chambre* of this history, he is too familiar with its déshabille and its offscourings; it can never be a hero to him." To remove a distinguished figure from the aura of public glory is often to diminish him, Thiers's compatriot and fellow historian Cousin had pointed out. "Every individuality, when it is detached from the general spirit which it expresses, is full of what is pitiful," reads a passage from his lecture on "Great Men"; "When we read the secret memoirs which we have of some great men, and when we follow them into the details of their life and conduct, we are always confounded to find them not only small, but, I am compelled to say, often vicious and most despicable."[17] So Thackeray discovered about Marlborough, the most conspicuous of the fallen idols in *Esmond*, whom he indicts for treachery and fraud on the basis of his reading of Torcy's *Memoirs* and *The Secret History of Great Britain*. Cousin distinguishes the memoirist from the historian who, like the classic dramatist, tries "to place in a clear light the idea which a great man represents," and therefore "ignores the purely individual and biographical side of man . . . [neglects] the description of weaknesses inherent in their individuality."[18] As he incorporates history into fiction (through his alter ego Henry Esmond), Thackeray leans more toward the "romantic drama" as defined by Cousin, which "takes man as a whole, not merely on his ideal side, but on the individual side; hence scenes the most burlesque and comic succeed scenes the most heroic and most pathetic, and heighten the effect."

A by-product of the newly emergent social and cultural history, the historical romance had come of age since the Waverley Novels and generally had gained acceptance by both critics and the public.

In the year when Queen Victoria came to the throne, the French critic Jules Janin observed in one of a series of articles he contributed to the *Athenaeum:* "From History to Romance we have but one step to make. History has descended so far from the pedestal on which she stood of old—and at the same time Romance has so elevated herself,—that, ere long, if care be not taken, History and Romance will stand face to face upon the same level. . . . History which formerly put on the lofty airs of majesty, has descended in our day to the character of a sprightly girl:—Romance, which was once, properly speaking, the mere running chronicle of our domestic manners, breaks out of its sphere, erects itself into a legislator—into a politician—into an historian—sways men and rebukes them—moralizes them—corrupts them."[19] An anonymous writer for *The Court Magazine and la Belle Assembleé*, commenting on Janin's article, declared that the historical novel had already achieved status as "the most prevailing class of fictions," was in fact "the bent of the age," and that consequently, "not a moment should be lost in analyzing its scope and tendency."[20]

The mingling of fact and fiction in the historical novel continued to meet with resistance in mid-century as it did in Scott's time. Carlyle once scoffed at the form as "nothing but a pasteboard Tree, cobbled together out of size and waste-paper . . . altogether unconnected with the soil of Thought . . . or at best united with it by some decayed stump and dead boughs." Disraeli made a character refer to historical novels as "insipidities . . . as full of costume as a fancy ball, and almost as devoid of sense."[21] As late as 1851, when Thackeray began work on *Henry Esmond,* the eminent archivist and historian of medieval England Sir Francis Palgrave denounced historical novels as "mortal enemies to history," attacked *Ivanhoe* in particular as "out of time, out of place, out of season, out of reason, ideal or impossible," and blamed writers of historical fiction in one sweep as responsible for the tendency of the common reader to look on history as "a splendid melodrama, set to the sound of kettledrums and trumpets."[22] Macaulay, on the other hand, was among the enthusiastic admirers of Scott, and no less a figure than the aforementioned Archibald Alison, writing for *Maga* in the mid-forties, welcomed the historical novel as an education both of the character and of the mind. In Alison's opinion, the two genres in vogue during the previous decade (to which Thackeray had made his contribution)—the "Almack" school, dealing with fashionable life, and its more sensational opposite number, the "Jack Sheppard" school—had pretty much exhausted themselves. Alison believed with Sir Joshua Reynolds that the province of the artist (pictorial or literary) lay not with any particular class of society, but with "general or common nature," and with Dr. Johnson that "whatever makes the Past or the Future predominate over the present, exalts us in the scale of thinking beings."[23] As far as Alison was concerned, the historical romancer, having all of time at his disposal as the travel writer had all of space, was better able to expand the reader's knowledge and human sympathies than was the novelist of contemporary life, confined to the temporal and the topical.

However historians may have argued over what some of them regarded as the bastard child of Clio, it is evident that the public took it to their bosoms. "The gods give them joy to their taste!— There are authors enough and to spare who write books reg- ulationwise," comments Mrs. Gore's coxcomb hero Cecil Danby; "As to your historical three volume novels per rule and compass, with a beginning, an end, and a middle, it strikes me that there is beginning to be no end to them, and they are all middling."[24] This observation is confirmed several years later by George Henry Lewes in a critical article. "To judge from the number yearly pub- lished, one may presume that there is a great demand for historical romance," complained Lewes, "and to judge by the quality of those published, one may suppose the readers very good-natured, or very ignorant; or both. We believe they are both."[25] Lewes's criti- cisms, however, are leveled not at the genre of the historical ro- mance, for which he had high regard, but at the all too typical writer of it who assumes that "he needs no style, no imagination, no fancy, no knowledge of the world, no wit, no pathos: he needs only to study Scott and the historical novelists; to 'cram' for the neces- sary information about costumes, antiquated forms of speech, and the leading political events of the epoch chosen; and to add thereto the art, so easily learned, of complicating a plot with adventures, imprisonments, and escapes." Lewes was opposed in general to the practice by writers of dragging in history to prop up a sagging tale, and to give their work adventitious prestige. The historical novel must stand on its own, he argued, meaning that it must be good history and a good story fused. Moreover "good" history for him did not mean simply accurate facts and straight chronology. Scott was criticized in his time, he points out, for mere "errors of detail" by the Dr. Dryasdusts of his time, unable to appreciate how he had "divined important historical truths which had escaped the sagacity of all historians." It is significant that whereas Scott himself had professed no greater intention than to provide an "amusing vehicle" for the conveyance of history to the ordinary reader, Lewes sees a larger function for the historical novelist: "When . . . a writer has so familiarized himself with the inward spirit and outward form of an epoch, as to be able to paint it with accuracy and ease, he may make that epoch a very useful and entertaining scene for his story. . . . Unfortunately it is only the outward form that most writers study; thinking with this outward form to compose splendid accessories. But, after all, what are accessories? Very much what splendid processions, gorgeous scenery, numerous attendants, and spangled dresses are to a tragedy: a panoply of ennui."[26]

Lewes's review indicates that more was hoped for from a historical novelist at this time than to furnish a colorful tableau as an aid to the teaching of history. Nor did potted knowledge suffice. M. Janin, in his *Athenaeum* piece, had already pointed to his countryman Alexis Monteil, "the very embodiment of patience, erudition, and exact and minute research . . . the learned half of Sir Walter Scott," who has "constructed an admirable theatre amid the history of France:—scarcely anything is wanting to it; palaces, cottages, churches, monasteries, fortresses, all are there—it wants only living men and their passions." Janin wondered if "the art of enchaining the interest, of putting the passions in play, of constructing a story at once true, chaste, simple and varied, out of the bloody and miry wrecks of real history" had been lost with the death of Scott.[27]

The chief inheritor of Scott's mantle in England was that "teeming parent of romance," G. P. R. James, not only the most prolific historical novelist of the Victorian age, but, with his appointment under William IV as Historiographer Royal, the most prestigious. A writer of omnivorous, if not always well digested, reading, James was widely regarded for his erudition—the "cram" parts of his books, in Lewes's phrase. In dedicating his *Saint James's; or, The Court of Queen Anne* to James, Harrison Ainsworth testified that "the amusement and instruction they have derived from your writings have endeared you to hosts of readers." So heavy was the demand, apparently, that in this same year, 1844, Smith, Elder (who were to be the publishers of *Henry Esmond*) commenced a collected edition of James's work to date, carefully revised by the author, and, as their advertisment reads, "got up in that superior style and size of type which renders it fit for every age and for every library."[28] The edition was successful, to judge by contemporary evidence. Smith, Elder's catalogue of 1845 quotes a comment in the

Literary Gazette on "the rapid absorption of a very large first edition," with a second moving fast: "This is as it should be, with a writer whose vraisemblance is always so perfect; and even what he invents so like truth, that we can never fancy we are reading fiction, nor, indeed, are we, in the historical portions of his publications,—and these form the far greater division,—which are all drawn from diligent research, deep study, and elaborate comparison." But for Lewes, as we have seen, diligence was not all, and the novels of James were in fact singled out in his review as conspicuous examples of uninspired task work. Before Lewes, another critic, R. H. Horne, raised a dissentient voice in the midst of the chorus of praise that greeted the Smith, Elder edition, in his *A New Spirit of the Age* (1844)—a book that Thackeray reviewed. Horne conceded that James's books, thanks to his conscientious research, are "admirable novels of costume; they may even lay claim to the higher distinction of being capital illuminations worthy of being let into the margins of history," but he added that "they must not be confounded with that class of historical or real-life novels in which all other considerations are subservient to the delineation of human nature."[29] "Accessories" and "outward form" did not make a novel for Horne any more than for Lewis.

James's pedantry and humorlessness made him a ripe candidate to hang in Thackeray's gallery of *Punch's Prize Novelists,* where his mannerisms are perfectly embalmed in "Barbazure. By G. P. R. Jeames, Esq., Etc." A lead-in to "Barbazure" is provided by an anonymous piece that appeared in Cruikshank's *Comic Almanack* the year before entitled "Hints to Novelists, for 1846," with a thumbnail parody of the "Read-up or Jamesonian" style that especially suggests Thackeray's hand. It begins with platitudinous moralizing on the lessons taught by the records left by the past, proceeds with the description of the two solitary horsemen that became identified as James's trademark, interrupted by the note: "At this point search the British Museum, and get up the costumes from pictures."[30] In "Barbazure" we take up the "two cavaliers" where we left them in the *Comic Almanack,* and by now their author has indeed "got up" the costumes ("Both were caparisoned in the fullest trappings of feudal war. The arblast, the mangonel, the demi-culverin, and the cuissart, of the period, glittered upon the neck and chest of the war-steed; while the rider, with chamfron and catapult, with ban and arrière-ban, morion and tumbrel, battle-axe and rifflard, and the other appurtenances of ancient chivalry, rode stately on his steel-clad charger, himself a tower of steel").[31] Thackeray was no one to scoff at painstaking research. While at work on *Esmond* he himself practically lived at the British Museum, reading up on the Age of Anne, and, particularly in the oft-quoted impression of Beatrix descending on the staircase at Walcote House, described down to the silver clocks in her scarlet stockings, shows himself to be quite exact in details of costume. However, in previous chapters we have noted how he joins his pictorial and dramatic skills to invigorate his portraits. It is evident too that for Thackeray clothes are important mainly as they make the man (as with Father Holt, a man of many disguises) as well as the woman. In fact, one of the more favorable of the early reviewers of *Esmond*, complaining that with the successors to Scott, accurate as they are in period dress, "no breathing, tangible body fills out these trophies of accoutrement . . . the plumed casques enclose only shadows," found Thackeray's novel refreshing by comparison. "Here are no laced coats and hoops enclosing names and no more," observed this reviewer. "His business lies mainly with men and women, not with high-heeled shoes and hoops and patches, and old china, and carved, high-backed chairs," wrote another.[32]

Contemporaneous reviewers of *Esmond* also made due note of Thackeray's success in suggesting the speech of a bygone century without archaism—idiomatic simplicity, vigor, and grace all combining "to transport us irresistibly to the days of Addison and Steele," in the words of one of them.[33] The convincing representation of the conversation of a past age remains *the* stumbling block of historical novelists even in our day, and Thackeray was quick to pounce on James's "antiquated forms of speech" (part of the stock in trade of the hack romancer, according to Lewes):

"Boy," said the elder, "thou hast ill tidings. I know it by thy glance. Speak: shall he who hath bearded grim Death in a thousand fields shame to face truth from a friend? Speak in the name of heaven and good King Botibol. Romané de Clos-Veugot will bear your tidings like a man!"

"Fatima is well," answered Philibert once again, "she hath no measles: she lives and is still fair."

"Fair, ay, peerless fair; but what more, Philibert? Not false? By Saint Botibol, say not false," groaned the elder warrior.

"A month syne," Philibert replied, "she married the Baron de Barbazure."

With that scream which is so terrible in a strong man in agony, the brave knight Romané de Clos-Veugot sank back at the words, and fell from his charger to the ground, a lifeless mass of steel.

We can easily gather that this parfait knyghte was pretty much a lifeless mass of steel even before his fit overcame him. With the example of James before him (and Scott did not fare too much better in *Ivanhoe*), Thackeray was probably well advised to abandon his attempt at a medieval romance, "The Knights of Borsellen." In the Age of Anne, at any rate, he had the advantage of a period that had left behind a record of its colloquial language. When James came to set novels in the eighteenth century, it is true that he shared Thackeray's high regard for the prose stylists of the age, but his model was Dr. Johnson,[34] not the "various, easy and delightful" conversation of Addison admired by Thackeray in common with Henry Esmond, along with the letters of Steele, "as artless as a child's prattle, and as confidential as a curtain lecture." In the lecture on Steele, Thackeray called particular attention to the "naturalness" of his writing: "He had a small share of book-learning, but a vast acquaintance with the world. He had known men and taverns. He had lived with gownsmen, with troopers, with gentlemen ushers of the Court, with men and women of fashion; with authors and wits, with the inmates of the spunging-houses, and with the frequenters of all the clubs and coffee-houses in the town."[35] Quite possibly Thackeray's imitating the conversational mode of the period, rather than its more formal writing, contributes to our feeling that we are really overhearing Lord Castlewood, for one example, discoursing on the very subject that agitates the breast of the knight in "Barbazure"—the infidelity of women: "'D——n it, Harry Esmond—you see how my lady takes on about Frank's megrim. She used to be sorry about me, my boy (pass the tankard, Harry), and to be frightened if I had a headache once. She don't care about my head now. They're just like that—women are—all the same, Harry, all jilts in their hearts. Stick to college— stick to punch and buttery ale: and never see a woman that's handsomer than an old cinder-faced bedmaker. That's my counsel'" (bk. 1, chap. 11). As Henry has informed us earlier, My Lord "was by no means reserved when in his cups, and spoke his mind very freely, bidding Harry in his coarse way, and with his blunt language, beware of all women . . . and using other unmistakeable monosyllables in speaking of them. Indeed 'twas the fashion of the day, as I must own." With a sense of decorum proper more to the audience of the next century than of his own, Henry manages to suggest the raciness of this gentleman's speech, if not in all its pungency.

Along with Thackeray's lively employment of period detail to enhance his narrative, and his adroit use of authentic-sounding eighteenth-century speech, we can infer from the early reception of *Esmond* that he satisfied reviewers with the "delineation of human nature" that R. H. Horne for one had found wanting in G. P. R. James. The reviewer for *Fraser's Magazine* noted "the predominance . . . of analysis and description over the dramatic element." Another critic elevated Thackeray above Dickens and Bulwer, his chief rivals at this time, as an author who does not merely "picture life," but has "seen into the mechanisms of life."[36] Lewes had praised some of the authors treated in his review article for their ability at "painting characters," but added: "We confess, however, that a little less painting, and a little more Shakesperian revelation of the 'inner being' would have charmed us more. But that is a gift few novelists possess. Scott wanted it. . . . The mass of novelists content themselves with 'objective' delineations."[37] Along these lines an early reviewer of *Esmond* observed: "Scott's heroes do not, like Esmond, tell their own story, or fill so large a portion of the canvas; neither are they endowed with those attributes of matured thoughtfulness, those ripened habits of calm reflection, with which Esmond is invested."[38] Even where critics felt that Thackeray carried introspection too far, or thought his hero overly melancholic, there was general agreement that he had advanced the historical romance intellectually beyond his greatest predecessor.

Whatever new that Thackeray brought to the historical novel, he also carried over much that was, by mid-century, old—and hence readily accessible to that legion of readers that Lewes deplored. Among the stock devices of the romancer according to Lewes was, as has already been mentioned, "the art, so easily learned, of complicating a plot with adventures, imprisonments, and escapes." Any reader of *Henry Esmond* is aware that Thackeray did not scorn this art, nor any of the other ingredients of the historical romancer's recipe as Lewes sets them out: "As for character, he need give himself no trouble about it: his predecessors have already furnished him with *types;* these he can christen anew. . . . If he has any reflections to make, he need only give them a sententious turn. . . . Sprinkle largely with love and heroism; keep up the mystery overhanging the hero's birth, till the last chapter; and have a good stage villain scheming and scowling through two volumes and a half, to be utterly exposed and defeated at last—and the historical novel is complete."[39] Though meant in disparagement, Lewes's formula describes not only a host of inferior novels, but that tale of "love and heroism" *Henry Esmond,* with its moral reflections, its hero who carries the stigma of the bar sinister, and its "stage villain" Lord Mohun, responsible directly for the murder of Lady Castlewood's husband, and indirectly for that of Beatrix's fiancé, himself eventually brought to an ignominious end. Among the fascinations of *Esmond* is Thackeray's ability to freshen up what had become the clichés of historical fiction, turning the "mystery overhanging the hero's birth," for example, to a moral rather than melodramatic purpose in making it the occasion for Henry's act of renunciation.

At the time when *Esmond* came out, its hero was characterized accurately by a reviewer as "a very noble type of the cavalier softening into a man of the eighteenth century."[40] Having depicted a typical gentleman of his own age in *Pendennis*, Thackeray, by an easy association, transferred his interest to the gentleman of the previous century, and the record makes clear that his predecessors among novelists had, as Lewes put it, "furnished him with types." The Stuart cavalier certainly was a familiar figure to mid-Victorian readers. Their parents had read Scott's *Woodstock; or, The Cavalier. A Tale of the Year Sixteen Hundred and Fifty-One* when it first came out in 1826, and this dramatic story of Prince Charles's intrigue-laden escape to the continent was still in print.[41] Other romances kept the events of 1651 and after before the reader of 1851, a year during which appeared in particular two works by the much lauded and lampooned G. P. R. James—*Henry Masterton; or, The Adventures of a Young Cavalier,* a Parlour Library reprint of a romance first published in 1832 that shared the limelight with *Henry Smeaton; a Jacobite Story of the Reign of George the First,* a new offering from the press of T. C. Newby.

Unlike some of James's popular works parodied by Thackeray in "Barbazure" that are set in medieval France (e.g. *Darnley; or, The Field of the Cloth of Gold,* where the "solitary horseman" makes his first appearance, *Corse de Leon, Philip Augustus, Henry of Guise,* and *Agincourt*), the two Henrys are concerned with later English history, the periods in fact immediately before and after the events narrated in *Henry Esmond.* Similarities among the respective heroes moreover extend beyond their names. The young cavalier-soldier in *Henry Masterton,* the earlier of James's romances, is caught up in a struggle between rival factions, in his instance the Puritans and the Roundheads, and the counterpart of Marlborough in his military career is George Goring, Lord Norwich. Lady Castlewood even is anticipated here by Lady Fleming, a widow who has been unhappily married and nourishes a repressed passion for the brother of the hero. Henry Smeaton, the hero of the later novel, is an earl (stepson of Bolingbroke) disguised as a commoner because of his involvement in political intrigue. "His clear hazel eyes, not without fire, nor even keenness, appeared to beam with a high generous soul," James tells us of this paragon. Thackeray did not make Esmond a twin of Smeaton—his hero has dark hazel eyes rather than light ones—but both physically and spiritually they could be brothers. Esmond seems to have been cut from the pattern that produced James's ideal gentleman, fusing puritan seriousness with cavalier grace: ". . . in his whole demeanour and carriage, was that sort of chivalrous aspect which had generally, in former days, distinguished the party called cavaliers; with a touch of their free and careless gaiety, but no appearance of their reckless licentiousness. There were moments . . . when he could be calm, thoughtful and grave enough; but the general tone of his conversation was gay, and even playful, with no touch of satire or persiflage—one of the great vices of the day. Much dignity, at times, was evident, but never any haughtiness of demeanour."[42]

Rachel Esmond's eulogy of her father that makes up the preface to his memoir embodies most of these traits. Certainly she does all she can to impress us with his generosity of soul, his "perfect grace and majesty of deportment," and particularly his dignity without haughtiness ("Though I never heard my father use a rough word, 'twas extraordinary with how much awe his people regarded him. . . . He was never familiar, though perfectly simple and natural; he was the same with the meanest man as with the greatest, and as courteous to a black slave girl as to the Governor's wife"). His own life history demonstrates that he is able when occasion demands to temper gravity with gaiety. His natural disposition is well brought out by his recollection of the "shade of melancholy" cast over his youth that has accompanied him through life (bk. 1, chap. 7). He refers to himself at one point as Our Knight of the Rueful Countenance; his fellow students at Cambridge nickname him Don Dismallo; his Dulcinea, Beatrix, dubs him My Lord Graveairs, and the Pretender later refers to him as Le Chevalier Noir. Yet Henry assures us that he "had his share of pleasures too, and made his appearance along with other young gentlemen at the coffee-houses, the theatres, and the Mall" (bk. 2, chap. 5), and several episodes represent him at these resorts of relaxation. His lighter side is brought out in his enjoyment of the humor of Fielding, his banter with the scholar-libertine Dick Steele, his literary jousts with Addison, and eventually his own mock *Spectator* paper.

His daughter Rachel sums up this dual nature neatly as her father's "grave satiric way."

Henry Esmond shares some of the adventures of Henry Smeaton as well as some of his moral character. James's hero, like Thackeray's, becomes embroiled, contrary to his own convictions, in a plot to depose William of Orange in favor of the pretender James III. Both are marked men as a result, but Esmond manages to avoid capture by escaping to Brussels, whereas Smeaton is imprisoned and saved from execution at the zero hour by a pardon from King William. Both young rebels come to accept the mandate of the people favoring the Hanoverian Succession, but themselves choose to emigrate. Thackeray's way with G. P. R. James is typical of his eclectic tendency (noted previously with Hook, Lever, and Mrs. Gore) to take what suits his purposes of an author's matter and reject excesses of manner. Obviously James's fine writing and pretentious platitude were not for Thackeray ("And what Briton can read without enjoyment the works of James so admirable for their terseness," he wrote in *The Book of Snobs*,[43] a bit of sarcasm best appreciated by his contemporaries). There are, however, more fundamental differences in the handling of their similar subject matter that reflect the divergent temperaments of the two writers. Much of James's three volumes, for example, is taken up with the "battles and bruises" that the pacifistic Thackeray compresses into his second volume. We learn nothing, on the other hand, about Henry Smeaton's mental and moral development—his childhood or education—the central concerns of the opening chapters of *Henry Esmond*. As opposed to the emotional sensitivity of Esmond's relationship with Lady Castlewood, only politics and war stand in the way of Henry Smeaton's eventual union with his beloved Emmeline, a love interest otherwise treated rather perfunctorily. Generally in his preoccupation with historical minutiae at the expense of narrative and character, James reminds us of a minor character in *Henry Smeaton*, the sculptor Van Noost, before whose eyes "monuments and carvings were seen in various different directions; and with true antiquarian enthusiasm, [he] soon forgot what was passing above in the examination of all that surrounded him." James can be called the Jonathan Oldbuck of the historical romance, as Thackeray became its John Evelyn.

An unlike likeness can be recognized too between *Esmond* and *Devereux*, a fictitious autobiography, set in the time of Swift and Bolingbroke, by Bulwer, another rival whom Thackeray parodied and respected. When Bulwer's novel first appeared in 1829,

Thackeray professed a strong dislike for it, asserting that he could do better. Eventually he proved that he could, but in some ways *Devereux* was a jumping-off place for *Esmond*.[44] Bulwer's intention "to portray a man flourishing in the last century with the train of mind and sentiment peculiar to the present" apparently was suggestive to Thackeray. The two novels also are linked by a similar didactic framework. *Devereux* is supposedly a posthumously published memoir dedicated to "children of an after century" by an ancestor whose life has been passed "in a stirring age, and not without acquaintance of the most eminent and active spirits of the time. . . . War—love—ambition—the scroll of sages—the festivals of wit—the intrigues of states—all that agitates mankind, the hope and the fear, the labour and the pleasure—the great drama of vanities, with the little interludes of wisdom;—these have been the occupations of my manhood; these will furnish forth the materials of that history which is now open to your survey." Henry Esmond's memoir too is exemplary autobiography addressed to posterity ("Master Grandson, who read this . . .") for their benefit.

To be sure, in another of *Punch's Prize Novelists*, "George de Barnwell. By Sir E. L. B. L., Bart.," an eighteenth-century cloudland revisited, Thackeray exaggerates certain features he did *not* like about the baronet's picture of the period. Again he comes down hard on intellectual pretension: "His [George's] bosom swells with ambition. His genius breaks out prodigiously. He talks about the Good, the Beautiful, the Ideal &c, in and out of all season, and is virtuous and eloquent almost beyond belief—in fact like Devereux, or P. Clifford, or E. Aram, Esquires."[45] Thackeray, as we have noticed, was drawn to the graceful, unbookish talk of Addison and Steele, from which nothing could be further removed than the pseudophilosophical jargon of Bulwer's alter egos. Also he was more interested in those who practiced the moral virtues than in those who merely talked about them. With his deep awareness of human limitations and self-delusion, Thackeray aims his shafts more at overblown characters than at inflated language. Bulwer's Augustan beau ideal Devereux "mingles in the world, which he is destined to ornament . . . outdoes all the dandies, all the wits, all the scholars, and all the voluptuaries of the age—an indefinite period of time between Queen Anne and George II—dines with Curll at St. John's Gate, pinks Colonel Charteris in a duel behind Montague House, is initiated into the intrigues of the Chevalier St. George, whom he entertains in his sumptuous pavilion at Hampstead." Thackeray places his hero in a definite time as "Col-

onel in the Service of Her Majesty Queen Anne" and does all else
he can to make him credible, rather than "beyond belief." Rachel
Esmond's description of her father as "of rather low stature, not
above five feet seven inches in height" does not leave a very imposing picture in our minds, and Henry's own modest recital of his
accomplishments tends to cut him down to mortal size. He mingles
with some of the celebrities of the time, as does young Morton
Devereux, but hardly shines as an "ornament" in their company.
He also engages in his share of dueling, and is "initiated into the
intrigues of the Chevalier de St. George," but with reluctance, it is
made clear, and out of love for Beatrix and loyalty to the
Castlewoods, for at heart he is a recluse. Generally Esmond's social
sphere and range of travel both are more contracted than those of
Bulwer's peripatetic hero (whose adventures carry him as far as St.
Petersburg), in line, one suspects, with Thackeray's desire to keep
his history more familiar and more domestic.

Far apart as Thackeray and Bulwer were in literary practice, they
were close together in their conception of the historical
romance—and together indicate the shift in emphasis the genre
had taken since Scott. Bulwer thought that he was departing from
Scott in his determination to write "fiction which deals less with the
Picturesque than the Real," an aim Thackeray certainly could sym-
pathize with, though, as has already been observed, he found
Scott's characters more "real" than Bulwer's. However well he
thought Bulwer succeeded at it, Thackeray could hardly quarrel
with the principle announced in the dedicatory epistle to *Devereux*
that the historical novelist should strive to achieve "that marked
individuality of character which distinguishes the man who has
lived and laboured from the hero of a romance."[46] Fundamentally
the two writers agreed in their emphasis on characterization and in
their subordination of history to human interest. In his prefatory
remarks Bulwer wrote that "the historical characters introduced [in
Devereux] are not closely woven with the main plot, like those in the
fictions of Sir Walter Scott, but are rather . . . designed to give a
greater truth and actuality to the supposed memoir," and serve
mainly as "an autobiographer's natural illustrations of the men and
manners of his time." As against Scott's way of slipping his characters into history or making them representative of historical ten-
dencies, Thackeray, with his interest in "men and manners," was
more inclined toward Bulwer's practice of intruding history from
time to time into lives of his fictitious characters who occupy central
stage.[47]

Of all the fictitious historical memoirs that Thackeray was aware
of, the one that seems to point most clearly in the direction he
moved with *Esmond* is *Sir Ralph Esher*, by Leigh Hunt. Here we find
the stately swashbuckling characteristic of *Esmond*, a turbulent age
represented through a refined and sensitive mind (Hunt prided
himself on his "reflecting exhibition of character"), the strong literary ambience to be expected from this "species of unconcealed
forgery, after the manner of a more cultivated and critical Pepys,"
and the overall subordination of politics and war to society, culture,
and religion. Ralph Esher, like Henry Esmond, is an orphan who is
entrusted to the care of relatives and becomes a page to an aristocratic family. Both young cavaliers, though peace-loving by nature,
endure battles by sea and land, and eventually denounce their
country's wars. Both also mingle in high society, become embroiled
in political intrigues in the course of which they shift allegiances,
and achieve happy marriages after prolonged love trials. The two
loves, profane and sacred, in Henry Esmond's life, moreover, have
their counterparts in Esher's gay cousin Miss Warmestre—who to
him embodies "the spirit of mirth"[48]—and one of his guardians, the
more dignified Miss Randolph, who eventually supersedes Miss
Warmestre in his affections when Ralph becomes convinced that
"the power of gravity in love promised a greater charm than
mirth." Ralph is also influenced by the other central character of
the book, Sir Philip Herne, whose Jesuit education has left him with
a "serious and suffering nature," a man "of mixed temperament
. . . in which sociability of disposition gave a playful discourse to his
very melancholy." Herne's reading of Saint Theresa "produced in
him a confusion respecting earthly and heavenly love" foreshadow-
ing Esmond's "*Dea certè*" Lady Castlewood, whom he surrounds
with a golden halo in his adolescence. Hunt's two heroes merge in
Thackeray's Henry Esmond, a source of the complexity of his
character.

On his religious side, Henry Esmond carries over an asceticism
and spirituality, a sublimated sexuality that manifests itself in the
beatification of women, associated more with the period dominated
by Crashaw, Milton, Marvell, and the great Anglican divines, into
the more robust Age of Anne and the Augustan wits. On his literary side he is more akin to the dilettantish Sir Ralph Esher. Young
Ralph believes himself (like his creator) to be "a hearty and a judicious admirer of wit and poetry," and virtually every literary worthy
of the time makes an appearance, from "merry St. Andrew" Marvell to the learned Dr. Sprat. He also puts pen to paper himself,

and although aware of his friend Sir Philip's idols Bunyan and Milton, he models himself on the playwrights and wits of the time, as does Henry Esmond. He writes a play (which has no more commercial success than Esmond's), short poems in imitation of Butler, and long ones in imitation of Dryden, whom he admires as much as Henry Esmond esteems Addison.

One of the few readers that *Sir Ralph Esher* has had in our century praises it for its portraiture of men and manners between the Commonwealth and the Restoration, commends Hunt for his ability to bring historical figures (like Lord Clarendon) to life, but finds his fictitious heroes Esher and Herne little more than "bundles of qualities."[49] On hindsight one agrees with the judgment that Hunt's lone novel "excels after the manner of [the memoirs of] Grammont and of his own books on the *Town*, and not after the manner of Scott and Thackeray." Nevertheless, Thackeray had before him the example of a "sham history" conveyed in the form of a colorful panorama, such as suited his own temperament as social historian, setting an adventure story against a large cultural milieu. Hunt also offered him as a character a model gentleman who manages to acquire some of the panache of the cavalier without the corruption. However, what Hunt turned into a literary pasticcio becomes with Thackeray a living memoir, owing to his superior ability to absorb his material into the developing consciousness of his hero.

We can gather from all the novels discussed so far that personal and familiar history were well established by the time Thackeray took up the writing of *Esmond*. It is evident furthermore that historical romancers at this time were sticking close to England for their inspiration, but this had not always been so. Among other observations made by Archibald Alison on historical romances in his *Maga* article, he deplored the tendency of novelists to seek exotic sources, turning to such remote areas as Persia, Russia, Poland, even the prairies of North America, when Scott had demonstrated what could be done with "events of national history," a source which was by no means exhausted.[50] Presumably the Bulwer of *Devereux* was to be emulated rather than the Bulwer of *The Last Days of Pompeii*, *Rienzi; or, The Last of the Tribunes*, and *Leila; or, The Siege of Granada*. From all evidence there were plenty of writers in readiness to respond to Alison's call for more national novels. Symptomatic perhaps is the turning of the shrewd and prolific G. P. R. James more and more during the 1840s to home soil for the scenes of his novels, after having oscillated between France and England, as well as his shift from medieval to modern history. His *Russell, a Tale of the Reign of Charles II* (1847) came out in the midst of an avalanche of tales dealing with various phases of Stuart history, such as Emma Robinson's *Whitefriars; or, The Court of Charles II*, her *Whitehall; or, The Days of Charles I*; G. W. M. Reynolds's *The Rye House Plot*; and Captain Marryat's *The Children of the New Forest* (taken up with the plight of a Royalist family near Lymington, one of Prince Charles's places of imprisonment). The beginning of the next decade brought forth such titles as Elizabeth M. Stewart's *Royalists and Roundheads; or, The Days of Charles the First* (1850) and the anonymous *The Royalist and the Republican: A Story of the Kentish Insurrection* (1852), both of which, along with *Henry Esmond*, employ the Scott formula of the hero torn between conflicting allegiances. Filling in the period between the Restoration and the Old Pretender were Joseph Sheridan Lefanu's second novel, *The Fortunes of Colonel Torlogh O'Brien* (1847), whose dashing hero is caught up in the Glorious Revolution and participates in the Battle of the Boyne; Isaac Butt's *The Gap of Bannesmore; a Tale of the Irish Highlands and the Revolution of 1688* (1848); and James Grant's *The Scottish Cavalier* (1851), which recalls the Battle of Killiecrankie. Most of this history is recapitulated in *Henry Esmond* through the successive generations of the Castlewood family. Scott correctly surmised that the novel was supplanting the drama in the nineteenth century as a means of teaching history to the large public. From the perspective of the 1850s, *Henry Esmond* stands at the crest of a wave of historical romances recreating the half-century from the Civil War to the Hanoverian Succession, just as Shakespeare and his contemporaries had staged the pageant of the establishment of the Tudor dynasty.

If to some of its first readers *Esmond* may have seemed, as a recent scholar puts it, "but one more in a long line of 'authentic' memoirs foisted on the reading public over the preceding decade,"[51] there is some reason to believe that it also filled a need at this time not adequately met. "Many are the tales of the present day; many are the tales of Cavaliers and Roundheads; many are the tales of the days of Chivalry," accurately observed another minor novelist contemporaneous with Thackeray, adding "but few, very few, are the tales of the *'talons rouge.'*" These words appear in the dedicatory preface of *The School for Fathers* (1852), an offering of Thackeray's publishers, advertised in the first edition of *Henry Esmond* as "a story of the *Tatler* and *Spectator* days . . . very fitly associated with that time of good English literature by its manly feeling, direct, unaffected manner of writing, and nicely managed, well-turned narrative."[52] The time evidently was ripe for Thackeray's own "red-heel" story. The author of *The School for Fathers*, appealing to those interested in "the polished days of swords and powder," sounds a nostalgic note: "In those days the difference between Town and Country manners, and Town and Country gentlemen was far greater than in these railway days: these days of rapidity, electric and submarine telegraphs." Her cautionary tale of the corruption of a young country squire in London, in pale imitation of Fielding and Goldsmith, anticipates *Esmond* only in its quaint trappings—"old face" typography and dedication to a patron—and in modeling its style after the *Spectator*. Interest, however, had been aroused in the social history of the eighteenth century in its more everyday aspects, which Thackeray was obviously in a good position to satisfy.

One of the first readers of *Henry Esmond*, Charlotte Brontë, complained to the editor whom she and Thackeray shared that the first and second volumes contained "too much history—too little story."[53] This criticism she did not have of the concluding part. "I have read the third volume of 'Esmond.' I found it both entertaining and exciting to me," she wrote to Williams a few days later; "it seems to possess an impetus and excitement beyond the other two; that movement and brilliancy its predecessors sometimes wanted never fail here." The romantic events connected with the ill-fated attempt to make the Chevalier St. George King James III, involving Henry, Beatrix, Lady Castlewood, and the young Lord Castlewood, strike most modern readers too as more "story" than "history." If for this section of his novel Thackeray seems to have allowed freer play to conjecture and his imagination, one good reason is that the sources then available to him failed him at this point. In one of his lectures he complains that Swift's history, which furnished him with some political and military background, "scarcely mentions, except to flout it, the great intrigue of the Queen's latter days, which was to have ended in bringing back the Pretender."[54] Even Macaulay made only the vaguest mention of the incident. Under the circumstances Thackeray made ingenious use of various fictitious sources to fill in the hiatus left by the records. Scott's *Woodstock* offered a prototype for the libertine displaced prince taking refuge in a castle and the plot to restore him to the throne, in which his hosts join. Other aspects of this part of the narrative—the cloak-and-dagger atmosphere, the incident of Frank Castlewood's breaking his sword in the presence of Prince James, a certain resemblance of Beatrix Esmond, aesthetic and moral, to Louise de la Vallière—make one understand why Robert Louis Stevenson dubbed the climax of *Esmond* "pure Dumas."[55] Thackeray's admiration and envy of G. P. R. James's principal continental rival is well known. "O Dumas! O thou brave kind gallant old Alexandre!" he exclaimed in one of the *Roundabout Papers*,[56] looking back over the reading of his boyhood and youth. His spoof of the creator of D'Artagnan in "The Legend of the Rhine" did not prevent him from borrowing the sword and cape when it suited him.

Echoes from France, never very far off in Thackeray's fiction, resound more loudly than usual in the climactic chapters of *Esmond* for the good reason that the chevalier comes from there. This courtly figure speaks mainly in French ("Assez, milord: je m'ennuye à la prèche") or in "Franglish" ("That which you do is unworthy, Monsieur": "I repose myself upon your fidelity"; "Eh! I know my history, Monsieur, and mock myself of frowning barons"). The prince is the Gallic gallant down to his final *beau geste* toward Frank Castlewood after the breaking of the sword:

> "Thus to lose a crown . . . to lose the loveliest woman in the world; to lose the loyalty of such hearts as yours, is not this, my lords, enough of humiliation?—Marquis, if I go on my knees will you pardon me?—No, I can't do that, but I can offer you reparation, that of honour, that of gentlemen. Favour me by crossing the sword with mine: yours is broke—see, yonder in the armoire are two. . . . Ah! you will? *Merci, monsieur, merci!*
>
> " . . .*Eh bien Vicomte!* . . . *il ne nous reste qu'une chose à faire.* . . . We have one more thing to do . . . you do not divine it? . . . *Embrassons nous!*" (Bk. 3, chap. 13)

It has been pointed out, among Thackeray's historical lapses in this section of the novel, that there is no factual basis for Prince James's foreign speech and inflection.[57] One doubts really whether the words Thackeray puts in the pretender's mouth were ever spoken anywhere on earth, except in unidiomatic translations of French *drames*—with which we could expect Thackeray to have been very well acquainted. The histrionic talk of the chevalier, together with the heightened emotions, melodramatic incidents, and dramatic confrontations characteristic of the episodes he figures in, impart a stagy atmosphere to them, of which the narrator is well aware. At one point Henry informs Beatrix "what her part of the comedy was to be"; the prince is called "the chief actor in it'" and later Beatrix is admonished that "[Prince James] is here on a great end, from which no folly should divert him; and, having nobly done your part of this morning . . . you should retire off the scene awhile, and leave it to the other actors of the play" (bk. 3, chaps. 9, 10). Historical drama, we are reminded, was still being staged at this time, and it is not surprising that history should have come into fiction by way of the proscenium arch as well as out of annals and chronicles. Scott utilized not only Shakespeare, but the German historical dramas of his day, notably those of Goethe and Schiller; Thackeray, for reasons of his own, turned to the popular Parisian stage, in which he had steeped himself the decade before as reviewer for the *Foreign Quarterly Review*.

In one of these articles, "English History and Character on the French Stage," Thackeray expressed his irritation with naïve misrepresentations of Englishmen by French writers,[58] and it is possible to see the Chevalier St. George as his perverse return in kind. He also uses the prince and the intrigue participated in by Henry and Beatrix to ridicule what he regarded as simplistic notions of history reflected in some of the plays he had reviewed. The play that bears most directly on *Henry Esmond* is Scribe's *Le verre d'eau; ou les effets et les causes*, which also takes place during the reign of Queen Anne, with the fortunes of the Duke of Marlborough in the foreground. The drama is set off by the quite unhistorical rivalry between Queen Anne and the Duchess of Marlborough for the affections of young Arthur Masham, who is married to the queen's favorite lady-in-waiting. Scribe utilizes this petticoat war to exemplify the maxim pronounced by Bolingbroke that gives the play its subtitle: "Les grandes effets produits par les petites causes . . . c'est mon système." Accordingly the plot is so contrived that the trifling incident of the Duchess of Marlborough's spilling a glass of water on Queen Anne's robe brings about not merely the fall from favor of the duchess, but the duke's loss of command as well, along with the overthrow of the Whig party, and concurrently the rise of Bolingbroke.[59] This drama particularly annoyed Thackeray, among the group he reviewed, and he denounced it in no uncertain terms as "in its conception . . . vulgar, and in its incidents, outrageously unnatural and absurd . . . a lie against history, as it is a lie against morals." Convinced in his own mind that "trivial circumstances are in this life pretexts, not causes," Thackeray pronounced Scribe "as bad a teacher of morals as he is an unwise and unsafe illustrator of history," and if he had his way would have removed him from the platform of the Comédie-Française to dispense his "sentimental opium" to the masses at the Gymnase.[60]

When he came to dramatize this period in *Henry Esmond*, Thackeray shows us that great events are propelled by more substantial causes than cat fights and petty jealousies. In so doing, he makes clear that he had not put Scribe or *Le verre d'eau* out of his mind, particularly in the episode where we are introduced to the pretender: "The impetuous young lad [Frank Castlewood] was for going down on his knees again, with another explosion of gratitude, but that we heard the voice from the next chamber of the august sleeper, just waking, calling out: *'Eh, la Fleur, un verre d'eau'*; his Majesty came out yawning:—'A pest,' says he, 'upon your English ale, 'tis so strong that, *ma foi*, it hath turned my head'" (bk. 3, chap. 9). Previously we have overheard this exchange between Swift and Bolingbroke (Scribe's grand manipulator), deep in his cups also:

> "Drink no more, my lord, for God's sake says he [Swift]. I come with the most dreadful news."
> "Is the Queen dead?" cries out Bolingbroke, seizing on a waterglass.
> "No, Duke Hamilton is dead: he was murdered an hour ago by Mohun and Macartney . . . . "(Bk. 3, chap. 5)

So Thackeray calls attention in his devious way to the fatefulness of this obscure episode of history, when almost simultaneously the hopes of the pretender were crushed and Bolingbroke ascended to the ministry. The detail of the water glass exposes James's moral flabbiness and the opportunism of Bolingbroke while it mocks Scribe's catchpenny theory of history ("the fortunes of England in the balance; the fate of France too as a nation; all depending upon the tremor of a hand which offered a glass of water," as he tauntingly remarked in his review). This motif returns briefly in an episode located in the very throne room where the crucial incident of *Le verre d'eau* takes place. Here Beatrix witnesses the sudden collapse of the Queen during the presentation of Prince James: "[Beatrix] came into the drawing-room in a great tremour and very pale; she asked for a glass of water as her mother went to meet her, and after drinking that and putting off her hood, she began to speak:—'We may all hope for the best,' says she, 'it has cost the Queen a fit'" (bk. 3, chap. 10). At this turn of events it appears that Prince James is destined for the crown, with a due reward for Beatrix as his current favorite. But such is not to be. The glass of water signalizes false hopes for Beatrix—just as for Bolingbroke, whose triumph proved short lived.

The incident that Swift reports to Bolingbroke—the violent murder of the Duke of Hamilton in Hyde Park by Lord Mohun—is analogous to the *verre d'eau* of Scribe's drama in its extended ramifications. Its immediate effect in Esmond's circle is to deprive Beatrix of her aristocratic fiancé, but its consequences reach throughout the realm by removing Prince James's principal champion in England. So it may seem that "les grands effets" arise out of "petites causes," as Scribe's Bolingbroke affirms, but Thackeray puts an effective rejoinder in Henry Esmond's mouth: "Men have all sorts of motives which carry them onwards in life, and are driven into acts of desperation, or it may be of distinction, from a hundred different causes" (bk. 3, chap. 5). And indeed the conflux of motives and cross-purposes that propels the prince's return, and eventually his failure—the timidity of his sister Anne, the self-seeking of her ministers, the ineffectualness and division among the pretender's supporters—emphatically refutes Scribe's elementary notions of historical causation. "We are willing to allow a very wide license to writers of fiction, when they take up incidents of history not clearly determined, or motives of character not positively ascertained," Thackeray wrote in his article "English History and Character on the French Stage."[61] He thought that Scribe overindulged this license, which he himself uses to probe the hidden roots of sin and virtue. "Fortune, good or ill, as I take it, does not change men and women. It but develops their characters," affirms Henry (speaking, one assumes, for his only begetter), and later he asks himself in the lonely darkness of his prison cell: "Who hath not found himself surprised into revenge, or action, or passion, for good or evil; whereof the seeds lay within him, latent and unsuspected, until the occasion called them forth?" (bk. 2, chap. 1).

In illustration of this theory of character, Henry is prompted against his better judgment to aid Prince James in what proves a foolhardy plot by a mixture of motives, selfish (to prove himself to Beatrix) and altruistic (his devotion to the Castlewood family). The downfall of Prince James in turn is brought about by a combination of human failing and circumstances—the Prince's own weakness of will, joined to evil companions, and abetted by "fate's surprises." "If ever a match was gained by the manliness and decision of a few at a moment of danger; if ever one was lost by the treachery and imbecility of those that had the cards in their hands, and might have played them, it was in that momentuous game which was enacted in the next three days, and of which the noblest crown was the stake," as Henry sums up these crucial events from the vantage point of forty years later (bk. 3, chap. 12). In this episode of "The Great Drama of the World," private history becomes absorbed into public history as Henry's disillusionment in love is linked with the falls of princes, betrayal in human and domestic relations related to betrayal writ large in politics and war. *Henry Esmond* is indeed a departure from "our orthodox history books" where "the characters move as on a gaudy playhouse procession; a glittering pageant of kings and warriors, and stately ladies, majestically appearing and passing away."[62] Rather than deck out his captains, kings, and ladies-in-waiting in the stilts and headdresses of the "old tragedies," he has conceived them in the image of the French drama of intrigue, at the same time teaching M. Scribe and company how to illustrate character through historical example. If Scribe could retort that Thackeray himself has perpetrated "a lie against history," Thackeray took care at least that his version of these events was not "a lie against morals."

With all his efforts to fix his fictitious memoir in its time—aided, as we have seen, by records as well as by the historians, historical romancers, and historical dramatists of his own time—Thackeray also endeavored, through his hero's vision, to view life under the aspect of eternity. "What can the sons of Adam and Eve expect, but to continue in that course of love and trouble their father and mother set out on?" sermonizes Henry as his chronicle gathers to its close. "Oh, my grandson! I am drawing nigh to the end of that period of my history, when I was acquainted with the great world of England and Europe; my years are past the Hebrew poet's limit" (bk. 3, chap. 5). We are constantly reminded of Henry's piety. The bells of Castlewood church ring in his ears when, as a boy, he is first introduced to Rachel Esmond and her husband, Lord Castlewood; virtually the last words of his memoir are a thanksgiving to God for the happy autumn of his life. Biblical cadence heightens his prose style, just as he finds biblical analogies in his own life—his years of waiting for Rachel Castlewood, for example, likened to the ordeal of Jacob and *his* Rachel in the Old Testament. Memorable episodes of the novel take place amid ecclesiastical surroundings, such as Henry's reconciliation with Lady Castlewood in Winchester Cathedral (bk. 2, chap. 6) and his meeting with Father Holt in the Church of Ste. Gudule in Brussels where he learns that he is legitimate (bk. 2, chap. 13). "So this is the little priest!" exclaims Lord Castlewood instinctively upon first seeing young Henry (bk. 1, chap. 1), and indeed for a time it seems that he is destined for the pulpit. As Henry sums up his vocational progress: "To please that woman [Beatrix] then I tried to distinguish myself as a soldier, and afterwards as a wit and politician; as to please another [Rachel] I would have put on a black cassock and a pair of bands, and had done so but that a superior fate intervened to defeat that project" (bk. 3, chap. 5).

Inevitably church as well as state intrudes into the life of the times Thackeray sets out to portray. Macaulay, upon whom he modeled himself to an extent, had defined as the province of the historian "the progress of useful and ornamental arts . . . the changes of literary taste . . . the manners of successive generations, and . . . even the revolutions which have taken place in dress, furniture, repasts, and public amusements"—all of which form part of the background of *Henry Esmond*, together with "the rise of religious sects,"[63] that Macaulay added to the secular aspects of life. The religious dimension makes *Henry Esmond* too, like many another Victorian historical romance, a novel of past and present. Religious disputes were no less rife under Queen Victoria than they had been under the Stuarts and Queen Anne, so that for its first readers *Henry Esmond* could have borne the subtitle Kingsley later pinned on *Hypatia:* "New Foes with an Old Face." With some exercise of empathy young men of the nineteenth century could have felt themselves reenacting Henry Esmond's religious experience.

"Page Esmond . . . good Father Holt will instruct you as becomes a gentleman of our name," Henry's aunt the Viscountess Castlewood informs him when he enters her service (bk. 1, chap. 3), thus introducing us to the earliest, and most significant, formative influence on Henry's religious sensibility. At first the impressionable young Henry, inspired by Father Holt's accounts of the courage and dedication displayed by the order, "thought that to belong to the Jesuits was the greatest prize of life and bravest end of ambition" (bk. 1, chap. 3). The mature Henry (like a number of his literary brothers, notably Morton Devereux and Philip Herne) wrenches himself free of Jesuit influence as he learns to think for himself on religious matters. Nevertheless Father Holt, even when removed from direct supervision over Henry's education, remains a presence in his life—turning up in Brussels when Henry is in the service of the Duke of Marlborough, in England once more when the conspiracy is afoot to place the Catholic pretender on the throne (just as he had aided Henry's aunt and uncle in their abortive attempt to restore James II), and he is even seen in America after Henry emigrates there.

The ubiquity of the disciples of Saint Ignatius had already been brought to the attention of Thackeray's generation. A book that Thackeray himself reviewed during the previous decade (and among those advertised in the first edition of *Henry Esmond*)—*The Novitiate; or, A Year among the English Jesuits*, the memoir of an ex-novice Andrew Steinmetz—was written in part as a caution to "pious young people . . . yearning after change, desirous of novelty, uncertain what to do with their souls."[64] They were put on their guard. "Let them not suppose that the Jesuits will be inactive spectators of any movement that takes place in the religious or political constitutions of the world," Steinmetz warned. "They are spread abroad over the earth; they are mixing in all societies; they have their institutions in the most crowded marts of life." Despite repressive measures, he was convinced, "the hydra will put forth more heads than have been lopped off; and . . . I will venture to predict machinations of the redoutable conspirators will, before very long, be found to have given them a pretty solid foundation even in this country, the bulwark of Protestantism." Young Arthur Pendennis, for one, is concerned; among his juvenile enterprises is the beginning of "a 'History of the Jesuits' in which he lashed that Order with tremendous severity, and warned his Protestant fellow-countrymen of their machinations" (chap. 3).[65]

Henry Esmond was written in the wake of the stir caused in 1850 when Pope Pius IX appointed Nicholas Wiseman a cardinal and first archbishop of Westminster in the newly organized English Catholic hierarchy. This move, popularly known as the Papal Aggression, must have seemed to some to confirm Steinmetz's prophecy. Thackeray commented on this event in *Punch*, and alluded facetiously to Catholic missionary zeal in his "Plan for a Prize Novel" that first appeared there. Among novelists with a purpose, whom "the eminent dramatist Brown" writes of to the aspiring novelist Snooks, is the sort who "with the most delicate skill insinuates Catholicism into you, and you find yourself all but a Papist in the third volume." Snooks himself cannot be so accused. "By the way, the scene in the 200th number between the Duke, his grandmother, and the Jesuit Butler, is one of the most harrowing and exciting I have ever read."[66] Brown writes in praise of Snooks's current sensation in parts, now concluding its run. Significantly, Thackeray's own variant on Snooks's "200th number" in *Henry Esmond* (bk. 1, chap. 5) finds young Henry himself in the midst of a conspiracy to depose William of Orange involving the Viscount and

Viscountess Castlewood along with their Jesuit chaplain Father Holt. This episode is exciting enough, but Holt, far from the sinister influence he would have been in the novels of Sue and company, is made an object of respect.[67] "By love, by a brightness of wit and good-humour that charmed all, by an authority which he knew how to assume, by a mystery and silence about him which increased the child's reverence for him, he won Henry's absolute fealty," recalls the hero, "and would have kept it doubtless, if schemes greater and more important than a poor boy's admission into orders had not carried him away" (bk. 1, chap. 4). As for those who feared the "insinuating" effect of the Jesuits and their literature, by the "third volume" of *Henry Esmond*, to be sure, Frank Castlewood has married into a German Catholic family, but the fact that Henry remains proof against Father Holt's silky persuasion to the very end should have been sufficient testimony to the power of free will.

For the conciliatory tone toward Jesuits, so evident in *Henry Esmond* in reaction against anti-Catholic writing of the time, Thackeray had the precedent of the Steinmetz memoir that he reviewed. In his review Thackeray noted that Steinmetz's revulsion from the fanaticism and furtiveness of the Jesuit order did not preclude his praising of individual members of it, or his respect in general for their intellect and moral courage. Steinmetz thought of himself as one who "has wrestled with the angel . . . gone through the fires of temptation," and hence could "look back dispassionately on the process through which he has passed; and, perhaps, instruct his fellow creatures with the narrative of his experience, without indulging any ill-will towards those who permitted him to try their method." One essential aim of this exemplary autobiography addressed to "serious and earnest minds" was to retrieve what Steinmetz felt worth retaining from his Jesuit education, while abjuring what he regarded as deleterious to mental or moral health. A strong personality emerges in *The Novitiate*, self-described as a soul endowed "with the keenest sensibility, the most passionate admiration of the beautiful in nature, in art, and, I will add, in woman" which felt itself stifled in the hampering atmosphere of the Jesuit monastery.[68] The interest that Thackeray took in it leads one to infer that this heartfelt *confessio* aided him in limning out the religious aspects of Henry Esmond's character.

Steinmetz makes much of the lasting effect of his novitiate on his habits of thought just as Esmond testifies to the continuing subliminal influence of his early Jesuit training. "Mr Holt obtained an entire mastery over the boy's intellect and affections," recalls Henry in later years (bk. 1, chap. 4). One recurring theme of his "history" indeed is the indelible trace left by early impressions: "It [a past love] becomes a portion of the man to-day, just as any great faith or conviction, the discovery of poetry, the awakening of religion, ever afterward influence him" (bk. 3, chap. 6). The mental and moral traits fostered by Jesuits that Steinmetz considers desirable—"self-restraint, self-command, the habit of thoughtfulness, the prostration of the will, and perfect familiarity with the themes of religion"—are easily recognizable in the make-up of Henry Esmond, with his introspection, constant self-examination, humility, and subordination of himself in devotion to others. His ultimate act of renunciation—giving up his claim to the Castlewood title in favor of his cousin Frank, thereby retaining the burden of the bar sinister—represents a complete conquering of pride and ambition, which incidentally has the full approval of Father Holt (bk. 2, chap. 13).

Steinmetz's candid appraisal of the cloistered life provides the key to what Esmond rejects as well as to what he chooses. In his final chapter, where he assesses the losses and gains of his religious education, Steinmetz concluded that "the labour for the body, occupation for the mind, and the stimulants for the heart or sentiment" are achieved at the cost of one's becoming "totally estranged from the common feelings of human nature." However elevating spiritually, to submit oneself to the Jesuit rule, he contends, is to starve the affections: "As a novice, the Jesuit lives in community without enjoying the heart's friendship: in the midst of many he is alone."[69] In his review Thackeray openly sympathized with the writer's antipathy toward monastic celibacy, and it is evident too that Henry, with all his self-abnegation, will not renounce the "common feelings of human nature"—friendship, love, and community. "As I think of the immense happiness which was in store for me, . . . I own to a transport of wonder and gratitude for such a boon—nay, am thankful to have been endowed with a heart capable of feeling and knowing the immense beauty and value of the gift which God hath bestowed upon me," his narrative concludes. "Sure, love *vincit omnia*; is immeasurably above all ambition, more precious than wealth, more noble than name. He knows not life who knows not that: he hath not felt the highest faculty of the soul who hath not enjoyed it. . . . To have such a love is the one blessing, in the comparison of which all earthly joy is of no value; and to think of her is to praise God." In the eclectic spirit of the author, Henry retains the Jesuitical spiritual zeal, while giving up its

asceticism. We learn furthermore that his union with Lady Castlewood has been blessed with a child, who becomes his biographer
and eulogist, testifying to his exemplary paternal love, bounty, and
charity. "All praise to the civilizers of humanity!" proclaimed the
renegade novice Andrew Steinmetz in commending the Jesuits
for their mission work to "mankind in its most degraded condition."
Henry Esmond, by converting a Virginia wilderness into a habitable plantation, and becoming a master of "negroes, the happiest
and merriest, I think, in all this country," seems also to carry forward this hallowed tradition.[70]

"Is the glory of Heaven to be sung only by gentlemen in black
coats? Must the truth be only expounded in gown and surplice, and
out of those two vestments can nobody preach it?" Thackeray in-
quired of the audience at his lectures, in connection with his much
admired Addison.[71] At the time when he leaves Cambridge, Henry
Esmond announces that he has given up any intention to take holy
orders, claiming that he lacks a "devout mind." However, sharing
Thackeray's admiration for the author of the *Spectator* papers, after
whom he models his life style as well as his literary style, he too can
be described as "a preacher without orders," a "parson in the tie-
wig," in whom "a sense of religion stirs through his whole being."
As such he serves appropriately as surrogate for the author himself, who had characterized himself as a "week-day preacher" in his
opening lecture. Esmond, like Thackeray, is led to seek God in the
world, rather than out of it, owing in his instance to influences that
supersede the instruction of Father Holt.

"After that first fervour of simple devotion, which his beloved
Jesuit-priest had inspired in him," Henry recalls, "speculative
theology took but little hold upon the young man's mind" (bk. 1,
chap. 9). Appropriately for his future destiny, his religious direction is taken over subliminally by his "*Dea certè.*" Lady Castlewood,
we learn through Henry, is "a critic, not by reason, but by feeling,"
with the "happiest instinctive faculty . . . for discerning latent
beauties and hidden graces of books." Among the books that
Henry reads under Rachel's tutelage are "famous British Divines of
the last age," inherited from the library of her father the Dean,
"who had been distinguished in the disputes of the late King's
reign; and, an old soldier now, had hung up his weapons of controversy." The writers mentioned were significant in their times
both as defenders of the Anglican faith and for their ecumenical
spirit. Simon Patrick, for one, was author of *Friendly Debate betwixt
. . . a Conformist and a Non-Conformist* (1669) and promoted the idea

of the *via media*. Edward Stillingfleet, another of Lady Castlewood's favorite writers, was the most eminent and erudite divine of the seventeenth century, author of *Irenicum, a Weapon Salve for the Church's Wound* (1659), intended to reconcile the Church of England with Presbyterianism, and became famous moreover for his friendly debates with men of all persuasions from atheists to Roman Catholics. The motto from the Epistle to the Phillipians, "Let your moderation be known to all men," that appears on the title page of *Irenicum* seems to be part of the message that Henry Esmond tried to convey to his grandchildren. At a time when the established church was being assailed from both within and without, when, as Newman reminded them in a series of lectures at the Oratory, the Anglicans were having their difficulties, Thackeray's main purpose in tracing "the rise of religious sects" was to eschew sectarianism.[72]

Lady Castlewood "hath admitted a certain latitude of theological reading which her orthodox father would never have allowed," observes Henry. Thackeray himself apparently was spiritually most at home among the Latitudinarians. It has been said of him that his was "a somewhat undogmatic Christianity. It would be difficult, if not quite impossible, to determine from his writings what precise tenets he held," and a relative who lived in his mother's household for a time referred years later to his "aspiration towards a religion that should be beyond the creeds."[73] His most explicit statement of belief, as expressed to a clergyman friend, is basic and elementary enough, if somewhat unsettling: "I want . . . to say in my way that love and truth are the greatest of Heaven's commandments and blessings to us; that the best of us, the many especially who pride themselves on their virtue most, are wretchedly weak, vain, and selfish, and to preach such a charity at least as a common sense of our shame and unworthiness might inspire to us poor people."[74] In the long run, as that scholar-libertine Dick Steele puts it: "'Tis not dying for a faith that's so hard, Master Harry. . . . 'Tis the living up to it that is difficult, as I know to my cost" (bk. 1, chap. 6). That this jolly backslider knows himself only too well is brought out in Thackeray's lecture on him where he is described writing his "ardent devotional work" *The Christian Hero* while "deep in debt, in drink, and in all the follies of the town,"[75] and Henry tells us that Ensign Dick is the laughingstock of his fellow Guards for "the Christian Hero was breaking the commandments constantly" (bk. 1, chap. 14). Even Henry, who comes closer to the ideal of the Christian Hero than its promulgator, sees himself as a lapsing one ("I look into my heart and think I am as good as my Lord Mayor, and know I am as bad as Tyburn Jack"). "The humorous writer professes to awaken and direct your love, your pity, your kindness—your scorn for untruth, pretension, imposture—your tenderness for the weak, the poor, the oppressed, the unhappy," declared Thackeray in the first of his lectures on the eighteenth century.[76] His vocation was united with "the parson's own" by the spirit of charity. "I hope men of my profession do no harm who take this doctrine out of doors to people in drawing-rooms and in the world" he declared later to a clergyman friend. He allied himself with Steele's friend and collaborator, another "preacher without orders," who brought philosophy out of the closet and religion out of the cloister.

"I take up a volume of Doctor Smollett, or a volume of the *Spectator*, and say the fiction carries a greater amount of truth in solution than the volume which purports to be all true," affirmed Thackeray in his lecture on Steele. "Out of the fictitious book I get the expression of the life of the time; of the manners, of the movement, the dress, the pleasures, the laughter, the ridicules of society—the old times live again and I travel in the old country of England. Can the heaviest historian do more for me?"[77] So he maintains his defence of "sham histories." He went even further in the notebook he compiled for his later series of lectures on the four Georges, where, under the heading "Lies in History," one comes upon this sentence: "Most histories with the exception of Holy Writ are just as false as romances with this exception that the latter are longer & more pleasantly written."[78] His attitude toward the "heavy" historians is best summed up perhaps in a caricature he drew in his copy of Rollin's *Ancient History*, known to many a Victorian schoolboy, representing Clio as a bird-beaked, bonnetted, blue-stockinged spinster standing on a pedestal made up of historic tomes, at the bottom of which is visible the name of Baron Münchausen.[79]

Actually, by the time that *Henry Esmond* came out, the climate was more favorable for historical romance than it had been when Scott began writing. Historians themselves were beginning to challenge the authority of history. At the end of the decade, the historian Prescott was quoted in a literary magazine, raising the question: "Who is there that does not derive a more distinct idea of the state of society and manners in Scotland from the Waverley novels than from the best of its historians; of the condition of the Middle Ages

from the single romance of Ivanhoe, than from the volumes of
Hume and Hallam?"[80] In this article the historical novel is regarded not simply as the adjunct to the teaching of history that
Scott and his disciples considered it, but as an essential "comple-
ment to history." It is noteworthy that not only Carlyle and
Macaulay, but also such distinguished historians as Prescott, Hallam, and Motley attended Thackeray's lectures, and that on the
basis of *Esmond*, Thackeray was invited by the editor of the *Encyclopedia Britannica* to contribute the article on the Age of Anne.[81]

Caricature of Clio drawn by Thackeray
in his copy of Rollin's *Ancient History*.
(From *Thackerayana*, ed. Joseph Grego
[London: Chatto & Windus, 1901].)

Not only were the accredited historians ready to admit that there
were aspects of the past that eluded them, but, as a writer for a
popular weekly in the late sixties put it: "The increased taste for
imaginary stories may have been considerably stimulated by the
doubts which have been thrown during the past twenty or thirty
years on so many that were accepted as real ones."[82] History, like
religion, was becoming less dogmatic as the century moved on.
With the pedestal of Clio resting on shifting sands as new sources
and documents came to light and old cities were newly discovered,
the historical novelist came to be recognized as a collaborator with

the formal historian in the revision of history. The writer just quoted suggests another favorable development—the fact that history writing had become "graphic and entertaining" thanks to Macaulay, Prescott, Froude, Motley, and their generation. As a result, this writer concludes, "persons who had an unexpressed idea that novels were trash because they gave a reader pleasure, and Hume, Robertson, Roscoe were improving because they bored him, got fairly puzzled. When the British public found itself taking precisely the same sort of interest, only intensified, in historical men and women that it did in the hero and heroine of a novel, the great barrier between Fiction and History was removed." From his side of the wall, Thackeray too helped to remove the barrier, by giving fictitious characters the reality of historical ones.

"Thackeray, in his heart, does not value political or religious intrigues of any date. He likes to show us human nature at home, as he himself daily sees it," was Charlotte Brontë's reaction on reading the first chapters of *Esmond* in manuscript.[83] A number of the early reviewers echo her opinion, one observing that "the main interest of the narrative is not dependent upon the progress of historical events, nor do the historical personages much advance the dramatic action of the piece"; another characterized it as "more like a family memoir than a novel," and thought that "the pathos is that of a secret home-sorrow, the incidents such as were happening everyday."[84] Such critics undoubtedly were not surprised to see Thackeray turn from historical memoirist to family chronicler in his next novel, *The Newcomes*. Moreover, when next we meet the Esmonds in *The Virginians* it is more in their home surroundings on both sides of the ocean. However, for him the domestic circle was a microcosm of society at large. Whatever form of "sham history" in which he chose to present his wisdom—"comic history" as in *Vanity Fair*, personal history as in *Pendennis*, or historical romance, as in *Henry Esmond*—his matter essentially remained "that strange and awful struggle of good and wrong which takes place in our hearts and in the world."

Of all the reviews that *Henry Esmond* received, obtuse and perceptive, there is no gainsaying the one that predicted that it "will endear itself to every reader of taste by an indescribable charm; and will probably survive in our literature almost every similar work of its time." It has survived but not quite as the same book, since it slipped out of its original "periwig and embroidery . . . beautiful type and handsome proportions"[85] into buckram boards and paperback. "Different classes of persons, at different times, make, of course, very various demands upon literature," as one of its later Victorian admirers, Walter Pater, remarked. He himself found in *Esmond* "a sort of cloistral refuge from a certain vulgarity in the actual world,"[86] the kind of appeal many of his generation found in the incense-laden atomosphere of its spiritual successor *John Inglesant*. Others read *Esmond* more as an adventure story on the order of *The Master of Ballantrae* and *Micah Clarke*. In our times, with Proust and Virginia Woolf behind us, it can be welcomed as an "attempt to capture the feeling of experience as it flows, to suggest the continuum of events by which we are carried along, shaped, or destroyed."[87] We are far removed from the time when it commended itself to "the attention of the thoughtful by its instructive exhibitions of the pathology of the heart, by many a grave lesson eloquently uttered."[88] Like the ordinary people of his "novel without a hero," those of Thackeray's "novel without a villain" hang on to "the skirts of history" rather than stride through her corridors of power, but through his most introspective hero he recapitulated for his first readers their collective past—its mingling of coarseness and refinement, its conflict of puritanism and joy of life, conservatism and revolution, and tried to aid them to reach a politics and religion of tolerance—the culmination for him, as for Victor Cousin, of the trial and error of history.

1. "Swift," *The English Humourists of the Eighteenth Century, Works*, 7:423.

2. No. 118, issued December 1849 (Michael Sadleir, *Nineteenth Century Fiction: A Bibliographical Guide*, 2 vols. [New York: Cooper Square Publishers, 1969], 2:102). This title, along with others by Hunt, was advertised in the first edition of *Henry Esmond*. In its first edition (1832, though probably written in 1830) it appeared in three volumes under the imprint of Colburn and Bentley and, like *Henry Esmond*, in Caslon type, with the subtitle *Adventures of a Gentleman in the Court of Charles II*. The two authors were close during these years. Thackeray wrote to congratulate Hunt on his Civil List Pension in 1847 (*Letters*, 2:307), and other letters document social engagements. Hunt sent Thackeray presentation copies of some of his books, notably the *Autobiography*, which came out in 1850, referred to by Thackeray as "those pleasant memoirs" (*Letters*, 2:711). Hunt reviewed Thackeray's first lecture favorably in the *Spectator*, 24 May 1851. Thackeray's letter of acknowledgment is reprinted in T. J. Wise's *The Ashley Library*, 11 vols. (London: Privately printed, 1922–36), 7:168 (see Gordon N. Ray, *The Age of Wisdom* [New York: McGraw-Hill, 1958], p. 455, n. 9).

3. Hunt makes much of the painstaking accuracy of the scholarship embodied in the book, recalling with satisfaction that a purchaser mistook it for an authentic memoir of the period. His name did not appear on the title page of the first edition. In a memorial tribute his son Thornton wrote, just after his death: "Of his one novel, *Sir Ralph Esher*, suffice it to say, that he had desired to make it a sort of historical essay—a species of unconcealed forgery after the manner of a more cultivated and critical Pepys; and that the bookseller [Colburn] persuaded him to make it a novel" ("A Man of Letters of the Last Generation," *Cornhill Magazine*, January 1860, p. 93).

4. "Congreve and Addison," *Works*, 7:463.

5. "Steele," *Works*, 7:489.

6. 17–19 April 1852, *Letters*, 3:38.

7. Thomas Macaulay, "History," *Miscellaneous Works*, ed. Lady Trevelyan, 10 vols. (New York: Putnam, 1898), 1:232 (originally appeared in *Edinburgh Review*, May 1828); *The History of England from the Accession of James II* (1849), introduction to chap. 1.

8. For a list of his primary sources, see the edition of T. C. Snow and William Snow (Oxford, 1912), p. xxvi. The manuscript (Trinity College Library, Cambridge University) has a long footnote that does not appear in printed editions, documenting the unscrupulousness of Marlborough with quotations from Macpherson's "Original Papers" and the memoirs of the Marquis de Torcy (Colbert).

9. 17–18? November 1815, *Letters*, 2:815.

10. Archibald Alison, "The Historical Romance," *Blackwood's Magazine*, September 1845, p. 351.

11. *Spectator*, 4 January 1840, p. 17.

12. Review of *Private Correspondence of Sarah, Duchess of Marlborough*, *Times*, 6 January 1838.

13. "Thieves' Literature of France," *Foreign Quarterly Review* 31 (April 1843); 231; *New Sketch Book*, p. 179.

14. Victor Cousin, lecture 10, *Course of the History of Modern Philosophy*, trans. O. W. Wight, 2 vols. (New York: Appleton, 1852), p. 203. It is amusing that Thackeray refined his presentation of Addison himself somewhat from manuscript to book. In the manuscript version of bk. 2, chap. 11, where Addison is introduced, he is first espied by Steele as he "came out of a little tavern near to Saint James's Church," but the passage is lined out and the present reading "was poring over a folio at a bookshop" substituted; some other diverting matter was deleted from the manuscript, including a slightly ribald exchange between Steele and Westbury in bk. 2, chap. 2 relating to Steele's wenching, and a taunt at Alexander Pope's opportunistic Catholicism by Mrs. Steele in bk. 2, chap. 15.

15. See F. S. Boas, "Thackeray on the Humourist as Hero," *Contemporary Review* 109 (January–June 1916): 223–30.

16. *Times*, 3 August 1837; *Works* (Furniss Ed.), 12:3–4.

17. Cousin, lecture 10, p. 203 (Wight).

18. Ibid., p. 204. See above, pp. 44–45.

19. Jules Janin, "Literature of the Nineteenth Century," *Athenaeum*, 6 May 1837, p. 321.

20. May 1837, p. 206.

21. Quoted in "Of Novels, Historical and Didactic," *Bentley's Miscellany* 46 (1859): 45, 46.

22. Quoted in James C. Simmons, "The Novelist as Historian: A Study of the Early Victorian Historical Fiction, 1828–1850" (Ph.D. diss., University of California, Berkeley, 1967), p. 225. I have found this thesis generally helpful in building up the background for this chapter. It has since been published (The Hague: Mouton, 1974).

23. Alison, "The Historical Romance," pp. 341–43.

24. Mrs. Gore, *Cecil a Peer* (1841), chap. 1.

25. George Henry Lewes, "Historical Romance," *Westminster Review* 45 (March–June 1846): 34.

26. Ibid., p. 37. "This false erudition," Lewes remarked "joined to a false imagination, produces an abortion, to which we prefer the flimsiest of novels."

27. Jules Janin, "Literature of the Nineteenth Century," *Athenaeum*, 22 April 1837, p. 285.

28. Inserted in the first edition of Andrew Steinmetz's *The Novitiate*, which Thackeray reviewed (discussed later in this chapter). The Smith, Elder catalogue quotes other favorable endorsements from the *Scotsman* and the *Atlas*. John Sutherland contends, however, that by the time of the publication of *Henry Esmond* the firm had found itself "badly out of pocket" in this deal with James (see "*Henry Esmond:*

The Shaping Power of Contract" in his *Victorian Novelists and Publishers* [London: Athlone Press, 1976], p. 107). Sutherland sees Smith's decision to go ahead with *Henry Esmond* as a sign of his faith in Thackeray.

29. R. H. Horne, "G. P. R. James," *A New Spirit of the Age* (London, 1844), pp. 134–35. Thackeray reviewed this book in the *Morning Chronicle*, 2 April 1844; *Contributions*, pp. 13–22.

30. *The Comic Almanack. An Ephemeris In Jest And Earnest, Containing Merry Tales, Humorous Poetry, Quips and Oddities*. By Thackeray, Albert Smith, Gilbert A' Beckett, The Brothers Mayhew. With many Hundred Illustrations By George Cruikshank And Other Artists (London: Hotten, 1846), p. 127. None of the items is signed, but evidence points to Thackeray's authorship of this item. It is attributed to him by Harold C. Gulliver in *Thackeray's Literary Apprenticeship*, pp. 127–30.

31. *Punch*, 10 July 1847, p. 2 (continued 17, 24 July); *Works*, 6:502. Thackeray was not the only writer who ridiculed James. His biographer quotes such mock advertisements as: "To be sold: *The Beauties of James* (very scarce), I Vol. . . ."; "A Catalogue of James's Novels. 9 vols. folio," and an announcement of his forthcoming two thousandth novel. For a summary of contemporaneous satire, see S. M. Ellis, *The Solitary Horseman* (Kensington: The Cayme Press, 1927), pp. 260–61.

32. *British Quarterly Review* 17 (1853): 267; *Spectator*, 6 November 1852. This reviewer, George Brimley, seems to have been familiar with *Catherine*, whose phraseology he echoes ("Our business is not with the hoops and patches, but with the divine hearts of man, and the passions which agitate them"). According to Gordon Ray, Thackeray considered this review "the best of many that appeared" (see his introduction to the Modern Library College Edition of *Esmond* [New York: Random House, 1950], p. xviii).

33. *British Quarterly Review* 17 (1853): 267. A reviewer in America wrote: "In point of style and skill in composition, *Esmond* is fully equal to its predecessors. The archaisms . . . are exquisitely managed" (*New York Times*, 19 November 1852, p. 2). K. C. Phillipps, in "The Language of *Henry Esmond*," *English Studies* 57 (February 1976): 19–42, stresses Thackeray's skill as "linguistic illusionist" rather than his literal period accuracy, pointing out that even when Thackeray is in error he conveys a convincing "quasi-archaic" sense.

34. According to Ellis, as a schoolboy James amused himself during holidays "with analysing and reconstructing some of the papers in *The Rambler*" (*The Solitary Horseman*, p. 31).

35. *Works*, 7:510.

36. "New Novels," *Fraser's Magazine*, December 1852, p. 623; "Our Schools of Fiction. Thackeray as a Depicter of Character," *Hogg's Instructor*, June 1853, pp. 638–40.

37. Lewes, "Historical Romance," p. 45.

38. *British Quarterly Review* 17 (1853): 269.

39. Lewes, "Historical Romance," pp. 34–35.

40. *Spectator*, 6 November 1852, p. 1067.

41. Parallels with *Henry Esmond* are pointed out by Andrew Lang in his introduction to *Woodstock* in the Illustrated Cabinet Edition of Scott's works (Boston, 1894), pp. xiv–xv. In "Scott and *Henry Esmond*," *Notes and Queries*, 17 June 1944, pp. 288–89, John Robert Moore points out what he believes to be a more striking parallel with *St. Ronan's Well*, in which the hero, Francis Tyrrel, foregoes his claim to legitimate birth, a title, and an English estate for the sake of a woman he loves, and goes into exile.

42. G. P. R. James, *Henry Smeaton* (1851), chap. 6.

43. "On Literary Snobs," *Works*, 6:358.

44. This point is made by John Loofbourow in his *Thackeray and the Form of Fiction* (Princeton, N.J.: Princeton University Press, 1964), p. 161—mainly to the detriment of Bulwer. For Thackeray's references to Devereux, see *Letters*, 1:95, 98. Actually, Thackeray felt that Bulwer's novel was "full of thoughts strong and deep, but that the author "has strung his pearls on a poor & fragile thread."

45. *Punch*, 3 April 1847 (continued 10, 17 April); *Works*, 6:471. John Sutherland discusses this parody in relation to Esmond in his introduction to the Penguin

English Library reprint of *Esmond* (Harmondsworth, Middlesex: Penguin Books Ltd., 1970), pp. 12–13. This reprint features "A Note on the Manuscript" and useful explanatory notes by Sutherland.

46. First published in 1829, in Colburn's Standard Novelists series, *Devereux* was reprinted in 1852, the year *Henry Esmond* came out, with an additional introductory note by the author, on which I have drawn.

47. Among modern critics, Georg Lukács has commented on Thackeray's obsession with "private manners" as against public events in dealing with history. He contrasts Thackeray's tendency to show us great people, institutions, and events in their "everyday manifestations" with Scott's tendency to make his characters stand for various historical movements or changes (see *The Historical Novel*, trans. Hannah and Stanley Mitchell [London: Merlin Press, 1962], pp. 201–2. In "Michael Angelo Titmarsh and the Knebworth Apollo" (*Costerus*, n.s. 2 [1974] pp. 75–76), Anthea Trodd links Esmond wth Bulwer's Devereux as figures withdrawn from public life looking back over the past in retirement, rather than as participants, in a meditative mood.

48. The characterization of Lady Castlewood could have been suggested also by Lady Vavasour, whom Philip Herne loves and eventually marries, the beautiful wife of a nobleman considerably older than she is, who is widowed after the Restoration. A historical character introduced in an early episode, incidentally, is Lady Castlemain, a favorite at the time of Charles II, whom Ralph admires from a distance in a parade.

49. Alexander Mitchell, "Notes on the Bibliography of Leigh Hunt," *Bookman's Journal*, series 3, no. 15 (1927), pp. 101–14. For further details, see the same writer's "The Problem of the First Edition of Leigh Hunt's *Sir Ralph Esher*," *Bookman's Journal*, series 3, no. 18 (1930), pp. 15–17. Ernest Baker dismisses *Sir Ralph Esher* briefly as a "pseudo-antique," a "minor work turning Leigh Hunt's knowledge of the town and of contemporary literature to profitable account" (*History of the English Novel*, 11 vols. [London: H. F. & G. Witherby, 1924–50], 7:91).

50. Alison, "The Historical Romance," pp. 348–49. Among the varied fare that Alison could have been referring to were Jane Porter's *Thaddeus of Warsaw* (first published in 1803, but revived in 1831 in Bentley's Standard Novels); Mrs. Gore's *Polish Tales* (1833); Morier's still popular *Hajji Baba of Isaphan*; Colonel Philip Meadows Taylor's *Confessions of a Thug* (1839) and *Tippoo Sultan: A Tale of the Mysore War* (1840); Thomas Colley Grattan's *The Heiress of Bruges; a Tale of the year 1600* (1830; Bentley's Standard Novels, 1834); and Charles Augustus Murray's *The Prairie Bird* (1844, concerned with the Indians of the Ohio Valley after their defeat by General Wayne; also reprinted in Bentley's Standard Novels). One of the romances reviewed by Lewes, Thornton Hunt's *The Foster Brothers*, centered on a war between Venice and Genoa.

51. James C. Simmons, "Thackeray's *Esmond* and Anne Manning's 'Spurious Antiques,'" *Victorian Newsletter* 42 (Fall 1972): 23. Simmons compares *Esmond* with two fictitious memoirs of Anne Manning in vogue at this time, *The Maiden and Married Life of Mary Powell* (1849) and *The Household of Sir Thomas More* (1851), as well as with Mrs. Rathbone's *Diary of Lady Willoughby* (1844), dubbed, with other works of the kind, "spurious antiques" by a *Fraser's* reviewer. The books already mentioned by Hunt, Bulwer, and G. P. R. James seem closer analogues to me, but it is significant that the *Diary of Lady Willoughby* was printed in "old face," like *Esmond*—instituting the so-called Caslon Revival. (For further discussion of the vogue for the revival of quaint typography at this time, see Andrew Sanders, "Clio's Heroes and Thackeray's Heroes: *Henry Esmond* and *The Virginians*," *English* 26 [Autumn 1977]: 212, n. 7.) Simmons gives the misleading impression that the contemporaneous reception of *Esmond* was predominantly unfavorable. Most of the reviews I have examined considered it superior to others of its kind.

52. Quoted from the review in the *Examiner*. The author was Josepha Heath Gulston, writing under the pseudonym of Talbot Gwynne. Michael Sadleir indicates that Gulston's next book, *Life and Death of Silas Barnstarke: A Story of the Seventeenth Century* (1853), was published exactly uniform with *Henry Esmond* by Smith, Elder (*Nineteenth Century Fiction*, 1:159).

53. Between 3 November and 6 November 1852, to W. S. Williams. *The Shakespeare Head Brontë*, 19 vols. (Oxford: B. Blackwell, 1931–38), *Life and Letters*, 4:17, 19.

54. "Steele," *The English Humourists of the Eighteenth Century, Works,* 7:488.

55. Robert Louis Stevenson, "A Gossip on Romance," *Works,* ed. Lloyd Osbourne and Fanny Van de Grift Stevenson, 26 vols. (London: William Heinemann; New York: C. Scribner's Sons, 1922–33), 12:194. Gordon Ray points out a specific analogue between the episode of Frank Castlewood's breaking of the sword before Prince James and a similar scene involving Athos and Louis XIV in chap. 197 of Dumas's *Le vicomte de Bragelonne (The Age of Wisdom,* p. 463).

56. "On A Lazy Idle Boy," *Roundabout Papers, Works,* 12:169. In "De Finibus" he writes: "No cares: no remorse about idleness: no visitors: and the Woman in White or the Chevalier d'Artagnan to tell me stories from dawn to night!" *(Works,* 13:373). "What wouldn't I give to have [Dumas's] knack of putting a story together," Thackeray wrote on one occasion to his mother *(Letters,* 2:568).

57. According to T. C. and William Snow, the Prince knew no French until he was seven; his tutors were English, and "his letters show no trace of the French idiom which Thackeray makes him use." They consider Thackeray unjust also in making the Prince a libertine, conjecturing that in the absence of records, he had to reconstruct James's character a priori, and "naturally he has constructed it on the models of his father, and his uncle, and his son" *(Henry Esmond,* ed. T. C. and William Snow, rev. ed. [Oxford: Clarendon Press, 1915], p. 570).

58. See also "French Dramas and Melodramas," *Paris Sketch Book.*

59. Calling for a glass of water is a secret signal agreed upon by the queen and Masham to indicate that the time is ripe for a private meeting, but the duchess learns of it through Bolingbroke, and this embarrassing accident occurs as the result of the shaking of her hand when she answers the queen's request. The title of the English version, "freely adapted" by W. E. Suter, is *A Glass of Water: Great Events from Trifling Causes Spring.* This version, first produced at the Queen's Theatre on 2 May 1863, is printed in Lacy's *Acting Editions of Plays,* vol. 79. In the introduction Bolingbroke's maxim is said, on the authority of Sainte-Beuve, to have originated in a theory of Voltaire. A more recent English version by De Witt Bodeen is anthologized in *Camille and Other Plays,* ed. Stephen S. Stanton (New York: Hill & Wang, 1957).

60. See above, pp. 93–95.

61. *Foreign Quarterly Review,* April 1843, p. 147. Another Scribe play adversely reviewed here, *Le fils de Cromwell,* seems to have given Thackeray suggestions for *Henry Esmond.* To Thackeray the title character, Richard Cromwell, who turns away from his father's politics and church, illustrates "early religious impressions acting upon a naturally amiable nature," and in the case of General Monk, another leading figure of this drama, "love of a gentle fair one . . . converted the old Roundhead into a cavalier, and so brought about the restoration" (ibid., pp. 140, 149).

Incidentally, Thackeray's strictures on Scribe did not inhibit him from seeking out the man himself during a Paris visit, as recorded in a letter to Mrs. Brookfield of 17–20 January 1851 *(Letters,* 4:428).

62. Review of *Correspondence of Duchess of Marlborough.*

63. Macaulay, *History of England,* introduction to chap. 1.

64. Andrew Steinmetz, *The Novitiate; or, A Year among the English Jesuits* (London: Smith, Elder, 1846), pp. 3–4. Thackeray's review appeared in the *Morning Chronicle,* 11 April 1846; *Contributions,* pp. 123–27.

65. Steinmetz followed up his memoir with a *History of the Jesuits, from the Foundation of Their Society to Its Suppression by Pope Clement IV* (1848)

66. *Punch* 20 (January–June 1851): 75; *Works,* 6:535. Another by-product of Steinmetz's memoir was his tale *The Jesuit in the Family* (1847), also published by Smith, Elder. "In 'The Novitiate' was exhibited the *Jesuit in training.* The present work is to display the *Jesuit in action,*" wrote Steinmetz in his preface, and accordingly he demonstrates the depths of "perjury, fraud, equivocation, falsehood" they will perpetrate in the name of their faith, and to win converts.

67. In a centenary tribute a Catholic writer commended Thackeray's portrait of Father Holt: "When it is remembered what the Jesuit figure was in English fiction up till his time," he wrote, "we can see how such a character that is merely human, and no mere Guy Fawkes night effigy, marks advance." He was pleased to note that though "Father Holt is shrewd and clever, he is not a monster of cunning, such as

Eugène Sue furbishes up. He has his limitations and weaknesses like other men; but he is amiable, adroit, supple, courageous, and entirely sincere in his devotion to his cause" (P. J. Gannon, "The Religion of Thackeray," *Dublin Review*, January 1912, p. 41). In reviewing Lever's *Saint Patrick's Eve*, Thackeray himself complained against various tendentious religious novels, specifically naming Sue's *Rodin*, which "has lately set all France against the Jesuits" (*Morning Chronicle*, 3 April 1845; *Contributions*, pp. 72–73). A popular English novel of the time was the Reverend William Sewell's *Hawkstone* (1845), depicting a depraved member of the order who eventually is eaten by rats.

68. Steinmetz, *The Novitiate*, pp. 1–3, 22, 68–69, 184.

69. Chap. 20. At one point Thackeray has his hero recall: "Esmond thought of his early time as a novitiate, and of this past trial as an initiation" (bk. 2, chap. 1—the prison episode).

70. The conclusion of *Esmond* seems also to reflect contemporaneous literature of emigration, e.g. Charles Rowcroft's *Tales of the Colonies; or, The Adventures of an Emigrant* (London, 1843), where it is pointed out that the growing difficulty of maintaining a family in England "has excited among all classes a strong attention towards the colonies of Great Britain, where fertile and unclaimed lands, almost boundless in extent, await only the labour of man to produce all that man requires" (p. v).

71. "Congreve and Addison," *Works*, 7:486.

72. William Sherlock and William Wake, also mentioned here, were other prominent divines of the time known for their latitudinarian disposition. Sherlock became prominent in the controversy attending the succession of William and Mary, at first a part of the resistance, eventually signing the oath of allegiance. Richard Baxter and William Law, also in Rachel's library, were noteworthy nonconformists. A lucid background for the religious controversies of this period, tending toward toleration, is provided in Gerald R. Cragg's *From Puritanism to the Age of Reason* (Cambridge: At the University Press, 1966).
Thackeray himself attended Newman's lectures at the Oratory in 1850. For his interest in Newman's career and in the controversy over the issues arising out of the Papal Aggression, see Ray, *The Age of Wisdom*, pp. 121–22, and p. 452, n. 10.

73. Gannon, "The Religion of Thackeray," pp. 30–31; Blanche Warre-Cornish, "An Impression of Thackeray in His Last Years," *Dublin Review*, January 1912, p. 21. In his lecture on Swift, Thackeray complained that his sermons "have scarce a Christian characteristic; they might be preached from the steps of a synagogue, or the floor of a mosque, or the box of a coffee-house almost" (*Works*, 7:441). He wouldn't carry latitudinarianism that far, nor was he one, like Swift, to write a paper on religion that is "merely a set of excuses for not professing disbelief."

74. *Memorials of the Reverend Joseph Sartain*, ed. Mrs. B. M. Sartain (London, 1861), pp. 322–23 (quoted in Ray, *Age of Wisdom*, pp. 368–69).

75. *Works*, 7:497. In one episode of *Henry Esmond*, Steele quotes from another nondogmatic religious thinker of the seventeenth century, the Cambridge Platonist, Ralph Cudworth: "A good conscience is the best looking-glass of heaven" (bk. 1, chap. 6).

76. "Swift," *Works*, 7:423–24.

77. *Works*, 7:489.

78. Unpublished "Autograph Notebook Used in Collecting Material for His Lectures on the Four Georges," 105 pp. (in various hands), in Library, The Philip H. and A. S. W. Rosenbach Foundation, Philadelphia, p. 35.

79. It is reproduced before the title page of *Relics from the Library of the Late W. M. Thackeray*, ed. J. H. Stonehouse (London, 1935), p. 62. The note to this item (present whereabouts unknown) indicates that there are thirty-nine "spirited illustrations of Ancient History, à la Titmarsh" interspersed through the text. This caricature is also reproduced in *Thackerayana*, ed. Joseph Grego (London: Chatto & Windus, 1901), p. 30.

80. "Of Novels, Historical and Didactic," p. 42.

81. The Fales Library, New York University, has an unpublished letter to the editor, Adam Black, dated 20 May 1853 from Paris, thanking him for the offer, but turning it down because of the pressure of other engagements.

82. "History and Fiction," *Once a Week*, 12 February 1868, p. 108. The writer of this article may have been E. S. Dallas, who was the editor at the time.

83. 14 February 1852, to George Smith, *Shakespeare Head Brontë, Life and Letters*, 3:314–15.

84. "'Esmond' and 'Basil,'" *Bentley's Miscellany* 37 (1862): p. 577; *British Quarterly Review* 17 (1853): 266.

85. *British Quarterly Review* 17 (1853): 271; Anne Thackeray, introduction to *Henry Esmond, Works*, 7:xxvi (in reference to the imitation of eighteenth-century typography and format in the first edition).

86. Walter Pater, "Style," *Appreciations, with an Essay on Style* (London, 1889), p. 14.

87. G. Robert Stange, introduction to *Henry Esmond* (New York: Holt, Rinehart, & Winston, 1962), p. x. Henri Talon, in "Time and Memory in Thackeray's *Henry Esmond*," *Review of English Studies*, n.s. 13 (May 1962): 147–56, characterizes it as "an attempt to understand the self through the rediscovery of his life and the reconstruction of time." He contrasts Thackeray's representation of time as "outer frame" with the "inner dimension" of time as reconstructed by Proust.

88. *British Quarterly Review* 17 (1853): 71.

THE NEWCOMES: FAMILIES RESPECTABLE
AND OTHERWISE

Chapter Eleven

"I THINK I HAVE BEGUN A NEW NOVEL IN numbers, giving up the idea of the lectures I had last week. But it is not worth while to write lectures for the Americans to rob them and any I do had best be for London hearers first," wrote Thackeray to his family late in the summer of 1852.[1] This is the first we hear of *The Newcomes: Memoirs of a Most Respectable Family*, which began to appear in October of the following year. It was headed "Mr. Thackeray's New Monthly Work," an indication that he was returning to his established format, after having tried out the three-decker with *Henry Esmond*, but illustrated this time by a former *Punch* colleague, Richard Doyle.[2] In announcing his new novel to his family, Thackeray had fresh in his mind his successful tour of the United States with his lectures on the eighteenth-century humorists. The nominal "editor" of *The Newcomes*, the now established writer Arthur Pendennis, also remembering this American tour, interrupts the "Overture" on themes from Aesop and Lafontaine to tell his readers: "Nay, since last he besought good-natured friends, a friend of the writer has seen the New World, and found the (featherless) birds there exceedingly like his brethren in Europe." To a young American friend he had met on his visit there, Sarah Baxter, Thackeray unburdened himself while at work on this most poignant and heartfelt of his books:

> I mean that [the] world is base and prosperous and content, not unkind—very well bred—very unaffected in manner, not dissolute—clean in person and raiment and going to church every Sunday—but in the eyes of the Great Judge of right & wrong what

rank will all these people have with all their fine manners and spotless characters and linen? They never feel love, but directly it's born, they throttle it and fling it under the sewer as poor girls do their unlawful children—they make up money-marriages and are content—then the father goes to the House of Commons or the Counting House, the mother to her balls and visits—the children lurk upstairs with their governess, and when their turn comes are bought and sold, and respectable and heartless as their parents before them. Hullo—I say—Stop! where is this tirade a-going to and apropos of what?[3]

It went of course into *The Newcomes*, where his "lectures" are carried on through his accustomed "confidential talk between writer and reader." "What a dreadful, dreadful place this great world of yours is, Arthur," says Laura Pendennis at one point, "where husbands do not seem to care for their wives; where mothers do not love their children; where children love their nurses best; where men talk what they call gallantry!" (chap. 49). After retreating to the Age of Anne, Thackeray was back in the world all too much with his readers, of getting and spending, of fathers and children, of marrying and giving in marriage. This time, however, his concern was not with people living without God in this world, as in *Vanity Fair*, but without love and charity. "I can bear it no longer—this diabolical invention of gentility which kills natural kindness and honest friendship," he had confided in his "Concluding Observations on Snobs," at the end of which he wrote: ". . . if Fun is good, Truth is still better, and Love best of all."[4] The thwarting of natural relations through the blighting of young love is a pervasive theme of Thackeray's tragicomedy of errors, given out first by Colonel Newcome's short-lived romance with Mademoiselle Blois, reiterated shortly after by Lady Ann Kew and Tom Poyntz, repeated in the next generation by their offspring Clive and Ethel, as well as by that ill-fated couple Lady Clara Pulleyn and Jack Belsize, and, in her sentimental histrionic way, by Madame la Duchesse d'Ivry, pining away after her lost Adolphes and Alphonses. This family chronicle is an extended paean to ideal love in its various manifestations—filial, parental, avuncular, romantic, marital, and spiritual.

Thackeray well knew where love and charity began. Charlotte Brontë's observation after reading *Henry Esmond* that Thackeray "likes to show us human nature at home" is borne out by a number

Following:
The Newcomes, page from the *Newcomes Advertiser* in part 4, showing books on domestic life advertised alongside works of Thackeray and fellow novelists. (The Heineman Collection, The Pierpont Morgan Library; reproduced by permission.)

of chapter headings in *The Newcomes:* "Mrs. Newcome At Home"; "Miss Honeyman's"; "Ethel And Her Relations"; "In Which Everybody Is Asked to Dinner"; "Park Lane"; "The Colonel At Home"; "In Which Benedick Is A Married Man"; "Mrs. Clive Is At Home." There are, to be sure, other more outgoing chapters that give this domestic history extension ("Describes A Visit To Paris . . ."; "In Which Clive Begins To See The World"; "Returns From Rome To Pall Mall"), but, generally speaking, Thackeray could say, along with Bulwer in *The Caxtons*, that here "man has been reviewed less in his active relations with the world than in his repose at his own hearth." *The Caxtons* and its sequel, *My Novel; or, Varieties in English Life*,[5] were two of numerous family novels publicized in *The Newcomes Advertiser*, such as Miss Mulock's *The Ogilvies* and *The Head of the Family;* Marmion Savage's *The Falcon Family*, Charles Lever's *The Dodd Family Abroad*; Cuthbert Bede's *The Adventures of Mr. Verdant Green*; Mrs. Oliphant's *Alieford: A Family History;* and Grace Aguilar's *Home Influence*, which was still in popular demand after its spinster author's untimely death. "Home influence" makes itself felt in many other books advertised in the monthly parts of *The Newcomes,* in a pictorial ambience of clothing, furnishings, aromatic teas, home remedies, and patent medicines. One number offers such useful works as *The Illustrated Family Friend Almanack and Housekeeper's Guide* (to which Martha Honeyman could have contributed) and Orr's series of Household Handbooks. Also introduced at this time was a new illustrated magazine called *The Home Companion.* Frederika Bremer's *Homes of the New World* in Mary Howitt's translation was recommended by one of the reviews for its "sound, clear views of the public and private life in America, mixed with expressions of comprehensive human kindness, and close family affection." On Mudie's current list was *Home Life in Germany.* Curiosity about home life in England at its upper reaches was satisfied by *Punch's Pocket Book for 1855* (advertised in number 14), which featured pieces on "The Royal Family," "The Queen's Household," "Prince of Wales' Household," and "Duchess of Kent's Household." Advertised in number 4 of *The Newcomes*—preceding chapter 14 where we participate with the family of Sir Brian Newcome in prayer—were *Daily Family Devotion; or, Guide to Family Worship* and *The Altar of the Household, a Series of Services for Domestic Worship.*[6] "God Bless the Home" could serve as a motto for many a novel then in vogue.

In *The Caxtons*, the best known of the predecessors to *The Newcomes,* Bulwer (through his alter ego Pisistratus Caxton) announces that he intends "to imply the influence of Home upon the conduct and career of Youth." Appropriately, and in line with Bulwer and other "domestic analysts"[7] of the age, Thackeray traces the "home influence" on youth Clive to its roots. "As the young gentleman who has just gone to bed is to be the hero of the following pages, we had best begin our account of him with his family history," writes Clive's biographer Arthur Pendennis, adding, to the presumed relief of his readers, "which luckily is not very long" (chap. 2).[8] Pendennis knew that he was writing to a genealogy-conscious generation represented in the novel itself by Clive's mother-in-law, The Campaigner, whom Pendennis recalls "it used to be my sport to entertain . . . with anecdotes of the aristocracy, about whose proceedings she still maintained a laudable curiosity" (chap. 78). Burke's Peerage is part of her favorite reading as well as of her daughter Rosey. The Mackenzies were only two of many, to judge by the popularity of Sir Bernard Burke's *Family Romance; or, Episodes in the Domestic Annals of the Aristocracy,* advertised along with humbler family romances in the first number of *The Newcomes.*

Sir Bernard really does not do the aristocracy proud, his theme, stated at the beginning of the second volume, entitled "The Vicissitudes of Great Families," being "the decadence of many a royal line . . . the withering of many a proud stem." He purposely confined himself to "such instances as have a historic halo around them," adding that "the vicissitudes of families less distinguished would extend the subject far beyond our limits." As can readily be surmised from the *Newcomes Advertiser,* numerous fictitious chroniclers of the 1850s took up where Burke left off, including *The Newcomes* itself with such innuendo-laden chapter headings as "Colonel Newcome's Wild Oats"; "Family Secrets"; "In Which Kinsmen Fall Out"; and "Barnes's Skeleton Closet." Charles Lever, as "editor" of the papers of the quite ordinary and much tried Dodd family, justifies himself in words that could have served for his fellow authors who were also prying into domestic arcana: "It is not in our present age of high civilisation that an Editor need fear the charge of having indulged family secrets, or made the private history of domestic life a subject for public commentary. Happily, we live in a period of enlightenment that can defy such petty slanders. Very high and titled individuals have shown themselves superior to similar accusations, and if the 'Dodds' can in any wise contribute to the amusement or instruction of the world, they may well feel recompensed for an exposure to which others have been subjected before them."[9] The "others" were not only those exposed by Burke, but also the likes of the Marlboroughs, the Bolingbrokes, the Walpoles, among illustrious clans, and, because of his recent death, the house of the Duke of Wellington, all of whose "family secrets" had been opened to readers in recent years. By now authors and the public seemed to agree with Bulwer that "every family is a history in itself and even a poem to those who know how to search its pages," to quote a motto from the title page of *The Caxtons*.[10]

The Newcomes are not, of course, merely *a* family, but "a Most Respectable Family." The term *respectability* was one much bandied about in popular reading at the time, one consequence presumably of middle-class families becoming subjected to the kind of scrutiny formerly reserved for their betters. It comes into the account of his lineage by one popular hero of the day: "If you will refer to the unpublished volumes of 'Burke's Landed Gentry' and turn to the letter G, article 'Green,' you will see that the Verdant Greens are a family of some respectability and of considerable antiquity. We meet with them as early as 1096, flocking to the Crusades among the followers of Peter the Hermit, when one of their name, surnamed Greene the Witless, mortgaged his lands in order to supply his poorer companions with the sinews of war."[11] Young Verdant Green finds himself the latest in a long line of "unsuspicious, credulous, respectable, easy-going people in one century after another, with the same boundless confidence in their fellow creatures, and the same readiness to oblige society by putting their names to little bills, merely for form's and friendship's sake."

Young Pisistratus Caxton takes himself more seriously. His father and uncle (a retired East India military officer) are given to arguing over whether they are descended from William Caxton, the printer, or from the warrior William de Caxton, but he describes them simply as "a family . . . old enough, but decayed." He is proud enough that his family lived "in what might be called a very respectable style for people who made no pretence to ostentation" and that their Queen Anne house "had an air of solidity, and well-to-do-ness about it—nothing tricky on the one hand, nothing decayed on the other."[12] Their neighbor Squire Rollick, however, has a somewhat more restricted view: "'Egad, sir, the country is going to the dogs! Our sentiments are not represented in parliament or out of it. The "Country Mercury" has ratted, and be hanged to it! and now we have not one newspaper in the whole shire to express the sentiments of the respectable part of the community!'" For "respectable part of the community," read, of course, "squirearchy." Uncle Jack Caxton, to whom this complaint is addressed, comes momentarily to the defense of the despised interlopers of this country, only to be summarily put down:

> "Yes, respectable fellow-creatures, men of capital and enterprise! For what are these country squires compared to our wealthy merchants? What is this agricultural interest that professes to be the prop of the land?"
> "Professes!" cried Squire Rollick—"it *is* the prop of the land; and as for those manufacturing fellows who have bought up the 'Mercury'—"[13]

The squire's unspoken expletive could have been directed at the "Screwcomes," scions of "manufacturing fellows," and now "men of capital and enterprise," who descend on London from their *rus in urbe,* and draw the scorn of the *Newcome Independent (The Newcomes,* chap. 14).

Try as he may, the conscientious chronicler of the Newcome family can find no authentic record of the clan before the reign of George III, when the father of Thomas, Brian, and Hobson Newcome "first made his appearance in Cheapside; having made his entry into London on a waggon, which landed him and some bales of cloth, all his fortune, in Bishopsgate Street" (chap. 2). He is determined to set the record straight, even to the embarrassment of the subjects of his memoir: "For though these Newcomes have got a pedigree from the College, which is printed in Budge's 'Landed Aristocracy of Great Britain,' [continues his account] and which proves that the Newcomes of Cromwell's army, the Newcome who was among the last six who were hanged by Queen Mary for protestantism, were ancestors of this house . . . and the founder slain by King Harold's side at Hastings, had been surgeon-barber to King Edward the Confessor; yet, between ourselves, I think that Sir Brian Newcome, of Newcome, does not believe a word of the story, any more than the rest of the world does, although a number of his children bear names out of the Saxon Calendar." The press is not so kind, as witness the lampoon by the *Newcome Independent* of Sir Brian as "Don Pomposo Lickspittle Grindpauper, Poor House, Agincourt, Screwcome, whose ancestors fought with Julius Caesar against William the Conqueror, and whose father certainly wielded a *cloth yard shaft* in London not fifty years ago" (chap. 14).[14]

In the eyes of Squire Rollick, with his £5,000 a year rent roll and his escutcheon extending back several centuries, the Newcomes might be excluded from "the respectable part of the community," but Colonel Newcome tries to place respectability on a basis more substantial than land or lineage. One of Clive's first disappointments is his discovery of what Pendennis brings to light—that his grandparents are not "swells." "And when I came back to school, where perhaps I had been giving myself airs, and bragging about Newcomes," he unburdens himself to his father during a visit to Grey Friars, "why you know I was right to tell the fellows." So the occasion arises for one of Clive's "early lessons" from his mentor:

> "That's a man," said the Colonel, with delight; though had he said, 'that's a boy,' he had spoken more correctly. . . . "That's a man," cries the Colonel, "never be ashamed of your father, Clive."
>
> "Ashamed of *my* father!" says Clive, looking up at him and walking on as proud as a peacock. "I say," the lad resumed, after a pause . . . "Is that all true what's in the peerage—in the baronetage, about uncle Newcome and Newcome; about the Newcome who was burned at Smithfield; about the one that was at the Battle of Bosworth; and the old old Newcome who was bar—that is, who was surgeon to Edward the Confessor, and was killed at Hastings? I am afraid it isn't; and yet I should like it to be true."
>
> "I think every man would like to come of an ancient and honourable race," said the Colonel in his honest way. "As you like your father to be an honourable man, why not your grandfather and his ancestors before him? But if we can't inherit a good name, at least we can do our best to leave one, my boy; and that is an ambition which, please God, you and I will both hold by." (Chap. 7)

In emphasizing through the colonel that respectability is something transmitted rather than inherited, Thackeray did his part to bring *gentillesse* within the purview of the middle class. By the same token, parentage becomes most crucial among the "first associates" of the rising generation, and in *The Newcomes* the character of Clive's father and principal mentor preempts even that of Clive himself in the interest of the family biographer. The outlines of this character could have been suggested to Thackeray in another book advertised in *The Newcomes—The Old Field Officer; or, The Military and Sporting Adventures of Major Worthington,* by J. H. Stocqueler, a military writer of prestige.[15] This hypothetical major recalls in his memoir, supposedly composed in retirement, an unhappy boyhood that began back in the eighteenth century. As a younger son of meager prospects, persecuted at school, and of a somewhat wild disposition, he leaves home to take up an army career in India, where he succeeds in moving up in the ranks. Here he becomes known for his kindliness, temperate disposition, and circumspection, except in money matters—his generosity leading him to make loans that are not repaid, and his trusting nature leading him to invest in tottering local banks.

With his gallantry and misguided idealism, Colonel Newcome suggests a modern Quixote. Cervantes's knight errant is in fact one of the colonel's literary heroes (along with Addison's Sir Roger de Coverley and Richardson's Sir Charles Grandison), and he is depicted in one of the historiated initials as the Man of La Mancha (chap. 66). It is evident that, as with honor, Thackeray meant for this old soldier to exemplify the aristocratic ideal of chivalry in a modern bourgeois setting. Such was the intention also of an earlier book by J. H. Stocqueler, *The British Officer: His Positions, Duties, Emoluments and Privileges* (1851), published the year before Thackeray began his writing of *The Newcomes.* "In our estimation, the British uniform should represent the generous and lofty sentiments of which the golden spurs of knighthood were once emblematical . . ." as Stockqueler sums up the ideal soldier in this conduct book. For him the military and civilian virtues are joined together in modern society:

> It is the character and conduct of the British gentleman that must secure this moral power for the British Officer [a bearing that inspires confidence]. He who seeks to obtain it must be urbane in manners and courteous to all; he must be just and honourable in his most trifling dealings. . . . Without being either a stoic or ascetic, he should look with scorn on that mindlessness which seeks for artificial excitement, or the worse gratification of avaricious rapacity. . . . But while scorning these low vices, our ideal, if grave with the grave, should be cheerful with the cheerful; should laugh with the gay and witty, but never with the envious and malicious. . . . In society, the British officer should be marked by unobtrusive courtesy and easy elegance of manners.[16]

The prototypical British officer, in short, should be "distinguished in ballrooms as well as in battlefields," and should be "as familiar with polite accomplishments as with professional attainments." Colonel Newcome tries his best amidst the assorted humbugs at Mrs. Hobson Newcome's "at Home" in her Bryanston Square mansion (chap. 8). The Doyle etching that accompanies this chapter shows the colonel poised and stately before the Hindustani guest paying respects to him. Two numbers later he is described kissing the hand of Ethel Newcome "with a great deal of grace and dignity" (chap. 15), the matching cut suiting the gesture to these words. Subsequently Arthur is pleased to see the colonel treat his wife, Laura, with a grace befitting Grandison (chap. 51).

The plate that illustrates chapter 56 catches the colonel acting with gallantry toward Rosey Mackenzie, and shortly afterward we "behold the stately grace . . . as he stepped out to welcome his daughter-in-law, and the bow he made before he entered her carriage" (chap. 62).

Stocqueler's model soldier is intended to be a pattern of morality as well as of courtesy, and the principle that he be "grave with the grave . . . cheerful with the cheerful" describes too the colonel's dual role of censor and companion to Clive. In early chapters we observe his capacity for innocent joy along with his sternness of disposition towards the intemperate (as in the Cave of Harmony episode), his sometimes pathetic attempts to share the pleasures of Clive's friends, as well as to participate in their literary and artistic conversation. The true soldier-gentleman, according to the ideal already set forth, scorns not only "artificial excitement," but also "the worse gratification of avaricious rapacity," and Colonel Newcome reacts accordingly against the greed and deceit of his brothers and other relatives. However, the colonel has certain chinks in his armor, as duly noted by his biographer. "He could believe all and everything a man told him until deceived once, after which he never forgave," Arthur comments on the colonel's first serious rift with his family, set off by Barnes's duplicity.[17] "And wrath being once roused in his simple soul and distrust firmly fixed there, his anger and prejudices gathered daily" (chap. 52). "Slow to anger and utterly beyond deceit himself," Arthur writes later, "when Thomas Newcome was once roused, or at length believed that he was cheated, woe to the offender!" (chap. 56).

Stocqueler's manual offered some counsel along these lines that the colonel should have taken in stride: "If gentlemen could see the undignified figure they make when in a towering passion, the chances are that they would endeavour to keep their temper a little more within bounds." In this rule book, "We may excuse anger, or even passion perhaps, when the name, fame, or character of friends and relatives are assailed," but a sense of proportion is urged, along with caution, in taking out this anger on others. "The fact is, that in nine cases out of ten, people only get in a towering passion when their self-love is assailed, when some selfish gratification is endangered," in Stocqueler's judgment, "when they strive to conceal error or littleness beneath an explosion of noble rage." This mirror for the perfect gentle knight of Victoria's golden days, then, anticipates not only Colonel Newcome's virtues but what proves to be his tragic flaw as well. The perceptive Arthur Pendennis is quick to assess the combination of righteous indignation and wounded pride that prompts the colonel's vendetta against Barnes and leads him, less justifiably, to malign Ethel, with sad consequences for Clive. He makes us aware too that his friend Clive, as "the inheritor of his father's blood, his honesty of nature, and his impetuous enmity against wrong" (chap. 62), although he becomes imbued with the colonel's ideas of respectability, also carries over the Newcome rashness of disposition.

"Train up a child in the way he should go; and when he is old, he will not depart from it," from Proverbs, appears as an epigraph on the title page of one of the family novels that had preceded Thackeray's home epic,[18] characteristic of the tendency of this genre to consecrate the hearthside as sanctuary and seminary. Colonel Newcome follows the counsel of the author of Proverbs, with his penchant, as we have already noticed, for "improving" each occasion with some moral lesson for Clive's benefit. The nurture of the Young Idea begins with the opening episode in the Cave of Harmony, where the colonel reproves Captain Costigan for his ribald songs: "For shame, you old wretch! Go home to your bed, you hoary old sinner! And for my part, I'm not sorry that my son should see, for once in his life, to what shame and degradation, and dishonour, drunkenness and whiskey may bring a man" (chap. 1). Later Clive's impulsive action of flinging wine in Barnes's face at the Oriental Club is turned by the colonel to his son's edification. The morning after, Clive finds his father at the foot of his bed, "reproving conscience to greet his waking," and following the soda water comes the sermon; "We ought to be ashamed of our doing wrong. . . . We must go and ask Barnes Newcome's pardon, Sir, and forgive other people's trespasses, my boy, if we hope forgiveness of our own" (chaps. 13, 14). Pendennis leads us to expect the colonel to become the censor of us all: " . . . that uplifted cane of the Colonel's had somehow fallen on the back of every man in the room," is his startling reaction to the abruptly terminated bacchanalian revel that concludes the first chapter. The catch is that the colonel's cane has fallen on his own back as well by the time he responds "Adsum," for both mentor and neophyte derive some harsh lessons from life.

The colonel's guiding hand over Clive is felt even beyond "home influence." In an early chapter (chap. 5) the colonel sets out a life program for Clive, beginning with the traditional gentleman's education, supplemented by educational travel, to be followed by choice of profession and a good marriage. Various chapter headings indicate stages of the colonel's scheme: "In Which Mr. Clive's School-Days Are Over"; "A School of Art"; "New Companions"; "Youth And Sunshine"; "In Which Clive Begins To See The World"; "Across The Alps"; "Clive In New Quarters"; "Mr. and Mrs. Clive Newcome"; "In Which Clive Begins The World." Furthermore, books promoted in various numbers of the *Newcomes Advertiser* seem sufficiently in keeping to have served as supplementary reading for those following the fortunes of this "respectable family." Along with Clive's school days one could have followed those of Mr. Verdant Green at Oxford; George Melly's *School Experiences of a Fag at a Public and a Private School* (". . . a vivid and striking picture of the brighter side of Public School Life," according to a review); *Revelations of School Life*, by "Cantab." (described in a blurb as a "Thorough Exposure of Our Scholastic System"); and Kay-Shuttleworth's pamphlets on education. The account of Clive's art lessons was framed by notices of Samuel Carter Hall's *Art Journal;* John Cassell's series *The Works of Eminent Masters;* and *Lectures on Architecture and Painting,* by John Ruskin, M.A., along with his *The Opening of the Crystal Palace: Considered in Some of Its Relations to the Prospects of Art.* It was easy to roam the continent vicariously with Clive and his companion John James Ridley through such offerings as *Purple Tints of Paris: Character and Manners in the New Empire,* Adam and Charles Black's Guide Books (illustrated on their borders with young men hiking with knapsacks and sketching), and Doyle's delightful picture book *The Foreign Tour of Messrs. Brown, Jones, and Robinson,* as well as Thackeray's *The Kickleburys on the Rhine.* Shortly after the first meeting of Clive and Ethel, readers were freshly apprised of Frank Smedley's *Harry Coverdale's Courtship And All That Came Of It,* with its Phiz-designed wrapper dominated by hoops in the form of wedding rings in which courting couples of various ages are depicted. This is a preoccupation also of *Punch's Pocket Book for 1855,* advertised in this same number, that included pieces on "Love's Rational Dream," "Marriage Ceremonies of the Great Britons," and "The Experiences of a Discontented Old Bachelor, Aetat. 64." Social life too plays its part in Clive's growing up, and prominent among novels that entertained and edified readers between numbes of *The Newcomes* was *Fortune: A Romance of London in the Nineteenth Century,* by David Trevenna Coulton, which at the time evoked comparison with the novels of Thackeray and Bulwer as a "biting satire of fashionable life, the moral anatomy of high society," and particularly as a scathing denunciation of materialism. So *The Newcomes* entered the stream of books of popular instruction, "rational amusements" pursued by cultural aspirants (like Mrs. Hobson Newcome, ever rushing to lectures, and the colonel's friend James Binnie, with his British Institution, Political Economy Club, and such), guides to the perplexed in the affairs of everyday life.

Doyle's decorated initials showing children at school or at play keep before us the focus of this novel on the formation of the young.[19] Pendennis too, in occasional asides ("And now, young people, who read my moral pages . . . "), is aware of his didactic function. He knows also that he is supposed to contribute to the moral education of the parents of his young readers ("I ask any gentleman and father of a family . . ."; "Do not let us be too angry with Colonel Newcome's two most respectable brothers. . . . I say, do not let us be too hard on them"; "Snooze gently in thy arm-chair, thou easy bald-head! play your whist, or read your novel, or talk scandal over your work, ye worthy dowagers and fogies!"). Now and then he brings his generations of readers together: "It may serve to recall passages of their early days to such of [Clive's] seniors as occasionally turn over the pages of a novel; and in the story of his faults, indiscretions, passions, and actions, young readers may be reminded of their own." So readers young and old are reminded that Clive's life history is supposed to be an exemplary biography, but they were warned in advance by the opening farrago of beast fables—which the design on the wrapper kept fresh in their minds from month to month[20]—with the confused and scrambled moral explications furnished by the author, not to expect any simplistic message from the real-life fable that follows.

Mothers and fathers looking for *the* way to train up their young could not have found much assurance from the relations between parents and children exhibited in this history. Colonel Newcome as a boy is subjected to an evangelical regimen, represented by, among others, his tutor, the Reverend T. Clack of Highbury College, "who was commissioned to spare not the rod neither to spoil the child" (chap. 2). The result, as the chapter title indicates ("Colonel Newcome's Wild Oats"), is to make young Tommy an unruly boy. One cut in this chapter shows him kicking the family butler in the shins; in one episode he is horsewhipped by his father for running away from home; and the chapter ends with his going off on his own to India. Reaction against his own stern upbringing leads the colonel to be more indulgent toward his son—not always to Clive's good. On the other hand, Martha Honeyman tells Arthur: "I have a brother [Charles] to whom my poor mother spared the rod, and who, I fear, has turned out but a spoilt child" (chap. 3). If gold will rust, what will iron do? we may ask with Chaucer. Not only the incumbent of Lady Whittlesea's Chapel, but also that peer of the realm and suitor to Ethel Newcome, Lord Farintosh, is a product of maternal pampering: "As an infant he had but to roar, and his mother and nurses were as much frightened as though he had been a Libyan lion. What he willed and ordered was law amongst his clan and family. During the period of his London and Paris dissipations his poor mother did not venture to remonstrate with her young prodigal, but shut her eyes, not daring to open them on his wild courses" (chap. 59). So much for permissiveness, but strictness does not fare better in the case of Lady Walham, whose son, and Ethel's first suitor, Lord Kew takes up his rakish course in revolt against his closely guarded childhood (chap. 37).

Not only are parents left somewhat confused by this particular *Familienroman* as to what course to take, but their very authority is undermined. "Children ought to consider themselves in the house of their father as in a temple where nature has placed them, and of which she has made them the priests and ministers that they might continually employ themselves in the worship of those deities who gave them being," reads the motto at the head of a chapter of one of the novels recommended by the *Newcomes Advertiser*.[21] But one can readily come away from a reading of *The Newcomes* itself convinced that father does *not* know best. "Who set her on the path she walked in?" asks the family historian, in connection with Ethel Newcome's betrothal to Lord Farintosh. "It was her parents' hands which led her, and her parents' voices which commanded her to accept the temptation set before her" (chap. 61). Circumstances, as it happens, compel Ethel to break off the engagement, sparing her the consequences of the family-arranged "Marriage in High Life" of Lady Clara Pulleyn to Barnes Newcome,[22] and of the relatively low life one of Clive to Rosey Mackenzie. However, the first readers of *The Newcomes* who took it in gradually over a period of two years were left in suspense as to whether Ethel was destined for the fate of the unfortunate Lady Clara, or of the Duchesse d'Ivry before her. The novelist Mrs. Oliphant, commenting on the novel before she knew the outcome, raised a question that must have been on many minds at that time: "Is Ethel to consume what remnants are left to her of that fresh girl's heart she had when we first knew her—when she first fell in love with her good uncle—and be a great lady, and blaze her youthful days away in barren splendour?"[23] Not too long before, Thackeray had cautioned Sarah Baxter, after whom Ethel Newcome was in part modeled, against making this very misstep:

> —Well—I was fancying my brave young Sarah (who has tried a little of the pomps & vanities of her world) transplanted to ours and a London woman of society—with a husband that she has taken as she has threatened to take one sometimes just because he is a good parti. No—go and live in a clearing—marry a husband masticatory, expectoratory, dubious of linen, but with a heart below that rumpled garment—let the children eat with their precious knives—help the help, and give a hand to the dinner yourself—yea, it is better than to be a woman of fashion in London, and sit down to a French dinner where no love is, Immense Moralist! . . . I see a chapter out of the above sermon and you know—I must have an i to the main chance—[24]

"Has Mr. Thackeray prepared this beautiful victim for Moloch, or is there hope for Ethel still?" asked Mrs. Oliphant in her essay. This sacrificial rite had been a leading topic of sermon and satire before Thackeray took it up. "We are a match-making nation," proclaimed Bulwer in *England and the English*; "the lively novels of Mrs. Gore have given a just and unexaggerated picture of the intrigues, the manoeuvres, the plotting, and the counter-plotting that make the staple of matronly ambition." As Thackeray's friend Horace Smith put it in *The Tin Trumpet*: "The difficulty of effecting marriage in these times of expensive establishments is one of the great evils of our social system, and the principal source of corrupt manners." The marriage mart was quite graphically displayed in the frontispiece to *Punch's Pocket Book for 1847*, consisting of a colored foldout entitled "The Matrimonial Tattersall's."[25] Here in a house in May Fair, under the hammer of two enterprising ladies who have taken the name of the Sisters Tattersall, after the emporium of that name, prospective wives and husbands are sold at auction. Among the human merchandise vividly portrayed by John Leech are: "A fine buxom widow, well off . . ."; "A sprightly young thing affectionate and tender"; "A Maid of Honour, under twenty-five, not proud"; "Governess, extremely clever, accustomed to children and work, warranted to endure every hardship . . ."; and "The younger daughter of a baronet, only came out last season." Leech's erstwhile colleague Richard Doyle gives us a visual reminder of "The Matrimonial Tattersall's" in the picture that heads chapter 54 of *The Newcomes* where we see Ethel, labeled "Lot 1.," being auctioned off by Lady Kew to a group of top-hatted bidders, just before we read of the party celebrating her engagement to Lord Farintosh.[26] Anticipating one of the most famous episodes of *The Newcomes* is another diverting detail of the *Punch* cartoon, a heavy-set, over-dressed female with her back to the reader, on which is conspicuous a tag marked £20,000. Ethel, in labeling herself with the green tag from the Suffolk Street Gallery, joins the market place that her family thrives in with the milieu of her cousin Clive.

"Ethel, at this time, was especially stubborn in training, rebellious to the whip, and wild under harness . . . ," we are told (chap. 32), in the imagery of educators of the period who tended to think of youth as animals to be tamed. "It is too much, grandmamma. Do please let me stay where I am: and worry me with no more schemes for my establishment in life," Ethel boldly tells off the formidable Lady Kew (chap. 38), who tries to supervise her as the colonel does Clive. The colonel slackens his reins over his young colt too, and his grand design for Clive is eventually balked, as are so many good intentions in this domestic tragedy where teenage rebellion comes into conflict with filial devotion. Clive may be said to signify for Thackeray what Pisistratus Caxton did for Bulwer: ". . . the specimen or type of a class the numbers of which are daily increasing in the inevitable progress of modern civilisation . . . the representative of the exuberant energies of youth, turning, as with the instinct of nature for space and development, from the Old World to the New." Exuberance is a trait we associate with Clive from our first introduction to him by Pen as he "jumped up from the table, bounded across the room, ran to me with his hands out . . ." (chap. 1). Pen continues to impress us with his friend's "kind and jovial disposition," that "good temper and gaiety which have seldom deserted him in life, and have put him at ease wherever his fate has led him" (chap. 18). Certainly it would be hard to conceive a greater antithesis to the "cut-throat melancholy" represented by Henry Esmond. In a larger sense Clive is the embodiment of mirth and joy of life opposing itself to the puritanism of the previous generation as represented by Colonel Newcome. As Pen sums him up, he reflects "the ardent and impulsive disposition . . . by whom all beauties of art and nature, animate or inanimate . . . were welcomed with a gusto and delight whereof colder temperaments are incapable" (chap. 27).[27]

A crucial question that arises in the course of Clive's training is to what useful end are his youthful energies going to be channeled. Advice of course is forthcoming. The colonel's intellectual and iconoclastic friend James Binnie has young Clive charted in advance according to the phrenological jargon of the day: "The imaginative and reflective organs are very large—those of calculation weak. He may make a poet or a painter, or you may make a sojer of him . . . but a bad merchant, a lazy lawyer, and a miserable mathematician. He has wit and conscientiousness, so ye mustn't think of making a clergyman of him" (chap. 8). The colonel soon resigns himself to the fact that Clive is no scholar: "As regarded mathematical and classical learning, the elder Newcome was forced to admit, that out of every hundred boys, there were fifty as clever as his own, and at least fifty more industrious" (chap. 17). Actually the choice of profession comes quite spontaneously, particularly since the colonel is determined that Clive should not follow in his military steps. Clive's peering into a volume of Hogarth engravings while his father is trying to interest him in Addison and Dr. Johnson confirms what the colonel has noticed from Clive's early years: ". . . his delight in the pencil was manifest to all. Were not his school-books full of caricatures of the masters? Whilst his tutor, Grindley, was lecturing him, did he not draw Grindley instinctively under his very nose? A painter Clive was determined to be, and nothing else" (chap. 17). The colonel proves no more influential on Clive's choice of profession than on his studies or literary taste, but he has the good sense to allow his son to "follow his own bent." The colonel in fact defends "the pictorial calling" against its disparagement by that pillar of respectability the Reverend Honeyman: ". . . as long as his calling is honest it becomes a gentleman; and if he were to take a fancy to play on the fiddle—actually on the fiddle—I shouldn't object" (chap. 12).

So, along with his healthy hedonism, Clive asserts the value of the arts in a philistine society. Clive's semibohemian student days enable Thackeray to relive vicariously the joy his own first vocation had brought him. "'Oh,' says Clive, if you talk to him about those early days, 'it was a jolly time! I do not believe there was any young fellow in London so happy!'" (chap. 16). Thackeray himself was moved by a visit to Paris in 1849 to write to Mrs. Brookfield: "I went to see my old haunts when I came to Paris thirteen years ago and made believe to be a painter—just after I was ruined and before I fell in love and took to marriage & writing. It was a very jolly time, I was as poor as Job: and sketched away most abominably, but pretty contented. . . . where is Art, that dear Mistress whom I loved though in a very indolent capricious manner, but with a real sincerity?"[28] Though forced himself for practical reasons to abandon this "dear mistress," in *The Newcomes* Thackeray pays tribute to those who remained faithful to her, as represented in particular by the painter Dick Tinto: "I love his honest moustache, and jaunty velvet jacket, his queer figure, his queer vanities, and his kind heart" (chap. 17). Tinto becomes a living paean to art itself: its vitality ("He is naturally what he is, and breaks out into costume as spontaneously as a bird sings, or a bulb bears a tulip"), its originality and mystery ("he gives his genius a darkling swagger, and a romantic envelope. . . . [he has] an instinct for the picturesque, which exhibits itself in his works, and outwardly on his person") combined with humane sympathies ("beyond this, a gentle creature loving his friends, his cups, feasts, merrymakings, and all good things").

Clive, like his creator, is attached to the artistic life because of its combination of nonconformity and elementary humanity. With Clive too Thackeray looks back over a time when the artist was struggling for status. Despite upholding his son's calling, the colonel has misgivings: "Newcome did not seem seriously to believe that his son would live by painting pictures, but considered Clive as a young prince who chose to amuse himself with painting" (chap. 27). Later we are told that he "felt secretly that his son was demeaning himself" (chap. 51). Other "respectable" people in the novel are of this opinion besides the Reverend Honeyman—Hobson Newcome, Major Pendennis, Lady Kew, and the Marquis of Farintosh, who thinks of Clive as a craftsman ready to "paint my dog Ratcatcher, by Jove! or my horse, or my groom, if I give him the order" (chap. 59).[29] Clive's biographer gives the impression that the situation has not changed much at the time of writing. At the beginning of the chapter describing Clive's training at Gandish's Academy, he remarks: "In walking through streets which may have been gay and polite when ladies' chairmen jostled each other on the pavement, and link-boys with their torches lighted the beaux over the mud, who has not remarked the artist's invasion of those regions once devoted to fashion and gaiety?" (chap. 17). He gives examples of such deteriorated neighborhoods taken over by artists, and the fanciful initial drawn by Doyle shows a shabbily dressed young painter pondering before his easel in a Soho garret, above him a former inhabitant of these quarters, an elegant lady being attended to by her hairdresser. Pendennis later observes: "The Muse of Painting is a lady whose social station is not altogether recognised with us as yet. The polite world permits a gentleman to amuse himself with her, but to take her for better or for worse! forsake all other chances and cleave unto her! to assume her name! Many a respectable person would be as much shocked at the notion, as if his son had married an opera-dancer" (chap. 27).

Alongside this discouraging testimony the *Newcomes Advertiser* provides some evidence of improvement of the artist's lot. The notice of the latest issue of the *Art Journal* (in no. 15) is accompanied by a retrospective note to subscribers by the editor, Samuel Carter Hall, calling attention to its success in achieving its initial purpose "to protect and advance the cause of Artists, and to extend a knowledge and appreciation of Art among all classes." Since the launching of this journal in 1839, Hall continues, "the Arts have been making large progress; the interest they create is no longer limited to the higher orders—it has spread among all ranks; the Manufacturers are now their liberal patrons,[30] and the Artizans are those that most profit by the lessons they teach. It cannot be presumptuous in us to believe that our exertions during so long a period have greatly aided the movement to which art has been subjected in England, nor that we have much assisted in the progress it has made." Behind Hall's sanguine words were such phenomena as the success of the Crystal Palace Exhibition, within the recent memory of these readers, and the popularity of Ruskin's *Modern Painters* and *The Seven Lamps of Architecture* (also duly noted in the *Newcomes Advertiser*). Against the complaint of Clive's master Gandish that "there is no patronage for a man who devotes himself to 'Igh art" (chap. 17), it is of additional interest that Hall quotes a commendation of the *Art Journal* by Prince Albert and announces for the following year a series of engravings from pictures in the private collections both of His Royal Highness and of Her Majesty.

Clive then might not have met with so much resistance had he set up his studio in the 1850s. There are other indications that the times were ripe for what he was doing. In his choice of profession, we watch him wrench himself free not only from the colonel's reins but, as has been noted in a previous chapter, from Gandish's "'Igh art" (what Thackeray called "the sham sublime") to take up the "pathetic and familiar." At an international art exhibition held in Paris in 1855 (coincidentally, the year when *The Newcomes* completed its run) no less a critic than Baudelaire isolated as a leading feature of the British work in view there its "intimate glimpses of home."[31] The British artist Richard Redgrave commented on this same show: "To pass from the grand salons appropriated in the Palais des Beaux Arts to the French and Continental works, into the long gallery of British pictures, was to pass at once from the

midst of warfare and its incidents, from passion, strife, and
bloodshed, from martyrdoms and suffering, to the peaceful scenes
of home."[32] Clive shows that he is moving in this direction in the
letter he writes to Arthur from the Louvre in Paris, where he has
gone to rest from his labors over "The Battle of Assaye": "Art
ought not to be a fever. It ought to be a calm; not a screaming
bull-fight or a battle of gladiators, but a temple for placid contemplation, rapt worship, stately rhythmic ceremony, and music solemn and tender. I shall take down my Snyders and Rubens, when I
get home; and turn quietist. To think I have spent weeks in depicting bony Life Guardsmen . . . and painting black beggars off a
crossing!" (chap. 22).

Unlike his friend John James Ridley who inspires him, and more
like Thackeray himself, Clive is not represented as a great painter.
"If Mr. Clive is not a Michael Angelo or a Beethoven," declares his
biographer, "if his genius is not gloomy, solitary, gigantic, shining
alone, like a lighthouse, a storm about him, and breakers dashing
about his feet, I cannot help myself; he is as Heaven made him,
brave, honest, gay, and friendly, and persons of a gloomy turn
must not look to him as a hero" (chap. 39). Recognizing his own
limitations Clive eventually abandons his imitations of the
"Imperio-Davido-classical school" and his copies of the masterpieces "in the heroic vein" in the museums of Paris and Rome to
find his subject matter in the streets.[33] "We walked out to see the
town, which I daresay you know, and therefore shan't describe," he
writes to Pen. "We saw some good studies of fishwomen with bare
legs; and remarked that the soldiers were very dumpy and
small. . . . Didn't I get up the next morning and have a good walk
in the Tuileries! The chestnuts were out, and the statues are shining: and all the windows of the palace in a blaze. . . . No end of
little children were skipping and playing in the sunshiny walks,
with dresses as bright and cheeks as red as the flowers and roses in
the parterres" (chap. 22). When he has to seek his livelihood by the
sweat of his brow, he sets himself, however reluctantly, to record
the life around him on canvas: "I am doing Mail Coaches . . . and
Charges of Cavalry; the public like the Mail Coaches best—on a
dark paper—the horses and milestones picked out white—yellow
dust—cobalt distance, and the guard and coachman of course in
vermilion"; "Crackthorp, and a half-dozen men of his regiment
came, like good fellows as they are, and sent me five pounds apiece
for their heads. . ." (chap. 74). By trial and error Clive eventually
comes round to Thackeray's own view that "it is the study of

Nature, surely, that profits us, and not of these imitations of her. A man, as a man, from a dustman up to Aeschylus, is God's work, and good to read, as all works of Nature are."[34]

Clive anticipates what is to be his metier when he sets up his first studio and invites the colonel to pose for him: "That's *your* key, sir . . . and you must be my first sitter, please, father; for though I'm a historical painter, I shall condescend to do a few portraits, you know" (chap. 22). At this point, Pen interposes: "Clive has never painted anything better than that head, which he executed in a couple of sittings; and wisely left without subjecting it to the chances of further labour." He shares Thackeray's own inclination for art that is spontaneous, for "small pictures" that "come straight to the heart," for faces expressive of "real nature, real startling home poetry."[35] Eventually Clive's drawing of his own baby son helps to cheer the colonel's last days in Grey Friars. Not the turbulent genius prized by the romantics, Clive, though temporarily deflected from his path by his ill-advised marriage, comes closer to the Victorian middle-class ideal of the artist. His conversion to "the peaceful scenes of home" is most clearly signaled in that moment of illumination in Baden when his spiritual and human loves merge in his consciousness: "As he looked at a great picture or statue, as the 'Venus' of Milo, calm and deep, unfathomably beautiful as the sea from which she sprung; as he looked at the rushing 'Aurora' of the Rospigliosi, or the 'Assumption' of Titian, more bright and glorious than sunshine, or that divine 'Madonna and divine Infant' of Dresden, whose sweet face must have shone upon Raphael out of heaven; Clive's heart sang hymns as it were, before these gracious altars; and somewhat as he worshipped these masterpieces of art, he admired the beauty of Ethel" (chap. 30). Clive may be said to represent the modern artist of "the bourgeois style," whose cause Thackeray had advanced in his art criticism, as well as the spirit of art itself domesticated and, like other former manifestations of "the unbought grace of life," accommodating itself to everyday life. Clive's conversion as an artist is illustrated on the title page of the second volume of *The Newcomes* (in its original format) where he is represented before the easel, his wife looking over his shoulder, his child at his feet playing with the sketches that have fallen on the floor.[36]

Along with Clive Newcome's hammering out of his "bourgeois style" of art we witness another significant coming of age—that of the domestic novelist incarnated in the chronicler of the Newcome family, Arthur Pendennis of the staff of the *Pall Mall Gazette: Journal of Politics, Literature, and Fashion.* By now he has left far behind him both the mooncalf of Chatteris and the bachelor-about-town. He has taken on a more staid character, in keeping with that of his creator, who at this stage was determined to dispense more heady stuff than "the brisk, sparkling champagne drink from the presses of Colburn, Bentley & Co." "Write sober books, books of history, leave novels to younger folks," Thackeray advised himself in the letter to Miss Baxter. Appropriately Arthur purports to be, not a teller of tales, but the editor of Clive Newcome's "logs" and the colonel's "papers," a historian who, "charged with the duty of making two octavo volumes out of his friend's story, dresses up the narrative in his own way" (chap. 24). Never other than a "veracious" chronicler, Pendennis attempts with his leisurely pace to give the illusion of the random quality of life: "In such a history, events follow each other without necessarily having a connection with one another" (chap. 24). Having got his adolescent misanthropy and *weltschmerz* out of his system with his apprentice work *Walter Lorraine,* he is ready to write the sort of books Laura approves of: "good books, kind books, with gentle, kind thoughts . . . such as might do people good to read." Ethel Newcome, who has read Arthur's first book (over Lady Kew's severe objections), also gives him ideas. "Why do you give such bad characters of women?" she asks him at a dinner party at the Hobson Newcome's mansion in Bryanstone Square. "Don't you know any good ones? . . . Why don't you put them into a book?" She adds: "Why don't you put my uncle into a book? He is so good that nobody could make him good enough" (chap. 24). Arthur takes up both challenges.

By the "good ones" Ethel refers not to herself but to Arthur's mother, Helen, and to Laura, whom indeed he marries midway through the book and whose supreme virtues he makes all too well known to us. But with Ethel, whom Clive elevates into an object of adoration, Arthur appears to be answering critics who thought that Thackeray himself had given "bad characters of women." Not too long before *The Newcomes* began coming out, Thackeray had been taken to task by an American magazine for dividing his feminine characters into "the good-foolish and the selfish-shrewd" with no gradations in between. Another American reviewer was perturbed to find that Thackeray's women are "either composites of vice or flattering slaves, and they are thus unnatural."[37] Back home, Mrs. Oliphant complained: "Mr. Thackeray does not seem acquainted with anything feminine between a nursery-maid and a fine lady—

an undiscriminate idolator of little children and an angler for a rich husband. The 'perfect woman nobly planned' has no place in the sphere of Mr. Thackeray's fancy."[38] Ethel is far from the "perfect woman," being all too imbued with the Newcome pride and willfulness that bring grief also to Clive and to the colonel. Lord Farintosh is rash as usual when he sums her up as "the finest girl in England—and the best-plucked one, and the cleverest and the wittiest, and the most beautiful creature, by Jove, that ever stepped . . ." (chap. 59), but he comes close to what made her at the time a novelty among Thackeray's heroines. As though determined to prove that these virtues were not really dissociated, Thackeray made her as clever as Becky, as tender-hearted as Amelia, as flirtatious as Blanche, and almost a match for Beatrix as a beauty. He also showed that one and the same woman could be artful and good-hearted, vain and unselfish, an "idolator of little children" as well as an "angler for a rich husband." This shift was noticed by an early reviewer of *The Newcomes* who pointed out: "Mr. Thackeray is not for the most part a flattering painter of women. The clever are artful, and wicked; the good are insipid. Ethel is a great exception, and has no counterpart in *Vanity Fair* or *Pendennis*."[39]

Most of Thackeray's characters, even his unscrupulous ones, reveal surprising glints of goodness from time to time, or unexpected resources, but Ethel is unique among his young women in developing with the passage of time, in being "improved" by her circumstances—as the moralists of Victoria's day would have it. Her elders having failed her as guides through life, Ethel becomes an autodidact in the school of hard knocks. "She has a generous nature, and the world has not had time to spoil it," Laura Pendennis observes to her husband. "Do you know there are many . . . problems that she has to work out for herself. . . . Life and experience force things upon her mind which others learn from their parents, or those who educate them" (chap. 49). Certainly she passes with honors the moral tests that life imposes on her: allowing Lord Farintosh to save his face by giving it out that he, rather than she, has broken off their engagement; taking over the care of the children of her brother Barnes and Lady Clara after their separation and divorce; attending to the poor and sick in the London slums. She really rises in our estimation when, prompted by moral scruples, she rejects, in Clive's favor, a family legacy to which she is entitled. (Here, incidentally, is the justification for the much criticized conventional device of the belated discovery of her paternal grandmother's will.) We can agree with Laura that "the trials, and perhaps grief, which the young lady . . . had to undergo have brought out the noblest qualities of her disposition," and with Arthur that by the end of this history, "She is a very different person from the giddy and worldly girl who compelled our admiration of late in the days of her triumphant youthful beauty, of the wayward generous humour, of her frivolities and her flirtations" (chap. 62). We are left guessing whether Ethel and Clive, after their respective trials and tribulations, actually achieve a "happy ever after," it being merely hinted at the conclusion that they are united "in Fable-land somewhere." The main point presumably is their biographer's conviction that they are "a great deal happier now than they would have been had they married at first, when they took a liking to each other as young people." They are both chastened by what they have known of spoiled human relations. What is more important—they have before them the noble example of Colonel Newcome.

"Why interest oneself in a personage who you know must, at the end of the third volume, die a miserable death?" Thackeray had asked the British public in a review ten years before.[40] At this time he was urging them to read that "good, cheerful, clever, kind-hearted, merry, smart, bitter, sparkling romance" called *Jérôme Paturot*, whose impact on *Vanity Fair* has already been noticed. With *The Newcomes*, however, we do indeed interest ourselves in a personage who dies abjectly, at the end of the second volume in this instance, one more sign of Thackeray's growing inclination toward "sober subjects." The colonel annoys some modern readers, but he was this novel's pinnacle to many of Thackeray's contemporaries. Mrs. Oliphant, who was critical of Ethel Newcome, found her most worthy of our regard "when we see her beautiful eyes shining with pride for her noble old uncle." To the reviewer in the *Times,* the colonel was "a noble creature, worthy of any age." The characterization of Colonel Newcome finally established Thackeray as a novelist of sympathy and human compassion, as well as of wit and intelligence. In America one reviewer praised him for at last creating a character who commands "our profound reverence"; and another found in *The Newcomes* ample refutation of the charges of misanthropy as well as of misogyny that had been laid at his door.[41] The words of Saintsbury written near the beginning of this century seem best to express the continuing appeal of this Christian soldier on those who have basked in his radiance: "The Colonel's end enchanted and enchants everybody who is susceptible to the sentimental, and appears to have disarmed, most of the anti-sentimentalists by the intensity of its humanity."[42]

Like Ethel, the colonel grows on us, but in a different way. At first he appears something of a prig and a bore, a figure for gentle ridicule. It is evident, in connection with the "improvement" program in progress throughout the novel, that in some respects Telemachus is ahead of Mentor: "Indeed [the colonel] spoke out his mind pretty resolutely on all subjects which moved or interested him; and Clive, his son, and his honest chum, Mr. Binnie, who had a great deal more reading and much keener intelligence than the Colonel, were amused often at his naive opinion about men, or books, or morals. Mr. Clive had a very fine natural sense of humour, which played perpetually round his father's simple philosophy, with kind and smiling comments" (chap. 14). A passage that follows in the manuscript of *The Newcomes* but was dropped in press goes further: "Lad as he was he had a shrewdness & experience w[h] the elder's 50 years had never attained. Clive with his young eyes looked more clearly at men & the world than his father who had seen it so long & so little: & the boy very soon began to keep his own opinion & to question the experience of w[h] his artless sire never doubted the value. In truth Thomas Newcome was but a child in the understanding of the world although he fancied himself becomingly versed in that science, imagining that a man of necessity acquired experience by age & took steps in knowledge, as he did in military rank, by seniority."[43]

Whatever the superiority of pupil to master, the upshot of the colonel's educational scheme for Clive is that the two learn from each other. One function of Pendennis, as surrogate for the author, is to act as eclectic moralist, reconciling the old and new generations:

> Between this pair of friends the superiority of wit lay, almost from the very first, on the younger man's side; but, on the other hand, Clive felt a tender admiration for his father's goodness, a loving delight in contemplating his elder's character, which he has never lost, and which in the trials of their future life, inexpressibly cheered and consoled both of them. *Beati illi*! O man of the world, whose wearied eyes may glance over this page, may those who come after you so regard you! O generous boy, who read in it, may you have such a friend to trust and cherish in youth, and in future days fondly and proudly to remember!

These are significant words coming from that "man of the world," the erstwhile skeptic Arthur Pendennis, who seems to discern in the "simple philosophy" of Colonel Newcome what M. Cousin referred to as "the authority of those general beliefs which constitute the common sense of mankind." The better part of wisdom in Thackeray's world blends the "reflective reason" (in Cousin's terms) as represented by the wit and sophistication of Clive with the "spontaneous reason" of the colonel.[44]

Of all the people in this novel with whom the colonel comes into contact, he makes the deepest impression on Arthur, through whose eyes we see and judge him. Those readers who had been watching with interest his development from the young coxcomb of *Pendennis* must have been gratified by Arthur's response to this pattern of "a gentleman, a Christian, and a man of honour," as he is referred to by Pen's journalist friend Frederick Bayham (chap. 12). Among Pen's various functions in this novel is that of impartial (if unsuccessful) arbiter in the family feud that propels the drama of this book. In this capacity he sees the colonel as "a man . . . simple and generous, . . . fair and noble in all his dealings," temporarily warped by a desire for revenge disguised as righteous indignation. It is poetic justice then that he rises to his true nobility in adversity, purged of his pride and vindictiveness. Stocqueler, to turn once more to his model after whom the colonel appears in a number of respects to have been fashioned, had written that "the manners of the British officer should invariably be those which Chesterfield delineated; his conduct and sentiments, those which in life and death Sir Philip Sidney illustrated."[45] It is fitting therefore that the example the colonel has set before us of holy living should be rounded off by an episode of holy dying, and indeed nothing becomes him in life like his leaving of it. For one who had been "but a child in his understanding of the world," there is a special appropriateness to his last moments as reported by Arthur: "At the usual evening hour the chapel bell began to toll, and Thomas Newcome's hands outside the bed feebly beat a time. And just as the last bell struck, a peculiar sweet smile shone over his face, and he lifted up his head a little, and quickly said 'Adsum!' and fell back. It was the word we used at school, when names were called; and lo, he, whose heart was as that of a little child, had answered to his name, and stood in the presence of The Master" (chap. 80).

Moving as the colonel's death remains to those of us who are susceptible, it had a special significance to Thackeray's contemporaries whose grief was still fresh over the passing three years before of one of Victorian England's most revered military heroes, the Duke of Wellington. The first readers of *The Newcomes* were reminded of this doleful occasion, not only through Tennyson's famous commemorative ode, but also through a published lecture by Samuel Warren (advertised in no. 1). "While my tears fell, in common with those of all present, including royalty itself; while music pealed mournfully, dissolving the very soul, and the gorgeous coronated coffin finally disappeared," lamented Warren, continuing in words that look forward to Colonel Newcome's fate: "there arose before my mind's eye a kindred yet different scene— the vision of some pauper burial, simple and rude, occurring perhaps at that very moment; the burial of some aged forlorn being, whose poverty-stricken spirit was at length safely housed *where the weary are at rest:* the poor dust unattended, save by those whose duty was to bury it—without a sigh, without a tear; with no sound but a reverend voice, and the gusty air, and no prolonged ceremonial."[46] These sentiments, and some of the words, are echoed by Thomas Newcome when Arthur discovers him clad in a black pensioner's gown among the congregation at the Grey Frairs chapel, where the colonel has taken refuge after the Bundlecund disaster—having fled also the wrath of The Campaigner, more than his match for high spirits and temper. The colonel tells him of a friend, another pensioner, veteran of the Peninsular War, "gone now . . . where 'the wicked cease from trembling, and the weary are at rest'; and I thought then . . . here would be a place for an old fellow when his career was over, to hang his sword up; to humble his soul, and to wait thankfully for the end" (chap. 75). Subsequently we witness with Arthur the stoicism with which this Christian warrior faces death, once his "fate decreed poverty, disappointment, separation, a lonely old age." We are spared his "pauper funeral," but attend his death bed along with Arthur, Laura, Clive, Ethel, Frederick Bayham and Mme de Florac, his lost Léonore, who has remained faithful to him in spirit through the years.

Just before Arthur spots the colonel among the old pensioners, he has participated in the service before the Founder's Tomb, which inspires him with an awesome sense of our common destiny: "A plenty of candles lights up this chapel, and this scene of age and youth, and early memories, and pompous death. How solemn the well-remembered prayers are, here uttered again in the place where in childhood we used to hear them! How beautiful and decorous the rite; how noble the ancient words of the supplications which the priest utters, and to which the generations of fresh children, and troops of bygone seniors have cried Amen under those arches!" (chap. 75). Colonel Newcome's humbler memorial becomes equated with the Founder's Tomb which, "with its grotesque carvings, monsters, heraldries darkles and shines with the most wonderful shadows and lights," and "Fundator Noster [Sir Thomas Sutton], in his ruff and gown, awaiting the great Examination" is united under the aspect of eternity with an old veteran remembered only by a few devoted ones and by God. So Samuel Warren in his panegyric on the Duke of Wellington reminded the mourners of the nation: "In the world of spirits, both these might already have met—the warrior-statesman and the pauper, each aware of the different dispersal of the dust he had left behind! Thus are we equally unable to evade death, to conceal or disguise its true and awful character. *One event happeneth to all* (Eccles. 11. 14). The words spoken on high, and great and mean are beside each other in the same darkness, with the same event before them."[47]

The chapel bell that accompanies Colonel Newcome's spirit out of this world tolls for us all. His cane falls lightly on our backs, too, as Arthur voices a belated apology: "The steps of this good man had been ordered thither by Heaven's decree: to this almshouse! Here it was ordained that a life all love, and kindness, and honour, should end! I heard no more of prayers, and psalms and sermon, after that. How dared I to be in a place of mark, and he, he yonder among the poor? O pardon, you noble soul! I ask forgiveness of you for being of a world that has so treated you—you my better, you the honest, and gentle, and good!"[48] (chap. 75). However, the family chronicler of the Newcomes means for us to look back on life properly chastened rather than to dwell on contrition and death, and so the passing of Thomas Newcome leaves us ultimately exhilarated.[49] "Though he fall, he shall not be utterly cast down, for the Lord upholdeth him," Arthur reads from the Bible at the colonel's bed, the very same psalm sung at the Founder's Day service: "And who that saw him then, and knew him and loved him as I did—who would not have humbled his own heart, and breathed his inward prayer, confessing and adoring the Divine Will, which ordains these trials, these triumphs, these humiliations, these blest griefs, this crowning Love?" (chap. 75).

New life is the theme of another episode where the colonel, Clive, and Clive's little boy Tommy come together in prayer: "So these three generations had joined in that supplication: the strong man, humbled by trial and grief, whose loyal heart was yet full of love;—the child, of the sweet age of those little ones whom the Blessed Speaker of the prayer first bade to come unto Him;—and the old man, whose heart was well nigh as tender and as innocent: and whose day was approaching, when he should be drawn to the bosom of the Eternal Pity" (chap. 79).[50] Not only young Tommy but others of the rising generation seem to be imbued with the colonel's spirit. "The boys of the school, it must be said, had heard the noble old gentleman's touching history, and had all got to know and love him," observes Arthur upon revisiting Grey Friars (chap. 80). Such is the intended effect of this history on all others who have come to know this noble old gentleman—boys, girls, men, women, of all generations, in or out of school. Within the world of these "Memoirs of a Most Respectable Family," at least, love conquers all, the spirit of charity transmitted by Sophia Alethea, the mother of Brian and Hobson Newcome, stepmother of Thomas, somehow triumphing over the dark angels of greed, pride, and materialism.

"Parbleu, what virtue, my friend! what a Joseph!" exclaims that *bon vivant* Paul de Florac: "One sees well that your wife has made you the sermon. My poor Pendennis. You are hen-pecked, my pauvre bon! You become the husband model" (chap. 57). Himself conditioned in the more easygoing marital morals of the continent—which we have already seen exemplified through the sordid intrigue involving Lord Kew with Madame la Duchesse d'Ivry[51]—Florac, if unintentionally, answers to the presumed satisfaction of Thackeray's readers of the time the question raised at the end of *Pendennis:* "And what sort of a husband would this Pendennis be?" If modern readers feel that they get a little too much of Pen as model husband and especially of his angel in the house,[52] perhaps that is because, as Tolstoy writes at the beginning of *Anna Karenina:* "Happy families are all alike; every unhappy family is unhappy in its own way." Somehow we interest ourselves more in the "Children dishonoured . . . honest families made miserable" (chap. 57) with whom Pen brings us into sympathy. By this time too he has matured not only into a young Darby, but into "a man of the world looking on" as well, who, as Dr. Watts advised, "has seen the men and morals of many cities" (chap. 74) and hence is in a position to write not merely about *a* family, but the human family, relating the "small ills" of the Newcomes to the "great ills" of the world. "In *The Newcomes* we have 'the form and pressure of the very age and body of the time' as regards huge masses of society," in the words of one of its first reviewers. Moreover, taking in not only his own society but the ancient Orient, the continent, and, by implication, "the (featherless) birds" of the New World, its sweep is not merely national but cosmopolitan.

With his enlarged views, Arthur tries to see the frustrations suffered by the parents in this book against a universe that baffles the mortal will: "Who can foresee everything and always? Not the wisest among us," he declares midway through his narrative. "We may be deep as Jesuits, know the world ever so well, lay the best ordered plans, and the profoundest combinations, and by a certain not unnatural turn of fate, we and our plans and combinations, are sent flying before the wind" (chap. 33). He is speaking here specifically of Lady Kew, who "brought a prodigious deal of trouble upon some of the innocent members of her family, whom no doubt she thought to better in life by her experienced guidance, and undoubted worldly wisdom." As with Colonel Newcome, we can infer that the elders of the tribe are not invariably the wise counselors, either in the domestic circle or in the family writ large in the state: "We may be as wise as Louis Philippe, that many-counselled Ulysses whom the respectable world admired so; and after years of patient scheming, and prodigies of skill, after coaxing, wheedling, doubling, bullying, wisdom, behold yet stronger powers interpose—and schemes and skill and violence are nought" (chap. 33). Old and young, high and low, stumble in the same darkness.

In keeping with his seriousness both as family man and as writer, Arthur even professes to "disdain, for the most part, the tricks and surprises of the novelist's art" (chap. 70), preferring to draw his matter from the vicissitudes of life itself. However, within the apparent random sequence of events and the talk of mischance and fortuity governing the world, in no other novel of Thackeray's do we become more convinced that character is destiny. Fate vies with free will through all of Thackeray's novels from *Catherine* on, but in *The Newcomes* we get more of a sense of men and women bringing ill on themselves than of ill being thrust upon them. Ultimately Arthur, as lawyer by training, writer by vocation, and moral philosopher by conviction, thinks of his role as surrogate for "the Judge who sees not the outward acts merely, but their causes, and views not the wrong alone, but the temptations, struggles, ignorance of erring creatures" (chap. 61). "Erring creatures" is the key phrase here, the vast gallery in *The Newcomes*, though it ranges wide through the moral spectrum, being free of the outlaws, scapegraces, and demireps who flash through most of his other novels. Hence while its predecessors may have more spark and color, *The Newcomes* comes closest to Thackeray's ideal of a novel made up of

"men and women of genteel society . . . living in no state of convulsive crimes, . . ."⁵³ As Arthur points out, "The wicked are
wicked no doubt, and they go astray, and they fall, and they come
by their just deserts, but who can tell the mischief which the very
virtuous do?" (chap. 20). Even the most depraved of these "erring
creatures," Barnes Newcome and Mrs. Mackenzie, are outwardly
"respectable" and in conformity with the social codes. It is this
moral realism, the grasp of the normality of sin as well as of the evil
that is performed unwittingly, that led Coventry Patmore, another
early reviewer of *The Newcomes,* to refer to its author as "the
Athanasius of human peccability" whose "discreditable characters·
have an unhapy trick of claiming kindred with us" at the same time
as "his good people confront us with a display of our own pos-
sibilities."⁵⁴

As the most accessible and least ironical of Thackeray's novels,
The Newcomes brought Thackeray his greatest prestige along with
the widest public esteem that he ever had, establishing his claim to
be taken seriously as a writer among respectable readers. Early in
our century George Saintsbury could still refer to it as "probably
. . . Thackeray's most popular book on the whole."⁵⁵ Such
episodes as the devotion of Clive and his father in adversity, the
humility of the colonel, and his reunion with and forgiveness of
Ethel, have led Saintsbury to remark further that "perhaps, there is
no book in which Thackeray has attained to such a Shakesperian
pitch of pure tragicomedy," an aspect of him missed by present-day
readers who have not ventured beyond *Vanity Fair.*⁵⁶ It obviously
engaged Thackeray himself deeply, even in the midst of his doubts
about his powers. In one letter to Miss Baxter written during its
composition, he told himself: "You are old, you have no more
invention &c. . . ."; but in another he wrote that the new novel
"torments me incessantly, and I wander about it with my interior,
lonely & gloomy, as if a secret remorse was haunting me."⁵⁷ His
absorption with these fictitious men and women seems to have
approached that of Dickens, as one gathers from his reluctance to
let them as well as the readers go at the end. It is known that he
took the pen from the hand of his daughter, who wrote down much
of *The Newcomes* at his dictation, when he came to the death of the
colonel, in order to write it himself in private.⁵⁸ What this most
penetrating of his novels meant to him is possibly best summed up
in a letter he wrote a few days after finishing the book: "Last
Thursday, the 28th at 7 o'clock in the evening, I wrote the last lines
of the poor old *Newcomes* with a very sad heart. And afterwards

what do you think I did? Suppose I said my prayers, and humbly prayed God Almighty to bless those I love and who love me, to help me to see and speak the truth and to do my duty? You wouldn't wonder at that would you? That finis at the end of a book is a solemn word."[59] "Damn all literary fellows—all artists—the whole lot of them!" growls the respectable Hobson Newcome (chap. 20). In defense of the calling that he and Clive have devoted themselves to, as professors at the pen and at the easel, Arthur could affirm: "Art is truth: and truth is religion; and its study and practice a daily work of pious duty" (chap. 65).[60]

1. 16 August 1852, from the Reform Club, *Letters*, 3:67.

2. Doyle had broken off his prosperous connection with *Punch* in 1850 taking objection, as a Roman Catholic, to their attacks on the Papal Aggression—one reason quite possibly why Thackeray is easier on Catholicism in *The Newcomes* than he had been in *Pendennis*. In his article "Pictures of Life and Character" (*Quarterly Review*, December 1854), devoted to Leech, Thackeray digresses on the great loss to *Punch* brought about by Doyle's defection. Thackeray at first planned to illustrate *The Newcomes* himself, but gave up this task for health reasons, turning to Doyle, whom he had already employed to delightful effect for *Rebecca and Rowena*.

3. 26 July 1853, *Letters*, 3:297; text taken from *Thackeray's Letters to an American Family*, ed. Lucy Baxter (London: Smith, Elder, 1904), pp. 85–91. Thackeray's friendship with the Baxters during his first American lecture tour is summarized in *Letters*, 1:lxxxvii–xc.

4. *Works*, 6:462, 464.

5. The narrator of *My Novel* is Pisistratus Caxton, hero of *The Caxtons*. This device gave Thackeray the idea for making Pendennis the chronicler of *The Newcomes* (see letter of 26 July 1853 to Sarah Baxter, *Letters*, 3:298). About a year after he began writing *The Newcomes*, and following upon a reprint of *The Yellowplush Papers*, Thackeray wrote to Bulwer to apologize for his ridicule of him in the earlier work (*Letters*, 3:278). In a letter to his mother, Thackeray praised the panoramic *My Novel* as "fresher & richer than any [Bulwer] has done" (*Letters*, 3:288).

6. With special appropriateness to the occupation of Brian and Hobson Newcome, advertisements for banks and insurance companies are also interspersed among the numbers.

7. This phrase is used in a family novel, Anna Harriet Drury's *Misrepresentation* (1850), to describe the function of the narrator. See Jane Miller Ross, "Minor English Novels of the Eighteen-Fifties," (Ph.D. diss., Columbia University, 1964), p. 18. This thesis is valuable generally for the literary context of *The Newcomes*.

8. Ross comments on the tendency of the family chronicles of the decade to spin out the narrative over several generations: "The presumed heroine of the first volume turns out to be the real heroine's grandmother. Often the dénouement of the love plot hinges upon a scandal or feud, which occurred two centuries before the fair seventeen-year old appears on the scene and threatens to blight her happiness and absolutions of the final pages." She quotes complaints about the prolixity of these novels by critics, the most extreme being this one from the *Athenaeum:* "Are we coming to the days when no tale will be complete unless it begins before the Flood and ends with the final consummation of things" ("Minor English Novels of the Eighteen-Fifties," pp. 35–36). Arthur more considerately breaks off the ancestral portion of his chronicle at the beginning of chap. 4: "If we are to narrate the youthful history not only of the hero of this tale, but of the hero's father, we shall never have done with nursery biography."

9. Charles Lever, *The Dodd Family Abroad* (London: Chapman & Hall, 1854), "A Word From The Editor."

10. This epigraph is attributed to Lamartine. Among recently published biographies were MacFarlane's *Life of the Duke of Marlborough* (1852), a new edition of Bolingbroke's *Works and Life* in four volumes (1849), and Warburton's *Memoirs of Walpole and Contemporaries* (1851). In the *Newcomes Advertiser* are listed *The Duke of Buckingham's Memoirs of the Court and Cabinets of George III. From Original Family Documents* and *Characteristics Of The Duke of Wellington Apart From His Military Talents* by the Right Honorable Earl De Gray. Anne Manning was among historical novelists who carried this trend over into fiction, e.g., *Ye Maiden and Married Life of Mary Powell Afterwards Mistress Milton* (1849) and *Ye Household of Sir Thomas More* (1851).

11. *The Aventures of Mr. Verdant Green, an Oxford Freshman. By Cuthbert Bede, B.A.* (London: Nathaniel Cooke, 1853), chap. 1. The author's real name was Edward Bradley.

12. Bulwer, *The Caxtons: A Family Picture* (Edinburgh and London: William Blackwood & Sons, 1849), bk. 1, pt. 2, chap. 3.

13. Ibid., chap. 4. To get in the good graces of Squire Rollick, the opportunistic Uncle Jack inaugurates a newspaper supporting the "agricultural interest" in opposition to the despised *Mercury* of the "manufacturing fellows" (cf. the attack on Sir Brian by the *Newcome Independent*, the source of which is left vague, though Barnes attributes it to "our infernal radicals of the press").

14. Some episodes of *My Novel* are set in Screwstown, whose "society . . . was, like most provincial capitals, composed of two classes—the commercial and the exclusive." A figure for satire is a tuft-hunting wealthy trader who maneuvers himself into the "sublime coterie" of landed aristocrats. They patronize him for his wealth and hospitality and also try to manipulate him politically (bk. 5, chap. 3). In a later chapter is introduced one Colonel Pompley of Screwstown, "stately in right of his military rank and services in India," who, unlike Colonel Newcome, is a snob who makes claim to aristocratic connections.

15. J. H. Stocqueler, *The Old Field Officer; or, The Military and Sporting Adventures of Major Worthington* (Edinburgh: Adam and Charles Black, 1853), advertised in no. 4, January 1854. Stocqueler was a prolific writer, credited on the title page with a biography of Wellington, *The Handbook of British India*, and *The Military Encyclopedia*. The advertisement for the *Encyclopedia Britannica*, 8th ed., that appears on the back of several numbers lists him as contributor of the article on military affairs. He also wrote under the name Joachim Heyward Siddons.

16. J. H. Stocqueler, *The British Officer: His Positions, Duties, Emoluments and Privileges* (London: Smith, Elder, 1851), pp. 2–3. This book was advertised, along with other Smith, Elder publications, in the first edition of *Henry Esmond*.

17. In chap. 65 the colonel refers to Barnes's "falsehood and rapacity . . . cruelty and avarice."

18. *The Two Families; an Episode in the History of Chapelton*, by Mrs. Sarah Whitehead (London: Smith, Elder, 1852).

19. Reference is made to children's fables: "When we read in the fairy stories that the King and Queen, who lived once upon a time, build a castle of steel, defended by moats and sentinels innumerable, in which they place their darling only child, the Prince or Princess, whose birth has blest them after so many years of marriage, and whose christening feast has been interrupted by the cantankerous humour of that notorious old fairy who always persists in coming, although she has not received any invitation to the baptismal ceremony: when Prince Prettyman is locked up in the steel tower, provided only with the most wholesome food, the most edifying educational works, and the most venerable old tutor to instruct and to bore him, we know, as a matter of course, that the steel bolts and brazen bars will one day be of no avail, the old tutor will go off in a doze, and the moats and the drawbridges will either be passed by his Royal Highness's implacable enemies, or crossed by the young scapegrace himself, who is determined to outwit his guardians, and see the wicked world" (chap. 10). Such analogies, along with the likening of Lady Kew to the wicked fairy of legend, remind us that Thackeray also composed *The Rose and the Ring*, his "Fireside Pantomime for Great and Small Children," during this period.

20. The design seems to be a carry-over from *Punch.* The title page of the 1851 volume, for example, represents Punch on a pedestal marked *The Modern Aesop* surrounded by humanized animals of various sorts—a lion in dress clothes, a donkey in sport suit and top hat, a bull sitting and reading, among others. *Punch's Pocket Book for 1852,* used by Thackeray as an engagement calendar during his first American tour, has a border designed by Tenniel made up of connecting circles containing performing animals.

21. Dinah Mulock, *The Ogilvies* (1849), chap. 4.

22. The ugly divorce suit resulting from Lady Clara's elopement with Jack Belsize, in which she was forced to give up her children to Barnes, was especially topical. The account comes in no. 19 (April 1855), the year after the publication of Caroline Norton's famous pamphlet *English Laws for Women In The Nineteenth Century* (London: Printed for Private Circulation, 1854) growing out of the suit brought against her for debt by her estranged husband, which eloquently denounced property and divorce laws that condoned the tyranny of husband over wives. She likened the situation of women at the time to slavery, invoking the name of Harriet Beecher Stowe (whose recent welcome in England is referred to in chap. 28 of *The Newcomes*). In a letter of 7 March 1855, Thackeray wrote to his mother that he had been to his club "to read the trial of Norton v. Melbourne having a crim-con affair coming on in the Newcomes" (*Letters,* 3:428). The 1850s was an active decade for divorce legislation. In 1850 a Royal Commission was appointed to examine the existing laws; Lord Cranworth's Marriage and Divorce Bill of 1855 (the subject of another pamphlet by Caroline Norton) transferred jurisdiction of these suits from ecclesiastical to civil courts; and in 1858 a more lenient law was passed.

Inevitably there was a spate of novels dealing with mismatings and unhappy marriages: e.g., *The Wife's Sister; or, The Forbidden Marriage* (1851); *Clara Harrington: A Domestic Tale* (1852); *May and December: A Tale of Wedded Life* (1854); *A Mother's Trials* (1859). Emma Robinson's *Mauleverer's Divorce: A Story of a Woman's Wrong* (1858) has for its heroine a novelist, possibly suggested by Mrs. Norton. For a discussion of these and others, see Ross, "Minor English Novels of the Eighteen-Fifties," chap. 5.

23. Mrs. Oliphant, "Mr. Thackeray and His Novels," *Blackwood's Magazine* 77 (January 1855): 86–96.

24. 26 July 1853, *Letters,* 3:297. According to Sarah's sister Lucy, who brought out this correspondence many years later, in Ethel Newcome some of Thackeray's impressions of Sarah were transferred from New York to London, especially Sarah's attitude toward New York society (*Thackeray's Letters to an American Family,* pp. 6–7; quoted in *Letters,* 1:lxxxviii–ix).

25. In chap. 31 of *The Newcomes,* reference is made to an analogous Parisian institution, the *bureaux de convenance.*

26. The theme of the marriage mart recurs in novels advertised in *The Newcomes. The Fair Carew; or, Husbands and Wives* opens: "Marriage . . . that stumbling block to many a family in its march to preferment proved in most instances a useful auxiliary to the Luttrels, a circumspect prudence governing their conduct in this as in other matters of business." Pisistratus Caxton is dismayed to hear the name of his ladylove bandied about at the Opera House as one of the most desirable heiresses in England by two young loungers who hope to marry wealth and who express the opinion that "one ought to be an earl at least to aspire to Fanny Trevanion." In Coulton's *Fortune* a group of cynics at an evening party exchange such pearls as: "The heart of every woman is for sale"; "Marriage is as much a barter as any transaction concluded between Baring and Rothschild"; "Cupid, blind though he be, does not look favorably on inequality of condition, and Hymen abhors it."

27. Richard Simpson saw in Clive a partial "autobiographical portrait" of his creator, representing "the reaction of youth and health, of the love of energy, of art, of beauty, against the pale cast of thought which sicklies over the portrait of Pendennis" ("Thackeray" [obituary], *Home and Foreign Review* 4 [April 1864]: 492).

28. February 1849, *Letters,* 2:503.

29. A number of novels of this decade deal with artists struggling either to find their vocation or to establish status: e.g. Lady Georgina Fullerton's *Lady Bird* (1852); Anna Harriet Drury's *Light and Shade; or, The Young Artist* (1852); Julia Kavanagh's

Daisy Burns (1853); and Amelia Edwards's *My Brother's Wife; a Life History* (1855), which deals with a Dionysian painter, the direct antithesis of Clive. See Ross, "Minor English Novels of the Eighteen-Fifties," chap. 7. The young Burne-Jones, reviewing *The Newcomes* as a student, was inspired by the elevated position Thackeray accorded the artist (*Oxford and Cambridge Magazine* 1 [January 1856]: 50–61).

30. Pendennis refers to "the magnificent bankers and manufacturers" of Newcome who "would give their thousand guineas for a picture or statue, and write you a cheque for ten times the amount any day" (chap. 55). Clive's uncles apparently are not among them.

31. Quoted in Graham Reynolds, *Victorian Painting* (London: Studio Vista, 1966), p. 94.

32. Quoted ibid. Redgrave was among the artists on whom Thackeray contributed an appreciative piece in Louis Marvy's *Sketches After English Landscape Painters*. Here he described Redgrave's work as "chiefly character pieces of the pathetic and domestic cast."

33. See above, p. 69.

34. "On the French School of Painting," *Works*, 5:45.

35. See above, p. 63. In "On Men and Pictures" Thackeray expressed the opinion that in portrait painting "our English painters keep the lead still" over their continental rivals (*Works*, 13:381).

36. The corresponding plate for vol. 1, entitled "J. J. in Dreamland," shows Clive's friend and companion in a trance surrounded by figures conjured up by his imagination. Thackeray at one time contemplated a sequel to *The Newcomes* centered on Ridley, who is represented as a more respected artist than Clive but remains a rather shadowy figure in this novel. J. R. Harvey has suggested that Ridley was intended as a representation of Doyle (*Victorian Novelists and Their Illustrators* [London: Sidgwick and Jackson, 1971], p. 95); see also Anthony Burton, "Thackeray's Collaborations with Cruikshank, Doyle, and Walker," *Costerus*, n.s. 2 (1974): 167–74.

37. *Putnam's Monthly Magazine* 1 (April 1853): 371–73; *Knickerbocker* 42 (August 1853): 155–59. Paraphrased in Dudley Flamm, *Thackeray's Critics* (Chapel Hill: University of North Carolina Press, 1967).

38. Mrs. Oliphant, "Mr. Thackeray and His Novels," p. 90.

39. Whitwell Elwin in *Quarterly Review* 97 (September 1855): 366.

40. "Jerome Paturot," *Works*, 13:386.

41. *Blackwood's Magazine*, January 1855, p. 93; *Times*, 29 August 1855, p. 5; *North American Review* 82 (January 1856): 284; Parke Godwin in *Putnam's Monthly Magazine* 6 (September 1855): 283–90.

42. George Saintsbury, introduction to *The Newcomes*, Oxford Thackeray, 15:xiv. For an intransigent antisentimentalist, see Russell A. Fraser, "Sentimentality in Thackeray's 'The Newcomes,'" *Nineteenth-Century Fiction* 4 (1949): 187–96. Fraser criticizes the novel completely out of the context of its period, and also fails to take into consideration that it is being told from the point of view of Arthur Pendennis, who is establishing his sympathy with the human condition.

43. Most of what has survived from the original manuscript (fourteen chapters of vol. 1, twenty-three chapers of vol. 2) is in the library of Charterhouse School, now in Godalming, Surrey. Why this significant passage should have been omitted cannot be determined—perhaps to allow for the paragraphs that conclude the chapter, beginning with Sir Brian's "'The spirit of radicalism is abroad in this country,'" which were added in press.

44. See above, pp. 31–32.

45. J. H. Stocqueler, *The British Officer*, p. 5.

46. Samuel Warren, *The Intellectual and Moral Development of the Present Age* (Edinburgh: William Blackwood & Sons, 1854), p. 11. This lecture was delivered before the Literary and Philosophical Society of Hull. Thackeray himself was in America at the time of the duke's funeral, but an ode, "Weep, Albion, weep!", that appeared in the *Globe* on the day of the ceremony (18 November 1852) has been attributed to him (see Harold C. Gulliver, *Thackeray's Literary Apprenticeship* [Valdosta, Ga.: Southern Stationery and Printing Co., 1934], pp. 164–67).

47. Warren, *The Intellectual and Moral Development of the Present Age,* p. 11.

48. This whole treatment of the colonel's death stands out in stark contrast to Lady Kew's funeral (chap. 55), quite fittingly headed by a picture of a weeping crocodile. Cf. also the brief dismissal of the last days of Major Pendennis at the end of chap. 49, a sure sign that Arthur has parted company with the "worldly philosophy."

49. In a letter written on Christmas Day 1849 to Mrs. Brookfield, he wrote: "I think that cushion-thumpers and high and Low Church exstatics have often carried what they call their love for △ to what seems Impertinence to me . . . the wretched canting Fakeers of Christianism, the Convent & conventicle dervishes they are only less unreasonable now than the Eremites and holy women who whipped & starved themselves, never washed, and encouraged vermin for the Glory of God. What a history that is in the Thos à Kempis book. The scheme of that book carried out would make the world the most wretched, useless, dreary, doting place of sojourn,—there would be no manhood, no love no tender ties of mother & child, no use of intellect, no trade, or science—a set of selfish beings crawling about avoiding one another, and howling a perpetual miserere" (*Letters,* 2:615–16). Although devout, Thackeray definitely kept his eye on things of this world, though he could be hard also on those who take the easy way (the Reverend Honeyman, a false "cushion-thumper").

50. The accompanying plate, the last in the book, shows Tommy kneeling in prayer at the colonel's bedside while the colonel sits hunched over and haggard in his chair and Clive looks sadly down at him.

51. The playing off by Madame d'Ivry of one lover against another, and the ensuing duel, are reminiscent of Horace de Viel-Castel's *Le faubourg St. Germain.* This type of intrigue figures also in Charles de Bernard's *Gerfaut.* See Thackeray's essay "On Some French Fashionable Novels" and above, pp. 249–50.

52. The first part of that supreme paean to marriage, *The Angel in the House,* by Coventry Patmore, came out in 1854. Its author was one of the most favorable reviewers of *The Newcomes* (see below, n. 54). Even Major Pendennis joins the throng of worshippers in his deathbed recantation: "I had other views for you, my boy, and once hoped to see you in a higher position in life; but I began to think now, Arthur, that I was wrong; and as for that girl, sir, I am sure she is an angel" (chap. 49).

We are assured that the reformed rake Lord Kew is settled down to marital bliss with the sister of Lady Clara, but are spared a visit to their household.

53. "On Some French Fashionable Novels," *Works,* 5:84.

54. Coventry Patmore, "Fielding and Thackeray," *North British Review* 55 (November 1855): 197–98. To illustrate the moral range of *The Newcomes,* Patmore classified its characters as "good" (Colonel Newcome, Ethel, Arthur and Laura, J. J. Ridley, Martha Honeyman, and the Countess of Florac), "mixed" (Bayham, Sherrick, De Florac, Lord Kew, Lady Walham), and "abominable" (Barnes, Mrs. Mackenzie, Mrs. Hobson Newcome, Lady Kew).

55. Saintsbury, introduction, Oxford Thackeray, 15:xv. Some of the unfavorable response that it met at the time of its publication, including that of Dickens who was then writing in *Household Words* against the administration of charity at Charterhouse, is summarized by Lionel Stevenson in *The Showman of Vanity Fair* (New York: Charles Scribner's Sons, 1947), pp. 299–300.

56. In John Dodds's judgment: "It is difficult to compare *Vanity Fair* and *The Newcomes.* Each is great in its own way, for similar and for different qualities. Thackeray never went higher than the former, nor deeper than the latter" (*Thackeray: A Critical Portrait* [New York: Oxford University Press, 1941], p. 210). Despite this praise, *The Newcomes* has been strangely neglected in critical discussion, but it is gratifying to see tribute paid to it in two more recent monographs, Juliet McMaster's *Thackeray: The Major Novels* (Toronto: University of Toronto Press, 1971) and Barbara Hardy's *The Exposure of Luxury* (London: Athlone Press, 1972). A stimulating article is Jean Sudrann's "'The Philosopher's Property': Thackeray and the Uses of Time," *Victorian Studies* 10 (June 1967): 359–88. R. D. McMaster analyzes its aesthetic theories in "The Pygmalion Motif in *The Newcomes,*" *Nineteenth-Century Fiction* 29 (June 1974): 22–39; in "'An Honorable Emulation of the Author of *The Newcomes*' . . .," *Nineteenth-Century Fiction* 32 (March 1978): 399–419, McMaster coun-

teracts the "loose baggy monster" stigma by pointing out evidence of the influence of *The Newcomes* on Henry James, notably in *Roderick Hudson* and *The American*. In "The Challenges of Serialization: Parts 4, 5, and 6 of *The Newcomes*," *Nineteenth-Century Fiction* 29 (June 1974): 3–21, Edgar F. Harden studies the changes Thackeray made in manuscript, necessitated sometimes by miscalculations about the lengths of numbers. Harden's investigation is continued for later numbers in *Huntington Library Quarterly* 39 (February 1976): 203–18, and *Studies in English Literature* 16 (Autumn 1976): 613–30. In a more recent textual study, "William Makepeace Thackeray's *The Newcomes* in America," *Proof* 5 (Columbia, S.C.: J. Faust & Co., 1977): 45–56, Elizabeth James points out the differences between the first American printing in *Harper's New Monthly Magazine,* based on the manuscript, and the first English edition, which incorporates Thackeray's revisions made in the proof stage.

57. 7 August 1853, *Letters,* 3:299; 4–5 July 1853, *Letters,* 3:284.

58. Introduction to *The Newcomes, Works,* 8:xxxviii. According to another received account, Thackeray was found weeping by a housekeeper after he had completed the writing of the colonel's death.

59. 2 July 1855 to Kate Perry, *Letters,* 3:459.

60. Toward the end of "Concluding Observations on Snobs," Thackeray wrote: "A court system that sends men of genius to the second table, I hold to be a Snobbish system. A society that sets up to be polite, and ignores Arts and Letters, I hold to be a Snobbish society" (*Works,* 6:464). Cousin's *Du vrai, du beau, et du bien,* incidentally, was reissued in 1853.

THE VIRGINIANS: THE OLD WORLD
AND THE NEW

Chapter Twelve

DURING THE SUMMER OF 1855, WITH "THE Newcomes" completed, Thackeray busied himself preparing another set of historical lectures that had been on his mind for some time, and by the fall of that year he was once more traveling around the eastern seaboard of the United States, this time, as he later wrote, "killing & eating the Georges."[1] This tour took him to the South, especially to Virginia, where, in his usual way, he benefited from association with fellow writers. While he was in Richmond, the consul there happened to be G. P. R. James, a close friend despite "Barbazure." According to contemporary report, the two conversed several times over cigars, but unfortunately what they talked about is not on record. In "The Esmonds of Virginia," the preface to *Henry Esmond* supposedly penned by Henry's daughter Rachel, readers had been led to expect a sequel involving Rachel's two sons, and perhaps now Thackeray was reminded of James's historical romance *Henry Masterton*, reprinted earlier in the decade, centering on two brothers of antithetical temperaments who, like George and Harry Warrington of *The Virginians*, find themselves on opposite sides in a revolution.[2] While lecturing in Virginia, Thackeray was friendly also with one of her native writers, John Esten Cooke, whose *The Virginia Comedians; or, Old Days in the Old Dominion*, a historical romance looking back over the sunset of the Tidewater aristocracy, had been published the year before. With its narrator whose imagination is carried back to the last century by ancestral portraits on his walls, and who purports to be editing a manuscript left behind by one of his kinfolk, *The Virginia Comedians* anticipates the framework of Thackeray's novel that grew out of his American experience.[3] Also evocative for Thackeray was a book by another of his literary hosts, John Pendleton Kennedy, *Swallow Barn; or, Days in the Old Dominion*, characterized by its author as "a book of travels, a diary, a collection of letters, a drama, and a history," preserving a rural Virginia that had faded from men's memories, "the mellow, bland, and sunny luxuriance of her old-time society—its good fellowship, its hearty and constitutional companionableness, the thrifty gayety of the people, their dogged but amiable invincibility of opinion, and that overflowing hospitality that knew no ebb" (some of which Thackeray tries to convey, particularly in his chapter entitled "Hospitalities").[4]

While in the last stages of composing *The Virginians*, Thackeray wrote to a friend about "all the trouble I take," and from all accounts it can rate as the most thoroughly researched of his novels. John Reuben Thompson, editor of the *Southern Literary Messenger*, made available the resources of the Virginia State Library, of which he was director.[5] John Pendleton Kennedy lent him several source books besides conducting him around plantations to give him the feel of the local topography.[6] Suggestions for the Lambert family, whose daughters are courted by George and Harry, have been traced to a book by another friend, the diplomat William Bradford Reed's *The Life of Esther de Berdt*, commemorating an English ancestor who emigrated to America as a young bride.[7] Reed also furnished Thackeray with information about old Virginia families. One of these accounts, concerned with two brothers, George and Bryan Fairfax, the first of whom went back to England in an attempt to take possession of an ancestral estate, supplied him with a part of his narrative line.

A surviving notebook that Thackeray compiled for the novel indicates a passion for fact rivaling Scott's.[8] Here one finds a table of the Hanoverian succession; samples of Queen Caroline's bad French spelling (both taken from Kemble's State Papers); notes on such customs as public bathing and the practice of removing boots before approaching the royal family; drawings of a sailor in the year 1761, of the Duke of Cumberland with a pigtail hanging down his back, and of the statesman William Pitt (whom George Warrington glimpses briefly on a visit to Kensington Palace); and notices copied from the *Public Advertiser* of 1756 (a newspaper read also by Harry Warrington) relating to productions at Drury Lane and Covent Garden (attended by George and Harry together with the Lamberts), a peruke sale in Lombard Street, and an eyewitness account of the execution of Dr. Dodd. A description of Southampton Row in 1759 is transferred from Thomas Gray's *Letters* to George Warrington's account of his lodgings near his favorite haunt, the newly opened British Museum (chaps. 59, 63, 67). From Robert Beverley's *History of Virginia*, Thackeray learns that Charles II was proclaimed king in Virginia by her royal governor before he was crowned in England (a detail used in chap. 3 of *The Virginians*).[9] Bancroft's *History of the American Republic* provides him with background on schooling in colonial Virginia (useful in connection with the schooling of George and Harry), and acquaints him with the clamor already manifesting itself in the colonies by 1754 for taxation by Parliament rather than by the king. If history tends to swamp story in *The Virginians* (". . . here is a third of the great story done equal to two-thirds of an ordinary novel—and nothing has actually happened except that a young gentleman has come from America to England," he remarked in connection with Harry's narrative that makes up the first section),[10] a concomitant reward is its solidity of texture and concreteness that accumulated out of painstaking documentation.

Thackeray had the projected sequel to *Esmond* on his mind in a letter he wrote to the publisher George Smith while on his lecture circuit: "On my own account I propose to sell you an edition of 'The Georges. Sketches of Courts, Manners, and Town Life,' and if I do a book of travels, I shall bring it to you, but this is hardly likely. I shall more likely do the Esmonds of Virginia, and it will depend on the size to which it goes whether it shall appear in 3 vols, or 20 numbers." Hence one is not surprised that the research that went into *The Four Georges* also entered, along with Thackeray's impressions of and reading about America, the ensuing novel, retitled *The Virginians: A Tale of the Last Century*, which began to emerge in November 1857 in the familiar yellow wrappers and was not completed until two years later, the author having gathered enough matter to stretch the book out over twenty-four numbers.[11] "Not about battles, about politics, about statesmen and measures of State, did I ever think to lecture: but to sketch the manners and life of the old world: to amuse for a few hours with talk about the old society: and with the result of many a day's and night's pleasant reading, to try and while away a few winter evenings for my hearers," opens the first of the lectures.[12] A good amount of this chat about "manners and life of the old world" is heard in the novel, more even than in *Henry Esmond*, and from a different perspective:

"Of a society so vast, busy, brilliant, it is impossible in four brief chapters to give a complete notion; but we may peep here and there into that byegone world of the Georges, see what they and their Courts were like; glance at the people round about them; look at past manners, fashions, pleasures, and contrast them with our own."

The lecturer's vantage point here is precisely that of the narrator of *The Virginians* who is not, like Henry Esmond, *of* the period he is writing about but apart from it, looking back over a world now dead: "Dear kind reader (with whom I love to talk from time to time, stepping down from the stage, where our figures are performing, attired in the habits and using the parlance of past ages . . .)" (chap. 62). As mediator between then and now, he makes us constantly aware of "that Old World from which we are drifting away so swiftly," represented by the Warrington brothers, whose papers he is supposedly editing. "And the high-road, a hundred years ago, was not that grass-grown desert of the present time," he takes occasion to observe in connection with Harry's visit to the mother country. "It was alive with constant travel and traffic: the country towns and inns swarmed with life and gaiety" (chap. 1). Life was slower moving then: "The ponderous waggon, with its bells and plodding team; the light post-coach that achieved the journey from the 'White Hart,' Salisbury, to the 'Swan with the Two Necks,' London in two days; the strings of pack-horses that had not yet left the road; my Lord's gilt post-chaise and six, with the outriders galloping on ahead; the country squire's great coach and heavy Flanders mares; the farmers trotting to market, or the parson jolting to the cathedral town on Dumpling, his wife behind on the pillion—all these crowding sights and brisk people greeted the young traveller on his summer journey." He calls attention to outmoded dress: "We must fancy our American traveller to be a handsome young fellow, whose suit of sables only made him look the more interesting." Charming period "characters" are quickened into life: "The plump landlady from her bar, surrounded by her china and punch-bowls, and stout gilded bottles of strong waters, and glittering rows of silver flagons, looked kindly after the young gentleman as he passed through the inn-hall from the post-chaise, and the obsequious chamberlain bowed him upstairs to the 'Rose' or the 'Dolphin.' The trim chambermaid dropped her best curtsey for his fee, and Gumbo, in the inn-kitchen, where the townfolk drank their mug of ale by the great fire, bragged of his young master's splendid house in Virginia."

"The question of Slavery was not born at the time of which we write," the author reminds his readers in a later chapter, touching on a rife social issue prompted by the recurrent presence of the servile Gumbo. "To be the proprietor of black servants shocked the feelings of no Virginia gentleman. . . . You might have preached negro emancipation to Madam Esmond of Castlewood as you might have told her to let the horses run loose out of her stables; she had no doubt but that the whip and the cornbag were good for both" (chap. 3). In England Harriet Beecher Stowe had spoken to crowds several years before[13] and an Emancipation Bill had been passed more than two decades earlier; in America north of the Mason-Dixon Line the abolition movement was active; south of it planters were still clinging to what the narrator describes as a "patriarchal" and "feudal" society. Thackeray was aware that he was writing to audiences variously disposed on this question, and he made some attempt to avoid ruffled feelings. He is quick to point out: ". . . nor in truth was the despotism exercised on the negroes generally a savage one." In his first chapter it is made clear that although the Esmonds of Virginia own slaves, they do not favor the slave trade. In reply to an offer by the trader and shipowner Mr. Trail for "any number of healthy young negroes before next fall," Harry declares: "We are averse to the purchase of negroes from Africa. . . . My grandfather and my father have always objected to it, and I do not like to think of selling or buying the poor wretches." (In the manuscript the last phrase originally read "poor devils.")[14] In a much later chapter he notes a greater tolerance on his side of the ocean: "I believe Europe has never been so squeamish in regard to Africa, as a certain other respected Quarter. Nay some Africans—witness the Chevalier de St. Georges, for instance—have been notorious favourites with the fair sex" (chap. 64). However, presumably in deference to his Southern readers, he lined out this passage that follows in the manuscript: "who love contrast doubtless and who rebuke the haughtiness of the owner by their tenderness towards the poor negro: They seem to say to his master: 'Tyrant': They consider this (coloured) gentleman is not only your Man, but he is your brother!"[15]

In England the affairs of the rakish Will Castlewood bring up a topic close to Thackeray's own interest—the shift of sensibility and taste in the area of "pleasures" from the last century to his own: "A hundred years ago his character and actions might have been described at length by the painter of manners: but the Comic Muse, now-a-days, does not lift up Molly Seagrim's curtain; she only indicates the presence of some one behind it, and passes on primly, with expressions of horror, and a fan before her eyes" (chap. 20). "Did you ever hear of such books as 'Clarissa,' 'Tom Jones,' 'Roderick Random': paintings by contemporary artists, of the men and women, the life and society of their day?" he queries his readers at the beginning of a number. "Suppose we were to describe the doings of such a person as Mr. Lovelace, or my Lady Bellaston, or that wonderful 'Lady of Quality' who lost her memoirs to the author of 'Peregrine Pickle.' How the pure and outraged Nineteenth Century would blush, scream, run out of the room, call away the young ladies, and order Mr. Mudie never to send one of that odious author's books again!" (chap. 41).

Such observations lead into the general question: "And in public and private morality? Which is better, this actual year 1858, or its predecessor a century back?" And he answers it in characteristic eclectic fashion:

> Do you remember our great theatres thirty years ago? You were too good to go to a play. Well, you have no idea what the playhouses were, or what the green boxes were, when Garrick and Mrs. Pritchard were playing before them! And I, for my children's sake, thank that good Actor in his retirement who was the first to banish that shame from the theatre. No, madam, you are mistaken; I do *not* plume myself on my superior virtue. I do not say that you are naturally better than your ancestress in her wild, rouged, gambling, flaring tearing days; or even than poor Polly Fogle, who is just taken up for shoplifting, and would have been hanged for it a hundred years ago. Only I am heartily thankful that my temptations are less, having quite enough to do with those of the present century.

In one respect at least he notes a sign of improvement: "Well, at any rate, Art has obtained her letters of naturalization, and lives on terms of almost equality. If Mrs. Thrale chose to marry a music master now, I don't think her friends would shudder at the mention of her name. If she had a good fortune and kept a good cook, people would even go and dine with her in spite of the *mésalliance*, and actually treat Mr. Thrale with civility."

The Virginians slowly unfolds a panorama of social life and manners on both sides of the Atlantic from the middle to the late eighteenth century, but it does not wholly ignore "battles, politics . . . statesmen and measures of State." We can barely hear ancestral voices prophesying war at the outset when Old England and the Old Dominion are still one:

> Mr. Esmond called his American house Castlewood, from the patrimonial home in the old country. The whole usages of Virginia,

indeed, were fondly modelled after the English customs. It was a loyal colony. The Virginians boasted that King Charles the Second had been King in Virginia before he had been King in England. English King and English Church were faithfully honoured there. The resident gentry were allied to good English families. They held their heads above the Dutch traders of New York, and the money-getting Roundheads of Pennsylvania and New England. Never were people less republican than those of the great province which was soon to be foremost in the memorable revolt against the British Crown. (Chap. 3)

By the time that George and Harry Warrington have reached full manhood they, along with their fellow colonists, have sung "The Last of God Save the King" (as chap. 67 is entitled), but during their boyhood:

> The gentry of Virginia dwelt on their great lands after a fashion almost patriarchal. For its rough cultivation, each estate had a multitude of hands—of purchased and assigned servants—who were subject to the command of the master. Their lands yielded their food, live stock, and game. The great rivers swarmed with fish for the taking. From their banks the passage home was clear. The ships took the tobacco off their private wharves on the banks of the Potomac or the James River, and carried it to London or Bristol, —bringing back English goods and articles of home manufacture in return for the only produce which the Virginian gentry chose to cultivate. Their hospitality was boundless. No stranger was ever sent away from their gates. The gentry received one another, and travelled to each other's houses in a state almost feudal. . . . The food was plenty, the poor black people lazy and not unhappy.

In its amplitude and plenitude, the sprawling new land is likened to the biblical promised land flowing with milk and honey, and at the same time is envisioned as an embryonic society struggling to be born. "It was the period of the culmination of the old social *régime*," Thackeray had read at the beginning of John Esten Cooke's *The Virginia Comedians*. Cooke also waxes nostalgic: "A splendid society had burst into flower, and was enjoying itself in the sunshine and under the blue skies of the most beautiful of lands. The chill winds of the Revolution were about to blow, but no one suspected it. Life was easy and full of laughter—of cordial greetings, grand assemblies, and the zest of existence which springs from the absence of care. . . . In town and country life was a pageant." And we can visualize it as this idyll continues: "His Excellency the Royal Governor went in his coach-and-six to open the Burgesses. The youths in embroidered waistcoats made love to the little beauties in curls and roses. The 'Apollo' rang with music, the theatre on Gloucester

Street with thunders of applause; and the houses of the planters were as full of rejoicing."

Here and there Thackeray affords us a glimpse of the "pageant" of life that Cooke displayed in his romance of these times—such as the grand governor's assemblies in Jamestown attended by Madam Esmond, and General Braddock's levees in Alexandria that George and Harry are invited to. In one of the pictorial initials a youth in embroidered waistcoat is shown kissing the hand of a beauty in curls and roses; in another a magnificently attired Rachel Esmond is shown receiving the young Colonel Washington in the covered gallery of her great house (chap. 8). But generally his picture of pre-Revolutionary Virginia stresses the plainer, more practical side of life. The initial C that opens chapter 2 encloses a sober Colonel Esmond in plain black braodcloth, black hat, black stockings, his young grandsons at his knees. In other initials we see a trapper in rough garb (chap. 7), two negro boys capturing barnyard fowl (chap. 10), an Indian scout peering through a tree (chap. 12), and a galloping post boy sounding his horn (chap. 30). The predominating impression we get of "homely simplicity" and primitivism in the New World falls in with Thackeray's intention of contrasting the vitality of the emergent country with the decadence of the aristocratic society across the sea. Moreover, George's military adventures in the armies of Colonel Washington and General Braddock presage the turbulence to come. The glamorous pageant and sunshine that Cooke described was only "what may be seen on the surface of society . . . but that social organization had reached a stage when the elements of destruction had already begun their work," as he was quick to point out in the introduciton to his *The Virginia Comedians*. To those with an ear to the ground, "new ideas were on the march. The spirit of change was under the calm surface. The political agitation soon to burst forth was preceded by the social. . . . On the surface the era is tranquil, but beneath is the volcano. Passions smoulder under the laughter; the home-spun coat jostles the embroidered waistcoat; men are demanding social equality, as they will soon demand a republic, and the splendid old *régime* is about to vanish in the storm of the Revolution."[16]

"I know the fatal differences which separated [my sons] in politics never disunited their hearts; and I . . . can love them both, whether wearing the King's colours or the Republic's," wrote Rachel Esmond in the preface to her father's memoir. So it was foreshadowed that the Revolutionary War would figure in the sequel, and *The Four Georges*, particularly the lecture "George the

Third," revived this great event in the memories of Thackeray's audiences on both sides of the ocean. Inevitably, then, the affairs of court and camp intrude on the lives of the Esmonds, but by his reliance on family documents, the author does all he can to lend human interest to his chronicle: "Their lot brought them into contact with personages of whom we read only in books, who seem alive, as I read in the Virginians' letters regarding them, whose voices I almost fancy I hear, as I read the yellow pages written scores of years since, blotted with boyish tears of disappointed passion dutifully despatched after famous balls and ceremonies of the grand Old World, scribbled by camp-fires, or out of prison: nay, there is one that has a bullet through it, and of which a greater portion of the text is blotted out with the blood of the bearer" (chap. 1). Appropriately we owe the preservation of these letters not to an archivist or scholar, but to the "affectionate thrift" of the mother of the two young men.[17] So the domestic history promised by Thackeray's original title becomes amalgamated with social, political, and military history.

In his approach to "battles, politics . . . statesmen and measures of state," Thackeray was moving with a trend well exemplified by one of the books promoted through the *Virginians Advertiser*, Charles Knight's widely read *Popular History of England*, written with the intent to "connect domestic matters with the course of public events and the political condition of various classes of society—to trace the essential connection between Government and the people, and to study events and institutions not as abstract facts, but as influencing the condition of the whole nation."[18] In *The Virginians* certainly every effort is made to establish these connections. The social classes are represented both in the mother country and in the colony, from slaves and servants to aristocrats. Of domesticity we get aplenty, beginning with the "training up" of Rachel's two boys, and following through with their flirtations, courtships, and, with George, early married life. We peep inside the homes of the Esmonds in Virginia, the Castlewoods both in town (London, Kensington) and country (Tunbridge Wells), the Miles Warringtons (from the other side of the family), as well as the Lamberts in Oakhurst, learning en route how they dress, furnish their rooms, and amuse themselves. It is left mainly to George and Harry, shunted from home to society to battlefield, to link up "domestic matters" with "the course of public events."

Not only is the domestic sphere enlarged by its absorption into the grand orbit of Anglo-American relations, but with the Esmond household we can "trace the essential connection between Government and the people," for it in itself constitutes a little nation:

> When the boys' grandfather died, their mother, in great state, proclaimed her eldest son George her successor and heir of the estate; and Harry, George's younger brother by half-an-hour, was always enjoined to respect his senior. All the household was equally instructed to pay him honour; the negroes, of whom there was a large and happy family, and the assigned servants from Europe whose lot was made as bearable as it might be under the government of the Lady of Castlewood. (Chap. 3)

Rachel Esmond, moreover, is monarch of all she surveys:

> Yonder I fancy [Rachel] enthroned in her principality of Castlewood, the country gentlefolks paying her court, the sons dutiful to her, the domestics tumbling over each other's black heels to do her bidding, the poor whites grateful for her bounty and implicitly taking her doses when they were ill, the smaller gentry always acquiescing in her remarks, and for ever letting her win at backgammon. . . . The truth is, little Madame Esmond never came near man or woman, but she tried to domineer over them. (Chap. 4)[19]

> Have we not read how Queen Elizabeth was a perfectly sensible woman of business, and was pleased to inspire not only terror and awe, but love in the bosoms of her subjects? So the little Virginian princess had her favourites, and accepted their flatteries, and grew tired of them, and was cruel or kind to them as suited her wayward imperial humour. There was no amount of compliment she would not graciously receive and take as her due. (Chap. 5)

As with many another tyrant, Rachel Esmond's authority does not go unchallenged. Quite early, in the chapter from which the above quotation is taken (entitled "Family Jars"), we indeed witness a palace revolt when George smashes a family heirloom in defiance of his mother, and Harry strikes their tutor and spiritual counselor who has attempted to cane George in punishment. At this point Rachel capitulates: "Her power over [George] was gone. He had dominated her. She was not sorry for the defeat; for women like not only to conquer, but to be conquered; and from that day the young man was master at Castlewood." In vain does Mr. Ward preach subsequently "on the beauty of subordination, the present lax spirit of the age, and the necessity of obeying our spiritual and temporal rulers" at a time when George and Harry defy both. "'For, my dear friends,' [Ward] nobly asked . . . 'why are governors appointed, but that we should be governed? Why are tutors engaged, but that children should be taught?'" Ward himself leaves Castlewood at the end of this episode, abdicating his spiritual rule over the boys, just as Rachel has had to give up her temporal authority. The rebellion of youth that engendered the domestic drama of *The Newcomes* takes on a grander significance in this novel. We see enacted on a small scale in this rural Virginia estate the larger, more encompassing political revolution that furnishes the background of the tale in which an emergent young nation finds its own strength and casts off the authority of an old nation.

Setting the coming of age of the prototypical Harry and George Warrington against the tumultuous background of the Seven Years' War and the War of Independence, *The Virginians* also grafts a novel of education onto a historical romance in the manner that nineteenth-century readers had grown accustomed to since *Waverley*. The opening episodes notified readers immediately that the twin sons of Rachel Esmond Warrington, no less than their counterparts in Thackeray's "modern" novels, are subjected to tutelage by their elders and others whom they brush against on the skirts of history. In this respect, too, *The Virginians* offers a diverting study in contrasts. Of the worldly Baroness Bernstein née Beatrix Esmond, whom Harry meets for the first time in her dotage on his visit to England, we are told in a delicious understatement: "She was not a rigorous old moralist, nor, perhaps, a very wholesome preceptress for youth" (chap. 28). As an urban libertine she is the direct antithesis to her countrified half sister Rachel, who in the New World has come under the influence of the evangelical pastor Mr. Ward: "To be for ever applying to the Sacred Oracles, and accommodating their sentences to your purpose—to be for ever taking Heaven into your confidence about your private affairs, and passionately calling for its interference in your family quarrels and difficulties—to be so familiar with its designs and schemes as to be able to threaten your neighbour with its thunders, and to know precisely its intentions regarding him and others who differ from your infallible opinion—this was the schooling which our simple widow had received from her impetuous spiritual guide, and I doubt whether it brought much comfort" (chap. 5).

As against the strictness represented by Madam Esmond, her father, Henry, "of a sceptical turn of mind on many points," leans more on the side of what our age calls permissiveness. If he still would not go along with the moral principles of his erstwhile inamorata Beatrix, and is still more Hebraist than Hellenist in his own code of life, he seems to side with the baroness when it comes to handling the young: "It was Colonel Esmond's nature, as he owned in his own biography, always to be led by a woman; and his wife dead, he coaxed and dandled and spoiled his daughter . . . indulging, and perhaps increasing her natural imperiousness of character, though it was his maxim that we can't change dispositions, and only make hypocrites of our children by commanding them over-much" (chap. 3). The ironical consequence of Henry's indulgence of his daughter is to make her a sterner parent.

The account of the revolution among the Esmonds of Virginia is followed by a chapter entitled "The Virginians Begin To See The World" (chap. 6), emphasizing that the most important education received by his two heroes comes when they are released from the guardianship of those three p's—parent, priest, and pedant. From among outsiders, the boys find a patron of permissiveness in, of all people, Rachel Esmond's gentleman caller George Washington, whom she naturally holds up to them as a model for emulation. When Madam Esmond expresses the hope that her son George, about to enter military service, will associate only with "gentlemen of honour and fashion," we learn through the family chronicler that Colonel Washington "had seen the gentlemen of honour and fashion in their cups, and perhaps thought that all their sayings and doings were not precisely such as would tend to instruct and edify a young man on his entrance into life; but he wisely chose to tell no tales out of school, and said that Harry and George, now they were coming into the world, must take their share of good and bad, and hear what both sorts had to say" (chap. 8). In late career, Thackeray is still having his wry way with copybook morality, these presumably being the last words his American readers must have expected to issue from the mouth of Parson Weems's pillar of sobriety and uprightness.[20]

It is George Washington nevertheless who predicts the course that the education of Harry and George is to take in the school of experience, most explicitly set forth in the chapter entitled "The Way of the World," where Harry luxuriates with his English relatives: "After a fortnight of Tunbridge, Mr. Harry had become quite a personage. He knew all the good company in the place. Was it his fault if he became acquainted with the bad likewise?" (chap. 28). We witness the trials and temptations of both George and Harry, the one initiated in a rough academy, the other in a polished one. While Harry lounges and disports himself among his kin at Castlewood Manor and Tunbridge Wells, George endures the hardships of frontier life in Penn's Woods. One vivid impression of what George goes through is conveyed by a ghastly plate (accom-

panying the false account of his death) showing him being saved
from a scalping by a redskin through the timely intervention of a
fellow soldier who plunges a sword through the savage's shoulder
(chap. 12).[21] In the next volume we learn of George's imprisonment in an Indian village (chap. 51), and a pictorial initial heading
a later chapter shows him adrift in an open boat (chap. 56). Harry's
ordeals during this period are moral rather than physical—"the
perils of gaming" and "the perils of gallantry" as the author puts it.
The pictures that head these chapters, accordingly, are more
analogical than literal. One depicts a little boy clinging to a tree on a
cliff edge, the sign in the distance reading "Man Traps" (chap. 20).
Others represent a hand holding playing cards (chap. 25); a group
of Hogarthian apprentices, framed by an initial L in the form of a
looped snake, dicing over a grave (chap. 27); a youth idling, oblivious to the church tower in the distance (chap. 29). An especially
stark one shows a young man being held up by a man in a black
mask, the initial T forming a gibbet. Then, by the lottery of life, the
situations of the two brothers are reversed, Harry joining Wolfe's
forces in America, George remaining behind in the "old Home,"
"penning sonnets to his mistress' eye-brow, mayhap . . ." (chap. 66),
until he gets briefly caught up once more in military affairs. By the
end of their respective adventures, both brothers have been educated, more or less, to perform the offices of both peace and war.

Critics of *The Virginians* commonly complain of its dissipation of
interest—the shifting of its center from Harry to George in the
midst of things, the change from omniscient to autobiographic
point of view toward the end. A greater source of dissatisfaction,
from the purely novelistic standpoint, is the slackening of tension
in the relations between the two heroes as the tale progresses. In its
early chapters, when Harry shows alternately affection, fear, and
deference toward George, we are led to expect some conflict to
build between this Jacob and Esau (to whom they are likened at one
point because of the circumstances of their birth) as they free themselves from apron strings and cassock. But if Thackeray had such
an intention he obviously gave it up,[22] for our interest in George
and Harry comes to be not so much as clashing personalities as
facets of their creator's "humorous ego." Hence the delights of the
book really spring from Thackeray's ingenuity in making Harry,
on one hand, his instrument for deflating social hypocrisy and
stuffiness, and in using George, on the other, as a spokesman for
his antiromantic outlook on life and literature.

"Society has this good at least: that it lessens our conceit, by teaching us our insignificance, and making us acquainted with our betters," interposes the narrator ironically in the midst of Harry's English adventure, to remind us that this young man is undergoing a course of continuing education in the world. "If you are a young person who reads this, depend upon it, sir, or madam, there is nothing more wholesome for you than to acknowledge and to associate with your superiors" (chap. 23). The naïve, convivial Harry, welcomed by the villagers of Castlewood for his "frank, cordial ways and honest face," is the perfect foil for his corrupt, "civilized" relatives. As we are told in the course of Harry's conversation with his "preceptress" the Baroness Bernstein at Tunbridge:

> . . . The lad had brought with him from his colonial home a stock of modesty which he still wore along with the honest home-spun linen. Libertinism was rare in those thinly-peopled regions from which he came. The vices of great cities were scarce known or practised in the rough towns of the American Continent. Harry Warrington blushed like a girl at the daring talk of his new European associates: even Aunt Bernstein's conversation and jokes astounded the young Virginian, so that the worldly old woman would call him Joseph, or simpleton. (Chap. 28)

The life-style of Harry's English cousins and their circle, to which he rapidly becomes accustomed, is graphically depicted in various plates and cuts that illustrate his capers, such as Harry taking a dancing lesson from Lady Fanny Castlewood, to the accompaniment of Lady Maria at the harpsichord (chap. 14); and Harry accepting a rose from Lady Maria on the terrace of Castlewood Manor beneath a statuette of Cupid (plate entitled "Gather Ye Rosebuds While Ye May" linking chaps. 17 and 18). The laxity of the age is suggested in the cut showing the convivial Parson Sampson sharing a bottle of burgundy with the rakish young Will Castlewood (chap. 15, "A Sunday at Castlewood"); its corruption by the plate entitled "The Ruling Passion" showing Harry with assorted "gentlemen" gathered around a card table (chap. 28), and by another, ambiguously entitled "The Vice-Queen" (chap. 34), introducing us to a buxom Lady Yarmouth, current mistress of George II, in full regalia.[23] "It was not a good time. That old world was more dissolute than ours," the narrator reminds us. "There was an old king with mistresses openly in his train, to whom the great folks of the land did honour. There was a nobility, many of whom the great folks of the land did honour. There was a nobility, many of whom were mad and reckless in the pursuit of pleasure; there was a looseness of words and acts which we must note, as faithful historians, without going into particulars, and needlessly shocking present readers" (chap. 28).

The narrator breaks off at a tantalizing point. The real shock, however, to the "present readers" must have been that, despite the analogy with "The Rake's Progress" (the title of chap. 41), Harry does not go down the inexorable road to perdition. "So if Harry Warrington rides down to Newmarket to the October meeting, and loses or wins his money there; if he makes one of a party at the 'Shakespeare' or the 'Bedford Head'; if he dines at White's Ordinary, and sits down to macco and lansquenet afterwards; if he boxes the watch, and makes his appearance at the Roundhouse," concludes the narrator in summing up the round of Harry's amusements and pleasures of the day, "if he turns out for a short space a wild, dissipated, harum-scarum young Harry Warrington; I, knowing the weakness of human nature, am not going to be surprised; and, quite aware of my own shortcomings, don't intend to be very savage at my neighbour's" (chap. 41). Once again he flouts the Grundys in his audience, those "honest readers" who may have expected him to make Harry an example: "O the Truthful, O the Beautiful, O Modesty, O Benevolence, O Pudor, O Morse, O Blushing Shame, O Namby Pamby—each with your respective capital letters to your honoured names!"

Out in the world Harry is certainly not deprived of advice from elders, both of the prudential sort, as with General Lambert and Colonel Wolfe, and the cynical, as with his cousins and his aunt, the Baroness Bernstein. Among those who take him in hand is Parson Sampson, chaplain to the Castlewoods, an earthen vessel, as we quickly recognize, unlike that disciple of George Whitefield, Mr. Ward, "keeper of the undoubted waters of Jordan," whom Rachel foists on her boys to tame their unruly spirits. We get vivid glimpses of him both on the pulpit: "Mr. Sampson . . . in his chapel in Long Acre . . . gave Sin no quarter; out-cursed Blasphemy with superior anathemas; knocked Drunkenness down, and trampled on the prostrate brute wallowing in the gutter; dragged out conjugal Infidelity, and pounded her with endless stones of rhetoric—"; and off the pulpit: "and, after service, came to dinner at the 'Star and Garter,' made a bowl of punch for Harry and his friends at the 'Bedford Head,' or took a hand at whist at Mr. Warrington's lodgings, or my Lord March's, or wherever there was a supper and good company for him" (chap. 41). However he may fall short as a man of God, Parson Sampson is no hypocrite. "I don't say, madam, my practice is good, only my doctrine is sound," he candidly admits to Lady Maria (chap. 35), and his point has already been made in the plate entitled "Preaching and Practice" (preceding chap. 29), where Harry happens upon him at cards with Will. Yet one gathers that with his determination to "speak as a one man of the world to other sinful people, who might be likely to profit from good advice" (chap. 15), Parson Sampson comes closer to Thackeray's own ideal of the "week-day preacher" than some of the more straitlaced clergymen we encounter in his novels and essays. The rub really is the inability of his congregation, particularly Harry, "to profit from good advice." The futility of all sermonizing is perhaps best demonstrated in the episode in "A Sunday at Castlewood," when the Good Parson preaches on the evils of gambling. On this occasion, Sampson piles example upon precept, relating "in a manner startling, terrible, and picturesque" an execution he had witnessed of a horse-thief. He reviews the life history of this culprit who had started life with good prospects but, tempted first by gambling and card playing, was led to crime, a course that eventually carried him down the road to Tyburn. Though the sermon is directed to Harry, with the intention of leaving him contrite, the episode ends with Harry's spirits lifted as he learns that a horse he has bet on against odds has just won that day's race (chap. 15).

The ultimate moral of this tale, as Harry is forced to fend for himself amidst the contradictory advice he receives from his "superiors," is that one learns morality from experience, not from sermons. For a while Harry seems to live a charmed life that earns him the label of The Fortunate Youth, but soon enough he learns that Lady Luck, who smiles on him for a time at the gaming table or the turf, is quick to withdraw her favors. A certain amount of Harry's success, it is true, verifies the wise observation of the wicked fairy of this fable, the Baroness Bernstein: "You are making your entry into the world, and the gold key will open most of its doors to you. To be thought rich is as good as to be rich" (chap. 24). His status as heir presumptive to the estate of the Esmonds of Virginia (the extent of which is magnified by his servant Gumbo) certainly breaks down barriers, accounting for the hospitality he enjoys from his English cousins, including the embarrassing pursuit by the Lady Maria, and the readiness of the society around Tunbridge to dance attendance upon him (even allowing him to win at cards?). Harry does follow one stage of the rake's progress—imprisonment for debt—but this turn of events serves really to expose the deficiencies of his relatives and drinking companions—all of whom let him down in his need. Naïve as he may be, Harry is clearly morally superior to his worldly companions. He gains something of a pyrrhic victory over them in addition. They become the victims of their own cupidity when Harry reverts to the status of second son with the unexpected appearance of his "dead" elder brother George. The return of George, which dramatically ends what was the first volume of *The Virginians* in its original format, also brings about the timely rescue of Harry from prison. By the caprice of fate, Harry's economic downfall brings about his moral rehabilitation. A collateral dividend is Harry's release from his rashly incurred engagement to his middle-aged cousin Maria when George informs her father Lord Castlewood that Harry is a pauper. Fortune, in the form of George, is cruel in order to be kind.

Harry serves to illustrate the observations made much later by F. Scott Fitzgerald's Nick Carraway: ". . . a sense of the fundamental decencies is parcelled out unequally at birth." At any rate Harry's "American" virtues of frankness, kindness, and honesty, together with his "modest blushing timidity," prove his saving graces, raising him in our esteem above his charming and more cultivated forebears. Having served his purpose of showing up his betters, the active Harry is displaced from center stage in favor of his more contemplative brother. Actually this shift is prepared for earlier. "I want to have a cheerful hero, though this is very difficult, for a cheerful character must have some deeper element to give dignity and interest," Thackeray confided to one of the most favorable reviewers of *The Newcomes* when he was contemplating its successor. "It is hardly possible to have a hero without a dash of melancholy. I think the cheerful man must be the second character—a good-humoured, pleasant rogue. But people are always complaining that my clever people are rascals and the good people idiots."[25] Harry is "good," but no idiot, as we have seen, and George, the "clever" brother, is no rascal. Essentially George provides the "dash of melancholy" that Thackeray felt was necessary to give dignity to his book, and it is he who lifts it above social comedy to serious commentary.

In some respects Thackeray divided himself between the two brothers, transferring different details from his own background to each. Whereas Harry had the gambling fever and squanders his patrimony, for instance, George is given to sketching, studies law in a desultory way, fritters away time reading novels, and struggles for a literary career. From the temperamental standpoint it is possible to see one aspect of Thackeray in the "good-humoured, pleasant" Harry—the naïve, convivial self that responds naturally to "what was tender, helpless, pretty, or pathetic." But surely the "peaceful, studious, and silent" George is closer to Thackeray's introspective, sophisticated, "grave-satirical" self. "'I never know whether you are laughing at me or yourself, George. . . . I never know whether you are serious or jesting,'" complains Harry at one point. "'Precisely my own case, Harry, my dear!'" is George's reply.

In the course of the novel we see something of George as soldier, as student, as courting swain, and as husband; but primarily he presents himself to us a a dramatist, memoirist, and amateur historian, and in these capacities is in a good position to express his creator's views on history, civilization, and "society in general." The characteristic iconoclasm asserts itself once more, provoked in this instance by George's disillusionment with his English cousins:

> "Are these the inheritors of noble blood?" thought George, as he went home quite late from his aunt's house, passing by doors whence the last guests of fashion were issuing, and where the chairmen were yawning over their expiring torches. "Are these the proud possessors of ancestral honours and ancient names, and were their forefathers, when in life, no better? We have our pedigree at home with noble coats-of-arms emblazoned all over the branches, and titles dating back before the Conquest and the Crusaders. When a knight of old found a friend in want, did he turn his back upon him, or an unprotected damsel, did he delude her and leave her? When a nobleman of the early time received a young kinsman, did he get the better of him at dice, and did the ancient chivalry cheat in horseflesh?" (Chap. 54)

George is not inclined to glorify himself either. Although Theo Lambert falls in love with him for the dangers he had passed, he manages to remove all the romance from his imprisonment at Duquesne, as narrated to his brother and the Lambert family. Despite expectations aroused by the Virgilian tags to these chapters ("Conticuere Omnes"; "Intentique Ora Tenebant"), George candidly affirms: "Ladies, I wish I had to offer you the account of a dreadful and tragic escape; how I slew all the sentinels of the fort; filed through the prison windows, destroyed a score or so of watchful dragons, overcame a million of dangers, and finally effected my freedom. But in regard of that matter, I have no heroic deeds to tell of, and own that, by bribery and no other means, I am where I am" (chap. 51). George suits his inaction to his word, his humdrum account (including his rescue from scalping not through his own derring-do but through that of a friend who intervenes out of an obligation incurred at cards) divesting his tale even of the excitement that Cooper might have brought to it. Furthermore, the Indian maid La Biche, of the "long straight black hair, which was usually dressed with a hair-oil or pomade by no means pleasant to approach,[26] with little eyes, with high cheek-bones, with a flat nose, sometimes ornamented with a ring . . . her cheeks and forehead gracefully tattooed, a great love of finery, and inordinate passion for . . . whisky," seems to possess a closer "fidelity to history" than Cooper's noble savages, or Chateaubriand's Atala.[27]

George tends to look with the same unglazed eyes at "battles, politics . . . statesmen" in the larger world. "How is it, and by what, and whom, that Greatness is achieved?" he asks after reading his brother's account of the Battle of Montmorenci, which brought General Wolfe glory out of defeat. "Is it Frolic or Fortune? Is it Fate that awards successes and defeats? Is it the Just Cause that ever wins? How did the French gain Canada from the savage, and we from the French, and after which of the conquests was the right time to sing Te Deum?" (chap. 74).

His subsequent animadversions on the American Revolution in the chapter entitled "In Which We Both Fight and Run Away" bring heroism in general under a cold, skeptical glare. One comment could have come out of Cousin's lecture on "Great Men," or out of Thackeray's own "near view" of history: "I pray my children may live to see or engage in no great revolutions, —such as that, for instance, raging in the country of our miserable French neighbours. Save a very few indeed, the actors in those great tragedies do not bear to be scanned too closely; the chiefs are no better than ranting quacks; the heroes ignoble puppets; the heroines anything but pure. The prize is not always to the brave."[28] George, though himself on the Loyalist side, concedes in retrospect that the victory went to the deserving, but even his tribute to the leadership of Washington emphasizes human failings: "His great and surprising triumphs were not in those rare engagements with the enemy where he obtained a trifling mastery; but over Congress; over hunger and disease; over lukewarm friends, or smiling foes in his own camp, whom his great spirit had to meet, and master" (chap. 90). The late war too leads George to philosophize on the fortuity of life's rewards: "Who has not speculated, in the course of his reading of his history, upon the 'Has been' and the 'Might have been' in the world? I take my battered old map-book from the shelf, and see the board on which the great contest was played; I wonder at the curious chances which lost it; and, putting aside any idle talk about the respective bravery of the two nations, can't but see that we had the best cards, and that we lost the game" (chap. 91). We are persuaded that "the excitement of metaphysics must equal almost that of gambling," as young Thackeray declared on first reading Cousin's *Cours de l'histoire.*

From his armchair George has been musing over the volatile half century that Thackeray looked back on from his lectern. "We have to glance over sixty years in as many minutes," opened the lecture on "George the Third." As Thackeray reminded his audience: "England has to undergo the revolt of the American colonies; to submit to defeat and separation; to shake under the volcano of the French Revolution." From this point he plunges ahead to the aftermath of these catastrophic times:

> The old society, with its courtly splendours, has to pass away; generations of statesmen to rise and disappear . . . the old poets who unite us to Queen Anne's time to sink into their graves; Johnson to die, and Scott and Byron to arise. . . . Steam has to be invented; kings to be beheaded, banished, deposed, restored. Napoleon is to be but an episode, and George III is to be alive through all these varied changes, to accompany his people through all these revolutions of thought, government, society; to survive out of the old world into ours.

The Virginians presents us then with one more episode in Thackeray's saga of "the progress of civilization and the mutations of manners," but whereas in *Vanity Fair, Pendennis,* and *The Newcomes* we have been witnesses to change taking place, *The Virginians* allows us to review and assess what has already come to pass. Arthur Pendennis's two histories gave us opportunity to contrast two generations as to ways of life and moral attitudes, but through George Warrington our historic imagination is stretched wider to take in two centuries, two countries, and two distinct cultures.

Toward the end of *The Virginians* George hails, if with some misgivings, the coming of age of the new nation in the midst of the destruction of the old order in Europe. Anne Thackeray has reminded us of the interest her father took in "that later time . . . when George III was king in England, and when America, throwing off kings altogether, preferred to elect Presidents in their place." The writing of *The Virginians* happened to coincide with Thackeray's own brief involvement with politics, which renewed his interest in the democratic process. During the summer of 1857, several months before *The Virginians* began to appear, Thackeray ran for the vacated Whig seat in Parliament from Oxford. "With no feeling but that of good will towards these leading aristocratic families who are administering the chief offices of the State," he declared in a manifesto addressed to the electors of Oxford, "I believe that it would be benefited by the skill and talents of persons less aristocratic, and that the country thinks so likewise." He would go even further, to "have the suffrage amended in nature as well as numbers, and hope to see many Educated Classes represented who have now no voice in Elections." Amidst the steeples and academic towers of this ancient seat of learning he sees a new city emerging, "peopled by thousands of hard-working, honest, rough-handed men," who "have grown up of late years, and have asserted their determination to have a representative of their own."[29] Thackeray apparently hankered at this time for a more resonant platform than the lecture circuit offered him, and to be more conspicuously in the public eye, but he lost out on his one campaign for elective office. He soon reconciled himself to this defeat, determined once more to "retire, and take my place with my pen and ink at my desk. . . ."[30]

To the Electors of the City of Oxford Thackeray had promised "to use my utmost endeavour to increase and advance the social happiness, the knowledge and the power of the people," and something of this populist zeal courses through the pages of *The Virginians* in which a stream of fresh air from the New World counteracts the odor of decay hanging over the Old. Early in the novel we have witnessed the spirit of revolt personified in young George and Harry throwing off authority; toward its end the new generation asserts its rights once more in the comely person of the countrywoman Lydia van den Bosch, heiress to the fortune of her grandfather, a self-made Dutch trader from New York. Miss van den Bosch exudes brash self-confidence in the plate where we glimpse her with head tossed back, body thrust forward as she "sailed into chapel" on the arm of her cousin George, backed up by two footmen carrying her folio-sized prayer book (chap. 73). This parvenu sails into society with equal alacrity. Her affluence provides her easy access to the abode of the Castlewoods, which she soon makes her own: "Over that apartment, and the whole house, domain and village, the new Countess speedily began to rule with unlimited sway. It was surprising how quickly she learned the ways of command; and if she did not adopt those methods of precedence usual in England among great ladies, invented regulations for herself, and promulgated them, and made others submit" (chap. 73). By this time she has literally been received into the bosom of the Castlewood family through marriage to Eugene, the eldest of the eligible sons, and proceeds to "take over": "She made the oldest established families in the country—grave baronets and their wives—worthy squires of twenty descents, who rode over to Castlewood to pay the bride and bridegroom honour—know their distance, as the phrase is, and give her the *pas*. She got an old heraldry book . . . and ere long she jabbered gules and sables, bends and saltires, not with correctness always, but with a volubility and perseverance." Before long she rivals Rachel Esmond as a power to be reckoned with: "She made little progresses to the neighbouring towns in her gilt coach and six, or to the village in her chair, and asserted a quasi-legal right of homage from her tenants and other clodpoles. She lectured the parson on his divinity; the bailiff on his farming; instructed the astonished housekeeper how to preserve and pickle . . . and as for physick, Madam Esmond in Virginia was not more resolute about her pills and draughts than Miss Lydia, the earl's new bride."

In her patronizing way Baroness Bernstein welcomes Miss van den Bosch for her "great fire and liveliness, and a Cherokee manner which is not without its charms." *"Nous la formerons cette petite,"* Beatrix proclaims with her customary assurance to nephew George; "Eugene wants character and vigour, but he is a finished gentleman, and between us we shall make the little savage perfectly presentable." The "little savage," however, has ideas of her own, as demonstrated particularly by her reaction to Harry's news of Wolfe's victory in Canada: " . . . and now we have turned the French king out of the country, shouldn't be at all surprised if we set up for ourselves in America." To her husband's shocked outcry that she is talking treason, she has a ready response:—"I'm talking reason anyhow, my lord. I've no notion of folks being kept down, and treated as children forever!" The baroness is sympathetic, admiring the "little Countess's courage and spirit in routing the Dowager and Lady Fanny," but she herself is destined also to go down in defeat. On one occasion Lydia determines to face up to "old Goody," as she calls her. "You are both afraid of her: and I ain't, that's all," she declares to George and Eugene. "I ain't a-going to bite her head off. We shall have a battle, and I intend to win." George and Eugene discretely remove themselves for some pheasant shooting, clearing the ground for the impending encounter. George's laconic dispatch set down after the event for the edification of his children reads: "Well, then, what happened I know not on that disgraceful day of panic when your father fled the field, nor dared to see the heroines engage; but when we returned from our shooting, the battle was over. America had revolted and conquered the mother country" (chap. 73).

With this mini–Revolutionary War anticipating things to come, George takes up the popular historian's obligation to "connect domestic matters with the course of public events." If his own patrician background makes Lydia's abrasive commonness somewhat repellent to him, he goes along with her protest against "folks being kept down, and treated as children forever." This attitude comes out in the somewhat unconventional advice he leaves to his children, and by extension to the rising generation as a whole. "I know that I ought to be very cautious in narrating this early part of the married life of George Warrington, Esquire, and Theodosia his wife," begins one section of his journal, "—to call out *mea culpa*, and put on a demure air, and, sitting on my comfortable easy-chair here, profess to be in a white sheet and on the stool of repentance, offering myself up as a warning to imprudent and hot-headed youth" (chap. 81). However, George thwarts the expectations of the parents among his readers by offering encouragement to the "hot-headed." He has carried his boyhood defiance of his mother into manhood by marrying a bride of his own choice rather than following her dictates. What is more, he has no regrets: ". . . truth to say, that married life, regarding which my dear relatives prophesied so gloomily, has disappointed all those prudent and respectable people. . . . To marry without a competence is wrong and dangerous, no doubt, and a crime against our social codes; but do not scores of thousands of our fellow-beings commit the crime every year with no other trust but in Heaven, health, and their labour?" In going through the family papers in his retirement, George recalls, "I found docketed and labelled with my mother's well-known neat handwriting, 'From London, April, 1760. My son's dreadful letter.'" He is referring to the letter announcing his engagement to Theo. He proceeds to explain why the letter is no longer extant: "When it came to be mine I burnt the document, not choosing that that story of domestic grief and disunion should remain amongst our family annals for future Warringtons to gaze on, mayhap, and disobedient sons to hold up as examples of foregone domestic rebellions. For similar reasons I have destroyed the paper which my mother despatched to me at this time of tyranny, revolt, annoyance, and irritation" (chap. 78).[31] So his own little declaration of independence disappears without a trace.

The youthful exuberance and rebellion that figure prominently in this "Tale of the Last Century" are harbingers in their small way of the "revolutions of thought, government, society" to come. As amateur historian, George recognizes the inevitability of change, while maintaining a lingering regard for the "Old World from which we are drifting away so swiftly." In the blunt, robust Miss van den Bosch of the "Cherokee manner" and her trading-class grandfather of "talk and appearance somewhat too homely" he shows us something of the less pleasant side of the emergent egalitarianism from the New World. However he may admire her spirit, George certainly does not share the young capitalist's contempt for tradition. "You tell me to respect old people. Why? I don't see nothin' to respect in the old people I know," Lydia protests to George just before her altercation with the baroness. "They ain't so funny, and I'm sure they ain't so handsome. Look at grandfather; look at Aunt Bernstein. They say she was a beauty once! That picture painted from her! I don't believe it nohow." Unlike his insensitive cousin by marriage George is gifted with historical imagination, which enables him to see more in Aunt Bernstein than meets the eye: "I would look in her face, and, out of the ruins, try to build up in my fancy a notion of her beauty in its prime." He rereads her life history as narrated by his grandfather Henry (more accurate, as he discovers, than her own oral account), "and my fancy wandered about in her, amused and solitary, as I had walked about her father's house at Castlewood, meditating on departing glories, and imagining ancient times" (chap. 73). The passing of an era is concentrated in a brief flash in George's mind's eye during his last glimpse of the dying Baroness Bernstein recollecting her youth in her delirium:

> Let us draw the curtain round it. I think with awe still of those rapid words, uttered in the shadow of the canopy, as my pallid wife sits by, her Prayer-book on her knee; as the attendants move to and fro noiselessly; as the clock ticks without, and strikes the fleeting hours; as the sun falls upon the Kneller picture of Beatrix in her beauty, with the blushing cheeks, the smiling lips, the waving auburn tresses, and the eyes which seem to look towards the dim figure moaning in the bed. (Chap. 83)

The plangency, mellow wisdom, and leisurely movement of this "Tale of the Last Century" was not destined to catch the crowd. "The Virginians is no doubt not a success," Thackeray wrote in a despondent mood to a friend as it was concluding its run. "It sadly lacks story, and people won't care about the old times, or all the trouble I take in describing them."[32] This novel, for which Thackeray initially received four times more than he had for *Vanity Fair*, eventually disappointed his publishers' hopes,[33] quite possibly for a reason he anticipates in an earlier letter to Mrs. Baxter: "The book's clever but stupid that's a fact. I hate story-making incidents, surprises, love-making, &c. more and more every day." It is true that he makes fewer concessions than ever here to "the lazy, novel-reading, unscientific world." The "story-making incidents," such as Harry's fall from a horse and rescue by the Lamberts and his later imprisonment, tend to be perfunctory, or, as has already been suggested in connection with George's capture by the Indians, to parody the staples of popular romances set in America. The main "surprise" of the book—George's return from the "dead"—could not have been so to any reasonably alert reader, being anticipated literally in Rachel's dream (chap. 13) and ironically in Harry's delusive prosperity.[34] The "love-making" introduced is mainly of the comic opera sort, like Lady Maria's pursuit of Harry and her subsequent marriage to the actor Hagan, or materialistic, like the rivalry of the Castlewood brothers for the hand and fortune of Lydia van den Bosch. A hint of romance is provided in such chapter headings as "The Course of True Love" and "Pyramus and Thisbe" (headed by a pictorial initial depicting these legendary lovers separated by a wall). However, interfering cousins rather than the vagaries of Eros slow the path to the altar of George and Theo, and the outcome is never much in doubt. Moreover, their courtship is glossed over in favor of their domestic difficulties ("Res Angusta Domi") on limited income. The other true love celebrated in the book—the courtship of Harry and Fanny Mountain—is briefly narrated in a letter.

The Virginians clearly is not a book one turns to for "story," as Thackeray surmised, but for much more—its thought and its rich evocation of "the old times." George as historian is clearly surrogate for Thackeray, torn between past and present, the Old World and the New, "meditating on departed glories, and imagining ancient times," yet with his double vision looking at once backward and forward, observing humanity "advance over ruins."[35] George refers toward the end of his memoir to two works in progress—a "History of the American War" and "Travels in Europe." According to his editor, "Neither of these two projected works of Sir George Warrington were brought, as it appears, to light," but it is reasonable to suppose that some of the notes for them spill over into the pages of *The Virginians*. Actually Thackeray could just as well have titled his book *The Anglo-American Sketch Book*, placing it alongside his earlier travel books with which it has much in common in its synthesis of "physical geography" with social and literary criticism, taking in "the history of religion, the history of art, the history of legislation, the history of wealth . . ." that Victor Cousin defined as the scope of the student of humanity.[36]

As with many another excursion into history, this book offers many attractive side trips. From the literary standpoint there can be no gainsaying Thackeray's aims as set forth in the opening, where the author explains his function:

> The letters of the Virginians, as the reader will presently see, from specimens to be shown to him, are by no means full. They are hints rather than descriptions—indications and outlines chiefly; it may be, that the present writer has mistaken the forms, and filled in the colour wrongly; but poring over the documents, I have tried to imagine the situation of the writer, where he was and by what persons surrounded. I have drawn the figures as I fancied they were; set down conversations as I think I might have heard them; and so, to the best of my ability, endeavoured to revivify the bygone times and people.

Little as the results may have been appreciated by his contemporaries, Thackeray opens out to view here his formula for the successful collaboration of romancer and scholar in fleshing out the "ephemeral repertories" of life. Historical memory combines with the mimetic arts, graphic ("I have drawn the figures as I fancied they were") and oral ("set down conversations as I think I might have heard them"). In their ambition "to revivify the bygone times and people," the "sham" historian and the true come together.

In this most transnational of his novels, fusing *Familienroman*, literary autobiography, and historical romance, Thackeray wrote with a distinct sense of audiences on both sides of the ocean.[37] In the letter to Mrs. Baxter remarking on the slow pace of the narrative that used up a third of its length to transport Harry from Virginia to England, Thackeray added: "I wish an elderly [gentleman] could do t'other thing, and have the strongest wish to come and see you all."[38] As things turned out, Thackeray never again got to the United States to carry out the study and observation "sur les lieux"[39] that he had begun during his tour with *The Four Georges*, to the detriment, as he was the first to concede, of the later American episodes, particularly the Revolutionary War, which seem cursory and truncated. Having already admitted to his readers his relief that Harry, during his tour on the continent, did not join the Prussian forces, "for then I should have had to describe battles which Carlyle is going to paint; and I don't wish you should make odious comparisons between me and that master" (chap. 62), Thackeray, one suspects, was just as happy not to become a rival to American military historians. He obviously feels kinship with George who, after brief participation in the battle of Fort Clinton, is *"Satis Pugnae"* and content to retire under vine and fig tree and learn war no more. His Anglo-American novel, if not the detailed history that he had originally planned, became nevertheless a substitute fulfillment of his desire "to come and see you all." It is dominated appropriately by a spirit of concord and conciliation epitomized most graphically in the wrapper design (subsequently reproduced on the title page of the second volume) showing an American and a British soldier literally extending hands across the sea. "Now my country is England, not America, or Virginia: and I take, or rather took, the English side of the dispute. My sympathies had always been with home, where I was now a squire and a citizen," George affirms, "but had my lot been to plant tobacco, and live on the banks of the James River or Potomac, no doubt my opinions had been altered. When for instance, I visited my brother at his new house and plantation, I found him and his wife as staunch Americans as we were British" (chap. 86). The "differences which separated them in politics," alluded to by their mother, prove in the long run not to be "fatal" after all.[40]

"Indeed, Mr. George has a lofty way with him, which I don't see in other people; and, in reading books, I find he chooses the fine noble things always, and loves them in spite of his satire. He certainly is of a satirical turn, but then he is only bitter against mean things and people. No gentleman hath a more tender heart I am sure." This shrewd summing up by Theo Lambert of her future husband can be taken also as Thackeray's apology for himself to his readers. George, alter ego for his creator as mediator between two eras and two generations, also afforded opportunity for Thackeray to view himself simultaneously as struggling young literary aspirant and as middle-aged armchair philosopher, fusing the themes of vitality and superannuation that run through the narrative as countermotifs. Against the comedy of youthful hope, confidence, error, and mishap is posed the pathos of age, represented at one extreme by the stoical Henry Esmond, left with some "bankruptcy of heart" as a result of which he "submitted to life, rather than enjoyed it"; at the other by his erstwhile lady love Baroness Bernstein who, sans teeth, clings to life ("I still have my cards—thank Heaven, I still have my cards!"). "To stay is well enough, but shall we be very sorry to go?" Thackeray himself wrote to a confidant, Dr. John Brown, late in 1858. "What more is there in life that we haven't tried? What that we have tried is very much worth repetition or endurance?" the letter continues, and proceeds on this tired note: "I have just come from a beefsteak and potatoes 1 f., a bottle of claret 5 f., both excellent of their kind, but we can part from them without a very severe pang. . . . What *is* a greater pleasure? Gratified ambition, accumulation of money. What? Fruition of some sort of desire, perhaps? when one is twenty, yes; but at 47 Venus may rise from the sea, and I for one should hardly put on my spectacles to have a look. Here I am snarling away on the old *poco curante* theme."[41] A certain autumnal aura that suffuses the pages of *The Virginians* reflects Thackeray's sense of time running out. A letter written during the summer of 1859 as he was bringing it to a close, makes his last major book sound almost like his elegy: "There has been nothing to say. We have gone jogging on in the old fashion. We dine out. We go to a few drums. I am ill every 5 weeks or so with my accustomed spasms—get well, plunge about while my number is in gestation—and so the moon fills and wanes, and the world wags. Next month (d.v.) Virginians will be done. Then a little rest: then next year begin again; and tomorrow and tomorrow comes until pallida mors ends them."[42] He did take up his pen again the following year, but the rest of what he had to say to his public came from the retreat of an editorial chair, and under a lengthening shadow.

1. 8 February 1857 to Frederick Cozzens, *Letters*, 4:18. These lectures are antici-pated in a satirical poem, "The Georges," that Thackeray contributed to *Punch,* October 1845, on the occasion of the unveiling of statues of these monarchs in the Parliament palace. His interest was renewed during a visit to Germany in 1852.

2. This conversation is mentioned by John Esten Cooke in "An Hour with Thackeray," *Appleton's Journal,* n.s. 22 (September 1879): 251. Cooke indicates that Thackeray had at first intended to make George and Harry rivals in love (as the brothers are in James's novel). In a speech delivered to fellow authors before setting sail for his second tour of America, Thackeray refers to the "kindly old chronicler of the lovely September or November evening when two horsemen were seen" who "serves her Majesty as one of the consuls in the United States, occupying his leisure moments by the composition & delivery of lectures of one of w^h it appears I myself have been the pleasing subject, coming in for a sound whipping as I read in a Virginia paper at the hands of that veteran romancer—and why not?—as Jack said when his 'old woman' boxed his ears—'It amuses her & it doesn't hurt me.'. . . ." (MS "Notes for a Literary Fund Speech," Taylor Collection, Princeton University).

It is amusing to note that the lecture "George the Second" opens in the G. P. R. James manner parodied in "Barbazure": "On the afternoon of the 14th of June

1727, two horsemen might have been perceived galloping along the road from Chelsea to Richmond. The foremost, cased in the jackboots of the period, was a broad-faced, jolly-looking, and very corpulent cavalier. . . ." Thus Thackeray introduces Sir Robert Walpole and his companion on their way to Richmond Lodge to announce the death of George I to the next in line.

3. *The Virginia Comedians* was published both in New York (D. Appleton) and in London in 1854. In the back of the first edition are advertised several of Thackeray's magazine writings that had been brought out in book form in Appleton's Popular Library, and the epigraph on the title page is a stanza from Thackeray's ballad "The End of the Play." The narrative is supposed to be based on a memoir left by Champ Effingham, the central figure. Cooke also refers to his book as "a family romance," allying it in genre with *The Virginians.*

4. The article on Kennedy in *Appleton's Cyclopedia of American Biography* (by John H. B. Latrobe) credits him with the writing of the episode of George's trip from Fort Duquesne to the coast to embark for England (chap. 52), but Kennedy himself recorded in his diary that Thackeray "partially incorporated" some notes he prepared for this chapter at Thackeray's request (see Lionel Stevenson, *The Showman of Vanity Fair* [New York: Charles Scribner's Sons, 1947], p. 354).

5. For most of my information on sources I am indebted to Jay B. Hubbell, "Thackeray and Virginia," *Virginia Quarterly Review* 3 (January 1927): 76–86, and Gordon N. Ray, *The Age of Wisdom* (New York: McGraw-Hill, 1958), pp. 381–86.

6. One of the books that Kennedy lent him, Graydon's *Memoirs of the Revolution,* apparently suggested a minor episode, the marriage of Lady Maria to the actor Hagan.

7. Esther's nickname, Hetty, is given to the younger of Major Lambert's daughters, who does not, however, marry either George or Harry Warrington. In a letter to Mrs. Baxter, Thackeray likened the two Lambert daughters to his own (*Letters,* 4:81).

8. "Ms. Notebook for *The Virginians,*" in the Beinecke Library, Yale University, passim. Also useful for the background of the novel is the Notebook for the Four Georges, now in the Rosenbach Library. One of the memoirists cited here, Poellnitz, appears in the Tunbridge Wells episode of *The Virginians* (chap. 26).

9. In chap. 16 Maria Castlewood consults "the 'History of Virginia' by R. B. Gent."

10. 10–23 April 1858 to Mrs. Baxter, *Letters,* 4:80–81.

11. *Letters,* 3:471. It concluded its run in October 1859, but the first volume in book form, consisting of the first twelve numbers, was published late in 1858. Bradbury and Evans, not Smith, Elder, were the publishers. The reasons for the change of format and publisher are unknown.

12. "George the First," *Works,* 7:621. The lectures were eventually published for the first time under the auspices of Smith, Elder in the *Cornhill Magazine* during Thackeray's editorship (July, August, September, October 1860).

13. In *The Newcomes,* chap. 28, the narrator refers to Lady Ann Newcome as one of those "who signed the address to Mrs. Stowe, the other day, along with thousands more virtuous British matrons."

14. The extant manuscript (about two-thirds of the novel) is in the Pierpont Morgan Library. It has been utilized by Gerald C. Sorensen in his Ph.D. dissertation, "A Critical Edition of W. M. Thackeray's *The Virginians* [Part I–III] [with] *The Virginians,* Volumes I and II, London: Bradbury and Evans, 1858" (University of Minnesota, 1966), which I have also drawn upon for its useful bibliographical history and annotation.

15. This sentence echoes the famous words uttered by Charles Yellowplush to a member of the nobility that serve as the caption for a sketch Thackeray drew for *The Book of Snobs;* cf. also the concluding sentence of *Pendennis.*

16. The hero of *The Virginian Comedians,* Champ Effingham, peruked, powered, and patched in his "figured satin waistcoat, *point de Venise* lace . . . feet cased in slippers of Spanish leather, adorned with diamond buckles," surrounded by furniture in the Louis Quatorze style, represents the decadent patrician class still clinging to Old World elegance. He is contrasted with the more virile agitators in the course of the Revolution.

17. Among these surviving letters is one by Horace Walpole to General Conway describing Henry in Tunbridge, not included in Peter Cunningham's then recent edition, this editor hastens to add (chap. 40).

18. Beginning his publishing career as printer to Lord Brougham's Society for the Diffusion of Useful Knowledge, Knight became one of the most famous autodidacts and promulgators of low-priced, serious reading of the Victorian age. His *Popular History of England* was also published by Bradbury and Evans. A review quoted in the *Virginians Advertiser* indicates that Knight followed the "familiar" approach to history advocated by Macaulay and Alison: "Mr. Knight prefers the pleasant to the stately. In his hands History lays aside her robes, her crown, and her majestic utterance; she delights to linger by the wayside, under shady branches or by old crosses or ivied porches. . . ."
Uniting the two worlds of *The Virginians* is another book advertised in no. 18 (and in vol. 2 of the first edition with Knight): *Civilized America*, by Thomas Colley Grattan, "Late Her Britannic Majesty's Consul for the State of Massachusetts." A quoted review reads: "As a book on the political and social aspects of the States, on government, society, literature, public men, manners, and morals, a very high commendation must be rendered."

19. The MS at this point originally indicated that Rachel succeeded her father in command after his death. This statement is lined out in favor of the present reading: "The management of the house of Castlewood had been in the hands of the active little lady long before the Colonel slept the sleep of the just." ("Active," incidentally, originally read "arbitrary.")

20. In chap. 9 he is represented according to the received traditions as "above levity and jokes." Obviously aware of Washington's prestige in America, Thackeray pays tribute to him intermittently through the novel. In chap. 81 George, though less enthusiastic than Harry, is made to say: "Indeed I allow the gentleman every virtue; and in the struggles which terminated so fatally for England a few years since, I can admire as well as his warmest friends, General Washington's glorious constancy and success." In the MS this sentence originally concluded "though I think there were many officers as good as he," but these words are lined out. Despite such tact, Thackeray's treatment of Washington was received with resentment by some of his American readers. They lost sight of the fact that George was supposed to represent Loyalist opinion; nor did they appreciate Thackeray's "familiar" approach to their hero.
In chap. 8 of the MS is deleted a reference to the scandalous past of another American culture hero, Benjamin Franklin.

21. His rescuer is an ancestor of M. Paul de Florac, whom we have met in *The Newcomes*.

22. There is various evidence of change in direction. Besides the anticipation of rivalry in love (see above, n. 2), Rachel's reference in the preface to *Esmond* of the "fatal differences" in politics suggests more serious consequences than actually ensue. The military disposition shown by George and Harry in chap. 7 ("Preparations for War") is hardly borne out in the rest of the novel. The situation in this chapter of the elder brother being selected to go to war to uphold the family honor while the younger must stay back is carried to a more tragic denouement by Stevenson in *The Master of Ballantrae*—a romance in which the influences of G. P. R. James and Thackeray converge. The only surviving plan, recently discovered in the Lockwood Memorial Library, State University of New York at Buffalo, apparently represents an early stage, without even the Tunbridge Wells episodes or the Lambert family introduced. See Edgar F. Harden, "A Partial Outline for Thackeray's *The Virginians*," *Journal of English and Germanic Philology* 75 (January–April 1976): 168–87.

23. The initial that heads chap. 34 ("In Which Mr. Warrington Treats The Company With Tea And A Ball") shows a clerical figure bent over to kiss the hand of Lady Yarmouth on this occasion.

24. F. Scott Fitzgerald, *The Great Gatsby* (New York: Charles Scribner's Sons, 1953), opening paragraph.

25. Conversation with the Reverend Whitwell Elwin, reported in Elwin's *Some Eighteenth Century Men of Letters* (London: Murray, 1902), 1:156–57; quoted in *Letters*, 3:619 n. Thackeray was accounting here for his decision to abandon his plan for a sequel to *The Newcomes* centering on the artist J. J. Ridley. In his eventual disposi-

tion of both George and Harry in *The Virginians,* Thackeray transferred a suggestion that the Reverend Elwin had made for the sequel to *The Newcomes:* "Why don't
you describe a domestic family, enjoying the genuine blessings of calm domestic
felicity, put in contrast with the vexations and hollowness of fashioanble life?"
(ibid.).

26. This is modified from the first version in the MS: ". . . a hair oil or pomade
of such an odour that I did not care to approach."

27. George later attributes the failure of his drama *Pocahontas,* based on the
best-known incident in the life of Sir John Smith, to its "fidelity to history."

28. Cf. Thackeray's review of *The Private Correspondence of Sarah, Duchess of
Marlborough* (quoted above, pp. 107–8). Harry's account of the Battle of Saint-
Malo, in which he participates, is equally iconoclastic (chap. 64). Military swagger
and American chauvinism are both parodied in the last of Thackeray's "Prize
Novels" for *Punch,* "The Stars and Stripes. By The Author of 'The Last of the
Mulligans,' 'Pilot,' Etc.," obviously aimed at Cooper with its heroes Leatherlegs and
Tom Coxswain.

29. Quoted in the introduction to *The Virginians,* 10:xxx–xxxiii. See *Letters,* vol. 4,
appendix 19 ("The Oxford Election, 1857"), for texts of Thackeray's campaign
speeches.

30. Although defeated by only a small margin, Thackeray came to the conclusion
that he was not suited for politics. In a late chapter of *The Virginians,* George records
in his journal: "I thought I might perhaps succeed to my uncle's seat in Parliament,
as well as to his landed property; but I found, I knew not how, that I was voted to be
a person of very dangerous opinions. I would not bribe, I would not coerce my own
tenants to vote for me in the election of '68" (chap. 85).

31. "Despatched," with its more military connotation, is substituted for "sent" in
the MS. Harry follows the course of his elder brother in marrying Fanny Mountain,
daughter of his mother's housekeeper, against Rachel's express wishes. The plate
that illustrates this episode is labeled "Flat Rebellion" (chap. 84).

32. Unpublished letter of December 1858, continued 16 July 1859, to William
Webb Follett Synge. The original (incomplete) is in the Morgan Library.

33. Actually, the book did reasonably well, the main cause for its financial failure
being Bradbury and Evans's overestimation of the demand. Apparently on the basis
of the sales of the first edition of *The Newcomes,* they printed twenty thousand copies
of the first number of *The Virginians* (as against about forty-five hundred of *Vanity
Fair* and ninety-five hundred of *Pendennis*). The print order was gradually reduced
for successive numbers, tapering off at thirteen thousand for numbers 18 through
24, still bringing the figure above those for individual numbers of both *Vanity Fair*
and *Pendennis.* Most of the sale of *Vanity Fair,* it should be remembered, was
achieved in its later cheap edition. *The Virginians* did not go into a cheap edition until
1863. Compounding the economic problem of *The Virginians,* of course, was the
generous payment advanced to Thackeray for each number—£250 (reduced volun-
tarily by Thackeray from £300, when sales lapsed), as against £60 for *Vanity Fair,*
£100 for *Pendennis,* and £150 for *The Newcomes.* The publication of *The Virginians*
marked Thackeray's parting of the ways with Bradbury and Evans. The most detailed financial account based on an examination of the extant records is Peter L.
Shillingsburg, "Thackeray and the Firm of Bradbury and Evans," *Victorian Studies
Association Newsletter,* March 1973, pp. 11–14, from which my information is mainly
drawn.

34. Some readers, however, may have been misled by the abrupt announcement
of George's death at the end of chap. 12 that echoes the famous one of George
Osborne's death in the field of Waterloo in *Vanity Fair.*

35. See above, pp. 47–48.

36. See above, pp. 36–37. In keeping with the documentary solidity of the book is
a style of illustration more literal than is characteristic of the earlier novels. Pictorial
initials tend toward the scenic rather than the emblematic, the figures in the plates
are engraved in finer detail than heretofore, and backgrounds in general seem to be
more filled up. The relationship of Thackeray's modes of illustration to his books
remains one of the neglected areas of scholarship.

37. *The Virginians* was published simultaneously in America in *Harper's Magazine,* netting Thackeray an additional $100 per month. Some numbers were pirated by the *New York Tribune,* leading to altercations between the publishers. For details see Frederick S. Dickson, "Bibliography of Thackeray in the United States," in James Grant Wilson's *Thackeray in the United States,* 2 vols. (London: Smith, Elder, 1904), 2:246–47; and Edgar F. Harden, "The Growth of *The Virginians* as a Serial Novel," *Costerus* (1974), pp. 235–36, n. 10a.

38. *Letters,* 4:81.

39. Letters of 23 January–25 February 1858 to William Duer Robinson, *Letters,* 4:66. In this letter Thackeray requested some historical details relating to George Washington and other military matters from Robinson, an American friend with whom he had stayed in New York.

40. A number of antagonistic remarks were deleted from the MS. In chap. 3 after "Ere the establishment of Independence, there was no more aristocratic country in the world than Virginia," the following passage is lined out: "no people more loyal or king loving, no place where the traditions of English home were more fondly cherished. The New England Puritans and Republicans were held in scorn by the cavalier inhabitants of the southern regions." From chap. 7 following upon the reference to the Duke of Cumberland's calling for help from the colonies in the Seven Years' War is lined out a long passage indicating that the provinces were laggard at the time and "seemed inclined to let the British Government fight their battles, fulfilled none of their engagements, and contributed neither men nor money nor horses, nor beef." This passage further states that the Pennsylvania farmers managed to find horses and wagons when Benjamin Franklin informed them that General Braddock would take what he wanted by force if he could not get it by fair means.

My discussion of the MS overlaps in some details that of John Sutherland in chap. 5 of his *Thackeray at Work* (London: Athlone Press, 1974), which I read after this chapter was written. Another detailed examination of the changes Thackeray made is Edgar Harden's "The Growth of *The Virginians* as a Serial Novel," pp. 217–66.

41. 4–10 November 1858, from Paris, *Letters,* 4:115; quoted inaccurately in Anne Thackeray's introduction to *The Virginians, Works,* 10:xli–xlii.

42. Unpublished letter of 16 July 1859 to Synge (continued from letter begun December 1858 quoted above, n. 32). Thackeray was apologizing here for the lapse of time between beginning the letter and concluding it. The world-weariness betrayed in this and other letters of this period is attributable in part to Thackeray's exhaustion from his lecture tours with *The Four Georges,* which proved lucrative but exacerbated his ill health and probably contributed to his premature death. Some resurgence of spirit is observable subsequently when he was freshly stimulated by his writing for *Cornhill Magazine.*

"THE PREACHER OF CORNHILL":
ROUNDABOUT AND RETROSPECT

Chapter Thirteen

AS FAR BACK AS 1844, THACKERAY HAD expressed an ambition to head up "a slashing, brilliant, gentlemanlike, sixpenny aristocratic literary paper."[1] It was not until late 1859, four years before his death, that he finally assumed the kind of editorial chair that he had dreamed of. The post came to him at the invitation of his publishers Smith, Elder, who now looked to his prestige to lend luster to the new shilling monthly they wished to launch.[2] This journal was named after the district of London where Saint Peter's Church was located—a site made much of by Thackeray in the editorial position he adopted as "The Preacher of Cornhill." As the original host of his most famous essays, as well as of his last three works of fiction, the *Cornhill Magazine* enveloped the entire sunset of Thackeray's literary career and provided his ultimate platform. At a time when he felt that his creative vein had been depleted, the new magazine offered him a free hand to indulge his tendency toward discourse without straining his powers of invention. Nostalgia consequently provides the linking thread through the writings of his silver age. Some stanzas from a poem of his late years called "The Past—Looking Back!" anticipate this mood:

> Alone in the evening's shadow-light
>   In the deepening gloom and sadness
> I roam the paths of past delight,
>   Of youth's wild dream of gladness.
>
> I see that panorama vast
>   That to these eyes is giving

The joyous scenes of that dead past
Still in my bosom living.

I call those thoughts and mem'ries back
That stern-faced toil banish'd,
And wander o'er the beaten track
Of happy days long vanish'd.[3]

The "dead past" indeed returns over and over again in the significantly titled *Roundabout Papers* that Thackeray contributed to the
Cornhill Magazine virtually at monthly intervals through early 1863
(though his editorship ceased in March 1862) under such heads as
"On A Lazy Idle Boy," "Nil Nisi Bonum," "Tunbridge Toys," "De
Juventute," "Round About The Christmas Tree," "On A Peal Of
Bells," and "Autour De Mon Chapeau." The "paths of past delight"
are retraced also in his serials in *Cornhill*'s pages, a harkening back
to his hack journalism and his earliest mode of publishing his
novels. If the least profound of his "sham histories," the novels that
appeared in *Cornhill* are valuable as Thackeray's final testaments on
his life as well as his art. It is not farfetched to read into the narrator of *Lovel the Widower* (called Mr. Batchelor), the first of the
Cornhill group, a literary portrait of Thackeray himself, both
bachelor and widower (in spirit if not in fact), looking at himself as
an observer of life. *The Adentures of Philip,* which reintroduces his
former alter ego Arthur Pendennis as narrator, has obvious connections with Thackeray's own school days, journalistic career, and
blighted marriage. *Denis Duval,* although historical in setting (the
eighteenth century once more), is the only purely autobiographical
novel in the Thackerayan canon after *Barry Lyndon* and surges also
with the vitality of "happy days long vanish'd." Moreover, for the
Duval family Thackeray is known to have drawn on records of his
own naval ancestors.[4] The fiction and the essays alike that Thackeray published in the *Cornhill Magazine* help to place his career in
perspective, representing his own assessment of his accomplishments, his literary ideals, and how he may have fallen short of
them. His last novel, of which unfortunately only about half was
completed, shows him simultaneously "on the beaten track" and
setting out in a new direction.

The *Roundabout Essays,* like the fiction that appeared in *Cornhill,*
proceed filament-like out of Thackeray's busy, self-examining consciousness. "In these humble essaykins I have taken leave to
egotise," he admits in one of them; and together they display his
"humorous ego" in its variety of moods:

> I daresay the reader has remarked that the upright and indepen-
> dent vowel, which stands in the vowel list between E and O, has
> formed the subject of the main part of these essays [begins "Ogres"].
> How does that vowel feel this morning?—fresh, good-humoured,
> and lively? The Roundabout lines, which fall from this pen, are
> correspondingly brisk and cheerful. Has anything, on the contrary,
> disagreed with the vowel?
>   . . . Under such circumstances, a darkling misanthropic tinge, no
> doubt, is cast upon the paper.[5]

Thackeray could well say along with his favorite Montaigne (also
mentioned in passing in these "humble essaykins") "reader, myself
am the matter of my book," but the self is viewed under controlled
conditions. Thackeray's subject really could be called what
Wordsworth referred to as "emotion recollected in tranquility."
The "little sermons" (another name Thackeray gives to these essays) are further linked to the novels by a bifocal vision of time in
which past and present coalesce. "When I come to look at a place
which I have visited any time these twenty or thirty years, I recall
not the place merely, but the sensations I had at first seeing it, and
which are quite different to my feelings today," he writes. "A man
can be alive in 1860 and 1830 at the same time, don't you see?"[6]
The past stirs up various emotions in him. One is contrition: "In
the midst of a great peace and calm, the stars look out from the
heavens. The silence is peopled with the past; sorrowful remorses
for sins and shortcomings—memories of passionate joys and griefs
rise out of their graves, both now alike calm and sad."[7] Another is
nostalgia for what seems an irrecoverable primal world once beautiful and new:

> I stroll over the Common and survey the beautiful purple hills
> around, twinkling with a thousand bright villas, which have sprung
> upon this charming ground since first I saw it. What an admirable
> scene of peace and plenty. What a delicious air breathes over the
> heath, blows the cloud—shadows across it, and murmurs through
> the full-clad trees! Can the world show a land fairer, richer, more
> cheerful? I see a portion of it when I look up from the window at
> which I write. . . . [My eyes] are looking backwards, back into forty
> years off, into a dark room, into a little house hard by the Common
> here, in the Bartlemytide holidays.[8]

Suspended between past and present, the editor of *Cornhill* sees
himself at the same time as on the verge of a new epoch: "The
pretty little city [of Chur] stands, so to speak, at the end of the
world—of the world of to-day, the world of rapid motion, and
rushing railways, and the commerce and intercourse of man."[9]

These "essaykins," besides furnishing Thackeray with occasions
for periodic self-examination, also enable him to continue the

dialogue with his public begun as early as his first novel, *Catherine*. The tone has become subdued, but the public is still alternately wooed, teased, flattered, and scolded. Keeping his promise to be candid with his readers, he kicks away the pedestal beneath his feet: "Some philosophers get their wisdom with deep thought, and out of ponderous libraries; I pick up my small crumbs of cogitation at a dinner-table; or from Mrs. Mary and Miss Louisa, as they are prattling over their five-o'clock tea."[10] He makes no great claim for these "rinsings" from his tired brain: "No, I do not, as far as I know, try to be port at all; but offer in these presents, a sound genuine ordinaire at 18 s per doz., let us say, grown on my own hillside, and offered *de bon coeur* to those who will sit under my *tonelle*, and have a half-hour's drink and gossip."[11] Behind this modesty lurks a sense of insufficiency, even of depletion: "It is none of your hot porto, my friend, I know there is much better and stronger liquor elsewhere. Some pronounce it sour; some say it is thin; some say that it has woefully lost its flavour. This may or may not be true. There are good and bad years, years that may surprise everybody; years of which the produce is small and bad, or rich and plentiful." Ultimately he falls back on the justification of sincerity: "But if my tap is not genuine, it is naught, and no man should give himself the trouble to drink it." Fear of superannuation, of redundancy, of wearing out his welcome—the occupational malaises that have overtaken many a writer—recur as motifs in Thackeray's swan songs.

One professional concern that carries over into the novels that Thackeray produced during these years is the consciousness that he is repeating himself. "And is it not with writers as with *raconteurs*?" he pointedly asks in one of the essays. "Ought they not to have their ingenuous modesty? May authors tell old stories, and how many times over?"[12] He quotes a letter from a hypothetical reader: "What a poverty of friends the man has! He is always asking us to meet those Pendennises, Newcomes, and so forth. Why does he not introduce us to some new characters? Why is he not thrilling like Twostars, learned and profound like Threestars, exquisitely humourous and human like Fourstars? Why, finally, is he not like somebody else?" Further on in this essay he confronts himself with a leading question: "Will it not be presently time, O prattler, to hold your tongue, and let younger people speak?"[13]

Between self-doubts, the occasional suspicion that he may have had his day, Thackeray's perennial impatience with obtuse readers is revived: "Now with respect to jokes—and the present company of course excepted—many people are as infants. They have little

sense of humour," he complains after a perusal of the morning
mail that has come to the editor's desk.

> They don't like jokes. Raillery in writing annoys and offends them.
> The coarseness apart, I think I have found very few women who
> liked the banter of Swift and Fielding. Their simple natures revolt at
> laughter. Is the satyr always a wicked brute at heart, and are they
> rightly shocked at his grin, his leer, his horns, hoofs, and ears? *Fi
> donc, le vilain monstre,* with his shrieks, and his capering, crooked legs!
> Let him go and get a pair of well-wadded black stockings, and pull
> them over those horrid shanks; put a large gown and bands over
> beard and hide; and pour a dozen of lavender-water into his lawn
> handkerchief, and cry, and never make a joke again.[14]

Thackeray recalls here his own conversion from satirist to "week-
day preacher." But neither are the "gown and bands" always welcome:

> Before the Duke of York's column, and between the "Athenaeum"
> and "United Service" Clubs, I have seen more than once, on the
> esplanade, a preacher holding forth to a little congregation of
> *badauds* and street-boys, whom he entertains with a discourse on the
> crimes of a rapacious aristocracy, or warns of the imminent period of
> their own souls. Sometimes this orator is made to "move on" by brutal
> policemen. Sometimes, on a Sunday, he points to a white head or two
> visible in the windows of the Clubs to right and left of him, and
> volunteers a statement that those quiet and elderly Sabbath-breakers
> will very soon be called from this world to another, where their lot
> will by no means be so comfortable as that which the reprobates
> enjoy here, in their armchairs by their snug fires.[15]

The way of the iconoclast is a hard one, whether the voice be one of
mirth or melancholy.

This clown-parson stoops to conquer, making himself a sounding
board to the great vox populi. "Our subject, I beg leave to remind
the reader's humble servant, is novel heroes and heroines," he
interrupts a reminiscence about his own school-boy reading. "How
do you like your heroes, ladies? Gentlemen, what novel heroes do
you prefer?" In their preferences his hypothetical readers are divided between the present generation and the one just past. "The
gentleman refers me to Miss Austen; the lady says Athos, Guy
Livingstone, and (pardon my rosy blushes) Colonel Esmond, and
owns that in youth she was very much in love with Valancourt." He
recognizes that there are readers to whom the very name Udolpho
is a mystery: "'Valancourt? and who was he?' cry the young people.
Valancourt, my dears, was the hero of one of the most famous
romances which was ever published in this country. The beauty

and elegance of Valancourt made your young grandmamas' gentle hearts to beat with respectful sympathy. He and his glory have passed away."[16] For the benefit of his younger readers he quotes a page from another favorite of yesteryear, *Evelina;* and in a footnote he offers an "updated" version, substituting the "present modern talk" for the "old perfumed, powdered D'Arblay conversation."

The pages of *Cornhill* furthermore offer Thackeray an open field to carry on his favorite sport of pelting away at rivals. "Some authors, who shall be nameless, are, I know, accused of depicting the most feeble, brainless, namby-pamby heroines forever whimpering tears and prattling commonplaces," he begins another bandying essay.[17] He visualizes an impossible paragon of beauty combined with erudition enough to "surprise and confound the bishop with her learning," who can also "outride the squire," outshoot a military officer, "rescue from fever and death the poor cottager's family whom the doctor had given up," and "draw tears from the professional Italian people by her exquisite performance (of voice and violoncello) in the evening." In another essay he regales his readers with a supernatural tale of horror that came to him in a nightmare after reading "one of those awful—those admirable sensation novels . . . which are full of delicious wonders."[18]

Assured of a captive audience and the largest he had ever gathered together at one time, Thackeray could now dart from essays to fiction with a freedom that he had not known before. Hence not merely hypothetical novels but his own are openly discussed with the subscribers to *Cornhill.* Among the "thorns in the cushion" are letters from dancers protesting against his treatment of one of their number, Elizabeth Prior, in *Lovel the Widower.*[19] He complains of the constant invasion of "the 'editor's private residence,' to which in spite of prayers, entreaties, commands, and threats, authors and ladies will send their communications," interrupting him in such "exquisite inventions" as how to rescue "Maria . . . from the unprincipled Earl," and how to thwart "the atrocious General . . . in his machinations." Here he was indirectly alluding to two of the plot mechanisms in his serial then in progress, *The Adventures of Philip.*[20] "How do you like your novels?" he asks in "De Finibus," and answers for himself: "I like mine strong, 'hot with,' and no mistake; no love-making, no observations about society . . . ,"[21] undoubtedly looking forward to the last of his tales, the swashbuckling *Denis Duval.* Such openness characterizes the fiction itself, with its informality, air of improvisation, and constant interruption by the author *in propria persona,* almost at times making the reader a collaborator.

Shortly before the appearance of *Lovel the Widower*, Thackeray wrote in a letter to Trollope inviting him to contribute to the new magazine: "Whatever a man knows about life and its doings, that let us hear about. You must have tossed a good deal about the world, and have countless sketches in your memory and your portfolio. Please to think if you can furbish up any of these besides a novel. When events occur, and you have a good lively tale, bear us in mind. One of our chief objects in this magazine is the getting out of novel spinning, and back into the world."[22] This attitude prepares us for a certain casualness about *Lovel* in which the narrator does not so much "spin" his plot as twirl it about, with the teller far more in the forefront than the tale. It begins tentatively: "Who shall be the hero of this tale? Not I who write it. I am but the Chorus of the Play. I narrate their simple story . . . the scene is in the parlour, and the region below the parlour. No: it may be the parlour and kitchen, in this instance, are on the same level. There is no high life, unless, to be sure, you call a baronet's widow a lady in high life; and some ladies may be, while some certainly are not." Pretending to draw his readers in as participants of a novel in the making, he solicits their approval of his selection of the cast of characters:

> The heroine is not faultless (ah! that will be a great relief to some folk, for many writers' good women are, you know, so *very* insipid). The principal personage you may very likely think to be no better than a muff. But is many a respectable man of our acquaintance much better? . . . I wish with all my heart I was about to narrate a story with a good mother-in-law for a character, but then, you know, my dear madam, all good women in novels are insipid. This woman certainly was not. She was not only not insipid, but exceedingly bad-tasted. She had a foul loud tongue, a stupid head, a bad temper, an immense pride and arrogance, an extravagant son, and very little money. Can I say much more of a woman than this?

At least he is able to assure "my dear madam" that the women of this story are not "the most feeble, brainless, namby-pamby heroines forever whimpering tears and prattling commonplaces."

Thackeray's familiar pose as stage manager in this instance betrays the literally theatrical origins of *Lovel* in his comedy *The Wolves and the Lamb* that he had not succeeded in getting commercially produced.[23] For the seminal situation of both play and novel, however, he went "back into the world," drawing on a real-life incident from his own experience. In a letter to his American friends the Baxters written during the summer of 1853 he referred to the prospect of a young girl coming to live in as governess and companion to his daughters. "But says I! No my dear you are a great deal too good looking," the letter continues. "Knowing the susceptibility of this aged heart I'm determined to put it to no more temptation than I can help—She is left behind and my heart is perfectly easy. I think of writing a book 'The Adventures of a Gentleman in Search of a Governess.'"[24] These adventures are projected into those of Lovel, the "muff" hero of the novel (Horace Milliken in the play), newly widowed, responsible for the upbringing of two children, hag-ridden and henpecked by his mother and mother-in-law who descend upon him to aid him in his difficulties, but only compound them. Unlike Thackeray, Lovel does succumb to the wiles of the pretty young governess, who enters his household when she ac-companies him and his children home from Naples upon the death of his wife and eventually becomes the second Mrs. Lovel.

Actually Thackeray's relationship to the titular character is con-fined to the initial domestic situation. (The lining out from the original manuscript of an oblique reference to his own wife, still living in a non compos state, indicates some attempt to deper-sonalize the narrative.)[25] More of his inner self undoubtedly went into the lonely wistful author Mr. Batchelor (Captain Touchit in the play), weekend guest of Mr. Lovel, who, as we learn, has loved and lost ("Ich habe genossen das iridische Glück—ich habe—geliebt!" he tells us in chap. 3 in words borrowed from Schiller). It is through Mr. Batchelor's sensibility that we get momentarily engaged with this country-house intrigue, giving Thackeray opportunity to play not only with the reader but with himself as author.

In presenting his various characters, Mr. Batchelor tends to adopt the viewpoint of the outsider looking in. He arouses our curiosity about a subsidiary character like Lovel's mother, who "takes a precious long time to dress for dinner": "And, indeed, on looking at Lady Baker, the connoisseur might perceive that her Ladyship was a highly composite person, whose charms required very much care and arrangement. There are some cracked old houses where the painters and plumbers and puttyers are always at work" (chap. 2), no less than the heroine: "I protest here is Miss Prior coming into the room at last. A pale face, a tawny head of hair combed back under a black cap: a pair of blue spectacles as I live! a tight morning dress buttoned up to her white throat; a head hung meekly down: such is Miss Prior" (chap. 2). His part in the events to come is set forth in the chapter aptly entitled "I Play The Spy"; "Now it may be that one of the double doors of the room which I inhabited was occasionally open, and that Mr. Batchelor's eyes and ears are uncommonly quick, and note a number of things which less observant persons would never regard or discover; but out of this room, which I occupied for some few days, now and subsequently, I looked forth as from a little ambush upon the proceedings of the house, and got a queer little insight into the history and characters of the personages round about me" (chap. 3). The growing rivalry between Lady Baker, Lovel's mother, and his mother-in-law Mrs. Bonnington, as witnessed by Mr. Batchelor, promises excitement:

> There was one point on which the two ladies agreed. A very wealthy widower, young still, good-looking, and good-tempered, we know can sometimes find a dear woman to console his loneliness, and protect his motherless children. From the neighbouring Heath, from Wimbledon, Roehampton, Barnes, Mortlake, Richmond, Esher, Walton, Windsor, nay Reading, Bath, Exeter, and Penzance itself, or from any other quarter of Britain from which your fancy may please to travel, families would come ready with dear young girls to take charge of that man's future happiness; but it is a fact that these two dragons kept all women off from their ward. An unmarried woman with decent good looks, was scarce ever allowed to enter Shrubland's gate. If such an one appeared, Lovel's two mothers sallied out, and crunched her hapless bones. (Chap. 3)

With the entrance of an additional contestant this stage really becomes a household arena:

> Here was Lovel, this willing horse; and what a crowd of relations, what a heap of luggage had the honest fellow to carry! How that little Mrs. Prior was working, and scheming, and tacking and flattering, and fawning, and plundering to be sure! And that serene Elizabeth, with what consummate skill, art, and prudence had she to act, to keep her place with two such rivals reigning over her! . . . Why, Elizabeth Prior, my wonder and respect for thee increase with every hour during which I contemplate thy character! How is it that you live with those lionesses, and are not torn to pieces? (Chap. 3)

Mr. Batchelor's general attitude of bemusement toward what he observes in this house in Shrublands, his looking on the situation as "an intricate problem," as "secrets of the house" to be unraveled, suggests gossipy interest rather than deep emotional involvement. "The great satirist has not yet exhausted himself, but he is beginning to choose rather trivial motives for his puppets," reads one of the few reviews that *Lovel* had. This reviewer observed accurately, if with some disappointment, that in this late story Thackeray had descended from "the stern realities of great evil" to the "petty pleasures and small sins" of life.[26] If no neglected masterpiece, *Lovel* can be enjoyed in the spirit in which Thackeray undoubtedly intended it—as the sport and recreation of a relaxed but by no means dry brain. That he could still address himself to "the stern realities of great evil" is attested by the next serial he composed for *Cornhill*, *The Adventures of Philip*, but at this time, as he wrote afterward to his friend Charles Lever, "I sang purposely small: wishing to keep my strongest suit for a later day." The main reason was a professional one: Trollope had accepted his invitation, and with *Framley Parsonage* on hand to open the first issue of *Cornhill Magazine*, Thackeray felt obliged in the name of editorial diplomacy to allow the author of *Barchester Towers* "all the honours of *Violono Primo*."[27]

Under these circumstances one understands why Thackeray should appear here to be "shadow-boxing with himself," as a modern critic complains.[28] Another way to put it is that he allows himself more than the usual freedom to talk about his story rather than to get on with it, and that consequently his creations become objects of inquiry rather than full-bodied characters—images projected upon a mental screen rather than palpable substances. The spotlight and the attentions of the men of the story (including Mr. Batchelor) center on Elizabeth Prior, of meek and prim exterior, behind which, it is suggested, lurk hidden depths and a calculating nature. Of obscure parentage and rather seedy background (a former dancer in "The Rose and the Bulbul" at the Prince's Theatre, it is rumored), she is a kind of transmogrification of Becky Sharp. She shares with her more glittering predecessor a fluency in French along with a refined manner and, like her, moves into genteel society through governessing, but goes Becky one better by marrying her wealthy employer, winning out over other candidates more to the manor born.

We have to take for granted the charm that Miss Prior exerts on all the men who fly into her orbit, for she remains a furtive and enigmatic personage. We see her only through the susceptible eyes of Mr. Batchelor, who admits to being an easy touch: "Pooh! I say, women will make a fool of me to the end. Ah! ye gracious Fates! Cut my thread of life ere it grow too long. Suppose I were to live till seventy, and some little wretch of a woman were to set her cap at me? She would catch me—I know she would" (chap. 4). Mr. Batchelor retains an infatuation for Miss Prior from an earlier acquaintance, which he mistakenly believes is reciprocated, and thus becomes more involved in the marriage game going on about him than he had intended. Eventually he loses out to his friend Lovel, but his affectionate nature makes him unusually forgiving. Confronted with what looks like evidence of cold opportunism and deceit on this governess's part (in a letter to another suitor that comes his way), rather than expose her, he justifies her: "In that dismal, wakeful night . . . I had thought her character and story over, and seen to what a life of artifice and dissimulation necessity had compelled her. I did not blame her. In such circumstances, with such a family, how could she be frank and open? Poor thing! poor thing!" (chap. 6). He gives his blessing to the engagement of Lovel and Elizabeth: "Miss Prior, I am delighted that my old friend should have found a woman of good sense, good conduct, good temper—a woman who has had many trials and borne them with a great patience—to take charge of him and make him happy. I congratulate you both. Miss Prior has borne poverty so well that I am certain she will bear good fortune . . ." (chap. 6).

"*Lovel,* I think, does not have any thoroughgoing partisans," George Saintsbury has remarked,[29] but it is not to be dismissed. This slightest of Thackeray's stories somehow teases us into thought. Ending with the conventional wedding bells, it still leaves us uncertain as to Lovel's future with his young bride, reminding us of Thackeray's apprenticeship in the Parisian Théâtre Ambigu-Comique. "We may hear of LOVEL MARRIED some other day, but here is an end of LOVEL THE WIDOWER," reads the epilogue. "*Valete et plaudite,* you good people, who have witnessed the little comedy. Down with the curtain; cover up the boxes; pop out the gas-lights. Ho! cab! Take us home, and let us have some tea, and go to bed. Good night, my little players. We have been merry together and we part with soft hearts and somewhat rueful countenances, don't we?" The nearest Thackeray ever got to the sequel hinted at was in a letter to a friend where he described his heroine as "a woman without a vice, but without the least heart" and spoke of his intention to carry her up the social ladder, "making her husband an Earl by her exertions." He thought too of having her first love turn up, "some low cad . . . for whom she has retained a sneaking affection through life while caring for nobody else."[30] What remains is an amusing *jeu d'esprit* in which Thackeray undermines even the authorial omniscience he had previously been at pains to defend: "Do we know anybody? Ah! dear me, we are most of us very lonely in the world," sighs Mr. Batchelor near the conclusion, putting himself in the solipsistic state of the ordinary reader rather than in that of the confident Manager of the Performance of *Vanity Fair* who "knows everything."[31] More to his purpose, Mr. Batchelor's soft heart and readiness to "pardon humanity" leave us with a certain glow of benevolence shining through a naughty world of scheming, deception, and self-serving.

In January 1861 Thackeray moved up to "Primo Violono" position in *Cornhill* with what was to prove his last completed novel, *The Adventures of Philip On His Way Through The World Showing Who Robbed Him, Who Helped Him, And Who Passed Him By*. A modern fable whose title echoes the biblical parable of the Good Samaritan, this presumably was the "strongest suit" that he was holding back until the conclusion of *Framley Parsonage*.[32] The story of *Philip* is a rather intricate, if not a particularly absorbing, one, an indication that Thackeray could still concoct a plot and busy himself with the techniques of narration when he set his mind to them, despite his scorn for "story-making incidents, surprises, love making, &c." However, even while immersed in "novel spinning," he enjoys his jokes about it. Though dependent upon the usual sources, such as letters and reports by eyewitnesses or friends, he gives up his old pretense that his story is taken entirely "from the life." "I could not, of course, be present at many of the scenes which I shall have to relate as though I had witnessed them; and the posture, language, and inward thoughts of Philip and his friends, as here related, no doubt are fancies of the narrator in many cases," he admits; "but the story is as authentic as many histories, and the reader need give only such an amount of credence to it as he may judge that its verisimilitude warrants" (chap. 3). So he turns the hoary "founded on fact" device upside down by casting doubt instead on what is received as truth.

In a similar perverse mood Thackeray's customary teasing of his readers for their hankering after escapism takes on a new twist: "He with whom we have mainly to do is a gentleman of mature age now walking the street with boys of his own. He is not going to perish in the last chapter of these memoirs—to die of consumption with his love weeping by his bedside, or to blow his brains out in despair, because she has been married to his rival, or killed out of a jig, or otherwise done for in the last chapter but one," he hastens to assure his readers very early in the story. "No, no; we will have no dismal endings. Philip Firmin is well and hearty at this minute, owes no man a shilling, and can enjoy his glass of port in perfect comfort. So, my dear miss, if you want a pulmonary romance, the present won't suit you. So, young gentleman, if you are for melancholy, despair, and sardonic satire, please to call at some other shop" (chap. 2). He implicitly joins forces with the author of *Guy Livingstone* (a current favorite mentioned in one of the Roundabouts)[33] in upholding the hearty hero against the sickly one. In this era of the sensational novel, moreover, the "tragic" ending rather than the happy one is associated with sham sentimentality.

Even when Philip's economic situation is temporarily at low ebb, the author immediately deprives his readers of suspense: "As yet there was not only content with his dinner, but plenty therewith; and I do not wish to alarm you by supposing that Philip will ever have to encounter any dreadful extremities of poverty or hunger in the course of his history. The wine in the jug was very low at times, but it never was quite empty. This lamb was shorn, but the wind was tempered to him" (chap. 16).

Although he had spoken of his readers' demands for "new characters" in one of his essays, we find Thackeray in his penultimate novel still dredging up "scraps, heeltaps, odds and ends of characters"[34] from the past. "I have exhausted all the types of character I am familiar with, and it's very difficult to strike out anything new," he had confessed to his friend the Reverend Elwin after the completion of *The Newcomes*. Instead he chose to put his familiar types through fresh inversions. Through his hero Philip, for example, we get a glimpse of the penny-a-liner phase of his early career rather than of the budding novelist, as with Pendennis, or of the apprentice artist, as with Clive Newcome. Arthur Pendennis, cut out of *Lovel the Widower*,[35] returns once more to chronicle the tribulations of Philip Firmin, like Clive Newcome a friend and schoolfellow, but by now Pen has evolved from neophyte to mentor. The filial devotion central to all Thackeray's domestic novels here has turned to gall, and in place of the over-mothering or overfathering of *Pendennis* and *The Newcomes*, we are presented in *Philip* with a monstrously selfish father and a much put-upon son.

For two of the principal characters in the new novel Thackeray went back to a much earlier uncompleted magazine tale, *A Shabby Genteel Story*. Readers of this tale had been introduced to Caroline Gann, "an innocent young woman in love with Brandon," and to this lover George Brandon, "a young gentleman, in love with himself." In tone it belongs among Thackeray's "comicalities and whimsicalities," an updating of the Cinderella story in the form of a burletta, but a serious note is intruded. "I should like to know how many such scoundrels our universities have turned out; and how much ruin has been caused by that accursed system which is called in England 'the education of a gentleman,'" moralizes the author in connection with this false Prince Charming: "My friend Brandon had gone through this process of education, and had been irretrievably ruined by it—his heart and his honesty had been ruined by it, this is to say; and he had received, in return for them, a small quantity of classics and mathematics—pretty compensation for all he had lost in gaining them!" (chap. 2). The hapless Caroline, browbeaten and kept in the shade by her stepmother and stepsisters, is all too easy a prey to the blandishments of this "rescuer," but the outcome of this seaside romance was kept in suspense, the story breaking off just at the point where Caroline elopes with Brandon, lured by a delusive promise of marriage. "God bless thee, poor Caroline!" the author takes abrupt farewell of her. "Thou art happy now, for some short space at least; and, here, therefore, let us leave thee." Dire things were presumably in store for this Margate Cinderella, and in fact when Thackeray resurrected the torso for his *Miscellanies* in 1857, he appended to it this advertisement: "It was my intention to complete the little story, of which only the first part is here written. Perhaps novel-readers will understand, even from the above chapters, what was to ensue. Caroline was to be disowned and deserted by her wicked husband: that abandoned man was to marry somebody else: hence, bitter trials and grief, patience and virtue, for poor little Caroline, and a melancholy ending—as how should it have been gay?" So readers were prepared for *The Adventures of Philip*, in which we meet the erstwhile rake George Brandon now matured into the respectable Dr. Firmin, Philip's father, and his cast-off Caroline Gann, reincarnated as the saintly Little Sister, who, as fate wills it, nurses young Philip in illness, and becomes something of an adopted mother to him.

The elegant scamp was a type that fascinated Thackeray from his beginnings as a writer. Ordinarily we might have expected George Brandon, if not to reform, at least to mellow with time, but in *The Adventures of Philip* this university "gentleman" has graduated into one of the most infamous scoundrels Thackeray ever conceived. From one digression in *Philip* it becomes obvious that Thackeray was still pondering the "diversities and fluctuations of crime" that had preoccupied him as far back as *Catherine*. We learn in a flashback that Brandon-cum-Firmin after he left the university "had lived in a wild society, which used dice and cards every night, and pistols sometimes in the morning. . . . When this century was five-and-twenty years younger, the crack of the pistol-shot might still occasionally be heard in the suburbs of London in the very early morning; and the dice-box went round in many a haunt of pleasure. . . . Now, the times are changed. The cards are coffined in their boxes. Only *sous-officiers*, brawling in their provincial cafés over their dominos, fight duels" (chap. 5).[36] If *The Adventures of Philip* is a falling off in some respects, it takes on significance as

Thackeray's final exploration of civilized evil. Here too he extends inquiries begun in his essays. "Ogres in our days need not be giants at all," he observed in one of the Roundabouts that appeared concurrently with *Philip*. "In former times and in children's books, where it is necessary to paint your moral in such large letters that there can be no mistake about it," continues this essay, "ogres are made with that enormous mouth and *ratelier* which you know of, and with which they can swallow down a baby, almost without using that great knife which they always carry." But no longer. "They are too cunning nowadays. They go about in society, slim, small, quietly dressed."[37] Such an ogre is Dr. Firmin, physician to nobility, member of learned societies, married to wealth and status, as registered in the consciousness of Arthur Pendennis, with his "very white false teeth, which perhaps were a little too large for his mouth, and these grinned in the gaslight very fiercely. On his cheeks were black whiskers, and over his glaring eyes fierce black eyebrows, and his bald head glittered like a billiard-ball" (chap. 1).

From outlawry Thackeray had moved up through his various "annals of human folly" to the kind of crime that is practiced within the confines of the social code. One leading theme in *Philip* is sounded in the title of another Roundabout paper: "On Being Found Out." As he reminds readers in a paper that appeared shortly after the conclusion of *Philip,* not all sinners are caught: "I will assume, my benevolent friend and present reader, that you yourself are virtuous, not from a fear of punishment, but from a sheer love of good; but as you and I walk through life, consider what hundreds and thousands of rascals we must have met, who have not been found out at all. In high places and in low, in Clubs and on 'Change, at church or the balls and routs of the nobility and gentry, how dreadful it is for benevolent beings like you and me to think these undiscovered though not unsuspected scoundrels are swarming!"[38] Thackeray's readers had already been in the company of one—"undiscovered" to society, that is, but revealed for what he is to his son Philip and to Philip's friend Arthur. So in his continuous probing of the "refinement" of crime, Thackeray progressed from verdicts of outright guilt to those of "not proven."

From its opening chapter, entitled "Dr. Fell" (suggesting an antipathy on the part of the narrator that is deep seated but unaccountable), to hints of Dr. Firmin's shady past, to evidence throughout the tale of his furtiveness and slipperiness, the reader of *Philip* finds himself wrapped in a thickening moral miasma. "Some of us have more serious things to hide than a yellow cheek

behind a raddle of rouge, or a white poll under a wig of jetty curls,"
declares the Preacher of Cornhill in one of his most trenchant
papers. "You know, neighbour, there are not only false teeth in the
world, but false tongues: and some make up a bust and an appearance of strength with padding, cotton, and what not? while another
kind of artist tries to take you in by wearing under his waistcoat,
and perpetually thumping, an immense sham heart."[39] Pendennis,
as narrator of *Philip,* anticipates this thought in distinguishing between "gentlemen with rough coats and good hearts, like Dr.
Goodenough; gentlemen with superfine coats and superfine
double-milled manners, like Dr. Firmin, and hearts—well, never
mind about that point . . . " (chap. 6). In essays and novel alike,
Thackeray probes moral evil more insidious than the humbug and
deceit that he had so expertly anatomized heretofore. The false
gentleman Dr. Firmin and his former accomplice the "Reverend"
Tufton Hunt are not merely "rascals enough," but, it is strongly
hinted, have lived in a "state of convulsive crimes." What we do
know is that Hunt, posing as a clergyman, aided Brandon in his
seduction of Caroline by performing a fake marriage ceremony.
Dr. Firmin, morally if not legally guilty of bigamy—having deserted Caroline and married the wealthy woman who becomes
Philip's mother in order to gain access to her estate—is likened by
Pen to Captain Macheath with his Lucy and Polly.

To Pen, moreover, Dr. Firmin is that most sinister of villains—an
unregenerate one. He is unimpressed by the doctor's humbling
before his wronged son: "'And am I a traitor to both of them
[Caroline and Mrs. Firmin]. Yes; and my remorse, Philip, my remorse!' says his father in his deepest tragedy voice, clutching his
hand over a heart that I believe beat very coolly," reports Pen as
witness of the incident (chap. 12). Far from making good to Philip
for having cast doubt on his son's legitimacy through his previous
"marriage," he compounds the wrong by dissipating his wife's estate (to which he has gained possession illegally) through various
fraudulent enterprises, impoverishes Philip as a result of his ex-
travagances, and climaxes his infamy by forging Philip's name to a
bill. The coup de grace comes when Dr. Firmin "forgives" his son
for failing to acknowledge the forged bill. The rationalization of sin
was among the moral topics that Thackeray interested himself in at
this time. "Do you imagine there is a great deal of genuine right-
down remorse in the world?" he asks the readers of *Cornhill* in an
essay that coincided with an episode of *Philip.* "Don't people rather
find excuses which make their minds easy; and endeavour to prove

to themselves that they have been lamentably belied and misunderstood?"[40]

As *Philip* was drawing to its close, Thackeray opened out his mind to his readers as to a proper disposition of its villain. In one of the Roundabouts he confided that he had considered drowning Dr. Firmin along with his one-time crony, now attempted blackmailer, at sea on their way to America, but relented. "Thou ghastly lying wretch, thou shalt not be drowned; thou shalt have a fever only; a knowledge of thy danger; and a chance—ever so small a chance—of repentance." He throws out a question to his readers, but leaves the answer open: "I wonder whether he *did* repent when he found himself in the yellow-fever in Virginia? The probability is, he fancied that his son had injured him very much, and forgave him on his death-bed."[41] All we learn of Dr. Firmin's demise in the novel is that he dies of the fever in Virginia three months after remarrying presumably another prosperous lady. We are left to puzzle over another unanswered query posed in one of the Roundabout Papers: "Is conscious guilt a source of unmixed pain to the bosom which harbours it? Has not your criminal, on the contrary, an excitement, an enjoyment within, quite unknown to you and me who never did anything wrong in our lives?"[42] Dr. Firmin has much in common with his prototype Don Juan. He may be taken as Thackeray's illustration of high-class evil at its most depraved—intransigent, unrepentant, and relishing itself.

If Dr. Firmin exemplifies at their most extreme what Thackeray referred to at the end of *Pendennis* as "flaws of vice and meanness, and stains of evil" in high places, his seduced and abandoned victim represents the "flowers of good" blooming in "foul places" or at least in very drab ones. By contrast with Philip's father who robs him, and with others who pass him by on his way through the world, "meek little Caroline . . . pale, freckled, thin, meanly dressed" (as she is represented in *A Shabby Genteel Story*), emerges in the sequel as the supreme good samaritan, revealing an unsuspected inner strength. Her filial devotion is tested like Philip's, but her sacrifice takes the form of standing by her failure of a father (the henpecked oil merchant's clerk of *A Shabby Genteel Story*, now a widower) even after her eyes have been opened to his pretensions and self-delusions, her admiration now diminished to compassion. Her moral courage is brought out more fully on two occasions when by the whirligigs of fate she has opportunity to protect her former betrayer. She is reliably informed that her marriage to Brandon is valid before the law as long as she believed it to be a true ceremony, even if his own intentions were dishonorable.[43] Nevertheless she testifies that she knew she was being deceived, realizing that to assert her rights would render Philip illegitimate. In the most "sensational" episode of the novel, her experience as a nurse enables her to stupefy the unscrupulous Reverend Tufton Hunt with chloroform in order to retrieve a paper that would have incriminated Dr. Firmin and disgraced Philip.[44] So Caroline stoops to duplicity for good purposes, in antithesis to her "husband," who conceals evil intentions under a benevolent exterior. First as nurse to Philip in one of his boyhood illnesses, then as benefactress in moments of crisis, Dr. Firmin's illegal wife, rather than his legal one, proves the true mother to Philip. Characteristically her death comes while she is ministering to a patient. The world of Philip is generally a harsh one, inhabited by "rascals . . . who have not been found out at all," but the serene presence of the Little Sister reminds us that there are also those who "are virtuous, not from a fear of punishment, but from a sheer love of good."

"'Philip' did not have the success it deserved. To me it seems to contain some of the wisest and most beautiful things my father ever wrote," asserted Anne Thackeray in the course of introducing it to a new generation.[45] As with Thackeray's late fiction in general, it is to be relished more for its digressions than for its story. His last completed novel offered full vent to his tendency both to moralize and to "egotise," as his daughter also reminds us: "I can remember his saying how much of his own early life was written down its pages." Its opening chapter gives us further glimpses of the Charterhouse of his boyhood and of the theatrical entertainments that enthralled him from his adolescence on. In Philip's marriage with the shallow Charlotte Baynes, Thackeray to an extent relives his own (but leaves Philip at the end in a marital haven that was never his), and with Mrs. Baynes we are treated to still another version of his own mother-in-law. Apart from domestic life, the profile of Philip stands out as possibly the most candid self-appraisal on record of the author as a young man:

> . . . Mr. Philip, in some things, was as obstinate as a mule, and in others as weak as a woman. He had a childish sensibility for what was tender, helpless, pretty, or pathetic; and a mighty scorn of imposture, wherever he found it. He had many good purposes, which were often very vacillating, and were but seldom performed. He had a vast number of evil habits, whereof, you know, idleness is said to be the root. Many of these evil propensities he coaxed and cuddled with much care; and though he roared out *peccavi* most frankly when charged with his sins, this criminal would fall to peccation very soon

after promising amendment. What he liked he would have. What he disliked he could with the greatest difficulty be found to do. He liked good dinners, good wine, good clothes, and late hours; and in all these comforts of life . . . he indulged himself with perfect freedom. He hated hypocrisy on his own part, and hypocrites in general. He said everything that came into his mind about things and people; and, of course, was often wrong and often prejudiced, and often occasioned howls of indignation or malignant whispers of hatred by his free speaking. (Chap. 6)

The rude belligerence displayed by Philip in parts of the novel that have made him somewhat less than endearing to readers can be taken as an aspect of Thackeray's own youthful character that he was making apology for. Hence this comment on Philip as fledgling journalist on the *Pall Mall Gazette* has a special pertinence. "His style was coarse, his wit clumsy and savage. Never mind characterising either now. He has seen the error of his ways, and divorced with the muse whom he never ought to have wooed" (chap. 16).

The Adventures of Philip ends with a reunion of the families of Thackeray's three autobiographic novels. It looks like literary endogamy with hints of marriages in the offing between Philip's children and those of Pen and Clive, and readers might well have been led to expect still more of "those Pendennises, Newcomes, and so forth." However, Thackeray intended this idyll not as prologue but as epilogue and farewell: "Dance on the lawn, young folks, whilst the elders talk in the shade! What? The night is falling: we have talked enough over our wine; and it is time to go home? Good-night. Good-night, friends, old and young! The night will fall: the stories must end: and the best friends must part." This was not, however, quite the end, though Thackeray was in his grave by the time the readers of *Cornhill* read the last story from his pen.[46]

We have seen Thackeray attempting various new twists and turns in his *Cornhill* fiction, but with *Denis Duval* he did a complete about-face. The period is one he had dealt with before—the eighteenth century of the times of the American Revolution—but the Cinque Ports setting is different and the viewpoint is that of an Englishman of Alsatian ancestry. In his last novel Thackeray can be said really to have honored his readers' requests for "some new characters," with not one holdover from previous novels to be found in its cast of characters. The wholesome, rather outgoing hero, moreover, is a kind of narrator that Thackeray's readers had become unaccustomed to. "I tell you I would like to be able to write a story which should show no egotism whatever—in which there

should be no reflections, no cynicism, no vulgarity (and so forth),"
he had assured them in "De Finibus," one of the last of the Roundabouts, "but an incident in every other page, a villain, a battle, a
mystery, in every chapter."[47] With its relentless pace, starting with
the flight of Denis's ancestors from religious persecution under
Louis XIV, and tapering off with a battle at sea, *Denis Duval* fulfills
this prescription almost too well. The narrator arouses us to a high
pitch of excitement at once. "Around her little cradle a double, a
triple tragedy was about to be enacted," he anticipates in recounting the birth of Agnes Saverne, who was to become his wife.
"Strange that death, crime, revenge, remorse, mystery, should attend round the cradle of one so innocent, and pure—as pure and
innocent, I pray Heaven now, as upon that day when, at scarce a
month old, the adventures of her life began" (chap. 2). "As I survey
it now, the curtain is down, and the play is long over; as I think of
its surprises, disguises, mysteries, escapes, and dangers, I am
amazed myself," he shudders out loud shortly afterwards. "What a
destiny it was! What a fatal tragedy was now about to begin!" (chap.
3). Accordingly, in the hurly-burly of the eight chapters that
Thackeray lived to complete we are drawn into a world of
smugglers, pirates and highwaymen; plunged at the outset into the
midst of a family feud whose consequences affect all the principal
characters; witness the escape of Agnes's harassed mother and the
infant Agnes in a storm, a duel followed by a violent death, the
funeral of Madame de Saverne, the shooting of a bandit by Denis,
all manner of espionage activities, and the outbreak of war. We get,
in short, "plenty of fighting, escaping, robbery, and rescuing," to
quote from another of the Roundabouts.[48]

"We do not claim to rank among the military novelists. Our place
is with the non-combatants," wrote Thackeray at the beginning of a
chapter of *Vanity Fair*. "When the decks are cleared for action we go
below and wait meekly. We should only be in the way of the manoeuvres that the gallant fellows are performing over head" (chap.
30). We can appreciate then what an effort of imagination must
have gone into the creation of a hero like Denis who joins His
Majesty's Navy and just as his narrative is interrupted is about to
engage in battle against the fleet of John Paul Jones as midshipman
aboard the *Serapis* under Captain Pearson.[49] The original manuscript indicates besides that to "write a story with no egotism whatever . . . in which there should be no reflections" required special
negative capability on Thackeray's part. A draft of the first chapter
that was eventually scrapped opens: "Is it Fate w[h] impels the man,

or is it man who brings the fate down on him?" This query, appropriate enough as an epigraph to Thackeray's work, was apparently not deemed suitable coming from Denis, a man more of action than of thought. Also rejected were other dicta that would have had too familiar a ring to Thackeray's devotees: "We spake anon of the fruit of the tree w^h our first mother ate and w^h caused the downfall of our race. Yes but the tree was there; and the first fruit hung tempting within reach. No tree, no temptation, it might have been, had Wisdom not ordained otherwise. I knock my head against that tree often & often"; "As for the Chevalier de la Motte, he always preferred to think he had no more control in the matter of existence than Punch has in the show. He is a puppet ruled by hands under the curtain. And if he kills his wife & the beadle, flings his baby out of a window, and is fetched up to Tyburn at last; it is all on account of Monsieur Fate behind the Curtain. Is this so?"[50] Thackeray had second thoughts about making Denis himself a ventriloquist's dummy.

In the first version Denis also is rather rambling and discursive. One discarded passage represents him in his anecdotage, musing half aloud from an armchair that once belonged to a doctor of his acquaintance: "As I lean back in the comfortable arms (not unmindful that the generation in which I belong is the next to be called) I hold on to the past w^h was present once to my faithful old study companion." Burke once sat in this chair, the narrator recalls, and its owner also knew Garrick, whom he liked to talk about. The good doctor's sons took part in the great wars of the century, and here he sat and read their letters. And so Denis leads into his preamble: "Good readers, if you will listen to a story of the old times, I will relate one, w^h must have come to pass when this old chair was new."

Gone are the maundering and the name dropping in the tale as it was published. Denis now begins his narrative in the brisk good spirits that characterize it throughout: "To plague my wife, who does not understand pleasantries in the matter of pedigree, I once drew a family tree of my ancestors, with Claude Duval, captain and highwayman, *sus. per coll.* in the reign of Charles II, dangling from a top branch. But this is only my joke with her High Mightiness my wife, and his Serene Highness my son. None of us Duvals have been *supercollated* to my knowledge. As a boy I have tasted a rope's end often enough, but not round my neck." He does not linger long over family history: " . . . the persecutions endured by my ancestors in France for our Protestant religion, which we early received and steadily maintained, did not bring death upon us, as upon many of our faith, but only fines and poverty, and exile from our native country." His few moral observations are apt, shrewd, and terse: "At my early age I could only be expected to obey my elders and parents, and to consider all things were right which were done round about me. . . . Of course, being a simple little fellow, I honoured my father and mother as became me—my grandfather and mother, that is—father being dead some years" (chap. 4); "That habit I had of speaking out everything that was on my mind, brought me, as a child, into innumerable scrapes, but I do thankfully believe has preserved me from still greater" (chap. 5). "On the matter of church I am not going to make any boast. That awful subject lies between a man and his conscience. I have known men of lax faith pure and just in their lives, as I have met very loud-professing Christians loose in their morality, and hard and unjust in their dealings" (chap. 6). *"Monsieur mon fils,"* Denis interrupts his narrative at one point, "if ever you marry, and have a son, I hope the little chap will have an honest man for a grandfather, and that you will be able to say, 'I loved him,' when the daisies cover me" (chap. 6), and the rest of his readers give ready assent. In his openness and candor this able seaman steers a middle course between the naïfs and windbags of Thackeray's early fiction and the melancholics and skeptics of the later.

> I shall not attempt to tell the story of the battle of the 23rd. September, which ended in our glorious Captain striking his own colours to our superior and irresistible enemy. Sir Richard [Pearson] has told the story of his disaster in words nobler than any I could supply, who, though indeed engaged in that fearful action in which our flag went down before a renegade Briton and his motley crew, saw but a small portion of the battle which ended so fatally for us. It did not commence till nightfall. How well I remember the sound of the enemy's gun of which the shot crashed into our side in reply to the challenge of the captain, who hailed her! Then came a broadside from us—the first I had ever heard in battle.

At this crucial moment of Denis Duval's baptism by fire his tale comes to a sudden halt, and so Thackeray was spared to the end the task of military reporter that heretofore he had ducked so adroitly. We take leave of his wise, ingenuous, and likeable hero with genuine regret. We are especially sorry to lose the thread of a story that "breaks off as his life ended—full of vigour, and blooming with new promise like the apple-trees in the month of May," as Frederick Greenwood, Thackeray's successor in the editorial chair of *Cornhill*, wrote.[57] His greatest rival, Dickens, was prompted to say in one of the obituary tributes: "In respect of earnest feeling, far-seeing purpose, character, incident, and a certain living picturesqueness blending the whole, I believe it to be much the best of his works."[52] Whether or not one is inclined to go as far as Dickens in praise, it cannot be disputed that Thackeray's half-told tale, in its incisiveness, dramatic sweep, and narrative drive, reveals his mastery purely as a literary artist, if not his full intellectual strength.

Thanks to the pains that Thackeray took with *Denis*, its development was not left so much to conjecture as was Dickens's own aborted *Edwin Drood*. In his eulogy, Dickens himself pointed out that "by reason of the singular construction of the story, more than one incident usually belonging to the end of such a fiction is anticipated in the beginning, and thus there is an approach to completeness in the fragment." We know virtually from the outset that, though they endure the ordeals of separation, Denis and Agnes are happily married at the time when the story is being written. We are led to expect rough times ahead: "But this dearest and happiest season of my life . . . was to come to an abrupt ending, and poor Humpty Dumpty having climbed the wall of bliss, was to have a great and sudden fall, which, for a while, perfectly crushed and bewildered him" (chap. 8). Denis's parting with his mother as he is about to go to sea looks ahead both to storms and to a safe haven: ". . . When I was in my bed she came and knelt down by it, and with tears rolling down her furrowed face, offered up a prayer in her native German language, that He who had been pleased to succour me from perils hitherto, would guard me for the future, and watch over me in the voyage of life which was about to begin. Now, as it is drawing to its close, I look back at it with an immense awe and thankfulness, for the strange dangers from which I have escaped, the great blessings I have enjoyed" (chap. 8). Thackeray's last letter to his publisher also foretells the end of sorrows: "Dear Smith.—I was just going to be taken prisoner by Paul Jones when I had to come to bed. If I could get a month's ease I should finish the eight numbers handsomely with the marriage of Denis and Agnes, after the capture of Toulon by the English. 'The Course of True Love' I thought of as a pretty name."[53]

We have some more idea of what was in store for Denis from the detailed notes Thackeray left behind that indicate that he still relished historical research fully as much as the challenge of spinning a rattling yarn. Among these notes is a chronology of the principal events of the novel. Excerpts from such sources as the *Annual Register*, the *Gentleman's Magazine*, records of criminal trials, and *Sussex*

Archaeological Collections (for notices of smuggling operations in that area) attest to his "conscientious effort to keep as near truth in feigning as possible," in Greenwood's words.[54] Thackeray is known also to have visited Winchelsea, where most of the early episodes take place, both to get the feel of the region and to investigate its past in local archives. This background contributes to the authenticity of the seaside atmosphere and pins the events of the story down to time and place. Although the hero and heroine of *Denis Duval* apparently are completely fictitious, the nefarious Weston family, whose involvement in smuggling is alluded to, came out of the Sessions Papers, and a true trial and execution for treason recorded in the *Annual Register* for 1781 gave Thackeray the basis for the mysterious Chevalier de la Motte. In the novel he becomes the adulterous lover of Agnes's mother, the murderer of her father, as well as the spy of historical record.

In a Roundabout essay recalling his earlier reading of Dumas and Scott, Thackeray admitted to a lingering relish for novels that are "strong, 'hot with' . . . plenty of fighting; and a villain in the cupboard, who is to suffer tortures just before Finis."[55] The Chevalier presumably was to fulfill this role, for we know from the *Annual Register* that he was betrayed by his accomplice Henry Lütterloh (also introduced in *Denis Duval*), and was eventually condemned to be hanged, drawn, and quartered for conspiring to sell British naval secrets to the French. However, the account of the trial of the Chevalier also states that "throughout the whole of this trying scene [he] exhibited a combination of manliness, steadiness, and presence of mind," that "his deportment was exceedingly genteel, and his eye was expressive of strong penetration," preparing us for the ambivalent figure we encounter fitfully in the story as it has come down to us. In the dramatic episode of the funeral of Agnes's mother, the Countess de Saverne, concluding with the Chevalier "weeping and crying that the curse—the curse of Cain was upon him," (chap. 5),[56] we recognize that here is no mere "villain in the cupboard." "I had the queerest feelings towards that man," Denis confesses, unaware at the time of the past of the Chevalier who has befriended him. "He was a perfect fine gentleman when he so wished: of his money most liberal, witty (in a dry *cruel* sort of way)—most tenderly attached to Agnes. *Eh bien!* As I looked at his yellow handsome face, cold shudders would come over me . . ." (chap. 6).

From these hints we are led to anticipate a character of power and dark fascination, perhaps the ultimate "refinement of cruelty" in

Thackeray's annals of civilized infamy. There can be no doubt that the paths of Denis and this tragic noble were destined to cross. In the last chapter that Thackeray wrote, Denis, who at this point had inadvertently become privy to the cloak-and-dagger escapades that de la Motte is engaged in, recalls: "The Chevalier, who had once been neutral, and even kind to me, was confirmed in a steady hatred against me, and held me as an enemy whom he was determined to get out of his way" (chap. 8). In addition to enduring much both by land and sea, through being caught up in the American and French Revolutions, Denis, we gather, was also to feel the wrath of the vengeful de la Motte, who was not above trying to pander off his ward Agnes on the rascally Lütterloh. But eventually the spirit of charity was to assert itself, with Denis forgiving his enemy at the scaffold: "Except my kind namesake, the captain and the admiral, this was the first *gentleman* I ever met in intimacy," reads one unpublished fragment, "a gentleman with many a stain—nay, crime to reproach him but not all lost I hope and pray. I own to having a kindly feeling towards that fatal man." With his "sneaking kindness" toward a man who had done so much to make his life wretched, Denis teaches us to "pardon humanity." We can also see in Denis's rise from his tradesman origins Thackeray's final incarnation of his ideal of a natural gentility. Furthermore, his moral integrity, maintained despite corrupt "first associates," demonstrates "flowers of good blooming in foul places." Clearly Thackeray had in mind much more than the "picturesque affair" that Henry James labeled this torso of a novel. James missed here the sophistication and high comedy of Thackeray's novels of manners that look forward to his own; but this serious adventure story, for a modern reader, links Scott and Captain Marryat to Stevenson and "Captain Conrad."

At the beginning of one of his essays, Thackeray describes himself as he "sits under Time, the white-wigged charioteer, with his back to the horses, and his face to the past, looking at the receding landscape and the hills fading into the grey distance,"[57] and appropriately the manuscript of *Denis Duval* contains a sketch of the hero reading in an armchair, the figure of Father Time with his scythe hovering in the background. The *Roundabout Papers* in their backward glance bridge the gulf between the two eras that Thackeray had witnessed. One of his early unsuccessful ventures into journalism concluded with good wishes "To the young Queen [for] a long reign and a merry one: to the People—the Franchise, with

Denis Duval manuscript: pencil sketch by Thackeray depicting the hero reading in the author's own armchair, figure of Father Time in the background. (Unpublished; The Pierpont Morgan Library; reproduced by permission.)

Lord Durham for a minister";[58] at the apex of his career he is able to congratulate the middle-aged Queen's son Prince Albert Edward on the occasion of his wedding to the Princess Alexandra. "I am sure hearty prayers were offered outside the gate as well as within for that princely young pair, and for their Mother and Queen," Thackeray wrote in celebration of this event. "The peace, the freedom, the happiness, the order, which her rule guarantees, are part of my birthright as an Englishman, and I bless God for my share. Where else shall I find such liberty of action, thought, speech, or laws which protect me so well?"[59] Some of the music performed at this wedding had been composed by the late husband of the Queen, moving Thackeray to remember Prince Albert as a patron of arts and learning as well as a model of integrity. "And as we trace in the young faces of his many children the father's features and likeness," he concluded his eulogy, "what Englishman will not pray that they may have inherited also some of the great qualities which won the Prince Consort the love and respect of our country?" That could not be said about any of the four Georges.

"The good-natured reader who has perused some of these rambling papers has long since seen . . . that the writer belongs to the old-fashioned classes of this world, loves to remember very much more than to prophesy," aptly wrote the Preacher of Cornhill.[60] His "rambling papers" gave him opportunity to review the period in which he came of age, obviously an improvement morally and politically over the Regency that had called forth his most biting satire. Here also he reviewed the literary calling that brought him both money and celebrity. Along the way significantly are commemorated the deaths of noted authors—of Scott earlier in the century ("Be a good man, my dear!" his alleged dying words to Lockhart, come to this devoted reader's mind), of Thomas Hood, a fellow writer for *Punch* memorialized by his children in time to be recalled by Thackeray in *Cornhill*, of Washington Irving and Lord Macaulay, "the Goldsmith and Gibbon of our time," in Thackeray's words, both of whom died in 1859.[61] The most poignant of these papers, perhaps, in view of its ironic prefiguring of Thackeray's own literary fate, is "The Last Sketch," his hail-and-farewell to Charlotte Brontë on the posthumous publication of a fragment of a novel in progress. "The trembling little hand was to write no more. The heart newly awakened to love and happiness, and throbbing with maternal hope, was soon to cease to beat," read his tribute in part; "that intrepid outspeaker and champion of truth, that eager impetuous redresser of wrong was to be called out of the world's fight and struggle, to lay down the shining arms, and to be removed to a sphere . . . where truth complete, and right triumphant, no longer need to wage war."[62]

"Yesterday is gone—yes, but very well remembered; and we think of it the more now we know that To-morrow is not going to bring us much," writes the narrator of *The Adventures of Philip* (chap. 6). These words might well have served as epigraph to these "little Essays which have amused the public and the writer," as Thackeray referred to them in a letter to his readers upon his relinquishing the "thorny cushion" of the editorial chair of *Cornhill*.[63] The Roundabouts add up to a diary of the heart arresting time in its course, very much like one he describes: "Here are the records of dinners eaten, and gone the way of flesh. The lights burn blue somehow, and we sit before the ghosts of victuals. Hark at the dead jokes resurging! Here are the lists of the individuals who have dined at your own humble table. The agonies endured before and during these great entertainments are renewed, and smart again."[64] *The Roundabout Papers* recapture transient pains and pleasures both, but in the midst of the roving, the holidaying, the party-going and playgoing, beyond his visions of "pantomime, pudding, and pie," Thackeray occasionally caught glimpses of eternity. "Look, through the windows jewelled all over with saints the light comes streaming down from the sky, and Heaven's own illuminations paint the book!" he exclaimed in an Antwerp cathedral. "A sweet touching picture indeed it is, that of the little children assembled in this immense temple, which has endured for ages, and grave teachers bending over them. Yes, the picture is very pretty of the children and their teachers, and their book—but the text? Is it the truth, the only truth, nothing but the truth?"[65] This epiphany came inevitably to him as an animated illustration, and it is equally characteristic that it should end with a question mark. So too he saw life as an ever continuing work in progress, as in the plangent coda to "De Finibus":

> So you are gone, little printer's boy, with the last scratches and corrections on the proof, and a fine flourish by way of Finis at the story's end. The last corrections? I say those last corrections seem never to be finished. . . . That turning back to the old pages produces anything but elation of mind. Would you not pay a pretty fine to be able to cancel some of them? Oh, the sad old pages, the dull old pages! Oh the cares, the *ennui*, the squabbles, the repetitions, the old conversations over and over again! But now and again a kind thought is recalled, and now and again a dear memory. Yet a few chapters more, and then the last; after which behold Finis itself come to an end, and the Infinite begun.

About a week before he was found dead in his bed on the morning of Christmas Eve, 1863, Thackeray had confided to his daughter Anne that his children were his only reason for going on living.[66] So, much profit and occasional joy as it had provided him, he did not regret his leaving of Vanity Fair. Neither did he ask to see the distant scene, but we can detect in his preoccupation with "the battle of life, with its chances, perils, wounds, defeats, distinctions," some concern for the future judgment—moral and literary: "And so we meet and part; we struggle and succeed; or we fail and drop unknown on the way"; "Ah, friend! may our coin, battered and clipped, and defaced though it be, be proved to be Sterling Silver on the day of the Great Assay!"[67] In his lament on the untimely passing of Charlotte Brontë, he made his plea for all—writers, artists, ordinary men— with regrets over what has been left undone: "Is there record kept anywhere of fancies conceived, beautiful unborn? Some day will they assume form in some yet undeveloped light? If our bad unspoken thoughts are registered against us, and are written in the awful account, will not the good thoughts unspoken, the love and tenderness, the pity, beauty, charity, which pass through the breast, and cause the heart to throb with silent good, find a remembrance too?"[68] He was about to be "found out" by posterity, and he was uncertain of the verdict.

1. See above, p. 57.

2. Thackeray's contract with Smith, Elder at first called for serial publication of "one or two novels of ordinary size," with rights to book publication afterward, for which he was to be paid £350 per month, the most generous offer he ever received. "I am not going to put such a document as *this* into my wastepaper basket," he is reported as saying. The offer of the editorship came from Smith as an afterthought and brought Thackeray an additional £1,000 per year. For details of the agreement, see Gordon N. Ray, *The Age of Wisdom* (New York: McGraw-Hill, 1958), pp. 293–94. Further background is supplied by Spencer L. Eddy, Jr., *The Founding of the Cornhill Magazine*, Ball State Monograph no. 19 (Muncie, Indiana, 1970).

3. *Unpublished Verses*. By William Makepeace Thackeray (London: W. T. Spencer, 1899), pp. 22–25. The poem is undated. The MS is in the Huntington Library.

4. Lionel Stevenson, *The Showman of Vanity Fair* (New York: Charles Scribner's Sons, 1947), p. 387.

5. "Ogres," *Works*, 12:309.

6. "Notes Of A Week's Holiday," *Works*, 12:243, 244.

7. "De Juventute," *Works*, 12:241.

8. "Tunbridge Toys," *Works*, 12:227–28.

9. "On A Lazy Idle Boy," *Works*, 12:167. This was the first of the Roundabout Papers, appearing in the opening number of January 1860. The reference is to the village in the Grisons where the martyr Lucius, founder of the Church of Saint Peter, Cornhill, lies buried.

10. "On A Hundred Years Hence," *Works*, 12:296.

11. "Small-Beer Chronicle," *Works*, 12:303.

12. "Notes Of A Week's Holiday," *Works*, 12:243.

13. "De Finibus," *Works*, 12:369, 372.

14. "Thorns In The Cushion," *Works*, 12:212.

15. "Strange To Say, On Club Paper," *Works*, 12:434. This is the opening paragraph of the last essay that Thackeray published in *Cornhill* (November 1863). Although not, strictly speaking, part of the Roundabout Papers, it appears with them in his collected works.

16. "On A Peal Of Bells," *Works*, 12:381.

17. "A Mississippi Bubble," *Works*, 12:331–32.

18. "The Notch On The Axe—A Story A La Mode," *Works*, 12:368. Saintsbury conjectured that here Thackeray was once again parodying Bulwer, this time his supernatural tale *A Strange Story*.

19. "Thorns In The Cushion," *Works*, 12:214. In the first chapter of *Lovel the Widower*, the narrator, Mr. Batchelor, makes fun of the affectation of Bessy Prior's mother in referring to the vaudeville theater where her daughter dances as an "academy."

20. "On A Chalk-Mark On The Door," *Works*, 12:279. The society doctor Dr. Firmin corresponds in a farfetched way to "the unprincipled Earl." "The atrocious General" could be either Charlotte Baynes's vicious mother (called "La Générale"), who tries to keep her daughter and Philip apart when she learns that he has been disinherited by Lord Ringwood, or her henpecked husband, General Baynes, who goes along with her machinations, against his better judgment.

21. "De Finibus," *Works*, 12:373.

22. 28 October 1859; quoted by Trollope in *An Autobiography* (London: Oxford University Press, 1923), p. 126.

23. It was given a private performance on 24 and 25 March 1862 as part of the housewarming celebration when Thackeray moved with his two daughters into his last home at 2 Palace Green. Among those taking part were Thackeray's younger daughter Minny as Mrs. Bonnington, and Thackeray himself in the mute role of Mr. Bonnington. The prompt copy of this version is in the British Musseum.

24. 25–30 June 1853, *Letters*, 3:280.

25. The original autograph MS, virtually intact, is in the Morgan Library. It is the least revised of the manuscripts that I have examined, but there has been some tinkering with the passage in chap. 1 that reads: "Though I am a steady and *confirmed* old bachelor (I shall call myself Mr. Batchelor, if you please, in this story; and there is one far-far away who knows why I will NEVER take another title). . . ." The MS originally read "one I know far far away who knows that I will NEVER, etc." Parts of the MS, incidentally, are written on the backs of *Cornhill* rejection slips. In his study of Thackeray's revisions, *Strokes of the Great Clock* (Athens: University of Georgia Press, forthcoming) (chap. 7), which I had the opportunity to read in typescript before this book went to press, Edgar Harden finds substantial alterations of various kinds on the proof sheets at Yale and Huntington.

26. [Richard Holt Hutton], "Mr. Thackeray's Satire," *Spectator*, 30 November 1861, p. 1314. The story ran in *Cornhill* from January through June 1860 (almost simultaneously in America in *Harper's Monthly Magazine*, February–July 1860). The lateness of the *Spectator* review suggests that it was based upon the first book publication.

27. 15 October 1861, unpublished, but partially quoted in Ray, *The Age of Wisdom*, p. 303. The original is in the Houghton Library.

28. John Dodds, *Thackeray: A Critical Portrait* (New York: Oxford University Press, 1941), p. 231.

29. Introduction to *Lovel the Widower*, Oxford Thackeray, 20:x.

30. "Some Letters of Whitwell Elwin-II," *Times Literary Supplement*, 25 September 1953, p. 620.

31. In "The Breakdown of Thackeray's Narrator: *Lovel the Widower*," *Nineteenth-Century Fiction* 32 (June 1977): 36–53, Ina Ferris interprets this open-mindedness as indecisiveness. In my opinion she takes this novel more seriously than Thackeray intended.

32. *Framley Parsonage* still had two more numbers to go, but once it had finished its run, *The Adventures of Philip* headed off almost every issue of *Cornhill* through June 1862, when, with two more installments left, it yielded place to George Eliot's *Romola*.

33. See above, p. 430. Thackeray's reference seems to be to Lawrence's later *Sword and Gown* (1859), in which the narrator protests in defense of his promulgation of the "physical force" doctrine: "Modern refinement requires that the chief character shall be made interesting in spite of his being dwarfish, plain-featured, and a victim to pulmonary or some more prosaic disease. . . . Let our motto still be 'Forward': we have pleasures of which our grandsires never dreamt, and inventions that they were inexcusable in ignoring." *Guy Livingstone* itself, incidentally, has a "dismal" ending, the hero dying in his prime.

34. "De Finibus," *Works*, 12:375.

35. In chap. 1 of the original MS there is lined out a reference to Lovel's meeting Arthur at his university. As Edgar Harden points out (*Strokes of the Great Clock*, chap.

7), there is evidence in this part of the MS that Thackeray at first intended for Pendennis to be the narrator, but changed his mind.

36. Cf. "Hints for a History of Highwaymen," quoted above, pp. 160–61.

37. "Ogres," Works, 12:314. This essay appeared in the issue of August 1861, along with chap. 17–18 of Philip, by which time the hero has been deserted by his father.

38. "On A Pear Tree," Works, 12:388. This essay appeared in the issue of November 1862. Philip had concluded its run in the August issue.

39. "On A Medal Of George The Fourth," Works, 12:433.

40. "De Finibus," Works, 12:373. Its original appearance was in the August 1862 issue of Cornhill.

41. Ibid.

42. "On A Medal Of George The Fourth," Works, 12:431.

43. Here is an instance where Thackeray utilized his legal knowledge to give credibility to what seems on the surface a strained plot device and turns a melodramatic situation into a case of conscience. The much-maligned ending of Philip, in which the hero's inheritance is restored through the discovery of a lost will found in a carriage, is based on a true eighteenth-century case that Thackeray recorded in his notebook for The Virginians and apparently had thought of using in the earlier novel.

44. Thackeray's physician, Sir Henry Thompson, contributed an article, "Under Chloroform," to the April 1860 number of Cornhill. This episode from Philip is quoted at length above, p. 104.

45. Introduction to The Adventures of Philip, Works, 11:xii.

46. With the conclusion of Philip, Thackeray fulfilled his contractual obligation to Smith, but in the letter announcing his resignation as editor, he wrote: "Whilst the present tale of Philip is passing through the press, I am preparing another, on which I have worked for intervals for many years past, and which I hope to introduce in the ensuing year" ("To Contributors and Correspondents . . . 18 March, 1862," Letters, 4:260). In his note to this letter, Gordon Ray identifies the announced new tale as "The Knights of Borsellen," a historical romance placed in the period of Henry V on which Thackeray worked intermittently but never actually completed. Why Thackeray came to substitute Denis Duval, or how he persuaded Smith to agree to a historical tale after he had completed the two modern ones stipulated in his agreement, is not known. The name Duval has been used by Thackeray in one of his Christmas books, Dr. Birch and His Young Friends, for the school bully young Duval dubbed "the pirate of Birch's," in obvious reference to the notorious seventeenth-century renegade numbered facetiously by Denis among his ancestry.

47. "De Finibus," Works, 12:374.

48. "On A Lazy Idle Boy," Works, 12:169.

49. Denis narrates the tale in retirement. In his letter to the readers of Cornhill (see above, n. 46) Thackeray reminded them of the first of the Roundabout Papers, "On A Lazy Idle Boy," in which he had likened himself to a sea captain, and carries on the naval image: "Those who have travelled on shipboard know what a careworn, oppressed, uncomfortable man the captain is. Meals disturbed, quiet impossible, rest interrupted—such is the lot of captains. This one resigns his commission. I had rather have a quiet life than gold-lace and epaulets: and deeper than did ever plummet sound I fling my speaking trumpet" (Letters, 4:259). With special aptness, Denis Duval can be called Thackeray's Tempest.

50. The rejected version of chap. 1 is preserved with most of the autograph MS (lacking parts of chaps. 6 and 7, and all of chap. 8) in the Morgan Library. For a careful analysis of the stages of revision of the opening chapter, see John Sutherland, Thackeray at Work (London: Athlone Press, 1974), chap. 6.

51. "Notes on Denis Duval," Cornhill Magazine 9 (June 1864): 655; Works, 12:555. This memorial appeared after the conclusion of Denis, which ran in four numbers of Cornhill, beginning with the previous March.

52. "In Memoriam," Cornhill Magazine 9 (February 1864): 129–32.

53. 17 December 1863, *Letters*, 4:295. Quoted by Anne Thackeray in her introduction to *Denis Duval, Works*, 12:xxxiii.

54. "Notes on Denis Duval," *Works*, 12:555–68. These are excerpts from the notebook in the British Museum that has never been published in full. Portions are reprinted in Sutherland, *Thackeray at Work*, "Appendix One: The Local Plans for *Denis Duval*."

55. "De Finibus," *Works*, 12:373.

56. This episode is quoted above, p. 105.

57. "On A Joke I Once Heard From The Late Thomas Hood," *Works*, 12:261.

58. *The Constitutional*, 1 July 1837 (announcement of termination of the paper); *Mr. Thackeray's Writings for the "National Standard" and "Constitutional,"* p. 297.

59. "On Alexandrines," *Works*, 12:424.

60. "On A Joke I Once Heard From The Late Thomas Hood," *Works*, 12:261.

61. "Nil Nisi Bonum" *Works*, 12:173–79.

62. *Cornhill Magazine* 1 (April 1860): 486; *Works*, 12:187–88. Although originally written as an introduction to Miss Brontë's "Emma," this piece is reprinted with the Roundabout Papers in collected editions of Thackeray.

63. "To Contributors and Correspondents . . .," *Letters*, 4:260.

64. "On Letts's Diary," *Works*, 12:335.

65. "Notes Of A Week's Holiday," *Works*, 12:246.

66. In a letter dated 1 May [1864] to Anna Smith Strong Baxter reporting her father's death, and its aftermath, Anne Thackeray wrote: "What we like to think about is a little expedition with Papa a week before Christmas. We went to the Temple Church together & then walked in the garden with all the sunsetting—and he was so well and in such good spirits—Just at the last week he was very sad & he said to me that if it was not for us he did not want to live much longer. But he was not near so ill as we had often seen him & Monday he was well again we thought. . . . It is almost more dreadful to think of these last days than of those which came after" (Maude Morrison Frank Correspondence, Rare Book and Manuscript Library, Columbia University).

67. "On Letts's Diary," *Works*, 12:340; "On A Medal Of George The Fourth," *Works*, 12:433.

68. "The Last Sketch," *Works*, 12:186–87. This thought was prompted by a recent visit to the studio of the late Charles Robert Leslie, a favorite artist of Thackeray's, whose painting of Titania and the fairy forest from *A Midsummer Night's Dream* lay on the easel uncompleted. "Some day our spirits may be permitted to walk in galleries of fancies more wondrous and beautiful than any achieved works which at present we see," this memorial essay continues, "and our minds to behold and delight in masterpieces which poets and artists' minds have fathered and conceived only." Thackeray then proceeds to his tribute to Charlotte Brontë.

CHRONOLOGY: SOME SIGNIFICANT EVENTS IN THACKERAY'S LITERARY CAREER

1811 (18 July)	Born in Calcutta.
1817	Sent to England by his parents to be educated.
1822–28	Student at Charterhouse School, London ("Cabbages," parody of L. E. L.'s "Violets," written for school paper, the *Carthusian*).
1824–28	Summers at Larkbeare, Devon (Fairoaks of *Pendennis*) (attributed publication in *Western Luminary:* parody of Moore's "Minstrel Boy," 1828).
1829 (February)	Matriculates at Trinity College, Cambridge (literary records: contributions to the *Snob* and the *Gownsman* under the signature θ; amateur theatricals recalled in *Letters*, 1:106).
1829 (July–September)	First trip to Paris.
1830 (June)	Leaves Cambridge without degree, after losing £1,500 in a gambling debt.
1830–31 (July–March)	In Weimar "for sport, or study, or society" (records: "Commonplace Book while in Weimar . . .," unpublished MS, Morgan Library; "Goethe in His Old Age," letter of 28 April 1855 to George Henry Lewes).

1831 (June 3)	Enters Middle Temple.
1832 (July 31– November 25)	Living in Paris (reading of Victor Cousin and other French writers recorded in Diary of 2 April–23 November 1832, *Letters*, 1:185–238).
1833 (May–August)	With the *National Standard* as partner and Paris correspondent (last number February 1834) (selection of Thackeray's contribution reprinted in *Mr. Thackeray's Writings for the "National Standard" and "Constitutional"*). Studies art in Paris (intermittently until 1837) at various ateliers, including that of Antoine-Jean Gros; copies paintings at the Louvre; sketches at the Life Academy. Suffers loss of considerable portion of his inheritance through bank failure in India.
1834 (May)	First identified contribution to *Fraser's Magazine:* "Il Etait un Roi d'Yvetot." Settles in Paris to study art (September).
1835	Meets Isabella Shawe.
1836	*Flore et Zephyr*, Thackeray's first book, published (series of comic lithographs of ballet dancers). Marries Isabella Shawe in Paris (20 August). First article appears (19 September) as Paris correspondent for the *Constitutional* (ceased publication 1 July 1837) (selection reprinted in *Mr. Thackeray's Writings for the "National Standard" and "Constitutional"*). Contributor to *Galignani's Messenger;* also to G. W. M. Reynolds's *Paris Literary Gazette* (see Jean Guivarc'h, "Deux journalistes anglaises de Paris en 1845 [George W. M. Reynolds et W. M. T.]," *Etudes anglaises* 28 [April–June, 1975]: 203–12).

1837	Settles in London (at 18 Albion Street). *Yellowplush Correspondence* in *Fraser's Magazine* (November 1837–August 1838).
1838	Moves to 13 Great Coram Street (neighborhood of *The Bedford-Row Conspiracy*).

Charles G. Addison's *Damascus and Palmyra* published, with illustrations by Thackeray.

Some Passages in the Life of Major Gahagan in *New Monthly Magazine* (February, March, November, December 1838; February, 1839).

1839   *Catherine; a Story* in *Fraser's Magazine* (May 1839–February 1840) (published posthumously in book form in 1869).

"Illustrations of the Rent Laws" in *The Anti–Corn Law Circular*, no. 8 (3 July).

"Captain Rook and Mr. Pigeon" in *Heads of the People*, drawn by Kenny Meadows.

"Stubbs's Calendar; or, The Fatal Boots" in *The Comic Almanack for 1839*.

Correspondent for the American magazine the *Corsair*, ed. Nathaniel P. Willis ("Letters from London, Paris, Petersburgh, Etc." signed T. T. for "Timothy Titcomb") (partially reprinted in *Paris Sketch Book*).

1840   *The Bedford-Row Conspiracy* in *New Monthly Magazine* (January, March, April).

A Shabby-Genteel Story in *Fraser's Magazine* (June–October) (left uncompleted; taken up later in *The Adventures of Philip*).

Essay, "George Cruikshank," in *Westminster Review* (June).

Paris Sketch Book, Thackeray's first book published in England.

First trip to Ireland; becomes aware of wife's incipient insanity.

Active as art critic for *Fraser's Magazine* (through 1847).

1841

The Second Funeral of Napoleon and The Chronicle of the Drum published (under pseudonym of M. A. Titmarsh, also illustrated by Thackeray).

Comic Tales and Sketches, edited and illustrated by Mr. Michael Angelo Titmarsh (contains *The Yellowplush Papers, Some Passages in the Life of Major Gahagan*, "The Professor" [from *Bentley's Miscellany*, September 1837], *The Bedford-Row Conspiracy, Stubb's Calendar*).

"The Fashionable Authoress" and "The Artists" in *Heads of the People*, New Series.

"Reading a Poem" [dramatic sketch on literary life] in *Britannia* (1, 8 May) (first published as a book, 1891).

The Great Hoggarty Diamond in *Fraser's Magazine* (September–December) (published as book, 1849).

1842

"The Legend of Jawbrahim-Heraudee," first identified contribution to *Punch* (15 June).

"Miss Tickletoby's Lectures on English History" in *Punch* (July–October).

Begins as contributor to *Foreign Quarterly Review* (intermittent through July 1844; first identified contribution: "The Rhine [by Victor Hugo]," April 1842).

Visits Ireland (4 July–1 November).

1843

The Irish Sketch Book, by Mr. M. A. Titmarsh (first book to contain his own name, in the dedication to Charles Lever, "laying aside for the moment the travelling title of Mr. Titmarsh").

Important articles for *Foreign Quarterly Review*, e.g., "English History and Character on the French Stage" (January); "Thieves' Literature of France" (April); "French Romancers on England" (October); reprinted in *New Sketch Book*.

Travels in Holland and Belgium (4–30 August) (record: "Notes of a Tour in the Low Countries," *Letters*, 2: 833).

"Jerome Paturot. With Considerations on Novels in General," in *Fraser's Magazine* (September).

1844   *Barry Lyndon* in *Fraser's Magazine* (January–December with interruption in October as "The Luck of Barry Lyndon") (first American ed. [Philadelphia: Appleton, 1852] reprints magazine version; revised as *The Memoirs of Barry Lyndon* in 1856, appearing both as a separate book and as vol. 3 of *Miscellanies*).

Reviewer for the *Morning Chronicle* (through 1848) (identified articles reprinted in *Contributions to the Morning Chronicle*).

European political correspondent for the *Calcutta Star* (until late 1845) (see "Letters from a Club Arm Chair . . .," ed. Henry Summerfield, *Nineteenth-Century Fiction* 18 [December 1963]: 205–33).

Commissioned by publisher Giraldon to translate Sue's *Les mystères de Paris*; project falls through (see *Letters*, 2:159).

Tour of the Mediterranean and the East (22 August–26 November).

1845   Submits first chapters of *Vanity Fair* to Colburn; they are turned down (see *Letters*, 2:198 n, 262).

Wife brought back to England from continent, placed in care of attendant.

1846

Notes of a Journey from Cornhill to Grand Cairo, by Mr. M. A. Titmarsh, Thackeray's last travel book.

The Book of Snobs in *Punch* (7 March 1846–27 February 1847, as "The Snobs of England, by One of Themselves").

Moves to 13 Young Street, Kensington, where much of *Vanity Fair, Pendennis*, and *Henry Esmond* were composed; later joined by his daughters Anny and Minny, who had been reared by his mother and stepfather.

Mrs. Perkin's Ball, by M. A. Titmarsh, Thackeray's first Christmas book.

1847

First number appears of *Vanity Fair. Pen and Pencil Sketches of English Society* (January) (20 parts through June 1848 [double number], published by Bradbury and Evans, publishers also of *Punch*; in book form as *Vanity Fair. A Novel Without a Hero*).

"Punch's Prize Novelists" in *Punch* (intermittently from 3 April through 9 October; in book form as *Novels by Eminent Hands*).

Our Street, second Christmas book.

1848

Vanity Fair concluded (29 June).

Begins writing of *Pendennis* (see letter to his mother, 18 July 1848, *Letters*, 2:401).

First number of *Pendennis* appears (November) (published in 24 parts through November 1850 [double number], with interruption noted below, by Bradbury and Evans).

Dr. Birch and His Young Friends, Christmas book.

1849

"Mr. Brown's Letters to a Young Man about Town" (analogue to *Pendennis*) in *Punch* (24 March–18 August; published in book form, 1853).

Illness interrupts composition of *Pendennis* (September–November).

Rebecca and Rowena, Christmas book (from *Fraser's Magazine*, August, September 1846).

1850   "The Dignity of Literature," *Morning Chronicle* (12 January).

Louis Marvy's *Sketches after English Landscape Painters* (text supplied by Thackeray).

Pendennis concluded (26 November).

Begins reading for lectures on the English humorists (see *Letters*, 2:692).

The Kickleburys on the Rhine, Christmas book.

1851   Lectures on the eighteenth-century English humorists in London (22 May–3 July).

Begins writing of *Henry Esmond* (August; see letter to Jane Brookfield, *Letters*, 2:736).

Resigns from *Punch* (December).

1852   Continues lectures on humorists in England and Scotland.

Esmond published (October) in three volumes by Smith, Elder.

Leaves for his first trip to America (30 October).

Lectures in New York (16 November–20 December).

1853   Lectures on humorists in various cities of East and South (13 January–1 April).

Returns to England.

Begins *The Newcomes* (9 July) while traveling with his daughters in Germany (see *Letters*, 1:lxi—"A Chronology of Thackeray's Life").

First number of *The Newcomes* published (October) (24 parts through August

1855 [double number], Bradbury and Evans).

1854   Begins *The Rose and the Ring* while in Rome with his daughters (January).

Moves to 36 Onslow Square, Brompton, where *The Virginians* and *The Adventures of Philip* were composed.

"John Leech's Pictures of Life and Character" in *Quarterly Review* (December).

The Rose and the Ring. A Fireside Pantomime for Great and Small Children, last of his Christmas books.

The Wolves and the Lamb, a comedy, composed (late 1854 or early 1855); later novelized as *Lovel the Widower*.

1855   Bradbury and Evans bring out most of Thackeray's fugitive writings to date in *Miscellanies: Prose and Verse* (4 vols., extending to 1857; simultaneous cheap edition in yellow wrappers imitative of the format of his novels in parts, 13 vols.).

Completes writing of *The Newcomes* in Germany (28 June) (see *Letters*, 3:459).

Composes lectures on the four Georges (August–October).

Leaves for second trip to America (28 October).

Lectures on the four Georges in New England and New York (December).

1856   Lectures on the four Georges in Philadelphia, various southern cities, Saint Louis, Cincinnati (January–April).

Returns to England (arriving 8 May).

Lectures in Scotland and northern England (November–December).

1857   Continues lecture tour through England and Scotland (January–May).

Campaigns for seat in Parliament from city of Oxford, is defeated (8–21 July)

(record: "The Oxford Election, 1857,"
Letters, vol. 4, appendix 19).

First number of *The Virginians* appears
(November) (24 parts through October 1859, Bradbury and Evans).

1858   "Garrick Club Affair" set off by insulting
article by Edmund Yates in *Town Talk*.

1859   Enters into agreement to write "one or
two novels of ordinary size" for the
Cornhill Magazine, founded by George
Smith (19 February).

Accepts editorship of the *Cornhill
Magazine* (7 August).

Completes writing of *The Virginians* (7
September).

1860   First number of the *Cornhill Magazine*
(January) (Thackeray's contributions:
Lovel the Widower [through June], "On
A Lazy Idle Boy" [first of the *Roundab-
out Papers*]).

"Vanitas Vanitatum" in *Cornhill
Magazine* (July).

"The Four Georges" in *Cornhill* (July–
October).

The Four Georges published in book form
(first edition in New York by Harper;
published in London by Smith, Elder
the following year).

1861   *The Adventures of Philip* begins in *Cornhill*
(January) (monthly through August
1862; published as book, 1862).

Roundabout Papers continue in *Cornhill*
(intermittently through November
1863; published as book by Smith, Elder, 1863).

1862   Resigns editorship of *Cornhill* (6 March).

Moves to 2 Palace Green, Kensington—
his last residence (31 March) (private
performance of *The Wolves and the
Lamb* given here).

Finishes writing of *The Adventures of
Philip*, last completed novel (3 July).

1863   Begins writing of *Denis Duval* (May) (see
                             Letters, 4:287).
                             "Strange to Say, on Club Paper," last of
                             Roundabout Papers, appears in *Cornhill*
                             (November).
                             Death (24 December).
                             Burial in Kensal Green Cemetery (29
                             December).

1864   Uncompleted *Denis Duval* appears in
                             Cornhill (March–June).

1867–69   Library Edition of Thackeray's *Works*
                             published by Smith, Elder, 24 vols.

THACKERAY'S PRINCIPAL POSTHUMOUS PUBLICATIONS

1864   *Denis Duval. Cornhill Magazine* (March–
                             June).

1867   *Denis Duval*. London: Smith, Elder.
                             Early and Late Papers, hitherto uncol-
                             lected. Boston: Ticknor and Fields.

1869   *Ballads and Tales*. London: Smith, Elder
                             (vol. 18, Library Ed. of *Works*).
                             Catherine; a Story. Boston: Ticknor and
                             Fields; London: Smith, Elder (vol. 22,
                             Library Ed.) (both are cut from origi-
                             nal version).
                             The Wolves and the Lamb. London: Smith,
                             Elder (vol. 22, Library Ed.).

1876   *The Orphan of Pimlico and Other Sketches*,
                             with some notes by Anne Isabella
                             Thackeray. London: Smith, Elder.

1886   *Contributions to "Punch"* (not previously
                             reprinted). London: Smith, Elder;
                             Philadelphia: J. B. Lippincott.

1887   *Sultan Stork and Other Stories and Sketches*.
                             London: George Redway.

1891   *Reading a Poem* (dramatic sketch). Lon-
                             don: Chiswick Press.
                             "The Heroic Adventures of M. Boudin"
                             (illustrated comic tale left uncom-
                             pleted in MS), *Harper's New Monthly*

	Magazine (February) (facsimile of MS in Cent. Biog. Ed. 26:1–24).
1894	*Loose Sketches. An Eastern Adventure of the Fat Contributor, Etc.* London: Frank T. Sabin.
1899	*Mr. Thackeray's Writings for the "National Standard" and "Constitutional,"* comp. Walter Thomas Spencer. London: W. T. Spencer. *Unpublished Verses.* London: W. T. Spencer.
1900	*The Hitherto Unidentified Contributions . . . To "Punch,"* Comp. M. H. Spielmann.
1901	*Stray Papers.* Ed. Lewis Melville. Philadelphia: George W. Jacobs.
1906	*The New Sketch Book.* Being Essays Now First Collected from "The Foreign Quarterly Review," Ed. Robert S. Garnett. London: Alston Rivers (more recent research has discovered that not all of these papers are by Thackeray; see *Wellesley Index*, vol. 2).
1908	*Catherine: A Story.* Oxford Thackeray, ed. George Saintsbury, vol. 3 (reprints version that appeared in *Fraser's Magazine*, together with Thackeray's original illustrations).
1911	"The Knights of Borsellen" (uncompleted historical romance). *Cornhill Magazine* (18 July) (reprinted in Cent. Biog. Ed., 25:3–46).

INDEX

This index locates the significant names and topics represented in this book. Thackeray's titles are indexed under *Thackeray—works*. Other titles are indexed under their authors' names. The only separate title entries are for a few anonymous works.